I0867021

Orbital Debris Prevention and Mitigation Efforts among Major Space Actors

Studies in Space Law

General Editor

F.G. von der Dunk (*University of Nebraska-Lincoln, College of Law, Space, Cyber and Telecommunications Law Program*)

Editorial Board

M. Ferrazzani (*Senior Legal Counsel, ESA, Paris*)
S. Freeland (*Bond University, Australia, Prof. Emeritus and Professorial Fellow*)
J. Gabrynowicz (*University of Mississippi, Prof. Emerita*)
S. Hobe (*University of Cologne*)
R. Jakhu (*Institute of Air and Space Law, McGill University*)
F. Lyall (*University of Aberdeen, Prof. Emeritus*)
K.U. Schrogl (*IISL, Paris*)
L.J. Smith (*Leuphana University, Luneburg*)

VOLUME 20

The titles published in this series are listed at *brill.com/slaw*

Orbital Debris Prevention and Mitigation Efforts among Major Space Actors

Commonalities and the Search for Customary International Law

Marc G. Carns

BRILL | NIJHOFF

LEIDEN | BOSTON

Library of Congress Cataloging-in-Publication DataNames: Carns, Marc G. author.

Title: Orbital debris prevention and mitigation efforts among major space actors : commonalities and the search for customary international law / Marc G. Carns.
Description: Leiden ; Boston : Brill Nijhoff, [2023] | Series: Studies in space law, 1871-7659 ; volume 20 | Based on author's thesis (doctoral - University of Nebraska, 2022). | Includes bibliographical references and index. | Summary: "In the absence of formal treaty law, orbital debris has grown exponentially in our most valuable orbital regions. To address this problem, many major spacefaring programs have implemented independent laws and policies meant to mitigate the release and overall threat of debris"– Provided by publisher.
Identifiers: LCCN 2022058745 (print) | LCCN 2022058746 (ebook) | ISBN 9789004535831 (hardback) | ISBN 9789004535848 (ebook)
Subjects: LCSH: Space debris–Law and legislation.
Classification: LCC KZD3608 .C37 2023 (print) | LCC KZD3608 (ebook) | DDC 341.4/7–dc23/eng/20230403
LC record available at https://lccn.loc.gov/2022058745
LC ebook record available at https://lccn.loc.gov/2022058746

Typeface for the Latin, Greek, and Cyrillic scripts: "Brill". See and download: brill.com/brill-typeface.

ISSN 1871-7659
ISBN 978-90-04-53583-1 (hardback)
ISBN 978-90-04-53584-8 (e-book)

Copyright 2023 by Koninklijke Brill NV, Leiden, The Netherlands.
Koninklijke Brill NV incorporates the imprints Brill, Brill Nijhoff, Brill Hotei, Brill Schöningh, Brill Fink, Brill mentis, Vandenhoeck & Ruprecht, Böhlau, V&R unipress and Wageningen Academic.
All rights reserved. No part of this publication may be reproduced, translated, stored in a retrieval system, or transmitted in any form or by any means, electronic, mechanical, photocopying, recording or otherwise, without prior written permission from the publisher. Requests for re-use and/or translations must be addressed to Koninklijke Brill NV via brill.com or copyright.com.

This book is printed on acid-free paper and produced in a sustainable manner.

It may be a pretty tough neighborhood in the not-too-distant future.[1]

1 General William Shelton, former Commander, Air Force Space Command, National Space Symposium, 12 April 2011.

Contents

Preface

This is the published version of a doctoral work that began in late 2019 and was successfully defended for my doctoral degree in February 2022 through the University of Nebraska. However, the concept of this work began much earlier, around 2015, when I first began pursuit of my LL.M. with a focus on space law. I had advocated in my earlier work that nations needed to be more aggressive in efforts toward the removal of space debris from our orbital environment, going so far as to argue that even absent formal treaties, there were grounds in customary international law for even non-consensual removal. I presented that theory at the International Astronautical Congress in 2017 to a receptive audience and was published by the United States Air Force Judge Advocate Law Journal that same year.

Over the next two years, I was fortunate to engage regularly with Professor von der Dunk, my eventual supervising attorney for this work, on advancing a portion of that original concept into a much larger undertaking. In particular, I was fascinated by the efforts of mature spacefaring nations and organizations in their attempt to address the problem of debris absent any formal guidance or requirements forcing their hand to do so. It became evident that these nations and organizations recognized that in the absence of formal rules, the preservation of the orbital environment remained critical for our advancement as a species. We rely heavily on our scarce orbital resources for much of the way we live out our lives. Without a deep respect for the health of our orbital environments, much of the necessities of our daily lives, such as GPS, banking, communications, healthcare, transportation, information ... all of it could come to an immediate halt with the right orbital disaster.

Based on that, I undertook to fill at least an initial gap in some of the available information, primarily assessing and comparing how the major spacefaring nations and the European Space Agency (ESA), absent any formal treaty law, have implemented their own orbital debris mitigation and prevention programs in an effort to do their part to preserve our most valuable orbital regions. My analysis then looked for common themes among them that might, without us having originally recognized it, risen to the level of establishing customary international law. Were that the case, our reliance on soft-law guidelines might be reduced, and our ability to aggressively advocate that there were existing legally binding rules would benefit the entire international community. This is by no means and end to the work, but my hope is that it is at least a kernel from which many discussions can be had and important conceptual advances can be made.

Much like that long road to establish the start of this concept, getting here was no easy feat and took an extraordinary amount of support. I owe so many so much appreciation. And while I am not able to name them all, I would be remiss if I did not take the opportunity to thank some. Most importantly, I would like to thank my wife Sandra and my children, Michael and Lauren, for their enduring support throughout this effort. My wife held everything together and gave me the greatest support I could possibly ask for. My children never complained about the time I was working and showed enormous appreciation for the time we did have together. I am so thankful for them every day. My parents, Michael and Victoria, sister Michelle and her family, my brother and sister-in-law, Kris and Sarah Williams, and my extended family Susan and Charles Kelley, also wholeheartedly supported me, offering encouragement and feedback whenever I needed it!

As I said, for many years Professor von der Dunk has been on this journey with me, through two advanced law degrees. I am thankful for his faith in me that I could successfully take this on. He has been endlessly available, answered hundreds of questions, and guided me through this at every step. In addition, I would like to thank the entire staff of the University of Nebraska, including my doctoral panel for their generous time in reviewing this work for my defense and the library staff in helping me navigate difficult searches for materials I would likely have never been able to do on my own. Additionally, my thanks to Deborah Howe who has provided enormous editorial support for me.

Finally, I would like to thank my fellow legal colleagues in my prior role whom I worked with from 2019-2022 through the duration of this work. They were endlessly supportive and responded to the needs of my clients when I was absent to focus on this effort. I owe special thanks to Mr. Brock Dahl, Mr. Ben Kastan, Mr. Brian Ryckman, Mr. Matthew Colson, Ms. Charity King and USAF Major Carolyn Carmody. Last but not least, the support staff, Ms. Shannon Nixson, Ms. Barbara Chavez and Ms. Laura Heatherly-Reiss, who navigated the demands on my schedule. Everyone involved helped make this possible without complaint and have my great respect and deep gratitude.

Disclaimer

Any opinions of the author expressed in this book are the author's alone and do not reflect any official position of the United States government or the Department of Defense.

Figures

Abbreviations

ADR	Active Debris Removal
AFB	Air Force Base
AFSPC	Air Force Space Command (US)
ASAT	Anti-Satellite
ASI	Italian Space Agency
BNSC	British National Space Agency
BSS	Broadcasting-Satellite Service
CASC	China Aerospace and Science and Technology Corporation
CCP	Chinese Communist Party
CGPHESE	Consultative Group of Potentially Harmful Effects of Space Experiments
cm	Centimeters
CNES	Centre National D'études Spatiales (French Space Agency)
CNSA	China National Space Administration
COSPAR	Committee on Space Research
CPR	Common Pool Resources
CSM	Conjunction Summary Message
CSpOC	Combined Space Operations Center (US)
DA-ASAT	Direct Ascent-Anti Satellite
DAMAGE	Debris Analysis and Monitoring Architecture to the Geosynchronous Environment
DART	Double Asteroid Redirect Test
DBS	Direct Broadcast System
DLR	Deutsches Zentrum für Luft- und Raumfahrt e.V. (German Space Agency)
DoD	Department of Defense (US)
DoS	Department of State (US)
DoT	Department of Transportation (US)
EAC	European Astronaut Center
ECSAT	European Centre for Space Applications and Telecommunications
ECSS	European Cooperation on Space Standardization
ELDO	European Launch Development Organization
EOM	End of Mission
EOMDP	End of Mission Disposal Plan
ESA	European Space Agency
ESAC	European Space Astronomy Center
ES-MCAT	Eugene Stansbury-Meter Class Autonomous Telescope
ESOC	European Space Operations Center
ESRIN	ESA Centre for Earth Observation

ESRO	European Space Research Organization
ESSTI	Ethiopian Space Science and Technology Institute
ESTEC	European Space Research and Technology Center
ETRSS	Ethiopian Remote Sensing Satellite
EU	European Union
FAA	Federal Aviation Administration (US)
FAA/AST	Federal Aviation Administration Office of Commercial Space Transportation (US)
FCC	Federal Communications Commission (US)
FMEA	Failure Mode and Effects Analysis
GDP	Gross Domestic Product
GEO	Geostationary Orbit
HAND	High Altitude Nuclear Detonation
HAPS	Hydrazine Auxiliary Propulsion System
HAX	Haystack Auxiliary Radar
HEO	High Earth Orbit
HUSIR	Haystack Ultra-wideband Satellite Imaging Radar
IAA	International Academy of Astronautics
IADC	Inter-Agency Debris Coordination Committee
IAEA	International Atomic Energy Agency
ICJ	International Court of Justice
ICSU	International Council of Scientific Unions
IGO	International Governmental Organization
ILA	International Law Association
ISO	International Organization for Standardization
ISS	International Space Station
ITSO/INTELSAT	International Telecommunications Satellite Organization
ITU	International Telecommunications Union
JAXA	Japanese Space Agency
JFSCC	Joint Force Space Component Commander
JSASS	Japan Society for Aeronautical and Space Sciences
JSpOC	Joint Space Operations Center (US)
kg	Kilogram
km	Kilometer
LEO	Low Earth Orbit
LTS	Long-term Sustainability
MEO	Middle Earth Orbit
MFA	Ministry of Foreign Affairs (China)
MIIT	Ministry of Industry and Information Technology (China)
mm	Millimeter

MOF	Ministry of Finance (China)
NASA	National Aeronautics and Space Administration (US)
NASDA	National Space Development Agency of Japan
NGSO	Non-Geostationary Orbit
nm	Nautical mile
NMI	NASA Management Instruction
NOAA	National Oceanic and Atmospheric Administration (US)
NPC	National People's Congress (China)
NRC	National Research Council (US)
NPRM	Notice of Proposed Rule Making
NSC	National Space Council (US)
NSP	National Space Policy (US)
NSPD	National Space Policy Directive (US)
NSS	NASA Safety Standard
ODMSP	Orbital Debris Mitigation Standard Practices (US)
ODPO	Orbital Debris Program Office
OMB	Office of Management and Budget
OOS	On-Orbit Servicing
OST	Outer Space Treaty
PCIJ	Permanent Court of International Justice
PECS	Plan for European Cooperating States
PLATO	Planetary Transits and Oscillations of Stars
RSA	Russian Space Agency
RRAMP	Re-entry Risk Assessment and Mitigation Plan
SASAC	State Owned Assets Supervision and Administration Commission (China
SASTIND	State Administration of Science, Technology, and Industry for National Defense (China)
SDA	State Data Association
SDARS	Satellite Digital Audio Radio System
SDMP	Space Debris Mitigation Plan
SDMR	Space Debris Mitigation Report
SKKP	Main Centre for Reconnaissance of Situation In Space (Russia SSA)
SPCS	Space Control Squadron
SPD	Space Policy Directive
SSA	Space Situational Awareness
SSC	Space Safety Coalition
SSN	Space Surveillance Network
SST	Space Surveillance and Tracking
STA	Science and Technology Agency (Japan)
STM	Space Traffic Management

SWE	Space Weather
TESS	Transiting Exoplanet Survey Satellite
TW&E	Threat Warning and Assessment
UCP	Unified Command Plan (US)
UN COPUOS	United Nations Committee on the Peaceful Uses of Outer Space
UN	United Nations
USD	United States Dollar
USSF	United States Space Force
USSPACECOM	United States Space Command
USSTRATCOM	United States Strategic Command

Introduction

Access for All

If you were to look at the shifting of the tectonic plates underneath our landmasses, you might be convinced that the distance between countries is expanding. While that may be physically true, the exact opposite is occurring technologically.[2] The result is that many countries that might otherwise be severely handicapped because of their nascent technological status have been able to achieve near-peer if not parity status, even if only sometimes in niche areas. One example is access to space, where countries which may lack infrastructure, technology, launch facilities, launch vehicles, or even the ability to manage their satellites once in space, can now do so if they simply have the desire and the financial resources to do so.

Ethiopia is a specific case of such an ability. As an economy, Ethiopia has a Gross Domestic Product[3] (GDP) of 96.108 billion USD (as of 2019). For context, the United States had a GDP of 19.39 Trillion for that same year.[4] [5] In terms of a competitive economy, the World Economic Forum put Ethiopia as the 126th most competitive nation out of 140 that were ranked.[6] Its economic problems are many, including extraordinary poverty for almost half of its 80 million person population, high food and other resource costs, drought, high illiteracy (approximately 49% of the population), rampant corruption and poor government policies.[7] And yet, in 2016, despite all of these challenges, Ethiopia established the Ethiopian Space Science and Technology Institute (ESSTI) intending to launch a satellite into space within 3–5 years.[8] In the shorter of the claimed

---

2 *How Far do Tectonic Plates Move Each Year?*, REFERENCE, https://www.reference.com/science/far-tectonic-plates-move-year-822add27f707b0cf (last visited Feb. 23, 2020).

3 Leslie Kramer, *What is GDP and Why is it So Important to Economists and Investors?*, INVESTOPEDIA, https://www.investopedia.com/ask/answers/what-is-gdp-why-its-important-to-economists-investors/ (last updated Dec. 2, 2019). Gross domestic product is a popular measurement used to track the health of a nation's economy and includes different variables to arrive at a general dollar value for everything that the country produces in goods and services over a period of time, which is then compared to previous time periods to give context.

4 U.S. GDP, GOOGLE, https://www.bing.com/search?q=us+gdp&form (search "U.S. GDP").

5 *Ethiopia*, THE WORLD BANK DATA, https://data.worldbank.org/country/ET (last visited Aug. 5, 2020).

6 *Ethiopia Competitiveness Rank*, TRADING ECONOMICS, https://tradingeconomics.com/ethiopia/competitiveness-rank (last visited Feb. 23, 2020).

7 *Major Problems Facing Ethiopia Today*, AFRICA W, https://www.africaw.com/major-problems-facing-ethiopia-today (last visited Jan. 20, 2020).

8 *Ethiopia Celebrates Launch of First Satellite*, PHYS.ORG (Dec. 20, 2019), https://phys.org/news/2019-12-ethiopia-celebrates-satellite.html.

© KONINKLIJKE BRILL NV, LEIDEN, 2023 | DOI:10.1163/9789004535848_002

timeframes, just three years, Ethiopia achieved its goal on 20 December 2019 with the launch of the ETRSS-1.[9]

Ethiopia did not achieve such a feat by being exceptionally technologically advanced or extraordinarily financially robust. Nor does it possess any exceptional space-centric infrastructure or any launch facilities or launch vehicles to speak of. Instead, Ethiopia managed to deliver its first-ever satellite into space by exploiting the training, facility, equipment, and financial support (upwards of USD 14 million) from China.[10] Despite being an arguably unlikely candidate to prioritize becoming a spacefaring nation, Ethiopia now has a functioning asset in space and under its control.[11]

This example demonstrates that ease of access to space is both a blessing and a danger. On the one hand, countries like Ethiopia stand a genuine chance of improving their economic development, achieving better planning for agricultural improvements, and potentially reducing the suffering of its population from drought and other natural disasters. But these benefits are not without potential cost beyond just Ethiopia. The ease of accessibility by more and more countries into space, including those like Ethiopia, has the accompanying risks of significantly increasing the catalog of debris entering and remaining in Earth's orbital environments. Meanwhile, unlike on Earth, the ramifications for increased pollutants in space are different because the ability to remove debris is considerably more challenging. On Earth, a piece of trash might be an eyesore or otherwise an irritant. But the remedy to its presence is simply to pick up the object and throw it in the nearest trash receptacle (and hopefully recycle it). For obvious reasons, the logistics of doing the same in space are exponentially more challenging.

We have known about the problem of debris for decades. It has been discussed as an eventuality among politicians, space agencies, lawyers, scientists, and other interested parties regularly since at least 1957, when the first mechanical space object (Sputnik) made its appearance on the 'grand stage.' The increasing debris population has been thoroughly documented ever since. Additionally, while warnings of the debris risk were being discussed early in the space race, little attention was paid until 1978, when scientists such as

9 *Ethiopia in Space*, GLOBALSECURITY.ORG, https://www.globalsecurity.org/space/world/ethiopia/index.html (last visited Feb. 23, 2020).

10 Elias Mesert, *Ethiopia's First Satellite Launch into Space by China*, ASSOCIATED PRESS NEWS (Dec. 20, 2019), https://apnews.com/37baf3f65b352e8b6480b43246ccbf77.

11 Peter Pedroncelli, *10 African Countries Which Have Launched Satellites into Space*, THE MOGULDOM NATION, (Jun. 20, 2019), https://moguldom.com/207725/10-african-countries-which-have-launched-satellites-into-space/.

Dr. Donald Kessler began sounding the alarm at the debris growth and corresponding potential risks. However, at least an additional 20 years passed before any notable steps toward mitigation were considered by States.

And while some States have taken steps to reduce their debris footprint, what is absent is a comprehensive set of internationally legally binding rules to force compliance. A series of voluntary guidelines instead have served as the *de facto* minimum standards, and States have taken it upon themselves to implement domestic limitations gratuitously. This is often not altruistic but merely a requirement for self-preservation to continue orbital operations. The 'three musketeers' mantra is true in this case, such that it is 'all for one and one for all' in space. If Athos were to lose operating access to space because of enormous debris fields, so too likely goes the opportunities of Porthos and Aramis. But for a problem that unsurprisingly impacts every spacefaring country and future hopeful, there remains no binding treaty to prevent debris growth.

The goal of this book is to illuminate how the most significant spacefaring countries, and one critical international organization, have approached the growing debris problem. In some cases, this may be only as signatories to the existing space law treaties. In many cases, the more mature spacefaring entities have made efforts to implement domestic law, policies, and programs to meet or exceed commitments made to the international community.

To advance the stated goal of illumination, three major elements will constitute the body of this analysis. First, this book will analyze the degree to which the problem of space debris exists and an examination of how serious the long-term effects can be. Second, this book reviews the body of efforts expended to create and advance the existing body of international space law, and space debris prevention and mitigation in particular. Last, with that high-level baseline, the third portion of this book will determine where legal gaps in the existing regulatory environment exist, and if so, whether customary international law has nonetheless been developed as a result of State practice and behavior. The conclusion will make some suggestions on what, if any, further legal measures could help protect this precious environment.

There is no single solution to the problem, nor will the efforts to prevent or mitigate debris ever likely reach a conclusion. Even small steps are often delayed for fear of overregulation and stymying potential technological developments that may save the environment when the time comes that it most needs saving. Some may even brush off this call to arms as 'fake news' and lambast those calling for action as just boys crying wolf.

Technology will indeed play a crucial and pivotal role in helping to solve this problem. We may be lucky that the technology of the future makes the threat less than it is today. But what technology cannot do is substitute for the clear understanding of the problem as it is now and the necessity for rule of law that must be at the forefront to stave off environmental disaster. A universal understanding can help level the playing field, illuminate the areas that have been the dark horse problems in the influx of debris, and bring to the fore the enormous lack of comprehensive implementation efforts that are causing this problem to proliferate. There is no limit to a desire to visualize the environment for how we want it to be and to dream of the technology we hope will one day be available to address this problem. Unfortunately, we are today limited to taking both our dreams and desires as just that and acknowledging the environment and risks to it as they are now.

If there is any 'benefit' to the amount of space debris in our orbits, it is that almost all global actors must acknowledge the debris' existence as having some effect on them one way or another. Whether a spacefaring country or a country dependent on others for the use of their satellites or services, the problem is common to everyone. The prospect of an inability to utilize LEO alone presents immediate problems with communications, weather, and navigation at a minimum. Beyond just the potential loss of LEO, it is foreseeable that a disaster in LEO could additionally hinder our ability to traverse through LEO. This could preclude our ability to access even more valuable orbits, such as MEO and GEO, where the debris problem has not yet shown significant impact due to their (relatively) limited use and specialized purposes.

If the international community alternatively chooses to ignore the severity of the problem, it will undoubtedly be unprepared to address the impact when it comes. Meanwhile, very near misses and unfortunate collisions that cause grave danger or damage to one or more satellites and the orbital environment have, and continue to, occur with frightening regularity. As Dr. Kessler warned, the impact on one satellite is but a foretelling of things to come. Entire orbital areas could be rendered unusable by a failure to control the amount of debris in the orbital space environment. Meanwhile, the technology to rehabilitate it may lag by many years. Passivity to address this problem is likely to have catastrophic outcomes.

CHAPTER 1

The Debris Problem

1 Introduction

At any given moment in space, there are millions of artificial objects circling Earth. Of those, only approximately 1,950 objects are known functioning satellites.[12] The remaining artificial objects are debris, estimated to total around 34,000 pieces larger than 10 centimeters (cm), 900,000 between 1 cm and 10 cm, and upwards of 128 million objects smaller than 1 cm.[13] This debris, both natural and unnatural, amounts to scattered junk and is orbiting in the many valuable orbital brackets of near-Earth space, including Low Earth Orbit (LEO), Middle Earth Orbit (MEO), Geostationary Orbit (GEO), High Earth Orbit (HEO) and populating graveyard orbits (See Figure 1).[14] [15]

The increase in the amount of space debris is not surprising. The engagement in space operations by governments worldwide, like the opportunities available to Ethiopia, continues to increase. And while there are currently only nine countries and the European Space Agency that have demonstrated independent orbital launch capabilities, the payloads that these vehicles carry are by no means limited to those nine.[16] Instead, utilizing the many options provided by these launch-capable countries, already an additional 68 countries have engaged in some form of space operations as countries are finding more and

12 *Space Debris by the Numbers*, EUROPEAN SPACE AGENCY, https://www.esa.int/Safety_Security/Space_Debris/Space_debris_by_the_numbers (last updated Feb. 2020).

13 *Id.*

14 The three most commonly discussed orbits are GEO, which according to NASA is greater than 35,780 kilometers (km) from Earth. The Mid-Earth Orbit (MEO) is approximately between 2,000 and 35,780 km from Earth, and Low-Earth Orbit (LEO) is approximately between 180 km and 2,000 km from Earth. The area of greatest congestion and high-risk particles is in the LEO orbit. Holli Riebeek, *Catalog of Earth Satellite Orbits*, NASA EARTH OBSERVATORY (Sept. 4, 2009), http://Earthobservatory.nasa.gov/Features/OrbitsCatalog.

15 *Space Debris by the Numbers, supra* note 12. *See also* Nivedita Raju, *A Proposal for a Ban on Destructive Anti-Satellite Testing: A Role for the European Union?*, NON-PROLIFERATION & DISARMAMENT PAPERS, no. 74, April 2021, at 5, https://www.sipri.org/sites/default/files/2021-04/eunpdc_no_74.pdf.

16 International Space Activities, *Launching Countries*, SPACEPOLICYONLINE.COM (Dec 9, 2020, 5:22 PM ET), https://spacepolicyonline.com/topics/international-space-activities/ (last visited Jun 17, 2020).

© KONINKLIJKE BRILL NV, LEIDEN, 2023 | DOI:10.1163/9789004535848_003

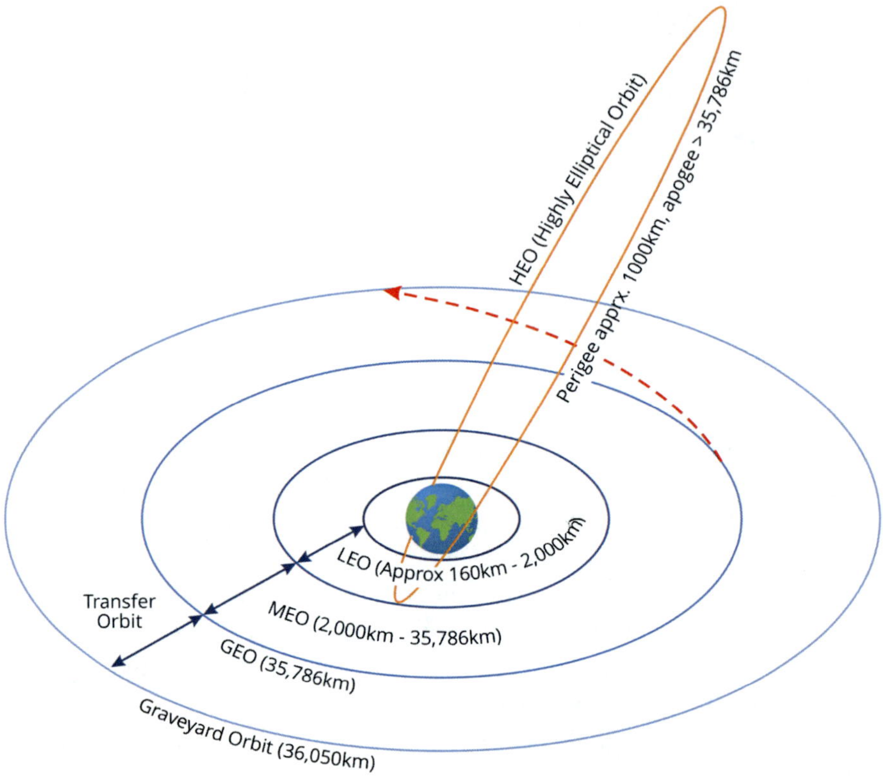

FIGURE 1 Visual depiction of the four main orbital areas, including the graveyard orbit above GEO, beginning at 36,050 km and beyond.

more ways to have active satellites operating in space.[17] Furthermore, the future is very bright for new applications, with the International Telecommunications Union (ITU) and the U.S. Federal Communications Commission's (FCC) applications for new spacecraft numbering approximately 107,000 in just the next ten years alone. The potential increase in the number of operating satellites, and the inevitable corresponding debris, is quite astounding.[18]

The consequence of the ease of accessibility to space has had a significant impact on the growth of debris orbiting Earth. The unfortunate cluttering of

17 *Satellites by Countries and Organizations*, N2YO.COM, https://www.n2yo.com/satellites/?c=&t=country (last visited Jan. 21, 2020).

18 Daniel L. Oltrogge, *The Contributions of Commercial Best Practices to the Global Space Governance Continuum*, Advanced Maui Optical and Space Surveillance Technologies Conference 3 (2020), https://amostech.com/TechnicalPapers/2020/SSA-SDA/Oltrogge.pdf.

the space environment, particularly in some of the most used orbits like LEO, has often resulted from irresponsible debris-creating actions by States, and/or a lack of recognition during early spacefaring activities of the problems associated with the accumulation of space junk. But the danger is extreme, with these debris particles flying around at extraordinary speeds, capable of destroying or disabling satellites and threatening the lives of astronauts operating in space on impact.[19] Some predictions put the estimate of close calls per year in the most congested orbital regimes in the next ten years at approximately 2.5 million annually.[20] Even worse, these estimates also predict over 40 actual collisions will occur annually if there is no improvement in the debris environment.[21] What to do about it, however, has remained a contentious point of debate around the world.

1.1 *Early Recognition of the Risk of Space Debris*

Before the early 1980s, States considered the possibility that the growing debris environment in space could hamper the future of navigation and use. Dr. Kessler and others had long since made public statements warning about the security of the space environment. But the expanse of space led to a generally dismissive attitude to how serious the problem was or could become. Instead, on balance, the size of space was believed to be capable of absorbing a huge number of debris before a serious threat might come to fruition. Therefore, a cavalier approach was taken toward the likelihood of a problem arising and the risk assessed as quite low.

Several reasons bolstered the legitimacy of this belief. Among them was that in the 1950s, only two countries could even launch satellites in the first place. Moreover, early space objects naturally did not remain in orbit for long periods. For example, Sputnik, after just 92 days in orbit, entered low-Earth atmosphere and disintegrated on 4 January 1958.[22] It was thought that this would be the likely outcome for most space objects since initial orbits into LEO were at very low altitude resulting in an atmospheric drag on the object affecting them very rapidly. Thus, over a long enough period of time, operators assumed

---

19 Because of the high impact speed between orbiting objects in space, debris as small as 0.2 millimeters (mm) poses real threats to Human Space Flight (EVA suit penetration, Shuttle window replacement, et cetera.) and other critical national space assets. *See Active Debris Removal Technologies*, SMALL BUS. INNOVATION RES., https://www.sbir.gov/content/active-debris-removal-technologies (last visited Feb. 28, 2016).

20 Oltrogge, *supra* note 18 at 3.

21 *Id.*

22 YANEK MIECZKOWSKI, EISENHOWER'S SPUTNIK MOMENT: THE RACE FOR SPACE AND WORLD PRESTIGE 18 (2013).

most, if not all, materials would inevitably decay and be destroyed in Earth's atmosphere. However, these theories did not appear to account for the advent of more spacefaring countries, advanced technology, and utilization of much higher altitudes in LEO and above, coupled with the opportunities presented by private companies. Space debris growth theories thus had to adapt to the growing congestion of debris developing in space and accept the reality that something would have to be done sooner rather than later if the environment was to be preserved.

'Sooner' unfortunately came in 1986, when a rocket body from an Ariane-1 rocket orbiting in LEO exploded and sent an estimated cloud of 492 large debris pieces into the environment.[23] This occurrence, among others, prompted a series of increased efforts by space organizations such as the National Aeronautics and Space Administration (NASA), the European Space Agency (ESA), the United Nations and the United Nations Committee on the Peaceful Use of Outer Space (UN COPUOS), and others to make concerted efforts to begin unified acknowledgment of the international need to take more significant steps to stem the threat to the space environment. Discussed more in Chapter 3, efforts of the United Nations and the Inter-Agency Debris Coordination Committee (IADC) made significant strides toward at least some understanding and actions among interested States through recognition of the IADC Space Debris Mitigation Guidelines (hereafter IADC Debris Mitigation Guidelines) endorsed by UN COPUOS in 2007.[24]

Despite these initial efforts, these guidelines did not mandate adherence nor provide for any enforcement mechanism. At best, the resolutions flourished with color but were lacking in substance. By 2011, as the seriousness became progressively evident, the US National Research Council (NRC) was requested to conduct a study to review NASA's efforts to address debris in space, both natural and artificial, and make recommendations whether the efforts of NASA were appropriate or should be vectored elsewhere.[25] Their analysis included a review of national and international models on space debris. They surmised that

23 Nicholas Johnson, *Origin of the Inter-Agency Space Debris Coordination Committee*, 16 ORBITAL DEBRIS Q. NEWS 4 (2012).

24 U.N. OFF. OF OUTER SPACE AFFAIRS, SPACE DEBRIS MITIGATION GUIDELINES OF THE COMMITTEE ON THE PEACEFUL USES OF OUTER SPACE, at III, U.N. Sales No. V.09-8857 (2010) *available at* https://www.unoosa.org/pdf/publications/st_space_49E.pdf.

25 NAT. RES. COUNCIL, COMMITTEE FOR THE ASSESSMENT OF NASA'S ORBITAL DEBRIS PROGRAMS, LIMITING FUTURE COLLISION RISK TO SPACECRAFT: AN ASSESSMENT OF NASA'S METEOROID AND ORBITAL DEBRIS PROGRAMS viii (2011).

even if complying with a 25-year deorbiting rule[26] or placing satellites in graveyard orbits[27] that will not generally interfere with the most valuable LEO, MEO and GEO orbits[28] within 25 years of end-of-mission, the amount of

26 This is a standard commonly acknowledged among spacefaring Nations, often seen reflected in some fashion through national legislations and domestic agency rulemaking as a standard practice. The '25-year' rule was originally proposed by the IADC in 2007. The IADC settled on 25 years as a 'reasonable and appropriate time' that space objects could remain in space post-mission without posing an unnecessary risk for collision and corresponding environmental debris growth and ideally to prevent them from orbiting in space 'forever.' As such, the IADC encouraged Nations to implement the rule that would establish an expectation among operators that post-mission, the operator will have placed the spacecraft in an orbit which would, through atmospheric drag and other environmental factors, cause the space object to otherwise decay into the atmosphere and burn up, or be placed in a location (such as a graveyard orbit) where the space object posed no further threat to other objects, within 25 years. *See* IADC SPACE DEBRIS MITIGATION GUIDELINES, INTER-AGENCY SPACE DEBRIS COORDINATION COMMITTEE, REVISION 3, para. 5.3.2. (2021), https://www.iadc-home.org/documents_public/file_down/id/5251.

27 Specifically, graveyard orbits are used when the change in velocity required to perform a de-orbit maneuver is too large. In general, graveyard orbits lie away from common operational orbits, such as the super-synchronous orbit that is well above or outside of the LEO, MEO, or GEO orbits so as not to interfere with those valuable orbits. The movement of satellites into these graveyard orbits is meant to reduce the probability that a satellite which is otherwise not able to be deorbited by atmospheric methods will collide with operational spacecraft. *See* Louis de Gouyon Matignon, *Parking Orbit and Graveyard Orbit*, SPACE LEGAL ISSUES (May 7, 2019), https://www.spacelegalissues.com/parking-orbit-and-graveyard-orbit/.

28 These orbits are extremely valuable for different reasons based on different uses. The highest, GEO, is so valuable because an object in GEO travelling at an altitude of 35,786 km at a speed of 3 km per second can hold a 'stationary' or 'fixed' position over Earth by rotating at the same speed as Earth. This can allow satellites, such as telecommunications satellites that must be above one particular place on Earth to properly operate, to maintain a fixed position. Additionally, as few as three equally-spaced satellites in GEO can provide near-global coverage. LEO, on the other hand, is relatively close to Earth's surface and satellites often do not need to follow specific paths, like in GEO. This allows them to have many more available routes. Additionally, it can be used effectively for satellite imaging because of its close proximity to Earth, which also allows for reduced latency for a host of other applications. It is also far cheaper to send something into LEO than to reach GEO allowing LEO to be much more cost-efficient. *See* Types of Orbits, Geostationary Orbit (GEO), THE EUROPEAN SPACE AGENCY (Mar. 30, 2020), https://www.esa.int/Enabling_Support/Space_Transportation/Types_of_orbits#GEO. *See also* GEO VS LEO—Quick Facts, AVANT, https://www.avantiplc.com/wp-content/uploads/2020/09/GEO-vs-LEO_Quick-Facts_Avanti-Communications.pdf. MEO represents a middle-ground, with varying advantages of both GEO and LEO. It allows access to high altitude with better reception than GEO satellites. It also hosts most global-positioning systems and has greater communications range as a result of its orbit. It can also provide global coverage with less total satellites (approximately 12) than required in LEO to cover the same area. This provides the advantage of offering reduced latency compared to GEO satellites and greater ground

debris created would continue to grow despite even the strictest adherence to the mitigation guidelines.[29] Their analysis, and their review of the available data, made it evident that "the rate of collision [in LEO below 2,000 km] had already reached the point that debris would be generated faster than it could be removed by natural forces, mainly atmospheric drag."[30] Furthermore, based on the most recent model of NASA, not only would it be necessary that nothing new be created, "it would be necessary to remove five large, intact objects per year over the next 100 years to prevent this future growth in the orbital debris population, assuming that 90 percent of future launches follow NASA's current mitigation guidelines including that no further explosions or other major releases of debris occur."[31] In short, in even the best of scenarios, at least the LEO environment in space is arguably already, or inevitably will be, supersaturated with dangerous debris.

In 2013, based on efforts initiated in 2009, the IADC also undertook a serious analysis of the problem presented by the debris accumulation in LEO. Their analysis also resulted in the conclusion that current mitigation efforts in the international space community, including those of their own body and the United Nations, "may be insufficient to stabilize the future orbital debris environment."[32] As such, they further concluded that mitigation was, if the current debris scenario continued, insufficient as a sole measure and "additional measures should be considered to better preserve the near-Earth space environment for future generations."[33]

It is also worth noting a few key points about the IADC analysis, which is a cautionary tale on the true magnitude of the threat. The presumptions within the analysis presented a self-proclaimed 'best-case scenario.' The assumptions identified in the IADC report, *Stability of the Future LEO Environment*, include that future launch traffic would be represented by the historical cycle of launches from 2001–2009.[34] Second, the mitigation measures were presumed

---

coverage than LEO, as well as its ability to access polar regions better, makes it an ideal middle-ground solution to a number of problems facing operators. *See Medium Earth Orbit Satellites*, CAPACITY (Dec. 31, 2010, 7:00 pm), https://www.capacitymedia.com/article/29ot47zfua7b7uq4z7g1s/news/medium-earth-orbit-satellites. *See also Is MEO Poised for New Growth as Satellite Market Shifts?*, KRATOS, https://www.kratosdefense.com/constellations-podcast/articles/is-meo-poised-for-new-growth-as-satellite-market-shifts.

29 NAT. RES. COUNCIL, *supra* note 25 at 10.

30 *Id.* at viii.

31 *Id.* at 13.

32 Inter-Agency Space Debris Coordination Comm., *Stability of the Future LEO Environment, IADC-12-08 Rev. 1*, at 1 (Jan. 2013).

33 *Id.*

34 *Id.* at 2.

to be well-implemented, such that "90% [complied] with the post-mission disposal 25-year rule[35] for payloads and a 100% success for passivation (no future explosion) were presumed.[36] In addition, an eight-year mission lifetime for payloads launched after 1 May 2009 was uniformly adopted."[37] It is not a stretch to imagine that with the increase in spacefaring actors, and advances in technology, it is unlikely that the launches between 2001–2009 will reflect that of the future, particularly with the increase of private operators in space. What is more, rarely has the best-case scenario ever become a reality in a given situation.

Still, by 2014, in the Fifty-Seventh session of UN COPUOS, it was recorded by members of the body that "the Committee noted the increasing amount of space debris."[38] Though satisfied with the acceptance of the mitigation recommendations from the previous session, there is ample evidence that the problem continues to grow. One such model scenario examined in 2019 provides support for this increase, particularly in LEO, despite mitigation efforts. The Southampton study found that even if operators were within a 90% compliance with the 25-year rule, the rate of injection is at least on par with the rate of decay at that compliance rate (if not even higher).[39] As such, any compliance rate at 90% at best meets equilibrium, whereas anything less than 90% compliance rate increases space debris in LEO, destabilizing the environment even faster.[40]

This theory was tested by Hugh G. Lewis at the University of Southampton Astronautics Research Group, which extended the typical simulation model for debris growth of 100–200 years in LEO orbit to a full 1,000 years.[41] In the analysis, his team found that the shorter of the two timeframes was failing to accurately reflect the most likely projections of the future debris populations in LEO for debris 10 cm or larger.[42] Using the Debris Analysis and Monitoring

35 The 25-year rule is discussed more in-depth in Chapter 8, section 4.1.

36 Inter-Agency Space Debris Coordination Comm., Rev. 1, *supra* note 32 at 2.

37 *Id.* at 2.

38 General Assembly, Rep. of Comm. on the Peaceful Uses of Outer Space, on Its Fifty-Seventh Session, U.N. Doc. A/69/20 at 41 (Jun. 2014), *available at* http://www.unoosa.org/pdf/gadocs/A_69_20E.pdf [hereafter Rep. on the Fifty-seventh session].

39 Hugh G. Lewis, Professor of Engineering and Physical Sciences and member of the Astronautics Research Group at the University of Southampton, paper presented at the First International Orbital Debris Conference, Houston, Texas: Understanding Long-term Orbital Debris Population Dynamics (2019).

40 *Id.*

41 *Id.* at 1.

42 *Id.* at 1, 3.

Architecture to the Geosynchronous Environment (DAMAGE) evolution model, the team actually found that the current methods of minimizing debris populations, through the use of graveyard orbits for example, had the potential to exacerbate the debris problem in LEO.[43] The team noted that in the first 200 years, the simulations indicated a relatively stable, though constant, growth rate of 5.48 objects per year, resulting in an overall increase in the orbital population of 13.88%.[44] However, when the system was left to run over a longer period of time, it showed that in the last 200 years of the projected period, the debris population grew at a rate of 48.28 objects per year, and the total orbital population increased by 134.1%.[45] One of the most significant contributors to this problem was the misunderstanding that the placement of objects into a graveyard orbit still allowed them a crossing trajectory into altitudes in lower LEO orbit (below 700km) for at least 25 years of the timeframe.[46] The findings of the 1000-year simulation were that compliance with the 25-year rule in the higher LEO altitudes still resulted in a significant number of catastrophic collisions over a 1,000 year time frame.[47] What is more, the effects of those upper collisions caused similar outcomes in lower altitudes of LEO as well, exacerbating the problem even further.[48]

2 Space Debris Defined

None of the existing space treaties provide a clear and concise definition of space debris. As a result of this omission, the spacefaring community has come up with some consensus on a helpful definition. This has primarily resulted from importing secondary sources, which has been very useful to fill the vacuum created by the absence of guidance within the international treaties. Secondary sources have also contributed to the discussion among interested parties within the space community. In August of 1994, the International Law Association (ILA) in Buenos Ares offered one of the first proposals for formal acceptance of a definition. The intent was that the proposals be submitted at the next session of UN COPUOS. That report of the ILA, touted as "the first concrete proposal for a legal instrument on space debris", defined space debris

43 *Id.* at 1, 9.
44 *Id.* at 1, 6.
45 *Id.* at 1, 6.
46 *Id.* at 1, 8.
47 *Id.* at 1, 10.
48 *Id.* at 1, 10.

as "man-made objects in outer space, other than active or otherwise useful satellites, when no change can reasonably be expected in these conditions in the foreseeable future."[49] However, some delegations did not feel that definition was adequate and proposed at the UN COPUOS meeting a more robust definition. It was suggested in the 12 August 1994 report to the United Nations General Assembly (hereafter UN General Assembly) that space debris should be defined as "all man-made objects in Earth's orbit or reentering the dense layers of the atmosphere which are non-functional with no reasonable expectation of assuming or resuming their intended functions or any other functions for which they are or can be authorized, including their fragments and parts."[50] At that same meeting, other delegations felt that it was inappropriate for UN COPUOS to establish a definition at the time since their own subcommittee, the Scientific and Technical Sub-Committee of UN COPUOS,[51] had yet to engage thoughtfully on the subject.[52] By 1999, the Scientific and Technical Sub-Committee of UN COPUOS had taken up the issue of defining space debris and proposed its definition for general understanding among Nations. It proposed space debris be defined as "all-man-made objects, including their fragments and parts, in Earth's orbit or reentering the dense layers of the atmosphere that are non-functional with no reasonable expectation of their being able to assume or resume their intended functions or any other functions for which they are or can be authorized."[53]

This offering was a major step in developing a 'general consensus' on the definition of space debris since it was one of the earliest written definitions

---

49 Joyeeta Chatterjee, *Legal Issues Relating to Unauthorized Space Debris Remediation*, 65 INT'L. ASTRONAUTICAL CONGRESS 1, 3 (2014), *available at* http://www.iislweb.org/docs/Diederiks2014a.pdf (citing Karl-Heinz Bockstiegel, *ILA Draft Convention on Space Debris*, 44 GERMAN J. AIR & SPACE L. 29 (1995)).

50 UN COPUOS Report to UN GENERAL ASSEMBLY, Supplement, at 18, U.N. Doc. A/49/20 (Aug. 12, 1994), https://www.unoosa.org/pdf/gadocs/A_49_20E.pdf.

51 The Committee on the Peaceful Uses of Outer Space has two subsidiary bodies. One is the Scientific and Technical Sub-Committee, which provides specific technical and scientific advice to the greater body, which was established in 1961, two years after its parent UN COPUOS was formed. The other is the Legal Sub-Committee which discusses legal questions related to the exploration and use of outer space, including legal mechanisms relating to space debris mitigation. *Committee on the Peaceful Uses of Outer Space*, UNITED NATIONS OFFICE FOR OUTER SPACE, http://www.unoosa.org/oosa/en/ourwork/copuos/index.html (last visited Aug 19, 2020).

52 UN COPUOS Report to UN GENERAL ASSEMBLY, *supra* note 50 at 18.

53 Comm. On the Peaceful Uses of Outer Space, Rep. of Sci. and Tech. Subcomm. On Its Thirty-Second Session, U.N. Doc. A/AC.105/605, at 17–18 (Feb. 24, 1995), *available at* http://www.unoosa.org/pdf/reports/ac105/AC105_605E.pdf.

by the United Nations. Other organizations were also developing their own definitions to further their own understanding of how to classify space debris and attempt to influence the general consensus. For example, in 2001 the International Academy of Astronautics (IAA) proposed a very comprehensive definition that space debris is "any man-made earth-orbiting object which is non-functional with no reasonable expectation of assuming or resuming its intended function, or any other function for which it is or can be expected to be authorized, including fragments and parts thereof. Orbital debris includes non-operational spacecraft, spent rocket bodies, material released during planned space operations, and fragments generated by satellite and upper-stage breakup due to explosions and collisions."[54]

By 2007, in the report to the UN General Assembly, UN COPUOS had incorporated a definition of space debris which represented an amalgamation of recommendations from various organizations.[55] In the annex to the report, UN COPUOS defined space debris as "all-man-made objects, including fragments and elements thereof, in Earth's orbit or reentering the atmosphere, that are non-functional."[56] Since then, many states have incorporated definitions of space debris into their own national legislation. While some reflect the United Nations definition, significant diversity remains between some states. For example, in the United States, NASA has defined space debris as "all-man-made objects in orbit about Earth which no longer serve a useful purpose."[57] In just a simple comparison to the UN COPUOS definition, a distinction can quickly be seen by the words used by UN COPUOS of "non-functional" contrasted against

54 Walter Flury & Jean-Michel Contant, *The Updated IAA Position Paper on Orbital Debris*, 2 PROC. OF THE THIRD EUR. CONF. ON SPACE DEBRIS 841, 842 (2001), *available at* http://adsabs.harvard.edu/full/2001ESASP.473.841F.

55 Part of the report submitted by the Scientific and Technical Sub-Committee of UN COPUOS was also based on the work of the IADC. This organization was formed in 1993 as a joint effort of ESA, Russia, the United States, and Japan. Some of their work in this area, the IADC Debris Mitigation Guidelines, were adopted by consensus of the Steering Group in October 2002 and were presented to the Scientific and Technical Sub-Committee of UN COPUOS in February 2003. These later served as a foundation for the development of the UN COPUOS Space Debris Mitigation Guidelines, which were adopted by UN COPUOS and later endorsed by the UN General Assembly resolution 62/217 in 2007. Inter-Agency Space Debris Coordination Comm., *20 Years of IADC: 51st Session of the Scientific and Technical Subcommittee*, at 3 (Feb. 2014), http://www.iadc-online.org/Documents/IADC-2014-04,%2051st_UN_COPUOS_STSC.pdf.

56 General Assembly, Rep. of Comm. On the Peaceful Uses of Outer Space, on Its Sixty-Second Session, U.N. Doc. A/62/20 (2007), *available at* http://www.unoosa.org/pdf/gadocs/A_62_20E.pdf.

57 *Frequently Asked Questions: Orbital Debris*, NASA ORBITAL DEBRIS PROGRAM OFFICE, https://orbitaldebris.jsc.nasa.gov/faq/ (last visited February 28, 2020).

NASA's use of the words "no longer serves a useful purpose."[58] In this singular case alone, the lack of an internationally legally binding definition can have immediately evident and widespread impacts on the way States behave.

3 Space Debris Creation

The issue of space debris was largely inconsequential when man first endeavored to travel among the stars. In the mid-1950s, only two countries were realistically within range of potentially launching the first satellites into space; the United States and the Union of Soviet Socialist Republics (hereafter Soviet Union from 1922 to 1991[59]).[60] As is well known now, the Soviet Union was the first to be successful when, on 4 October 1957, Sputnik was launched into orbit.[61] By January of 1958, Sputnik had deteriorated in orbit and reentered the atmosphere, leaving nothing of its prior existence in space.[62] That same year the United States launched its own satellite into space, Explorer 1, on 1 January

58 The United Nations defines space debris as "all man-made objects, including fragments and elements thereof, in earth's orbit or re-entering the atmosphere, that are non-functional." U.N. Off. of Outer Space Affairs, Space Debris Mitigation Guidelines of the Committee on the Peaceful Uses of Outer Space, *supra* note 24 at III. Contrast that with NASA, which defines space debris as "all man-made objects in orbit about Earth which no longer serve a useful purpose." *Frequently Asked Questions: Orbital Debris*, *supra* note 57.

59 The Soviet Union, a union of 15 states including Russia, was established in 1922, following the Russian Revolution of 1917. The term 'Soviet Union' and 'Soviets' is appropriate for discussions prior to 25 December 1991. Since that date, Russia has stood alone as an independent State. On that date, the flag of the Soviet Union, the hammer and sickle, was lowered from the Kremlin in Moscow and replaced by the Russian tricolor flag. Mikhail Gorbachev resigned as President of the Soviet Union, and Boris Yeltsin was appointed President of the independent Russian State. *See* Celine, *Difference Between Soviet Union and Russia*, DifferenceBetween.net, http://www.differencebetween.net/miscellaneous/politics/political-institutions/difference-between-soviet-union-and-russia/ (last visited Dec. 7, 2021). *See also* The Collapse of the Soviet Union, U.S. Dep't of State, Office of the Historian, https://history.state.gov/milestones/1989-1992/collapse-soviet-union (last visited Dec. 7, 2021).

60 The White House, National Space Policy of the United States of America, 4 (June 28, 2010), *available at* https://obamawhitehouse.archives.gov/sites/default/files/national_space_policy_6-28-10.pdf.

61 *Sputnik Launched*, History (2009), http://www.history.com/this-day-in-history/sputnik-launched.

62 *Id.*

1958.[63] With that, the space race had begun. And, as the space race between the two superpowers heated up, debris began accumulating as well. Explorer 1 did not reenter Earth's atmosphere for over a decade after its launch, finally decaying in the atmosphere on 31 March 1970.[64]

Since then, the amount of space debris has increased exponentially for several reasons. First is the collection of formerly operating satellites which are now defunct but not properly disposed of. NASA currently estimates that approximately 2,400 non-operational spacecraft of variable sizes are still in Earth's orbit.[65] Second, there are numerous vehicle stages used to launch satellites and spacecraft into orbit that were also not properly disposed of. According to NASA, there are approximately 1,700 stages still in orbit, ranging in mass from 100 kg to as large as eight metric tons.[66] A third cause is from smaller parts of launch vehicles that break away during some point between the launch and placement of the spacecraft into its proper orbit. This debris often included weights, straps, and even covers to certain parts of the spacecraft. While modern launches have now mitigated much of this type of debris, the prior existing pieces before design advancement are still pollutants in various orbits.[67]

Last, but among the greatest threats, is debris caused by fragmentation of spacecraft and component parts. The primary causes of this type of debris are generally the result of explosions, collisions, or anomalous events.[68] Arguably the most mysterious anomalous event was the Cosmic Background Explorer, which released 76 debris pieces of at least 10 cm in size each. Meanwhile, the satellite still remained functional and the mystery of what caused the satellite to dispel the debris is unsolved.[69] Collisions or explosions round out the threat of fragmentation, due to either one spacecraft colliding with another or explosions due to remaining fuel violently expelling. One of the more notable explosions was caused by the breakup of the STEP II hydrazine propulsion system in 1996 at an orbit of 586 km.[70] During the STEP II mission, the hydrazine

---

63 Elizabeth Howell, *Explorer 1: The First U.S. Satellite*, SPACE.COM (Aug. 11, 2017), http://www.space.com/17825-explorer-1.html.

64 *Id.*

65 NASA, *Orbital Debris Management and Risk Mitigation*, at 6, https://www.nasa.gov/pdf/692076main_Orbital_Debris_Management_and_Risk_Mitigation.pdf (last visited Dec. 11, 2019).

66 *Id.*

67 *Id.*

68 *Id.*

69 *Id.* at 8.

70 Mika McKinnon, *A History of Garbage in Space*, GIZMODO (May 7, 2014, 7:00 PM), http://space.gizmodo.com/a-history-of-garbage-in-space-1572783046.

auxiliary propulsion system (HAPS) failed to burn all of the fuel to depletion leaving hydrazine and nitrogen in the tanks of the stage rocket (and subsequently caused the rocket to fail to achieve the intended orbit as well).[71] While the cause of the explosion remains a mystery, the resulting explosion from the remaining fuel was estimated to create over 700 pieces of debris which, at the altitude of explosion, will likely remain for decades.[72] A second major explosion, this one intentional by China, was caused when China successfully conducted an anti-satellite (ASAT) missile system test on their own weather satellite in January of 2007.[73] Estimates put the resulting debris total in excess of 37,000 pieces of varying size into LEO.[74] Because of the altitude of the explosion, it is estimated that the resulting debris could also last for decades or even centuries.[75] A third event, one of the most significant collision events between satellites, occurred between the Iridium 33 and Cosmos 2251 satellites in 2009.[76] This event was estimated to create almost 2,000 large debris pieces and untold amounts of smaller debris[77] Most recently, India has also joined

---

71 Email from Paul Maley to John C. Broman, Jr., Orbital Launch Services Project Office (June 26, 1996, 3:02 PM), http://www.satobs.org/seesat/Jun-1996/0299.html (last visited Aug. 6, 2020).

72 McKinnon, *supra* note 70.

73 *Chinese Anti-satellite Test Creates Most Severe Orbital Debris Cloud in History*, ORBITAL DEBRIS Q. NEWS, April 2007, at 1, 2–3, http://orbitaldebris.jsc.nasa.gov/newsletter/pdfs/ODQNv11i2.pdf.

74 T.S. Kelso, Analysis of the 2007 Chinese ASAT Test and the Impact of its Debris on the Space Environment, 2007 AMOS Conference, https://celestrak.com/publications/AMOS/2007/AMOS-2007.pdf.

75 On 11 January 2007, the Chinese successfully tested an anti-satellite system on its own meteorological spacecraft, the Fengyun-1C (960kg/2,116lbs), which was orbiting at approximately 845 km above Earth. It was struck by a ballistic interceptor, and the debris created extended from approximately 200 km to 4000 km in altitude. This is significant since the altitude at which this debris exists is commonly transited by hundreds of operational spacecrafts that also fly at an altitude known for long duration orbits, from decades to centuries, since Earth's gravitational pull is not significant enough to draw it into the atmosphere. At the time of the incident, the debris created was singularly responsible for comprising over 15% of the known debris in orbit at the time. *Chinese Anti-satellite Test Creates Most Severe Orbital Debris Cloud in History*, *supra* note 73 at 1, 2–3.

76 NASA, *Satellite Collision Leaves Significant Debris Cloud*, ORBITAL DEBRIS Q. NEWS, April 2009, at 1, https://orbitaldebris.jsc.nasa.gov/quarterly-news/pdfs/odqnv13i2.pdf.

77 Unlike the Chinese ASAT Test of 2007, this involved the inadvertent collision of two very large satellites on 10 February 2009 at an altitude of approximately 790 km. *Id.* This incident was unforeseen and therefore the functioning Iridium 33 satellite (560kg/1,234lbs), a US communication satellite, could not take evasive maneuvers to avoid the Cosmos 2251 satellite (900kg/1,984lbs), a decommissioned Russian communications satellite. *Id.* If the word 'lucky' can be fairly used, it is estimated that the objects did not collide head-on (which could have created tens of thousands of debris particles) but instead at a right

what was previously only a trio of ASAT capable countries, launching its own ASAT test on 27 March 2019 against its own specifically placed satellite.[78] This event, because it was conducted at an altitude of approximately 300 km, did cause the debris cloud impact to be more minimal than previous tests.[79] The Indian government implied that most of the fragments would be gone in less than 45 days both as a result of the low altitude of the test and also how it was conducted.[80] Despite these assurances and evidence that much of the debris did deteriorate, some of the pieces still ended up at altitudes at or exceeding 1,000 kilometers, crossing even into the path of the International Space Station. This only makes clearer that even the best plans rarely end up being as successful as intended.[81]

Those are only a few of the many debris-creating incidents that have occurred in the various orbits. Aside from those four, NASA estimates that between 1961 and 2018, there have been more than 242 satellite fragmentations and 78 anomalous events. NASA specifically noted that the breakups and anomalous[82] debris

---

angle and on top of the Iridium satellite, thus leaving Iridium 33 largely in-tact. *Id.* Still, it was estimated by the United States Space Surveillance Network (SSN) that at least 528 pieces of debris from Iridium 33 and 1,347 from Cosmos 2251 greater than 10 cm were produced. *Id.* And, while a few pieces have decayed into the atmosphere, it is believed that over half of the debris will remain in orbit for at least 100 years. *Id. See also* Brian Weeden, *2009 Iridium-Cosmos Collision Fact Sheet*, SECURE WORLD FOUNDATION, http://swfound.org/media/6575/swf_iridium_cosmos_collision_fact_sheet_updated_2012.pdf (last updated Nov. 10, 2010).

78 Express Web Desk, *What is Mission Shakti—ASAT?*, THE INDIAN EXPRESS, (Mar. 27, 2019, 3:44 PM), https://indianexpress.com/article/what-is/mission-shakti-asat-missile-5645166/.

79 *Space Debris from Anti-Satellite Test to "Vanish" in 45 Days: Defence Research Body Chief*, NDTV (Mar. 28, 2019, 6:03 PM), https://www.ndtv.com/india-news/mission-shakti-space-debris-from-anti-satellite-test-to-vanish-in-45-days-defence-research-body-chie-2014301.

80 *Id.*

81 Loren Grush, *More than 50 Pieces of Debris Remain in Space after India Destroyed its own Satellite in March*, THE VERGE (Aug. 8, 2019, 1:27 PM), https://www.theverge.com/2019/8/8/20754816/india-asat-test-mission-shakti-space-debris-tracking-air-force. *See also* Ashley J. Tellis, *India's ASAT Test: An Incomplete Success*, CARNEGIE ENDOWMENT FOR INTERNATIONAL PEACE (Apr. 15, 2019), https://carnegieendowment.org/2019/04/15/india-s-asat-test-incomplete-success-pub-78884 (last visited Aug. 6, 2020).

82 NASA, in this case, defines an anomalous event as the "unplanned separation, usually at low velocity, of one or more detectable objects from a satellite, which remains essentially intact. Anomalous events can be caused by material deterioration of items such as thermal blankets, protective shields, solar panels, or by the impact of small particles." *See* PHILLIP D. ANZ-MEADOR, JOHN N. OPIELA, DEBRA SHOOTS & J.C. LIOU, HISTORY OF ON-ORBIT SATELLITE FRAGMENTATIONS 3 (5th ed. 2018), https://ntrs.nasa.gov/archive/nasa/casi.ntrs.nasa.gov/20180008451.pdf (last visited Mar. 3, 2023).

have accounted for 65% of the total catalog growth observed since 2007.[83] The significance of these events, and their unfortunately common occurrences, cannot be understated. Between August 2015 and March 2016, NASA additionally noted that there were four significant satellite breakups which accounted for over a hundred pieces of debris.[84] This included the Russian *Fregat* Upper Stage breakup on 3–4 August 2015, accounting for at least 24 pieces of debris,[85] the US National Oceanic and Atmospheric Administration (NOAA)-16 satellite breakup in November 2015 accounting for at least 136 pieces of debris,[86] the Russian *Briz-M* Core stage fragmentation on 16 January 2016 accounting for at least ten pieces,[87] and the Russian Sistema Obespecheniya Zapuska motor on 26 March 2016 accounting for at least 21 pieces.[88] Complicating the problem is that all four of these incidents count those pieces which are large enough to be tracked. There remains the likelihood of numerous more pieces simply too small to track but could be decidedly more dangerous.

These incidents, and other regularly occurring incidents, increase the probability of existing pieces colliding to create even more debris. This is commonly referred to as the Kessler Syndrome.[89] First suggested by Donald J. Kessler and Burton G. Cour-Palais in the Journal of Geophysical Research in 1978, this theory suggests that as debris accumulates in a particular area, over time, the chances of collision between debris pieces increases.[90] For each piece that collides with another piece, more debris is created.[91] Kessler and Cour-Palais eventually arrived at the inevitable conclusion that "with time, enough collisional fragments could be produced to become important in producing new collision fragments.[92] When these conditions apply, the number

83 *Id.* at i.

84 NASA, ORBITAL DEBRIS Q. NEWS, 1, 1–4, April 2016, https://orbitaldebris.jsc.nasa.gov/quarterly-news/pdfs/odqnv20i1-2.pdf.

85 *Fragmentation of* Fregat *Upper StageDebris*, ORBITAL DEBRIS Q. NEWS, April 2016, at 2, https://orbitaldebris.jsc.nasa.gov/quarterly-news/pdfs/odqnv20i1-2.pdf.

86 *Recent NOAA-16 Satellite Breakup*, ORBITAL DEBRIS Q. NEWS, April 2016, at 1, https://orbitaldebris.jsc.nasa.gov/quarterly-news/pdfs/odqnv20i1-2.pdf.

87 *Briz-M Core Stage Fragments Near Geosynchronous Orbit*, ORBITAL DEBRIS Q. NEWS, April 2016, at 3, https://orbitaldebris.jsc.nasa.gov/quarterly-news/pdfs/odqnv20i1-2.pdf.

88 *Russian SOZ Unit Breaks Up in March*, ORBITAL DEBRIS Q. NEWS, April 2016, at 4, https://orbitaldebris.jsc.nasa.gov/quarterly-news/pdfs/odqnv20i1-2.pdf.

89 Donald J. Kessler & Burton G. Cour-Palais, *Collision Frequency of Artificial Satellites: The Creation of a Debris Belt*, 83 J. OF GEOPHYSICAL RES., 2637, 2642 (June 1, 1978), *available at* http://www.castor2.ca/07_News/headline_010216_files/Kessler_Collision_Frequency_1978.pdf.

90 *Id.*

91 *Id.*

92 *Id.*

of objects will increase exponentially with time, even though no new objects may be placed into orbit ..."[93] And yet, considering the continual occurrence of debris-creating events, especially deliberate actions like ASAT tests, there is no indication that the lessons are being learned. This is evidenced as recently as March 2019 by India's ASAT test and November 2021 by Russia's ASAT test.

Finally, there is little opportunity for natural decay once created except for the lowest altitudes in LEO orbit. The United Nations suggested that as of 2009, at the estimated rate of decay of 10 cm or larger objects in LEO, only approximately 5 objects naturally decay annually.[94] At the same time, about seven times that amount are being injected into space yearly.[95] If relying only on natural decay for the removal of space debris, the evidence is mounting that the environment in space will continue to be increasingly polluted and at high-risk for aggravation.

4 Identifying the Degree of Space Debris Accumulation—What Is Space SSA?

As previously mentioned, the first satellite launched by the United States, Explorer 1, quickly convinced the United States of the need to understand the location, trajectory, and speed at which satellites would travel and potentially cross paths with other space objects. That recognition led to an immediate effort by the United States to establish a network of sensors to track and identify space objects. Development of this network has allowed the United States to create a picture of the congestion in space and assist operators to ensure the most accurate safety of flight profiles. This includes assisting with the deconfliction of space objects for collision avoidance at initial launch stages via launch conjunction assessments,[96] collision avoidance

---

93 *Id.*

94 Comm. On the Peaceful Uses of Outer Space, Rep. of the Int'l Interdisciplinary Congress on Space Debris Remediation and On-Orbit Satellite Servicing on Its Forty-Ninth Session, *Active Debris Removal—An Essential Mechanism for Ensuring the Safety and Sustainability of Outer Space*, at 19, U.N. Doc. A/AC.105/C.1/2012/CRP.16 (Jan. 27, 2012) *available at* http://www.unoosa.org/pdf/limited/c1/AC105_C1_2012_CRP16E.pdf.

95 *Id.*

96 Launch conjunction assessment is the process of identifying close approaches between the planned trajectory of a launch vehicle and other man-made objects on orbit, to include active and inactive satellites, rocket bodies, debris, and analyst objects that are not in the public catalog, as well as the International Space Station and vehicles transiting to and from it. Trajectories include all objects associated with the launch vehicle, such as booster segments, payloads, jettisoned components and debris. 18th Space Control

guidance[97] during insertion, and orbital deconfliction and warning for the space object (if any) after insertion.[98]

This tracking ability, better known as Space Situational Awareness (SSA) and the elements comprising Space Surveillance Network (SSN), is defined differently by agencies and organizations. US military doctrine from the United States Air Force defines SSA as the "requisite foundational, current, and predictive knowledge and characterization of space objects and the operational environment upon which space operations depend, including physical, virtual, information, and human dimensions, as well as all factors, activities and events of all entities conducting or preparing to conduct space operations."[99] The Space Foundation defines SSA as an activity that "refers to keeping track of objects in orbit and predicting where they will be at any given time."[100] Finally, ESA states that SSA comprises three different aspects of space object information. First, Space Surveillance and Tracking (SST), which is the surveillance and tracking of objects in Earth's orbit.[101] Second, Space Weather (SWE), which obtains information on environmental conditions that can have a harmful effect on space and ground-based structures and organic health.[102] Finally, near-Earth objects, focusing on those objects that can have an impact on the planet and its inhabitants.[103]

Within Air Force doctrine, SSA falls into four general disciplines related to the management of space operations: Detect, track and identify space objects to ensure that understanding of the location of space objects and their identity; Threat Warning and Assessment to understand the risks to satellites and what the origins of those risks are (for example, nefarious versus naturally occurring threats); Characterization, which is the ability to assess the "strategy, tactics, intent and activity of all space capabilities and threats posed by those capabilities"; and finally, Data Integration and Exploitation, which is the ability

---

Squadron, *Launch Conjunction Assessment Handbook*, at 2 (Dec. 2018) https://www.space-track.org/documents/LCA_Handbook.pdf.

97 Launch collision avoidance is the decision to mitigate the risk of predicted conjunctions by altering planned launch times to avoid or resolve the close approaches. *Id.*

98 *Id.*

99 Curtis E. Lemay Center, *Space Situational Awareness*, https://www.doctrine.af.mil/Portals/61/documents/Annex_3-14/3-14-D04-SPACE-SSA.pdf (last updated Aug. 27, 2018).

100 The Space Foundation, *The Space Briefing Book* (2019), https://www.spacefoundation.org/wp-content/uploads/2019/10/SpaceFoundation_Space101.pdf.

101 *SSA Programme Overview*, EUROPEAN SPACE AGENCY, https://www.esa.int/Safety_Security/SSA_Programme_overview (last visited Feb. 28, 2020).

102 *Id.*

103 *Id.*

to take all-source data and compile it into a digestible form for space operations decision-makers.[104] Put simply, SSA is collectively the effort to find, track, and predict in the future where objects will be at any given time and the risks posed to them from any source.

4.1 *Who Is Responsible for SSA Management?*

In the United States, the United States Strategic Command (USSTRATCOM) is the designated US government entity responsible for SSA. Assuming this role in 2009, USSTRATCOM began the SSA sharing program to provide a series of services to support the entire lifetime of a satellite's operation, from pre-launch through post-mission disposal.[105] These services, intended to provide a holistic approach to the management of satellite operations from birth to death, include support for launch conjunction assessment, satellite life collision avoidance, and deorbit support.[106]

USSTRATCOM delegated management of the SSA sharing program down to 14th Air Force at Vandenberg Air Force Base, a United States Air Force Numbered Air Force, which oversees the two major organizations responsible for maintaining the catalog of space objects and notification responsibilities.[107] These two organizations are the 18th Space Control Squadron (SPCS) and the Combined Space Operations Center (CSpOC), also both co-located at Vandenberg Air Force Base, California.[108] The CSpOC reports directly to the Joint Force Space Component Commander (JFSCC) to ensure their ability to execute the command and control of space forces to achieve theater and global objectives, specifically tailoring space effects on demand to meet the national security objectives of Combatant Commanders globally, 24/7.[109]

To ensure an entire sight picture of the space environment, the 18th SPCS is ultimately responsible for the day-to-day responsibilities assigned from USSTRATCOM to meet the taskings required by the United States Air Force for SSA missions, other responsibilities to the United States Department of

104 Curtis E. Lemay Center, *supra* note 99.

105 18th Space Control Squadron, *supra* note 96 at 3.

106 *Id.*

107 Sandra Erwin, *U.S. Space Command Eager to Hand Over Space Traffic Duties to Commerce Department*, SPACE NEWS (Nov. 17, 2019), https://spacenews.com/u-s-space-command-eager-to-hand-over-space-traffic-duties-to-commerce-department/ (last visited Aug. 6, 2020).

108 18th Space Control Squadron, *supra* note 96 at 2.

109 COMBINED SPACE OPERATIONS CENTER/164TH AIR OPERATIONS CENTER, U.S. STRATEGIC COMMAND FACT SHEET (current as of July 2018), https://www.stratcom.mil/Portals/8/Documents/CSpOC_Factsheet_2018.pdf (last visited Aug. 8, 2020).

Defense (DoD), as well as interagency and global space partners.[110] While the United States is arguably the leader in the effort for SSA and ultimately its uses, such as conjunction warning, there are a number of governments and organizations similarly involved in the attempt to create whole pictures of the space object environment.

4.2 *Other SSA Programs*

Joining the efforts of the United States, ESA's SSA program similarly works to track objects that could have a significant effect on the operation of other satellites or pose a threat to locations on Earth.[111] Third, the Russian Military Space Surveillance Network (SKKP), the equivalent in Russia of the USSTRATCOM SSA, perform all the same functions of cataloging and tracking space objects.[112] Finally, the Space Data Association (SDA) is an effort led by commercial satellite operators to provide a degree of 'self-help' for collision warnings.[113] The SDA is a private not-for-profit association, and while unique because it is the only well-established non-governmental organization engaged in SSA, it still similarly supports the ingestion of flight dynamics from member companies and other available resources to enhance the safety of space flight as well as improve the accuracy and timeliness of collision warning notifications.[114]

In many cases, while one or more of these governments have made individual efforts to establish conjunction warning and SSA, there are also several countries that work with the United States and other governments in an effort to share information to create a more comprehensive orbital picture. For

110 18th Space Control Squadron, *supra* note 96 at 2. In carrying out the SSA mission on behalf of the United States, it is also worth noting that the Secretary of Defense is authorized under US law to specifically share situational awareness data and information, and receive such information in return, not just from government entities. As long as the Secretary of Defense determines that such action is consistent with US national security, the Secretary is authorized to share and receive data from non-United States Government entities, including 1) States, 2) political subdivisions of States, 3) United States commercial entities, 4) governments of a foreign country, and 5) foreign commercial entities. *See* 10 U.S.C. § 2274, paras. (a) & b(1)-(5), https://www.govinfo.gov/content/pkg/USCODE-2011-title10/pdf/USCODE-2011-title10-subtitleA-partIV-chap135-sec2274.pdf. For additional discussion, *see also* DANIEL MORGAN, CONG. RSCH. SERV. R. 45416, COMMERCIAL SPACE: FEDERAL REGULATION, OVERSIGHT AND UTILIZATION 19–20, https://fas.org/sgp/crs/space/R45416.pdf (updated Nov. 29, 2018).

111 *Space Briefing Book: Space Situational Awareness*, SPACE FOUNDATION, https://www.spacefoundation.org/space_brief/space-situational-awareness/ (last visited Jan. 22, 2020).

112 *Id.*

113 *Id.*

114 *Space Data Center*, SPACE DATA ASSOCIATION, https://www.space-data.org/sda/space-data-center-3/ (last visited Jan. 22, 2020).

example, as of April 2019, USSTRATCOM reached an agreement with Romania for SSA sharing.[115] This marked the 20th nation to enter an agreement with USSTRATCOM for the sharing of SSA information and marked the 100th total sharing agreement overall between USSTRATCOM and all sharing partners.[116]

4.3 *How Are Space Objects (and Debris) Identified and Tracked?*

At the outset, it is critical to understand that in any discussion about the extent to which orbital debris occupies space around Earth, there is no one tool which gives a comprehensive picture of all of the debris surrounding Earth at any given time. Instead, there are several different systems that, when working together, can provide a reasonably accurate image of debris of a specific size (orbit dependent) or can at least offer a predictive model to assist in establishing a likely estimate of the environmental threats.

Generally, three major categories of systems are utilized to provide a snapshot of the space environment. First, ground based radars, consisting of both a transmitter and receiver, propagate signals into space and interpret the returns to identify the motion of an object and a representation of its shape.[117] This is an effective method of information gathering depending on the proximity to the object, but can be costly and complex, particularly the further the distance to the object that the operator is desiring to target.[118] Because of the distance limitations of ground based radars, the limits for the effectiveness of modeling for radars generally terminates at approximately 1,000 km.[119] For example, as used by the NASA Orbital Debris Program Office (ODPO) for LEO measurements, accurate sampling of the debris in that range is approximately 3 cm with the Haystack Auxiliary Radar (HAX) radar, 5 mm with the Haystack Ultra-wideband Satellite Imaging Radar (HUSIR), and the Goldstone radar, which

115 Karen Singer, *100th Space Sharing Agreement Signed, Romania Space Agency Joins*, U.S. STRATEGIC COMMAND (Apr. 26, 2019), https://www.stratcom.mil/Media/News/News-Article-View/Article/1825882/100th-space-sharing-agreement-signed-romania-space-agency-joins/.

116 The 100 sharing agreements include 20 partner Nations, ESA and the European Organization for the Exploitation of Meteorological Satellites, as well as 78 commercial space interests that partners shared between USSTRATCOM and partner Nations in the effort to provide total space picture. *Id.*

117 Brian Weeden, *Space Situational Awareness Fact Sheet*, SECURE WORLD FOUNDATION, https://swfound.org/media/205874/swf_ssa_fact_sheet.pdf (last updated May 2017).

118 *Id.*

119 NASA Orbital Debris Program Office, *Haystack Ultra-Wideband Satellite Imaging Radar Measurements of the Orbital Debris Environment: 2014–2017*, 1 (Jul. 2019), https://ntrs.nasa.gov/api/citations/20190028719/downloads/20190028719.pdf.

provides additional amplifying data to the HUSIR radar to increase the debris data known for objects to about 2–3 mm at or below approximately 800 km.[120]

Another major category of systems to snapshot the orbital environment are optical telescopes. These systems collect light or other electromagnetic radiation from an object and translate that information into an image using a series of lenses and mirrors.[121] Most often, these are used to identify the debris population beyond LEO, focusing largely on GEO or near-GEO environments where radar struggles to accurately receive returns.[122] The Eugene Stansbury—Meter Class Autonomous Telescope (ES-MCAT) at Ascension Island in the South Atlantic Ocean is one of the newest additions to the Optical Telescope network.[123] This telescope can provide accurate measurements of debris in order to assess the debris environment by comprehensive examination and tracking through all altitudes from LEO up to GEO.[124] Optical telescopes can also help support radar in instances where materials occasionally used in a space object, such as plastic, may make detection and identification harder.[125] An optical telescope can mitigate these challenges by providing very accurate images of larger objects.[126] There are some drawbacks to optical telescopes, such that ground-based optical telescopes do remain susceptible to environmental interference, such as weather and light pollution, which can cause distortion or complete image interference.[127]

The last major system to support cataloguing the orbital environment are '*in situ*' (or in-place) tools for debris measurements, which usually focus on presenting a characterization of the submillimeter orbital debris environment, which would otherwise not be reasonably detectable by radar or optical methods.[128] Analysis from *in-situ* materials can provide environmental information for altitudes based on an analysis of the time with which they are exposed

---

120 *Id.*

121 Weeden, *supra* note 117.

122 Mark Matney, *Measuring Small Debris—What You Can't See Can Hurt You,* NASA ORBITAL DEBRIS PROGRAM OFFICE, https://ntrs.nasa.gov/archive/nasa/casi.ntrs.nasa.gov/20160011226.pdf (last visited Feb. 28, 2020).

123 S.M. Lederer, et al., *NASA's Optical Program on Ascension Island: Bringing MCAT to Life as the Eugene Stansbury-Meter Class Autonomous Telescope (ES-MCAT)*, NASA ORBITAL DEBRIS PROGRAM OFFICE 1, https://ntrs.nasa.gov/archive/nasa/casi.ntrs.nasa.gov/20170008560.pdf (last visited Jan. 23, 2020).

124 *Id.*

125 Weeden, *supra* note 117.

126 *Id.*

127 *Id.*

128 *In Situ Measurements*, ORBITAL DEBRIS PROGRAM OFFICE, https://orbitaldebris.jsc.nasa.gov/measurements/in-situ.html (last visited Jan. 23, 2020).

to the orbital environment compared with the damage they receive during that time.[129] For example, for many years when the United States operated the Space Shuttle, damage to certain aspects of the shuttle, such as the windows, were analyzed upon its return to Earth after a voyage.[130] The information gleaned helped to characterize the debris content in the common operating altitudes of the space shuttle, below 600 km generally.[131] While not intended to be a debris measuring tool, the Space Shuttle became a very good 'canary in the coal mine', demonstrating that toward the end of its operations, the damage from orbital debris was becoming so common that it required window replacements after almost every mission that it went on.[132]

4.4 *How Does SSA Work*

The US SSA system is organized into three categories.[133] The first is dedicated sensors, which are those operationally controlled sensors with a primary mission of space surveillance support.[134] Second, collateral sensors are operationally controlled sensors with a primary mission other than space surveillance but provide information regarding SSA as a secondary function to its primary mission.[135] Finally, auxiliary (sometimes called contributing) sensors are those sensors neither dedicated at a primary or secondary mission to SSA for the United States but will provide information upon request from the United States; usually as a result of a request from the CSpOC specifically.[136]

In combination, these sensors are utilized by an array of systems that collate the data and allow for both tracking, and in the event of a potential collision, potential notification through the CSpOC to satellite operators.[137] In the event that a potential incident is discovered by one of these various methods, when possible under the US SSA system, the CSpOC will issue a Conjunction Summary Message (CSM).[138] The message contains a combination of alphanumerics with six different elements: first, the catalog number for the first

---

129 *Id.*
130 Matney, *supra* note 122.
131 *Id.*
132 *Id.*
133 SAFETY DESIGN FOR SPACE OPERATIONS, ch. 8, para. 8.1 (Firooz A. Allahdadi & Tommaso Sgobba eds., 2013).
134 *Id.*
135 *Id.*
136 *Id.*
137 *Id.*
138 *Conjunction Summary Message Guide*, SPACE-TRACK.ORG, https://www.space-track.org/documents/CSM_Guide.pdf (last visited Feb. 20, 2020).

object; second, the catalog number for the potentially colliding object; the next three elements comprise the predicted month, year, and day of the collision; finally, the last element indicates if there are one or more possible conjunctions on any given day.[139] Additional amplifying information is contained in the body of the message, including the time of closest approach, the estimated speed, and information on how recent the information was in relation to the last observation from the SSN.[140] From this information, operators can make more informed decisions whether there is a likelihood of collision requiring them to expend extremely valuable resources, such as fuel, to decrease or eliminate entirely the possibility of collision with that particular object. They must also consider second-order effects that one maneuver may put them at risk of a separate threat.

One such warning was issued on 7 January 2017 by the Joint Space Operations Center (JSpOC). At the time, there were two satellites on a potential collision course over Antarctica in a sun-synchronous[141] orbit.[142] CSpOC did not publicly release the names of the two satellite owners, indicating only that the owners were notified of the potential collision.[143] However, correlating information with NASA indicated that one of the satellites was likely a 1,220 Kg DMSP F15 Block 5D-3 spacecraft (inserted in 1999), a US Defense Meteorological Satellite used to provide an array of environmental sensing data, which was operated under a joint US Air Force Space Command (AFSPC) and NOAA program.[144] The second satellite was likely a Meteor 1–26 Soviet-era weather satellite with a mass of approximately 2.2. metric tons (inserted in 1976).[145] In both cases, neither of the satellites were under current operational control and were therefore unable to maneuver. As a result, it was a 'wait and see' by the satellite operators, with the JSpOC estimating the probability of the collision being as high

139 *Id.*

140 *Id.*

141 A sun-synchronous orbit is an orbit in which the satellite's orbital plane is at a fixed orientation to the sun. In other words, where the orbit precesses about Earth at the same rate that Earth orbits the sun. It has the characteristics of maintaining similar sun angles along its ground trace for all orbits, and typically has an inclination from 96 to 98 degrees, depending on the orbit altitude and orbit shape (eccentricity). *Sun-synchronous orbit*, The Free Dictionary, *available at* https://www.thefreedictionary.com/sun-synchronous+orbit (last visited Feb. 20, 2020).

142 *Update: High-Risk Satellite Conjunction Passes Without Incident*, SPACEFLIGHT101.COM (Jan. 7, 2017, 11:15PM), http://spaceflight101.com/close-orbital-encounter-january-7-2017/.

143 *Id.*

144 *DMSP—Block 5D-3 Spacecraft Overview*, SPACEFLIGHT101.COM, http://spaceflight 101.com/spacecraft/dmsp-block-5d-3/ (last visited Feb. 20, 2020).

145 *Update: High-Risk Satellite Conjunction Passes Without Incident*, *supra* note 142.

as 44%.[146] Thankfully, reporting indicated that the two satellites remained as 'single objects' as they passed each other, indicating no collision occurred.[147]

Also, critically important in the SSA discussion is that avoidance maneuvers are not currently mandatory in international law.[148] While unfortunate, there is no international organization dedicated to avoidance maneuvers nor for instituting any specific requirements. Additionally, identification of exactly when a maneuver should be conducted still remains a judgment call in many cases. Ultimately, it remains that satellite operators are eligible to receive conjunction warnings from the United States or private providers, and coordinate with other operators at their discretion for deconfliction. But this deconfliction has not always gone smoothly. Disagreements have occurred over whether a potential collision justifies the expenditure of fuel to reduce collision risk and a question as to who should ultimately be responsible, if not required, for conducting a maneuver. This problem was evident in late 2019. On 2 September 2019, at an altitude of approximately 320 km above Earth in LEO orbit, ESA's Aeolus Earth Observation Satellite took action to maneuver away from a SpaceX Starlink constellation satellite, referred to as Starlink 44.[149] Aeolus, notably, had held the potential collision orbit for nine months previous to Starlink 44 entering its altitude.[150] SpaceX had been operating the Starlink series of satellites at an altitude much higher than Aeolus, but moved '44' into the orbit Aeolus was using in order to practice deorbit techniques.[151]

In late August 2019, the presence of both satellites in the same orbit at the same altitude triggered a SSA warning from the Air Force to both ESA and SpaceX that the two satellites had a 1 in 50,000 chance of colliding.[152] The industry standard to justify using fuel for a maneuver is 1 in 10,000, so the relevant parties discussed that at that probability, a maneuver was not necessary.[153] However, shortly after, the Air Force updated its assessment to show a probability higher than 1 in 10,000.[154] At the time, SpaceX did not move their

146 *Id.*

147 *Id.*

148 Jonathan O'Callaghan, *SpaceX Declined to Move a Starlink Satellite at Risk of Collision with a European Satellite*, FORBES (Aug. 22, 2018), https://www.forbes.com/sites/jonathanocallaghan/2019/09/02/spacex-refused-to-move-a-starlink-satellite-at-risk-of-collision-with-a-european-satellite/#36e043e11f62 (last visited Aug. 5, 2020).

149 *Id.*

150 *Id.*

151 *Id.*

152 *Id.*

153 *Id.*

154 *Id.*

satellite even though they were second to enter the orbit, which might have otherwise justified them being the ones to move.[155] Instead, without SpaceX moving, ESA was forced to conduct the maneuver including a second post-maneuver to return to the original orbit.[156]

Interestingly, this specific incident demonstrates that SSA is a knowledge tool, but not a control method or an ability to force actions by any party. And while SpaceX later said that the incident was merely a result of a failure on the part of SpaceX's system to notify them of the updated Air Force warning (and also evidently not seeing ESA's correspondence on the need for a maneuver), this incident raises the question of what happens (other than the potential for the worst outcome of a collision) if neither side wants to expend resources to conduct a maneuver (or hopes to hold out long enough that the other gives up on the game of 'chicken').

This current method of CSpOC SSA notification and coordination presents a weakness but is not the only one. Additionally, the SSN is not directly fed information from a satellite itself. Therefore, it is reliant on imaging from some separate technology, which may be located on Earth and therefore not be able to provide as accurate a positioning and orientation picture as possible.[157] This could result in an inaccurate geolocational assessment from the time between the last evaluation and the renewed target acquisition.[158] Additionally, it could lead to confusion whether the object is in the same place it was previously known to be or if it is in an entirely new location based on active repositioning.[159] Second, there are delays between when the data was accumulated and the time at which the satellite is given the commands to maneuver and can execute the change. Third, it is entirely possible that the change in maneuver eliminates one threat but puts the satellite in a different degree of orbit which could present new threats from different objects. Finally, the SSN is limited in what it can 'see' and even more limited on what it can regularly 'track.' For example, while objects smaller than a softball in LEO may pass through multiple observation points in the SSA array, this does not translate in an ability to regularly track the object at all times.[160] As such, if the objects are on a

155 *Id.*

156 *Id.*

157 BRETT HEMENWAY, WILLIAM WELSER & DAVE BAIOCCHI, ACHIEVING HIGHER-FIDELITY CONJUNCTION ANALYSIS USING CRYPTOGRAPHY TO IMPROVE INFORMATION SHARING 1 (2014).

158 *Id.*

159 *Id.*

160 *Space Debris 101*, AEROSPACE, https://aerospace.org/article/space-debris-101 (last visited Aug. 6, 2020).

collision course with other objects, the tracking may not be consistent enough to see and warn of the potential destructive collision course.[161] In practice, you could imagine objects, such as a golf ball or smaller, travelling at hypervelocity and yet too small to regularly track.[162] What is worse, there are potentially millions of objects like this in orbit between LEO and GEO.[163] Any of these objects could have the potential to completely debilitate a satellite.

5 Conclusion

There are several reasons why the space debris problem continues to perpetuate itself, and the models indicate that the environment will continue to grow. As well, the forecast may be much worse than we currently believe. At the same time, some efforts are ongoing to continue to monitor and track the debris, notify potential stakeholders of the risks associated with potential conjunctions, and efforts to ensure that it is understood what needs to be done to try to reduce the number of debris that continues to be injected into the environment. Meanwhile, this is an important issue for Nations to tackle. It is not just the preservation of the environment that is at stake, but as just discussed, there are liability issues that each Nation faces due to their objects presenting real threats to other space objects.

In most cases, these individual national efforts are subject to international law and understandings and therefore require an understanding of the existing environment of international law. The legal and regulatory environment that exists in space, most pertinent to the space debris discussion, will be covered in the next section.

161 *Id.*
162 *Id.*
163 *Id.*

CHAPTER 2

International Law and the Formal Space Treaties

1 Introduction

The formal body of space law as it stands today reflects international agreements, and in many cases, corresponding domestic law implementing necessary provisions of those global understandings. A thorough analysis of the existing treaties on space law establishes that while no specific formal international agreements regarding the creation or mitigation of space debris currently exists, ongoing efforts may lead to formal agreement(s) in the future. Meanwhile, there are enormously important existing space treaties that set the foundation for all international, and most national, space laws. Therefore, any future solution for the prevention and mitigation of space debris will require an understanding of how these formal international agreements shaped the body of law for this subject area.

International law has commonly been understood to be reserved mainly as the province of sovereign Nations and their representing international organizations, authorizing States to enter into binding agreements recognized by the signatory parties and by those who would otherwise be witness to the agreements.[164] Much of early 'international law' as it is known today was borne out of a need to establish very basic understandings between countries. There are a number of examples in history of just such efforts as early as 3100 B.C., in a borderline agreement between the countries of Umma and Lagash used to identify the boundaries where the two Nations were divided.[165] Other early treaties, such as those of Egyptian or Hittite rulers concerned alliances and boundary lines.[166] Finally, in 1291 B.C., the Egyptian King Ramses II and the Hittites King, Hattusili II, concluded an early extradition treaty, providing for the expulsion

164 Fact Sheet # 1, United Nations, 2011 Treaty Event Towards Universal Participation and Implementation, https://treaties.un.org/doc/source/events/2011/Press_kit/fact_sheet_1_english.pdf (last visited Feb. 17, 2020).

165 The Umma/Lagash treaty even included a novel concept of a requirement for arbitration within the treaty, possibly to be conducted by the presumed overlord of Lagash and Umma, King Mesilim of the neighboring Kish. *See* Arthur Nussbaum, A Concise History of the Law of Nations 8-10 (1947). *See also* C.H. Alexandrowicz, An Introduction to the History of the Law of Nations in the East Indies (1967).

166 Nussbaum, *supra* note 165 at 8–10.

© KONINKLIJKE BRILL NV, LEIDEN, 2023 | DOI:10.1163/9789004535848_004

of internal foes who take safe harbor within the other country.[167] Other early examples can be found throughout history, particularly surrounding international conflict, sovereignty, trade, and national security interests.[168]

Further understanding of international law developed out of the Roman system of recognition of international law. The Romans developed the '*jus gentium*', Latin for the 'law of nations', a recognition of early binding international understandings between Roman citizens and those citizens of other countries.[169] This Roman view of internationally applicable laws were eventually reflected in later international agreements between European Nations and similarly interested merchant trade Nations.[170] As the wealth of these countries grew, coupled with a need to establish rules to regulate trade interactions, Nations drew on the Roman model to gain a deeper understanding of

---

167 *Id.*

168 *Id. See also* GEOFFREY G. BUTLER & SIMON MCCOBY, THE DEVELOPMENT OF INTERNATIONAL LAW (1928) discussing extensively early English treaties surrounding commerce and the ability of the English merchants, in cases of dispute, to negotiate settlements under the treaties. Butler also discusses early commercial arrangements with the Duke of Burgundy and treaties in connection with the Netherlands, English and Castilian agreements, and the *Intercursus Magnus* (discussed further on page 213) of 1496 between England and Burgundy, the Anglo-Spanish treaty of July 1499, and treaties between the Duchy of Saxony and England in 1505. *Id.* at 211–213 (1928). *See generally* ELMER PLISCHKE, INTERNATIONAL RELATIONS: BASIC DOCUMENTS (1962).

169 William Conklin, *Myth of Primordialism*, 23 LEIDEN J. INTL'L L. 479 (2010) discussing Greek Philosopher Marcus Tullius Cicero's early writings on international relations between Roman citizens and citizens of other countries. History.com Editors, *Marcus Tullius Cicero*, HISTORY.COM (Dec. 16, 2009, updated Jun. 10, 2019), https://www.history.com/topics/ancient-history/marcus-tullius-cicero. As described by Conklin, 'the *jus gentium* manifests and guards the extent to which inhabitants reciprocally recognize each other in their social relationships.' Conklin, 23 LEIDEN J. INTL'L L. at 487. Conklin further describes Cicero's assessment of *jus gentium* as the nature of humans to be able to 'comprehend the cause of things … and by seeing with ease the whole course of life to prepare whatever is necessary for living', particularly an order and law to things. *Id.* at 489 (2010). *See also Character, Essence, Origin and Content of the Jus Gentium According to Vico and Suares*, 16 PERIODICALS ARCHIVE ONLINE 167 (Jan. 1, 1936). Interestingly, Nussbaum raises the point that Roman law was often bereft of significant discussions on references to foreign law, largely a result of Rome having conquered much of the known world, and therefore leaving very few legal systems other than Roman systems to apply to 'foreign' engagements. *See* ARTHUR NUSSBAUM, PRINCIPLES OF PRIVATE INTERNATIONAL LAW, Section 2, p. 10 (1943).

170 Emily Kadens, *The Medieval Law Merchant: The Tyranny of Construct*, 7 J. LEGAL ANALYSIS 251, 253 (2015) (highlighting early notions of customs of merchant guilds that predate flourishing of international laws). *International Law*, ENCYCLOPEDIA BRITANNICA, *available at* https://www.britannica.com/topic/international-law/Historical-development, (last visited Feb. 17, 2020).

international law and methods of more formal recognition of its contours.[171] That formalization has progressed into the rules we commonly see today, primarily under the establishment and leadership of international organizations like the United Nations.

Today, the United Nations has been among the most significant partners in establishing a broader recognition and formalization of international law and a greater acceptance among the international community.[172] Under its preamble, the United Nations set as one of its major tenets to "establish conditions under which justice and respect for the obligations arising from treaties and other sources of international law can be maintained …"[173] Further, in the United Nations Charter, Article 13(1)(a), Nations are encouraged to support "the progressive development of international law and its codification."[174] The 'progressive development' of international law is generally recognized in two broad categories; formal law, known as public international law or the law of nations (colloquially called 'Hard' or 'Treaty' law), and customary international law. Neither of these types of law are new. Still, the United Nations helped to usher in a more clearly understood definition supported by a greater community working under one all-encompassing international organization.

As discussed more below, some of the most significant challenges in space law have been ultimately, and thankfully, resolved by formal international law. For example, jurisdiction over debris is one of the foundational issues that must be addressed for any law to apply. In international law, jurisdiction means "the

171 *International Law*, ENCYCLOPEDIA BRITANNICA, *available at* https://www.britannica.com/topic/international-law/Historical-development, (last visited Feb. 17, 2020).

172 Responding to the outbreak of the Second World War (WWII), 26 Nations committed to each other to fight against Hitler's Germany and the Axis Powers. US President Franklin D. Roosevelt coined these 26 countries as representative of the 'United Nations.' Following the conclusion of WWII, the 'United Nations', then comprising 50 countries, was established from the United Nations Conference on Organization in San Francisco, California, in 1945. On 26 June 1945, the original 50 countries, and later Poland, became Member-States of the original Charter. On 24 October 1945, the Charter was ratified bringing the United Nations into formal existence. *See History of the United Nations*, UNITED NATIONS, https://www.un.org/en/sections/history/history-united-nations/ (last visited Feb. 17, 2020). *See also* B.G. RAMCHARAN, THE INTERNATIONAL LAW AND PRACTICE OF EARLY-WARNING AND PREVENTIVE DIPLOMACY: THE EMERGING GLOBAL WATCH (1991). "Facing global problems hitherto never experienced in the history of the international community, States are now discovering that if they are to protect their interests, they will need to entrust to the international community, through the agency of international organizations-notably the United Nations-competences to protect the common interest and human welfare and to act for the prevention of new threats to human welfare." *Id.* at 2.

173 U.N. Charter, *Preamble*, available at https://www.un.or/en/about-us/un-charter/full-text.

174 *Id.* at art. 13(1)(a). *See also Id.* at *Preamble.*

power of a State to exercise its sovereignty and authority and is based on the principle of effectiveness."[175] This is primarily focused on the powers of a state as they relate to those things under its control: persons, property or events.[176] Furthermore, the State's right of jurisdiction rests in its sovereignty.[177] The formal space treaties addressed these and other issues to set the standard rules necessary for functioning law in space.

2 Public International Law

Public international law comprises the legal rules, norms and standards that are recognized to apply between and among sovereign States and other legally recognized international entities. As indicated earlier, it comprises two bodies of law: formal treaty law and customary international law. The former we will discuss now, and the latter will be discussed later.

These formal legal rules are typically memorialized in international conventions, including treaties or agreements, which outline the specific provisions of the understandings between international parties.[178] They often include the list of consenting and ratified signatory countries and the specific roles and responsibilities expected of each member, and are typically registered and recognized by international institutions. Once a treaty is signed, these Nations demonstrate themselves legally bound in several different ways, but most commonly through acts including signature, ratification, acceptance, approval and accession.[179] The latter three are generally considered synonymous in an agreement, whereas signature followed by ratification reflects the strongest indication of an intent to be bound by the agreement.[180]

---

175 Sergio Marchisio, Professor at Sapienza University of Rome, National Jurisdiction for Regulating Space Activities of Governmental and Non-Governmental Entities, presentation at the 2010 United Nations/Thailand Workshop on Space L. at 1–3 (Nov. 16–19, 2010), http://www.unoosa.org/pdf/pres/2010/SLW2010/02-02.pdf.

176 *Id.*

177 *Id.*

178 *Soft Law*, USLEGAL, https://definitions.uslegal.com/s/soft-law/ (last visited Feb. 20, 2020).

179 Vienna Convention on the Law of Treaties, 1155 U.N.T.S. 331, arts. 11–15 (1969), https://treaties.un.org/doc/publication/unts/volume%201155/volume-1155-i-18232-english.pdf. *See also* STEPHEN P. MULLIGAN, CONG. RESEARCH SERV., RL 32528, INTERNATIONAL LAW AND AGREEMENTS: THEIR EFFECT UPON U.S. LAW (updated Sept. 19, 2018) *available at* https://fas.org/sgp/crs/misc/RL32528.pdf.

180 MULLIGAN, *supra* note 179.

However, the fundamental expectation under public international law is that States are expected to express a formal willingness to enter into the agreements and consider themselves to be legally bound by the agreement.[181] The typical development of this type of law is a treaty, whether involving two (bilateral) or more (multilateral) countries and involves a number of steps. This includes the development of the treaty elements through drafting and negotiation, signatory events by the authorized parties, and for full recognition and binding legal obligation if intended, ratification by governing bodies of the agreements within their domestic legal apparatuses followed by implementation.[182] The most significant remaining question is if the ratifying country recognizes the treaty as self-executing or non-self-executing. If an agreement is self-executing, it is generally taken whole cloth as binding on the signatory country. If an agreement is non-self-executing, additional steps such as implementing legislation are required by the signatory country to make the agreement binding in its own domestic law.[183]

For example, in the United States, once a treaty is negotiated between the United States and one or more countries, the US President will sign the agreement and then (under normal circumstances) transmit it to the United States Senate.[184] Under Article II, Section 2, Clause 2 of the Constitution of the United States, the United States Senate will provide its advice and consent to the agreement, and the treaty will pass if two-thirds majority of the Senate votes in favor of the agreement.[185] Assuming a favorable vote, the US President must then proclaim the treaty by ordering the release of an official statement acknowledging that the treaty is now in effect.[186] It is then the responsibility of the United States Congress to examine which provisions of the agreement will require the passage of domestic law to put into effect the elements of the agreement and those which it views as self-executing, if any. This process is where the key distinction between 'self' and 'non-self' executing treaties

181 Fact Sheet # 1, *supra* note 164.

182 Andrew T. Guzman, *The Design of International Agreements*, 16 EUR. J. OF INT'L L. 579 (2005), *available at* http://ejil.org/pdfs/16/4/310.pdf.

183 David Sloss, *Non-Self-Executing Treaties: Exposing a Constitutional Fallacy*, 36 U.C. DAVID L. REV. 1, 9 (2002).

184 *Treaties and International Agreements*, UNIVERSITY OF RICHMOND SCHOOL OF LAW, https://law-richmond.libguides.com/treaties (last updated Jun. 18, 2019, 11:57AM).

185 U.S. CONST. art. II, § 2, cl. 2.

186 Sloss, *supra* note 183 at 59.

becomes clear. These non-self-executing treaties trigger some final implementation of domestic recognition and creation of domestic law.[187]

2.1 *Development of Public International Law Related to Space*

The flyover of Sputnik was an affirmation of what many countries already predicted was the future of 'air-law.' By the early 1950s, most countries were already eagerly awaiting the moment when humans became spacefaring in some capacity. The result was a sense among major space powers that there needed to be a body of law governing conduct in space. Fortunately, the building blocks had already been provided by the development of air law ever since

187 One significant example of non-self-executing treaties is the Migratory Bird Convention. Between 1916 and 1918, the United States and Great Britain entered into the Migratory Bird Convention. This agreement was meant to address the concerns of various interest groups, including hunters worried about the diminishment of bird species, farmers concerned about the increase of pest threats to their crops, and wildlife organizations generally worried about the natural environment. But as a non-self-executing treaty, it had no means of enforcement absent some domestic legislation. In response, the United States passed the domestic Migratory Birds Convention Act of 1918, implementing federal law and enforcement of the agreement's provisions to the United States Bureau of Biological Survey. Today, that act prohibits in federal law the ability, among other things, to possess, export, or sell migratory birds (or derivative parts such as eggs) without a specific federal permit. And since the original enactment, the convention has been extended to include similar provisions with Mexico, Russia, and Japan, recognizing that the migration of birds does not occur in just one country. As distinguished from self-executing, it was necessary to implement US federal law since the interpretation of the Supremacy Clause did not give self-executing weight to the convention when agreed to by the United States and Great Britain; instead it required domestic law be implemented for its enforcement and supremacy over any State law which might have otherwise conflicted. *See* National Audubon Society, *The Migratory Bird Treaty Act, Explained*, AUDUBON (Jan. 26, 2018), https://www.audubon.org/news/the-migratory-bird-treaty-act-explained. *See also* Sunil Sonkar, *The 1916 Migratory Bird Convention*, FUNENDER.COM, (Sept. 15, 2018), https://funender.com/wildlife/the-1916-migratory-bird-convention.html. *See also Missouri v. Holland*, 252 U.S. 416 (1920), *available at* https://www.law.cornell.edu/supremecourt/text/252/416, Justice Holmes, addressing whether or not a treaty negotiated by the United States and Canada to protect the killing of migratory birds was an infringement of the Tenth Amendment to the detriment of States within the United States. Justice Holmes stated that "Acts of Congress are the supreme law of the land only when made in pursuance of the Constitution, while treaties are declared to be so when made under the authority of the United States." *Id.* at 433. Justice Holmes articulated that when a national interest is involved, that can be protected only by national action in joint effort with another national power. The treaty and statute prohibiting the killing of migratory birds must be upheld since nothing in the constitution compels the Government to sit by on a national issue properly enacted at the national level. *Id. at* 433, 456.

the Wright Brothers first took off on 17 December 1903.[188] But interesting challenges arose as space law was in its infancy. For example, one of the first challenges was a fundamental question over whether the sovereignty of States extended indefinitely into the heavens, or instead if there was a finite point where sovereignty over airspace ended and outer space, and a corresponding new set of rules, began.

There were then, and continue to be now, differences in the view to that challenging question. In response, at the ILA meeting at the New York Conference of 1958 it was proffered that air space was synonymous with atmospheric space.[189] Other attempts to provide clarity included that the term 'air space' was the height at which the elements of air can be found, leaving the actual altitude of that definition to be wherever scientist might determine the difference between its presence or absence exists.[190]

Likely one of the most well-known concepts is that outer space begins at approximately 62 miles (100 km) above sea level.[191] Commonly referred to as the Karman line, this measurement was coined based on a proposal of Austrian and German physicist Theodore von Karman.[192] At around 62 miles, von Karman proposed that the atmosphere is too thin to support flight unless the aircraft would have to go faster in flight than the speed required to achieve orbit.[193]

188 Joe Bullmer, *The Power of a Picture: The Wright Brothers Take Off*, AIR FORCE TIMES (Dec. 17, 2018), https://www.airforcetimes.com/veterans/military-history/2018/12/18/the-power-of-a-picture-the-wright-brothers-take-off/?utm_expid=.jFR93cgdTFyMrWXdYEtvgA.1&utm_referrer=https%3A%2F%2Fwww.bing.com%2Fsearch%3Fq%3D-wright%2Bbrothers%2Bfirst%2Btakeoff%26form%3DEDGTCT%26qs%3DPF%26cvid%3Dbd9144640096498a8dc424e9a89bc2f2%26refig%3D9d772a2a7ccb4300e3fbaad2f9160012%26cc%3DUS%26setlang%3Den-US%26plvar%3D0%26PC%3DHCTS#jwvideo.

189 Daniel Goedhuis, *Conflicts of Law and Divergencies in the Legal Regimes of Air Space and Outer Space*, *in* ACADEMIE DE DROIT INTERNATIONAL [ACADEMY OF INTERNATIONAL LAW], RECUEIL DES COURS [COLLECTION OF COURSES] 283 (1963) (citing *Air Sovereignty and the Legal Status of Outer Space*, Report of the 48th Conference of the International Law Association, 324 (1958)).

190 *Id.* at 284.

191 Nadia Drake, *Where, Exactly, is the Edge of Space? It Depends on Who You Ask*, NATIONAL GEOGRAHIC (Dec. 20, 2018), https://www.nationalgeographic.com/science/2018/12/where-is-the-edge-of-space-and-what-is-the-karman-line/#close.

192 John Spacey, *What is the Karman Line*, SIMPLICABLE (May 14, 2016), https://simplicable.com/new/karman-line (last visited Aug. 19, 2020).

193 *Id.* There is considerable literature that challenges the notion that 100 km is the proper delimiter, that another may be more useful, or that even establishing such a line is irrelevant entirely. In contrast to 100 km, many have argued that 80 km (50 mi) may be a more appropriate official altitude. This altitude has been recognized by the United States (with

Whatever the case, the debate continues where the proper altitude should be established.[194]

While a 'final answer' remains elusive, the reality is that by 4 October 1957, it had certainly been established that at least at 143 miles above Earth, the Soviet space satellite Sputnik was traveling in Earth's orbit, including taking numerous passes over the United States; a feat that would have been otherwise illegal according to general air law at the time.[195] In response, the United States launched the first US satellite on 31 January 1958, cementing the need for an international understanding of the rules for space.[196] The United Nations

---

one now notable exception; see below) and NASA for functional purposes. *See* Johnathan C. McDowell, *The Edge of Space: Revisiting the Karman Line*, 151 ACTA ASTRONAUTICA 668 (2018), https://arxiv.org/pdf/1807.07894.pdf. On the other hand, NASA Mission Control uses the point at which a vehicle will first encounter some identifiable degree of atmospheric drag, or approximately 76 miles above sea level. *See* Drake, *supra* note 191. What is more, the merit of 80 km is emboldened by research from Jonathan McDowell of the Harvard-Smithsonian Center for Astrophysics. Johnathan C. McDowell, *The Edge of Space: Revisiting the Karman Line*, 151 ACTA ASTRONAUTICA 668 (2018), https://arxiv.org/pdf/1807.07894.pdf. He proposes that von Karman's logic is sound for the effects on aircraft, but alternatively places the appropriate altitude somewhere between 66 km to 88 km (versus the 100 km attributed to von Karman). *Id.* Beginning around 66 km altitude, depending on the craft, aerodynamic forces transition from dominant to negligible. *Id.* Hence, in McDowell's opinion, von Karman's principal reasoning remains sound for the delimiter, but the scientific data still indicates a much lower proper altitude in the 66 km-88 km range. *Id.* As late as 2018, there has also been efforts by the World Air Sports Federation, the Federation Aeronautique Internationale, to also consider recognizing 80 km as the delimiter between airspace and outer space. *See Statement about the Karman Line*, FÉDÉRATION AÉRONAUTIQUE INTERNATIONALE (Nov. 30, 2018), https://www.fai.org/news/statement-about-karman-line (last visited Aug. 5, 2020). Wherever the final altitude is officially established internationally, if ever, the practical outcome is that States and organizations are utilizing a specific delimiter less for the practical impact on flight, and instead for defining the differences between where one's roles and responsibilities end, and another begins. For example, the United States is currently establishing the delimitation for use between the area of responsibility for the United States Air Force, and that of the United States Space Force (USSF). Specifically, the US Unified Command Plan (UCP) now defines where space begins as 100 km above sea level to make the area of responsibility for the new USSF clear. *See* Theresa Hitchens, *SPACECOM to Write New Ops War Plan: 100km and Up*, BREAKING DEFENSE (Sept. 16, 2019, 11:23 AM), https://breakingdefense.com/2019/09/spacecom-to-write-new-ops-war-plan-100km-and-up/ (last accessed Aug. 5, 2020). For a comprehensive analysis of the (in)accuracy of the Karman Line theory, see Thomas Gangale, The Non Karman Line: An Urban Legend of the Space Age, 41 J. Space L. 151 (2017).

194 The outcome of this is likely to have a significant impact if and when any specific treaty on space debris goes into effect. Essentially, what rules apply to orbital debris in 'outer space' is going to need to be defined at some altitude, which will make this topic even more pertinent over time as these discussions on debris develop.

195 *Sputnik Launched*, *supra* note 61.

196 Howell, *supra* note 63.

was quick to respond to the activities demonstrated by the Sputnik launch and the likely following activity that the United States publicly acknowledged. The unanimous adoption by the UN General Assembly of Resolution 1348 (XIII) on 13 December 1958 established an ad hoc UN COPUOS, with representatives from 18 countries[197] comprising the initial cadre.[198] The United Nations charged the committee with reporting back to the UN General Assembly on which efforts the United Nations could take in encouraging international cooperation and programs to benefit all countries.[199] By 1959, UN COPUOS was established as a permanent United Nations body, and its mandate for actions was established in a unanimous vote on Resolution 1472 (XIV) on 12 December 1959.[200] Among the responsibilities imposed on UN COPUOS was a charge to study and report on the legal problems which would arise from the exploration of outer space.[201]

To carry out the legal responsibilities and examine the legal ramifications of activities within space, in 1961 UN COPUOS established two subsidiary bodies to assist in meeting the obligations expected by the United Nations. The first was the Scientific and Technical Sub-Committee of UN COPUOS and the second was the Legal Sub-Committee of UN COPUOS.[202] In their respective roles, the Scientific and Technical Sub-Committee of UN COPUOS is charged with addressing questions related to the scientific and technical aspects of space activities, including space weather, near-Earth objects, the use of space technology for socio-economic development, disaster management support, global navigation satellite systems, and the long-term sustainability of outer space activities.[203] The Legal Sub-Committee of UN COPUOS is charged with addressing legal questions related to the exploration and use of outer space,

---

197 These countries included Argentina, Australia, Belgium, Brazil, Canada, Czechoslovakia, France, India, Iran, Italy, Japan, Mexico, Poland, Sweden, the Union of Soviet Socialist Republics, the United Arab Republic, the United Kingdom of Great Britain and Northern Ireland, and the United States of America. G.A. Res. 1348 (XIII) (Dec. 13, 1958), *available at* http://www.unoosa.org/pdf/gares/ARES_13_1348E.pdf.

198 *Id.*

199 *Id.*

200 *COPUOS History*, UNITED NATIONS OFFICE FOR OUTER SPACE AFFAIRS, http://www.unoosa.org/oosa/en/ourwork/copuos/history.html (last visited Mar. 1, 2020).

201 G.A. Res. 1348 (XIII) (Dec. 13, 1958), *available at* http://www.unoosa.org/pdf/gares/ARES_13_1348E.pdf.

202 *Committee on the Peaceful Uses of Outer Space*, UNITED NATIONS OFFICE OF OUTER SPACE AFFAIRS, http://www.unoosa.org/oosa/en/ourwork/copuos/index.html (last visited Feb. 19, 2020).

203 *Committee on the Peaceful Uses of Outer Space and its Subcommittees*, UNITED NATIONS OFFICE OF OUTER SPACE AFFAIRS, http://www.unoosa.org/oosa/en/ourwork/copuos/comm-subcomms.html (last visited Feb. 19, 2020).

including the status and application of the major space treaties, the definition and delimitation of outer space, national space legislation, legal mechanisms relevant to space debris mitigation, and international mechanism for cooperation in the exploration and use of space.[204]

Between 1959 through 1961, on the basic principle of the application of international law in space, there appeared to be consensus at the United Nations that regardless of where the conduct of Nations occurred, whether on the *terra firma* of Earth or beyond its boundaries, the conduct remained governed by international law.[205] However, there was open debate regarding whether a nation could claim sovereignty over celestial bodies.[206] By 1961, these debates were resolved at the 1085th plenary meeting of the United Nations.[207]

During that meeting, two specific principles were laid out by the delegations. First, an articulation of the first point for which there was very little remaining debate; that international law governed the activities of Nations, even in space.[208] Second, that outer space and celestial bodies are free for exploration and use by all states in conformity with international law and are not subject to national appropriation.[209] However, beyond those two points, there were significant gaps in agreement regarding an overall operating legal

---

204 *Id.*

205 Goedhuis, *supra* note 189 at 285. US President John F. Kennedy felt particularly strongly about this point in his address to the United Nations on 15 September 1961. During this speech to the UN General Assembly, he said "As we extend the rule of law on Earth, so must we also extend it to man's new domain—outer space … All of us salute the brave cosmonauts of the Soviet Union. The new horizons of outer space must not be driven by the old bitter concepts of imperialism and sovereign claims. The cold reaches of the universe must not become the new arena of an even colder war. To this end, we shall urge proposals extending the UN Charter to the limits of man's exploration of [in] the universe, reserving outer space for peaceful use, prohibiting weapons of mass destruction in space or on celestial bodies, and opening the mysteries and benefits of space to every nation. We shall propose further cooperative efforts between all Nations in weather prediction and eventually in weather control. We shall propose, finally, a global system of communications satellites linking the whole world in telegraph and telephone and radio and television. The day need not be far away when such a system will televise the proceedings of this body to every corner of the world for the benefit of peace." *A Timeline of the Exploration and Peaceful Use of Outer Space*, UNITED NATIONS OFFICE FOR OUTER SPACE AFFAIRS, http://www.unoosa.org/oosa/en/timeline/index.html (last visited Feb. 19, 2020).

206 Goedhuis, *supra* note 189 at 285.

207 G.A. Res. 1721 (XVI) (Dec. 20, 1961), *available at* http://www.unoosa.org/oosa/en/ourwork/spacelaw/treaties/resolutions/res_16_1721.html.

208 *Id.*

209 *Id.*

document for the use and exploration of space, with the Legal Sub-Committee of UN COPUOS being unable to reach any specific agreements during its first meeting in 1962.[210]

In Resolution 1802 (XVII), the UN General Assembly urged the Legal Sub-Committee of UN COPUOS to continue its efforts to establish the baseline of basic legal principles for the activities in space by Nations. Some advancements were made, if only in general acceptance of the already agreed understanding of the need for supremacy of international law over space activities.[211] But many of the possible advancements in cooperation at the United Nations were affected by the space activities of the United States and the Soviet Union. While on the one hand the language coming from the United States and Soviet Union indicated a desire for cooperation, their corresponding space activities seemed to indicate that the exploration of space, particularly its use for only peaceful purposes, was a point of contention. For example, on 9 July 1962, the United States launched a thermonuclear weapon (Starfish Prime) into space to possibly disrupt, and allegedly to learn from, the effect such a detonation would have on the Van Allen belts (named after the discoverer and physicist James Van Allen).[212] This activity caused problems with existing satellites in space and contributed to blackouts on Earth in locations in Hawaii as a result of the ensuing electromagnetic pulse from the detonation (it also had zero effects on the Van Allen belts for the record).[213] In another instance, the United States launched 19 kilograms of thin copper needle dipoles into space in an attempt to use a near-circular, near-polar orbit at approximately 2,200 km above Earth to serve as an artificial scattering medium for radio signals.[214] This experiment failed when the needles did not deploy causing the delivery rocket to become additional space junk.[215] Activities like these highlighted the

---

210 Goedhuis, *supra* note 189 at 294.

211 *Id.*

212 M. Admin, *The Nuclear Rainbow Bomb Parties of 1962*, KNOWLEDGENUTS (Jun. 16, 2014), https://knowledgenuts.com/2014/06/16/the-nuclear-rainbow-bomb-parties-of-1962/.

213 The Van Allen radiation belt is comprised of zones of highly energetic charged particles trapped at high altitudes in the magnetic field of Earth. The belt consists of highly energetic protons that move in spiral paths along the lines of force of Earth's magnetic fields. *Van Allen Radiation Belt*, ENCYCLOPEDIA BRITTANICA, https://www.britannica.com/science/Van-Allen-radiation-belt (last visited Mar. 1, 2020).

214 *Project West Ford*, NASA SPACE SCIENCE DATA COORDINATED ARCHIVE, https://nssdc.gsfc.nasa.gov/nmc/experiment/display.action?id=1961-028A-03 (last visited Mar. 1, 2020). *See also* Michael C. Mineiro, *FY-1C and USA-193 ASAT Intercepts: An Assessment of Legal Obligations Under Article IX of the Outer Space Treaty*, 34 J. SPACE L. 321, 327 (2008).

215 *Project West Ford, supra* note 214. *See also* Mineiro, *supra* note 214 at 321. As an interesting note, not to be deterred from its potentially damaging activity, the United States still

conflict between the goals of the United Nations for cooperation and the betterment of humanity in the uses of space and the actual competition brewing between the United States and the Soviet Union.[216]

The Soviet Union, for its part, complained vehemently about the behavior of the United States, arguing that the activity of the United States was not in any way in line with the Legal Sub-Committee of UN COPUOS's developing language that outer space shall be free from activities that would otherwise hinder the exploration or use of outer space for peaceful purposes.[217] Responding, the United States leveled its own accusations against the Soviet Union, arguing that while the United States socialized its experiments in space and sought scientific input, the Soviet Union had engaged in similar activities, including high altitude nuclear tests between 1961 and 1962, with zero announcements to the scientific community or regard for the scientific impact the activity could have on the environment.[218]

Regardless of the political posturing by the two major spacefaring countries, the efforts of the Legal Sub-Committee of UN COPUOS continued. By 1963, the formations of what would be the principal space treaty and follow-on treaties were taking shape. In the report of UN COPUOS that year, its Legal Sub-Committee had established that there was a receptiveness to a treaty-type document to establish the general principles expected of states in the exploration of outer space.[219] Additionally, discussions were advancing on rescuing of astronauts, emergency landing of space vehicles, and liability for activities occurring because of space activities. In each case, it was agreed among the members that the instruments to memorialize these principles should utilize formal international agreements.[220] The following year, the Legal Sub-Committee of UN COPUOS had reiterated that it recommended that "consideration should be given to incorporation in international agreement form, in

---

managed to succeed in 1963, launching another mission that successfully injected over 350 million copper needles into orbit. *See MIDAS 6*, NASA Space Science Data Coordinated Archive, https://nssdc.gsfc.nasa.gov/nmc/spacecraft/display.action?id=1963-014A (last visited Mar. 1, 2020).

216 Admin, *supra* note 212.

217 Goedhuis, *supra* note 189 at 298.

218 *Id.*

219 U.N. General Assembly, *Agenda Item 28: International Co-operation in the Peaceful Uses of Outer Space* (1963), *available at* http://www.unoosa.org/pdf/gadocs/A_5549E_and_A_5549Add1E.pdf.

220 *Id.*

the future as appropriate, legal principles governing the activities of States in the exploration and use of outer space."[221] The Legal Sub-Committee of UN COPUOS also identified that advances had been made in a convention on returning astronauts and liability for damage by space objects, but noted it did not have time to formalize any of these agreements.[222] Instead, it pushed these issues to the next session.[223] In 1965, UN COPUOS was further encouraged by the UN General Assembly to advance the two principal draft agreements under development: the *Declaration of Legal Principles Governing the Activities of States in the Exploration and Use of Outer Space* (Resolution 1962 (XVIII)) (hereafter Principles of Exploration) and the *International Cooperation in the Peaceful Uses of Outer Space* Resolution 1963 (XVIII).[224]

By 1966, genuine progress had been made, with a draft "Treaty Governing the Exploration of the Moon and Other Celestial Bodies" being submitted by the United States and the Soviet Union."[225] In the report of the Legal Sub-Committee of UN COPUOS, there were 12 major points to be included in a subsequent treaty, which had been socialized and supported by the United States and the Soviet Union.[226] They included specific points from early discussions that international law should govern activities (point 1) and that celestial bodies should not be subject to sovereignty (point 2).[227] Additionally, goals of peaceful uses in space, including collaboration and notification to other States, were considered important elements.[228]

Concurrently to these drafting efforts, a full draft of the proposed *Treaty Governing the Exploration of the Moon and Other Celestial Bodies* was submitted by the Legal Sub-Committee of UN COPUOS with a request that it be provided to the UN General Assembly and circulated as a UN document for presentation in the Fall of 1966.[229] It was submitted to the UN General Assembly in Resolution 2222 (XXI), based largely on resolution 1962 (discussed previously),

221 U.N. General Assembly, *Report of the Committee on the Peaceful Uses of Outer Space*, U.N. Doc. A/5785 at 9 (Nov. 13, 1964), *available at* https://www.unoosa.org/pdf/gadocs/A_5785E.pdf.

222 *Id.*

223 *Id.*

224 U.N. General Assembly, U.N. Doc. A/C.1/L.363/REV.1 at 5 (Dec. 18, 1965), *available at* http://www.unoosa.org/pdf/gadocs/A_6042E.pdf.

225 U.N. General Assembly, U.N. Doc. A/6431 at 5 (Sept. 22, 1966), http://www.unoosa.org/pdf/gadocs/A_6431E.pdf.

226 *Id.* at 13–14.

227 *Id.* at 14.

228 *Id.* at 14.

229 *Id.* at 14.

but with some amplifications.[230] By January 1967 the *Treaty on Principles Governing the Activities of States in the Exploration and Use of Outer Space, Including the Moon and Other Celestial Bodies* was opened for signature by the United Kingdom, the Soviet Union, and the United States.[231] Four additional key treaties would follow through 1973. These treaties are the international baseline documents establishing the critical provisions from which both treaty and customary international space law draws today.

3 International Space Treaties

3.1 *Treaty on Principles Governing the Activities of States in the Exploration and Use of Outer Space, including the Moon and Other Celestial Bodies*

The first and most well-known of all the space treaties, the *Treaty on Principles Governing the Activities of States in the Exploration and Use of Outer Space, including the Moon and Other Celestial Bodies* (hereafter Outer Space Treaty (OST)) was adopted by the UN General Assembly as Resolution 2222 (XXI), opened for signature on 27 January 1967, and entered into force on 10 October 1967. The treaty contains 17 different articles and is specific enough to outline relevant expected behaviors during space exploration, while at the same time was general enough to gain widespread acceptance. Included within the text were the critical provisions of freedom of exploration, prohibition on national appropriation, the applicability of international law to activities undertaken by States, and a prohibition on the placement of weapons of mass destruction in outer space in any manner (to include positioning on celestial bodies).[232] The Outer Space Treaty additionally addressed the foundations for the development of the four future space treaties, to include initial provisions for the treatment of astronauts (Article IV), for liability for damage arising from space activities (Article VII), and for the registration of space objects (Article VIII).[233]

230 *Treaty on Principles Governing the Activities of States in the Exploration and Use of Outer Space, Including the Moon and Other Celestial Bodies*, U.N. Off. for Outer Space Affairs, https://www.unoosa.org/oosa/en/ourwork/spacelaw/treaties/introouterspacetreaty.html (last visited Feb. 19, 2020).

231 *Id.*

232 G.A. Res. 2222 (XXI), at 13–14 (Dec. 19, 1966), https://www.unoosa.org/pdf/gares/ARES_21_2222E.pdf.

233 *Id.*

The Outer Space Treaty, while comprehensive in many respects, still had some omissions. As alluded to earlier, the treaty makes no mention of space debris or specific prohibitions on the creation of debris. It can even be argued that since the word 'debris' is entirely absent from the Outer Space Treaty, the treaty was not meant to include any binding behaviors by States to address debris. Granted, the amount of debris orbiting Earth in 1967, when the Outer Space Treaty was signed, was insignificant compared to the amount today or the corresponding threat. Still, it would be equally flawed to assume that the Outer Space Treaty did not contemplate the threat of debris to spacefaring Nations during its development and that those Nations were not expected to minimize debris creation in the course of their operations. This can be opined from several provisions of the Outer Space Treaty.

3.1.1 Outer Space Treaty, Article I

Article I of the Outer Space Treaty states that "outer space, including the Moon and other celestial bodies, shall be free for exploration and use by all States ... and there shall be free access to all areas of celestial bodies."[234] Further, it states that "there shall be freedom of scientific investigation in outer space, including the Moon and other celestial bodies."[235] The implication of this first article, relating to space debris, is that the framers understood that among the host of things that could inhibit the exploration of space and celestial bodies, space debris was among them. Ideally, addressing space debris directly would have likely been the best solution. But at the same time, as a treaty, the language needed to be generic enough to be widely accepted. But though the creation of space debris was not specifically mentioned in Article I does not mean the drafters did not consider debris as one of the things that could hinder the free exploration and use of space. Furthermore, the activities of the United States and the Soviet Union in the years preceding the finalization of the Outer Space Treaty had raised enough concern that the current character of activities could begin to have very harmful effects on the ability to explore outer space. Specifically, in just a few years during the Outer Space Treaty development, numerous nuclear detonations had occurred above Earth's atmosphere, two occasions had seen the attempted injection of copper needles into the orbital environment (albeit only one successful one), and other 'volatile' ongoing experiments meant the framers were aware that the trajectory of activity was putting navigation in space at risk. Addressing the myriad of potentially

234 *Treaty on Principles Governing the Activities of States in the Exploration and Use of Outer Space, Including the Moon and other Celestial Bodies*, Jan. 27, 1967, 610 U.N.T.S. 205.

235 *Id.*

negative behaviors under the auspices of obligations to protect the environment indicates a commission, versus omission, as a way to address many issues, including creating space debris.

Over time, the true meaning of Article I came under additional scrutiny because of what was perceived to be a conflict between paragraphs one and two of Article I. Under paragraph one, the exploration of space was to be carried out for the benefit and in the interests of all countries, regardless of their economic or scientific development.[236] However, the second paragraph indicated that exploration of space and the Moon was to be free for exploration and use by all States and there shall be free access to all areas of celestial bodies.[237] At issue was which of the two paragraphs in Article I was of preeminent importance? Developing countries understandably advocated for paragraph one as the priority, which had enormous impact and benefit for them. As to be expected, industrial spacefaring countries were not so supportive of what they believed might be interpreted as a wealth redistribution scenario of their efforts.

Between 1988 and 1996, a series of meetings occurred in the international community, with proposals being offered to explore a possible solution to the question and find a cooperative result between the competing interests.[238] In particular, Germany and France presented a proposal titled *Declaration on International Cooperation in the Exploration and Use of Outer Space for the Benefit and in the Interests of all States, Taking into Particular Account the Needs of Developing Countries* (hereafter the Space Benefits Declaration).[239] The paper offered two solutions. The first was that it opened to Nations the right to determine the entire degree to which they would cooperate internationally, including which and how many agreements they engaged in among other countries and the commercial or non-commercial nature of those agreements.[240] Second, Nations were free to choose the most efficient method of cooperation to be able to allocate their resources effectively.[241] By 1996, the culmination of the German and French efforts resulted in a final text developed by the main committee of UN COPUOS and was sent to the UN General

236 *Id.*

237 *Id.*

238 Marietta Benko & Kai-Uwe Schrogl, *History and Impact of the 1996 UN Declaration on Space Benefits*, 13 SPACE POL'Y 139, 139 (1997).

239 *Id.* at 141.

240 *Id.*

241 *Id.*

Assembly as a formal resolution with the same original title.[242] The UN General Assembly adopted it as Resolution 51/22 in 1996.[243]

The main tenets of the Space Benefits Declaration are to stress freedom of cooperation in accordance with international law while still respecting developing countries and their needs. It reiterates that States are free to determine the parameters of their participation in international cooperation and should be advocates for ensuring an equitable basis among international partners. As related to space debris, these main tenets put the onus on developed countries to conduct their activities in such a manner that balances two things relative to the creation of space debris. On the one hand, it leaves them free to explore space in a manner that suits them and with whom they choose to engage internationally. But in the same respect, their actions must consider all international partners to maintain a healthy environment that will allow space to remain accessible, useful, and free for exploration.[244] If a State chooses to act irresponsibly, it would be evidence that they were not complying with both the spirit and the demand of the resolution. For example, the well-known Chinese 2007 ASAT test has rendered certain areas of LEO quite dangerous (at least in the near future).[245] This, in and of itself, is contrary to the principles outlined in the Space Benefits Declaration such that it hinders operations for both current and future spacefaring Nations. But, despite these efforts, Article I still lacks any specificity related to space debris.

3.1.2 Outer Space Treaty, Article II

While the shortest of all articles within the Outer Space Treaty, Article II is one of the most confounding; its brevity and simplicity often only raises more questions. Article II reads, "Outer space, including the Moon and other celestial bodies, is not subject to national appropriation by claim of sovereignty, by means of use or occupation, or by any other means."[246] On its face, several questions arise immediately. What can (or cannot) be appropriated? What does appropriation mean? If 'national' appropriation is specifically

242 G.A. Res. 51/122, (Dec. 13, 1996) https://www.unoosa.org/oosa/en/ourwork/spacelaw/principles/space-benefits-declaration.html (last visited Aug. 8, 2020).

243 Benko, *supra* note 238 at 141.

244 Pierfrancesco Breccia, *Article III of Outer Space Treaty and its Relevance in the International Space Legal Framework*, 67th Int'l Astronautical Congress, September 26–30, 2016, at 5, https://iislweb.org/docs/Diederiks2016.pdf.

245 William J. Broad & David E. Sanger, *China Tests Anti-Satellite Weapon, Unnerving U.S.*, N.Y. TIMES (Jan. 18, 2007), https://www.nytimes.com/2007/01/18/world/asia/18cnd-china.html (last accessed Aug. 8, 2020).

246 G.A. Res. 2222(XXI), art. II (Dec. 19, 1966).

prohibited, but 'non-national' appropriation is omitted, does that mean some non-national appropriation may be authorized? Or is this remedied by later international agreements?

The meaning of Article II has come under even more scrutiny as of late, particularly in light of changes to United States law. Most notably, the *Commercial Space Launch Competitiveness Act*, adopted by the United States Congress in 2015, has raised serious challenges to the interpretation of appropriation. It authorizes any US citizen to "possess, own, transport, use and sell (any) asteroid resource or space resource obtained in accordance with applicable law."[247] And there is no doubt these space resources are valuable.[248] However, most legal scholars believe that the act of mining (whenever it first occurs) is walking a legal tight rope under current international law. Scholars, such as Professor Frans von der Dunk of the University of Nebraska, argue that the common approach to justifying the activity is by viewing it in line with the 'global commons' theory of the high seas: "no State may colonize the Atlantic Ocean, yet anyone can harvest its fish."[249] And while it is true that mining the resources of a celestial body may not qualify as national appropriation to avoid Article II issues on their face (the Moon and other celestial bodies are not subject to national appropriation), what happens if, for example, an asteroid is completely consumed in a mining operation? Would that continue to qualify only as having mined a celestial body to complete exhaustion, or by extinguishing the celestial body, has it in fact been appropriated?[250] Some might say the answer is obvious, but it is still up for interpretation.

---

247 51 U.S.C. § 51303.

248 Values of asteroids are, in fact, cataloged and ranked in terms of value by 'Asterank', from small amounts in the millions, to amounts exceeding trillions. *See* ASTERANK, http://www.asterank.com/.

249 Jesse Dunietz, *Space Law Needs to Catch Up with Asteroid Mining*, SCIENTIFIC AM. (Aug. 28, 2017), https://www.scientificamerican.com/article/floating-treasure-space-law-needs-to-catch-up-with-asteroid-mining/. *See also* Armel Kerrest, *New Development and the Legal Framework covering the Exploitation of the Resources of the Moon*, Proceedings of the 47th Colloquium on the Law of Outer Space, 534, 2005.

250 For a general overview of this issue, *see* Wi Xiaodan, *China's Lunar Exploration and Utilization: Positive Energy for International Law or Not?*, 15 ANUARIO MEXICANO DE DERECHO INTERNACIONAL 137, 145–49 (2015), https://reader.elsevier.com/reader/sd/pii/S1870465415000057?token=35192F535207F6EE6539B158703C38A297055EDA8022204A228BBB20B094A3F7651936EC9D3EC3B2370E5B7315AC6692. *See also* Olusoji Nester, Africa in Space: Legal Issues and Responsibilities Related to Space Technology Development, U.N./S. Africa Symposium on Basic Space Tech., at 53, Dec. 11–15, 2017, https://www.unoosa.org/documents/pdf/psa/activities/2017/SouthAfrica/slides/Presentation53.pdf.

While these issues of appropriation are not dispositive to the issues of space debris, it raises important questions about whether space debris itself can constitute national appropriation of outer space.[251] The most specific example is debris fields created by human activities. For example, the 2007 China ASAT test (discussed previously)[252] was responsible for creating at least 37,000 pieces of debris smaller than 10 cm (some estimates say as high as 150,000), and another 2,500 pieces larger than 10 cm; trackable debris in circuitous orbit which will likely remain there for centuries.[253] 12 years later in 2019, India also performed an ASAT test that sent over 400 hundred pieces of debris into orbit, including endangering the LEO altitude in which the International Space Station (ISS) operates.[254] That debris will also likely remain for years.[255] It is also believed that China has been preparing for a possible GEO ASAT test, even if it has no intent of actually intercepting a target in such orbit.[256] However, should China do so for any reason, or should a catastrophic accidental collision occur, the most valuable orbit that supports extensive Earth operations could be rendered entirely unusable for the realistic future.

This raises the question of whether creating a debris field as a result of an ASAT test, and thereby making it unusable, can constitute an appropriation of space by a nation. However, it is true that in conducting such an activity, the debris field renders the orbit unusable to everyone *including* the offender. But it is apparent that the intent of the Article was that States should not engage in activities that would prevent others from being able to use them. Thus, in such a case, it may make a fair argument that Article II also pertains to States creation of orbital debris, particularly in the case where the act is intentional and not simply an act of negligence.

3.1.3 Outer Space Treaty, Article III

Article III binds States to execute their activities in space in accordance with international law in the interests of maintaining peace and security. While relatively brief, the inclusion of this Article, specifically for future space debris

---

251 Raising all these questions, *see generally* Stephen Gorove, *Interpreting Article II of the Outer Space Treaty*, 37 FORDHAM L.R. 349 (1969), https://ir.lawnet.fordham.edu/cgi/viewcontent.cgi?article=1966&context=flr (last visited Sept. 10, 2020).

252 See Chapter 1, section 3.

253 Gregory Wischer, *A Proposal to Counter the Greatest Space Threat*, INT'L POL'Y DIGEST (Feb. 4, 2020), https://intpolicydigest.org/2020/02/04/a-proposal-to-counter-the-greatest-space-threat/ (last visited Sep. 10, 2020).

254 *Id.*

255 *Id.*

256 *Id.*

mitigation and prevention, was possibly a stroke of genius. As discussed previously, the Outer Space Treaty was the first treaty specifically developed to address activities in space, arguably among the first formal *lex specialis*[257] of space law. However, States involved in the development of the Outer Space Treaty recognized that the end result of the treaty would not be wholly encompassing and capable of addressing all legal issues that had arisen in space, nor that would arise in the future. As a result, it was necessary to provide for gaps in the law that the Outer Space Treaty would fall short of addressing. Pertaining to the space environment, this meant that where Article I, II, IX, and XI of the Outer Space Treaty may fall short for environmental protection, general international law could either supplement, or in the absence of an applicable provision, stand in for international law (*lex generalis*[258]).

In practice, this turned out to have considerable foresight into future problems that would prevent adequate environmental protection provisions within governing international space law. The failure of *The Agreement Governing the Activities of States on the Moon and Other Celestial Bodies* (hereafter the Moon Agreement) was just such a demonstration of the benefit of Article III of the Outer Space Treaty. While no new space treaties have been signed, the fact that international law where *lex specialis* is absent in the body of space law creates a gap, environmental efforts applicable to the activities of States has continued to develop in *lex generalis*. For example, the United Nations held two global environmental conferences resulting in environmental declarations for the preservation of Earth's environment; the *Declaration of the United Nations Conference on the Human Environment* (hereafter Stockholm Declaration) in Stockholm, Sweden, in 1972 followed by the *Rio Declaration on Environment and Development* from the United Nations in Rio de Janeiro in 1992 (hereafter the Rio Declaration).[259] Both of these conferences resulted in major environmental landmark declarations which, though not formally legally binding in international law, still established general principles in international understanding of obligations towards the preservation of Earth's environment.

---

257 *Lex Specialis Law and Legal Definition*, USLEGAL, https://definitions.uslegal.com/l/lex-specialis/ (last visited Sept. 24, 2020).

258 *Lex Generalis*, OXFORD REFERENCE, https://www.oxfordreference.com/view/10.1093/acref/9780195369380.001.0001/acref-9780195369380-e-1243?rskey=OB8GGU&result=7 (last visited Sept. 24, 2020).

259 Gunther Handl, *Declaration of the United Conferences on the Human Environment (Stockholm Declaration, 1972 and the Rio Declaration on Environment and Development, 1992*, AUDIOVISUAL LIBRARY OF INT'L L. https://legal.un.org/avl/ha/dunche/dunche.html (last visited Sept. 24, 2020).

More specifically, provisions resulting from both conferences imposed a responsibility to protect the environment that exceeded the boundaries of a State's national jurisdiction that are reflected in the general body of international law related to sovereignty. Principle 21 of the Stockholm Declaration, and similarly Principle 2 of the Rio Declaration, both affirm the applicability of State's responsibilities in conformity with the Charter of the United Nations and obligations under international law. As such, under the provisions of both declarations, States must ensure that activities undertaken within their jurisdiction do not cause damage to the "environment of other States or of areas beyond the limits of national jurisdiction."[260] Outer space, being a jurisdiction outside of the control of any national jurisdiction, thus falls under the protections that are intended under the principles of these two international declarations.

Thus, the inclusion of Article III is among the most important of all the provisions of the Outer Space Treaty. Furthermore, as far as space debris and the outer space environment is concerned, it serves the additional purpose of ensuring Nations understand that the absence of a specific law prohibiting environmental irresponsibility (or others for that matter) within the body of space law does not mean that no law exists at all for environmental responsibility generally. However, applying terrestrial environmental law to outer space debris is not an area that has yet been implemented, though current academic discussions are now being explored for benefits that may be derived from doing so.[261]

3.1.4 Outer Space Treaty, Article IX

Article IX is another important Article of the Outer Space Treaty that attempts to address environmental problems, such as space debris. The relevant excerpts state that 'in the exploration and use of outer space … States Parties to the treaty … shall conduct all their activities in outer space, including the Moon

---

260 U.N. Conference on Environment and Development, Rio Declaration on Environment and Development, U.N. Doc. A/CONF. 151/26/Rev. 1 (Vol. I), annex I, at Principle 2 (1992), https://www.jus.uio.no/lm/environmental.development.rio.declaration.1992/portrait.a4.pdf. *See also* U.N. Conference on the Human Environment, U.N. Doc. A/CONF.48, at Principle 21 (1972). *See also*, Louis B. Sohn, *Stockholm Declaration on Human Environment*, 14 HARVARD INT'L L.J. 423 (1973), https://wedocs.unep.org/bitstream/handle/20.500.11822/28247/Stkhm_DcltnHE.pdf?sequence=1&isAllowed=y. *See also* report of the UN on the Human Environment, Rep. of the U.N. Conference on the Human Environment U.N. Doc. A/CONF.48/14/Rev. 1 (1973).

261 Edwin Kisiel, *Law as an Instrument to Solve the Orbital Debris Problem*, 51 ENV'T L. 223 (2021).

and other celestial bodies, with due regard to the corresponding interests of all other States Parties to the Treaty.'[262] It further says that "States Parties to the Treaty shall pursue studies of outer space, including the Moon and other celestial bodies, and conduct exploration of them to *avoid their harmful contamination* and also *adverse changes in the environment of Earth* resulting from the introduction of extraterrestrial matter and, where necessary, shall adopt appropriate measures for this purpose."[263]

If Article IX were ideally drafted, the language would state clearly that activities conducted by States Parties should attempt to avoid the harmful contamination of space in general. However, a strict reading of the sentences, some of the historical background, and the later attempt of subsequent agreements (particularly the Moon Agreement[264]) indicate that addressing space debris was not a paramount concern of the parties during drafting. However, examining the circumstances and background may help illuminate what the context was at the time of the drafting.

At the outset, we first note that there is no evidence that use of the words 'harmful contamination' was meant to refer to some specific threat. Nor is there any specific definition for 'harmful contamination.' In the effort to interpret a treaty where ambiguity exists, the Vienna Convention on the Law of Treaties, Article 31, provides that a treaty shall be interpreted in good faith in accordance with the ordinary meaning to be given to the terms of the treaty in their context and in light of its object and purpose.[265] However, in this case, there is no amplifying information on the meaning of harmful contamination within the document from which to rely on. Absent a specific definition within the document (ambiguity), Article 32 of the Vienna Convention allows for the investigation of supplementary means of interpretation, including "preparatory work of a treaty and the circumstances of its conclusion" to divine an answer.[266]

The Outer Space Treaty does give some background information in the preamble, pointing to the Principles of Exploration and its subsequent

262 Outer Space Treaty, *supra* note 234 at art. IX.

263 *Id.*

264 G.A. Res. 34/68 (1979), https://www.unoosa.org/oosa/en/ourwork/spacelaw/treaties/moon-agreement.html.

265 Vienna Convention on the Law of Treaties, 1155 U.N.T.S. 331, 340 (1969), https://treaties.un.org/doc/publication/unts/volume%201155/volume-1155-i-18232-english.pdf.

266 *Id.*

adoption in 1963 as UN Resolution 1963 (XVIII).[267] A reading of the Principles of Exploration twice references harmful interference.[268] However, it offers no definition of what that means. Instead, the Principles of Exploration only identifies that if a State believes that an activity may occur which would cause harmful interference, it may request a consultation with the potentially offending State.[269] UN Resolution 1963 (XVIII) also does not provide amplifying information to define harmful interference. In fact, it does not even use the same words. Instead, it references the potentially harmful effects of activity in space, specifically pointing to space experiments versus debris or other pollution.[270] In short, neither UN Resolutions address space debris specifically, nor appear to contemplate space debris in either variance of harmful space activity. Furthermore, notably absent from both are any use of the words 'harmful contamination', which seem to point to a specific concern for the health of the space environment itself.[271] Those words do not show up until the actual drafting of Article IX of the Outer Space Treaty.[272] Therefore, both UN Resolutions do not answer the question where the language 'harmful contamination' comes from or its specific meaning.

The documents mentioned earlier were not the first time concerns over activity in space and its potentially harmful effects has been raised, particularly in light of experiments being conducted by the Soviet Union and the United States in outer space. For example, four years earlier in 1958, the United States had initiated the world's first High Altitude Nuclear Detonation (HAND).[273] Under the Argus Series tests, the United States conducted HANDs at between 240 km and 540 km altitude with 1.5 kiloton plutonium explosions.[274] In 1961, the Soviets also engaged in their own HANDs, conducting a similar series of 1.2 kiloton explosions between 150 km and 300 km altitude.[275] In 1962, recalling

267 For the 1962 resolution, *see* G.A. Res. XVIII (Dec. 13, 1963), https://www.unoosa.org/pdf/gares/ARES_18_1962E.pdf (last visited Nov. 8, 2021). For the 1963 resolution, *see* G.A. Res. XVIII (Dec. 13, 1963), https://www.unoosa.org/pdf/gares/ARES_18_1963E.pdf (last visited Nov. 8, 2021).

268 *Id.*

269 *Id.* at 6.

270 *Id.*

271 *Id.*

272 Outer Space Treaty, *supra* note 234 at art. IX.

273 Robert Johnston, *High-Altitude Nuclear Explosions* (updated Jan. 28, 2009), http://www.johnstonsarchive.net/nuclear/hane.html (last visited Aug. 16, 2020).

274 *Id.*

275 *Id.*

the previous discussion, other experiments were also cause for concern, such as the West Ford dipole experiment and discussions of engaging in similar experiments in the future.[276] In response, questions were voiced in the international community regarding the impacts of these and other experiments.[277] There were even calls to refrain from any further launches that might have negative environmental effects until it was established that there would not be any impact on future research as a result of such actions.[278] At the same time, the International Council of Scientific Unions (ICSU) called on the Committee on Space Research (COSPAR) to examine experiments in space that might have negative effects on scientific activities in space and to make the results available to interested parties.[279] COSPAR drafted Resolution 1 (1962) and created the Consultative Group of Potentially Harmful Effects of Space Experiments (CGPHESE).[280] CGPHESE in turn began an examination of the effects of scientific activities which were underway, such as the environmental effects of rock exhaust, high-altitude nuclear explosions and projects like West Ford.[281]

By 1962, with the backdrop of these HAND experiments and others, the Soviets were first to draft a declaration addressing activities that might cause harmful interference in space. The Soviet position was that "the implementation of any measure that in any way hinders the exploration or use of outer space for peaceful purposes by other countries shall be permitted only after prior discussion of, and agreement upon, such measures between the countries concerned."[282] This provision would fail, but not because countries were clamoring to engage in harmful interference against each other. Instead, countries such as the United States, the United Kingdom, and France all refused to

276 Gunter D. Krebs, *West Ford Needles*, Gunter's Space Page, https://space.skyrocket.de/doc_sdat/westford.htm (last visited Dec. 7, 2021).

277 Mineiro, *supra* note 214 at 328 (citing Z. Niemirowicz, *A Marriage to COSPAR:Part I– 1957–1967*, 1993 COSPAR INFORMATION BULLETIN 77–88.)

278 *Id.* (citing Z. Niemirowicz, *A Marriage to COSPAR:Part I– 1957–1967*, 1993 COSPAR INFORMATION BULLETIN 77–88.)

279 HOMER E. NEWELL, JR., BEYOND THE ATMOSPHERE: EARLY YEARS OF SPACE SCIENCE, ch. 18 (2010), https://history.nasa.gov/SP-4211/ch18-2.htm (last visited Aug. 16, 2020).

280 *Id.*

281 *Id.*

282 Comm. on the Peaceful Uses of Outer Space, Union of Soviet Socialist Republics: Draft Declaration of the Basic Principles Governing the Activities of States Pertaining to the Exploration and Use of Outer Space, U.N. Doc. A/AC.105/L.2 (Sept. 10, 1962), https://www.unoosa.org/pdf/limited/l/AC105_L002E.pdf.

support the potential of a veto ("and agreement upon") being introduced into the 'definition' of 'consultation' as the use was proffered in the draft.[283]

Meanwhile, France additionally supported efforts not to "obstruct outer space activities of other States" while concurrently also joining the United States and others in rejecting the veto provisions originally proposed by the Soviet Union.[284] A series of negotiations ensued over the following year preceding the drafting of Principle 6 of the Principles of Exploration.[285] However, the haggling that ensued was not related to the types of debris that may be created or the activities that might have harmful impacts.[286] Instead, the discussions continued to focus on the negotiations and consultations which were desired, or not, between the parties prior to engaging in certain activities that could be considered harmful to the corresponding interest of other States.[287] Additionally, to what degree consultation might be required for any potential harmful interference which may occur as a result of activities conducted during the peaceful exploration and use of outer space.[288]

What was abundantly evident, as alluded to earlier, is that the final version of the Principles of Exploration was without any discussion of contamination in the space environment, and instead limited to concerns over harmful interference with activities of other States' peaceful exploration and use of outer space.[289] It was not until 1966 that the harmful contamination provision was added into the draft language of Article IX of the Outer Space Treaty. Up to that point Article IX had been a mirror reflection of paragraph 6 of the Principles of Exploration verbatim (with no mention of contamination).[290]

283 For a comprehensive review of the deliberations between the countries on this provision, *see* Mineiro, *supra* note 214 at 328–29. The final arbitration was settled by UN COPUOS, including the language that States considering engaging in behavior which may constitute harmful interference with activities of other states shall undertake "appropriate international consultations before proceeding with any such activity or experiment" and that any country believing that another State may engage in such interference may request "consultation" by that country involving the proposed activity.

284 *Id.* at 328 (citing Opening Statement by the Chairman, GA 18th Sess., Annex II, U.N. Doc. A/5482, at para. (e) (1963)).

285 *Id.* at 328–29.

286 *Id.* at 328–29.

287 *Id.*

288 *Id.*

289 G.A. Res. XVIII (Dec. 13, 1963), https://www.unoosa.org/pdf/gares/ARES_18_1962E.pdf (last visited Aug. 18, 2020).

290 Outer Space Treaty, *supra* note 234 at art. IX. *See also* G.A. Res. XVIII (Dec. 13, 1963), https://www.unoosa.org/pdf/gares/ARES_18_1962E.pdf (last visited Aug. 18, 2020).

Still lacking a definitive explanation for the addition of the harmful contamination language and what it was vectored towards solving, some scholars have offered one possible explanation.[291] In the Eighteenth Session of the UN General Assembly report of UN COPUOS, several countries were in the process of debating what the final draft of the Principles of Exploration would look like.[292] Among the many debates of the proposed articles, Canada acknowledged that Principle 6 of the Principles of Exploration addressed potential harmful interference with activities of other States in outer space.[293] However, Canada criticized that Principle 6 did not address whether or not consultation was required if an experiment would have the potential to "modify the natural environment of Earth likely to be prejudicial to the well-being of human life."[294] Canada added that, in its view, any experiment that would affect Earth's environment would also meet the "harmful interference standard."[295] Were that the case, the experiment or activity would accordingly require consultation equivalent to that expected in space.[296] Interestingly, the Canadians did not require such specificity to be addressed in the current proposed Principles of Exploration, but did state that they "trust that when it proves possible to elaborate this principle, this important omission might be rectified."[297]

It is a prevailing view that the rectification of the Canadian concern was addressed with the inclusion of 'harmful contamination' in Article IX of the Outer Space Treaty four years later.[298] However, the inclusion of the additional language still does not answer if the Canadian concern was meant to cover more than just the potential of harmful contamination on Earth.[299] Again, a further examination of Article IX states that "Parties … shall pursue studies of outer space, including the Moon and other celestial bodies, and conduct exploration of them to avoid their harmful contamination and also adverse changes in Earth's environment."[300] Special attention being paid to the word "*them*" reinforces the point that the framers, even taking into account context

291 Mineiro, *supra* note 214 321.
292 Rep. of Comm. On the Peaceful uses of Outer Space, U.N. Doc. A.5549 and Add.1 (Sept. 24, 1963), https://www.unoosa.org/pdf/gadocs/A_5549E_and_A_5549Add1E.pdf.
293 *Id.* at 17.
294 *Id.*
295 *Id.*
296 *Id.*
297 *Id.*
298 Outer Space Treaty, *supra* note 234 at art. IX.
299 Rep. of Comm. On the Peaceful uses of Outer Space, at 17, U.N. Doc. A.5549 and Add.1 (Sept. 24, 1963), https://www.unoosa.org/pdf/gadocs/A_5549E_and_A_5549Add1E.pdf.
300 Outer Space Treaty, *supra* note 234 at art. IX.

per the Vienna Convention, were referring to 'celestial bodies including Earth' as compared to concerns for the outer space environment. Had they meant to include the space environment, it is more likely they would have either specifically used the words 'outer space' or used the words 'it' instead of 'them.'[301]

That being the case, there is still the second provision of Article IX, which potentially supports the argument that the environmental protection of outer space was envisioned beyond just celestial bodies. Article IX also says that if an activity a State is considering may give the State reason to believe it would cause 'potentially harmful interference' with the activities of another State, then the State should undertake consultations before doing so.[302] Did the language 'harmful interference' envision the creation of space debris? There are two supporting arguments, but it remains an unsettled legal matter.

The first argument supporting that environmental protection in outer space from space debris was understood as being 'included but unspecified' in both the Principles of Exploration and the Outer Space Treaty is a commonsense approach to reading the documents. First, it is difficult to imagine that the document framers did not contemplate that space debris could be a problem. Unfortunately, it must also be acknowledged that attempting to include space debris at the time of drafting specifically and its limitations presented too much of a challenge. For example, were the framers to identify debris caused by nuclear explosions, and therefore try to ban such activity in this document, it could be later argued that the framers named the specific threats that must be considered between the States Parties. That, to the exclusion of all other unnamed threats. In fact, we do have evidence that nuclear detonations were soon afterward addressed from the prequel to the Outer Space Treaty, without having to make modifications to the Principles of Exploration nor acknowledged specifically in the Outer Space Treaty. The *Treaty Banning Nuclear Weapon Tests in the Atmosphere, in Outer Space, and Under Water* (hereafter the Nuclear Test Ban Treaty) was signed in Moscow on 5 August 1963 and went into effect on 10 October 1963.[303] Among many provisions, the Nuclear Test Ban Treaty prohibited nuclear weapons tests or any other nuclear explosions in outer space, full stop.[304] There was no mention, as stated, of that being a prohibited activity in the Principles of Exploration, nor in the later Outer Space

301 *Id. See also* Breccia, *supra* note 244 at 5.

302 Outer Space Treaty, *supra* note 234 at art. IX.

303 Treaty Banning Nuclear Weapon Tests in the Atmosphere, in Outer Space, and Under Water, 480 U.N.T.S. 43 Oct. 15, 1963, https://2009-2017.state.gov/t/avc/trty/199116.htm (last visited Aug. 18, 2020).

304 *Id.*

Treaty. And yet, the relevant States took it upon themselves around the same time as the Principles of Exploration resolution to draft an agreement in space meant to limit environmental damage. This provides support to the proposition that all parties understood that the intent of the Outer Space Treaty was not limited to just celestial bodies, but to space generally.

The second argument is that the framers of the original Principles of Exploration constructed them so that they acknowledged environmental threats of all kinds; hence the use of the words "harmful interference". But it also acknowledged that no one could draft an all-encompassing provision at the time that would satisfy all stakeholders. As a result, it could be argued that the framers decided on a general provision within the documents that would allow for addressing environmental threats as they arose separately. That would ensure that each threat could be reviewed once fully recognized and the full scope and threat understood. We see this again through the Nuclear Test Ban Treaty. The signatories had at least five years of history to understand the potential effects and address the individual debris issues on a case-by-case basis.

Were the Nuclear Test Ban Treaty signatories to accomplish the same degree of specificity on 'harmful interference' in the Principles of Exploration, it would be very challenging. Among those challenges was that if the drafters were to create a parent document with specificity, it could be argued by construction that anything then not specifically included was allowed. Second, all the potential environmental dangers at the time could not possibly be envisioned anyway. Most space technologies remained nascent, only a limited number of experiments had been conducted, and the international community recognized that they were limited on their overall understanding of space. This was specifically acknowledged by the representative of the United States, speaking to UN COPUOS at the 24th meeting on 22 November 1963.[305] Mr. Francis Plimpton, on behalf of the United States, said that "a comprehensive codification of legal rules for outer space would not at this stage be appropriate. The world's experience in exploring outer space had been entirely too brief to make any such codification possible yet."[306]

Left in the unenviable position of trying to gain international consensus without having all the facts at hand, paragraph 6 of the Principles of Exploration, and Article IX of the Outer Space Treaty that followed, represent diluted environmental protection provisions. However, they still serve

305 Rep. of Comm. On the Peaceful uses of Outer Space, U.N. Doc. A.5549 and Add.1 (Sept. 24, 1963), https://www.unoosa.org/pdf/gadocs/A_5549E_and_A_5549Add1E.pdf.

306 *Id.* at 15.

as adequate markers that did not preclude, and in fact encouraged, further development of smaller, more specific environmental protection provisions under the umbrella of the larger treaties. Modern adoption by many States of the IADC Debris Mitigation Guidelines into their own domestic practices is one such example of recognition by States of the need to engage in debris prevention and mitigation practices irrespective of specific provisions of the Outer Space Treaty or other international agreements. It would not be difficult to credit such successes back to the early efforts of UN COPUOS and UN Resolutions 1962 (XVIII) and 1963 (XVIII).

There still remains reasonable counterarguments that the framers 'meant what they said' and that the environment they were trying to protect was simply the celestial bodies with little real concern about the overall environment. One way to measure their intent could be to look at any potential repercussion of engaging in such an activity. An actor often engages in negative social behavior by making a value judgment between the benefits of doing something compared to the repercussions and risks in the actor's assessment. In the case of Article IX, should a state wish to engage in activity that may cause harmful contamination of the space environment, the only obligation it is required to meet is to 'undertake appropriate international consultation before proceeding with any such activity or experiment.'[307] This is a provision with no enforcement mechanism. First, it only requires consultation *if* the State believes (or admits) that harmful contamination will occur. Second, even if a State does believe harmful contamination will occur, once it has consulted other States, there is nothing to prevent the State from moving forward regardless of contrary opinions. Certainly, there is no actual preventative measure against the State insofar as the Outer Space Treaty sets out. Third, it doesn't say whom must be consulted. The State could, based on the writing, choose to consult anyone it wanted, including a limited list of friends and allies who might be unlikely to raise any resistance. Furthermore, even if a State had the audacity to call out a potential harmful incident, the 'accusing' State can only ask for a consultation with the 'offending' State. Again, there is no mandate that the offending State respond or cease its activity. There is also not an agreed definition of what is harmful for a standard by which the accusing State can either substantiate or measure a violation. In fact, it would be within the realm of the possible that the offending State simply ignored the request entirely and wholly failed to respond to the requesting State.[308]

---

307 Outer Space Treaty, *supra* note 234 at art. IX.

308 It is worth noting that there are standards and expectations regarding what 'consultation' is meant to mean when used in the context of the United Nations. According to United

The crux of the issue with Article IX is that, even if we were to point to it as the most specific provision related to debris generation (or attempt at reigning in the potential), the Outer Space Treaty has no clarity on its meaning nor any 'stick' to influence the risk or reward calculus. In fact, there is evidence that it was the intent of the drafters that Article IX be without repercussions. There is at least some commentary indicating that Japan proposed a specific modification to the consultation's requirement prior to the final language that would have required consultation with the UN Secretary-General between parties before any harmful activity could be pursued.[309] Essentially, this would be to create an arbiter of sorts, even if no actual veto were to be implemented. It would also likely require the specific adversarial parties to be present, or at least represented, before the UN Secretary-General for some accountability.[310] As we know, such an addition never came to pass. Again, the point being that had the framers been serious about protecting the environment at all beyond the actual celestial bodies, they certainly gave no indication in the form of negative repercussions on States for engaging in any polluting activities.

A second argument that the environment was not a primary concern was that the framers established obligations on States if debris caused damage to the property of another State Party, whether in outer space or on Earth. Under the Outer Space Treaty Article VI, "States Parties bear international responsibility for national activities in outer space."[311] Under Article VII, each State

---

Nations practice, the United Nations acknowledged that the use of the word consultation was frequently used throughout all legal documents of the United Nations, such as the UN Charter, resolutions, and international agreements. Generally, the expectation acknowledged by the United Nations was that consultation was understood by UN Members to impose an obligation for the "consulting party to seek the views of the party which was to be consulted and to give due consideration to the views expressed in reaching the decision as to the specific action to be taken." However, it was still acknowledged by the United Nations that the "consulting party was considered as having the sole responsibility for taking such final decision as it considered appropriate in the light of the consultations it previously held." To distinguish the obligations of consultation (minimal) from actual obligatory actions, the United Nations highlighted that where statements such as 'agreement, concurrence, or consent' could be found, this was a distinguishing marker between an obligation to act, and the former where there was simply an expectation that the other party be 'heard.' For a complete discussion, see *Meaning of the Expressions "in consultation with" and "after consultation with" in the Practice of the United Nations*, 1962 U.N. Jurid. Y.B. 268, U.N. Doc. ST/LEG/8, https://legal.un.org/unjuridicalyearbook/pdfs/english/volumes/1962.pdf.

309 Stephen Gorove, *Contamination and the Outer Space Treaty*, 14 PROC. L. OUTER SPACE 63, 65 (1971).

310 *Id.*

311 Outer Space Treaty, *supra* note 234 at art. VI.

Party from whose territory or facility an object is launched is 'internationally liable for damage to another State Party to the Treaty ... by such object or its component parts ...'[312] The 'component' language was additionally repeated in Article VIII, when referencing the requirement to register an object by a State Party for retention of jurisdiction or control over an object or its component parts.[313] These provisions, in combination, provide compelling evidence that had the framers intended for the environments beyond the celestial bodies to remain pristine, there would not have likely been a need to establish liability provisions.

3.1.5 Outer Space Treaty, Article XI

The last article indicating some obligation toward mitigation and prevention for space debris under the Outer Space Treaty is Article XI.[314] It states, in part, that to promote the peaceful exploration of outer space, States agree to notify the United Nations (Secretary-General specifically) as well as the public and the international scientific community of the 'nature, conduct, locations and results of' their exploration activities 'to the greatest extent feasible and practicable.'[315] The original drafting of this provision was meant to be much more stringent, with an expectation of mandatory notification to States by other States on their activities in space.[316] Were that to have been the ultimate outcome, Article XI may have found a much more prominent and respectable position as a prevention and mitigation Article for space debris within the Outer Space Treaty. Instead, the history of the development of the Article demonstrates that while the United States and some allies, such as Japan, pushed hard for a mandatory requirement, the Soviet Union was having none of it.

As originally proposed, the United States had argued that there should be mandatory reporting to the UN Secretary-General of 'the nature, conduct, and locations' of activities on celestial bodies.[317] This was in line with the United States theme during the development of the Outer Space Treaty as a whole that the more transparency between Nations and scientific communities on space

---

312 *Id.*

313 *Id.*

314 *Id.*

315 *Id.*

316 Outer Space Treaty, *supra* note 234 at art. V & XI. *See also* Paul G. Dembling & Daniel M. Arons, *The Evolution of the Outer Space Treaty*, 33 J. AIR L. & COM. 419, 441 (1967), https://digitalcommons.unl.edu/cgi/viewcontent.cgi?article=1002&context=spacelawdoc.

317 Dembling & Arons, *supra* note 316 at 445.

activities, the less likely that space would become a threat for all involved.[318] As such, the original language proposed by the United States suggested that in addition to the mandatory reporting to the UN Secretary-General, that States were also required to make the findings of their activities 'freely available to the public and scientific community.'[319] And, while the Soviet Union did not indicate objection to the release of information, their position was that the provisions of mandatory reporting were a non-starter.[320] Dissemination of information would occur by the UN Secretary-General, in the opinion of the Soviets, only in the event that States like the Soviet Union volunteered to provide it in the first place.

Other efforts by States attempted to bridge the gap between the United States and the Soviet Union by proposing compromises that were close to imposing some obligations, without being outright.[321] For example, the United Arab Republic proposed that "all information shall be promptly submitted, preferably in advance … or immediately after" the activities.[322] However, any language that went beyond voluntariness was met with skepticism by the Soviet Union.[323] Even the United States retained some aversion with the United Arab Republic's proposal in its whole form.[324]

The Soviets ultimately indicated that the only mandatory provision within the Outer Space Treaty that the Soviets were willing to consider, and that was ultimately included, rested in the mandatory provisions of Article V, which required that States 'shall immediately' inform others of any threats that could 'constitute a danger to the life or health of astronauts.'[325] In an effort to at least

318 *Id.*

319 *Id.*

320 *Id.*

321 *Id.*

322 *Id.*

323 *Id.*

324 *Id.*

325 Outer Space Treaty, *supra* note 234 at art. V & XI. *See also* Dembling & Arons, *supra* note 316 at 441. There are additional explanations why the Soviet's were such stalwarts against mandatory provisions. One of the more significant concerns was that the military aspect of the provision was not specifically addressed. Should reporting have been required for all space activity, absent language otherwise, that would have included military activities. While many military activities, as peaceful endeavors, would likely be offered in transparency, the developing space competition at the time undoubtedly left the Soviet Union unwilling to hinder their potential desires in space over such an outright transparency requirement. *See* Bin Cheng, *Properly Speaking, Only Celestial Bodies Have Been Reserved for Use Exclusively for Peaceful (Non-Military) Purposes, but Not Outer Void Space*, 75 INT'L L. STUD. 81, 91–91 (2000).

advance the discussion, the United States compromised during the deliberations by agreeing to a voluntary reporting standard so long as language was included in the final provisions that States "to the extent feasible and practicable" will communicate their activities to the UN Secretary-General.[326]

As drafted, Article XI cannot necessarily be said to advance the efforts of space debris prevention or mitigation. However, it could be said at least that under the best circumstances, the provisions within Article XI could result in reporting of debris creation as a result of State activity to the UN Secretary-General under the 'results of such activities' provisions.[327] For example, if an experiment of any sort results in some type of equipment destruction resulting in debris creation, that would arguably be the 'result of such activities' in space. In turn, under the provisions of Article XI, fellow States might have a valid expectation that the result of that activity, and the dangerous debris now in the environment, should be reported in accordance with the language of Article XI 'to the greatest extent feasible and practicable.' While again the provision to do so remains voluntary, States may be at least a little hesitant to engage in potentially destructive behavior because of an expectation they should inform the UN Secretary-General if the results are less than desirable.

One last note on an issue touched above provides at least some context to the recognition that space debris was a concern during the drafting and remained one in the ensuing years after both the Principles of Exploration and the Outer Space Treaty were signed. The Moon Agreement, albeit a ratification failure, reflects an attempt to preserve not only the Moon, but also the environment around the celestial body and its orbits in particular.[328]

In Article 7, the Moon Agreement says that "in exploring and using the Moon, States Parties shall take measures to prevent the disruption of the existing balance of its environment … [including] by its harmful contamination through the introduction of extra-environmental matter or otherwise."[329] While a cursory review might assume that meant just the Moon as a celestial body, Article 1 of the agreement states that "reference to the Moon shall include orbits around or other trajectories to or around it."[330] As such, it can be seen that the two provisions in concert (the Moon includes its external environment, and a

326 Dembling & Arons, *supra* note 316 at 447.

327 Outer Space Treaty, *supra* note 234 at art. XI.

328 G.A. Res. 34/68 (1979), https://www.unoosa.org/oosa/en/ourwork/spacelaw/treaties/moon-agreement.html.

329 *Id.* at art. 7.

330 *Id.* at art. 1(2).

prohibition on introducing foreign matter) combine to create a ban on orbital debris being introduced.

It is worth noting that of all the existing space treaties, the Moon Agreement has been particularly 'unsuccessful' if measured in terms of ratifying countries. In fact, the Moon Agreement struggled to even achieve the number of ratifications necessary to enter into force. The Legal Sub-Committee of UN COPUOS developed the agreement from 1972–1979, and it was adopted in that final year under Resolution 34/68.[331] However, by 1984, it had only achieved five ratifications (the fifth being in that same year by Austria) but this was the number sufficient to allow it to enter into force, which it didn't accomplish until July 1984.[332]

It appears that the failure of the Moon Agreement can be largely attributed to language within Article 11 of the agreement. The language in that article precludes the natural resources of the Moon from becoming the property of any State.[333] The only exception is if the resources are extracted according to a (not-yet created) international regime to govern the exploitation of the natural resources of the Moon (Article 11, section 5).[334] Many countries foresaw potential unacceptable limitations on the potential for utilizing physical resources of the Moon, including the United States, Russia, and China. Between foresight, and also with the help of some pressure from industry groups and other special interests that saw the possibilities for exploitation and profitability of lunar resources in the future, most major spacefaring nations declined to sign the agreement.[335] That does not mean that the Moon Agreement is not still a culmination of the ideal provisions that many States have been attempting to impose since the earliest treaty discussions began. Because of these ideals, there still may be hope for the Moon Agreement principles if the issues in contention can still be sufficiently modified in the future to address concerns like resource use, especially as the interest in exploration of the Moon renews again.

331 *Agreement Governing the Activities of States on the Moon and Other Celestial Bodies*, U.N. OFF. OUTER SPACE AFFAIRS, https://www.unoosa.org/oosa/en/ourwork/spacelaw/treaties/intromoon-agreement.html (last visited Feb. 19, 2020).

332 *Id.*

333 G.A. Res. 34/68 (1979), 11, https://www.unoosa.org/pdf/gares/ARES_34_68E.pdf.

334 Outer Space Treaty, *supra* note 234 at art. 11, § 5.

335 *See generally L5 News: UN Moon Treaty Falling to US Opposition Groups*, NAT'L SPACE SOCIETY (Mar. 1982), https://space.nss.org/l5-news-un-moon-treaty-falling-to-us-opposition-groups/ (last visited Feb. 19, 2020).

3.2 *The Remaining 'Big 4' International Space Treaties*

As discussed, the Outer Space Treaty provided the baseline for conduct in space and created a need for more specificity in certain operational areas. As a result, additional treaties were borne out of the Outer Space Treaty to address specific activities of States in space that required more granularity than the Outer Space Treaty could provide.

The space treaties that followed the Outer Space Treaty include the *Agreement on the Rescue of Astronauts, the Return of Astronauts and the Return of Objects Launched into Outer Space* in 1968 (hereafter the Rescue Agreement), the *Convention on International Liability for Damage Caused by Space Objects* of 1972 (hereafter the Liability Convention), the *Convention on Registration of Objects Launched into Outer Space* of 1976 (hereafter the Registration Convention), and finally, as touched on already, the *Agreement Governing the Activities of States on the Moon and Other Celestial Bodies* of 1984.[336] Each of these treaties address expected behaviors in space including, but not limited to, how space should be used and expectations for its use.

4 Jurisdiction of Space Objects

Even absent the Moon Agreement, these treaties have tackled some of the most challenging issues. As discussed above, one of the foundational issues, for example, is jurisdiction over debris to begin with. In action, Article VIII of the Outer Space Treaty addressed jurisdiction by providing that a State "shall retain jurisdiction ..." over objects.[337] The Registration Convention also elaborates this point, such that it refers in its own Article II back to Article VIII

336 The Rescue Agreement is formally known as the *Agreement on the Rescue of Astronauts, the Return of Astronauts and the Return of Objects Launched into Outer Space*. The UN General Assembly adopted it in Resolution 2345 (XXII), opened for signature on 22 April 1968, and entered into force on 3 December 1968. The Liability Convention followed it, adopted by the UN General Assembly in Resolution 2777 (XXVI), opened for signature on 29 March 1972, and entered into force on 1 September 1972. The Registration Convention, formally known as the *Convention on Registration of Objects Launched into Outer Space*, was adopted by the UN General Assembly in Resolution 3235 (XXIX), and opened for signature on 14 January 1975. It entered into force on 15 September 1976. The last, and signed by the fewest States, is the *Agreement Governing the Activities of States on the Moon and Other Celestial Bodies*, adopted by the UN General Assembly in its Resolution 24/68, opened for signature on 18 December 1979, and entered into force on 11 July 1984. *See Space Law Treaties and Principles*, UNITED NATIONS OFFICE FOR OUTER SPACE AFFAIRS, http://www.unoosa.org/oosa/en/ourwork/spacelaw/treaties.html (last visited Feb. 29, 2020).

337 Outer Space Treaty, *supra* note 234 at art. VIII.

of the Outer Space Treaty, utilizing the language of jurisdiction that in the case of two or more launching States, one of the States must determine who will retain jurisdiction.[338] In both cases, the State(s) must establish jurisdiction over objects, thus asserting the privileges, and in turn, obligations for the space object. This stands independent of registration, such that, as discussed below, registration does impose obligations. However, not all cases have the same launching State and State of registry, such as in cases where agreements between the States specifically dictate otherwise.

5 Registration of Space Objects

Currently, ownership of space objects, whether operating or not, exists in perpetuity. The basis for this begins with an analysis of Articles VI, VII, and VIII of the Outer Space Treaty. At a basic level, these articles establish that a State which has launched an object into space will always own and be responsible for it. Article VI imposes several obligations on States, including, but not limited to, responsibility for national activities, ensuring that activities are conducted in conformity with the treaty, authorizing and continually supervising the activities and sharing international responsibility for which the State is a participant.[339] Based on this, whether activities are being conducted by the State itself or by private entities within its jurisdiction, States retain responsibility for the activities.[340] Article VII adds that damage created by an object of a State in space will incur liability for the object by the State.[341] Finally, Article VIII concludes that a State party on whose registry an object is launched into outer space shall retain jurisdiction and control over such object and all personnel.[342] The article further states that ownership of an object launched into outer space, including those landed or constructed on a celestial body, and

338 United Nations Office for Outer Space Affairs, United Nations Treaties and Principles on Outer Space and Related General Assembly Resolutions, 9–10, U.N. Sales No. E.08.I.10 (2008).

339 Outer Space Treaty, *supra* note 234 at art. VI.

340 Frans G. von der Dunk, *The Origins of Authorization: Article VI of the Outer Space Treaty and International Space Law*, 69 Space, Cyber & Telecomm. L. Program, Faculty Publ'n (2011), https://digitalcommons.unl.edu/cgi/viewcontent.cgi?article=1068&context=spacelaw (discussing breadth of State activities and what are considered national activities, including private enterprises).

341 Outer Space Treaty, *supra* note 234 at art. VII.

342 *Id.* at art. VIII.

their parts, are not affected by their presence in outer space.[343] If they return to Earth it will remain theirs if it can be identified and claimed.

Bolstering Article VIII of the Outer Space Treaty is the Registration Convention. Article II, Section 2, provides that where there are two or more launching States regarding one object, the States will resolve who will register the object. By doing so, the launching State of registry will retain jurisdiction and control over the space object and any personnel thereof.[344] Therefore, by launching an object under the Outer Space Treaty and registering the object under the Registration Convention, the international treaties have created a rubric by which ownership is determined. Meanwhile, in all cases of registration under the two Treaties, neither provides any mechanism for removing a State from a registry.

It is not to say that there is no ability to change some of the obligations of an original launching and registry State, but those options are limited. For example, company A of State A that launched a satellite could transfer ownership of the satellite to company B of State B. But while the contract may transfer ownership per se, the registering State still have obligations pertinent to that object and will retain those for the entirety of the satellite's existence, only some of which can be indemnified. Therefore, State A will always retain much of the obligations for the object that it had by launching and registering the object. Even contractual indemnification for liability as a launching State can be agreed to in such a transfer, however that still would still not absolve the original State of the obligations which were incurred upon the launch and registry of the original object. Ultimately, even a transfer of rights does not disavow at least one State from being responsible, liable, and the owner in perpetuity of a space object and arguably any debris derived therefrom.

6 Conclusion

These five international treaties reflect important steps in the establishment of the body of international space law and the most important provisions for operations in space. However, they fall short when it comes to 'precision and definition', especially on the issue of space debris mitigation and how to address the problem.[345] As discussed, when it comes to space debris guidelines

343 *Id.*

344 *Id.*

345 Chatterjee, *supra* note 49 at 5 (citing Nicolas Mateesco Matte, *Outer Space Treaty*, *in* 3 ENCYCLOPEDIA OF PUBLIC INTERNATIONAL LAW, 836, 838 (R. Bernhardt, ed., 1992).

for mitigation, there are no specific treaties that have been agreed to about limiting the creation of space debris. Instead, there have been discussions among the many interested countries and guidelines which have been published. Many of these discussions have resulted in provisions being included in the domestic law of States or provided as influential voluntary guidelines. As these guidelines exist, they are not public international law formed via treaty. Instead, they comprise a series of influential recommendations. But, it is possible that there may be an argument that some of these provisions stand, even absent treaty, as internationally binding law. We refer to this type of non-treaty law as customary international law. The next chapter will highlight the importance of this body of law. In particular, understanding customary international law will be crucial to determining if there exists binding legal provisions pertaining to the prevention or mitigation of space debris even absent a treaty on the subject.

Matte stated in reference to the drafting of the Outer Space Treaty, it "contains[sic] general principles for which the peaceful exploration and use of outer space, including the Moon and other celestial bodies ... was not to deal with all contingencies that might arise from the exploration and use. It is not a perfect instrument. Some of its principles are obscurely stated. Nevertheless, it represents the most important source of space treaty law." *Id.*

CHAPTER 3

Development of Customary International Law—Space Law and Debris Mitigation

1 Introduction

Complementing public international law are international rules with the force of law that neither follow formal written requirements nor the generally accepted treaty law characteristics for establishment. This alternate form of law is called customary international law. And, while tangible written documents such as formal treaties are very powerful international tools (clear, written, symbolic and so forth), customary international law is understood and treated with equal weight among Nation-States.

The strength of customary international law exists because though it may lack some of the same hallmarks of formal treaty law, it still equally reflects a full understanding and meeting of the minds (through practice and indications of assent) between States as formal written documentation does. Additionally, it has distinct advantages, such as establishing a working practice in much less time than typical treaty processes have taken to achieve the same result. Another advantage is that often formal treaties are required to be drafted to the level of the 'lowest common denominator.'[346] In other words, typically to get a treaty agreed upon by all interested States, drafters are often forced to write the instruments in a manner most agreeable to the least cooperative State. As a result of this 'dilution', the final formal treaty product often becomes more symbolic than actually clear and compelling.[347] This flaw rarely exists in customary international law since its very formulation is the direct result of cooperation among States to agree to a binding set of rules. Furthermore, it doesn't

346 Chatterjee, *supra* note 49 at 5 (citing Nicolas Mateesco Matte, *Outer Space Treaty*, *in* 3 Encyclopedia of Public Int'l L., 836, 838 (R. Bernhardt, ed., 1992)).

347 Michael P. Scharf, *Accelerated Formation of Customary International Law*, 20 ILSA J. Int'l & Comp. L. 305, 310 (2014) (citing H.L.A. Hart, The Concept of Law 130 (1961) (referring to the possibility of ambiguity as the "penumbra of uncertainty resulting from the differences in cultures as they come together to form treaties, including different languages cultural beliefs, legal beliefs, and political divides").

© KONINKLIJKE BRILL NV, LEIDEN, 2023 DOI:10.1163/9789004535848_005 require the logistical ratification by some set of States for enactment; in fact, most States actually need to do absolutely nothing but acquiesce.[348]

2 Basic Requirements of Customary International Law

Traditionally, two elements are required to establish customary international law: a subjective element and an objective element. As the late Professor Bin Cheng, Professor Emeritus of Air and Space Law of the University College London, once stated:

> The orthodox view is that a rule of customary law has two constitutive elements: (I) *corpus*, the material or objective element, and (II) *animus*, the psychological or subjective element. The *corpus* of a rule of customary law is the existence of a usage (*consuetudo*) embodying a rule of conduct. The *anuimus* consists in the conviction on the part of States that the rule embodied in the usage is binding (*opinio juris*).[349]

These two elements developed from the decisions of the predecessor to the International Court of Justice (ICJ), the Permanent Court of International Justice (PCIJ) in the 1929 *S.S. Lotus* case.[350] This case first established that international law was either reflected in expressed rules or those generally accepted as principles of law.[351] Further elaboration can be found in the famous *North Sea Continental Shelf Case*[352] decided by the ICJ. The objective element was

---

348 Lance Helfer & Ingrid Wuerth, *CIL as an Instrument Choice Perspective*, 37 MICH. J. INT'L L. 563 (2016), https://repository.law.umich.edu/cgi/viewcontent.cgi?article=1340&context=mjil. *See also* Jonathan I. Charney, *Universal International Law*, 87 AM. J. INT'L L. 529 (1993).

349 Bin Cheng, *United Nations Resolutions on Outer Space: "Instant" International Customary Law?*, 5 INDIAN J. INT'L L. 23, 35 (1965).

350 This case was borne out of a collision of two ships, one belonging to France (the *S.S. Lotus* mail ship) and another to Turkey (the *S.S. Boz-Kourt*). The *Boz-Kourt* was struck and sunk, and eight Turkish nationals were killed. In the discussion, the Court said of international law that it "governs relations between independent States. The rules of law binding upon States therefore emanate from their own free will as expressed in conventions or by usages generally accepted as expressing principles of law and established to regulate relations between these co-existing independent communities or with a view to the achievement of common aims. Restrictions upon the independence of States cannot therefore be presumed." *SS "Lotus"* (Fr. v. Turk.), Judgment, 1927 P.C.I.J. No. 9, at 18 (Sept. 7).

351 Scharf, *supra* note 347 at 311 (citing SS "Lotus" (Fr. v. Turk.), Judgment, 1927 P.C.I.J. No. 9, at 18 (Sept. 7)).

352 *North Sea Continental Shelf* (Ger. v. Den. & Ger. v. Neth.), Judgment, 1969 I.C.J. Nos. 51 & 52 (Feb. 20). In 1967, the issue of the proper apportionment of the continental shelf

that "the acts concerned amount to a settled practice, [and] they must also be such, or be carried out in such a way, as to be evidence of a belief that this practice is rendered obligatory by the existence of a rule of law requiring it."[353] The Court went on to say that "States concerned must therefore feel that they are conforming to what amounts to a legal obligation."[354] This means that there is a widespread and consistent State practice and behaviors reflecting that at least some Member-States of the international community act as though a behavior is a law, even if not enumerated, hence making it 'law' in practice. Second, there has to be what is called the '*opinio juris*', or the subjective element, generally meaning that there is an understanding by States that, written or not, they are obligated to follow the rule as understood.[355] This can manifest itself in several recognized ways, such as in the legislative body of work of a State, diplomatic statements consistent with the understanding, political statements indicating an adherence or recognition of the law or by simply acting accordingly.[356]

Collectively, where these two elements exist (the *corpus* and *animus*), under customary international law States are considered bound.[357] However,

---

extending from a country and the delineation with others came to a head in the ICJ between the Federal Republic of Germany and Denmark, and concurrently between the Federal Republic of Germany and the Netherlands.

353 *Id. See also* VAUGHAN LOWE, INTERNATIONAL LAW para. 2.1.2 (2015). *See also* International Law Association, *Report of the 69th Conference*, Committee on the Formation of Customary Int'l L., para. 10, page 729 (London, 2000), setting out a clear customary international law-making process.

354 NORTH SEA CONTINENTAL SHELF, *supra* note 352.

355 *Id.*

356 Nie Jing Jing & Yang Hui, *Revisit the Concept of International Custom in International Space Law,* 54 PROC. INT'L INST. OF SPACE L. 348, 348–356 (2013).

357 As it stands today, this is a straightforward application of a classic view of customary international law, and for the purposes of this book focusing on space debris, the view applied to the practice of ESA and the States assessed. That is not to say that this author does not recognize that both elements of customary international law are coming under increasing scrutiny for their sufficiency to truly reflect understanding of nations. To the first element, what is State practice, many scholars have been recently challenging both what a State is for the purposes of making a determination, and even if determined, which practices of the States are applicable to the determination of practice for the elements of customary international law. Furthermore, should varying weight for influence be given to certain practices over others, such as between words versus actions. As to the second requirement that States engage in the practice of the understood rule with a belief that they are legally bound to do so (*opinio juris*), again there is considerable modern literature that critiques exactly how to substantiate this element. This includes attempting to assess which State organs should be examined to determine applicable State practice, and even more, what acts of those organs specifically; Public proclamations, physical acts, or even legal implementations of rules reflecting the practice? All of these are valid criticisms.

what is most important is that the States themselves understand the binding nature of customary international law and enforce it internally and among all other international partners. It is true that in rare circumstances, exceptions to conformity do exist. Though rare, the phenomenon of a 'persistent objector' is tacitly recognized in customary international law. Under this practice, so long as a State clearly expresses its objection at the time of apparent formation of customary international law, publicly and clearly maintains its objection, and acts accordingly, it is not considered bound by the developing customary international law.[358] It is also worth noting that there is no solid evidence of any

---

However, for the purposes of this book, the classic focus does not ignore these concerns, but embraces the classical approach while these concerns are debated and slowly resolved. For an extensive discussion of the questions at issue, and the scholars embroiled in challenging these classical notions, *see* REEXAMINING CUSTOMARY INTERNATIONAL LAW (Brian D. Lepard ed. 2017).

358 G.A. Res. 73/203 part six, Annex, conclusion 15, Identification of Customary International Law (Dec. 20, 2018). *See also* Int'l Law Comm'n, Third Rep. on Identification of Customary International Law, Michael Wood, Special Rapporteur, U.N. Doc. A/CN.4/682 (Mar. 27, 2015), citing the International Court of Justice discussion in *North Sea Continental Shelf*, that rules of customary international law must have "equal force for all members of the international community," but recognizing that an "emerging rule which is persistently objected to, and maintains its objection after the rule has 'crystallized', is not bound by it." *See also* Statement of Principles Applicable to the Formation of General Customary International Law, Rep. of Comm. On Formation of Customary (General) Int'l L., INT'L LAW ASSOC. at 27 (2000), https://www.law.umich.edu/facultyhome/drwcasebook/Documents/Documents/ILA%20Report%20on%20formation%20of%20Customary%20Internati"nal%20Law.pdf (last visited Aug. 5, 2020). According to the ILA, the persistent objector rule generally states that if a State disagrees and overtly fails to both indicate and act in accordance with a rule during its formation and after, and therefore "manifest their dissent, the requisite [consent/formation] condition is not fulfilled." Therefore, the customary rule as it is established cannot be applied to that State. *See also* Scharf, *supra* note 347 at 309. Scharf provides a number of examples of recognition by the ICJ to the persistent objector rule. In the *Asylum* (Colombia v. Peru) Judgment, 1950 I.C.J. 7, at 276–278 (Nov. 20), the ICJ recognized Peru's adamant stance against a rule conceded by other Latin American States. Also, in *Fisheries Jurisdiction* (U.K. v. Iceland) Judgment, 1951 I.C.J. 55, at 131 (Feb 1973), the ICJ recognized persistent objector status by Norway against a claim by the United Kingdom that there was an international customary law limiting closing lines in bays to a length of ten miles. Scharf also recognizes the limits mentioned that recognition hinders on an objection from inception to the rule (not just when it then suits) and also binding on new states since there is no 'subsequent objector' rule available (citing Maurice H. Mendelson, *Formation of Customary International Law, in* 272 RECUEIL DES COURS 159, 227–244 (1998), https://files.pca-cpa.org/pcadocs/bi-c/2.%20Canada/4.%20Legal%20Authorities/RA-97%20-%20Formation%20of%20Customary%20International%20Law,%20M.%20Mendelson%20(1998).pdf. Furthermore, according to the ILA, "there is widespread agreement that, even if there is a persistent objector rule in international law, it applies only when the customary rule is in the process of

State expressing 'persistent objector' status for any current law in the body of space law.[359]

2.1 *Time Requirement of Customary International Law*

Because of the importance and impact the development of customary international law has, it is generally understood that the formation of these laws should occur over an extended period of years. This extended duration of time has the added benefit of ensuring that the 'custom' is widely understood and known. It also allows for an opportunity to develop in actual practice such that the absence of a written document does not diminish the understanding of the law's parameters. How long a period must pass remains a point of debate, but some States have articulated general guidelines. For example, the Supreme Court of the United States considered "decades or even centuries" to be appropriate.[360] The International Law Commission was less clear, but still addressed their expectation that customary international law develop "over a considerable period of time."[361] Others, such as Germany and France, have been

---

emerging. *See* Statement of Principles Applicable to the Formation of General Customary International Law, Rep. of Comm. On Formation of Customary (General) Int'l L., INT'L LAW ASSOC. at 27 (2000), https://www.law.umich.edu/facultyhome/drwcasebook/Documents/Documents/ILA%20Report%20on%2"Formation%20of%20customary%20International%20law.pdf (last visited Aug. 5, 2020). Therefore, it does not benefit States that came into existence only after the rule matured or which became involved in the activity in question only at a later stage. Still less can it be invoked by those who existed at the time and were already engaged in the activity but failed to object at that stage. In other words, there is no 'subsequent objector' rule. The rule, if it exists, is available only for those who object before the rule has fully emerged." For arguments countering Scharf and other scholars that the persistent objector theory is unsound, *see* J. Patrick Kelly, *Customary International Law in Historical Context, in* REEXAMINING CUSTOMARY INTERNATIONAL LAW 47, 78, Section 2.5 (Brian D. Lepard, ed. 2017), arguing that the theory of the persistent objector is fundamentally anathema to the concept of the consensus (actively or passively) that characterizes customary international law. Additionally, arguing that examples discussed above in *Fisheries* and *Asylum* are either more contractual arrangements (*regional custom*) in the case of *Asylum* or that reference in *Fisheries* in dicta to the persistent objector is merely a 'one-off' deviation or error, and not meant to be a recognition of the existence of the persistent objector.

359 Scharf, *supra* note 347 at 309.

360 Manley O. Hudson, *Article 24 of the Statute of the International Law Commission*, 2 Y.B. Int'l L. Comm'n 24, U.N. Doc. A/CN.4/16 (1950)).

361 *Id.* at para. 11(b). The more recent ILC report (2018) still demonstrates consistency with this theme, specifically dismissing the concept of 'instant custom' and instead indicating that while a short period of time is not prohibitive of the creation of a customary international law, a long duration may result in more extensive practice. However, 'time immemorial' or considerable or fixed duration of a general practice is not a condition for the existence of a customary rule. *See* Int'l Law Comm'n, Rep. on the Work of its Seventieth

much more specific, setting expectations at 30 years and 40 years respectively, whereas the International Court of Justice has noted that 'the duration of time required for the generation of customary law cannot be mathematically and uniformly decided.'[362]

2.1.1 How Important Is the Time Element of Customary International Law in Modern Times

The question of how much time must pass before the establishment of customary international law has come under further scrutiny recently. For the development of space law, this may be a positive. Specifically, with the recent rapid expansion of actors in space, especially the private sector, classic customary international law is unlikely to provide the adaptive rule-making that modern space activities will need. Modern times may increasingly call for recognition of laws that can be fashioned and executed in a shorter and more effective timeframe. And while traditional customary international law has been effective at filling the gap in time between when Nations accept a course of conduct and any eventual formal treaty, the significant duration of time for development of customary international law remains a hinderance.

The leading argument that duration of time should not be a dispositive element argues that, in effect, the first element on its own allows for customary international law to be developed almost, if not actually, instantaneously. Dean Scharf would call States that might subscribe to this approach as 'custom pioneers', such that there are those who are "first" to test the waters of a possible new action which might develop into customary international law.[363] Though not exact analogies, the requirements remain the same in theory as traditional customary international law, that there are subjective and objective elements. However, the duration of time may no longer be as relevant.

Session, Supplement No. 10 (1/73/10), U.N. Doc. A/73/10, at Conclusion 8, para. 9, page 135/149, https://legal.un.org/ilc/reports/2018/english/a_73_10_advance.pdf.

362 Franceso Parisi and Daniel Pi, *The Emergence and Evolution of Customary International Law*, University of Minnesota Law School Legal Research Paper Series Research Paper No. 12–40, pg. 16 (citing Gregory I. Tunkin, *Remarks on the Juridical Nature of Customary Norms in International Law*, 49 CA L. R. 419–430 (1961); Nicolas M. Mateesco, La Coutume Dans Les Cycle Juridiques Internationaux (1947)). *See* NORTH SEA CONTINENTAL SHELF, *supra* note 352, dissenting opinion of Justice Tanaka pg. 176.

363 Scharf, *supra* note 347 at 313.

2.1.2 Continuous Claim and Response

In supporting this position, Dean Scharf examined the proposals of Professor Myres McDougal of Yale Law School and Professor Anthony D'Amato of Northwestern University as they related to the inception of instant customary law. According to Dean Scharf, Professor McDougal posited an approach called "continuous claim and response."[364] In such a system, one State acts upon another, and then analyzes the response of the State acted upon. If favorable, the development of customary international law begins, especially if other States either passively or actively indicate concurrence with the behavior.[365] As Dean Scharf puts it, this is a backward-looking formulation, relying on 'jumping in' to test if the waters are hot or cold and determining the answer once in the water.[366]

Contrasting is the approach discussed by Dean Scharf posited by Professor D'Amato. He proposes what is called an "articulation and act."[367] In this formulation, the test is somewhat opposite, akin to a State hinting that it intends to jump in the water, and either following up by doing so or asking the State who owns the water what it thinks about that. This can take the form of a draft instrument, a broad statement in the UN General Assembly, or some other indication of a proposed action. It is essentially equivalent to getting a towel and heading to the pool if attempting to signal that you are going for a swim. This approach has been called the "modern custom" approach since it reflects a more forward-looking approach.[368] The articulation is intended to provoke a response for which the initiating State can then gauge the acceptability or reception to the act; "I wonder what everyone will think of me going for a swim … I am going to get my towel and find out."

2.1.3 Harry S. Truman and the Continental Shelf—Testing the Time Requirement

This modern theory of 'heading to the pool' was tested by President Harry S. Truman in 1945. On 28 September of that year, President Truman made the following Proclamation:

364 *Id.* at 306 (citing M.S. McDougal & N.A. Schlei, *The Hydrogen Bomb Tests in Perspective: Lawful Measures for Security*, 64 YALE L.J. 648 (1955)).

365 See *generally Id.*

366 *Id.* at 314.

367 Antony D'Amato, *Groundwork for International Law*, 108 AMER. J. INT'L L. 4, 650 (2014). *See also* Scharf, *supra* note 347 at 318–329.

368 D'Amato, *supra* note 367 at 650. *See also* Scharf, *supra* note 347 at 318–329.

> I, Harry S. Truman, President of the United States of America, do hereby proclaim the following policy of the United States of America with respect to the natural resources of the subsoil and sea bed of the continental shelf. Having concern for the urgency of considering and prudently utilizing its natural resources, the Government of the United States regards the natural resources of the subsoil and sea bed of the continental shelf beneath the high seas but contiguous to the coast of the United Sates as appertaining to the United States, subject to its jurisdiction and control. In cases where the continental shelf extends to the shores of another State, or is shared with an adjacent State, the boundary shall be determined by the United States and the State concerned in accordance with equitable principles. The character as high seas of the waters above the continental shelf and the right to their free and unimpeded navigation are in no way thus affected.[369]

The lead-up to the moment that the President acted was the only thing that was anything but instant. Before the United Nations Conference on the Law of the Sea beginning in 1958, maritime law had been largely governed by custom bolstered by a few small agreements between a minority of countries. Since Roman times, the sea was considered "*res communis*", belonging to everyone, but not owned by anyone.[370] This approach would be challenged through the centuries, some arguing for a much more controlled and partitioned environment, while others argued the contrary.[371] It was not until 1608 that the Dutch Statesman and Scholar Hugo Grotius argued that ownership of the

369 Proclamation No. 2667, 10 FED. REG. 12, 303 (Sept. 28, 1945).

370 U.N. Convention on the Law of the Sea art. 87, Dec. 10, 1982, 1833 U.N.T.S. 397, available at https://www.un.org/depts/los/convention_agreements/texts/unclos/part7.htm, "The high seas are open to all States, whether coastal or land-locked" and "shall be exercised by all States with due regard for the interests of other States in their exercise of the freedom of the high seas …". *See also* BARRY BUZAN, SEABED POLITICS 1 (1976), stating that early Roman thinkers were already "developing the notion of *res communis*" (belonging to everyone, and therefore open to use but not to appropriation).

371 BUZAN, *supra* note 370 at 1–4, highlighting that as early as the ninth century, there was evidence that this philosophy of openness was under pressure, as the Byzantium's claimed jurisdiction over fishery and salt resources, continuing through to 1493–1494, "when Spain and Portugal divided up most of the world's oceans between themselves on the basis of a Bull pronounced by Pope Alexander VI." This would continue into the 16th and 17th centuries, as the English and Dutch naval powers became more prominent and challenged the supremacy of Spanish and Portuguese claims over the oceans. Such challenges would not be unique, occurring on a regular basis into modern times.

seas was inappropriate, and that there should be the free use of the seas by everyone.[372]

During the 17th century, the scholarship of Hugo Grotius would be reflected largely in the "freedom of the seas" philosophy, such that oceans were considered an "infinite resource, and that anyone could exploit them, or use for travel and transport … outside a territorial sea of about 3 nautical miles from land."[373] This was generally accepted as the custom through the early 1900's, with countries exerting control over waters conjoined with their coasts. The three-mile rule would evolve to reflect a more 'war-like' approach, limited to reflect not just a three-mile rule, but also reflective of the "distance that a cannon could shoot from shore."[374] This distance remained a 'rule of thumb' and while some States treated it differently, the general rule persisted limiting control to some variance of relative proximity to the shore of the countries through the early 1900s.[375]

Because of this history, when the Proclamation was issued, it clearly went against well-established custom. However, the concept appealed to some countries because it was not without considerable benefit to them even if against existing customs[376] First, it made sense to other countries, and was advantageous to them in their own claims for resources and wealth that were beyond the customary three-mile rule. Second, it was replicable by any State, such that it did not require any change or expense in operations to claim the additional land conjoined with their coasts. It simply 'was.'[377] This was a

372 ALEXANDROWICZ, *supra* note 165 at 61–66, providing an extensive discussion of the basis for which Grotius likely based the development of his concept of freedom of the seas. It was clear that the early European traders preferred a controlled fee (permit) based approach. But prior trading routes in Asia and India had been very successfully conducted well before European models were imposed, thus likely influencing Grotius in his argument to revert to earlier models of free maritime navigation and trade.

373 Bill Mansfield, *Law of the Seas,* TE ARA (Jun. 12, 2006), http://www.teara.govt.nz/en/law-of-the-sea/page-1 (last updated July 13, 2012).

374 MICHAEL P. SCHARF, CUSTOMARY INTERNATIONAL LAW IN TIMES OF FUNDAMENTAL CHANGE: RECOGNIZING GROTIAN MOMENTS 104 (2013) (citing JAMES B. MORELL, THE LAW OF THE SEA: AN HISTORICAL ANALYSIS OF THE 1982 TREATY AND ITS REJECTION BY THE UNITED STATES (2013)).

375 *See generally Id.* at 109. Today, "Every state has the right to establish the breadth of its territorial sea up to a limit not exceeding 12 nautical miles, measured from baselines determined in accordance with [the United Nations Convention on the Law of the Sea]." *See also* U.N. Convention on the Law of the Sea section 2 art. 3, Dec. 10, 1982, 1833 U.N.T.S. 397, available at https://www.un.org/depts/los/convention_agreements/texts/unclos/unclos_e.pdf.

376 SCHARF, *supra* note 374 at 114 (referencing the preamble of Proclamation 2667).

377 *See generally Id.*

powerful advantage for countries both big and small to be able to replicate and benefit from an action without having to take on any additional responsibilities or obligations.

Thus, in what amounted to a page of text, President Truman, and the United States of America collectively, had demonstrated to the world its resolve to act in a manner contrary to history and without clear pre-approved international consent.[378] At the same time, it also demonstrated the ability to rapidly evolve customary international law in a way that both suited the United States and made sense for the rest of the world. It was not lost on history that the Proclamation received no opposition from any State.[379] Furthermore, many States quickly declared the Truman Proclamation to be valid and mirrored its premise. Hence, by 1950, 30 coastal States had enacted some declaration extending their territory past historical boundaries.[380] By 1950, scholars, including Sir Hersch Lauterpacht, concluded that the actions taken by the United States, and adopted by members of the international community, had the effect of establishing a virtually 'instant' customary international law.[381] By 1958, the Proclamation of President Truman had taken up permanent roots formally in the 1958 Convention on the Continental Shelf.[382]

---

378 It is worth noting that Dean Scharf observed that while there was not a request for consent, the United States did attempt to set at least a basic groundwork with a few major States prior to issuing the Proclamation. Scharf notes that there was 'behind the scenes diplomacy' that prevented most major countries from either feeling blindsided or outwardly objecting to the action by the United States. In particular, Canada, Mexico, the United Kingdom, and the Soviet Union all received some notification of the action, though it was made clear that the United States was not requesting any permission. So, while it was still an act without consent, it was not, at least, without some advance notification to a handful of countries. SCHARF, *supra* note 374 at 104, 115 (citing D.P. O'CONNELL, THE INTERNATIONAL LAW OF THE SEA 31–2, n. 58, (Oxford University Press 1983).

379 BUZAN, *supra* note 370 at 7–8, stating that "despite its radical nature, the Truman Proclamation encountered no open opposition from any other state, and this greatly increased its validity as a precedent." The reasoning behind this, according to Buzan, was the result of the proclamation being carefully worded, avoiding the contentious issues of waters 'superjacent to the continental shelf', avoided any discussion of sovereignty, and claimed jurisdiction over resources which allowed it to avoid acting as a territorial claim.

380 SCHARF, *supra* note 374 at 117 (citing JAMES B. MORELL, THE LAW OF THE SEA: AN HISTORICAL ANALYSIS OF THE 1982 TREATY AND ITS REJECTION BY THE UNITED STATES 2 (2013)).

381 Hersch Lauterpacht, *Sovereignty Over Submarine Areas*, 27 BRIT. Y.B. INT'L L. 376, 394 (1950).

382 Convention on the Territorial Sea and the Contiguous Zone, Apr. 29, 1958, 516 U.N.T.S. 205.

2.1.4 Legitimacy of Instant Customary International Law in the Courts

Not only by proclamation and action, but also by case law has the theory of instant customary international law been tested. In the 1967 *North Sea Continental Shelf Case*, discussed previously, the ICJ took specific note of the actions of President Truman's Proclamation. In doing so, the Court identified that there had long been various theories about the rights that countries had over the continental shelves extending from their land. However, the Court identified that the Truman Proclamation was the "starting point of the positive law on the subject, and the chief doctrine it enunciated … came to prevail over all others."[383] Thus, though many theories abounded for treatment of the continental shelf, the act of President Truman, both by later codification into a Convention and recognition as the starting point of positive law on the matter, recognized that in the instant of the proclamation, the law had been largely established. The court also addressed a critical issue in the development of customary international law which the court recognized would be of increasing importance in the modern age. The Court stated,

> With respect to the other elements usually regarded as necessary … it might be that, even without the passage of any considerable period of time, a very widespread and representative participation in the convention might suffice of itself.[384]

The Court further elaborated that:

> As regards the time element … although the passage of only a short period of time is not necessarily, or of itself, a bar to the formation of a new rule of customary international law on the basis of what was originally a purely convention rule, an indispensable requirement would be that within the period in question, short though it might be, State practice … should have occurred in such a way as to show a general recognition that a rule of law or legal obligation is involved.[385]

---

383 North Sea Continental Shelf, *supra* note 352.
384 North Sea Continental Shelf, *supra* note 352.
385 North Sea Continental Shelf, *supra* note 352.

The Court, therefore, recognized in one of the first instances that the time factor was not as controlling for customary international law as it might have once been thought to be. As a result, in the *North Sea Continental Shelf Case*, time only served to cement law further. It did not determine its applicability or validity nor did the lack of the passage of time "constitute an obstacle to recognizing its principles and rules, including the equidistance rule,[386] as part of general law."[387]

3 Instant Customary International Law in Space Law

In Space Law, the existence of instant customary international law is also evident.[388] Professor Cheng put forth what is among the most persuasive and commonly recognized academic arguments of the existence, or possibility, of instant customary international law in evolving space law. Professor Cheng

386 The equidistance rule is defined in Article 6 of the Convention on the Continental Shelf, 1958, as the median line, every point of which is equidistant from the nearest points of the baselines from which the breadth of the territorial sea of each State is measured. *See* Continental Shelf Convention art. 6(1), Jun. 10, 1964, 499 U.N.T.S. 311, *available at* https://legal.un.org/ilc/texts/instruments/english/conventions/8_1_1958_continental_shelf.pdf. The Court itself described the equidistant line as a line that "may be described as one which leaves to each of the parties concerned all those portions of the continental shelf that are nearer to a point on its own coast than they are to any point on the coast of the other party. An equidistance line may consist either of a 'median' line between 'opposite' States, or of a 'lateral' line between 'adjacent' States." *See* North Sea Continental Shelf, *supra* note 352.

387 Edward McWhinney, Judge Manfred Lachs and Judicial Law-Making 230 (1995).

388 This author recognizes that this is a minority view, particularly in more modern scholarship on the subject, and that some scholars argue that there is no such thing as 'instant customary international law.' Scholars such as Krivokapic Boris argue that any act of a State, to become customary international law, must be repeated several times by other States, so that finally the belief matures that is legally obligatory. In short, he states "customs which arise spontaneously cannot occur instantly." *See* Krivokapic Boris, *On the Issue of So-Called 'Instant' Customs in International Law*, 9 Acta Universitatis Danubius 81, 84 (2017), https://media.proquest.com/media/hms/PFT/1/eIOY7?_s=vNOFSBJdGlNbOsjjSrrQ3fBc%2BkY%3D. However, as presented here and throughout, it is the opinion of this author that while the 'time element' is debatable, in practice there are demonstrable cases of instant customary international law which are evident. This does not imply opposing scholars are wrong, only that there is space for differentiating views on the importance of the time element to ascertain understanding among States, such that it appears some scholars may be hesitant to use the word 'instant' more so than the actual acts of States might otherwise indicate such custom is formed.

began his analysis with an examination of the two space resolutions preceding the Outer Space Treaty; Resolution 1721 (XVI), *International Co-operation in the Peaceful Uses of Outer Space*[389] of 20 December 1961 and Resolution 1962 (XVIII), *Principles of Exploration*.[390] In his analysis, Professor Cheng recognized the previously established tradition of the two-fold requirements of customary international law; the objective and subjective elements.[391] But while both were predicates to the normal development of customary international law, Professor Cheng did not see that they were both required in all cases of establishing customary international law. Professor Cheng argued that the prolonged time requirement to establish customary international law historically stressed by courts and the international community was the element which 'needed the least adherence in the right circumstance'.[392] Instead, Professor Cheng argued that what is critical is the understanding of the States at the time. If States treated a custom as if it were law, regardless of the arbitrary lapse of some period of time, then as between these specific countries, such a customary law would exist between them immediately.[393] Additionally, if other Nations acted accordingly upon awareness of such a rule, then the time factor would be even more immaterial.[394]

The argument provided by Professor Cheng brings to focus the ability of custom to become established in almost real-time. The key is focusing on the understanding of the countries that agree to be bound when they are coming to the agreement. If it is immediately struck, then no documents or actual practice would be logically required to establish a law between those countries. At a minimum, it would exist as a bilateral customary international law, instant or otherwise.[395] If other countries then adhered to the same understanding, they too would equivalently establish a customary international law by which they chose to be bound. It then follows that if either the predominance of those

389 G.A. Res. 1721 (XVI) (Dec. 20, 1961).

390 G.A. Res. 1962 (XVIII) (Dec. 13, 1963).

391 Cheng, *supra* note 349 at 35.

392 *Id.* at 36.

393 *Id.* at 35.

394 *Id.*

395 Such arrangements are recognized by the UN General Assembly. Under Resolution 73/203, part seven, Conclusion 16, called 'particular customary international law', it is a rule of customary international law that applies only among a limited number of States. To determine the existence and content of a rule of particular customary international law, it is necessary to ascertain whether there is a general practice among the States concerned that is accepted by them as law (*opinio juris*) among themselves. *See* G.A. Res. 73/203, Conclusion 16 (Dec. 20, 2018).

who have an interest, or if those who have an interest pose no objection, the customary international law would arguably be binding on all States under customary international rule norms. Duration of time, under this presumption, is not always limited to extended periods for customary international law development.

3.1 *Post-Truman—Sputnik as the Next Use Case*

Applied to the first launch of a satellite, the existence of instant customary international law comes into focus. The Soviets, in fact, were arguably the first to demonstrate a resolve to act as a "Customary Pioneer" with the launch of the Sputnik satellite and to develop the first instant customary international law in space.[396] To fly over the airspace of any country, before the launch of Sputnik, would historically have required some minimum degree and expectation of permission. But the Soviets neither asked for, nor received, such authority. Instead, they shocked the world by transiting over States in space and established the seeds of the space race. Concurrently, they arguably established an instant customary international law. Instead of States raising alarms at the act of the Soviets (other than the shock of the Soviet ability to launch a satellite into orbit), within the following year the United States did the exact same thing. As Judge Manfred Lachs of the ICJ said:

> The first instruments that man sent into outer space traversed the airspace of States and circled above them in outer space, yet the launching States sought no permission, nor did the other States protest. This is how the freedom of movement into outer space, and in it, came to be established and recognized as law within a remarkably short period of time.[397]

This act had the effect of immediately establishing the freedom of movement in space, that is, an instant customary international law since others immediately followed it and did so without notable objection. What is even more important, it happened literally overnight.

396 *Sputnik and the Dawn of the Space Age*, NASA, http://history.nasa.gov/sputnik/ (last updated Oct. 10, 2007).

397 McWhinney, *supra* note 387 at 230.

4 International Efforts in Space Debris Mitigation—on the Cusp of Customary International Law

As discussed in Chapter two, an ideal scenario in international law is a development of a concept of law, some form of formal binding international instrument crafted in short order, and a formal agreement proposed, signed, and ratified in a timely manner. But where such a linear case for the development of law does not exist, customary international law can still provide the necessary development of law between States. Often these have humble beginnings, developing from academic writings, conferences, and proffers contributed by concerned domestic or international organizations. As these concepts gain traction, they can find elevation by the United Nations, most strongly in the form of UN Resolutions which, while not having the immediate force of law in most cases (excepting UN Security Council resolutions), are considered formal expressions of the opinion or will of organs of the United Nations.[398] The passing of these resolutions, particularly the 'who' and 'how many' aspects of these votes, provide indicators of the seriousness with which the international community begins to acknowledge the concept. This development also allows states to 'spot-check' as a litmus test to the proposal as it progresses. In other cases, it is possible that States instantly develop customs between themselves, as discussed above.

But we know that the five established international treaties do not specifically impose any clear rules on debris mitigation. As a result, customary international law is likely to be the most critical tool that the international community must use to advance any binding interests of space debris mitigation. To what extent, if any, the efforts in space debris have risen to the level of customary international law is still an open question. However, this book argues that through the IADC[399] Debris Mitigation Guidelines and other voluntary efforts

398 *UN Resolutions*, UNITED NATION, LIBRARY, http://research.un.org/en/docs/resolutions (last visited Apr. 25, 2020).

399 It is important to acknowledge that the IADC, as it pertains to customary international law, is a particularly influential entity when examining if customary international law is in some stage of formation. As will be thematic throughout this book, customary international law has the two requirements for development; understanding and practice as a law and some element, however brief, of duration. But additionally, those that do show evidence of acceptance generally must have more than simply a passing interest in the subject. For example, a non-spacefaring nation may have credibility in discussing space law as a country, but its influence is not as strong (for well-founded reasons) in shaping law as it would be for an active spacefaring country directly affected by the results of such law. That said, the IADC, originally comprised of just NASA and ESA beginning in 1986, has now grown to comprise 12 agencies that represent 11 Member-States and ESA.

(often referred to as 'soft-law' since they are guidance that is neither legally binding nor constitute binding 'law'), there is persuasive evidence that a valid body of customary international law is developing in the area of space debris mitigation.

The importance of examining where these areas may currently be forming cannot be overstated. The key rests in identifying the efforts that the international community has pursued in establishing debris mitigation guidelines, if and how those have been implemented into domestic law, and whether the actions of States because of these implementations have created what we understand to be the basis for forming actual international law through custom. Seeing that there was no specific formula for a binding set of rules to force debris mitigation, a series of efforts were initiated internationally beginning in the late 1980s and into the early 1990s. These first steps laid the groundwork for the international guidelines adopted by the United Nations that exist today. At the same time, the lack of international guidelines 40 years ago did not preclude several States from implementing mitigation guidelines. These States

---

See Johnson, *supra* note 23 at 1. The States which have organizations representing them are Italy, France, China, Canada, Germany, India, Japan, Korea, the United States, Russia, Ukraine, and the United Kingdom. *See Member Agencies*, Inter-Agency Space Debris Coordination Comm., https://www.iadc-home.org/ (last visited Aug. 6, 2020). Importantly however, even though these agencies represent their states, the IADC is not a formal intergovernmental organization. One of the distinguishing characteristics of ESA, on the other hand, is that unlike the IADC, it is an intergovernmental organization, created in 1975, and comprises 22 actual Member-States. Three States are 'repeats' whose space agencies are also members of the IADC; the United Kingdom, Italy, and France. But the remaining 19 are also influential space actors. They include Germany, the Netherlands, Spain, Austria, and Denmark among others. *See Member States & Corporate States*, Eur. Space Agency, https://www.esa.int/About_Us/Corporate_news/Member_States_Cooperating_States (last visited Aug. 6, 2020). *See also About the European Space Agency*, Eur. Space Agency https://www.esa.int/Newsroom/About_the_European_Space_Agency. Pertinent to the decisions of the IADC, the development of customary international law must also look at the influence of large organizations, since they represent a large 'voting and influence' block comparable to their peers. As well, the IADC put forth in 2007 what has become one of the most influential documents on space debris and has been the foundation for many domestic laws; the IADC Debris Mitigation Guidelines. It is fair to say that these mitigation guidelines carry significant 'weight' in the international community towards the acceptance and development of customary international law as a result of the Member-States putting them forth as a 'block.' It is also critical to consider that the 'original' IADC technically only comprised two members (ESA and NASA, followed by Japan and Russia). Johnson, *supra* note 23 at 4. That the organization has grown to represent so many countries, and the nearly universal respect for the IADC Debris Mitigation Guidelines, is evidence of both its value and its legitimacy in the international community.

recognized early the degree of the problem and decided that they could not wait for the international community to step in before some small domestic steps had to be taken.

4.1 *The United Nations Space Debris Mitigation Guidelines of the Committee on the Peaceful Uses of Outer Space*

On 8 December 1989, the UN General Assembly acknowledged in its annual summation that the issue of space debris needed to be addressed and was a problem that affected all Nations.[400] It recommended from that session two overarching themes that would lay the groundwork for the next few years in the effort to grapple with the debris problem.[401] First was a high level position that the outer space environment must be preserved.[402] The United Nations stated unequivocally that "more attention should be paid to all aspects related to the protection and the preservation of the outer space environment, especially those potentially affecting the Earth's environment."[403] Second, at a more granular level, it addressed Member-States directly, advising them that the solution to space debris was likely to originate at their level.[404] Specifically, it considered it "essential that Member-States pay more attention to the problem of collisions with space debris and other aspects of space debris, and call[ed] for the continuation of national research on that question."[405]

The following year, 1990, the Scientific and Technical Sub-Committee of UN COPUOS took note of the interest in space debris mitigation posed by the United Nations. The Scientific and Technical Sub-Committee of UN COPUOS recognized that unless advancements were made toward understanding the threat to Earth's environment posed by debris, and unless States took more responsibility in addressing the problem, it would only continue to grow.[406] However, at the time, there was no concise agreement within the Scientific and Technical Sub-Committee of UN COPUOS on what the best approach should be to address the problem. Some delegations believed the issue was urgent and all efforts should be exerted to immediately address the problem.[407]

---

400 G.A. Res. 44/46, preamble, *available at* https://undocs.org/en/A/RES/44/46.

401 *Id.*

402 *Id.*

403 *Id.* at paras. 23–24.

404 *Id.* at para. 24.

405 *Id.* at para. 23.

406 Comm. on the Peaceful Uses of Outer Space, Rep. of Sci. and Tech. Subcomm. on Its Twenty-Seventh Session, U.N. Doc. A/AC.105/456, at para. 98 (Mar. 12, 1990), *available at* https://www.unoosa.org/pdf/reports/ac105/AC105_456E.pdf.

407 *Id.* at para. 99.

Other delegations felt that while the subject of space debris was important and should be included as a Scientific and Technical Sub-Committee of UN COPUOS agenda item, the lack of available data to substantiate the extent of the problem made focusing on it as a Sub-Committee a premature endeavor.[408]

At the end of the March 1990 meeting of the Scientific and Technical Sub-Committee of UN COPUOS, the delegations reiterated the concern about debris, but made no specific commitments to take any action. In August of the same year, UN COPUOS similarly acknowledged that the United Nations considered this issue to be important. UN COPUOS stated that space debris was an "issue of concern to all Nations and that it could be an appropriate subject for discussion by UN COPUOS in the future."[409] Like the Scientific and Technical Sub-Committee of UN COPUOS, no specific action was taken by UN COPUOS that year, but the topic did remain a subject of consideration on the agenda going forward. In December at the UN General Assembly, Resolution 45/72 was passed.[410] That resolution charged UN COPUOS with keeping the subject of space debris at the fore.[411] The UN General Assembly addressed the efforts of UN COPUOS and indicated that space debris "could be an appropriate subject for discussion by UN COPUOS in the future."[412]

Over the next two years, the UN General Assembly, UN COPUOS, and the Scientific and Technical Sub-Committee of UN COPUOS continued to stress the risks presented by space debris and the potential harm to the environment it could create. However, despite these efforts, space debris remained a relatively unfocused effort. But by August of 1993, a shift occurred in the UN COPUOS report to the UN General Assembly. While prior action had indicated passive acknowledgement, UN COPUOS made a genuine commitment to investigate the problem and provide substantial information to the UN General Assembly on the space debris threat.[413] As an outcome of their August 1993 meeting, UN COPUOS officially agreed that space debris should be a subject regularly addressed by the United Nations.[414] More specifically, UN COPUOS stated that at the next session of its Scientific and Technical Sub-Committee, information

408 *Id.* at para. 101.

409 Rep. of Comm. on the Peaceful Uses of Outer Space, on Its Forty-Fifth Session, U.N. Doc. A/45/20, at para. 96 (Aug. 31, 1990) *available at* https://www.unoosa.org/pdf/gadocs/A_45_20E.pdf.

410 G.A. Res. 45/72, *available at* https://undocs.org/en/A/RES/45/72.

411 *Id.* at paras. 21–23.

412 *Id.* at 23.

413 Rep. of Comm. on the Peaceful Uses of Outer Space, U.N. Doc. A/48/20, para. 85 (Aug. 16, 1993) *available at* https://www.unoosa.org/pdf/gadocs/A_48_20E.pdf.

414 *Id.* at para. 85.

should be provided to UN COPUOS on space debris, including "studies, mathematical modelling, and other analytical work on the characterization of the space debris environment."[415] Furthermore, UN COPUOS tasked its Scientific and Technical Sub-Committee to officially add "Space Debris" as a formal agenda item to its regular activities beginning in 1994.[416] The UN General Assembly acknowledged in its 10 December 1993 meeting minutes that it both 'welcom[ed]' the decision of the Committee to consider the matter of space debris as a specific agenda item and 'endorse[d]' the selection of the Scientific and Technical Sub-Committee of UN COPUOS to spearhead the effort.[417]

4.1.1 Leading to the Mitigation Guidelines—Initial Assessments of Nation-State Efforts

UN COPUOS was quick to reach out to Member-Nations to request data to assess the current mitigation efforts already underway. Since 1991, the UN General Assembly had been laying the groundwork for this request, with the body including a provision within Resolution 46/45 requesting that the UN "Secretary-General invites Member-States to provide information on their national research on space debris to the Scientific and Technical Subcommittee."[418] On 13 July 1994, the UN Secretary-General did so, inviting Member-Nations to communicate to the Secretariat by 30 November 1994 with information that would be of use to UN COPUOS regarding ongoing domestic space debris efforts in several different categories.[419] By 30 November, UN COPUOS had received ongoing research information on space debris efforts, the safety of nuclear powered satellites with an eye to the potential for debris issues, and problems of collisions of nuclear-power sources with existing space debris from eight Member-States and three intergovernmental and international organizations.[420]

---

415 *Id.* at para. 87.

416 *Id.* at para. 87.

417 G.A. Res. 48/39, para. 8, *available at* https://undocs.org/en/A/RES/48/39.

418 *Id.* at para. 25.

419 Comm. on the Peaceful Uses of Outer Space, *National Research on Space Debris Safety of Nuclear-Powered Satellites Problems of Collisions of Nuclear-Power Sources with Space Debris, Notes by the Secretariat*, U.N. Doc. A/AC.105/593, para. 4 (Dec. 1, 1994) *available at* https://www.unoosa.org/pdf/reports/ac105/AC105_593E.pdf.

420 *Id. See also* Comm. on the Peaceful Uses of Outer Space, *Note by the Secretariat*, U.N. Doc. A/AC.105/731, at para. 2 (Dec. 20, 1999) *available at* https://www.unoosa.org/pdf/reports/ac105/AC105_731E.pdf. On 20 December 1999, the Secretariat compiled additional responses submitted to the UN General Assembly after the initial 30 November 1999 deadline which therefore did not make the first report. Cyprus, Ireland, Israel, the Republic of Korea, the Netherlands, and the United Kingdom of Great Britain and Northern Ireland

The resulting UN COPUOS report provided significant insight into the current debris mitigation efforts among countries involved in space activities or otherwise participants in UN COPUOS. Belgium, Canada, Hungary, Japan, Malta, Poland, Sri Lanka, and the United Kingdom all responded by the deadline.[421] Responses from intergovernmental and international organizations included the International Atomic Energy Agency (IAEA), COSPAR, and the International Telecommunications Satellite Organization (ITSO, now INTELSAT).[422] Notably absent from this document were the major spacefaring Nations at the time. This is likely because many of these Nations, specifically Russia and the United States, were already on record with their understanding of the debris problem and efforts toward mitigation. While this absence did diminish the weight of the UN COPUOS report to some degree, those who did respond still provided valuable contributions. Specifically, Canada, Japan, and the United Kingdom all expressed considerable interest in, and efforts toward, identifying the degree of the problem and making concerted efforts toward implementing specific mitigation measures in current operations.

Canada reported that its first commercial Earth observation satellite, RADARSAT, had already instituted two efforts specific to space debris mitigation in the report.[423] The first involved system designs that precluded debris from being released by the spacecraft during deployment of the satellite.[424] The second involved designs on the protection of the satellite itself, such that

---

(repeat) submitted comments. Cyprus, Ireland, Israel, and the Netherlands offered no opposition to efforts, but proffered little in their own advances. The Republic of Korea focused on the costs to stabilize the existing environment and proposed that those that created the debris should be technologically and fiscally responsible for finding ways to remove debris. Finally, Great Britain amplified several of the points they had initially submitted on 30 November, touting their efforts in advancing the analysis of the space debris threat through modelling, engineering, hypervelocity impact testing and survivability to name a few.

421 Comm. on the Peaceful Uses of Outer Space, *National Research on Space Debris*, *supra* note 419.

422 *Id.*

423 *What is Radarsat-1*, CANADA.CA, https://www.asc-csa.gc.ca/eng/satellites/radarsat1/what-is-radarsat1.asp (date modified Jan. 21, 2022).

424 Comm. on the Peaceful Uses of Outer Space, *National Research on Space Debris*, *supra* note 419 at 4.

it would be more resilient against existing space debris to avoid succumbing to damage and becoming debris itself.[425]

Japan also contributed significantly to the report, demonstrating leading-edge efforts to fully understand the debris problem. Japan noted that until as late as 1989, they had not addressed debris mitigation, but beginning in 1990 they took strides to rectify the oversight. In 1990, The Japan Society for Aeronautical and Space Sciences (JSASS) organized the Space Debris Study Group in September of that year.[426] Following their report, two additional groups were created: the Study Group on Space Debris Prevention Design Standards and the Study Group on Space Debris and Micrometeoroid Impact Detection.[427] By July 1993, both groups had initiated efforts on their respective tasks, and by August, the Japanese Space Agency (JAXA) (then known as the National Space Development Agency of Japan (NASDA)), had created a third organization, the in-house Space Debris Working Group.[428]

Similarly, Great Britain outlined several efforts in both defense and academia that were at the early stages of development since at least 1993. Three major areas had captured Great Britain's attention, including understanding the debris problem, predicting the long-term growth of the debris population, and a focus on the potential for the occurrence of Kessler syndrome effects.[429] In fact, Great Britain went so far as to make an ominous prediction that the year 2040 lent itself to the most likely year in which a catastrophic cascading of debris growth would occur.[430]

International and intergovernmental organizations also made substantial contributions to the understanding of the current global efforts. Specifically, (now) INTELSAT identified two practices adopted to minimize the creation of space debris.[431] One involved sending satellites into graveyard orbits (minimum 150 km above GEO).[432] The other involved INTELSAT applying pressure on its manufacturers to discourage spacecraft design that would inject post-launch spacecraft parts into orbit, particularly the extremely valuable GEO.[433] COSPAR also submitted a position paper published in 1993 to summarize their

425 *Id.*
426 *Id.* at 5.
427 *Id.*
428 *Id.*
429 *Id.* at 16.
430 *Id.*
431 *Id.* at 21.
432 *Id.*
433 *Id.*

view.[434] This report highlighted a number of valuable considerations, specifically focusing on reviewing the growth of the current debris population and recommending preventive measures for debris reduction. But one of its most important guiding principles was the notion that there is "no net benefit if only one of the presently active spacefaring Nations introduces preventive measures."[435] Instead, COSPAR insisted that a 'commons' model of effort among Nations should be adopted, such that the orbital environment must be protected to allow for the continued use of space.[436] Further acknowledging the potential dangers of satellite breakups, collisions, explosions, and other threats to the space environment, COSPAR made a number of reduction recommendations. Among them was post-mission disposal of spacecraft and material into maximum (atmospheric) drag orbits (ideally below 600–700 km), 'safing' the remaining fuel of upper stages and spacecraft in any orbit, and emphasizing engineering as one of the best ways to develop cost-effective satellite designs for minimum debris creation.[437] Finally, if all else was unavailable, and as the technology became feasible, efforts toward active debris removal (ADR) to reduce the overall debris threat should be considered, particularly among larger pieces of debris.[438] ADR offers many attractive options as the technology continues to advance, including the option of utilizing grappling hooks, harpoons, nets, and other methods of capture to actively utilize 'hunt' satellites to go out and physically capture other dead satellites, defunct space objects, and pieces of debris in the orbital environment.[439]

Following the 1994 publication, UN COPUOS undertook an ambitious plan to further canvass States for debris programs and information and make further recommendations to the UN General Assembly. At their meeting in September of 1995, UN COPUOS set out to formulate a multi-year plan to analyze the space debris problem. It found inspiration for collaboration from the partnership of the IADC, NASA, ESA, Japan's Science and Technology Agency/National Space Development Agency (STA/NASDA), and the Russian Space Agency (RSA),

434 *Id.* at 22, Annex.

435 *Id.* at 23.

436 *Id.*

437 *Id.* at 31.

438 *Id.* Active debris removal, as will be discussed extensively later in this book, involves utilizing various technologies to approach, capture, and dispose of non-functioning space objects, including debris, which are otherwise serving no useful purpose in orbit and present a threat to operational spacecraft. This can include, but is not limited to, harpoons, nets, grappling arms, foams, drag sails, and powered attachment devices. *See also* discussion of ADR *infra* at Chapter 9.

439 *See* discussion of ADR *infra* at Chapter 9.

which had formed two years prior and was engaged in information partnership and sharing facilitation.[440]

Advantageously, just seven months earlier, in February of 1995, the Scientific and Technical Sub-Committee of UN COPUOS had met and developed a roadmap to meet UN COPUOS's needs in this area. At their February meeting, the Scientific and Technical Sub-Committee formulated a multi-year plan to be executed between 1996 and 1998 that would allow it to advance its comprehensive understanding of the space debris problem.[441] In the plan, the Scientific and Technical Sub-Committee outlined an expectation for 1996 that it would review how space debris is measured through ground and space-based sensors.[442] 1997 would see the Scientific and Technical Sub-Committee involve modelling of the space debris environment and compiling risk assessments of the debris environment based on that modelling.[443] The last year of the proposed plan, 1998, involved an examination of the space debris mitigation measures, including best practices for how to reduce the existence of space debris and protect functioning satellites through shielding or collision avoidance.[444] Based on this roadmap, UN COPUOS endorsed the plan from its Scientific and Technical Sub-Committee in September of 1995 and determined that the findings should be reported back to UN COPUOS regularly as outlined in their February 1995 submission.[445]

Based on that multi-year plan, in 1999 the Scientific and Technical Sub-Committee published the culmination of the three previous years of effort on addressing the space debris problem in the *Technical Report on Space Debris*.[446] Among the main goals was to establish a baseline among all Nations to ensure a common understanding of the problem that space debris presented to orbital operations and to assist in prompting an informed discussion among States about how to address the problem.[447] The report was organized

440 Rep. of Comm. on the Peaceful Uses of Outer Space on Its Fiftieth Session, U.N. Doc. A/50/20, at para. 78, (1995) *available at* https://www.unoosa.org/pdf/gadocs/A_50_20E.pdf.

441 Comm. on the Peaceful Uses of Outer Space, Rep. of Sci. and Tech. Subcomm. on Its Thirty-Second Session, *supra* note 53 at para. 83.

442 *Id.*

443 *Id.*

444 *Id.*

445 *Id.* at para. 96.

446 Comm. on the Peaceful Uses of Outer Space, Rep. of Sci. and Tech. Subcomm., U.N. Doc. A/AC.105/720, (1999) *available at* https://www.unoosa.org/pdf/reports/ac105/AC105_720E.pdf.

447 *Id.* at para. 6.

according to the multi-year plan originally proposed in 1995. The first section addressed the ability to identify and measure the space debris problem, using both space and ground-based radars, and distinguishing the advantages and drawbacks of each method.[448] The second section focused on the modelling of the debris environment, with the intent to provide a mathematically reliable description and distribution of the known objects in space.[449] This information could then be utilized to assist States in several areas, including prediction of debris detection rates, risk and damage assessments, and whether or not any efforts in debris mitigation were reducing the congestion in orbit.[450]

The final aspect of the report resulted in the compilation of a review and critique of measures that should be taken to reduce the number of debris.[451] This was proffered in two ways. The first was through design enhancements during pre-launch, improved engineering to reduce particles that would detach from main bodies and also hardening of the space objects themselves to resist destruction if impacted by debris.[452] The second involved post-launch measures and end-of-life, to include accurate SSA to improve avoidance techniques for threatened satellites, 'safing' the satellites and delivery vehicles to reduce the possibility of in-orbit explosions and finally, end-of-life actions to reduce the amount of mission remnants loitering indefinitely in orbit.[453] Their final conclusions to UN COPUOS stated that they did not view space debris as much of a threat to the active spacecraft operating at the time. While such a lighthearted view of the threat may seem careless, it might be forgivable considering that only approximately 600 active spacecraft were in orbit at the time of the 1999 assessment.[454] Today, arriving at the same conclusion would seem unlikely considering the approximately 4,850 operating satellites (as of 1 January 2022).[455]

4.1.2 From Analysis to Understanding—the Development of the Debris Mitigation Guidelines

Through 2002, the Scientific and Technical Sub-Committee of UN COPUOS continued its efforts as an agenda item to contribute to the body of knowledge

448 *Id.* at para. 10.
449 *Id.* at para. 61.
450 *Id.*
451 *Id.* at section III.A.1.a.
452 *Id.* at section III.B.1.
453 *Id.* at section III.A.3.
454 *Id.* at para. 136.
455 *UCS Satellite Database*, UNION OF CONCERNED SCIENTISTS (Dec. 8, 2005, updated Jan. 1, 2022), https://www.ucsusa.org/resources/satellite-database.

of the space debris threat and to encourage States to include debris prevention and mitigation in their space programs to reduce the threat. Importantly, at the 39th session of the Scientific and Technical Sub-Committee in February 2002, a technical presentation was made by the IADC to the Scientific and Technical Sub-Committee.[456] In this presentation, the IADC submitted a series of mitigation guidelines for the consideration of the Scientific and Technical Sub-Committee.[457] Following the presentation, the Scientific and Technical Sub-Committee noted that the IADC had, in addition to their general presentation, reached a consensus on specific mitigation guidelines that were under final review by IADC members.[458] In response, the IADC was invited to present the debris mitigation recommendations the following year, at which point the Scientific and Technical Sub-Committee would review and make recommendations on whether or not to endorse the IADC guidelines.

On 29 November 2002, the IADC submitted its mitigation recommendations to the Scientific and Technical Sub-Committee. At the time, while the IADC felt that the threat to spacecraft from debris was relatively low, it acknowledged the number of debris was growing.[459] For the environment to be available to future generations, actions needed to be taken sooner rather than later to prevent the worst possible outcome of areas of outer space becoming inaccessible. The IADC also recognized that a series of national debris mitigation standards had been implemented by several States as well as international organizations.[460] To establish a common set of rules, the IADC looked at the different State programs currently in effect and identified a number of common principles to all of them. The fundamental ideas identified were included as their three principal ideas:

---

456 Comm. on the Peaceful Uses of Outer Space, Rep. of Sci. and Tech. Subcomm. on Its Forty-Fifth Session, U.N. Doc. A/AC.105/786, at 18 (Mar. 15, 2002) *available at* https://www.unoosa.org/pdf/reports/ac105/AC105_786E.pdf.

457 *Id.*

458 Rep. of Comm. on the Peaceful Uses of Outer Space on Its Fifty-Seventh Session, U.N. Doc. A/57/20, at 14 (2002) *available at* https://www.unoosa.org/pdf/gadocs/A_57_20E.pdf.

459 Comm. on the Peaceful Uses of Outer Space, Sci. and Tech. Subcomm. on Its Fortieth Session, *Inter-Agency Space Debris Coordination Committee Space Debris Mitigation Guidelines*, U.N. Doc. A/AC.105/C.1/L.260, at 4 (Nov. 29, 2002) *available at* https://www.unoosa.org/pdf/limited/c1/AC105_C1_L260E.pdf.

460 *Id.*

> Principle 1: Efforts should be made in the course of designing spacecraft and associated launch vehicles to limit the number of objects that must be released as debris during the normal course of operations.[461]

The IADC approached the first principle as a holistic effort covering the entire lifecycle of the space system, including mission planning, design, and operation (launch, mission, disposal).[462] In the initial design stage, the IADC encouraged engineering advances to reduce the potential number of parts which needed to be included in the design or adjusting how those parts might be configured to prevent their release during insertion (stage separations). Following design, during normal operations, the expectation was that there would not be a need to release debris. However, in the event that such a case existed, the IADC advocated that planning should include an environmental impact assessment and a determination if the debris can be limited in orbit to the shortest duration possible.[463] During post-mission disposal planning, efforts should be made to minimize the remainder of hazardous material such as propellants and fluids that could cause a catastrophic event (explosion) within the spacecraft.[464] Other 'safing' mechanisms should include reduction of high pressure containers,

---

461 *Id. See also* Comm. On the Peaceful Uses of Outer Space, Sci. and Tech. Subcomm. on Its Forty Second Session, *Report of the Inter-Agency Space Debris Coordination Committee Activities on IADC Space Debris Mitigation Guidelines & Supporting Documents*; Inter-Agency Space Debris Coordination Committee Space Debris Mitigation Guidelines Update, Comm. on the Peaceful Uses of Outer Space, Rep. of Sci. and Tech. Subcomm. on Its Forty-Fifth Session, https://www.unoosa.org/pdf/pres/stsc2008/tech-35E.pdf. *See also* Comm. on the Peaceful Uses of Outer Space, Sci. and Tech. Subcomm. on Its Fortieth Session, *Inter-Agency Space Debris Coordination Committee Space Debris Mitigation Guidelines, supra* note 459.

462 Comm. on the Peaceful Uses of Outer Space, Sci. and Tech. Subcomm. on Its Fortieth Session, *Inter-Agency Space Debris Coordination Committee Space Debris Mitigation Guidelines, supra* note 459. *See also* Comm. On the Peaceful Uses of Outer Space, Sci. and Tech. Subcomm. on Its Forty Second Session, *Report of the Inter-Agency Space Debris Coordination Committee Activates on IADC Space Debris Mitigation Guidelines & Supporting Documents. See also* IADC Space Debris Mitigation Guidelines *Update, supra* note 461.

463 Comm. on the Peaceful Uses of Outer Space, Sci. and Tech. Subcomm. on Its Fortieth Session, *Inter-Agency Space Debris Coordination Committee Space Debris Mitigation Guidelines, supra* note 459 at 4. *See also* Comm. On the Peaceful Uses of Outer Space, Sci. and Tech. Subcomm. on Its Forty Second Session, *Report of the Inter-Agency Space Debris Coordination Committee Activates on IADC Space Debris Mitigation Guidelines & Supporting Documents*, https://www.iadc-home.org/documents_public/file_down/id/4112. *See also* IADC Space Debris Mitigation Guidelines *Update, supra* note 461.

464 Current suggestions for reducing post-mission material focus on the ability to potentially reuse many of the satellite parts as the kernels for new satellites. If there is the potential

removal of flywheel power and de-activation of any remaining battery power to the spacecraft.[465] Finally, in conjunction with engineering, the overall management plan should actively address mitigation activities, including planning and assessment for minimizing the hazards that could cause malfunctions which would generate debris, cross comparing the guidelines to the compliance of the space design, and justifying a specific selection with mitigation in mind if several options existed.[466] The IADC recommended that planning forecasts should begin at the management planning stage well in advance of initial development, and involve a considerable investment in pre-planning for all aspects of the mission.[467]

> Principle 2: Prevention of on-orbit breakups was a critical factor in preventing increases in the amount of space debris in the orbital environment.[468]

The IADC approached this second principle in two parts: planning and monitoring. The planning part required that the engineering for the spacecraft reduce the probability of an accidental breakup to the greatest extent possible.[469] However, understanding that some risks will always exist, the second part encouraged regular monitoring of the system that would identify any

for compartmenting certain pieces and joining them with new additions to create 'refurbished' satellites, that would both be a considerable reduction in potential space junk and could be a very cost-effective method of reusing existing material already located in space. 3D printing 'factories' positioned in space might also potentially increase the possibility of replacing worn out parts and extending aging satellites' life. Other suggestions for reducing the potential for catastrophic events include changing the type of fuel from highly combustible liquid to a lower combustible solid, such as a paraffin wax. See suggestions from Danielle Wood, Massachusetts Institute of Technology (MIT) Media Lab in Megan Bartels, *Changing How we Build Satellites Could Do More Than Reduce Space Junk*, SPACE.COM, January 24, 2019, https://www.space.com/43098-satellite-design-engineering-equity-justice.html (last visited Aug. 5, 2020).

465 Comm. on the Peaceful Uses of Outer Space, Sci. and Tech. Subcomm. on Its Fortieth Session, *Inter-Agency Space Debris Coordination Committee Space Debris Mitigation Guidelines, supra* note 459 at 4. *See also* Comm. On the Peaceful Uses of Outer Space, Sci. and Tech. Subcomm. on Its Forty Second Session, *Report of the Inter-Agency Space Debris Coordination Committee Activates on IADC Space Debris Mitigation Guidelines & Supporting Documents*, https://www.iadc-home.org/documents_public/file_down/id/4112; IADC Space Debris Mitigation Guidelines *Update, supra* note 461.

466 *Id.*

467 *Id.*

468 *Id.*

469 *Id.*

problems as they arose. In such cases, the goal was that if the malfunction could cause a catastrophic loss of the spacecraft, measures could be taken to engage in post-mission disposal efforts to reduce the probability that the spacecraft would explode or otherwise end up as uncontrollable debris.

> Principle 3: Spacecraft and stages from spent rockets should not be allowed to remain in the most critical and high traffic orbital regions.[470]

Finally, the IADC focused guidance specific to the disposition of spacecraft operating in the most valuable and utilized orbital regions: LEO and GEO. In LEO, the IADC recommended that spacecraft should be deorbited after their mission.[471] If immediate deorbit cannot be accomplished, the spacecraft should be oriented to a position where the orbital drag would cause the spacecraft to deorbit within 25 years.[472] The IADC considered this to be a 'reasonable and appropriate' amount of time.[473] Within GEO, the possibility of entry into Earth's atmosphere was an unreasonable expectation due to the fuel required to conduct such a deorbit maneuver. Instead, the IADC recommended that no object should remain in GEO if no longer actively utilized and should be moved into a graveyard orbit where the spacecraft will avoid interference with existing functioning GEO systems.[474]

4.1.3 From Understanding to Action—Drafting the Debris Mitigation Guidelines

With the principles established, the IADC submitted recommendations on proposed mitigation guidelines in draft form. The next course of action was for participant Nations to review the IADC proposals and to provide feedback to UN COPUOS before the 41st session of the Scientific and Technical Sub-Committee.[475] Following that, recommendations could be made whether to endorse the mitigation guidelines or what other actions should be taken.[476] Among those future actions, delegations additionally expressed a desire that the Legal Sub-Committee also be included in the deliberations.

---

470 *Id.*

471 *Id.*

472 *Id.*

473 *Id.*

474 *Id.*

475 Rep. of Comm. on the Peaceful Uses of Outer Space, on Its Forty-Eighth Session, U.N. Doc. A/58/20, at 22, para. 125, (2003) *available at* https://www.unoosa.org/pdf/gadocs/A_58_20E.pdf.

476 *Id.* at 22, para. 126.

Critics of involving the Legal Sub-Committee expressed that they felt that the States should weigh in first, followed by the Legal Sub-Committee.[477] UN COPUOS settled the dispute, identifying a new item for its Legal Sub-Committee at their next meeting, titled "proposals to the Committee on the Peaceful Uses of Outer Space for new items to be considered by the Legal Sub-Committee of UN COPUOS at its forty-fourth session."[478] Thus, the issue was settled at least as a potential matter for legal consideration the following year.[479]

Through 2004, Member-States were, as discussed, given the opportunity to submit comments to the IADC and UN COPUOS. On 4 October 2004, the IADC held a meeting with interested States regarding the debris mitigation measures and submitted two letters to the UN General Assembly Secretariat describing the outcome of that meeting.[480] The first letter, sent by the Secretariat of the IADC, indicated that further work needed to be done, as well as additional documentation to be submitted to the Scientific and Technical Sub-Committee the following year at the 42nd session (2005).[481] The second letter was sent to UN COPUOS. The letter outlined that there were several issues raised, notably by Russia, India and Turkey, that warranted further technical study and consultation relative to the use of nuclear power in space.[482] India additionally raised concerns over what they felt were limitations on their use of GEO, as well as the time limit allowed for disposal of spent rocket-stages within GEO.[483] UN COPUOS, for its part, determined that its Scientific and Technical Sub-Committee Working Group on Space Debris (hereafter the Scientific and Technical Working Group) would review the issues submitted by the IADC.[484] In doing so, the intent, according to the IADC, was to address these issues at their following meeting scheduled for April 2005.[485]

In the interim, the Scientific and Technical Working Group on Space Debris met in February 2005, with one of their agenda items focusing on the previous

477 *Id.* at 34, para. 208.
478 *Id.* at 35, para. 209(11).
479 *Id.*
480 Comm. on the Peaceful Uses of Outer Space, Sci. and Tech. Subcomm. on Its Forty-Second Session, *Note by the Secretariat*, U.N. Doc. A/AC.105/C.1/L.279, at 2 (Feb. 7, 2005) *available at* https://www.unoosa.org/pdf/limited/c1/AC105_C1_L279E.pdf.
481 *Id.* at 3.
482 *Id.* at 4.
483 *Id.* at 7.
484 *Id.* at 1, para. 2.
485 *Id.* at 7.

year's work by the IADC and Member-States that had been referred over to it for resolution. In its review, the Scientific and Technical Working Group developed a set of proposed principles, adopting several aspects of the IADC Debris Mitigation Guidelines, to create a formal set of United Nations guidelines for debris mitigation.[486] The Scientific and Technical Working Group relied heavily on the IADC efforts that had already been conducted, capitalizing on the fact that the IADC guidelines already reflected the will of most interested States.[487]

As the name implies … ('guidelines') … the Scientific and Technical Working Group also established that their proposal would remain as guidelines, and not attempt to create binding international law.[488] This provided the flexibility to encourage states to act voluntarily, but also allowed for exceptions to be justified where necessary without undue burden.[489] Additionally, the document could always be updated to reflect any common customs that were developing among Nations as a result of domestic changes and implementations in response to the changing practices.[490] Ultimately, the Scientific and Technical Working Group summarized the planned document to be based on the IADC guidelines, but more 'concise, high-level, and qualitative.'[491]

Following the initial review, the Scientific and Technical Sub-Committee set out to accomplish the review over three years. Beginning immediately, the plan for 2005 was for the Scientific and Technical Working Group to consider all the materials and concerns submitted by States for adjustments to the guidelines.[492] This was significant considering that many of the major States had submitted considerable language changes for each of the specific principles. For example, in Principle 1 alone, the United States wanted it to read "The release of long-lived debris during the deployment and operation of spacecraft and launch vehicle orbital stages should be avoided."[493] The following year, 2006, involved further revisions to the draft IADC guidelines, adjusting them according to the concerns raised by States, and ultimately drafting the

486 Comm. on the Peaceful Uses of Outer Space, Rep. of Sci. and Tech. Subcomm. on Its Forty-Second Session, *Draft Report of the Working Group on Space Debris*, U.N. Doc. A/AC.105/C.1/SD/2005/L.1, at 1 (Mar. 3, 2005) *available at* https://www.unoosa.org/pdf/limited/c1/AC105_C1_SD_2005_L1E.pdf.

487 *Id.* at 2.

488 *Id.*

489 *Id.*

490 *Id.*

491 *Id.*

492 *Id.*

493 Comm. on the Peaceful Uses of Outer Space, Rep. of Sci. and Tech. Subcomm. on Its Forty-Eighth Session, *Intersessional Meeting of the Working Group on Space Debris of the Scientific*

core Scientific and Technical Sub-Committee document.[494] Finally, in 2007, the goal was to complete the document with an intent to submit the final draft for consideration to the Scientific and Technical Sub-Committee at the 44th session.[495] If all went well, the document would be submitted for adoption by UN COPUOS at their 50th session in 2007.[496]

Efforts by the Scientific and Technical Working Group continued from 2005 into 2006 as planned. In early 2006, the Scientific and Technical Working Group had a revised draft of the guidelines which had incorporated or addressed the concerns expressed by States during the development of the guidelines, and largely reflected the principles as drafted by the IADC.[497] The consensus final draft of the Scientific and Technical Working Group was approved in February of 2006, and reflected the following seven specific guidelines:[498]

1. Limit debris released during normal operations.[499]
2. Minimize the potential for breakups during operational phases.[500]
3. Limit the probability of accidental collision in orbit.[501]
4. Avoid intentional destruction and other harmful activities.[502]

---

and Technical Subcommittee, U.N. Doc. A/AC.105/2005/CRP.8, at 6 (Jun. 10, 2005) *available at* https://www.unoosa.org/pdf/limited/l/AC105_2005_CRP08E.pdf. It is worth noting the language 'long-term' debris did not appear to be an 'endorsement' that debris *generally* was fine by the United States, but more an acceptance that some debris is likely to be unavoidable, and the key would be to minimize the impact, in particular by duration of time in the areas where it was likely to be the greatest threat in congested orbital regimes. *Id.* at Guideline 2, at 6. The International Relations Committee of the European Space Agency also reflected this position, specifically, under 'Recommended Practice 1', in its proposal for a space debris mitigation document stating that 'space systems should be designed not to release debris during normal operations', but that there are cases where it simply was 'not feasible.' *Id.* at 2, Recommended Practice 1: Limit Debris Released During Normal Operations. When 'not feasible', the intent was to reduce the impact to some level that was 'acceptably low.' *Id.*

494 *Id.* at 2.

495 *Id.* at 3.

496 *Id.*

497 Comm. on the Peaceful Uses of Outer Space, Rep. of Sci. and Tech. Subcomm. on Its Forty-Third Session, *Progress Report of the Working Group on Space Debris, submitted by the Chairman of the Working Group*, U.N. Doc. A/AC.105/C.1/L.284, at 2 (Feb. 28, 2006) *available at* https://www.unoosa.org/pdf/limited/c1/AC105_C1_L284E.pdf.

498 *Id.* at 3–4.

499 *Id.* at Guideline 1, page 3.

500 *Id.* at Guideline 2, page 3.

501 *Id.* at Guideline 3, page 3.

502 *Id.* at Guideline 4, page 4.

5. Minimize the potential for post-mission breakups resulting from stored energy.[503]
6. Limit the long-term presence of spacecraft and launch vehicle orbital stages in the LEO region after the end of their mission.[504]
7. Limit the long-term interference of spacecraft and launch vehicle orbital stages within the GEO region after the end of their mission.[505]

Following approval by the Scientific and Technical Working Group, the guidelines were submitted to the Scientific and Technical Sub-Committee and were incorporated into their formal report from their February 2007 meeting.[506] By the time UN COPUOS met in Vienna in June of 2007, the finalized mitigation guidelines had been submitted by the Scientific and Technical Sub-Committee. At their 572nd meeting, UN COPUOS had endorsed the draft space debris mitigation guidelines and reported on it in their general 50th session. According to UN COPUOS, the guidelines "would increase mutual understanding on acceptable activities in space and thus enhance stability in space-related matters and decrease the likelihood of friction and conflict."[507]

4.1.4 Reviewing the Impact: Debris Mitigation Guidelines

The endorsement by UN COPUOS was a significant step toward acknowledging the need to reduce the amount of space debris being created and therefore reduce the potential for friction and conflict among States. However, even with the seven or eight years of concerted effort and compromise, there remained delegations who found these guidelines unsatisfactory.[508] It was noted by UN COPUOS that some delegations were frustrated by the simple fact that the guidelines were voluntary, and thus put emerging countries at a disadvantage over highly developed spacefaring ones.[509] Others felt that even though the guidelines were voluntary, and though mandatory guidelines may

503 *Id.* at Guideline 5, page 4.

504 *Id.* at Guideline 6, page 4.

505 *Id.* at Guideline 7, page 4.

506 Comm. on the Peaceful Uses of Outer Space, Rep. of Sci. and Tech. Subcomm. on Its Fiftieth Session, U.N. Doc. A/AC.105/890, at 7, para. G, (Mar. 6, 2007), *available at* https://www.unoosa.org/pdf/reports/ac105/AC105_890E.pdf.

507 General Assembly, Rep. of Comm. on the Peaceful Uses of Outer Space, on Its Sixty-Second Session, *supra* note 56 at 17. *See also* U.N. OFF. OF OUTER SPACE AFFAIRS, SPACE DEBRIS MITIGATION GUIDELINES OF THE COMMITTEE ON THE PEACEFUL USES OF OUTER SPACE, *supra* note 24 at III.

508 General Assembly, Rep. of Comm. on the Peaceful Uses of Outer Space, on Its Sixty-Second Session, *supra* note 56 at 18, para. 123.

509 *Id.*

be impractical, acceptance at the UN COPUOS level remained inadequate to exemplify the importance of these measures.[510] Instead, dissenting States felt the guidelines should be adopted as a resolution by the UN General Assembly to message the importance of the document.[511] Finally, regardless of whether the guidelines ended up being mandatory, other delegations still believed that they were insufficient to cover all debris-producing issues and would need to be constantly updated.[512]

There is certainly merit to the proposal that the guidelines did not, and to this day do not, go far enough to reduce debris creation or mitigate its impacts significantly. However, the establishment of the Space Debris Mitigation Guidelines of UN COPUOS set a United Nations level standard, albeit voluntary, for the minimum standards that all States should attempt to achieve in their space exploration. What is more, these mitigation measures were coordinated on a mass scale among a host of nations which encouraged greater consensus and buy-in from States, especially the most important ones.

UN COPUOS and the United Nations generally is not the only international organization with influence and impact on the health of the orbital debris environment, nor the only organization implementing persuasive pressure over global space operations to reduce the overall impact to some areas of the orbital debris environment (and establish some persuasive impact on customary international law formation). Another international organization with influence is the International Telecommunications Union (ITU), which in particular has implemented some voluntary guidelines to highlight the need to dispose of satellites properly to reduce the risk of debris due to collisions, and or the potential to render defunct large satellites as a result of debris fragments. Not only is this relevant for establishing the community standards for debris mitigation efforts,

510 *Id.* at 18, para. 125.

511 *Id.* at 18, para. 125. *See also* BRIAN D. LEPARD, CUSTOMARY INTERNATIONAL LAW, A NEW THEORY WITH PRACTICAL APPLICATIONS (2010). It is worth noting that even though many States desired that the guidelines be adopted as a resolution, it would stress the importance but still, as Professor Lepard points out, not establish legally binding requirements, but also provide persuasive weight. *Id.* at 209. Furthermore, as persuasive evidence, Professor Lepard identifies that it would contribute to significant evidence of *opinio juris*. *Id.* Specifically, "because many General Assembly resolutions purport to announce general principles or rules, they can be strong evidence that member states believe that these principles or rules should be universally applicable. They are also expressions of the views of a large number of states." *Id.* These factors all are contributing elements of establishing the *opinio juris* prong of formulation of customary international law.

512 General Assembly, Rep. of Comm. on the Peaceful Uses of Outer Space, on Its Sixty-Second Session, *supra* note 56 at 18, para. 128.

but also another organization with influence on the overall body of customary international law development. Let us turn to look the ITU efforts.

5 International Telecommunications Union[513]

The ITU is not normally an organization considered as having a role or concern for space debris. However, its mission makes the health of orbital space a top priority. The ITU was founded in 1865 as an intergovernmental organization, established initially as the International Telegraph Union (becoming the International Telecommunications Union in 1932).[514] By the early 1990's, in response to ever-growing demands on technology, communications regulation and coordination it formalized an ITU Constitution and Convention to regulate its activities, and utilized the Radio Regulations establishing the extended details of how to coordinate the international use of the frequency spectrum.[515] It currently has a membership of 193 countries and 700 private sector entities.[516]

One primary responsibility of the ITU is to minimize unintentional cross-border interference by various technical and legal means. In executing that overarching responsibility, the ITU impresses upon Member-States that the radio frequencies are limited resources that must be used in a rational, efficient, and economical way so that there may be equitable access to them based on the needs of individual countries and their unique situations.[517] In doing so, one focus of the ITU is to avoid harmful interference between users of frequencies by managing the prioritization of signals and ensuring separation of frequencies among users as appropriate.[518]

The ITU has also taken an interest in ensuring telecommunication and frequency harmony by paying close attention to the relative health of GEO,

513 For a broad, in-depth discussion on the ITU, recommend *Chapter 8, in* HANDBOOK OF SPACE LAW 456 (Frans von der Dunk & Fabio Tronchetti eds., 2015).

514 History, INT'L TELECOMM. UNION, https://www.itu.int/en/about/Pages/history.aspx#:~:text=ITU%20was%20founded%20in%20Paris,agency%20of%20the%20United%20Nations (last visited Sept. 10, 2020). *See also* HANDBOOK OF SPACE LAW, *supra* note 513 at 461.

515 HANDBOOK OF SPACE LAW, *supra* note 513 at 463.

516 History, INT'L TELECOMM. UNION, *supra* note 514.

517 *Chapter VII: Special Provisions for Radio, in* COLLECTION OF THE BASIC TEXTS OF THE INTERNATIONAL TELECOMMUNICATIONS UNION ADOPTED BY THE PLENIPOTENTIARY CONFERENCE, 49, art. 44, para. 2 (2019), http://search.itu.int/history/HistoryDigitalCollectionDocLibrary/5.22.61.en.100.pdf.

518 *Id.* at art. 45, para. 1.

where the bulk of critical communications satellites reside because of the extremely beneficial nature of the orbit. Since only 1,800 total practical slots exist in GEO, overcrowding is an enormous risk.[519] In response, the ITU adopted Recommendation ITU-R, S.1003–2, *Environmental Protection of the Geostationary Satellite Orbit*.[520]

Originally drafted in 1993, it has since been redrafted two times with the latest version being issued in 2010.[521] It is important to note again that the regulation is only a recommendation. But among the most forceful aspects of the regulation, it highlights the need to dispose of satellites properly to reduce the risk of debris due to collisions or the potential to render large satellites defunct as a result of debris fragments.[522] Ultimately, because of the distance and nature of GEO, without active measures to remove satellites into graveyard orbits where they are not a threat to functioning satellites, geostationary debris will remain in orbit almost indefinitely.

The ITU recognized that satellites in GEO have little chance of survivability in the event of a collision, telecommunications could suffer greatly if this occurred, and any debris from the collision could put all other satellites at risk or could block links of active satellites.[523] Based on these risks, the ITU made four specific recommendations to protect the environment:

1. In the course of GEO insertion, as little debris as possible should be released into the environment,[524] and
2. Efforts should be made to minimize the time any debris exists in elliptical transfer orbits with apogees at or near GEO altitude,[525] and
3. As part of post-mission disposal, actions should be taken to ensure that the satellite has enough propellant to move the satellite to no less than 200 km above the GEO orbit,[526] and

519 Chloe Billing, *There's a Parking Crisis in Space—and You Should be Worried About it*, THE CONVERSATION (Sept. 29, 2017 9:40 am), https://theconversation.com/theres-a-parking-crisis-in-space-and-you-should-be-worried-about-it-83479.

520 Recommendation ITU-R S.1003, Environmental Protection of the Geostationary-Satellite Orbit, INT'L TELECOMM. UNION, at Scope, paras. a-e (Dec. 2010), https://www.itu.int/dms_pubrec/itu-r/rec/s/R-REC-S.1003-2-201012-I!!PDF-E.pdf.

521 *Recommendation S.1003, Environmental Protection of the Geostationary-Satellite Orbit*, INT'L TELECOMM. UNION (Dec. 2010), https://www.itu.int/rec/R-REC-S.1003/en (last visited Apr. 10, 2020).

522 *Id.* at Foreword.

523 *Id.* at Scope, paras. a-e.

524 *Id.* at Recommendation 1.

525 *Id.* at Recommendation 2.

526 *Id.* at Recommendation 3.

4. Any post-mission activities should ensure minimal risk to radio-frequency interference with other active satellites.[527]

Ultimately, the ITU recognizes the enormous risk of threats to GEO and indeed the limitations on understanding the full complexity of the environment since Earth-based resolution quality in GEO only allows for visualization of objects of a size slightly less than 1 meter.[528] Therefore, the ITU, through both its recommendations and its recognition of GEO as such a scarce resource, has taken a particular interest in the environmental protection from debris of this extremely important orbit.

6 Conclusion

This chapter outlined the development of customary international law related to space law and debris mitigation. Unlike treaty law, customary international law does not have the exact same hallmarks. Instead, it relies on a meeting of the minds among States regarding rules for an activity, adherence to those rules, and to such a degree that it is equivalent to hard law.

There is the additional historical requirement of time as an element, though as discussed in this chapter, there is evidence that under the right circumstances, that period can be very short, if not 'instant.' In practice, the Truman Proclamation, and subsequent behavior of States regarding the continental shelf, is demonstrative of the formation of the understandings required for customary international law, the corresponding behaviors, and the need for time, however short. Courts have also recognized the time requirement, though the 'instant custom' argument remains the minority view. In space, the launch of Sputnik and how it defined the rules for national overflight in space is a perfect follow-on example of the development of customary international law and the spontaneity under which it can form.

Having established the understanding of the requirements for development of customary international law, this chapter then examined the lack of formal

527 *Id.* at Recommendation 4.

528 *Id.* at Annex 1. There has been some improvement since this regulation was written in 2010 on observation in GEO, such that according to ESA, ground-based telescopes can now detect debris down to about 10 cm in size. However, the threat posed by even 10 cm can be devastating at hypervelocity and any maneuvers to avoid potential impacts could also use up precious fuel that may be needed for effective post-mission disposal. *See Scanning and Observing*, EURO. SPACE AGENCY, https://www.esa.int/Safety_Security/Space_Debris/Scanning_and_observing2.

treaties related to space debris. Absent formality, the development of the understandings and practice among States has developed primarily through voluntary guidelines, most notably through the United Nations Space Debris Mitigation Guidelines of the Committee on the Peaceful Uses of Outer Space (hereafter UN COPUOS Space Debris Mitigation Guidelines) and in the most recognized guidelines, the IADC Debris Mitigation Guidelines. Reviewing the historical development of these efforts provided the opportunity to understand States' concerns in the development of these guidelines, which will help color the way this book examines State responses to these guidelines in their domestic law. This will help to identify if there are State practices and behaviors in debris mitigation and prevention behaviors that are both consistent and evident among States that some, if not all, of the guidelines have become customary international law.

The next chapters will explore how the major spacefaring Nations have approached debris mitigation and prevention in their practice and behaviors, and how this is colored by historical debris mitigation efforts on the international stage. Furthermore, how impactful the United Nations' advocacy for the IADC Debris Mitigation Guidelines has been to influence State practice and behaviors. Once this book establishes that baseline among the major spacefaring Nations for how their programs operate, the book will then pivot to comparing each State practice and behavior and ultimately address whether any practices and behaviors rise to customary international law. The second part of this book focuses on those efforts through the major spacefaring countries and ESA to make the debris mitigation guidelines a reality in their own domestic operations. The following chapter will begin with the analysis of the United States.

CHAPTER 4

The United States—Space Debris Mitigation, Prevention, and Policy

1 Introduction—US Space Debris Policy

As UN COPUOS and its subcommittees were making initial strides in the early 1990s on debris remediation and management recommendations, several countries were already well on their way to developing sophisticated orbital debris management programs. The United States was among the most aggressive to recognize the threat that debris posed to US national security interests and demonstrate an understanding of its obligations under the Outer Space Treaty. This made taking positive efforts toward debris remediation prudent. In response, around the same time the Scientific and Technical Sub-Committee of UN COPUOS was beginning to organize its efforts, the United States began establishing a mature series of expectations for its debris mitigation and prevention requirements to apply to space operations.

United States action was prompted by information that began maturing in the late 1970s, led by the warnings of Dr. Kessler and others, that the amount of space debris could lead to a catastrophic problem. Furthermore, the congestion was increasing without any serious checks and balances on the total number of injections into orbital areas versus removal of debris. It was also unlikely that the number of debris would decline going forward. Instead, it was clear the opposite was true considering the growth of annual spacefaring activity. Between 1980 and 1987, the efforts of NASA to highlight the issues in the space environment, and a series of debris-creating events occurring in space during this period, did raise the attention on the problem to the highest levels of the US government.

1.1 *Development of National-Level US Space Debris Policy*

Efforts at a tangible US space policy to address space debris began in 1988, when US President Ronald Reagan, shortly before he departed from office, indicated his interest to create a policy for how the United States would address the growing debris problem. This was largely uncharted territory since no country, including the United States, had taken any significant steps toward debris control or mitigation. In fact, before 1988, no US President had raised the issue of debris, or even the word itself, in any of their Presidential national space

© KONINKLIJKE BRILL NV, LEIDEN, 2023 | DOI:10.1163/9789004535848_006

policies nor indicated it was an issue requiring attention at that level. However, as President Reagan began to recognize the changing landscape and the potential threat that debris posed, he drafted changes into his second iteration of his National Space Policy (NSP) for 1988 (the previous being in 1982).[529] According to his 1988 NSP, "all space sectors will seek to minimize the creation of space debris. Design and operations of space tests, experiments, and systems will strive to minimize or reduce the accumulation of space debris consistent with mission requirements and cost-effectiveness."[530]

President Reagan's successor, President George H.W. Bush, assumed office in 1989. Continuing his predecessor's efforts, President G.H.W. Bush focused on the same bedrock principles with some updates of his own in National Space Policy Directive-1 (NSPD-1). Beyond the original language from the 1988 NSP, NSPD-1 added that "The United States government will encourage other spacefaring Nations to adopt policies and practices aimed at debris minimization."[531] This was significant, indicating that not only was the United States focused on ensuring that its own space actors implemented debris minimization procedures, but that the United States was also going to engage internationally to persuade foreign space participants to do the same.

By the time UN COPUOS attempted to tackle the debris problem and recommendations in late 1994, they were already behind the proverbial 'power-curve.' The United States, the year before, had moved on from debris policy rhetoric regarding 'encouragement to strive to reduce debris' to establishing tangible expectations upon US operators.[532] In 1993, NASA Management Instruction (NMI) 1700.8 positioned NASA at the forefront of efforts to limit the creation of orbital debris in line with the space directives of President Reagan and President G.H.W. Bush.[533] NASA's first effort that year only required 'that a debris assessment must be conducted during the development of NASA programs to assess the potential to generate orbital debris resulting

529 The White House, Office of the Press Secretary, Fact Sheet, Presidential Directive on National Space Policy, at 4 (Nov. 16, 1989), *available at* https://aerospace.csis.org/wp-content/uploads/2019/02/NSPD-1-Bush-I-National-Space-Policy.pdf.

530 *Id.*

531 *Id.*

532 *Id. See also* The White House, Office of the Press Secretary, Fact Sheet, Presidential Directive on National Space Policy, at 4 (Feb. 11, 1988), *available at* https://aerospace.org/sites/default/files/policy_archives/National%20Space%20Policy%20Feb88.pdf.

533 NASA Office of Safety and Mission Assurance, Guidelines and Assessment Procedures for Limiting Orbital Debris (Aug. 1995), *available at* https://ntrs.nasa.gov/archive/nasa/casi.ntrs.nasa.gov/19960020946.pdf.

from normal operations and malfunction conditions as well as on-orbit collisions.'[534] Additionally, it required that the assessment must also address post-mission disposal. However, this guidance was too vague to stand alone.

In response, the NASA Office of Safety and Mission Assurance tasked the NASA Johnson Space Center to develop the necessary guidelines that would allow for the implementation of the expectations established by the NMI 1700.8.[535] Published in August of 1995, NASA's Safety Standard (NSS) 1740.14, *Guidelines and Assessment Procedures for Limiting Orbital Debris*, provided "specific guidelines and methods to comply with the NASA policy to limit orbital debris generation."[536] It further established guidelines for three specific debris management requirements. First, making efforts to limit the creation of debris.[537] Second, assessing the risk of collision with existing debris in the orbital environment.[538] Third, requiring an assessment of the potential that debris generated from spacecraft might result in fragments landing on the Earth's surface.[539] Probably most impactful, NASA recognized that the sheer amount of debris that had accumulated in the orbital environment (at the time *only* 2 million kilograms of debris) was a direct result of the historical practice of abandoning spacecraft after the mission were complete or there was no functional use for the spacecrafts anymore.[540] The well-founded fear was that continuing the current modus operandi would create a threat to future operations that could reach a point where the growth was impossible to control.[541]

NSS 1740.14 set out the guidelines in five specific areas, which provided an organized template used by later debris limiting instructions. The five areas were 1) debris released during normal operations, 2) debris generated by explosions and internal breakups, 3) debris generated by on-orbit collisions during mission operations, 4) safe disposal of space systems after mission completion, and finally, 5) if disposal by atmospheric decay would result in re-entry survival, an assessment must be conducted to determine the re-entry risk to the surface of Earth.[542]

---

534 R.C. Reynolds, J.P. Loftus, & D.J. Kessler, *Issues Arising from the NASA Safety Standard to Control Orbital Debris*, 19 ADVANCES IN SPACE RSCH. 381 (1997).

535 *Id.*

536 NASA Safety Standard 1740.14, NASA Office of Safety and Mission Assurance, Guidelines and Assessment Procedures for Limiting Orbital Debris, at 7 (Aug. 1995), *available at* https://ntrs.nasa.gov/archive/nasa/casi.ntrs.nasa.gov/19960020946.pdf.

537 *Id.*

538 *Id.*

539 *Id.*

540 *Id.* at 39.

541 *Id.* at 71.

542 *Id.* at 5.

In each section, if these guidelines could not be met, there were additional expectations for the implementation of mitigation steps in the planning. Specifically, for post-mission disposal, NSS 1740.14 was very sensitive to an immediate effort to reduce the amount of debris accumulation in space. Therefore, the instruction outlined three particular options for post-mission disposal.[543] The first involved the direct retrieval and deorbit of the spacecraft.[544] The second allowed for positioning the spacecraft where the natural atmospheric drag would eventually cause the structure to burn up or safely reenter Earth, so long as that occurred within 25 years post-mission.[545] The last option was to utilize a graveyard orbit where the spacecraft, once positioned, would no longer pose any threat to ongoing operations.[546]

In 1996, President Bill Clinton remained true to the path of his Presidential predecessors. He continued to recognize that orbital debris was an ongoing threat and efforts must be made to minimize the creation of new debris. Additionally, the private sector was becoming increasingly capable and important as a player in space. As a result, President Clinton encouraged the DoD, NASA, and the Intelligence Community to work with their civilian

---

543 *Id.* at 39.

544 *Id.* at 39.

545 *Id.* at 39.

546 *Id.* at 39. It is important to note that NSS 1740.14 was superseded by NASA-STD 8719.14 in 2007. *See NSS 1740.14, NASA Safety Standard: Guidelines and Assessments for Limiting Orbital Debris (Aug 1995)*, EVERY SPEC, http://everyspec.com/NASA/NASA-NSS-PUBS/NSS_1740--14_2276/ (last visited Jul 25, 2020). NASA-STD 8719.14 was subsequently superseded by Revision A in 2011, Revision B in 2019, and subsequently Revision C in November of 2021, NASA-STD 8719.14C. *See* NASA Technical Standard, Process for Limiting Orbital Debris, NASA (Nov. 5, 2021), available at https://standards.nasa.gov/standard/nasa/nasa-std-871914. Like its predecessors, the current version provides technical requirements for limiting orbital debris and methods to comply with the requirements for limiting orbital debris generation for all NASA headquarters and NASA centers, as well as anyone that NASA has cooperative agreements with that are involved in programs and projects for NASA or NASA-sponsored objects. *Id.* at foreword. The most recent version aligns the NASA standards with the National Space Policy of the United States, Space Policy Directive-3, The National Space Traffic Management Policy, the US Government Orbital Debris Mitigation Standard Practices, the Inter-Agency Space Debris Coordination Committee, and the Space Debris Mitigation Guidelines of the United Nations Committee on the Peaceful Uses of Outer Space. *Id.* at foreword. The current version details four specific objectives of the updated technical standards. First, limiting the creation of debris; second, assessing the risk of collisions between debris currently in orbit; third, assessing the risk of objects colliding with the Earth; and last, addressing the risks associated with the end-of-mission parameters for space objects as well as attempting to limit those risks. *Id.* at para. 1.1.3.

counterparts to bring the necessary tools to bear to advance the exploration of space safely.[547]

Concurrently, President Clinton continued the historical emphasis on testing and experiments that would minimize or reduce the accumulation of space debris.[548] In doing so, President Clinton encouraged continued advocacy among other spacefaring Nations and organizations to reduce debris injection.[549] Additionally, he also added to the policy the prerogative of the United States to cooperate internationally and to exchange information on research and mitigation efforts relevant to debris.[550] With the IADC and other international organizations becoming more heavily involved in mapping out the direction that debris control and mitigation needed to go, this was a valuable grant of authority and encouragement by the President for agencies like NASA and other US departments and agencies.

By the time President George W. Bush took office and issued his NSP in August of 2006, the efforts on orbital debris management were robust in the United States. Beyond the established directives to coordinate and expend effort in reducing the creation of orbital debris by both government and civilian operations, President G.W. Bush also impressed upon agencies that they were directed to follow the US Government Orbital Debris Mitigation Standard Practices (ODMSP).[551] He also empowered the Secretaries of Commerce and Transportation, and well as the Chairman of the FCC, to manage debris creation through their administrative levers of power.[552] This empowerment would have a lasting impact in the management of orbital debris, when President Obama, followed by President Trump, began (and continued respectively) significant shifts of space-related responsibilities over to the Secretary of Commerce.

Once President Obama took office, his 2010 space policy was reflective of his immediate predecessor's commitment to the UN COPUOS Space Debris

547 The White House Nat. Sci. and Tech. Council, Fact Sheet: National Space Policy, at 12 (Sep. 19, 1996), *available at* https://aerospace.org/sites/default/files/policy_archives/National%20Space%20Policy%20Sep96.pdf.

548 *Id.* at 14.

549 *Id.*

550 *Id.*

551 U.S. National Space Policy, AERO SPACE, 9 https://aerospace.org/sites/default/files/policy_archives/Natl%20Space%20Policy%20fact%20sheet%2031Aug06.pdf (last visited Aug. 1, 2020).

552 *Id.*

Mitigation Guidelines as well as the US ODMSP.[553] However, his NSP had an additional layer of international policing to it, such that he included language that the United States would use its SSA capabilities to seek out irresponsible actions of actors in space and attribute that behavior (the implication being, at minimum, public embarrassment).[554] Furthermore, President Obama had promised broader international partnerships in two ways. First, regarding the removal of debris, hazard reduction, and environmental understanding, he tied together the Administrator of NASA and the Secretary of Defense by requiring they act as partners in the effort to research and develop solutions to the problem.[555] Second, he again partnered the Administrator of NASA and the Secretary of Defense, but this time added the Director of National Intelligence, and any other departments as appropriate, to work with industry and foreign Nations to improve understanding of the space threat environment and improve orbital debris tracking efforts.[556]

Within two years, President Obama issued another policy to further advance the theme that debris management was a whole of government effort. In November of 2013, President Obama issued his National Space Transportation Policy. This new policy gave the Secretary of Transportation two key responsibilities. The first was to authorize and provide safety oversight for non-federal launch and re-entry operations.[557] Second, it gave the Secretary the exclusive authority to address orbital debris mitigation practices for US licensed commercial launches, including the launch vehicle itself, through the licensing procedures that belonged to the Secretary of Transportation.[558] Not to be left out, the Secretary of Commerce was also given responsibilities as a dual partner with the Secretary of Transportation for encouraging commercial space transportation activities generally.[559] As such, the body of interested agencies in the debris mitigation efforts, whether through procurement, licensing, or operations grew and now required cooperation from a very robust team of powerful agencies for success.

---

553 EXEC. OFF. OF THE PRESIDENT, National Space Policy of the United States of America, 7 (Jun. 28, 2010), *available at* https://aerospace.org/sites/default/files/policy_archives/National%20Space%20Policy%2028Jun10.pdf (last visited Jul. 22, 2020).

554 *Id.*

555 *Id.*

556 *Id.* at 8.

557 EXEC. OFF. OF THE PRESIDENT, National Space Transportation Policy, 5 (Nov. 21, 2013), *available at* https://obamawhitehouse.archives.gov/sites/default/files/microsites/ostp/national_space_transportation_policy_11212013.pdf (last visited Jul. 22, 2020).

558 *Id.* at 5.

559 *Id.*

Following President Obama, President Trump's administration recognized both the severity of the debris problem and the need to implement definitive orbital debris prevention and mitigation efforts into the future. Space Policy Directive-3 (SPD-3), *National Space Traffic Management Policy*, issued on 18 June 2018, is largely dedicated to laying out the Trump Administration's specific debris reduction and mitigation policies. In his new SPD-3 announcement speech, President Trump criticized the prior handling of the debris problem by his predecessors and indicated his intent to solve the problem. He stated that the "two previous administrations tried and failed to develop a system to deal with congested conditions in orbit. We are finally going to get it done."[560]

SPD-3 focuses on several general points, but two stand out. The first addresses mitigation. The policy recognizes that the increase of debris in the orbital environment is to the detriment of all operators.[561] Furthermore, it argued that the existing ODMSP, dating back to 2001, was insufficient to meet the growing debris threat.[562] As a result, the Trump Administration established that the ODMSP should not stand alone.[563] Instead, it should incorporate additional minimum safety standards and best practices, which in turn, should be incorporated into Federal law to ensure proper enforcement of the principles.[564] This is especially important for end-of-life procedures. To further advance this effort, SPD-3 sets out that owners should participate in a pre-launch certification process which would, at a minimum, seek to prevent a collision, enhance the reliability of the objects, and ensure proper disposal in a timely manner upon mission conclusion.[565]

Once again, all US Presidents since Ronald Reagan relied on the buy-in (even if required) of several disparate interests to advance this goal. Among them, the expectation was that the Administrator of NASA,[566] Secretaries of State,

---

560 Remarks on Signing a Memorandum on National Space Traffic Management Policy 2018 DAILY COMP. PRES. DOC. (Jun. 18, 2018), *available at* https://www.govinfo.gov/content/pkg/DCPD-201800430/pdf/DCPD-201800430.pdf (last visited Jul. 22, 2020).

561 Memorandum on National Space Traffic Management Policy, 2018 DAILY COMP. PRES. DOC. (Jun. 18, 2018), *available at* https://www.govinfo.gov/content/pkg/DCPD-201800431/pdf/DCPD-201800431.pdf (last visited Jul. 22, 2020).

562 *Id.*

563 *Id.*

564 *Id.*

565 *Id.*

566 It is worth noting for clarity that NASA does not have regulatory authority generally. Instead, it provides technical consultation as needed during the interagency coordination process. This is especially important related to the ODMSP standards which require the coordination between so many disparate interests. Daniel L. Oltrogge & Ian A. Christensen, *Space Governance in the New Space Era*, 7 J. SPACE SAFETY ENG'G 6

Defense, Commerce, and Transportation, as well as the Director of National Intelligence would lead efforts to update the ODMSP and establish new guidelines for satellite design and operation.[567]

The second key point involves Space Traffic Management (STM). The Trump administration assessed that the debris problem could not necessarily be fixed in the near-term.[568] Instead, STM must adapt to have the technology necessary to provide expansive and accurate situational awareness coverage.[569] In particular, the need to more accurately identify very small debris was critically important, as well as making sure that the existing debris did not hinder overall operations.[570] To do that required the ability to identify the debris with the appropriate sensors and tools, which SPD-3 encourages investment and partnership development in. As a result, the focus on science and technology to advance the capability to identify and avoid debris was a key component of the overall management plan.[571]

1.2 *Orbital Debris Mitigation Standard Practices and SPD-3*

The original ODMSP were drafted in 1997 and finally approved in 2001.[572] The original objectives were to address the increased accumulation of orbital debris in near-Earth space.[573] The original standards consisted of four main objectives. In addition, specific mitigation guidelines were included to increase the likelihood of success for a particular objective. The current version, and the only update since the original document was approved,[574] occurred in 2019

(2020), https://www.researchgate.net/publication/342609732_Space_governance_in_the_new_space_era.

567 Memorandum on National Space Traffic Management Policy, *supra* note 561.

568 *Id.*

569 *Id.*

570 *Id.*

571 *Id.*

572 *Frequently Asked Questions: Orbital Debris*, *supra* note 57, at question 18.

573 *U.S. Government Orbital Debris Mitigation Standard Practices*, NASA ASTROMATERIALS RESEARCH & EXPLORATION SCIENCE, ORBITAL DEBRIS PROGRAM OFFICE, at para. 1–1, *retrievable from* https://www.hsdl.org/?abstract&did=722493 (last visited Jun. 20, 2022).

574 In 2010, a review at the request of Congress was conducted by the Office of Science and Technology under the Executive Office of the President to determine if the existing guidelines for mitigation of orbital debris were adequate and if the practices of US launch providers were adhering to the guidelines. The findings indicated that the guidelines were, at the time, adequate to slow the growth of orbital debris within the space environment. EXEC. OFF. OF THE PRESIDENT, OFF. OF SCI. & TECH. POL'Y, Letter from Ted Wackler, Acting Director, to Congress Reporting the Status of the Orbital Debris Mitigation Strategy, at 3 (Aug. 14, 2017), *available at* https://trumpwhitehouse.archives.gov/wp-content/uploads/2017/12/08-14-17-OSTP-Orbital-Debris-Report.pdf.

from SPD-3 guidance. The four original objectives and corresponding principles were as follows:

1. *Control of Debris Released During Normal Operations* requires that "spacecraft and upper stages should be designed to eliminate or minimize debris released during normal operations."[575] If the release of debris (5 mm or larger) was unavoidable, and if it would remain in orbit more than 25 years, it required that the reasoning be evaluated and justified.[576] The explanation would have to demonstrate the need for non-compliance based on cost-effectiveness and mission requirements.[577]
2. *Minimizing Debris Generated By Accidental Explosion* requires that "programs and projects will assess and limit the probability of accidental explosion during and after completion of mission operations."[578] This focuses on a requirement that in the development stage of spacecraft design, including its components, there is not a credible likelihood that an accidental explosion will occur.[579] If such a failure possibility exists, then the expectation is that the design or operational procedures for the mission will limit the probability that there will be such an occurrence.[580]

---

575 *U.S. Government Orbital Debris Mitigation Standard Practices*, *supra* note 573 at para. 1.

576 *Id.* at para. 1–1.

577 *Id.*

578 *Id.* at para. 2.

579 *Id.* at para. 2–1.

580 *Id.* A Failure Mode and Effects Analysis is a procedure by which methodologies are designed to identify potential failure modes for a product or process, assess the risk associated with those failure modes, rank the issues in terms of importance, and to identify and carry out corrective actions on the most serious concerns. *See Failure Mode and Effect Analysis (FMEA) and Failure Modes, Effects and Criticality Analysis (FMECA)*, WEIBULL.COM https://www.weibull.com/basics/fmea.htm (last visited Apr. 21, 2020). *See also Flight Assurance Procedure P-302–720, Performing a Failure Mode and Effects Analysis*, THE ELSMAR COVE MISSION, *available at* https://elsmar.com/pdf_files/FMEA%20Examples/FMEA_Nasa_spacecraft.pdf (last visited Apr. 21, 2020). *Standard for Performing a Failure Mode and Effects Analysis (FMEA) and Establishing a Critical Items List (CIL)* NASA RAPID SPACECRAFT DEVELOPMENT OFFICE, (Draft Procedures), *available at* https://rsdo.gsfc.nasa.gov/documents/Rapid-III-Documents/MAR-Reference/GSFC-FAP-322-208-FMEA-Draft.pdf (last visited Apr. 21, 2020). This also raises an important point that space is unique, such that many additional factors must be considered beyond the manufacturing and proper operation of an item, which is otherwise assumed from the beginning. Items under consideration must also factor in the harshness of space, such as the effects of shock and vibration from launch, orbital injection, deployment of power sources, instruments, et cetera.

3. *Selection of Safe Flight Profile and Operational Configuration* requires that "programs and projects will assess and limit the probability of operating space systems becoming a source of debris by collisions with man-made objects or meteoroids."[581] Specifically, both the probability of collision must be estimated, and spacecraft must, within cost constraints, limit the likelihood that debris a centimeter or smaller will cause a loss of control (and resulting inability to dispose of properly).[582]
4. *Post-mission Disposal of Space Structures* is the last of the original four guidelines. It requires effective planning for the disposal of all space vehicles and components at the end-of-mission life to minimize the impact on future space operations.[583] It offers three methods by which disposal may occur: 1) atmospheric re-entry, with a caveat that it must decay into orbit within 25 years of mission completion, 2) entry into a storage orbit and away from an operational orbit, and finally, 3) direct retrieval as soon as practicable after the mission is complete.[584]

As stated earlier, the issuance of President Trump's SPD-3 indicated a desire by the administration to update the ODMSP. By November 2019, that desire had been realized and a fifth objective was added.[585] The impetus for the addition focused on the view of the administration that the ODMSP's original four objectives were adequate for the time which they were issued, but no longer met the needs under the current environment.[586] Additionally, looking forward, the increase in private space enterprise further identified a need to add some considerations.[587] The language of the fifth, and newest, incorporation into the ODMSP practices, is as follows:

5. *Clarification and Additional Standard Practices for Certain Classes of Space Operations* requires that large constellations and small satellites are bound by the original four mitigation standard practices.

581 *U.S. Government Orbital Debris Mitigation Standard Practices*, *supra* note 573 at para. 3.

582 *Id.* at para. 3–2.

583 *Id.* at para. 4.

584 *Id.* at para. 4.

585 *U.S. Government Orbital Debris Mitigation Standard Practices, November 2019 Update*, NASA ASTROMATERIALS RESEARCH & EXPLORATION SCIENCE, ORBITAL DEBRIS PROGRAM OFFICE, at para. 5, *available at* https://orbitaldebris.jsc.nasa.gov/library/usg_orbital_debris_mitigation_standard_practices_november_2019.pdf (last visited Jun. 20, 2022).

586 *Id.* at 1.

587 *Id.*

> Additionally, rendezvous and on-orbit servicing operations should limit the probability of accidental collision or accidental explosion, and generally limit the potential for debris creating events according to objective one of the original standards. Last, when active debris removal operations become a reality, planning should ensure that the risks of damage to the crafts are minimal, the probability of accidental collision is low, and the accidental explosion probabilities are minimized, all in accordance with the objectives of the original guidelines.[588]

The new mitigation standard has made some additional substantive changes to the original objectives as well. The first objective saw the addition of a total debris object-time limitation in LEO below 100 years, such that the total time all planned debris releases from operations remain in orbit should not exceed 100 years total time in LEO.[589] The second objective moved away from the original Failure Mode and Effects Analysis (FMEA) model for determining failure considerations, and moved to a generic requirement that "commonly accepted engineering and probability assessment methods" be utilized.[590] Furthermore, a requirement that the probability of debris-generating explosions for all potential failures be less than 1 in 1,000.[591] Similar to objective one, objective three saw the same addition of the 100 years of total orbital lifetime for space objects to reduce the probability of collision, and furthermore, a specific inclusion of a requirement that the probability of a collision with objects 10 cm or larger be .001 (or less than 1 in 1,000).[592] It also added a probability requirement of less than .01 (or 1 in 100) that collisions with objects smaller than 1 cm will cause catastrophic damage such that post-mission disposal becomes impossible.[593] Finally, objective four saw the addition of a proper disposal reliability percentage of 90% with a goal of 99% or better.[594]

1.3 *2020 US National Space Policy*

Following SPD-3, President Trump, just prior to his departure from office, implemented the newest US NSP on 9 December 2020, published in the Federal

588 *Id.* at para. 5.
589 *Id.* at para. 1–1.
590 *Id.* at para. 2–1.
591 *Id.* at para. 2–1.
592 *Id.* at para. 3–1.
593 *Id.* at para. 3–2.
594 *Id.* at para. 4–2.

Register on Wednesday, 16 December 2020.[595] The new policy sets out six principles and eight goals to advance the interests of US space operations.[596]

1.3.1 The Six Principles of President Trump's National Space Policy

The specific principles include that all Nations should act responsibly for the sustainability of space in the future,[597] a strong commercial space sector will help the United States remain strong and exert global influence,[598] partnerships among friendly Nations should be encouraged,[599] and a reaffirmation of the Outer Space Treaty principles.[600] It did, however, caveat that while the United States respects the Outer Space Treaty, it still maintains the interpretation that it is not a violation of the Treaty to extract resources from the Moon and celestial bodies.[601] It also reaffirmed the intent of the United States that space remains peaceful[602] and a reaffirmation of the right of free use and exploration of space.[603]

1.3.2 The Eight Goals of President Trump's National Space Policy

The 8 goals from President Trump's NSP are that the United States shall:

1. Promote and incentivize private industry.[604]
2. Encourage and uphold the rights of Nations to use space responsibly and peacefully.[605]
3. Lead, encourage, and expand international cooperation.[606]
4. Create a safe, stable, secure, and sustainable environment for space activities.[607]
5. Increase the assurance of national critical functions.[608]

---

595 The National Space Policy, 85 Fed. Reg. 81755 (2020), https://www.federalregister.gov/documents/2020/12/16/2020-27892/the-national-space-policy.

596 *Id.* at § 2.

597 *Id.* at § 2(1).

598 *Id.* at § 2(2).

599 *Id.* at § 2(3).

600 *Id.* at § 2(4).

601 *Id.* at § 2(4).

602 *Id.* at § 2(5).

603 *Id.* at § 3(1).

604 *Id.* at § 3(1).

605 *Id.* at § 3(2).

606 *Id.* at § 3(3).

607 *Id.* at § 3(4). This goal addresses space debris specifically, indicating that collaboration with industry to improve a number of practices is important, but there also needs to be a way to accurately identify measures to mitigate orbital debris.

608 *Id.* at § 3(5).

6. Extend human economic activity into deep space.[609]
7. Increase the quality of life for all humanity.[610]
8. Preserve and expand United States leadership.[611]

1.3.3 President Trump's National Space Policy and Orbital Debris

The policy does address the concerns of the United States with the ongoing space debris problem. Specifically, the Policy highlights the need to preserve the space environment by minimizing the space debris created during US operations and use. As a result, several provisions were mandated (see 'shall'). They include:

1. Continue leading the development and adoption of industry and international standards, including the UN COPUOS Long-Term Sustainability Guidelines (UN COPUOS LTS Guidelines) and the UN COPUOS Space Debris Mitigation Guidelines.[612]
2. Make basic space SSA data available and assist with coordination, free of direct fees.[613]
3. Use SSA to detect activities that are inconsistent with safety, stability, security, and long-term sustainability of space.[614]
4. Maintain safety of flight standards and best practices.[615]
5. Comply with international obligations for the registration of space objects.[616]
6. Limit the creation of new debris, while still balancing mission requirements and costs, during all phases of space operations. This includes procurement, launch, testing and operations. Meanwhile, ensure adherence to the ODMSP.[617]
7. Ensure proper regulation and licensing of commercial space activities.[618]

---

609 *Id.* at § 3(6).
610 *Id.* at § 3(7).
611 *Id.* at § 3(8).
612 *Id.* at § 4(3)(a)(I).
613 *Id.* at § 4(3)(a)(II).
614 *Id.* at § 4(3)(a)(III).
615 *Id.* at § 4(3)(a)(IV).
616 *Id.* at § 4(3)(a)(V).
617 *Id.* at § 4(3)(a)(VI).
618 *Id.* at § 4(3)(a)(VII).

8. Develop technologies and techniques to mitigate the risks from orbital debris, as well as take steps to reduce hazards, while concurrently increasing the understanding of the current debris environment.[619]
9. Evaluate ADR as a potential long-term solution to maintaining safety of flight in long-term orbital regimes.[620]
10. Require approval of exceptions to the ODMSP.[621]
11. Continue to foster an environment that encourages the application of best practices to prevent orbital collisions, including working with like-minded partner Nations, and advancing the interests of long-term stability through communication with partner and friendly Nations.[622]

There is considerable importance to this document to ongoing debris mitigation efforts, the least of which is the obvious fact that even though President Trump's time in office is over, his administration continued its focus on space policy and interests even among their final administrative acts. Furthermore, the document is quite 'modern' reflecting the recently (as of 2019) published UN COPUOS LTS Guidelines and the intent of the United States to reflect the best practices of both those guidelines and the 2007 IADC Debris Mitigation Guidelines. The importance was further bolstered by President Trump's own comments, stating that "this policy reaffirms our leadership in the space domain and our status as the world's foremost spacefaring nation. This policy represents a whole-of-government approach that recognizes space as a national imperative."[623]

1.4 *Impact of ODMSP Changes and US Policy*

Whether the changes to the ODMSP will make a difference is yet to be determined. Brian Weeden, Director of program planning at the Secure World Foundation, called the changes "underwhelming."[624] Specifically, he cites that while the quantitative limits on events that cause debris were a favorable addition to the guidelines, the update fell short in many ways. In particular, a debate

619 *Id.* at § 4(3)(a)(VIII).
620 *Id.* at § 4(3)(a)(IX).
621 *Id.* at § 4(3)(a)(X).
622 *Id.* at § 4(3)(a)(XI).
623 Mike Wall, *Trump Unveils New National Space Policy for US Leadership off the Earth*, SMALL.COM (Dec. 10, 2020), https://www.space.com/trump-unveils-national-space-policy-us-leadership.
624 Jeff Foust, *U.S. Government Updates Orbital Debris Mitigation Guidelines*, SPACENEWS (Dec. 9, 2019) https://spacenews.com/u-s-government-updates-orbital-debris-mitigation-guidelines/ (last visited Apr. 22, 2020).

has arisen over whether or not the 25-year rule for proper post-mission disposal is still a viable timeframe or if instead it should be significantly reduced.[625] When the 25-year rule was first instituted, the debris within LEO was considerably less. In light of the current congestion, coupled with the soon-to-be addition of enormous amounts of constellation satellites by SpaceX and other companies, there are arguments that a 25 year deorbiting standard may be much too long under the current circumstances.[626]

As each administration has developed its own space policies and goals, the regulatory mechanisms that they have utilized to further their objectives have been varied. However, as seen in the space policy developments, United States regulation has been limited to that necessary to facilitate space activity through NASA. Before the 1980s, there was virtually no commercial space industries available globally. If a foreign government or interested actor wanted something launched into space, NASA was almost exclusively the delivery agency (the exception being for Soviet spacecraft).[627] Accordingly, NASA exerted considerable influence on the drafting and ultimate success of most regulatory implementation. However, as commercial competitors eroded NASA's exclusive launch monopoly, other agencies received regulatory authority over certain sectors of space operations.

Congress memorialized the change to the previous power held by NASA by legislating regulatory authority and empowerment to multiple government agencies. For example, the Department of Transportation was initially designated as the "lead agency for encouraging, facilitating and licensing commercial expendable launch vehicle activities."[628] Over time, the corresponding delegations to different agencies by Congress have caused considerable diversity of authorities and responsibilities through multiple agencies, including NASA, but many others as well. The FCC, FAA, Department of Commerce, Department of State (DoS), and others all now have a piece of the administrative and regulatory puzzle for space development, flight, and activity. As a result, each also has a 'vote' on the conditions in space for the use and protection of the environment. Discussed more below, these agencies create a patchwork of regulations specific to space debris that space actors must navigate to ensure regulatory compliance prior to their ability to conduct commerce in space.

---

625 *Id.*

626 This is discussed much more in depth, *infra* at Chapter 8, Section 4.1.

627 MORGAN, *supra* note 110 at 5.

628 *Id.* (citing Exec. Order No. 12465, *Commercial Expendable Launch Vehicle Activities*, 49 Fed. Reg. 7211, § 1 (Feb. 24, 1984) *available at* https://www.archives.gov/federal-register/codification/executive-order/12465.html).

2 Federal Aviation Administration

Since its inception in 1958 under the *Federal Aviation Act*, the FAA has been at the forefront of regulating and promoting civil aviation.[629] Today, the FAA falls under the Department of Transportation (DoT). As the 'parent' department of the FAA, the DoT has a wide range of responsibilities focused on supporting, maintaining, and advancing the most efficient and modern transportation systems in the world.[630] The FAA supports certain components of the DoT mission, including regulation of civil aviation to promote safety, encouraging and developing civil aeronautics, researching and developing the National Airspace Systems and civil aeronautics, and importantly, regulating US commercial space transportation.[631]

The National Space Transportation Policy directs the Secretary of Transportation to, among other responsibilities, "execute exclusive authority, consistent with existing statutes and executive orders" as well as "to address orbital debris mitigation practices for US licensed commercial launches, to include launch vehicle components such as upper stages through its licensing procedures."[632] The Federal Aviation Administration Office of Commercial Space Transportation (FAA/AST[633]) is the office of primary responsibility for the FAA to issue licenses for US commercial launch and re-entry activities and the operation of launch and re-entry sites by US citizens or other activities otherwise conducted in the United States.[634] Established under the *Commercial Space Launch Act of 1984*, the AST was originally situated under the Office of the Secretary of Transportation within the DoT.[635] However, in 1995, the AST and

629 *What We Do*, FED. AVIATION ADMIN., https://www.faa.gov/about/mission/activities/ (last visited Jul. 24, 2020).

630 *What We Do*, U.S. DEPT. OF TRANSP., https://www.transportation.gov/about (last visited Jul. 24, 2020).

631 *Safety: The Foundation of Everything We Do*, FED. AVIATION ADMIN. (last modified Nov. 6, 2019), https://www.faa.gov/about/safety_efficiency/ (last visited Jul. 24, 2020).

632 EXEC. OFF. OF THE PRESIDENT, National Space Transportation Policy, 5 (Nov. 21, 2013), *available at* https://obamawhitehouse.archives.gov/sites/default/files/microsites/ostp/national_space_transportation_policy_11212013.pdf.

633 MORGAN, *supra* note 110 at 5.

634 John Sloan, *FAA International Workshops on Commercial Space Transportation*, 68th International Astronautical Congress, 2 (Sept. 2017), https://www.faa.gov/space/additional_information/international_affairs/media/workshops_on_cstransportation_by_faa_for_intl_iac_adelaide_sloan_sept_2017_508.pdf.

635 *About the Office of Commercial Space Transportation*, FED. AVIATION ADMIN. (last modified Jul. 6, 2020), https://www.faa.gov/about/office_org/headquarters_offices/ast/ (last visited Jul. 24, 2020).

its responsibilities were transferred under the FAA.[636] The FAA/AST focuses on 'facilitation of a safe, efficient, and successful US commercial space transportation industry.'[637]

2.1 *Roles of the Federal Aviation Administration Office of Commercial Space Transport*

Specifically, the roles and responsibilities of the FAA/AST include the authority to:

1. Regulate the US commercial space transportation industry, ensure compliance with international obligations of the United States, and to protect the public health and safety, safety of property, and national security and foreign policy interests of the United States.[638]
2. Encourage, facilitate, and promote commercial space launches and reentries by the private sector.[639]
3. Recommend appropriate changes in Federal statutes, treaties, regulations, policies, plans, and procedures;[640] and
4. Facilitate the strengthening and expansion of the United States space transportation infrastructure.[641]

2.2 *Federal Aviation Administration Office of Commercial Space Transport Licensing*

The FAA/AST issues licenses under its authority derived from title 51 U.S.C. §50922 and promulgated in 14 C.F.R. Chapter 3, parts 400–460.[642] A license is required for the commercial launch of a launch vehicle[643] from the United

636 *Id.*

637 Oltrogge & Christensen, *supra* note 566.

638 *About the Office of Commercial Space Transportation*, *supra* note 635.

639 *Id.*

640 *Id.*

641 *Id.*

642 51 U.S.C. § 50922(a)(2)-(4) & (b)(1)-(3) (2011), https://www.govinfo.gov/content/pkg/USCODE-2011-title51/html/USCODE-2011-title51.htm. *See also Fact Sheet—Commercial Space Transportation Activities*, FED. AVIATION ADMIN., (Jun. 19, 2020), https://www.faa.gov/news/fact_sheets/news_story.cfm?newsId=19074 (last visited Jul. 25, 2020).

643 Launch vehicle is defined as a vehicle built to operate in, or place a payload in, outer space or a suborbital rocket. 51 U.S.C. § 50501(8) (2011), https://www.govinfo.gov/content/pkg/USCODE-2011-title51/html/USCODE-2011-title51.htm.*Seealso*Definitions,14C.F.R. § 401.5 (2003), *available at* https://www.ecfr.gov/cgi-bin/text-idx?SID=1e0feb88ce75b65ff5446cbb52c959f5&mc=true&node=pt14.4.401&rgn=div5issues or transfers under 14 C.F.R. §§ 400–460.

States or the operation of a launch site[644] within the United States, or for the reentry of a re-entry vehicle[645] from space in the United States, or to operate a re-entry site[646] within the United States.[647] Exceptions to FAA licensing include launch vehicles that would otherwise be properly licensed instead by the FCC, NOAA, or those owned or operated by the US Government.[648] To meet the commercial licensing requirements of the FAA, a launch operator must meet both FAA policy requirements and FAA safety requirements.

2.3 *Requirements for Initial Licensing Considerations*

The FAA has three specific policy requirements which must be met as an initial licensing consideration. First, the issuance of a license must not jeopardize US national security.[649] In doing so, the FAA will consult with interagency

---

644 A Launch site is defined as the location on Earth from which a launch takes place (as defined in a license by the Secretary) and necessary facilities at that location. *See* Definitions 51 U.S.C. § 50902(7) (2011), https://www.govinfo.gov/content/pkg/USCODE-2011-title51/html/USCODE-2011-title51.htm. *See also* Definitions, 14 C.F.R. § 401.5 (2003), *available at* https://www.ecfr.gov/cgi-bin/text-idx?SID=1e0feb88ce75b65ff5446cbb52c959f5&mc=true&node=pt14.4.401&rgn=div5issues or transfers under 14 C.F.R. §§ 400–460.

645 A re-entry vehicle is defined as a vehicle designed to return from Earth's orbit or outer space to Earth substantially intact. A reusable launch vehicle that is designed to return from Earth's orbit or outer space to Earth substantially intact is a re-entry vehicle. *See* Definitions 51 U.S.C. § 50902(16) (2011), https://www.govinfo.gov/content/pkg/USCODE-2011-title51/html/USCODE-2011-title51.htm. *See also* Definitions, 14 C.F.R. § 401.5 (2003), *available at* https://www.ecfr.gov/cgi-bin/text-idx?SID=1e0feb88ce75b65ff5446cbb52c959f5&mc=true&node=pt14.4.401&rgn=div5issues or transfers under 14 C.F.R. §§ 400–460.

646 A re-entry site means the location on Earth where a re-entry vehicle is intended to return. It includes the area within three standard deviations of the intended landing point. *See also* Definitions, 14 C.F.R. § 401.5 (2003), *available at* https://www.ecfr.gov/cgi-bin/text-idx?SID=1e0feb88ce75b65ff5446cbb52c959f5&mc=true&node=pt14.4.401&rgn=div5issues or transfers under 14 C.F.R. §§ 400–460.

647 *Fact Sheet—Commercial Space Transportation Activities*, *supra* note 642.

648 Payloads not Subject to Review, 14 C.F.R. § 415.53 (2012), *available at* https://www.ecfr.gov/cgi-bin/text-idx?SID=1e0feb88ce75b65ff5446cbb52c959f5&mc=true&node=pt14.4.415&rgn=div5#se14.4.415_153.

649 For general National Security consideration requirements, *see* 51 U.S.C. § 50918 (2011), https://www.govinfo.gov/content/pkg/USCODE-2011-title51/html/USCODE-2011-title51.htm. Under § 50918, Consultation, subsection a, the Secretary of Transportation shall consult with the Secretary of Defense on a matter under this chapter affecting national security. The Secretary of Defense shall identify and notify the Secretary of Transportation of a national security interest relevant to an activity. *See also* 14 C.F.R. § 415.21 (2012), *available at* https://www.ecfr.gov/cgi-bin/text-idx?SID=1e0feb88ce75b65ff5446cbb52c959f5&mc=true&node=pt14.4.415&rgn=div5#se14.4.415_121.

partners, including specifically NASA and the DoD at a minimum, to ensure no issues exist that the FAA needs to consider as part of its analysis.[650] Second, issuance of a license must not jeopardize foreign policy interests.[651] In making this determination, the FAA will coordinate with the State Department to determine if any multinational partners would otherwise be affected by a license being issued.[652] Last, issuance must not adversely affect or violate any international obligations of the United States.[653] Again, the State Department is among the most central departments to assist in this analysis.[654] If those three policy thresholds are not violated, then the proposed launch can be further considered for whether or not it meets the safety requirements demanded of all license seekers.

Once the policy requirements are met, the FAA looks at the plan specifics for the proposed activity, from launch to post-mission disposal, to make the safety determination. While there are a myriad of safety requirements overall, the primary interest of the FAA in this analysis is 1) the ability of the launch operator to be able to launch, and 2) can the launch operator do so without jeopardizing the public health and safety of property during all phases of launch operations.[655] One of the critical overarching elements of this analysis is the risk threshold for the potential loss of life or damage to property as a result of launch operations. The measurement of risk to persons and properties is a series of thresholds measured by the expected average number of casualties to the collective members of the public exposed to debris hazards from any

650 Payload not Subject to Review, 14 C.F.R. 415.53 (2012), *available at* https://www.ecfr.gov/cgi-bin/text-idx?SID=1e0feb88ce75b65ff5446cbb52c959f5&mc=true&node=pt14.4.415&rgn=div5#se14.4.415_153.

651 For general Foreign Policy consideration requirements, *see* 51 U.S.C. § 50198 (2011), https://www.govinfo.gov/content/pkg/USCODE-2011-title51/html/USCODE-2011-title51.htm. Under 51 U.S.C. § 50918, Consultation, subsection b, The Secretary of Transportation shall consult with the Secretary of State on a matter … affecting foreign policy. The Secretary of State shall identify and notify the Secretary of Transportation of a foreign policy interest or obligation relevant to an activity. *See also* 14 C.F.R. § 415.21.

652 For general Foreign Policy consideration requirements, *see* 51 U.S.C. § 50918 (2011), https://www.govinfo.gov/content/pkg/USCODE-2011-title51/html/USCODE-2011-title51.htm. Under Section 51 U.S.C. § 50918, Consultation, subsection b, the Secretary of Transportation shall consult with the Secretary of State on a matter … affecting foreign policy interest or obligation. *See also* Policy Review, 14 C.F.R. § 415.23 (2012), *available at* https://www.ecfr.gov/cgi-bin/text-idx?SID=1e0feb88ce75b65ff5446cbb52c959f5&mc=true&node=pt14.4.415&rgn=div5#se14.4.415_123.

653 14 C.F.R. § 415.21.

654 Policy Review, 14 C.F.R. § 415.23.

655 14 C.F.R. § 415.31 (2006), *available at* https://www.ecfr.gov/cgi-bin/text-idx?SID=1e0feb88ce75b65ff5446cbb52c959f5&mc=true&node=pt14.4.415&rgn=div5#se14.4.415_131.

specific launch.[656] For the debris risk analysis for an orbital launch, the FAA examines the operational risk analysis for each stage of the operational lifecycle. This encompasses an analysis that the launch operator must perform from the time of the potential lift-off through orbital insertion, and then to post-mission safety and disposal.

2.4 *Assessing Launch Risk*

When assessing the risk to members of the public under the required FAA analysis, there are generally four specific groupings of analyses that must be done depending on 1) where the launch will be conducted from and 2) where any debris, whether planned or not, could impact Earth. The first is the potential risk to members of the public or property at the launch site. The second is the risk to people and ships in the ocean along the flight path where the launch vehicle will travel which might be in danger if debris is inadvertently released during flight and lands in the ocean. The third is the same risk to people or property along the flight path or re-entry where a piece of debris may return to dry land. Last, the potential risk along the flight path to aircraft from the launch vehicle or components both during the upward insertion into orbit or for the return of the launch vehicle or components.

Evaluations for each of these stages must be accomplished and submitted to determine the risk to people or property during the different stages of operations, with specific analysis requirements for each type of grouping. The risk to members of the public in all four situations must also consider the potential for exposure to debris impact, toxic materials, and far-field blast overpressure.[657] If the risk to persons and property do not exceed specified levels, the FAA will look to the elements of the desired license.

---

656 *Id.*

657 Flight Safety, 14 C.F.R. § 417.107(b)(1) (2016), *available at* https://www.ecfr.gov/cgi-bin/text-idx?SID=1e0feb88ce75b65ff5446cbb52c959f5&mc=true&node=pt14.4.417&rgn=div5#se14.4.417_1107. Blast overpressure, also known as high energy impulse noise, is a damaging outcome of explosive detonations, which creates a shock wave issuing out from the point of blast detonation. The shock waves caused by these blasts can cause injury to humans, particularly to the brain, organ, auditory and respiratory systems. *Overpressure*, WIKIPEDIA, https://en.wikipedia.org/wiki/Overpressure (last visited Jul. 25, 2020). *See also* Dorothy L. Dobbins & Xiaoping Pan, *Neurological Effects and Mechanisms of Blast Overpressure Injury*, *in* HANDBOOK OF TOXICOLOGY OF CHEMICAL WARFARE AGENTS 159, 159 (Ramesh C. Gupta ed. 2d ed. 2015).

2.5 *Launch Application and License*

The process to apply for a license also follows four general stages. The initial step involves a review of the concept of operations and assignment of a commercial space transportation point of contact.[658] Following the initial assessment, the second step involves a pre-application consultation for the applicant to ensure that the licensing documents are initiated and a full review of the application for any concerns by the FAA or other concerned parties exists (airspace, coast guard, et cetera.).[659] Once all the documents are in order, an application evaluation is conducted between four and six months (depending on the type of request) prior to the launch date.[660] This involves a full review of all of the considerations, including safety, environmental, policy, payload review, airspace deconfliction, and the financial ability of the applicant to execute on the plan.[661] If a favorable determination is made on the launch, then a license (or permit) is issued.[662] Following the issuance, continued partnership occurs between the applicant and the FAA to ensure adherence to the plan, responding to any modifications, and issuing any necessary renewals.[663]

There are two types of licenses that may be obtained through the FAA licensing process. The first type of license is a launch-specific license. This type of license authorizes one or more individually identified launches or reentries, using the same site and the same type of vehicle.[664] It identifies, by

658 *Commercial Space Transportation Assistance Tool*, FED. AVIATION ADMIN. (last modified Jun. 11, 2020), https://www.faa.gov/space/licensing_process/ (last visited Jul. 25, 2020). *See also* Pre-Application Consultation, 14 C.F.R. § 413.15 (2012), *available at* https://www.ecfr.gov/cgi-bin/text-idx?SID=1e0feb88ce75b65ff5446cbb52c959f5&mc=true&node=pt14.4.413&rgn=div5#se14.4.413_115.

659 *Commercial Space Transportation Assistance Tool, supra* note 658. *See also* Acceptance of an Application, 14 C.F.R. § 413.11 (2007), *available at* https://www.ecfr.gov/cgi-bin/text-idx?SID=1e0feb88ce75b65ff5446cbb52c959f5&mc=true&node=pt14.4.413&rgn=div5#se14.4.413_111.

660 *Commercial Space Transportation Assistance Tool, supra* note 658. *See also* Pre-Application Consultation, 14 C.F.R. § 413.15 (2012), *available at* https://www.ecfr.gov/cgi-bin/text-idx?SID=1e0feb88ce75b65ff5446cbb52c959f5&mc=true&node=pt14.4.413&rgn=div5#se14.4.413_115.

661 *Commercial Space Transportation Assistance Tool, supra* note 658.

662 *Id. See also* Issuing a License or Permit, 14 C.F.R. § 413.19 (2007), *available at* https://www.ecfr.gov/cgi-bin/text-idx?SID=1e0feb88ce75b65ff5446cbb52c959f5&mc=true&node=pt14.4.413&rgn=div5#se14.4.413_119.

663 *Commercial Space Transportation Assistance Tool, supra* note 658. *See also* Licenses or Permit Renewals 14 C.F.R. § 413.23 (2007), *available at* https://www.ecfr.gov/cgi-bin/text-idx?SID=1e0feb88ce75b65ff5446cbb52c959f5&mc=true&node=pt14.4.413&rgn=div5#se14.4.413_123.

664 MORGAN, *supra* note 110 at 3.

name or mission, each activity authorized under the licenses and, so as long as the activity has the same operational parameters, the license is good until all launches and reentries are complete or the expiration date of the license, whichever comes first.[665] The second type of license is a launch-operator license. This type of license authorizes an unspecified number of launches or reentries using a family of similar, but not necessarily identical, vehicles over a period of years.[666] It typically remains in effect for two to five years from when it was issued.[667]

2.6 *Licensing and Orbital Debris*

There are, understandably, numerous requirements to obtain a launch license from the FAA overall. For the purposes here, the potential creation of debris in all aspects of a launch through post-mission disposal operations plays a significant role. There are good reasons for this, considering the damage which can occur to the space environment from a disaster or the risk to people and property on Earth in the course of operations. As such, the FAA has implemented a series of standards that the launch operator must address to mitigate the potential for debris creation through each phase of normal operations.

Under the FAA license analysis, the authority to grant or withhold a license rests in the FAA authority to conduct a safety review to determine whether the applicant is capable of launching a vehicle with appropriate safeguards for the health and safety of people and property from potential debris fallout from operations.[668] First, as a preliminary matter, the operator must minimize the risk to persons or property near the launch site and among the launch equipment.[669] Second, the operator must minimize the risk of danger posed by failures in the launch vehicle, components, and payload at downrange operational areas during flight.[670] Last, specific to the public, the licensed operator must make a series of calculations to ensure it is not exceeding risk thresholds

---

665 *Launch or Reentry Vehicles*, FED. AVIATION ADMIN., (last modified Jun. 27, 2016), https://www.faa.gov/about/office_org/headquarters_offices/ast/licenses_permits/launch_reentry/ (last visited Jul. 25, 2020).

666 MORGAN, *supra* note 110 at 3.

667 *Launch or Reentry Vehicles, supra* note 665.

668 General, 14 C.F.R. § 415.31 (2006), *available at* https://www.ecfr.gov/cgi-bin/text-idx?SID=1e0feb88ce75b65ff5446cbb52c959f5&mc=true&node=pt14.4.415&rgn=div5#se14.4.415_131.

669 Flight Safety, 14 C.F.R. § 417.107(a)(1) (2016), *available at* https://www.ecfr.gov/cgi-bin/text-idx?SID=1e0feb88ce75b65ff5446cbb52c959f5&mc=true&node=pt14.4.417&rgn=div5#se14.4.417_1107.

670 *Id.* at (a)(2).

to people or property. Specifically, the licensed operator must ensure that the risks account for the following:

1. The risk associated with the total flight to all members of the public, excluding persons in waterborne vessels and aircraft, does not exceed an expected average number of 0.0001 casualties from impacting inert and impacting explosive debris, for toxic release, and for far-field blast overpressure.[671]
2. For an individual member of the public, the standard is more stringent, such that the risk of injury to any individual member of the public cannot exceed a casualty expectation of 0.000001 per launch for each hazard.[672]

In addition, a launch operator must implement waterborne vessel hazard areas that provide an equivalent level of safety to that provided by waterborne vessel hazard areas implemented for launches from a federal launch range.[673]

---

671 Flight Safety, 14 C.F.R. § 417.107(b)(1) (2016), *available at* https://www.ecfr.gov/cgi-bin/text-idx?SID=1e0feb88ce75b65ff5446cbb52c959f5&mc=true&node=pt14.4.417&rgn=div5#se14.4.417_1107.

672 *Id.* at (b)(2).

673 *Id.* at (b)(3). For computing an aircraft hazard area, the launch operator must determine an aircraft hazard area in the vicinity of each planned impact location from the surface of Earth to an altitude of 100,000 feet MSL that wholly contains the launch vehicle's calculated impact dispersion with a 5 nm buffer and the normal trajectory. The entire calculation essentially requires determining the planned trajectory of the object from 100,000 feet altitude to the projected impact zone, then creating a safety box around the trajectory at all points that would otherwise pose a risk to transiting aircraft. That determines the hazard area of the object. *See* Launch Site Responsibility, 14 C.F.R. app. § B417.9 (2006), *available at* https://www.ecfr.gov/cgi-bin/text-idx?SID=1e0feb88ce75b65ff5446cbb52c959f5&mc=true&node=pt14.4.417&rgn=div5#se14.4.417_19. Similarly, for a ship hazard area analysis, a flight hazard area analysis must establish the trajectory of the object, its presumed landing location, and establish a 5 nm buffer in the vicinity of a planned downrange impact location, accounting for the largest ship that could be present in the ship hazard area, or default to a ship size of 120,000 square feet. The probability of impacting the reference ship must be no less than or equal to .00001. *See* 14 C.F.R. app. § B417.11 (2006), *available at* https://www.ecfr.gov/cgi-bin/text-idx?SID=1e0feb88ce75b65ff5446cbb52c959f5&mc=true&node=pt14.4.417&rgn=div5. For computing a land hazard area analysis, a similar analysis is required for both the launch site and the probable landing location of each debris piece. The risk that a member of the public being struck by debris in these areas must not exceed .000001. *See* 14 C.F.R. § B417.13 (2006), *available at* https://www.ecfr.gov/cgi-bin/text-idx?SID=1e0feb88ce75b65ff5446cbb52c959f5&mc=true&node=pt14.4.417&rgn=div5.

Whether an operator meets these criteria for their proposed activity is determined on a case-by-case basis.[674]

During the flight stage, the launch operator must account for any potential debris that could be created by the elements that compose the launch vehicle. This could include inert mechanisms, explosive elements, or other hazardous launch vehicle aspects that are part of normal operations. Debris potential from possible malfunctions must also be considered at every stage of operations.[675] This requires a thorough review and assessment of the potential results of a launch vehicle failure, subsequent break-up possibilities and the threat that these possible debris creation scenarios may cause.[676] In particular, a licensing requirement includes the need to ensure that a debris fragment list for each potential breakup is provided as well as an in-depth analysis of the fragment characteristics and potential harmful risks of each piece.[677]

If there is a release of debris from normal operations, or specific malfunctions are otherwise foreseeable, the operator must address and identify the following potential debris creation events and provide supporting evidence of the potential for each:[678]

1. Debris fragment data assessment from launch to insertion and achievement of orbital velocity.[679]
2. Listing of all inert and non-inert fragments, such as staging, payload fairing jettison and other normal hardware that will become debris but that do not burn or explode under normal or malfunctioning conditions.[680]
3. Identification of all propellant fragments that are explosive or non-explosive upon impact.[681]

---

674 Flight Safety, 14 C.F.R. § 417.107(b)(1) (2016), *available at* https://www.ecfr.gov/cgi-bin/text-idx?SID=1e0feb88ce75b65ff5446cbb52c959f5&mc=true&node=pt14.4.417&rgn=div5#ap14.4.417.0000_onbspnbspnbsp.

675 Debris Analysis, 14 C.F.R. § 417.211 (2006), *available at* https://www.ecfr.gov/cgi-bin/text-idx?SID=1e0feb88ce75b65ff5446cbb52c959f5&mc=true&node=pt14.4.417&rgn=div5#ap14.4.417.0000_onbspnbspnbsp.

676 *Id.*

677 *Id.*

678 14 C.F.R. app. § A417.11(c) (2016), *available at* https://www.ecfr.gov/cgi-bin/text-idx?SID=1e0feb88ce75b65ff5446cbb52c959f5&mc=true&node=pt14.4.417&rgn=div5#ap14.4.417.0000_onbspnbspnbsp.

679 *Id.*

680 *Id.* at (c)(2) & (c)(4).

681 *Id.* at (c)(2).

4. Assessment of the weight of any breakup fragments and the maximum velocity each fragment will achieve due to potential explosion or pressure rupture.[682]
5. Fragment projected area, ballistic coefficient (axial, transverse, and tumble orientation), fragment count, and fragment classes (if possible).[683]

2.7 *Debris Avoidance from Collision*

In addition to the debris risk posed by the flight if it were to be destroyed, some conditions must be met for collision avoidance. Under FAA rules for collision avoidance, the license seeker must ensure that any parts of the launch vehicle, including jettisoned components, do not come any closer in proximity than 200 km to an inhabitable orbital object throughout the entire launch to insertion phase (or return for suborbital flight) including, for orbital launches, maintaining that distance for at least one orbital rotation.[684] The 200 km rule also applies during maneuvers either to move into an appropriate new orbital location or movement from an initial park orbit.[685] Furthermore, launch operators must also ensure that they are knowledgeable on the potential threats within the orbits they intend to insert into by obtaining a conjunction assessment before launch.[686] There are also requirements throughout the planning process to ensure that the safety concerns are addressed, primarily required through descriptions of risk assessment and debris hazard thresholds throughout the flight plan.[687]

---

682 *Id.* at (c)(5) & (c)(6).

683 *Id.* at (c)(7)-(c)(10).

684 Flight Safety, 14 C.F.R. § 417.107(e) (2016), *available at* https://www.ecfr.gov/cgi-bin/text-idx?SID=1e0feb88ce75b65ff5446cbb52c959f5&mc=true&node=pt14.4.417&rgn=div5#ap14.4.417.0000_onbspnbspnbsp.

685 *Id.* at (e)(1)(B). *See also* Collision Avoidance Analysis, 14 C.F.R. § 417.231(b).

686 Launch Safety Rules, 14 C.F.R. § 417.113(b) (2006), *available at* https://www.ecfr.gov/cgi-bin/text-idx?SID=1e0feb88ce75b65ff5446cbb52c959f5&mc=true&node=pt14.4.417&rgn=div5#ap14.4.417.0000_onbspnbspnbsp.

687 For example, under 14 C.F.R. § 417.111(b)(4), *Launch Plans*, a requirement is included that there must be a description of the launch trajectory for each expendable launch vehicle including the planned orbital parameter, all planned stage impact times, locations, and downrange and cross-range dispersions. Other sections require detailed analysis be provided for the type of hazardous fuels that are on board for explosive risk analysis (*see* 14 C.F.R. § 417.111(c)(2)) and general launch safety rules (14 C.F.R. § 417.113), https://www.ecfr.gov/cgi-bin/text-idx?SID=1e0feb88ce75b65ff5446cbb52c959f5&mc=true&node=pt14.4.417&rgn=div5#ap14.4.417.0000_onbspnbspnbsp.a.

Once the satellite is placed in orbit, the FAA addresses the final risks of the functioning satellite becoming debris. However, it is not necessarily through the licensing process, but instead through obligations imposed on satellite operators to report all of the operating parameters of the satellite within 30 days of launch.[688] Included is the nodal period, the inclination, the apogee, and the perigee.[689] The requirement for this reporting action serves two purposes. First, it guarantees that the United States meets its obligations under international law for the registration of the space object under the Registration Convention.[690] Second, it ensures that under the obligations to supervise continually, the United States is always capable of determining the location of the object and assessing the possibility of any risk factors for collision with other known objects. In essence, this requirement makes sure that the FAA, in addition to the four licensing requirements for compliance with debris mitigation, can also determine that the likelihood of the satellite colliding with others after initiation of operations is effectively mitigated. If the United States is aware of its location and orbital parameters, SSA allows the government to monitor the possibility of a debris-creating event.

2.8 *End of Operations*

The FAA has a series of end of launch requirements for all launch vehicle stages or components that reach Earth's orbit. Common sense is at the forefront, such that the first requirement is that no unplanned physical contact occurs between the vehicle or any of its components after payload separation.[691] Second, that there is not a reaction from the conversion of energy sources that would otherwise cause an explosion or cause, in any manner, fragments or parts of the spacecraft to unintentionally end up as free-floating debris.[692]

The last requirement recalls the obligations for 'safing' a spacecraft at the end-of-life. The requirements from the FAA is that the spacecraft must be removed of its remaining fuel and leave all fuel valves open, depressurize any pressurized systems to reduce the threat of explosion, leave all batteries completely void of power without an ability to recharge, and to check for any other remaining sources of stored energy.[693] The condition of the remaining

688 Registration of Space Objects, 14 C.F.R. § 417.19(b) (2006).

689 *Id.* at (b)(4).

690 Safety at End of Launch, 14 C.F.R. § 417.129(a) (2006).

691 Safety at End of Launch, 14 C.F.R. § 417.129 (2006), *available at* https://www.ecfr.gov/cgi-bin/text-idx?SID=1e0feb88ce75b65ff5446cbb52c959f5&mc=true&node=pt14.4.417&rgn=div5#ap14.4.417.0000_0nbspnbspnbsp.

692 *Id.*

693 *Id.*

spacecraft should be entirely inert so that it should not be capable of fragmenting in the future as a result of remaining on-board energy or pressurized systems.

3 Federal Communications Commission

The Federal Communications Commission was established in 1934 as a result of Congressional enactment of the *Communications Act of 1934* (hereafter The Communications Act).[694] The Commission was originally charged with regulating interstate and international communications that occurred by wire and radio to provide a rapid and cost-effective method to ensure communication services could advance the needs of national defense, the safety of life and property, and centralizing the authority with respect to these goals under one organization.[695] Since then, the forms of communication falling under the purview of the FCC have expanded considerably, to include not only wire and radio, but also television, satellites, and cable.[696] Today, the FCC stands as an independent agency of the United States, capable of setting its own policies and procedures and is not subject to Executive Branch policy guidance.[697] Oversight of the agency is conducted by Congress.[698]

As early as 2000, the FCC began to initiate orbital debris licensing requirements for certain types of satellite[699] systems but had refrained from doing

694 Communications Act of 1934, 47 U.S.C. §§ 151–614 (1934), *available at* https://transition.fcc.gov/Reports/1934new.pdf.

695 47 U.S.C. § 151 (1996).

696 The Federal Communications Commission, NAT. TELECOMM. AND INFORMATION ADMIN., *available at* https://www.ntia.doc.gov/book-page/federal-communications-commission-fcc (last visited Aug. 2, 2020).

697 Oltrogge & Christensen, *supra* note 566 at 5.

698 *Id.*

699 The issue of whether the FCC appropriately regulated satellites was raised by the FCC itself beginning in 1966. *See* Establishment of Domestic Communications-Satellite Facilities by Nongovernmental Entities, 22 F.C.C. 2d 86 (1970) (report and order). For obvious reasons, the original mandate of the FCC under the Communications Act of 1934 did not specifically state that the FCC was responsible for authorizing domestic communications satellite facilities to nongovernmental entities. *Id.* In 1966, the FCC initiated a review of its authorities to determine the policy implications of authorizing domestic communications satellite facilities to nongovernmental entities and whether the FCC was charged with doing so. By 1970, the FCC answered both questions in the affirmative, finding that the FCC 'was designated by Congress the ability to authorize any non-Federal Government entity … to construct and operate communications satellite facilities for domestic use.' *Id.* at app. C. In its determination, the FCC specifically found that through

an 'across-the-board' implementation.[700] Therefore, any non-federal satellite operator wishing (or needing) to obtain a license from the FCC was subject to potential additional oversight regarding any creation of space debris during their operations. The FCC had, up until this point, opted to include these rules on a case-by-case basis while still reserving the potential for future guidance for all FCC license seekers. But the FCC had a problem with applying mitigation rules. Most notably, it continued to lack a statutory basis authorizing it to require licenses for orbital debris mitigation actions.

3.1 *Authority to License*

To remedy this, the FCC set out to review its boundaries by examining the authority it did have. It opined from a combination of statutory language and inferences that its existing authorities allowed it to impose orbital debris management expectations as part of its licensing process. The FCC first assessed that it had the authority because the Communications Act authorized the FCC to license radio frequency uses by satellites.[701] Second, the FCC highlighted that the Communications Act charged the FCC with advancing the "larger and more effective use of radio in the public interest."[702] The combination of these provisions convinced the FCC that orbital debris and debris mitigation plans of satellite operators were a critical component of assessing whether or not the

---

a series of challenges to its authority, Congress and the Courts had ultimately determined it was empowered with several forward-looking authorities, including to "develop the most desirable deployment and utilization of the Nation's communications facilities." *Id.* at app. C, para. 4 (citing *Connecticut Committee Against Pay TV v. F.C.C.*, 301 F. 2d 835, 837 (D.C. Cir. 1962), cert. denied. 371 U.S. 816 (1962)). Additionally, in *National Broadcasting Company v. United States*, the US Supreme Court discussed the expansive authority the FCC held over radio communications to utilize its power over newly developing technologies. *Nat'l Broadcasting Co. v. U.S.*, 63 S. Ct. 997 (1943). Ultimately, the Court found that so long as the FCC was meeting its foundational requirements to authorize communications systems in accordance with the public interest it was acting appropriately. All the evidence supports that position. *See Establishment of Domestic Communications-Satellite Facilities by Nongovernmental Entities*, 22 F.C.C. 2d at app. C, para. 6.

700 *Mitigation of Orbital Debris*, 19 F.C.C.R. 11567, 11571 (2004), *available at* https://docs.fcc.gov/public/attachments/FCC-04-130A1.pdf. According to the FCC, in 2000, the Commission required orbital debris mitigation rules for licenses issued in the 2 GHz mobile-satellite service and in the following years between 2000 and 2004, had additionally implemented rules for the Ku- and Ka- bands for NGSO fixed-satellite service.

701 Mitigation of Orbital Debris in the New Space Age, Fact Sheet, F.C.C., 8 (Apr. 2, 2020), *available at* https://docs.fcc.gov/public/attachments/DOC-363486A1.pdf (citing Communications Act of 1934, as amended, 47 U.S.C. § 151 (1996).

702 *Id.* (citing 47 U.S.C. § 303(g) (2010)).

public interest was served by approving any satellite-based communications system.

The second, and complementary, argument for the broad power to impose orbital debris limitation requirements into the licensing process rested in the connection between the radiocommunication functions and the physical operations of the spacecraft.[703] In the view of the FCC, part of the licensing responsibility included the obligation to ensure that satellites with radiocommunication functions can operate in space in a reliable, safe, and cost-effective manner for the specific satellite and for all commercial and other satellite operations authorized by the FCC.[704] Additionally, the FCC determined that the risk posed by orbital debris could also have an impact on the 'availability, integrity, and capabilities' of existing and new satellites.[705] The potential for impacting the ability of these satellites to operate would also affect their ability to utilize the full spectrum of radiocommunications that the FCC had licensed them to use.[706]

Ultimately, the FCC concluded that both the statutory language and their responsibility to manage the availability of the spectrum to satellite users effectively could be threatened by the existence of orbital debris. To reduce the risk of this possibility, the FCC determined that even if not explicitly articulated as an authorized regulatory area, the FCC was dependent on the authority to carry out their other mandated missions. Therefore, the FCC set about to implement oversight of orbital debris planning for satellites under their licensing purview.[707]

3.2 *Licensing Requirements*

Starting in 2002, the FCC began to examine the possibility of implementing formal rules for broad-scale orbital debris licensing requirements for all satellites. By 2004, the FCC had conducted its rule-making process and was convinced of the need to establish expectations for satellite licenses that fell under its purview.[708] This would formalize processes applicable to all operators that could address the FCC's concerns over the increase of orbital debris in

---

703 *Id.* at 9 (citing *Mitigation of Orbital Debris*, 19 F.C.C.R. 11567, 11575 (2004), *available at* https://docs.fcc.gov/public/attachments/FCC-04-130A1.pdf).

704 *Id.*

705 *Id.*

706 *Id.*

707 *Id.*

708 *Mitigation of Orbital Debris*, 19 F.C.C.R. 11567 (2004), *available at* https://docs.fcc.gov/public/attachments/FCC-04-130A1.pdf.

particularly vulnerable orbits including LEO and GEO.[709] As with most agencies involved with space, the FCC was becoming increasingly aware that the growth of orbital debris could have a highly detrimental effect on the responsibilities the FCC was charged with meeting.

The 2004 Orbital Debris Order provided both new guidelines and the FCC's justification for establishing their authority to enact the new rules.[710] Specifically, it stated that adoption of these rules "will help preserve the United States' continued affordable access to space, the continued provision of reliable US space-based services—including communications and remote sensing satellite services for US commercial, government, and homeland security purposes—as well as the continued safety of persons and property in space and on the surface of Earth."[711] The FCC established the requirement that any space operator desiring to receive FCC authorization, or any entity requesting a FCC approval for access to a non-US licensed space station, would be required to submit a plan to address any creation of orbital debris, and corresponding mitigation, as part of the licensing submission.[712] Additionally, not only were there requirements for the satellite operation, but there were also requirements that the FCC would review the plans for the post-mission disposal of the satellites.[713]

Following the issuance of the 2004 orbital debris order, the FCC recognized that it needed to update the licensing requirements based on the increasing number of spacefaring entities and requests for licenses, particularly for operations in the increasingly congested LEO.[714] Under this authority, as of 24 April 2020, the FCC conducted a comprehensive rule-making review and overhaul of the existing FCC satellite rules on orbital debris mitigation in over 15 years.[715] At the same time, the FCC indicated that the existing steps were only one of several future efforts to review and improve the orbital debris requirements to attempt to reduce the threat to satellites and inhabitable spacecraft in space, as well as minimize the risk of falling debris on persons and property on Earth.[716]

709 *Id.*

710 *Mitigation of Orbital Debris*, 19 F.C.C.R. 11567, 11568 (2004), *available at* https://docs.fcc.gov/public/attachments/FCC-04-130A1.pdf.

711 *Id.*

712 *Id.*

713 *Id.*

714 FCC Updates Satellite Orbital Debris Mitigation Rules, FC NEWS FROM THE F.C.C., 1 (Apr. 23, 2020), *available at* https://docs.fcc.gov/public/attachments/DOC-363947A1.pdf.

715 *Id.*

716 *Id.*

Generally, the FCC indicates that the new rules are an effort to improve the 'specificity and clarity' for satellite companies of the requirements imposed to address debris and debris mitigation plans.[717] Among the requirements are new expectations that applicants assign numerical values to collision risk, assess and explain the likelihood that their satellite will comply with post-mission disposal as required, and identify any risks to Earth for satellites that have selected, as a post-mission disposal plan, atmospheric re-entry.[718] Additionally, there are also new requirements for deployment of devices that would result in debris, the release of persistent liquids, trackability requirements, and information sharing for situational awareness.[719]

Specifically, the new FCC order replaces several existing provisions to tighten the rules or to expand the expectations for reporting.[720] But importantly, the order listed five specific objectives as an outcome of the new rulemaking:

1. The order incorporates metrics for risk assessment of collision with both large and small objects, and re-entry casualty risks.[721]
2. The order sets out additional requirements for reporting on the protection of inhabitable spacecraft (the ISS primarily), the maneuverability of the satellite and the capabilities to do so, the trackability such that they are equipped with systems that 'report' their location or have a signature which can be visibly or technologically tracked, space-station identification, and expectations that the information will be shared regarding the location of initial deployment, any planned maneuvers, and ephemeris[722] data.[723]
3. For Non-Geostationary Orbit (NGSO) space stations, a requirement that the application indicates that the success of post-mission disposal choice is 0.90% or greater for any individual space station, and preferably higher for larger systems.[724]

---

717 *Id.*

718 *Id.*

719 *Id.*

720 *Mitigation of Orbital Debris in the New Space Age*, No. 18–313, 2020 W.L. 2740496 *8 (F.C.C. Apr. 23, 2020), https://docs.fcc.gov/public/attachments/FCC-20-54A1.pdf (at p. 11 in PDF).

721 *Id.*

722 Ephemeris references the trajectory of naturally occurring astronomical objects as well as artificial satellites in the sky (the position and potentially the velocity of the object over time). *See Ephemeris*, WIKIPEDIA, https://en.wikipedia.org/wiki/Ephemeris (last visited Jul. 25, 2020).

723 *Mitigation of Orbital Debris in the New Space Age*, *supra* note 720.

724 *Id.*

4. Memorializes an ongoing expectation that license extensions will be considered/granted for five years;[725] and finally
5. Additional rules related to proximity operations, use of deployment devices from the original craft (and subsequent debris implications), and plans for disposal of space stations.[726]

The impact of these objectives is outlined in the new rules derived from Title 47 C.F.R. Parts 5, 25, and 97. Taken in turn, each of these sections has a significant impact on the information operators must now provide to obtain licensing when addressing the potential creation of space debris.

3.3 *Title 47 C.F.R. (Telecommunication) and New Orbital Debris Rules*

3.3.1 Title 47 C.F.R. Part 5—Experimental Radio Service, 47 C.F.R. §5.64(b)-Special Provisions for Satellite Systems

Under 47 C.F.R. §5.64(b), *Special Provisions for Satellite Systems*, the FCC established new rules in 2021 requiring that applicants for an experimental authorization involving a satellite system must submit a description of the design and operational strategies the satellite system will use to mitigate orbital debris.[727] It must include the following:

1. A statement that the operator has assessed and limited the number of debris released in a planned manner during normal operations.[728]
2. A statement indicating whether the space station operator has assessed and limited the probability that the space station will become a source of debris because of collision with small debris.[729]
3. A statement attesting that the operator has limited the probability of accidental explosions or release of liquids that will persist in droplet form. Additionally, the statement must indicate debris generation will not be caused by energy from the spacecraft causing damage. An assessment should include how the spacecraft will be 'safed' post-mission.[730]

---

725 *Id.*

726 *Id.*

727 47 C.F.R. § 5.64 (b) (2013), *available at* https://www.ecfr.gov/current/title-47/chapter-I/subchapter-A/part-5/subpart-B. The amendments to 47 C.F.R. §§ 5.64(b) and 97.207(g)(1), published at 85 Fed. Reg. 52422 on August 25, 2020, are effective October 20, 2021. *See* 85 Fed. Reg. 52422 (Aug. 25, 2020), *available at* https://www.govinfo.gov/content/pkg/FR-2021-09-20/pdf/2021-20193.pdf.

728 *Id.* at 47 C.F.R. § 5.64 (b)(1).

729 *Id.* at 47 C.F.R. § 5.64 (b)(2).

730 *Id.* at 47 C.F.R. § 5.64 (b).

4. A statement that the space station operator has assessed the probability of the space station becoming debris because of impact with large objects or other space stations. Additional requirements exist if the space station will be in an NGSO location.[731]
5. A statement addressing how the space station will be trackable, as well as additional requirements for space stations in NGSO.[732]
6. Disclosure of any proximity operations, if expected, and potential for debris generation as a result.[733]
7. A statement detailing disposal plans and an indication of fuel that will be preserved to conduct the post-mission disposal. Additional specificity is required depending on the orbit in which the space station is currently operating.[734]

3.3.2 Title 47 C.F.R. Part 25—Satellite Communications

There are five sections under 47 C.F.R. Part 25 that are relevant to the FCC's regulation of orbital debris through licensing requirements. As will be discussed in each, four of them were subject to recent rule-making notices and were otherwise finalized as rules. However, they were not given effective dates yet subject to Office of Management and Budget (OMB) approval. The final section was passed under the same rule-making notice, but it went into effect in September of 2020. This book will look at each in turn to identify the relevant regulatory requirements applicable for licensing of space objects and how the rules (and FCC authority) are increasing.

3.3.2.1 *Title 47 C.F.R. §25.114—Applications for Space Station Authorizations*

47 C.F.R. §25.114 has been subject to a number of Notice of Proposed Rule Making (NPRM) activities by the FCC since 2020 and is pending significant changes upon the approval of OMB for 47 C.F.R. §25.114(d)(14). To be thorough, this section will first review the law as it pertains to space stations and debris mitigation requirements currently. It will then outline the changes that will occur in late 2021 or early 2022 upon OMB approval.

As the law currently stands, 47 C.F.R. §25.114(d)(14) lays out four requirements for applications for space station authorizations. Generally, it requires that each application provide a description of the design and operational

731 *Id.* at 47 C.F.R. § 5.64 (b)(4).
732 *Id.* at 47 C.F.R. § 5.64 (b)(5).
733 *Id.* at 47 C.F.R. § 5.64 (b)(6).
734 *Id.* at 47 C.F.R. § 5.64 (b)(7).

strategies that will be employed to ensure that there is sufficient mitigation of orbital debris from the operation of the spacecraft. Specifically, it requires:

1. A statement that the space station operator has assessed and limited the amount of debris released during normal operations, including limiting the chances that collisions with small debris or meteoroids will render the spacecraft incapable of functioning. The particular concern is that the space station is expected, regardless of small impacts, to be able to conduct its post-mission disposal plan.[735]
2. A statement that the space station operator has limited the chances of accidental explosion throughout the satellite's lifecycle. This includes a demonstration that on-board energy sources can be successfully passivated as necessary so that the energy sources do not cause fragmentation of the spacecraft. Regarding passivation, there is an expectation that the exact methods of passivation will also be identified, including the methods of removal of the remaining energy sources.[736]
3. An assessment that limits the probability of the spacecraft colliding with large debris or another spacecraft. For any known variables, such as spacecraft operating in co-located or similarly oriented altitudes and orbits, the plan must include an assessment of the mitigation efforts and coordination that has been accomplished to prevent the possibility of collision. This applies both to LEO and GEO. Additionally, satellites in either orbit that may lack propulsion systems for potential mitigation maneuvers must account for the potential degradation of the station over time and the potential of collisions with future spacecraft or debris.[737]
4. A detailed post-mission disposal plan, including remaining fuel for the maneuver. If selected for atmospheric removal, a re-entry risk assessment must be conducted. Alternatively, if selected for a graveyard orbit, the proposed altitude and orbital plan must be identified.[738]

735 47 C.F.R. § 25.114 (d)(14)(I) (2020), *available at* https://www.ecfr.gov/current/title-47/chapter-I/subchapter-B/part-25.

736 *Id.*

737 *Id.* at (d)(14)(III).

738 *Id.* at (d)(14)(IV).

There is a fifth requirement, though it pertains to non-US licensed space stations and only requires that the design and operational strategies meet the effective regulatory oversight of whomever is the national licensing authority.[739]

One of the reasons this current version of 47 C.F.R. §25.114 came under scrutiny is because it focused only on the main satellite system, designating that a space station operator was only responsible for assessing and limiting the amount of debris released during normal operations.[740] The new pending FCC licensing requirements state that for space systems, if there will be a separate deployment device, the license request must include "an orbital debris mitigation disclosure for any separate deployment devices, distinct from the space station launch vehicle, that may become a source of orbital debris."[741]

Second, the prior FCC rules under 47 C.F.R. §25.114 addressed the need to assess the probability of the space station becoming a source of debris if it were to collide with other debris or another functional object.[742] While useful, the new version of the rules requires specificity regarding whether the "probability for an individual space station to become a source of debris by collision with small debris or meteoroids that would cause loss of control and prevent disposal is .01 (1 in 100) or less."[743]

Third, the prior version did not include any specific statements related to the release of liquids. In the new requirements, the FCC implemented an expectation that the likelihood of the release or potential explosions of liquids that would otherwise remain in droplet form be addressed.[744] Furthermore, the FCC implemented a very specific requirement that the energy sources within

739 *Id.* at (d)(14)(v).

740 The original NPRM for the rule proposal to change to, among other sections, 47 C.F.R. § 25.114, was released 24 April 2020. Mitigation of Orbital Debris in the New Space Age, Report and Order and Further Notice of Proposed Rulemaking, FCC 20–54 (Apr. 23, 2020). The NPRM was officially accepted as a Final Rule on 25 August 2020, under the Mitigation of Orbital Debris in the New Space Age FCC Final Rule, Part 25—Satellite Communications, specifically Section 25.114(d)(14), found at Mitigation of Orbital Debris in the New Space Age, 85 Feb. Reg. 165 (Aug. 25, 2020) (to be codified at 47 C.F.R. §§ 5, 25 & 97), *available at* https://www.govinfo.gov/content/pkg/FR-2020-08-25/pdf/2020-13185.pdf. However, as specified under the official recordkeeping of the C.F.R., the changes to Section 25.114(d)(14) remain ineffective until approval has been given by the Office of Management and Budget. However, it is included as an additional section of the current law for reference and convenience. 47 C.F.R. § 25.114(d)(14).

741 Processing Applications in the Digital Broadcast Satellite Service, 86 Fed. Reg. 49484 (Sept. 3, 2021) (to be codified at 47 C.F.R. § 25.114(d)(14)(i)).

742 47 C.F.R. § 25.114(d)(14)(iii).

743 *Id.* (to be codified at 47 C.F.R. § 25.114(d)(14)(ii)).

744 *Id.* (to be codified at 47 C.F.R. § 25.114(d)(14)(iii)).

a spacecraft be prevented from combining in such a way that the likelihood of release or explosion was increased.[745] The license must also address what will happen to the remaining fuel at the end of the mission and how the remaining power sources will be rendered inert.[746]

The fourth significant change requires an assessment of the potential that the station becomes debris in NGSO's due to impact or other events. If the license requests insertion outside of GEO, additional information is required. This includes:

1. Assessments that the probability of collision with an object 10 cm or larger in diameter is limited to less than a 0.001 probability (1 in 1,000).[747]
2. An analysis of the proposed orbits and any risk of collision with other objects based on the proposed orbit, as well as any pre-coordination that has been conducted with potential threats.[748]
3. A description of operational strategies used to minimize risk to other stations if the post-mission plan or deorbit phase will pass through inhabited orbits.[749]
4. The capability of the satellite to maintain its orbit under the proposed plan under the original licensing requests.[750]
5. Certification of responsiveness in the event of a conjunction warning, and that the operator will take all steps possible to assess the threat and mitigate if necessary.[751]

To improve the awareness of the spacecraft while operating in space, the FCC under 47 C.F.R. §25.114(d)(14) also implemented an additional trackability requirement, specifically for NGSO space stations or systems. By default, the FCC indicated that operations in LEO would be presumed trackable for any object that is already 10 cm or larger.[752] As discussed earlier in this book, at that size in LEO, most objects are already easily tracked based on current technology. However, the FCC, in the new rule-making, still implemented expectations that within the application submission, the operator will disclose the method

745 *Id.* (to be codified at 47 C.F.R. § 25.114(d)(14)(I)).
746 *Id.* (to be codified at 47 C.F.R. § 25.114(d)(14)(III)).
747 *Id.* (to be codified at 47 C.F.R. § 25.114(d)(14)(IV)).
748 *Id.* (to be codified at 47 C.F.R. § 25.114(d)(14)(IV)(A)(2)).
749 *Id.* (to be codified at 47 C.F.R. § 25.114(d)(14)(IV)(A)(3)).
750 *Id.* (to be codified at 47 C.F.R. § 25.114(d)(14)(IV)(A)(4)).
751 *Id.* (to be codified at 47 C.F.R. § 25.114(d)(14)(IV)(A)(5)).
752 *Id.* (to be codified at 47 C.F.R. § 25.114(d)(14)(V)).

of identifying the space station (that is, by size or technological reporting system), whether the space station will be registered with an SSA tracking entity, such as the 18th SPCS (or future entity within the Commerce Department), and last, the extent to which the operator will be forthcoming with data regarding all phases of the satellite or station lifecycle.[753]

47 C.F.R. §25.114 also adds specific requirements to post-disposal plans and disclosures. Included are requirements for maintenance and reporting of fuel reserved for end-of-life requirements, disposal orbit and altitude (for GEO satellites), and specifications for any atmospheric planned destruction or re-entry recoveries for all spacecraft.[754] There must also be a demonstration in all cases that the likelihood of success of the chosen disposal method will be 0.90% or greater for any individual station, and for any system which includes multiple systems, the expectation is that the operators will exceed the 0.90% threshold, with an ideal level of 0.99% success or better.[755] There is also an expectation for stations that will terminate missions utilizing atmospheric re-entry and destruction that disposal must occur within 25 years of mission conclusion, with outliers using a non-traditional disposal method being assessed on a case-by-case basis.[756] As well, in the event of atmospheric disposal, operators must disclose whether the action is controlled or uncontrolled, and how much of the spacecraft, if any, will survive re-entry and impact Earth.[757] If there is survivability, a corresponding assessment must be conducted regarding a calculated casualty risk less than 0.0001 (or 1 in 10,000).[758]

3.3.2.2 *Title 47 C.F.R. §25.121—License Term and Renewals*

Unlike the previous section, which was a modification to the existing rules, the second of the five relevant Part 25 sections will add an entirely new paragraph, 'f', under the '*License Terms and Renewals*' section of 47 C.F.R. §25.121.[759] This original section focuses on the licenses for both ground and space-based

753 *Id.* (to be codified at 47 C.F.R. § 25.114(d)(14)(v)(A)-(C)).

754 *Id.*

755 *Id.* (to be codified at 47 C.F.R. § 25.114(d)(14)(vii)(D)(1)).

756 *Id.*

757 *Id.* (to be codified at 47 C.F.R. § 25.114(d)(14)(vii)(D)(2)(I)-(II)).

758 *Id.* (to be codified at 47 C.F.R. § 25.114(d)(14)(vii)(D)(2)(I)-(II)).

759 Similar to the prior section, the amendment to 47 C.F.R. § 25.121 also has a similar provision within the final rule that the provisions of the final rule specific to 47 C.F.R. § 25.121 are also not effective until approved by the Office of Management and Budget. *See* Mitigation of Orbital Space Debris in the New Space Age, 85 Fed. Reg. 52451, https://www.govinfo.gov/content/pkg/FR-2020-08-25/pdf/2020-13185.pdf (proposed amendment to 47 C.F.R. § 25.121 that would add (f)).

stations. Generally, licenses for these stations will be between eight and ten years.[760] For example, the Direct Broadcast Stations (DBS) (except DBS's not licensed as broadcast facilities which instead receive ten years), the Satellite Digital Audio Radio System (SDARS), and the Broadcasting-Satellite Service (BSS) all receive an initial eight year license.[761] The prior version did address that extensions could be applied for, but did not address any specificity for the renewal of licenses except the form and time period in which the licenses must be submitted.[762]

The new paragraph, 47 C.F.R. §25.121(f), when enacted, will add that an extension is authorized in increments of five years or less for GEO space stations that received an initial issuance term of 15 years.[763] These modifications also address orbital debris concerns in several ways. The applicant is required to provide information that will assist the FCC in determining if the risk of the space object becoming debris is increased by the extension offered in section 47 C.F.R. §25.121(f).[764] To be successful, the applicant must specify the duration of the request and the estimated total remaining space station lifetime of the craft.[765] Second, malfunctions and risks, defects, or anomalies that might affect the end-of-life disposal plan must be disclosed.[766] Third, a certification that even with the extension, the craft will still have the remaining fuel necessary to complete the pre-planned end-of-life deorbiting.[767] Finally, the operator must certify that all of the communications links, including telemetry, tracking, and command, are fully functional.[768]

3.3.2.3 *Title 47 C.F.R. §25.122—Applications for Streamlined Small Space Station Authorization*

The third of the five Part 25 sections, 47 C.F.R. §25.122, provides a process for streamlined small space station authorizations.[769] 47 C.F.R. §25.122(c)

---

760 47 C.F.R. § 25.121(a) (2014), *available at* https://www.ecfr.gov/current/title-47/chapter-I/subchapter-B/part-25.

761 *Id.* at (a)(2).

762 *Id.*

763 *Mitigation of Orbital Space Debris in the New Space Age*, 85 Fed. Reg. 52452, https://www.govinfo.gov/content/pkg/FR-2020-08-25/pdf/2020-13185.pdf (proposed amendment to 47 C.F.R. § 25.122(f)(1)).

764 *Id.* (proposed amendment to 47 C.F.R. § 25.122(f)(2)).

765 *Id.* (proposed amendment to 47 C.F.R. § 25.122(f)(2)(I)-(II)).

766 *Id.* (proposed amendment to 47 C.F.R. § 25.122(f)(2)(III)).

767 *Id.* (proposed amendment to 47 C.F.R. § 25.122(f)(2)(IV)).

768 *Id.* (proposed amendment to 47 C.F.R. § 25.122(f)(2)(V)).

769 47 C.F.R. § 25.122 (2020), *available at* https://www.ecfr.gov/current/title-47/chapter-I/subchapter-B/part-25/subpart-B/subject-group-ECFRe2bd70fc6b2eea0/section-25.122.

addresses certifications. In submitting a request for licensing under the FCC, operators of small space stations must attest to several requirements that will reduce the likelihood of objects being rendered debris. Among the most relevant, operators must certify that, in addition to operating only below GEO, the space stations will also:[770]

1. Have a total lifetime not to exceed six years.[771]
2. Operate no higher than 600 km altitude or will have a propulsion system capable of making collision avoidance and deorbit maneuvers.[772]
3. Be no smaller than 10 cm at its largest dimension, with a mass (including propellant) no larger than 180 kg.[773]
4. Maintain an identifiable unique telemetry marker distinct from other objects.[774]
5. Refrain from any release of operational debris.[775]
6. Ensure an assessment is conducted to reduce the potential of accidental explosion.[776]
7. Ensure the collision probability with any large object is 0.001 or less.[777]
8. Utilize atmospheric re-entry for disposal and that the probability of human casualty because of object survivability from re-entry is zero.[778]
9. Operate within authorized frequency bands.[779]
10. Retain the capability on the craft to terminate transmission if required and to eliminate harmful interference if necessary.[780]

47 C.F.R. §25.122(c) is also pending amendment, subject to the approval of OMB.[781] The first of the two sections provide additional considerations for

770 *Id.* at (c)(1).
771 *Id.* at (c)(2).
772 *Id.* at (c)(3).
773 *Id.* at (c)(11)-(12).
774 *Id.* at (c)(4).
775 *Id.* at (c)(5).
776 *Id.* at (c)(6).
777 *Id.* at (c)(7).
778 *Id.* at (c)(8).
779 *Id.* at (c)(9).
780 *Id.* at (c)(10).
781 The original NPRM for the rule proposal to change to, among other sections, 47 C.F.R. § 25.122, was released 24 April 2020. Mitigation of Orbital Debris in the New Space Age, Report and Order and Further Notice of Proposed Rulemaking, FCC 20–54 (Apr. 23, 2020). The NPRM was officially accepted as a Final Rule on 25 August 2020, under the

47 C.F.R. §25.122(c)(7). That section, as identified in '7' above, articulated an expectation that the collision probability with any large object is .001 (1 in 1,000) or less.[782] The new section specifies that not only must collision with large objects be addressed, but also that collision with small debris will not likely result in loss of control:

> The probability that any individual space station will become debris as a result of a collision with small debris or meteoroids that would either cause the station to lose control or otherwise preclude disposal should be 0.01 (1 in 100) or less.[783]

As well, the final addition to the amendment for 47 C.F.R. §25.122(c) is a section to address conjunction warnings. The current version imposes no requirements for the operators of a space station if they receive a conjunction warning and an expected response to such a receipt. The amendment, when enacted, will provide for the following:

> Upon receipt of a SSA conjunction warning, the operator will take all possible steps to assess the collision risk and take mitigating steps if necessary. This includes, but is not limited to, communication with other involved spacecraft, sharing data as appropriate with any operators, and modifying altitudes or operations as appropriate.[784]

In addition to subsection 'c' and amendments, subsection 'd' of the current law directs that in addition to the streamlined application, a narrative section is

---

Mitigation of Orbital Debris in the New Space Age FCC Final Rule, Part 25—Satellite Communications, specifically to 47 C.F.R. § 25.122(c) which added two additional sections, sections 13–14, found at *Mitigation of Orbital Space Debris in the New Space Age, supra* note 763. However, as specified under the official recordkeeping of the C.F.R., the changes to 47 C.F.R. § 25.122(c) remain ineffective until approval has been given by the Office of Management and Budget.

782 47 C.F.R. § 25.122(c)(7).

783 Mitigation of Orbital Debris in the New Space Age FCC Final Rule, Part 25—Satellite Communications, specifically to 47 C.F.R. § 25.122(c)(13) found at *Mitigation of Orbital Space Debris in the New Space Age, supra* note 763. As discussed, under the official recordkeeping of the C.F.R., the changes to 47 C.F.R. § 25.122(c)(13) remain ineffective until approval has been given by the Office of Management and Budget.

784 *Mitigation of Orbital Space Debris in the New Space Age, supra* note 763. As discussed, under the official recordkeeping of the C.F.R., the changes to 47 C.F.R. § 25.122(c)(14) remain ineffective until approval has been given by the Office of Management and Budget.

also required with amplifying information as identified by the FCC. The current version of 47 C.F.R. §25.122 does not ask for amplifying information pertinent to orbital debris, except for general inquiries regarding maneuverability and deorbit systems,[785] as well as general strategies for avoiding in-orbit[786] collisions. However, the amendment provides an expansive set of questions, aimed at control of the station and debris-related questions, both of which coincide with enhancing the safety of space through requiring debris-prevention descriptions. The additional relevant sections proposed in the amendments to 47 C.F.R. §25.122(d)[787] are as follows:

1. If, during a mission or deorbit, the station will transit through orbits occupied by inhabited spacecraft (such as the ISS), a description of risk strategies will be provided to minimize the possibility of collision and avoid operational constraints to the inhabited spacecraft.[788]
2. A description of the steps taken to coordinate with other spacecraft or systems, or collision avoidance measures considered, for any space station orbits that the station will operate in that might present a collision risk.[789]
3. A statement identifying how the station will be tracked (active or passive), whether it will be registered with the 18th SPCS, and the extent to which the operator plans to share the deployment characteristics with any STM entities.[790]
4. A description of any planned proximity operations, and specific details addressing any potential debris generation that could result from the operation. That could include debris from the operation

785 47 C.F.R. § 25.122 (d)(4).

786 47 C.F.R. § 25.122(d)(5).

787 *Mitigation of Orbital Space Debris in the New Space Age*, *supra* note 763, specifically to 47 C.F.R. § 25.122(d). As discussed, under the official recordkeeping of the C.F.R., the changes to 47 C.F.R. § 25.122(d) remain ineffective until approval has been given by the Office of Management and Budget.

788 *Id.* (specifically to 47 C.F.R. § 25.122(d)(4)). As discussed, under the official recordkeeping of the C.F.R., the changes to 47 C.F.R. § 25.122(d)(4) remain ineffective until approval has been given by the Office of Management and Budget.

789 *Id.* (specifically to 47 C.F.R. § 25.122(d)(5)). As discussed, under the official recordkeeping of the C.F.R., the changes to 47 C.F.R. § 25.122(d)(5) remain ineffective until approval has been given by the Office of Management and Budget. Note also that this particular subsection, unlike the others under the amendment, is a modification of the current rule, 47 C.F.R. § 25.122(d)(5), versus an entirely new addition.

790 *Id.* (specifically to 47 C.F.R. § 25.122(d)(6)). As discussed, under the official recordkeeping of the C.F.R., the changes to 47 C.F.R. § 25.122(d)(6) remain ineffective until approval has been given by the Office of Management and Budget.

itself, or debris as a result of accidental explosion or collision during the proximity operations. A thorough explanation will include measures taken to mitigate those risks.[791]

5. A demonstration that the probability of disposal success is 90% or better for any individual space station. An exception to this provision exists if, in the event of station failure, the station is located in an orbit where atmospheric drag would cause it to enter the atmosphere for destruction in less than 25 years.[792]

As discussed, these additional provisions from the amendment await the approval of OMB. However, they are drafted in a way that highlights the overall effort by the FCC, as seen through these modifications, to take a serious position to ensure that it is aware of the potential debris-creating events posed by these operations. The FCC is demanding more thorough descriptions for the operations prior to licensing in order to execute this objective.

3.3.2.4 *Title 47 C.F.R. §25.123—Applications for Streamlined Small Spacecraft Authorization*

The final two parts of 47 C.F.R. Part 25 relevant to this discussion are 47 C.F.R. §25.123 and 47 C.F.R. §25.271. 47 C.F.R. §25.123 is very similar to 47 C.F.R. §25.122, though where the latter addresses small space *station* authorizations (unique such that it must be 180 kg or less), the former addresses small *spacecraft* (up to 500 kg, but could include space stations) authorization.[793] The current rules under 47 C.F.R. §25.123, generally limited to those addressing debris concerns, have the following requirements which must be provided for licensing requests:

1. The space station must operate and be disposed of beyond earth's orbit (versus 47 C.F.R. §25.122(a), which only requires it operate outside of GEO).[794]
2. Total lifetime must be six years or less (same as 47 C.F.R. §25.122(c)(2)).[795]

---

791 *Id.* (specifically to 47 C.F.R. § 25.122(d)(8)). As discussed, under the official recordkeeping of the C.F.R., the changes to 47 C.F.R. § 25.122(d)(8) remain ineffective until approval has been given by the Office of Management and Budget.

792 *Id.* (specifically to 47 C.F.R. § 25.122(d)(9)). As discussed, under the official recordkeeping of the C.F.R., the changes to 47 C.F.R. § 25.122(d)(9) remain ineffective until approval has been given by the Office of Management and Budget.

793 47 C.F.R. § 25.123 (2020), *available at* https://www.ecfr.gov/current/title-47/chapter-I/subchapter-B/part-25/subpart-B/subject-group-ECFRe2bd70fc6b2eea0/section-25.123.

794 *Id.* at (b)(1).

795 *Id.* at (b)(2).

3. The space station will release no operational debris (same as 47 C.F.R. §25.122(c)(5)).[796]
4. No debris will be generated in an accidental explosion resulting from energy conversion on board that fragments the spacecraft (same as 47 C.F.R. §25.122(c)(6)).[797]
5. Collision probability with another large object (10 cm or larger) must be 0.001 or less (same as 47 C.F.R. §25.122(c)(7)).[798]
6. Each station must be 10 cm or larger in its smallest dimension (same as 47 C.F.R. §25.122(c)(11)).[799]
7. It must have a mass of 500 kg or less, including propellant (as compared to 47 C.F.R. §25.122(c)(12) requiring mass of 180 kg or less).[800]
8. It must also identify either active or passive means of maneuverability, the design of deorbit systems, and have strategies to avoid in-orbit collision with any crewed spacecraft.[801]

Like the sections discussed above, 47 C.F.R. §25.123 was also subject to the FCC recent rule-making activity. However, in the case of spacecraft, only one additional requirement was added. The new provision is exactly the same as the addition in the amendment to 47 C.F.R. §25.122(c) related to conjunction warnings. The current version for spacecraft similarly made no accountability for operators of small spacecraft to take any specific actions in the event they received a conjunction warning. The amendment accounts for this, adding in (when approved by OMB) section 47 C.F.R. §25.123(b)(11), which states:

1. Upon receipt of a SSA conjunction warning, the operator will take all possible steps to assess the collision risk and take mitigating steps if necessary. This includes, but is not limited to, communication with other involved spacecraft, sharing data as appropriate with any operators, and modifying altitudes or operations as appropriate.[802]

---

796 *Id.* at (b)(4).
797 *Id.* at (b)(5).
798 *Id.* at (b)(6).
799 *Id.* at (b)(9).
800 *Id.* at (b)(10).
801 In accordance with 47 C.F.R. § 25.123(c), licensing under this provision also requires the additional narrative expectations of 47 C.F.R. § 25.122(d) (2020), *available at* https://www.ecfr.gov/current/title-47/chapter-I/subchapter-B/part-25/subpart-B/subject-group-ECFRe2bd70fc6b2eea0/section-25.122. The provisions relevant for this discussion are contained in 47 C.F.R. §§ 25.122(d)(4)-(5) (2020).
802 *Mitigation of Orbital Space Debris in the New Space Age*, *supra* note 763, specifically to 47 C.F.R. § 25.123(b)(11). As discussed, under the official recordkeeping of the C.F.R., the

3.3.2.5 *Title 47 C.F.R. §25.271—Control of Transmitting Stations*

47 C.F.R. §25.271 focuses on the facility that controls the spacecraft and the licensee's obligations for control of the facility. This includes adding a security requirement to the physical security of facilities of the operators.[803] Specifically, one of the concerns is that the objects could be 'hijacked' by an unauthorized user and ultimately used for nefarious or otherwise dangerous purposes (for example, destruction of the object or another object).[804] Because of this, facilities must be properly secured, and even in the event of a breach, unauthorized satellite commands should be precluded from access and use by unauthorized personnel.[805] Additionally, the personnel necessary to ensure proper operation must be readily available for both potential service needs or to shut off the Earth-station within the controlling network if it is causing harmful interference.[806]

3.3.3 Title 47 C.F.R. Part 97—Space Station

The last of the three parts that address orbital debris by the FCC is 47 C.F.R. §97.207.[807] This section applies to amateur operators, allowing them under proper licensing to operate space stations subject to appropriate rules and limitations.[808] Specific to orbital debris, within 30 days after the determination of the launch vehicle, but no later than 90 days, the operator must submit a notification to the FCC which, among other things, includes a design description and operational strategies that the space station will use to mitigate orbital debris.[809] The following, which is reflective of most, if not all, of the prior

---

changes to 47 C.F.R. § 25.123 (2020) remain ineffective until approval has been given by OMB.

803 47 C.F.R. § 25.271 (2020), *available at* https://www.ecfr.gov/current/title-47/chapter-I/subchapter-B/part-25/subpart-D/section-25.271. Unlike the prior sections within 47 C.F.R. § 25, this was modified under the original NPRM released 24 April 2020. *Mitigation of Orbital Debris in the New Space Age*, Report and Order and Further Notice of Proposed Rulemaking, FCC 20–54 (Apr. 23, 2020). The NPRM was officially accepted as a Final Rule on 25 August 2020, under the *Mitigation of Orbital Debris in the New Space Age*, 85 Fed. Reg. 165 (Aug. 25, 2020) (to be codified at 47 C.F.R. §§ 5, 25 & 97), *available at* https://www.govinfo.gov/content/pkg/FR-2020-08-25/pdf/2020-13185.pdf. However, this was one of two rules that did not require OMB approval had an effective date of 24 September 2020.

804 47 C.F.R. § 25.271(c)(2) (2020).

805 47 C.F.R. § 25.271(d) (2020).

806 47 C.F.R. § 25.271(c)(4)-(5) (2020).

807 47 C.F.R. § 97.207 (2020), *available at* https://www.ecfr.gov/current/title-47/chapter-I/subchapter-D/part-97/subpart-C/section-97.207.

808 47 C.F.R. § 97.207 (a) (2020).

809 47 C.F.R. § 97.207 (g)(1) (2020).

orbital debris rules applicable to space stations and spacecraft, must additionally be addressed. This includes, but is not limited to:

1. A statement that an assessment has been conducted, and the amount of debris released in a planned manner is minimal as a result of normal operations. In the event of separate deployment devices from the space station launch vehicle, a debris mitigation disclosure must also accompany the statement if the separate device could also become a source of debris.[810]
2. A statement that an assessment and limitation of the probability of collision with small debris that would cause loss of control or disposal has been conducted. The statement must indicate if the probability of the station becoming debris is .01 (1 in 100) or less.[811]
3. A statement that the operator has assessed and limited the probability, during all phases, of accidental explosions or release of liquids that will persist in droplets. Passivation should also be addressed and the method of doing so.[812]
4. A statement that collision is minimized to avoid the craft becoming debris itself.[813]
5. A statement for trackability of the space station, active or passive, the registration entity for SSA, and what information will be shared.[814]
6. Disclosure of any planned proximity operations.[815]
7. Detailed disposal plans, particularly for those that will remain in orbit as part of the disposal plan, and the probability of success for those plans (with an expectation of .90% or greater).[816]

Additional information must also be reported for NGSO spacecraft. This includes that the probability of collision with other large objects is less than .001 (1 in 1,000),[817] identifiable collision risks,[818] minimization of risks to other spacecraft and inhabited stations,[819] how orbital parameters will be

810 47 C.F.R. § 97.207 (g)(1)(I) (2020).
811 47 C.F.R. § 97.207 (g)(1)(II) (2020).
812 47 C.F.R. § 97.207 (g)(1)(III) (2020).
813 47 C.F.R. § 97.207 (g)(1)(IV) (2020).
814 47 C.F.R. § 97.207 (g)(1)(V) (2020).
815 47 C.F.R. § 97.207 (g)(1)(VI) (2020).
816 47 C.F.R. § 97.207 (g)(1)(VII) (2020).
817 47 C.F.R. § 97.207 (g)(1)(IV)(A)(1) (2020).
818 47 C.F.R. § 97.207 (g)(1)(IV)(A)(2) (2020).
819 47 C.F.R. § 97.207 (g)(1)(IV)(A)(3) (2020).

maintained,[820] and a responsiveness plan to conjunction warnings.[821] If the request is for a GEO station, then additional information must identify if there are any existing stations within the projected position that are at risk of collision, and a plan to avoid that.[822]

3.4 *Evolution of FCC Efforts toward Addressing Orbital Debris Mitigation Efforts*

The FCC continues to publish new NPRM's seeking input on a series of new initiatives which, if implemented, should lead to improved orbital debris reduction from US licensed operators. In particular, following the promulgation of the new rules on 3 September 2021, following the NPRM Final Order in the 24 April 2020 announcement, the FCC has proposed a new section, tentatively titled 47 C.F.R. §25.166, under which the FCC seeks comment related to the imposition of a surety bond tied to successful post-mission disposal.

Under Title 47 C.F.R. §25.165, there already exists a bond required for licensing related to the operational lifetime of the satellite.[823] However, post-mission disposal had not been addressed. The NPRM seeks comment on whether or not those seeking space station licenses should be required to post a surety bond during licensing for successful post-mission disposal.[824] Under the new proposal, for an NGSO licensee, the required surety bond would be determined according to the following formula: BA=(TM)*((Y-25)(TO)).[825] *BA* is the amount of the bond in dollars, *TM* is the total mass of the satellite system, *Y* is the number of years that an individual satellite will remain in orbit if it fails in the deployment orbit, and *TO* is the total number of objects in orbit.[826] Under this formula, *BA* could not exceed $100,000,000.

If a satellite is not successfully deorbited, the amount of actual payment that would be required for remit will follow a different formula (rounded to the nearest $10,000).[827] The formula is FA=(M-EM)*((Y-25)*(O-EO)).[828] *FA* is the amount to be paid in dollars, *M* is the total undisposed mass in orbit in

820 47 C.F.R. § 97.207 (g)(1)(IV)(A)(4) (2020).
821 47 C.F.R. § 97.207 (g)(1)(IV)(A)(5) (2020).
822 47 C.F.R. § 97.207 (g)(1)(IV)(B) (2020).
823 47 C.F.R. § 25.165 (2018), *available at* https://www.govregs.com/regulations/47/25.165.
824 *Mitigation of Orbital Debris in the New Space Age*, No. 18–313, 2020 W.L. 2740496, *80 (F.C.C. Apr. 23, 2020), https://docs.fcc.gov/public/attachments/FCC-20-54A1.pdf (at p. 123–24 in PDF).
825 *Id.*
826 *Id.*
827 *Id.*
828 *Id.*

kilograms, *EM* is the expected undisposed mass in orbit in kilograms, *Y* is the mean of the remaining years in orbit for any individual undisposed object, up to a maximum of 200 years per object, *O* is the total number of undisposed objects in orbit, and *EO* is the expected number of undisposed objects in orbit.[829]

For a GEO licensee, the rules for bonding are somewhat different, such that there is not a formula, but instead a set amount that must be obtained. In the case of GEO licenses, a surety bond is required for payment in the event of default in the amount of $5,000,000.[830] If the length of the licensee is extended, the amount is doubled for every five-year extension.[831] In the event of a default, the GEO licensee will then be responsible according to the following formula: FA=$5M*(Y), where *FA* is the amount to be paid in dollars, and *Y* has a sub-formula.[832] *Y*=1 if the satellite operates for less than 15 years, *Y*=2 for between 15 and 20 years of operation, and if the satellite operates for more than 20 years, *Y*=2 plus the total number of operational years, and then subtract 20.[833]

As of this moment, the only evidence of modification to surety bonds that have been implemented is in accordance with 14 C.F.R. §25.165 under the NPRM, FCC Final Order, stating in part that 'failure to post a bond, or obtain one within a specified time after licensing, will render the license null and void automatically.'[834]

3.5 *FCC and the Way Ahead*

The FCC is demonstrating both an aggressive interest in updating its current existing debris mitigation requirements for licensing and feedback for a broad series of proposals they are currently considering. Overall, the proposal to set bond requirements for post-mission disposal is novel, providing a path to penalize non-compliance with a considerable monetary fine. Whether this will come to pass remains to be seen. Meanwhile, the current outlook for the FCC is a continued attempt to push the envelope for debris-reducing requirements for those seeking licenses. This should ensure that the orbital areas being used

829 *Id.*
830 *Id.*
831 *Id.*
832 *Id.*
833 *Id.*
834 Processing Applications in the Digital Broadcast Satellite Service, 86 Fed. Reg. 49489 (Sept. 3, 2021) (to be codified at 47 C.F.R. § 25.165), *available at* https://www.govinfo.gov/content/pkg/FR-2021-09-03/pdf/2021-18043.pdf.

will either require operator diligence to ensure a reduction in pollution, or alternatively, allow for aggressive fines for non-compliance.

4 The US National Space Council

One institution that has not currently been discussed, but is worth mentioning, is the US National Space Council (NSC). This body is important for many reasons, but primarily for the efforts of coordination that it advances among all interested space entities within the United States. Pertinent to space debris, any advancements going forward, whether it be adherence to the ODMSP, further implementation of the IADC Debris Mitigation Guidelines, or consideration of new UN COPUOS proposals, the NSC brings together all of the important US entities to be able to assess and implement any necessary policies effectively.

The NSC has fluctuated between high degrees of use and relative hibernation depending on which US administration is at the helm. The council originated because of the act which established NASA in 1958, creating an advisory council to the president (the NSC) made up of the Secretary of Defense, the NASA Administrator, the Chair of the Atomic Energy Commission, and additional appointees as the President deemed necessary.[835] While underutilized during the Eisenhower administration, the following Kennedy administration revitalized it and modified the charter to make the US Vice President a member and Chair-person among other modifications.[836] Through the following years, the influence ebbed and flowed, seeing little change through the Reagan administration.[837] It was not until President G. H. W. Bush that the NSC was well-received, establishing it fully in 1989 to address the full range of civil, military, and commercial space issues.[838] Alas, through the Clinton, G. W. Bush, and Obama era's, the NSC did not flourish.[839]

In 2017, however, the NSC was reestablished as an office for space policy development and coordination among the Executive Branches under the Trump administration. The participants include the US Vice President, serving as Chair, and a virtual 'who's who' of members. This includes the Secretaries of State, Defense, Commerce, Transportation, Energy, and Homeland Security,

---

835 James A. Vedda, *National Space Council, History and Potential*, CTR. FOR SPACE POL'Y & STRATEGY POL'Y PAPER, 2 (Nov. 2016).

836 *Id.*

837 *Id.*

838 *Id.* at 3.

839 *Id.* at 3–4.

as well as the Directors of National Intelligence, Office of Management and Budget, Office of Science and Technology Policy, the NASA Administrator, the National Security Advisor, the Chairman of the Joint Chiefs of Staff, the Assistant to the President for Economic Policy, and finally the Assistant to the President for Domestic Policy.

Arguably, as discussed earlier, the US policy that was produced in December 2020 was a derivative of the efforts of the National Space Council. President Trump himself indicated its importance in establishing policy within the administration, stating that "The National Space Council will be a central hub guiding space policy within the administration. And I will draw on it for advice and information and recommendations for action."[840] Among that advice was the recommendation to initiate a review and update of the ODMSP, which was subsequently updated in 2019.[841]

How the current Biden administration will approach the NSC has yet to be determined. However, the direction that US space policy, and US space debris policy especially, will take is likely to be heavily influenced by the receptiveness of the Biden administration to the NSC. So far, it appears that the administration has not taken steps to undo some of the previous Trump administration's more significant space-related decisions. For example, the Biden administration confirmed that it is not seeking to revisit the decision to implement the new United States Space Force military service.[842] On the other hand, there appears to be a growing consensus that the Biden administration will likely revert many of the responsibilities that were being performed by the NSC and place them instead with the National Security Council.[843] Ultimately, with a current agenda packed with pressing problems, how important space and

840 Space News Staff, *President Trump Reestablishes National Space Council*, SPACE NEWS (June 30, 2017), https://spacenews.com/breaking-president-trump-reestablishes-national-space-council/.

841 Oltrogge & Christensen, *supra* note 566 at 7.

842 Valerie Insinna, *With Biden's "Full Support," the Space Force is Officially Here to Stay*, DEFENSE NEWS ((Feb. 3, 2021), https://www.defensenews.com/space/2021/02/03/with-the-full-support-of-the-biden-adminisration-the-space-force-is-officially-here-to-stay/. *See also* Marina Koren, *What Happens to the Space Force Now?*, ATLANTIC (Jan. 26, 2021), https://www.theatlantic.com/science/archive/2021/01/space-force-trump-biden/617812/.

843 According to 'Breaking Defense', language in the National Security Executive Order seems to indicate this responsibility change, where National Space Policy Directives will be replaced with National Security Study Memoranda, a product of the National Security Council versus the National Space Council. Theresa Hitchens, *NSC Memo May Spell End of National Space Council*, BREAKING DEFENSE (Feb. 5, 2021, 12:11 PM), https://breakingdefense.com/2021/02/nsc-memo-may-spell-end-of-national-space-council/.

corresponding space debris efforts are in the priority list of President Biden remains an open question mark.

5 Conclusion

The United States stands as one of the most important international leaders in preventing the proliferation of space debris. It was among the first to acknowledge that space debris is a problem and set out to implement within its domestic policies a recognition of (and responses to) that fact. Licensees are subject to several requirements addressing all aspects of operations, from initial concept to post-mission disposal. Included among those licensing standards are the requirement to find solutions at all stages to reduce the potential that any debris still created will not remain indefinitely in outer space if possible.

These preventative efforts are admirable. However, in practice, while the licensing requirements are mandatory to obtain licensing, the reality is that they are all 'plans.' While they all purport to impose strict requirements to obtain a license for operations, they do not have the subsequent follow through for failures if a plan does not go accordingly. For example, a licensee would obviously not be issued a license if they simply said they will not comply with the rules. However, there is currently no indication that a licensee, once licensed, has suffered any notable penalty if it is later discovered that their satellite or launch vehicle has become space debris.

On the other hand, such an intentional scenario wouldn't make much sense. It would be highly unusual for a satellite operator to invest the time and money necessary to get a satellite into space only to purposely abandon it as space debris. On the other hand, for those injecting satellites into space, it can also be said that the real issue with creating space debris is not collisions and explosions. They occur, to be sure, but they are more the exception to the rule than the standard. Instead, the bulk of debris is simply the result of satellites failing to operate properly, rocket bodies being jettisoned at altitudes that do not naturally decay in a reasonable amount of time, and other planning and operational failures. In so far as the prevention of space debris is concerned, it is not to say that the operators in such a situation did not try to implement debris mitigation procedures to reduce risk of destruction. In fact, it is likely much less expensive to implement preventive measures than to lose a satellite after launch. And while unintentional outcomes do still occur, those destructive events that could even be qualified as the result of deliberate negligence (at worst) do not appear to result in any repercussions because of these failures. Going forward, part of the solution will have to consider implementing significant penalties for failures resulting in the creation of space debris, a form of strict liability, regardless of culpability.

One problem lies in the fact that there are simply different rules related to space debris, and licensing, for different agencies. One licensee may be subject to the FCC rules, whereas another may be subject to a different one. None are 'pushovers' but there are differences that can present challenges. And while there is some discussion about attempting to align the rules across the agencies, the will and coordination required to do so simply have not come to pass. As envisioned by the FCC licensing, this has caused some agencies to forge ahead with their licensing expectations and plans, while the others have not necessarily kept up. Thus, the potential for an 'uneven' playing field is real and likely to persist because of an apparent lack of consistency across all federal agencies. In the future, this is an area for improvement, particularly as the technology and testing standards become better. In the interim, the United States continues to make considerable strides toward ensuring that it creates a legal, policy, and educational regime regarding space debris that increases the likelihood of it being considered a good steward of the space environment. It remains to be seen what the Biden administration will do in this area, but it is unlikely that it will significantly roll back any of the efforts of the prior administrations, which have done a lot to support space endeavors.

CHAPTER 5

China

1 Introduction to the Chinese Space Program[844]

The history of Chinese success in space is as storied as it is complicated. From the earliest years of the Chinese space-age, China's leaders felt the only way to gain parity with the West was through two key technologies. The first was nuclear weapons. However, only owning nuclear weapons was not enough. They also needed the technology to deliver them. China felt that being able to access and utilize outer space was a great equalizer; a way to put China and its new government in the early 1950s on an equal footing with the likes of the Soviet Union and the United States, even if only in one or two technological areas.

To say that China's space program journey from the 1950s to now was simple and linear would be anything but the truth. Even today, China's space program is not comprehensive, but instead highly successful in some areas and significantly lacking in others. For example, though highly technologically skilled at launching rockets and satellites into space, China still has no official national space law. Furthermore, the dual-use construct of its space program makes defining the lines between military and civilian control like drawing chalk lines in the rain.[845] And, with so many different agencies having a hand in the

844 It is important to note that considerable effort has been taken to obtain relevant source documents. However, there are areas in which secondary sources discussing source documents were the only resources available to obtain the necessary information. Appropriate credit was given to the authors of this material to identify where the reference was from a secondary source. Specifically unavailable, though with diligent effort, is the 2006 China National Industry Standard, Orbital Debris Mitigation Requirements (QJ321–2005), in force in 2006, referenced by Professor Zizheng Gong, Activities of Space Debris Mitigation and Protection in China, Beijing Space Sustainability Conference, Oct. 13–41, 2011, slide 34, https://swfound.org/media/50864/gong_mitigationchina.pdf, and there may be an update to that regulation as well. For the record, communication efforts were expended to reach Professor Gong at the last known e-mail address as of 2019, but no response was received. Additionally, attempts were made to contact other researchers and academics in China familiar to this area of law but no responses have been received as of the date of this publication.

845 China has increasingly leveraged the advancements of its private enterprise into military applications, and vice versa, making the regulatory landscape even more challenging for commercial programs. Referenced as 'civil-military fusion', departments like the *Chinese Strategic Support Force*, which is the People's Liberation Army branch with the

© KONINKLIJKE BRILL NV, LEIDEN, 2023 | DOI:10.1163/9789004535848_007

development of all aspects of its space program, even high-level officials are sometimes in the dark as to how it all works. One example of the challenges was demonstrated in an interview Dr. Joan Johnson-Freese conducted with a vice-president of the China Aerospace Corporation.[846] In that interview, the vice-president struggled to explain from whom he received supervision for policy guidance and funding requirements.[847]

Regardless, there is no doubt that space has played a critical role in China's technological and social development and will increasingly do so in the future. China's latest National Security Strategy (China NSS) in 2015 demonstrates the increased importance of space to China. It states that China considers the exploration and use of space critical to its ability to conduct domestic operations, scientific investigation, development, and protection of activities and assets in outer space.[848]

However, as China's space program grows, there appears to be an increased recognition that it must address some of the more fundamental aspects of a maturing space program. While the development of its program early on allowed for often reckless abandon in its use of space, China appears to conclude that it must respect the environment that it is operating in. Access to the resources that space provides, and that China so desperately desires to exploit, will be limited should it fail to take steps to protect the space environment. And, without a doubt, China is becoming increasingly dependent on the social, agricultural, national security, and technological advancements that the utilization of space provides. To continue its success, China recognizes the need to take care of the environment and prioritize the sustainability of its

---

primary responsibility for space, have been heavily engaged in efforts that blend the civil and military programs. *See* Lorand Laskai, *Civil Military Fusion and the PLA's Pursuit of Dominance in Emerging Technologies*, CHINA BRIEF, Apr. 9, 2018, https://jamestown.org/program/civil-military-fusion-and-the-plas-pursuit-of-dominance-in-emerging-technologies/ (last accessed Sep. 25, 2020).

846 ROBERTO RODRIGUEZ, THE SPACE PROGRAM OF THE PEOPLE'S REPUBLIC OF CHINA 3 (2011), available at https://www.researchgate.net/publication/215828158_The_Space_Program_of_the_People's_Republic_of_China (citing JOAN JOHNSON-FREESE, THE CHINESE SPACE PROGRAM: A MYSTERY WITHIN A MAZE 55 (1988)).

847 *Id.* (citing JOAN JOHNSON-FREESE, THE CHINESE SPACE PROGRAM: A MYSTERY WITHIN A MAZE 55 (1988)).

848 National Security Law of the People's Republic of China, promulgated by the Standing Comm. Nat'l People's Cong., Jul. 1, 2015, Art. 32, *available at* https://www.chinalawtranslate.com/2015nsl/?lang=en#_Toc423592312. *See also* Teruhisa Tsunjino, *Teruhisa Tsunjino, Chapter 4: Role of Space Development in the National Security of China, in* INT'L SYMPOSIUM ON SECURITY AFFAIRS 2015, (Nov. 5, 2015), available at http://www.nids.mod.go.jp/english/event/symposium/pdf/2015/E-04.pdf.

access to space. To China's credit, just the last ten years or so have seen a series of efforts to contribute to the preservation of space for 'all mankind.'

2 Background of the Development of the Chinese Space Program

The China of the early 1950s was a consolidated power of the Chinese Communist Party (CCP) led by Chairman Mao Zedong. For the preceding 30 to 40 years, China had survived decades of war, conflict, and internal political upheaval. In addition to two World Wars, internal strife between the ruling Chinese Nationalist Party and the CCP had grown since the early 1920s.[849] While the Nationalist Party managed to keep primary control of China and the government for decades, the following 30 years saw their control of China steadily eroded by the CCP.[850]

The tension between the Nationalists and the CCP boiled over after World War II. While the CCP had been a diminished threat between the late 1920s and 1930s, the post-World War II CCP was anything but weak. Boasting a standing army of just under 1 million soldiers and almost 2 million militia, by October of 1949 the CCP had overtaken almost all of mainland China, declaring it the People's Republic of China with Chairman Mao,[851] an early leader in the party, ascending from party leadership to control over the entire country.[852] The remaining Nationalist Party retreated to the island of Taiwan in a bid to maintain its legitimacy.[853]

With this backdrop, China was a nation empowered, but still had reason to be cautious as a newly established government. In particular, both the Korean

---

849 *Northern Expedition*, ENCYCLOPEDIA BRITANNICA (last updated Dec. 29, 2020), https://www.britannica.com/place/China/The-Northern-Expedition.

850 *Resumption of Fighting*, ENCYCLOPEDIA BRITANNICA (last updated Dec. 29, 2020), https://www.britannica.com/place/China/Resumption-of-fighting.

851 Chairman Mao (also known as Chairman Mao Tse-tung or Mao Zedong) rose through the ranks of the CCP in the early 1920s and 1930s as a charismatic leader and guerilla leader and fighter against the Nationalist Party. By 1935, Mao Zedong had been elevated to the position of Chairman within the CCP. Yet, for all his later fame, as a young guerilla leader, he was surprisingly unsuccessful. His eventual retreat to the central areas of China to reorganize by the CCP was ultimately known as the 'Long March'. This is interesting as it was later used as the descriptor for the line of rockets that would send much of China's materials into space. *See generally Mao Tse-tung*, BIOGRAPHY, (last updated Sept. 1, 2020), https://www.biography.com/political-figure/mao-tse-tung.

852 *Resumption of Fighting*, *supra* note 850.

853 *What's Behind the China-Taiwan Divide?*, BBC NEWS (Sept. 28, 2020), https://www.bbc.com/news/world-asia-34729538 (last visited Jan. 17, 2021).

war and the United States and Taiwan Mutual Defense Treaty in 1954 gave the CCP reason to pause.[854] There was concern that any aggression by China against Taiwan, and the remaining Nationalist Party in exile there, could be met with nuclear deterrence from the United States.[855]

To address this perceived threat, Chairman Mao set upon a missile program capable of supporting nuclear weapons as a deterrent from aggression against the homeland.[856] Chairman Mao was so convinced that he needed nuclear weapons that he was quoted in 1955 saying "We need the atom bomb. If our nation does not want to be intimidated, we have to have this thing."[857]

Chairman Mao's statement was evidence of a perception that as long as the United States and Russia both had atomic bombs, China's place in the world and its security was under threat if China was left without it. As such, China began a diligent effort to develop both nuclear weapons and the missile technology necessary to deliver them. By 1958, Chairman Mao, with his fledgling technology in development,[858] not only advanced his military's missile program, but also decreed that China would develop its space program and launch

---

854 *Chinese Nuclear Program*, ATOMIC HERITAGE FOUNDATION (Jul. 19, 2018), https://www.atomicheritage.org/history/chinese-nuclear-program.

855 *Id.*

856 *Id.*

857 *Id.* (quoting Monika Chansoria, *The Political History of China's Nuclear Bomb*, 6 CLAWS *J. 79, 80* (2013)). Additional scholars, such as Teruhisa Tsujino, referred to this policy as a development from the earlier mantra of Mao Zedong's 'two bullets and one star' policy (sometimes referenced as 'two *bombs* and one star'). The two bullets signified the two types of bombs, atomic and hydrogen, and the one star was representative of a satellite in space. *See* Teruhisa Tsunjino, Chapter 4: Role of Space Development in the National Security of China, in INTERNATIONAL SYMPOSIUM ON SECURITY AFFAIRS 2015, (Nov. 5, 2015), available at http://www.nids.mod.go.jp/english/event/symposium/pdf/2015/E-04.pdf.

858 While fledgling, it would also be untrue to say Chairman Mao started from zero. In fact, he had the help of an extremely capable scientist at the inception of his program. Qian Xuesen had been among the pioneers of US rocket technology, studying at the Massachusetts Institute of Technology (MIT) and later teaching at the California Institute of Technology (CALTECH) as well as being a founding member of the Jet Propulsion Laboratory. He would serve the United States in several capacities after the war, including debriefing German scientists (such as Werner von Braun) and analyzing the famous V-2 rockets. However, as tensions with China rose, he was stripped of his security clearance and placed on house arrest in the United States for five years until 1955. He was eventually returned to China in 1955 and became the foremost engineer and leader of the Chinese rocket and space program. *See* Michael Wines, *Qian Xuesen, Father of China's Space Program, Dies at 98*, N.Y. TIMES (Nov. 3, 2009), https://www.nytimes.com/2009/11/04/world/asia/04qian.html#:~:text=BEIJING%20%E2%80%94%20Qian%20Xuesen%2C%20a%20brilliant,died%20on%20Saturday%20in%20Beijing.

an artificial satellite into space.[859] By 1970, Chairman Mao made good on his promise, overseeing the launch of China's first artificial satellite into space on 24 April of that year.[860] The *Dong Fang Hong I* was a scientific test satellite which successfully engaged in communicating various information to the ground, while also including a tune generating device that played the music, 'The East is Red.'[861]

3 The Modern Chinese Space Program

Today, China has grown exponentially from its early missile and spacecraft development programs and achieved several significant accomplishments in outer space. For example, in 2003, China launched its first manned spaceflight on the Shenzhou 5, with its Taikonaut Yang Liwei orbiting Earth 14 times.[862] Demonstrating highly advanced missile technology (withholding a discussion on the propriety of the underlying activity until later), China managed to intercept one of its own orbiting satellites with its own ballistic missile in 2007 (discussed earlier in Chapter 1, section 3).[863] And most recently, on 3 January 2019, the Chinese landed a robotic spacecraft on the South Pole-Aitken Basin area of the Moon, also called the 'far' or 'dark' side of the Moon.[864] Finally, China is looking forward and, like the United States, has its eyes on reaching Mars.[865] It is currently operating a 'Mars Base 1' mock operational base in China's Gobi Desert as it continues to develop its understanding of the demands which will

859 Sirui Zhu, *China's Long March to Space*, REUTERS GRAPHICS (Jul. 24, 2019, last updated Dec. 27, 2019), https://graphics.reuters.com/SPACE-EXPLORATION-MOON/0100B0BH0NZ/index.html?fbclid=IwAR1kdi84loyGvILV0vsPxaOFYTulH8Wn2L1HcUBMP2hY3jvvtO5LAa2us6g.

860 Wei Long, *China Celebrates 30th Anniversary of First Satellite Launch*, SPACE DAILY (Apr. 25, 2000), https://www.spacedaily.com/news/china-00u.html.

861 DFH-1, ASTRONAUTIX, http://www.astronautix.com/d/dfh-1.html (last visited Jan. 10, 2021).

862 The Editors of Encyclopedia Britannica, *Meet the People: Yang Liwei*, SPACE NEXT 50, https://www.britannica.com/explore/space/yang-liwei/ (last visited Jan. 10, 2021).

863 SHIRLEY KAN, CONG. RSCH. SERV., RS22652, CHINA'S ANTI-SATELLITE WEAPON TEST (2007).

864 Sarah Pruitt, *China Makes Historic Landing on 'Dark Side' of the Moon*, HISTORY (Jan. 3, 2019), https://www.history.com/news/china-plans-historic-landing-on-dark-side-of-the-moon#:~:text=The%20Chinese%20spacecraft%20is%20the%20first%20to%20ever,or%20%E2%80%9Cdark%20side%E2%80%9D%20of%20Earth%E2%80%99s%20only%20natural%20satellite.

865 Charlie Campbell, *From Satellites to the Moon and Mars, China is Quickly Becoming a Space Superpower*, TIME (Jul. 17, 2019), https://time.com/5623537/china-space/.

be required for sustaining life.[866] It is targeting a possible unmanned visit to Mars in this decade.[867]

China has also dedicated considerable resources towards the advancement of its modern space program. In 2017, China was estimated to have spent approximately $8.4[868] billion (USD) on its space budget.[869] While that may not be as significant compared to the United States' $19.65[870] billon (USD), it is still the second-largest individual country expenditure with the nearest competitor, Russia, coming in at third place at only $1.5[871] billion (USD).[872] In 2019, the program numbers again show the commitment to space by China, with the US budget remaining nearly the same, but China adding almost $3 billion (USD) more for operations.[873]

Responsibility for properly executing these funds falls on a series of different Chinese space organizations. But China's governing structure, as it relates to space, is largely a 'blended' system, with the 'civil' side of operations sometimes having very little autonomy from the military arm. The intersection of the different governing bodies and space management programs creates a complicated web that has colored much of the development (or as we will see, lack thereof) in the space law of China. Having some understanding of this will be critical to understanding the implementation of their space debris standards.

4 The Legislative Governance Elements of the Chinese Space Program

At the national level, China's governance system can generally be described as a "party government system" or "party-state".[874] The CCP has been, and remains,

866 *Id.*

867 *Id.*

868 Brian Wang, *China's Space Budget is Nearly Triple Russia's Budget but Far Less than the USA Budget*, NEXT BIG FUTURE, (Jul. 24, 2019), https://www.nextbigfuture.com/2019/07/chinas-space-budget-is-nearly-triple-russias-budget-but-far-less-than-usa.html.

869 *Id.*

870 Jeff Foust, *NASA Receives more than $19.6 Billion in 2017 Omnibus Spending Bill*, SPACE NEWS, (May 1, 2017), https://spacenews.com/nasa-receives-more-than-19-6-billion-in-2017-omnibus-spending-bill/.

871 Government Space Budgets: Russian Government Space Budget, THE SPACE REPORT ONLINE, https://www.thespacereport.org/?taxonomy=topic&term=russian-government-space-budget (last visited Jan. 10, 2021).

872 Wang, *supra* note 868.

873 *Space Agencies and Their Budgets*, RADIO FREE EUROPE RADIO LIBERTY, (Feb. 12, 2019), https://www.rferl.org/a/space-agencies-and-their-budgets/29766044.html.

874 Zhili Bai & Juan Liu, *China's Governance Model and System in Transition*, 9 J. CONTEMP. E. ASIA STUD. 65, Mar. 24, 2020, https://www.tandfonline.com/doi/full/10.1080/24761028.2020.1744229.

the most powerful political organization in the country, comprising approximately 92 million members,[875] and represents a highly vetted group of government, military, and civilian personnel.[876] It is also where almost all of the relevant governance and influence in China originates.[877] At the very top of the legislative arm of the governance structure, populated by members of the CCP, is the National People's Congress[878] (NPC).[879] It is the only body that has the power to legislate changes to the Chinese Constitution (adopted in 1982) and has only amended its Constitution five times since.[880] The Constitution serves to outline the responsibilities of the NPC for the country and serves as its highest body of law. Below the NPC and Constitution, there are generally four levels of legislative making bodies.

First, there are laws which the NPC and, as appropriate in certain circumstances, its Standing Committee[881] enact.[882] These include the basic laws governing regulations such as criminal offenses, civil affairs and State civil procedural laws.[883] Next, there are a series of administrative regulations which are drafted and executed by the State Council, the highest administrative organ

---

875 This is not, of course, representative of the Chinese population as a whole.

876 Ban Xiao, *Current and Former Chinese Communist Party Members Explain their Motivations for Joining*, ABC NEWS (Jul. 24, 2020, 3:33 PM), https://www.abc.net.au/news/2020-07-25/chinese-communist-party-members-motive-join-us-travel-ban/12485530.

877 *Id.*

878 For the full list of NPC responsibilities, *see* State Institutions, THE NATIONAL PEOPLE'S CONGRESS FOR THE PEOPLE'S REPUBLIC OF CHINA, http://www.npc.gov.cn/english npc/statestructure2019/201911/fa2deebf75264effa68df01cfecfb60c.shtml (last visited Jan. 10, 2021).

879 National People's Congress, THE NATIONAL PEOPLE'S CONGRESS FOR THE PEOPLE'S REPUBLIC OF CHINA, http://www.npc.gov.cn/englishnpc/c2846/column2.shtml (last visited Jan. 10, 2021).

880 Functions and Powers of the NPC, THE NATIONAL PEOPLE'S CONGRESS FOR THE PEOPLE'S REPUBLIC OF CHINA, http://www.npc.gov.cn/englishnpc/c2846/201903/b149298c33b24f1e8aaa7b8b0e45fa77.shtml (last visited Jan. 10, 2021).

881 The Standing Committee exercises joint power with the National People's Congress (NPC) and may enact and amend all laws, except those such as the constitution which the NPC may only amend. When the NPC is not in session, laws that the NPC has enacted may be partially supplemented to support necessary inclusions, so long as the modifications do not otherwise contravene the existing law or intent. *See* Functions and Powers of the Standing Committee, THE NATIONAL PEOPLE'S CONGRESS FOR THE PEOPLE'S REPUBLIC OF CHINA, http://www.npc.gov.cn/englishnpc/c2847/201903/bcc988763e4140d298515047a9c1549a.shtml (last visited Jan. 10, 2021).

882 Fabio Tronchetti, *Space Law and China*, OXFORD RES. ENCYCLOPEDIA, PLANETARY SCI., at 3, Feb. 2019.

883 Functions and Powers of the NPC, *supra* note 880.

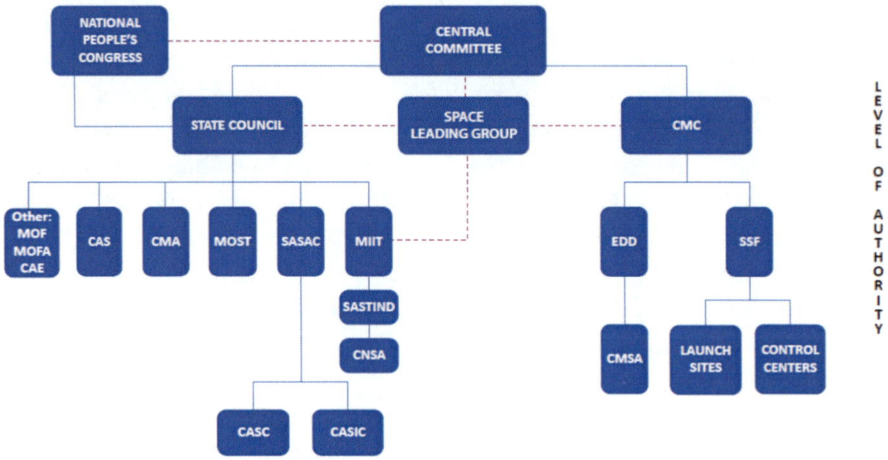

FIGURE 2 Organizational chart for China's space program
Note: Alexander Bowe, China's Pursuit of Space Power Status and Implications for the United States, U.S.-China Economic and Security Review Commission (Apr. 11, 2019), https://www.uscc.gov/sites/default/files/Research/USCC_China%27s%20Space%20Power%20Goals.pdf.
Acronyms: From top left to right, then down from left to right: China Military Commission (CMC); Ministry of Finance (MOF); Ministry of Foreign Affairs (MOFA); China Academy of Engineering (CAE); China Academy of Sciences (CAS); China Meteorological Administration (CMA); Ministry of Science and Technology (MOST); State-owned Assets Supervision and Administration Commission (SASAC); Ministry of Industry and Information Technology (MIIT); Equipment Development Department (EDD); Strategic Support Force (SSF); State Administration of Science, Technology, and Industry for National Defense (SASTIND); China National Space Administration (CNSA); China Manned Space Agency (CMSA); China Aerospace Science and Technology Corporation (CASC); China Aerospace Science and Industry Corporation (CASIC).
SOURCE: ADOPTED FROM MARCO ALIBERTI, WHEN CHINA GOES TO THE MOON, 10 (2015).

in China.[884] Below that, ministerial regulations are created by the Ministries and Commissions of the State Council.[885] Finally, the least influential are local decrees issued by the Local People's Congresses, and other administrative and local rules that are issued by organizations supporting local governments.[886]

884 Tronchetti, *supra* note 882 at 3.
885 Tronchetti, *supra* note 882 at 3.
886 Tronchetti, *supra* note 882 at 3.

The State Council, mentioned above, plays a central role in the development of space policy. In particular, the Information Office of the State Council publishes the Chinese space 'white papers' which (as will be discussed below) are critical documents outlining the purpose and vision of the Chinese space program issued approximately every five years. All the different agencies that make up the Chinese space program report to the State Council. Seen in the diagram, there are a significant number of these organizations with delegated responsibilities from the State Council and are responsible for some portion of drafting, implementing, and executing each regulation governing Chinese space activities (See Figure 2).

Among all the regulatory bodies in China, as stated before, the State Council is the pinnacle of policy-making bodies. Below the State Council, several less influential ministries and agencies are responsible for setting policy and guidance for the space program. This 'multi-departmental' approach contributes to a large number of different agencies exerting influence over the legislative process related to space activities as well as for interpretation, supervision, and enforcement of the resulting rules.[887] Among them, aspects of the military play an important role based on the dual nature of some space programs, such as the Central Military Commission and the General Armaments Department.[888] But otherwise, a host of agencies on the civil side, such as the State Administration of Science, Technology, and Industry for National Defense (SASTIND), the Ministry of Foreign Affairs (MFA), and the Ministry of Finance (MOF) all additionally influence the legislative and policy process.[889] Of course, as always, all power to formulate official State space law remains with the NPC and the Standing Committee.[890]

Of these important agencies, the SASTIND reports directly to the Ministry of Industry and Information Technology (MIIT).[891] It is responsible for drafting the guidelines, policies, laws, and regulations related to science, technology, and industry for national defense, including scientific development of dual-use

887 Caixia Yang & Guozhu Gai, *Overview of the Current Situation and Improvement of Chinese Space Legislation*, 38 ANNALS AIR & SPACE L. 385, 394 (2013).

888 *Id.*

889 *Id.*

890 *Id.*

891 State Administration for Science, Technology and Industry for National Defense (SASTIND), NUCLEAR THREAT INITIATIVE (last updated Jul. 13, 2012), https://www.nti.org/learn/facilities/781/.

systems (such as satellites).[892] Its additional responsibilities include developing production and technology policy, developing plans for nuclear, aerospace, aviation, shipping and ordinance industries, research on developing policies, laws, and regulations on the defense industry and for conversions of equipment to serve in dual-use roles.[893] It is also responsible for maintaining the national registry provided by operators with the name of the owner and the basic orbital parameters of the space object as well as using that information to register the objects internationally that are launched by China.[894]

4.1 *China's Civil Space Program Management*

There are two organizations responsible for executing the Chinese civil space program: the China National Space Administration (CNSA) and the China Aerospace and Science and Technology Corporation (CASC). The lines of responsibility divide somewhere between the CNSA being responsible for policy and the CASC being responsible for the execution, but they are in effect a single organization with split responsibilities for policy and executive decisions, as well as sharing personnel between the two agencies at the senior levels.[895]

CNSA, for its part, is the national agency for China to coordinate its space activities and is subordinate to SASTIND.[896] Formed in 1993, largely as a result of China taking some steps to distinguish its military and civil space programs, CNSA today is responsible for fulfilling China's international obligations under the international space treaties and is the governmental entity designated to sign national agreements for space on behalf of the Chinese government.[897] It is also responsible for planning and developing space activities, with piloted space flight its first priority followed by specific application satellites.[898] Additionally, CNSA serves as China's interface with other space agencies, and the corresponding focal point for bilateral and multilateral cooperation agreements and activities with other Nations.[899]

---

892 *Id.* Often, SASTIND engages with several different ministries and agencies, such as the General Armaments Department and the Ministry of Foreign Affairs, to formulate rules that fulfill the needs of the space programs and meet the international obligations of China to the United Nations and other international bodies.

893 *Id.*

894 Tronchetti, *supra* note 882 at 3.

895 *China National Space Administration* (CNSA), GLOBALSECURITY.org, https://www.globalsecurity.org/space/world/china/cnsa.htm (last visited Jan. 10, 2021).

896 *Id.*

897 Yang & Gai, *supra* note 887 at 391.

898 *China National Space Administration* (CNSA), *supra* note 895.

899 Yang & Gai, *supra* note 887 at 394.

CASC, on the other hand, is a large State-owned enterprise that serves as the execution arm of the space program under the supervision of the State-owned Assets Supervision and Administration Commission (SASAC), which in turn falls under the direct supervision of the State Council.[900] It is comprised of over 130 organizations focused on research and development, manufacturing, and supplying spacecraft launch vehicles and tactical missiles, giving it the ability to launch LEO, GEO, and sun-synchronous rockets, as well as developing communication, meteorological, Earth resource, and scientific experimental satellites.[901]

As indicated above, there is independence and integration at all levels of development for space operations and for the development of law and policy. Especially in the example of CASC and CNSA, the integration allows for dual leadership and guidance in the development of programs and integration of international cooperation and obligations into operations. Meanwhile, there is also the independence of some military and civilian aspects of space operations which allow for centralization of effort, when necessary, and decentralization of activity where warranted.

As the major policy-making elements, each of these organizations plays a part in developing the applicable regulatory governance model. As will become evident, however, there are drawbacks to the number of different agencies that have an input in the regulatory development.[902] Among them, there are varying departmental interests, especially between international cooperation objectives on the civil side and the desire for secrecy on the military side.[903] Also, there is no single authoritative decision-maker to regulate space activities until arriving at a very high level of government.[904] This can make coordination and decision-making a long and arduous process. And last, the booming growth of China has made space important, but a standardized regulatory national scheme is not among the most pressing issues.[905] Therefore, most of the guidance and decisions that exist are not high-level controlling guidance, but instead low-level directives created in reaction to immediate needs.

---

900 Liheng Want, *China Aerospace Science and Technology Corporation* (CASC), FEDERATION OF AMERICAN SCIENTISTS (Sept. 8, 2020), https://fas.org/nuke/guide/china/contractor/casc.htm.

901 *Id.*

902 Yang & Gai, *supra* note 887 at 398.

903 *Id.* at 398.

904 *Id.*

905 *Id.*

5 Chinese Regulatory Efforts toward Sustainability and Orbital Debris

5.1 *China and International Space Agreements*

China is a party to several international space agreements. In 1967, the Republic of China signed on to the Outer Space Treaty and deposited ratification on 24 July 1970.[906] The Government of the People's Republic of China submitted an instrument of accession on 30 December 1983, assuming responsibility for the international rights and obligations arising from the application of the Treaty, including applicability and responsibility to the Hong Kong Special Administrative Region.[907] Five years later China acceded to the Rescue Agreement, the Liability Convention, and the Registration Convention in 1988.[908]

Like most other countries, China has not ratified the Moon Agreement. In addition to the international space treaties, China has also been an international advocate for the continued peaceful uses of outer space and for cooperation among Nations, including a call to resist the placement of weapons of mass destruction in outer space.[909] However, as mentioned earlier, though China has obligated itself under international regimes, it has still failed to implement comprehensive national space legislation to effect many of its goals. But, it has taken steps at the administrative level to implement some provisions of the Outer Space Treaty, Liability Convention, and Registration Convention through its lower level-regulations. The result of commitments to these international treaties and agreements has bolstered China's robust space goals and significant successes.

5.2 *Chinese Regulations Based on International Commitments*

China has demonstrated national-level concern with pollution and has made efforts to make public-facing proposals that imply it is a good steward of the environment. As early as the 1970s, China recognized its high population

---

906 Status of International Agreements Relating to Activities in Outer Space as of 1 January 2020, U.N. Office of Outer Space Affairs, at 6, https://www.unoosa.org/documents/pdf/spacelaw/treatystatus/TreatiesStatus-2020E.pdf.

907 *Id. See also China: Accession to Outer Space Treaty*, United Nations Office for Disarmament Affairs (Dec. 30, 1983), http://disarmament.un.org/treaties/a/outer_space/china/acc/washington.

908 *Id. See also* Yun Zhao, *National Space Law in China; An overview of the Current Situation and Outlook for the Future*, 10 Studies in Space Law, at 42–46 (2015), https://brill.com/view/title/27093.

909 *Id.*

density put a strain on the available resources which places further importance on protecting a fragile environment.[910] The path to the first two relevant regulations is a result of a recognition by China on the importance of environmental sustainability starting over 50 years ago.

Beginning in the 1980s, China appreciated that its survival and success in the future would be largely impacted by treatment of its own environment.[911] Therefore it moved forward with establishing environmental protection and stewardship as one of its foundational national policy priorities.[912] Throughout the 1980s, China initiated a series of at least 18 laws aimed at addressing efforts toward protection of natural resources in air, sea and land.[913] This movement culminated in 1989 with the passage of the Environmental Protection Law of the People's Republic of China, which laid out the priorities of environmental stewardship at the highest levels of government and that "plans for environmental protection formulated by the State must be incorporated into the national economic and social development plans."[914] Furthermore, the State was required to "adopt economic and technological policies and measures favorable for environmental protection."[915]

In short, environmental protection was thus required to be weaved into the planning of all conduct of Chinese economic and societal advances. As a result, many of the documents China has issued, or agreements it has subjected its domestic activities to, reflect this concern. In furtherance of their environmental objectives, China became one of the original members of the

---

910 Information Office of the State Council of the People's Republic of China, *Environmental Protection in China*, PERMANENT MISSION OF THE PEOPLE'S REPUBLIC OF CHINA TO THE UNITED NATIONS OFFICE AT GENEVA AND OTHER INTERNATIONAL ORGANIZATIONS IN SWITZERLAND (Jun. 1996), https://www.mfa.gov.cn/ce/cegv//eng/bjzl/t176940.htm.

911 *Id.*

912 *Id.*

913 Rui Lin Jim & Wen Liu, *Environmental Policy and Legislation in China*, Proceedings of the Sino-American Conference on Env't L., at 6–7 (Aug. 16, 1987), https://scholar.law.colorado.edu/cgi/viewcontent.cgi?referer=https://www.google.com/&httpsredir=1&article=1009&context=proceedings-of-sino-american-conference-on-environmental-law#:~:text=In%201979%2C%20the%20%22Environmental%20Protection,tal%20management%20by%20legal%20means.&text=Since%20the%20beginning%20of%20the,of%20the%20Chinese%20legal%20system.

914 Environmental Protection Law of the People's Republic of China, CHINA.ORG.CN, http://www.china.org.cn/english/environment/34356.htm (last visited Sept. 11, 2020).

915 *Id.*

IADC in 1995.[916] Recalling the earlier discussion in Chapter 3, the IADC's efforts are focused on assessing the debris threat and the potential remedies that spacefaring countries could implement to reduce the accumulation of debris in orbit.

Second, China engaged in efforts to assess the impact of space debris domestically. As early as 2001, China developed plans to set up a monitoring and research program to minimize space debris originating from its launchers and satellites.[917] The effort involved a five-year action plan which would initiate the development of a SSA network of satellites, develop a tracking database for space debris, create policies and procedures to assess the risk of debris as well as emergency avoidance systems, develop proper simulation and modelling techniques to assess threats, and take steps to mitigate space debris generation, especially for post-mission disposal activities.[918] This five-year plan built on earlier efforts by the Chinese to focus on the dangers posed by orbital debris which they learned from their involvement with the IADC and other orbital debris research efforts.[919]

5.3 *Domestic Departmental-Level Regulations*

The goal to establish some degree of domestic space legislation in response to their five-year plan was therefore a normal iteration of Chinese development of their environmental policies. In the form of departmental laws, two principal regulations were issued. However, as will be discussed further, the departmental laws do not rank high in the hierarchy of Chinese laws. There are at least three reasons the Chinese developed them at that level.

The first reason is that the departmental level regulations are simpler than the more onerous high level national laws.[920] The second is departmental level regulations are also much faster to develop than higher-level laws.[921] The third reason is more complicated and may explain, at least to some extent, why

---

916 Nicolas L. Johnson, *Saving Space: The multilateral Approach to Orbital Debris*, 15 GEORGETOWN J. INT'L AFFAIRS 130, 133 (2014), *available at* https://www-jstor-org.libproxy.unl.edu/stable/pdf/43134273.pdf.

917 *China Plans Space Debris Monitoring and Research Program*, MOOD DAILY, (Mar. 7, 2001), https://www.moondaily.com/reports/China_Plans_Space_Debris_Monitoring_and_Research_Program.html (last visited Sept. 6, 2020).

918 *Id.*

919 *Id.*

920 U.N. Int'l Institute of Air and Space Law Workshop on Capacity Building in Space Law, U.N. Doc. ST/Space/14 (2003), 167–68, https://www.unoosa.org/pdf/publications/st_space_14E.pdf.

921 *Id.*

national-level legislation is unlikely to materialize soon. Specifically, Chinese space activity has numerous areas where the dual-use nature of space objects end up requiring coordination over a number of different agencies, with several different disparate groups having an interest in the activities and regulations governing the activities.[922] What may be good for the civil sector may be contrary to the interests of the military, which further complicates who controls a particular activity between the two.[923] Additionally, because so many different levels of government have some involvement in all stages of satellite operation, it is very difficult under Chinese law to implement a law that would reflect consensus among all the relevant stakeholders.[924] Thus, because of at least these three reasons, China indicated early on that while there was an intent to upgrade the departmental regulations into administrative law or higher when more is known, for now, the regulations as issued have offered the flexibility to be responsive to the international obligations and needs of China without being overly burdensome to develop.[925]

The first of the two space regulations implemented to meet international obligations (and among other things, address environmental protections) is the 2001 *Measures for the Administration of Registration of Objects Launched into Outer Space*. The second is the 2002 *Interim Measures on the Administration of Licensing the Project of Launching Civil Space*. For context, both measures were created as departmental regulations, which is the lowest form of law in China.[926] But, while the primary administrative regulations may be low level, it would be a mistake to consider them to be insignificant.

5.3.1 China's Existing Space Regulations—2001 Measures for the Administration of Registration of Objects Launched into Outer Space[927]

In 1988, as previously discussed, the People's Republic of China acceded to the Registration Convention with the United Nations, thus taking on the

922 Bin Li & Haifeng Zhao, *Governmental Regulations on Commercial Aspects of China's Space Activities*, 3 INDIAN J. OF INT'L ECON. L. 28, 35 (2010), http://docs.manupatra.in/newsline/articles/Upload/DC5083B1-356C-4E2D-BE48-7A2909DAB086.pdf.

923 *Id.*

924 *Id.*

925 U.N. Int'l Institute of Air and Space Law Workshop on Capacity Building in Space Law, *supra* note 920.

926 Tronchetti, *supra* note 882 at 3.

927 It is extremely important to note that China has at least eight regulations of varying governmental levels of importance relevant to space debris. Again, despite extensive effort, none of these became available nor were repeated inquiries into possible avenues for obtaining the information responded to. However, QJ3221–2005, revised 2015, is the

obligations imposed within it.[928] Specifically, Article II requires that a launching State has two obligations pertinent to the launch of a space object.[929] One, it must register the space object by means of entry into an appropriate registry which the launching State shall maintain.[930] Second, the Member-State shall inform the Secretary-General of the United Nations of the creation of such registry.[931] Having done so, Article IV further requires that the registering State shall additionally furnish to the UN Secretary-General pertinent information concerning the space object, such as its basic orbital parameters, designator, date, and territory of launch and the name of the launching State.[932] China

---

China National Industry Standard, *Requirements for Orbital Debris Mitigation*, and is the overall controlling document. Below that are at least seven lower-level regulations, KJSP-T-1-01 chronologically through KJSP-T-1-06, and KJSP-M-1-01. *See* Zizheng Gong, Chief Scientist, China Practices on Satellites Post-Mission Disposals Toward Space Long-Term Sustainability, UN COPUOS Scientific and Technical Subcomm., 53rd Session, Vienna (Feb. 15–26, 2016), at 9, https://www.unoosa.org/documents/pdf/copuos/stsc/2016/tech-21E.pdf. For reference, Chinese standards exist at four levels. The highest are *national standards*, followed in cascade by *professional, local,* and then *enterprise* standards. "QJ" is a designator used within the professional standards to reference 'Space', demonstrating the second-highest level of standards and are often reflective of "industry standards." These standards are developed when no national standard (designated as "GB" standards) exist, but where a unified technical requirement is needed for a specific industry sector. Importantly, a subcontext of Chinese standards indicates that if a standard is 'voluntary', the standard designator will have a '/T' following it. So, if the primary debris standard for China, QJ, was voluntary, it would be '*QJ/T*.' The fact that it is not indicates that those requirements, which secondary sources appear to conclude are based heavily on the UN COPUOS Space Debris Mitigation Guidelines and IADC Debris Mitigation Guidelines, absent specifics, are mandatory for Chinese operators. *See PRC Standards System: Standards Used in China*, AM. NAT'L STANDARDS INST., https://www.standardsportal.org/usa_en/prc_standards_system/standards_used_in_china.aspx (last visited Aug. 8, 2021). The remaining standards, it would appear, are all in some sort of draft and utilize the 'KJSP' designator, which is otherwise not specifically clarified in the available literature to its exact meaning (only identified as 'under approved'). *See* Zizheng Gong, CASC Efforts on Dealing with Space Debris Toward Space Long Term Sustainability, UN COPUOS Scientific and Technical Subcomm., 50th Session, Vienna (Feb. 11–22, 2013), at 25, https://www.unoosa.org/pdf/pres/stsc2013/2013lts-03E.pdf. As a note, it does appear that there is a national level standard which may be equivalent to ISO 24113–2019, though designated as voluntary; *Space Debris Mitigation Requirements, The Standardization Administration of the People's Republic of China* GB/T 34513–2017.

928 Yang & Gai, *supra* note 887 at 403.

929 G.A. Res. 3235 (XXIX), at Art. II, Registration Convention (Jan. 14, 1975), *available at* https://www.unoosa.org/pdf/gares/ARES_29_3235E.pdf.

930 *Id.*

931 *Id.*

932 *Id.* at Art. IV.

did not establish a national registry until 2001.[933] Prior to that time, China had relayed to the UN Secretary-General the pertinent information on launched space objects to keep it generally compliant with the Registration Convention, even if it was not technically in accordance with the specific expectations.[934] Between 1990 and 2000, China relayed information to the United Nations on twenty-seven space objects launched from China.[935]

Recognizing the shortfall in compliance, and having established the national registry by 2001, China then endeavored to become completely compliant with the requirements of the Registration convention by promulgating the *Measures for the Administration of Registration of Space Objects Launched into Outer Space* (hereafter China Registration Measures) on 8 February 2001. This was a joint effort drafted by SASTIND and the MFA, and officially established the first administrative regulation in China regarding civil space activities. In addition to making China compliant with its international obligations, it also incorporated much of the additional elements of the Registration Convention into Chinese regulatory vernacular, such as the definition of a launching State and space object, including going at least a step ahead on the definition of a space object.[936]

5.3.2 China's Existing Space Regulations—the Interim Measures on the Administration of Licensing the Project of Launching Civil Space

The second regulation, the *Interim Measures on the Administration of Licensing the Project of Launching Civil Space* (hereafter China Interim Licensing Measures) entered into force on 21 December 2002.[937] The China Interim Licensing Measures provides guidance on government expectations for

933 Yang & Gai, *supra* note 887 at 403.

934 *Id.*

935 *Id.*

936 According to the 2001 China Registration Measures, a 'space object' refers to 'artificial satellites, crewed spacecraft, space probes, space stations, launch vehicles and parts thereof, and other man-made objects launched into outer space.' It did not regard temporarily transiting objects as space objects, such as sounding rockets and ballistic missiles. *See* Yang & Gai, *supra* note 887 at 405. Compare that to the Registration Convention, which simply defines a space object as 'component parts of a space object as well as its launch vehicle and parts thereof.' *See* G.A. Res. 3235 (XXIX), at Art. I(b), Registration Convention (Jan. 14, 1975), *available at* https://www.unoosa.org/pdf/gares/ARES_29_3235E.pdf.

937 Guoyu Wang, Associate Prof. Institute of Space Law, China's Space Regulations: Registration and Licensing, UN COPUOS Legal Subcomm., 53rd Session, Vienna (Mar. 2014), at 5, https://www.unoosa.org/pdf/pres/lsc2014/tech-05E.pdf. *See also* Laws of the People's Republic of China, *Interim Measures on the Administration of Permits for Civil Space Launch Projects* (Nov. 21, 2002), http://www.asianlii.org/cn/legis/cen/laws/imotaopfcslp771/.

commercial operators to obtain a license for launch. The 28 Article document sets out the standards that administrative civil space launch projects will follow to promote the development of the space industry, ensure that State security is not compromised and that there are public benefits to the activities, and that all activity will meet internationally agreed-upon norms.[938] It does apply only to civil activity, not military, and establishes China's jurisdiction and expectations for submissions to obtain a permit to launch objects into space, either from Chinese territory or abroad for Chinese citizens.[939]

5.3.2.1 *Licensing Requirements*

Licensing, as would be expected, does require submissions of commonly expected information, such as launch location, time, technical requirements of the payload, orbital parameters, reports on landing or recovering locations (if applicable) and radio station licensing (if applicable).[940] There are also Articles (or sections thereof) which relate to protection of the environment, which include obligations to reduce the potential for the creation of space debris.

Article 5(b) requires that any request for licensing may not 1) endanger State security, 2) damage benefits of the State, or 3) violate Chinese obligations under diplomatic policies or international conventions.[941] As a result, the obligations of the Outer Space Treaty apply to the licensing requirements, such that elements of the Outer Space Treaty (Articles I, II, and IX especially) are reflected in China's domestic regulatory space law.

From an environmental perspective, China reinforces these international obligations, and also highlights their own interest in the protection of the environment, through Article 5.[942] That provision states that activities will not cause "irremediable danger to the health, safety or properties of the public."[943] While this does apply to all phases of operations, it especially applies to conduct in space since space debris could be considered an 'irremediable danger' to any future operations to properties of the public.[944]

---

938 Laws of the People's Republic of China, *Interim Measures on the Administration of Permits for Civil Space Launch Projects* (Nov. 21, 2002), Art. 1, http://www.asianlii.org/cn/legis/cen/laws/imotaopfcslp771/.

939 *Id.* at Art. 2.

940 *Id.* at Art. 6(c).

941 *Id.* at Art. 5(b).

942 *Id.* at Art. 5(c).

943 *Id.*

944 *Id.*

To China's credit, it also directly addresses space debris in the licensing requirements in Article 6(d).[945] It provides that the safety design must meet several safety considerations to obtain a permit. Among them, the requestor must indicate that the materials being used provide for public security, the safety systems are reliable, and any assessments that indicate possible malfunctions of the rocket during launch have been publicized.[946] Importantly, the requestor must also indicate in the permit how the operator intends to avoid pollution and space debris.[947] What it does not do, however, is define what constitutes space debris or pollution.[948] But, considering the regulation was promulgated in 2002, China deserves credit for making space debris risks part of its licensing regime well in advance of when the IADC published their guidelines five years later.[949]

5.4 *The 2010 Interim Instrument on Space Debris Mitigation and Management Instrument*

A separate and more recent legislative effort, distinct from the regulations issued because of the original 'five-year' plan, is the 2010 *Interim Instrument on Space Debris Mitigation and Management* Instrument (hereafter the China Debris Mitigation Measures). The China Debris Mitigation Measures have been enacted to implement the domestic technical standards and the recommended practices that have been established in order to reduce environmental pollution during all stages of a spacecraft lifecycle in China.[950] It was not only issued by SASTIND, but also charged SASTIND with the duty of supervising and administering the mitigation of, and protection against, space debris.[951] Under the China Debris Mitigation Measures, SASTIND defined space debris as 'all non-functional man-made objects, including fragments and elements thereof, which are in Earth's orbit or re-entering the atmosphere.'[952] The China Debris Mitigation Measures remained in such status until 2015, when it was formally adopted as the *Measures on the Administration of Space Debris Mitigation and Protection*.[953]

---

945 *Id.* at Art. 6(d).
946 *Id.*
947 *Id.*
948 *Id.*
949 *Id.*
950 Tronchetti, *supra* note 882 at 7.
951 Yang & Gai, *supra* note 887 at 422.
952 *Id.*
953 Xinmin Ma, Deputy Director-General of the Department of Treaty and Law Ministry of Foreign Affairs for China, China's Space Diplomacy: Policies and Practices, UNISPACE+

Up to this point, while existing licensing requirements addressed space debris, they did not necessarily limit the debris creation. Instead, they simply required that an operator explain the safety and protective aspects that might be at issue. The China Debris Mitigation Measures, on the other hand, implement a regulatory scheme that closely resembles the IADC Debris Mitigation Guidelines.[954] According to Professor Fabio Tronchetti, the technical standards force operators to control debris released during normal operations, minimize debris generated by accidental explosions and choose a flight path that provides a safe flight profile.[955] Additional requirements include passivation requirements for any residual propellants from the launch vehicle and deorbiting of the upper stages of the rocket delivery systems.[956] Finally, operators must ensure proper post-mission deorbit of satellites, either through atmospheric deorbiting or graveyard orbits, particularly for GEO satellites.[957]

For space debris, according to Professor Tronchetti, Articles 8 and 9 of the China Debris Mitigation Measures also impose two specific space debris responsibilities.[958] Article 8 requires that, as part of the licensing requirements, space debris mitigation measures must be described to obtain a permit.[959] Article 9 imposes a duty to constantly monitor for risks to the spacecraft from a potential collision with another craft, and subsequent space debris risks.[960] This is in line with the registration requirements, such that an operator must provide the orbital insertion and parameters of orbital trajectory as part of registering the space object through SASTIND.

50, High Level Forum (HLF), Dubai, (Nov. 20–24, 2016), at 18, https://www.unoosa.org/documents/pdf/hlf/1st_hlf_Dubai/Presentations/73.pdf.

954 Gong, China Practices on Satellites Post-Mission Disposals Toward Space Long-Term Sustainability, *supra* note 927 at 2.

955 Tronchetti, *supra* note 882 at 7; IADC Interim Debris Mitigation Guidelines, Arts. 6–7.

956 Gong, China Practices on Satellites Post-Mission Disposals Toward Space Long-Term Sustainability, *supra* note 927 at 25. Of note, according to China at the UN COPUOS Scientific and Technical Sub-Committee at the 53rd session in 2016, there are only 1800 available locations to put satellites in the GEO region. Failure to properly remove satellites out of GEO, as a result, could have disastrous effects long term because of the limited nature of the locations and the resource generally. *See also* Louis de Gouyon Matignon, *Orbital Slots and Space Congestion*, SPACE LEGAL ISSUES (Jun. 8, 2019), https://www.spacelegalissues.com/orbital-slots-and-space-congestion/.

957 Gong, China Practices on Satellites Post-Mission Disposals Toward Space Long-Term Sustainability, *supra* note 927 at 25. *See also* Matignon, *Orbital Slots and Space Congestion*, *supra* note 956.

958 Tronchetti, *supra* note 882 at 7.

959 *Id.*

960 *Id.*

6 China's Space Policy—the Chinese White Papers

In addition to actual regulatory guidance, China has been telegraphing its intentions in space through "White Papers" that it began issuing in 2000 and have re-issued an update approximately every five years. These documents reflect China's goals, ambitions, strategies, and principles covering a range of topics, including its current vision of space use, technological applications, and goals for international cooperation.[961] Importantly, these documents are not binding; they are neither law nor constitute an issued regulation of any department.[962] However, they do provide general transparency of the view of China towards space activities and a projection of the direction in which China is moving, including the need for a sustainable space environment.[963] They also discuss China's views on international policy and the international regulatory environment.[964] Finally, the White Papers acknowledge that while space-related laws may not exist at the national level, China understands the importance of at least memorializing the national strategy on its growing space program for both domestic and international audiences.[965]

6.1 *The 2000 China Space White Paper*

The first official issuance of the white paper, the 2000 Space White Paper, set out China's basic position in regards to international space obligations that space should be used for peaceful purposes and for the benefit the whole of humanity.[966] Importantly, it also set out the overarching aims of China's national efforts in space.[967] First, to explore space and learn more about Earth as a result.[968] Second, in the course of utilizing space for peaceful purposes, an intention to promote the betterment of mankind.[969] Third, to meet the growth of China, as well as its security, to advance the scientific

961 Rongping Mu & Yonggang Fan, *An Overview of Chinese Space Policy*, *in* HANDBOOK OF SPACE SECURITY 413, at 422–423 (2015).

962 *Id.*

963 *Id.*

964 *Id.*

965 *Id.*

966 China National Space Administration, *China's Space Activities, a White Paper*, SPACE REF, at § I (Nov. 22, 2000), http://www.spaceref.com/news/viewsr.html?pid=7107. *See also* Irina Liu et al., *Evaluation of China's commercial Space Sector*, SCI. & TECH. POLY INST. at 11–13 (Sept. 2019), https://www.ida.org/-/media/feature/publications/e/ev/evaluation-of-chinas-commercial-space-sector/d-10873.ashx.

967 China National Space Administration, *China Space Activities*, *supra* note 966 at § I.

968 *Id.*

969 *Id.*

and technological development to protect China's national interests as well as enhance its strength in the world.[970]

The 2000 White Paper, in line with the discussion on the importance of environmental protection to China and its national security, also addressed a series of principles that would guide its national space activities. In particular, the first principle was to ensure that there was "long-term, stable and sustainable development" of space activities.[971] Additional principles included articulating the importance of being self-sufficient, while still being engaged in the international community to tackle significant problems and make breakthroughs in space technology.[972] This is very closely reflective of China's early efforts in the IADC to tackle orbital debris issues in the previous years before the issuance of this paper.[973] Similarly, it again addressed environmental concerns as a principle requiring that "necessary measures should be adopted to protect the space environment and space resources" in the course of its operations.[974] Also, the principles included a focus on activities to drive modernization of the technology that would allow for overcoming major difficulties that would arise in the course of space exploration.[975] Finally, to advocate for engaging in long-term planning to find efficiencies in the exploration of space to promote comprehensive and coordinated development in the advancement of space activities.[976]

The remainder of the 2000 White Paper served as a roadmap of where China had been, where it was at the time, and where it wanted to go.[977] In particular, China indicated its focus on future scientific and technological developments that would orient it to meet the 21st century demands for national development and growth in the space industry.[978] Recalling the two regulatory efforts that were being issued at the same time as the White Paper, there was considerable alignment between the sustainability aspects reflected in the parallel efforts.[979] As such, the White Paper served as an initial roadmap and closely choreographed the future regulatory issuances just a year later.

970 *Id.*
971 *Id.*
972 *Id.*
973 *Id.*
974 *Id.*
975 *Id.*
976 *Id.*
977 *Id.*
978 *Id.* at III.
979 *Id.*

6.2 *The 2006 China Space White Paper*[980]

The 2006 Space White Paper had many of the hallmarks of the 2000 issuance, though more succinct. It looked back at some of the successes and efforts of the space program, its 'eye-catching' achievements, and its continued peaceful efforts in space toward the betterment of all mankind.[981] Importantly, it also reiterated the focus on environmental protection that was stressed in the first White Paper, discussing the continued intention of China to "protect the space environment, and develop and utilize space resources in a rational manner", alluding to an interpretation that 'rational' implies a management of the resources so as to preserve them and ensure their continued access and availability.[982]

6.3 *The 2011 China Space White Paper*[983]

The third publication of the White Paper, issued in 2011, again addressed the issue of protecting the space environment. However, the language in this White Paper had a 'tone' that was different, likely because of the political fallout from the 2007 environmentally disastrous Chinese ASAT test (discussed earlier in Chapter 1, section 3). It is somewhat hard to reconcile the language with the actual activities, but the White Paper does state that China "develops and utilizes space resources in a prudent manner and takes effective measures to protect the space environment."[984]

Importantly, the way China crafted the statement made it appear to be speaking to an international, versus domestic, audience. The first line, "China always adheres to the use of outer space for peaceful purposes", appears defiant to the international community, as if in response to some perceived slight.[985] The following use of the words, "The country develops and utilizes space resources in a prudent manner", again reflects a statement not meant for a domestic audience in appearance, but is addressed to the international community regarding how China goes about its business.[986] Even more interesting is that while

980 *White Paper on China's Space Activities Published*, CHINA.ORG.cn (Oct. 12, 2006), http://www.china.org.cn/english/2006/Oct/183588.htm.

981 *China's Space Activities in 2006*, CHINA NATIONAL SPACE ADMINISTRATION, § 1 (Dec. 12, 2006), http://www.cnsa.gov.cn/english/n6465645/n6465648/c6477657/content.html. *See also* Liu et al., *supra* note 966 at 13–14.

982 *China's Space Activities in 2006*, *supra* note 981 at § 1.

983 *White Paper on China's Space Activities in 2011*, CHINESE EMBASSY, § 1 (Dec. 30, 2011), http://bg.chineseembassy.org/eng/dtxw/t891870.htm.

984 *Id. See also* Liu et al., *supra* note 966 at 13–14.

985 *White Paper on China's Space Activities in 2011*, *supra* note 983 at § 1.

986 *Id.*

China mentioned many of the activities of 2007, including numerous space launches and efforts, it never mentioned the 2007 ASAT test, and the damaging environmental effects, at all. As arguably one of the most significant events in the five preceding years of this report, that is a notable absence.

Also significant is that a new section was added into the 2011 White Paper which addressed Space Debris for the first time.[987] It outlined several efforts China has been making to address the space debris threat.[988] First, it noted Chinese accomplishments in monitoring space debris through advancements in SSA radars, providing early warning for two lunar probes and one manned spaceship.[989] Furthermore, China touted its efforts in post-mission disposal, including rendering inert the 'Long-March' rockets that had been sent into space and remained.[990] Furthermore, it noted China's repositioning of some aging satellites out of GEO and into graveyard orbits.[991] Finally, it very briefly addressed protection of manned spaceships from space debris.[992] This was likely alluding to efforts that it had made to understand the effects and dangers of hypervelocity impacts in space through its university efforts.[993]

6.4 *The 2016 China White Paper*[994]

The 2016 White Paper demonstrated an evolution in the format of the White Papers, offering significant clarity on the purpose, vision, and principles of China's space ambitions.[995] It also reads like a further awakening of the strength and ambition of the Chinese program.[996] In fact, in no ambiguous terms, it states that its vision is to "build China into a space power in all respects."[997] It also reduced the general principles to four major themes;

987 *Id.* at § II(9).

988 *Id.*

989 *Id.*

990 *Id.*

991 *Id.*

992 *Id.*

993 *See generally* Zizheng Gong, CASC *Efforts on Dealing with Space Debris Toward Space Long Term Sustainability*, UN COPUOS Sci. & Tech. Subcomm., Fiftieth Session, at 31-32, Vienna (Feb. 11–22, 2013).

994 *Full Text of White Paper on China's Space Activities in 2016*, ENGLISH.GOV.CN (last updated Dec. 28, 2016), http://english.www.gov.cn/archive/white_paper/2016/12/28/content_281475527159496.htm.

995 *Id. See also* Liu et al., *supra* note 966 at 13–14.

996 *Full Text of White Paper on China's Space Activities in 2016*, *supra* note 994 at § I.

997 *Id.*

innovative development, coordinated development, peaceful development and open development.[998]

China's acknowledgment of the space debris threat remained, with a dedicated section continuing in the 2016 iteration.[999] Among the notable achievements in this area, China highlighted its continued success with SSA, and advancements in early warning for the safe operation of satellites and spacecraft seeing enhanced protections as a result.[1000] It also addressed advancements in scientific technologies, specifically in hypervelocity impact protection implemented in its spacecraft to prevent damage to its operational satellites.[1001] Last, it identified that all of its 'Long-March' rockets that remained in orbit now had procedures to ensure complete passivation preventing their combustion and destruction by internal mechanisms, as well as efforts geared to move retired spacecraft into a graveyard or other orbits to ensure the protection of the space environment.[1002]

6.5 *The 2021 China White Paper*

The 2021 China White Paper is indicative of a very aggressive space program on the part of China, particularly focused on exerting a global reach and influence among the major spacefaring nations. Its breadth is extensive, focusing on a broad array of areas, including maintaining a strong space presence, developing systems and technology to improve its space capabilities, advancing its commercial space capabilities, research, governance, and legal issues among the broad areas it addresses.

In executing its goals, space debris features prominently in this new White Paper. At a high level, China acknowledges its obligation for facilitating a global consensus on its shared responsibility in "utilizing outer space for peaceful purposes and safeguarding its security for the benefit of all humanity."[1003] It also highlights its long history of involvement in the advancement of debris management, sustainability, and other space management efforts through its international efforts, including its participation in the Space Debris Working Group of the China-Russia Space Cooperation Sub-Committee, and the Sino-US Expert Workshop on Space Debris and Space Flight Safety.[1004] Through

998 *Id.*
999 *Id.* at § II(9).
1000 *Id.*
1001 *Id.*
1002 *Id.*
1003 *Id.* at § I(1).
1004 *Id.* at § VI(1).

these efforts, China uses the White Paper to argue that it remains a strong advocate for the control of space debris to ensure the continued peaceful use and benefit of space for humanity. This consistent theme throughout its previous White Papers is enhanced here with more specificity in two main areas. First, space debris and the corresponding technology. Second, an improved regulatory scheme for imposing more stringent requirements.

Regarding space debris, China proposes to advance its interests through a series of efforts. First, an advancement of new technologies. As a precursor to operations, China highlights that it intends to improve its space debris monitoring systems and SSA, to improve cataloging of existing objects in space and providing early warning services to prevent collisions and the resulting debris.[1005] Second, China specifies its interests in developing technologies that will allow it to conduct in-orbit service and maintenance of spacecraft, thus extending their useful life and preventing them from becoming useless debris.[1006] When that is not possible, China has indicated its interest in 'space debris cleaning', presumably through methods of active debris removal, though it does not specifically use that term.[1007]

Importantly, the effort to respond to the prevention and mitigation of space debris will require a more stringent regulatory scheme. That is a second area that China has highlighted in the White Paper to specifically improve. Critically, it points out that it intends to finally produce a national space law and a space legal system. This is an issue that was identified earlier; that they lack both a national level program and the regulatory scheme they do have exists at very low levels of government. China's specific commitment to 'speed up the formulation of a national space law' will likely be well received in the international community and will finally place China's program on legal par with its peer-nation counterparts.[1008]

China also highlights its continued adherence to the IADC Space Debris Mitigation Guidelines and to the UN COPUOS LTS Guidelines, both of which advocate for mitigation and prevention of debris during all stages of space planning, flight, and post-mission operations.[1009] China further advocates for setting goals beyond the efforts of its peers. Specifically, China has indicated that it intends to apply upper stage passivation to all its carrier rockets, which is a significant contribution toward the effort of reducing debris overall.[1010]

1005 *Id.* at § II(7).
1006 *Id.* at § II(6).
1007 *Id.* at § II(6).
1008 *Id.* at § V(5).
1009 *Id.* at § II(7).
1010 *Id.*

Consistent with its theme overall of being a global leader in the space environment, the 2021 White Paper is a considerable evolution from previous versions. It arguably contains more specificity, more advanced goals, and with a new regulatory scheme, a significant improvement in how China provides oversight at the senior level to its space program. Considering the advancement of technologies which utilize outer space generally, this is no surprise. Nor is it a surprise that China is expending more effort in this area, considering its clear domestic and national security interests in the continued advancements in space. This White Paper is yet another reflection of China's commitment to space, and its attention to space debris mitigation and prevention is a very positive element of its goals.

6.6 *Words versus Actions—Are the Chinese Actually Committed to the Space Sustainability Discussed in Their White Papers?*

Though the Chinese addressed space debris directly in the 2016 White Paper and demonstrated a different 'tone' to their actions, their actual behavior has not necessarily aligned with some of their White Paper policy positions. Importantly, even in the years leading up to its 2016 White Paper, China continued to appear to maintain ASAT technology as part of its counter-nation conflict strategy. Irrespective of the backlash from the 2007 ASAT test, China pressed forward with what appeared to be advanced ASAT technologies. For example, it is alleged by the United States Department of State that China conducted another (non-destructive) ASAT test in 2014.[1011] Additional ASAT tests were noted both before and after publication of the 2016 White Paper, with new higher orbit suspected ASAT missile tests in 2015, 2016, 2017, and 2018.[1012] And these are only the tests that the United States publicly alleges.

There are other suspicious tests which were also likely ASAT tests. For example, in 2010, China launched what they labeled a "ground-based midcourse missile interception technology" against a ground-launched ballistic missile target.[1013] In early 2013, China again executed a 'mid-course missile interception

1011 Marcia Smith, *U.S. Accuses China of Conducting Another ASAT Test*, SPACEPOLICYONLINE.COM (July 25, 2014, 12:00 AM), https://spacepolicyonline.com/news/u-s-accuses-china-of-conducting-another-asat-test/#:~:text=The%20full%20statement%20from%20the,missile%20designed%20to%20destroy%20satellites.

1012 *Space Threat 2018: China Assessment*, AEROSPACE (Apr. 12, 2018), https://aerospace.csis.org/space-threat-2018-china/.

1013 Brian Weeden, *Anti-Satellite Tests in Space—The Case of China*, SECURE WORLD FOUNDATION, https://swfound.org/media/115643/china_asat_testing_fact_sheet_aug_2013.pdf (updated Aug. 16, 2013).

test' which resembled the 2007 and 2010 ASAT system tests.[1014] Potentially more disturbing is that in mid-June of 2013, China launched a rocket to over 10,000 km that they called a 'high-altitude scientific experiment' that released a canister of barium powder.[1015] While their scientific explanation may be true, there were some who insist that the launch was simply another ASAT test, showing China's continued development of rocket technology aimed at destroying satellites orbiting as high as the geosynchronous orbit[1016] Overall, it is assessed that China is regularly testing new higher orbit ASAT missiles.[1017] However, it is also true that while China continues its development and testing of these technologies, it appears they have not conducted an ASAT test resulting in debris since the 2007 test.

Meanwhile, China has not publicly acknowledged the existence of any new ASAT tests since the 2007 ASAT test. However, the evidence of their launches, the influence of the military over the Chinese space program, and the writings of Chinese academics all tend to support the theory that China views the development of ASAT systems as critical to its strategic plans against any superpower such as Russia or the United States.[1018] Most likely, China has assessed that the Achilles heel of the United States is space-based technology which gives it a military and diplomatic advantage.[1019] Any successful direct conflict with the United States likely will require minimizing the influence of these US

1014 *Id.*

1015 *Id. See also* Mike Gruss, *Pentagon Says 2013 Chinese Launch May Have Tested Antisatellite Technology*, SPACE NEWS (May 14, 2015), https://spacenews.com/pentagon-says-2013-chinese-launch-may-have-tested-antisatellite-technology/.

1016 Weeden, *supra* note 1013. This was later confirmed to be a believed ASAT test in public statement as the US position, notably by Air Force Lt. Gen. Jay Raymond, in 2015. *See* Colin Clark, *Chinese ASAT Test was "Successful:" Lt. Gen. Raymond*, BREAKING DEFENSE (Apr. 14, 2015, 6:34 PM), https://breakingdefense.com/2015/04/chinese-asat-test-was-successful-lt-gen-raymond/.

1017 *Space Threat 2018: China Assessment*, *supra* note 1012.

1018 According to Sandra Erwin of Space News, Chinese scholars have exerted considerable effort to outline the need to 'destroy, damage, or interfere with the enemy's reconnaissance and communications satellites, including navigation and early warning, to blind and deafen the enemy.' These academics, coupled with the military's strategic goals, make Chinese ASAT ambitions logical to achieve a strategic and tactical advantage in any conflict. Sandra Erwin, *Pentagon Report: China's Space Program "Continues to Mature Rapidly"*, SPACE NEWS (Aug. 20, 2018), https://spacenews.com/pentagon-report-chinas-space-program-continues-to-mature-rapidly/.

1019 Andrew Sveda, *The U.S. Military's Achilles Heel*, OBSERVER (Sept. 23, 2019), https://ndsmcobserver.com/2019/09/the-u-s-militarys-achilles-heel/. *See also* FRANK A. ROSE, MANAGING CHINA'S RISE IN OUTER SPACE 5 (Apr. 2020), https://www.brookings.edu/wp-content/uploads/2020/04/FP_20200427_china_outer_space_rose_v3.pdf.

advantages. ASAT technology probably figures heavily into the Chinese strategic calculus.[1020] If this is the case, the concern would be that for a near-term advantage, China may be willing to sacrifice the long-term sustainability of space for everyone (even itself) and render some altitudes and orbits almost completely inaccessible.

7 Conclusion—the Future of China's Space Program

Without question China is making extraordinary strides in space exploration. As recently as 23 November 2020, the launch of the Change'e-5 mission, and its apparent wild success in returning Moon soil and rocks in under 3 weeks, is a testament to the technological ability of China.[1021] Much of this, as noted by Professor Tronchetti, is likely due to four major factors. The Chinese are investing heavily in space and space-related activities; China has the capabilities to offer services globally; China is beginning efforts toward some privatization of space activities; and, there is interest developing in the rest of the world to engage in space commerce with the Chinese.[1022]

As discussed, potentially hindering achieving total success in all four areas for China is the lack of a unified national space law. However, efforts are ongoing to finalize one, which has been in development for several years. According to Professor Yeshchuk and Ms. Vasina, the 'model' Chinese law will need to

---

1020 Some analysts believe that the United States is not up to the task of winning a high-end conflict, which encourages countries like China to develop these ASAT types of weapons systems. According to David Ochmanek, a RAND think tank warfare analyst, and Robert Work, a former deputy Secretary of Defense, the US space-based systems would be crippled, which serve as the "brain and the nervous system that connects all of these [military] pieces" together. If they were to be destroyed, the likely outcome is that the "aggressor force often obliterates US stealth fighters on the runway, sends US warships to the depths, destroys US bases, and takes out critical US military systems." *See* Ryan Pickrell, *The U.S. Has Been Getting "it's ass Handed to it" in War Games Simulating Fights Against Russia and China*, BUSINESS INSIDER (Mar. 8, 2019, 10:26 AM), https://www.businessinsider.com/the-us-apparently-gets-its-ass-handed-to-it-in-war-games-2019-3.

1021 Kim Lyons, *China's Chang'e 5 Completes Docking Mission on its way Back to Earth*, THE VERGE (Dec. 5, 2020, 5:54 PM), https://www.theverge.com/2020/12/5/22156311/china-change-5-docking-mission-moon-lunar-samples. *See also* Leonard David, *China's Chang'e 5 Moon Samples are Headed to the Lab*, SPACE.COM https://www.space.com/china-chang-e-5-moon-samples-lab (last visited Jan. 14, 2020).

1022 Tronchetti, *supra* note 882 at 8.

address a series of foundational concerns.[1023] It must comply with the norms of international space law; it must standardize all aspects of aerospace activities; and it must introduce a system of administration of all aspects of space operations, promote privatization, and advance China's overall national goals.[1024]

While this may seem straightforward, even the development of a national law has its challenges. It is noted that the military may see much of the space operations and administration as something that should fall within their purview.[1025] The more it is handed over to civilians and private companies, the more the program becomes less secretive.[1026] That has created, at least in some assessments, a fear among the Chinese military that they will lose influence over the Chinese space program compared to the civilian sector.[1027] Where the CCP will fall on the final determination will likely have a huge impact on the success of China's space efforts going forward. In the interim, however, several significant and impactful regulations and requirements continue to allow China to advance its program while still demonstrating some respect for the environment.

Meanwhile, there is reason for caution. The continued ASAT tests demonstrate that the policy of China may not be entirely aligned with its stated goals. Furthermore, there is evidence to demonstrate a degree of carelessness even under its existing debris regulations. For example, as recently as May of 2020, China demonstrated a lack of control over a massive 21 metric-ton Long March 5B rocket, which entered uncontrolled into the Earth's atmosphere from LEO.[1028] In the rocket's last rotation over Los Angeles and New York in the United States, some of its pieces crossed and ultimately landed in Cote D'Ivoire in West Africa.[1029] And while it would likely be too early to assume that this degree of carelessness indicates a lack of adherence to its own stated

1023 Olga Yeshchuk & Anna Vasina, *Chinese Space Law: Problems and Areas of Reforming*, 3 Advanced Space L. 140 (2019), *available at* https://www.researchgate.net/publication/335597379_Chinese_Space_Law_Problems_and_Areas_of_Reforming.

1024 *Id.* (citing Xi Jinping, *Strengthening the Party's Leadership over the Rule of Law in a Comprehensive Manner*, (Feb. 15, 2019), http://www.xinhuanet.com/politics/2019-02/15/c_1124120391.htm (google translated)).

1025 *Id.* at 147.

1026 *Id.*

1027 *Id.*

1028 Loren Grush, *An Out-of-Control Rocket May Have Dumped Debris in Africa After Falling From Space*, The Verge (May 13, 2020 9:28 PM), 20, 2020 7:13 PM), https://www.theverge.com/2020/5/13/21256484/china-rocket-debris-africa-uncontrolled-reentry-long-march-5b (last visited Dec. 9 2021).

1029 *Id.*

responsibilities within its national policy, it is something to watch to determine if China's words versus actions deviate further in the future.

As the privatization of Chinese space programs sees continued growth, the activities of China toward environmental protection will likely continue to be one of the pillars of Chinese space operations. With the issuance this year of the next iteration of the Chinese space White Paper, we see China moving closer and closer to developing a national space law. The implementation of any national law will have a considerable impact on the degree to which companies moving forward will need to comply with standards. Additionally, such a development will help to identify potential areas of Chinese behavior which will support analysis going forward whether there are elements of customary international law that have formed. As discussed, with the establishment of a more mature legal regimen, China's State behavior will be more evident as well as the legal obligations they have imposed domestically. What the standards for China ultimately look like, and how that might affect the international regulatory regime for space debris, will be highly anticipated by the international community.

CHAPTER 6

Russia

1 Introduction[1030]

No discussion about the history of Russia's space aviation begins properly without acknowledging one of the all-time greatest accomplishments of mankind; the launching of a small, artificial satellite into orbit around Earth.[1031] And while other amazing feats by mankind would follow, such as Neil Armstrong's first steps on to the Moon, it is hard to completely capture the shock and awe around the world when, at 10:29 PM (Moscow time) on 4 October 1957, from Tyuratam launch base in the Kazakh Republic, this tiny satellite called Sputnik[1032] began its journey into outer space.[1033] Over the next four months, people on Earth could look up at the sky with binoculars and view the small metal object traveling at 18,000 miles an hour![1034] In January 1958, Sputnik deteriorated into Earth's atmosphere, but while it descended and burned up, the space age (and race) was now ascending with the Soviet Union firing a startling initial salvo.[1035]

A deep bench of brilliant scientists enabled the Soviet Union's technological leap from air to space flight. Considered the father of Soviet rocketry science, Konstantin E. Tsiolkovsky was a teacher, inventor, physicist, and aviation engineer.[1036] While rudimentary rockets had been in existence for thousands of

1030 Yuri Karash: "I am under the impression that the drafters of the (Russian 2030 Space) strategy were guided by the same principle as the housewife making a vegetable soup and thinking, 'I will put in all the veggies available, mix them, and hope that the soup will come out more or less decent.'" Victor Zaborskiy, *Russia: From Space Programs to Space Strategy*, SPACE News (May 2, 2012), https://spacenews.com/russia-space-programs-space-strategy/.

1031 *This Day in History: October 4*, HISTORY, https://www.history.com/this-day-in-history/sputnik-launched (last visited Jan. 15, 2021).

1032 In Russian, the word *Sputnik* comes from Russian спутник meaning "*companion of road*" or "*satellite*." *See* Louis de Gouyon Matignon, *Sputnik and the Birth of Space Law*, SPACE LEGAL ISSUES (Jan. 16, 2019), https://www.spacelegalissues.com/space-law-sputnik-and-the-birth-of-space-law/ (last visited Oct. 28, 2020).

1033 *This Day in History: October 4*, *supra* note 1031.

1034 *Id.*

1035 *Id.*

1036 Konstantin E. Tsiolkovsky, NASA (Sept. 22, 2010), https://www.nasa.gov/audience/foreducators/rocketry/home/konstantin-tsiolkovsky.html.

© KONINKLIJKE BRILL NV, LEIDEN, 2023 | DOI:10.1163/9789004535848_008

years,[1037] Tsiolkovsky used mathematics and physics to harness the knowledge necessary to study and model rocket dynamics.[1038] By the time of Tsiolkovsky's death in 1935, many other Soviet scientists had built on his contributions in the field of rocket science. Friedrich A. Tsander developed the idea of using the rocket ship components as fuel.[1039] Yuri V. Kondratyuk developed the idea of aerodynamically braking a rocket returning from a space voyage.[1040] And, Nikolai Rynin was a prolific publisher of treatises on aeronautics.[1041] Through the late 1920s and early 1930s, these scientists had published and shared enormous technical advances among themselves and other scientists while advancing the field of rocket propulsion and space flight.[1042] Meanwhile, other scientists, such as Valentin P. Glushko, were putting those concepts and designs into action developing rocket engines. From humble beginnings of 110 pounds of thrust in early rockets, Soviet efforts by 1933 demonstrated varying fuel combinations resulting in thrusts of almost 2000 pounds in some rocket models and an ability to achieve altitudes of almost six miles by 1935.[1043]

Recognizing the applications presented by the quickly developing technology, the Soviet government, and especially the military, showed great interest in the accomplishments of these rocket scientists. By 1934, the Soviets had organized a government-sponsored rocket research program well ahead of its

---

1037 The first reported use of true rockets was in the early 1200s. According to NASA, during the battle of Kai-Keng, the Chinese were able to succeed against the Mongol invaders by firing large amounts of 'arrows of flying fire.' They were described as a tube capped at one end and filled with gunpowder and a small opening at the other end. Once tied to a stick with a fuse, the rocket flew forward as would be commonly understood today. Their destructive effects are largely unknown (their sheer velocity might have been particularly damaging in flight if colliding with a target, but otherwise unlikely a serious weapon of mass destruction). However, the inception led to many advancements through the 12th century. Others took the concept and attempted to advance it further, ultimately creating versions that supported everything from war (rocket-bombs) to entertainment (fireworks). *See Brief History of Rockets*, NASA, https://www.grc.nasa.gov/www/k-12/TRC/Rockets/history_of_rockets.html#:~:text=The%20date%20reporting%20the%20first,of%20a%20solid%2Dpropellant%20rocket (last visited Oct. 11, 2020). *See also* Major Burton "Ernie" Catledge, *Space History*, *in* AU-18 SPACE PRIMER, 1 (2009).

1038 Tsiolkovsky, *supra* note 1036.

1039 STAFF OF THE COMM. ON ASTRONAUTICS AND SPACE EXPLORATION, 58TH CON. REP. ON SPACE HANDBOOK: ASTRONAUTICS AND ITS APPLICATIONS AT SECTION IV. ASTRONAUTICS IN OTHER COUNTRIES, *available at* https://history.nasa.gov/conghand/astrussr.htm.

1040 *Id.*

1041 *Id.*

1042 *Id.*

1043 *Id.*

competitors, leading the German development by five years and the United States Army by at least eight years.[1044] The onset of World War II in 1939 provided fertile development grounds for advancing Soviet technology even further, enhanced by pilfered German technology after the war, such as the state-of-the-art German V-2 rockets.[1045] The intellectual property transfer from the Germans to the Soviets post-WWII allowed the Soviets to advance existing V-2 technology to increase the thrust by 22,000 pounds (increasing the travel distance from 200 to 700 miles) and develop a separate super-rocket engine boasting 265,000 pounds of thrust.[1046]

Within four years after the conclusion of World War II, the Soviets were able to parlay their rocket advancements into upper atmosphere rocket programs.[1047] By May of 1957, that allowed a Soviet rocket to raise an instrument payload of 4,840 pounds to an altitude of 131 miles above Earth facilitating the launch of Sputnik just five months later.[1048] The rest is history.

2 Russian Interpretation of International Law Influencing Russian Space Law

Discussed more thoroughly in earlier chapters, Russia's prolific activity in space made it a key partner in developing future space law, especially the Outer Space Treaty. The need for the treaty was a natural consequence of the success of their space activity coupled with the advent of the space race in which the United States and Soviet Union suddenly found themselves engaged. Beginning in the 1950s and through the early 1960s, the ongoing discussions about what should be allowed in the use of outer space were under continuous debate. The United States and its allies wanted to focus on the peaceful and scientific purposes of

1044 *Id.*

1045 *Id.*

1046 *Id. See also* Carolyn Collins Petersen, *A Short History of Roscosmos and the Soviet Space Program*, ThoughtCo (Jul. 3. 2019), https://www.thoughtco.com/soviet-space-program-history-4140631. *See also* Anatoly Zak, *The Russian Space Agency, Roskosmos*, RussiaSpaceWeb.com, 1 (last updated Sept. 18, 2018), http://russianspaceweb.com/roskosmos.html.

1047 Staff of the Comm. On Astronautics and Space Exploration, 58th Con. Rep. on Space Handbook: Astronautics and its Applications at Section iv. Astronautics in Other Countries, *available at* https://history.nasa.gov/conghand/astrussr.htm.

1048 *Id.*

space.[1049] However, the Soviets had already sent up Sputnik by 1957 and had further (secret) designs on more capable ballistic missiles and other artificial satellites.[1050] The result is that the Soviets were publicly[1051] very disinterested in agreeing to any limitations on the use of space without clear definitions of what that would mean for their space program.[1052] Through 1963, a number of United Nations resolutions tried to initiate a dialogue on the necessity of formal discussions, and hopefully formal documents, that would address the contentiousness with the Soviet Union.[1053]

Ultimately, on 27 January 1967, after years of discussion among the major space powers, the Soviets signed the final version of the Outer Space Treaty and obligated itself to the accompanying requirements and limitations. Following that, the Soviet Union signed three more of the five major international space treaties: the Rescue Agreement, the Liability Convention, and the Registration Convention. Like almost all major spacefaring countries, the Soviet Union declined to sign the fifth international space treaty, the Moon Agreement.[1054]

Although the Soviets signed these agreements, and other 'activity-focused' space treaties such as the Limited Test Ban Treaty of 1963,[1055] it would be impossible to paint with a precise brushstroke a clear picture of modern-day Russia's perspective on its resulting international law obligations in space operations. According to Professor Leon Lipson, former Paul C. Tsai Professorial Lecturer in Law at Yale, in some areas, Russia has demonstrated a persona as a hardened

---

1049 Daryl Kimball, *The Outer Space Treaty at a Glance, Fact Sheets & Briefs*, ARMS CONTROL ASSOCIATION, (Last updated Oct. 2020), https://www.armscontrol.org/factsheets/outerspace#:~:text=UN%20Resolution%201962%20set%20out,General%20Assembly%20in%20June%201966 (last visited Oct. 28, 2020).

1050 *Id.*

1051 *Id.* (Indicating the Russian hesitance to sign on to any treaty without fully understanding what would be prohibited in light of its at-the-time secret progress on Sputnik and ballistic missiles).

1052 *Id. See also* Casandra Steer, *Global Commons, Cosmic Commons: Implications of Military and Security Uses of Outer Space*, 18 GEORGETOWN J. INT'L AFFAIRS 9, 10 (2017). Ms. Steer discusses that a combination of events, such as nuclear testing in outer space (Starfish Prime), caused both superpowers to recognize that while achieving superiority in space had enormous benefits, weaponization of space could be equally disastrous for both.

1053 Kimball, *supra* note 1049.

1054 *International Legal Agreements Relevant to Space Weapons*, UNION OF CONCERNED SCIENTISTS (Feb. 11, 2004), https://www.ucsusa.org/resources/legal-agreements-space-weapons. *See also* NATALIIA R. MALYSHEVA, SPACE LAW AND POLICY IN THE POST-SOVIET STATES 15 (2018).

1055 Treaty Banning Nuclear Weapon Tests in the Atmosphere, in Outer Space and Under Water ("Test Ban Treaty"), 480 U.N.T.S. 6964, Oct. 10, 1963, *available at* https://www.ourdocuments.gov/doc.php?flash=false&doc=95.

advocate, arguing for specific and precise treaty law with no ambiguity.[1056] In other areas, Russia is a vociferous objector to any international regulation, arguing that any interpretation that would impinge on the sovereignty of the State would be fundamentally illegal.[1057] In attempting to walk both sides of the line, Russia appears to be 'consistently inconsistent.' In turn, Russia has been equally quick to share barbs with the rest of the international community when it finds it suitable.[1058] But Russia's approach to international law can be partially credited to the Soviet Union's experience through and after the Bolshevik revolution under Vladimir Lenin. These Bolsheviks would ultimately become the Communist Party of the Soviet Union and shape the experience and behaviors of the Soviet Union (and later Russia) in the international community.[1059]

2.1 *Overview of Russian Approach to International Law*

The Russian Revolution, beginning on 8 March 1917, was the result of compounding economic, political and social failures in Russia.[1060] The Russian king, Czar Nicholas Romanov had failed, despite promises from the early 1900s, to improve conditions, and the impact of World War One had only exacerbated already overwhelming suffering in all aspects of Russian life.[1061] Between 8 and 11 March 1917, uprisings among the people ultimately led the Duma (Russia's Parliament) to create a provisional government on 12 March 1918.[1062] Within a

---

1056 Leon S. Lipson, *The Soviet View on International Law*, 61 INT'L L. STUD. 101, 101–103, https://digital-commons.usnwc.edu/cgi/viewcontent.cgi?article=1831&context=ils#:~:text=Current%20Soviet%20foreign%20policy%20is,policies%20may%20have%20been%20abandoned.&text=Thus%20every%20utterance%20from%20a,the%20source%20must%20be%20considered. *See also* Frans G. von der Dunk, *Two New National Space Laws: Russia and South Africa*, Proceedings of the Forty-Eighth Colloquium on the Law of Outer Space, 251, 253 (1995), *available at* https://digitalcommons.unl.edu/cgi/viewcontent.cgi?article=1046&context=spacelaw.

1057 Lipson, *supra* note 1056 at 101–103. *See also* Brian Zachary Mund, In Defense of Sovereignty: An Analysis of Russian Voting Behavior in the United Nations Security Council (1995–2012) (Arp. 1, 2013) (B.A. thesis, University of Pennsylvania), *available at* https://repository.upenn.edu/cgi/viewcontent.cgi?article=1188&context=curej.

1058 Lipson, *supra* note 1056 at 101–103.

1059 *This Day in History, March 9, 1918, Russian Bolshevik Party Becomes the Community Party*, HISTORY (Nov. 6, 2019, last updated Nov. 12, 2019), https://www.history.com/this-day-in-history/russian-bolshevik-party-becomes-the-communist-party.

1060 *Russian Revolution*, HISTORY (Nov. 9, 2009, last updated Feb. 28, 2020), https://www.history.com/topics/russia/russian-revolution (last visited Oct. 12, 2020).

1061 *Id.*

1062 *Id.*

few days, Czar Romanov had abdicated the throne.[1063] The Duma immediately attempted to implement a number of social reforms, including a liberal program of freedom of speech, legal equality, and support to unions.[1064] However, these reforms were insufficient to quell the unrest in Russia.[1065] By November of the same year, Vladimir Lenin led a coup d'état against the Duma and ultimately ousted the Duma while concurrently implementing a Communist State.[1066] By 1922, despite challenges to his rule, both internally and from external influences, Lenin consolidated power and established the Soviet Union.[1067]

It is important to appreciate that the challenges to Lenin's power consolidation were not just from internal threats. Professor Lipson further identified that some of the challenges were from external influences, including some 14 States in the course of the five years from 1917 to 1922.[1068] Reasons varied, including continuing the war against Germany, protecting foreign assets in the country, and opposing Lenin generally.[1069] But regardless of the reason, Lenin and the Bolsheviks took cues on the status of international relationships.[1070] Their observations led them to find some common ground to support economic partnership, territorial sovereignty, and social accommodation among fellow countries.[1071] However, many of the agreements the Soviets made, according to Professor Lipson, focused on respecting international rules when it suited them and otherwise ignoring them, and their international partners, when laws inconvenienced the goals of the State.[1072] The 'consistently-inconsistent' activities of the Soviets in the early formative years of post-Soviet rebellion marked a general practice by the Soviet Union of taking what it liked and rejecting that which it did not.[1073] A second trait of early Soviet international law was to treat international law as an inherent system of tension, such that at times it is cooperative and collaborative.[1074] At other times, it conflicts and creates a struggle.[1075] Ultimately, according to Professor Lipson, the constant

1063 *Id.*
1064 *Id.*
1065 *Id.*
1066 *Id.*
1067 *Id.*
1068 Lipson, *supra* note 1056 at 102.
1069 *Id.*
1070 *Id.*
1071 *Id.*
1072 *Id.*
1073 *Id.*
1074 *Id.*
1075 *Id.*

tension facilitated the creation of treaty relations, recognition of international contracts and exchange of goods, and allowed the Soviet Union to engage in the international community, but still retain the Leninist façade of the proletariat holding the true power within the country.[1076]

Through the 1970s, the Soviet Union remained resistant to many of the obligations of international law unless it was specifically beneficial,[1077] and even then was still viewed domestically as only holding limited importance.[1078] Instead, the Soviet approach to international law relied on the doctrine of transformation, allowing it to retain influence in the international community by being a signatory on numerous international documents, but avoiding implementing some or all of them by a principle that they would only hold force if they were separately recognized by the Soviet legislature.[1079] This is often referred to as a 'dualist' approach to governance, defined by a system in which "no treaties have the status of law in the domestic legal system; all treaties require implementing legislation to have domestic legal force."[1080]

But the 1980s to early 1990s saw a greater recognition of international norms and values, likely credited to the Soviet's Perestroika shift. Beginning in 1986, Perestroika was a program led by the Soviet Union's President, Mikhail Gorbachev, which involved shedding the legacy (and chains) of the Leninist totalitarian State model which was choking the country to death.[1081] Instead, the Soviet Union began a shift to a program of economic, political, and social restructuring.[1082] While initially a program of limited success, its impact allowed for at least some private ownership among Soviets and enabled greater

---

1076 *Id.*

1077 Dr. Gennady Danilenko notes, for example, that the "former Soviet Union never considered international law, especially international law of human rights, as something that might be invoked before, and enforced by, its domestic courts. Furthermore, the 1977 USSR Constitution did not allow the direct operation of international law within the domestic setting." GENNADY M. DANILENKO, IMPLEMENTATION OF INTERNATIONAL LAW IN RUSSIA AND OTHER CIS STATES 2 (1998), *available at* https://www.nato.int/acad/fellow/96-98/danilenk.pdf.

1078 *Id.*

1079 *Id.* at 3.

1080 David Sloss, *Domestic Application of Treaties*, SANTA CLARA L. DIGITAL COMMONS, 2–3 (Apr. 29, 2011), https://digitalcommons.law.scu.edu/cgi/viewcontent.cgi?article=1620&context=facpubs#:~:text=Used%20in%20this%20sense%2C%20dualist,to%20give%20effect%20to%20them.

1081 *Revelations from the Russian Archives, Perestroika, in* Library of Congress Soviet Archives, https://www.loc.gov/exhibits/archives/pere.html.

1082 *Id.*

access international goods and services (and consequently the influence of the international norms).[1083]

2.2 *Modern Russian Approach to International Law*

By 1991, the Soviet Union was dissolving and was now the Russian Federation.[1084] Its new Constitution, Article 15(1) (pre-2020 version) provided that, "the Constitution of the Russian Federation shall have supreme juridical force, direct action, and shall be used on the whole territory of the Russian Federation."[1085] Regarding international law, within the same paragraph, Article 15(4) stated that "universally-recognized norms of international law and international treaties and agreements of the Russian Federation shall be a part of its legal system. If an international treaty or agreement of the Russian Federation fixes other rules than those envisaged by law, the rules of the international agreement shall be applied."[1086]

There is now yet another shift in Russia with the current President, Vladimir Putin, pushing modifications to the Russian Constitution that will no longer recognize international law as 'supreme' to the Constitution.[1087] Specifically,

---

1083 *Id.*

1084 *Russian Federation's Constitution of 1993 with Amendments Through 2008*, CONSTITUTEPROJECT.ORG, (1993, updated 2008), https://www.constituteproject.org/constitution/Russia_2008.pdf.

1085 Konstitutsiia Rossiĭskoĭ Federatsii [Konst. RF] [Constitution] art. 15(1) (Russia) *available at* http://www.constitution.ru/en/10003000-02.htm.

1086 *Id. See also* Sloss, *supra* note 1080 at 2–3. Interestingly, as discussed earlier, Russia now reflects a dualist system in the event that there is any conflict between international law and domestic law, or in the event that a new international law presents itself. However, in the period between 1991 and 2020, Russia reflected what Mr. Sloss would likely have argued was close to a version of the Monist state, which is one in which 'some treaties have the status of law in the domestic legal system, even in the absence of implementing legislation.' Russia post-2020 reflects something of a hybrid, such that, as discussed in the body, international law and treaties can be valid, arguably even absent domestic implementation, as long as they don't restrict the rights of Russians or contradict the Russian Constitution.

1087 Alexandra Svetlicinii, *Can Russia's Constitution be above International Law*, CGTN (Jan 20, 2020, 7:13 PM), https://news.cgtn.com/news/2020-01-20/Can-Russia-s-Constitution-be-above-international-law--NppxZNaSTS/index.html (last visited Oct. 12, 2020). *See also* Andrew Higgins, *The Theatrical Method in Putin's Vote Madness*, THE NEW YORK TIMES (Jul. 1, 2020), https://www.nytimes.com/2020/07/01/world/europe/putin-referendum-vote-russia.html. *See also* Morgan Lewis & Bockius LLP, *Russia Adopts Major Amendments to its Constitution* (Ju. 13, 2020), https://www.lexology.com/library/detail.aspx?g=9173f461-a6e0-4b5d-9964-c2632abc2fc6. *See also Attorney: Constitutional Amendment on International Law Could Give Russia a "Red Button"*, CURRENT TIME (Jun. 25, 2020), https://en.currenttime.tv/a/30690618.html.

President Putin stated that "I [Vladimir Putin] truly believe that ... requirements of international law and treaties as well as decisions of international bodies can be valid on the Russian territory only to the point that they do not restrict the rights and freedoms of our people and citizens and do not contradict our Constitution."[1088]

The net effect of this change is likely minimal. It is probable that if there was a true contradiction in international law, Russia would have either withdrawn from any corresponding treaty that was averse to its interests, never signed it in the first place, or otherwise largely ignored the provisions in its domestic policy.[1089] Why it is important, however, is that it arguably brings history full circle. As originally pointed out, the skepticism with which Lenin and the Bolsheviks approached international law, and the 'consistently inconsistent' approach, is now a renewed sentiment. The changing provisions in the Russian Constitution point to a renewed policy that Russia will support and follow international law ... as long as it is beneficial to the Russian people.[1090] Absent that, it is not to say that they will not still find ways to at least create a perception of adherence to certain agreements, but President Putin has made clear that there are very real limitations to Russia's compliance. If nothing else, what

---

1088 Svetlicinii, *supra* note 1087.

1089 *Id.*

1090 Recent events bear this out as well, from accusations of interference with US elections, the annexation of Crimea, alleged activities in Georgia, and separatist activity support in eastern Ukraine. *Russia Doesn't Just Violate International Law—It Follows and Shapes it Too*, THE CONVERSATION (Mar. 23, 2018, 10:38 AM), https://theconversation.com/russia-doesnt-just-violate-international-law-it-follows-and-shapes-it-too-92700. *See also* Abigail Abrams, *Here's What we Know so Far About Russia's 2016 Meddling*, TIME (Apr. 18, 2019, 8:20 AM), https://time.com/5565991/russia-influence-2016-election/, describing alleged actions of Russia to undermine the confidence in the 2016 elections and provide support to the candidacy of US President Donald Trump, seen as largely supportive of Putin's regime. *See also* Anastasia Mgaloblishvili, *Russian Interference in Georgia's Elections, How Will the Government Respond*, NEW EASTERN EUROPE (Sept. 28, 2020), https://neweasterneurope.eu/2020/09/28/russian-interference-in-georgias-elections-how-will-the-government-respond/, discussing interfering in the elections of Georgia as well as creating constant instability operations in the region. *See also* Sam Sokok, *Russian Disinformation Distorted Reality in Ukraine. Americans Should Take Note*, FOREIGN POLICY (Aug. 2, 2019, 4:40 PM), https://foreignpolicy.com/2019/08/02/russian-disinformation-distorted-reality-in-ukraine-americans-should-take-note-putin-mueller-elections-antisemitism/, describing Russia's alleged efforts to distort Ukrainian perceptions and regional stability. Much of Russia's defense appears to rest on a 'hypocrisy' defense, accusing those who would otherwise try to take Russia to task for its activities of engaging in exactly the same type of behavior. *Russia Doesn't Just Violate International Law—It Follows and Shapes it too*, THE CONVERSATION (Mar. 23, 2018, 10:38 AM), https://theconversation.com/russia-doesnt-just-violate-international-law-it-follows-and-shapes-it-too-92700.

was likely a matter of Russian psychological skepticism towards international law borne from its history is now clearly out in the open as a Constitutional State position.

3 Russia's Domestic Implementation of Obligations under International Space Law

The narrowing of Russia's reception to international law and its applicability today demonstrates a preference for adherence to the UN Charter and UN Security resolutions beyond what would be considered simply international norms.[1091] Contrasting that perspective is the view of the West, which is generally more flexible and situational based, finding more opportunities for existing laws and norms to be interpreted to cover the activity versus requiring specific approval or consensus of the UN Security Council.[1092] Furthermore, the West's interpretation is expansive, including a host of commitments by leaders that constitute more political commitments than legal ones.[1093] This perspective supports at least one of the reasons for the recent Russian Constitutional changes.

Regardless, Russia today does value the United Nations, if for nothing else than Russia's perception that influence over countries within the United Nations equates to raw power and national prestige, two things President Putin values very highly. And, as discussed above, Russia is a party to four of the five major spacefaring treaties, excepting the Moon Agreement.[1094] Moreover, as

---

1091 Philip Remler, *Russia at the United Nations: Law, Sovereignty, and Legitimacy*, CARNEGIE ENDOWMENT FOR INT'L PEACE, 3–4 (Jan 22, 2020).

1092 *Id.*

1093 *Id.* at 4. Additionally, for general background on licensing, *see* Sergey P. Malkov & Catherine Doldirina, *Regulation of Space Activities in the Russian Federation, in* NATIONAL REGULATION OF SPACE ACTIVITIES Sec. 4, para. I & Section II, para. A (Ram S. Jakhu ed., 2010), *available at* https://doi.org/10.1007/978-90-481-9008-9_13.

1094 *Agreement Governing the Activities of States on the Moon and Other Celestial Bodies (Moon Agreement)*, NTI (last updated Oct. 26, 2011), https://www.nti.org/learn/treaties-and-regimes/agreement-governing-activities-states-moon-and-other-celestial-bodies-moon-agreement/. In fact, only 18 States are party to the Moon Agreement, none of which are major space programs. That is not to say that its spirit is dead, particularly with the recent signing by the United States and other allies of the Artemis Accords. While many of the sticking points with the Moon Agreement revolve around the potential exploitation of resources, the Artemis Accords are a good first step in establishing some multilateral agreements (short of international law, but potentially influential in the future). *See* Christopher Newman, *Artemis Accords: Why Many Countries are Refusing to Sign Moon Exploration Agreement*, THE CONVERSATION (Oct. 19, 2020, 7:45 AM),

a result of its international obligations, and its own advancements in space, Russia has undertaken to formally recognize and implement much of its international commitments into its own domestic law. Surprisingly, it has also begun instituting some non-binding guidance and principles as well, discussed more shortly, with a specific focus on Russia's attempts to address the threat posed by space debris and efforts to mitigate it.

3.1 *Russian Domestic Space Debris Regulatory Scheme*

The overarching regulatory space legislation is the *Law of the Russian Federation About Space Activity, Decree No. 5663–1* (as amended 15 April 2019[1095]). This body of law sets the foundational legal principles for space activities in the interest of encouraging efforts in space by scientific and industry partners to solve challenging problems facing the Russian Federation.[1096] And while this document does not address every aspect of space activity, it does lay down the legal and organizational foundations of space activities which fall under the jurisdiction of the Russian Federation.[1097]

In addition to identifying the executive structure of the Russian Space Program, it also establishes the current Russian space agency, Roskosmos, dictates licensing for space activities, establishes a fund to support and promote space science and industry, and covers technology development, use, and export, among many other responsibilities.[1098] Importantly, in all space activities, it recognizes the legal obligations under international law that Russia has agreed to. Therefore, Russian law prohibits any activity contrary to both its domestic and international legal commitments that fall under the jurisdiction of the Russian Federation.[1099] Accordingly, related to the environmental concerns of orbital debris, Russia provides clear guidance to prohibited activity which would potentially create damage to the environment.

---

https://theconversation.com/artemis-accords-why-many-countries-are-refusing-to-sign-moon-exploration-agreement-148134.

1095 Федеральный закон Российской Федерации о космической деятельности [The Law of the Russian Federation About Space Activities], ukazy [Decrees] Aug. 20, 1993 (as amended Apr. 15, 2019), No 5663–1, *available at* https://cis-legislation.com/document.fwx?rgn=1531.

1096 *Id.*

1097 *Id.*

1098 *Id.*

1099 *Id.* at art. 4(2). For a more detailed discussion of the additional aspects of the law related to liability, insurance, second-party partnerships, et cetera. *see* Frans von Der Dunk, *International Space Law, in* HANDBOOK OF SPACE LAW, *supra* note 513 at 146–147.

3.1.1 Russian Domestic Regulatory Scheme—Decree No. 5663–1, about Space Activities

Specifically, Decree No. 5663–1, Article 4, addresses environmental concerns. Article 4(1) states that space activities should be carried out in conformity with several principles, including, but not limited to, safely engaging in space activity and calls out the principles of safety including the 'protection of the environment.'[1100] For example, Article 4(1) discusses the need for international cooperation that is equal and mutually beneficial to the parties.[1101] The implication is that engagement in the behavior, such as that which would be detrimental to the environment, would logically be to the detriment of both parties. Additionally, Article 4(1) discusses that the development of space should be for scientific, social, and economic purposes to benefit the defense and safety of the Russian Federation. Again, while not clearly stating the importance of protecting the environment, it is impossible to imagine the advancement of any of these goals should the environment be polluted to such an extent that areas of space are rendered unusable.[1102]

One additional provision of the regulation that addresses environmental concerns of debris is Article 22. This article states that "space activities shall be performed taking into account levels of permissible anthropogenous[1103] loads on the environment and near-Earth space."[1104] While this does not specifically identify the limits that would constitute an impermissible 'load' on the environment, it does indicate a requirement that an assessment be done to determine the possible negative outcomes of excessive injection of material into the outer space environment that could ultimately constitute a debris threat to the environment and operations.

It is worth noting that the current version of Article 4 is a far cry from the specificity of protection to the environment provided by its predecessor.[1105] In the 2015 version, the Russian government clearly outlined prohibitions within

1100 Федеральный закон Российской Федерации о космической деятельности [The Law of the Russian Federation About Space Activities], *supra* note 1095 at art. 4(1).

1101 *Id.*

1102 *Id.*

1103 *Anthropogenic*, Free Dictionary, *available at* https://www.dictionary.com/browse/anthropogenic (last visited Jun. 24, 2021).

1104 Федеральный закон Российской Федерации о космической деятельности [The Law of the Russian Federation About Space Activities], *supra* note 1095 at art. 22(1).

1105 Федеральный закон Российской Федерации о космической деятельности [The Law of the Russian Federation About Space Activities], ukazy [Decrees] Aug. 20, 1993, No 5663–1, art. 4(2) (outdated), *available at* https://www.unoosa.org/oosa/en/ourwork/spacelaw/nationalspacelaw/russian_federation/decree_5663-1_E.html.

outer space and its commitments to many of the provisions of international law. Specifically, the prior version of Article 4(2) viewed the threat to the space environment from a strategic and ecological security perspective.[1106] It prohibited the creation of 'harmful contamination of outer space' which could lead to unfavorable changes in the environment.[1107] It also prohibited any deliberate destruction of a space object in outer space, which recognized the long-term damage that could occur as a result of such destructive activity.[1108] Additionally, it precluded the destructive elimination of space objects in outer space, as well as testing nuclear (or other kinds of weapons of mass destruction) in outer space, in addition to the general requirement prohibiting the placement of either in an orbit around Earth.[1109] Finally, section 4(2) held a general provision that any activity which is prohibited by international treaties of the Russian Federation was also prohibited.[1110] As stated above, much of this was in support of protecting the outer space environment from activity which could create additional debris. It is no longer included, nor does the 2019 update reshuffle these provisions, elsewhere within the law.[1111]

3.2 *Licensing in Russia*

The Federal Law of the Russian Federation of 4 May 2011, No. 99-FZ, *About Licensing of Separate Types of Activity* (as amended on 31 July 2020), is the overarching law that establishes the requirements and specific provisions for licensing certain activities and outlines the environmental concerns which must be addressed.[1112] As a general provision, Russian law requires licensing for any activity to ensure it is conducted in a way that prevents danger or damage to the rights, legitimate interests, life or health of citizens, the environment, objects of cultural heritage, defense, and safety of the people of the Russian

1106 *Id. See also* von der Dunk, *supra* note 1056 at 256.

1107 Федеральный закон Российской Федерации о космической деятельности [The Law of the Russian Federation About Space Activities], *supra* note 1105 at art. 4(2) (outdated).

1108 *Id.*

1109 *Id.*

1110 *Id.*

1111 At least one of the direct impacts of the removal of many of the prohibitions on destructive activities in Space by Russia was laid bare when the Russians engaged in an ASAT test on 15 November 2021 against their Cosmos 1408 satellite. Discussed more in depth in Chapter 8, the point is that the removal of the rules against destructive tests was shortly after exploited by the Russians to engage in such destructive behavior in space.

1112 Federal Law of the Russian Federation, About Licensing of Separate Types of Activity, No. 99-FZ, May 4, 2011 (as amended on 31 July 2020), https://cis-legislation.com/document.fwx?rgn=43154.

Federation.[1113] Among the list of activities requiring licensing, space activities are to be regulated by the Russian space agency, *Roskosmos*.[1114] [1115]

Roskosmos' responsibilities include both the development of space policy and commercial space projects, but also any other responsibilities as assigned by the Russian government.[1116] To carry out its responsibilities, Roskosmos

---

1113 *Id.* at art. 2(1).

1114 It is important to note that the requirements for licensing by Roskosmos are additionally identified in the origination document for Roskosmos itself, Федеральный закон Российской Федерации о Государственной корпорации космической деятельности [Federal Law of the Russian Federation on the State Corporation for Space Activities] Sobranie Zakonodatel'stva Rossiĭskoĭ Federatsii [SZ RF] [Russian Federation Collection of Legislation] Jul. 13, 2015, No. 215-FZ (with changes and additions of 30 August 2017, introduced by the Federal Law of 29 July 2017, No. 267-FZ). *See* Nataliia R. Malysheva, *Federal Space Program of Russia for 2016–2017*, *in* SPACE LAW AND POLICY IN THE POST-SOVIET STATES 149 (2018). The establishment of Roskosmos (a.k.a. the Russian Federal Space Agency), Article 7(11), established that Roskosmos' (referred to also as the "Corporation") powers and functions include conducting licensing of outer space activities and the maintenance of the register of issued licenses and license controls (in accordance with Russian Federation law). *See* Федеральный закон Российской Федерации о Государственной корпорации космической деятельности [Federal Law of the Russian Federation on the State Corporation for Space Activities] Sobranie Zakonodatel'stva Rossiĭskoĭ Federatsii [SZ RF] [Russian Federation Collection of Legislation] Jul. 13, 2015, No. 215-FZ (with changes and additions of 30 August 2017, introduced by the Federal Law of 29 July 2017, No. 267-FZ). It is also important to note that the implementation of Roskosmos in this role is not new to Russia. In fact, it is more recognizable as a return to the original model of all space responsibilities falling under one agency under government control. *See* Bruce McClintock, *The Russian Space Sector: Adaptation, Retrenchment, and Stagnation*, 10 SPACE & DEFENSE 3 (2017) *available at* https://www.rand.org/content/dam/rand/pubs/external_publications/EP60000/EP67235/RAND_EP67235.pdf. *See also* A.V. Shaskova, K.A. Polovchenko & A.G. Volevodz, *Questioning State Corporations as Special forms of Legal Entities*, 1 INT'L J. ECON. & BUS. ADMIN. 186, 198–200 (2019).

1115 Федеральный закон Российской Федерации о лицензировании отдельных видов деятельности [Federal Law of the Russian Federation About Licensing of Separate Types of Activities], *supra* note 1112 at art. 1(1.1). This is further identified by the provisions of those activities, which require licensing, 99-FZ, Article 12(55) which lists space activity as one of the specific activities requiring licensing. Thus, 99-FZ establishes that space activities require licensing and Roskosmos is the corporation authorized to engage in such licensing. The Law of the Russian Federation, 5663–1, *About Space Activities*, 20 August 1993 (as amended on 4 April 2019) also cross-references these responsibilities. Article 6 imposes the responsibility on the corporation on space activities, Roskosmos, to perform licensing of space activities. Article 9 states that space activities are subject to licensing according to the aforementioned law, 99-FZ.

1116 Федеральный закон Российской Федерации о Государственной корпорации космической деятельности [Federal Law of the Russian Federation on the State Corporation for Space Activities] Sobranie Zakonodatel'stva Rossiĭskoĭ Federatsii [SZ RF] [Russian Federation Collection of Legislation] Jul. 13, 2015, No. 215-FZ.

implemented a regulatory licensing scheme to ensure proper oversight of commercial space activities in accordance with the Order of the Government of the Russian Federation No. 298, *About Licensing Space Activities*.[1117]

Under regulation No. 298, Roskosmos implemented the procedures for licensing legal entities engaged in space activities occurring either within the territory of the Russian Federation or those areas for which the Russian Federation exercises jurisdiction.[1118] Additionally, in enacting both No. 298 as well as No. 5663–1, Russia established that the licensing requirements must meet both Russian Federal law and international law.[1119]

Under the licensing regime, an entity is required to submit an application to Roskosmos to obtain authorization to engage in activities in space.[1120] [1121] There are two major categories of activities that must be addressed under the licensing regime and cover a broad range of requirements from inception to mission completion.[1122] The first major category covers the spacecraft and components of launch.[1123] The second covers the services that accompany the

1117 Under regulation No. 298, Roskosmos implemented the procedures for licensing legal entities engaged in space activities occurring either within the territory of the Russian Federation or those areas for which the Russian Federation exercises jurisdiction. Order of the Government of the Russian Federation About Licensing of Space Activities, No. 298, Appendix, § II, para. 13 (Mar. 18, 2020, effective Apr. 18, 2020) (hereafter Licensing Space Activities Order) (invalidating the Order of the Government of the Russian Federation About Licensing of Space Activities, No. 160 (Feb. 22, 2012) (The Russian Federation Code 2012, No. 10, the Art. 1248)).

1118 *Id.*

1119 *Id. See also* Outer Space Treaty, *supra* note 234 at art. IV. *See also* Федеральный закон Российской Федерации о космической деятельности [The Law of the Russian Federation About Space Activities], ukazy [Decrees] Aug. 20, 1993 (as amended Aug. 12, 2020), No 5663–1, *available at* https://cis-legislation.com/document.fwx?rgn=1531.

1120 In accordance with Decree No. 5663–1, space activity is defined as any activity immediately connected with operations to explore and use outer space, including the Moon and other celestial bodies. Space activity shall include space research, remote sensing of Earth from outer space, navigation use, topographical and geodesic satellite systems, piloted space missions, manufacturing of materials and other products in outer space, and other kinds of activity perforce with the aid of space technology. Furthermore, space activity comprises creating as well as issuing and transferring of space techniques, space technology, other products and services necessary for carrying out space activity. *See* Федеральный закон Российской Федерации о космической деятельности [The Law of the Russian Federation About Space Activities], ukazy [Decrees] Aug. 20, 1993 (as amended Aug. 12, 2020), No 5663–1, art. 2, *available at* https://cis-legislation.com/document.fwx?rgn=1531.

1121 Order of the Government of the Russian Federation About Licensing of Space Activities, *supra* note 1117.

1122 *Id.* at Appendix, §§ I–II.

1123 *Id.* at Appendix, § I.

launch.[1124] There is a third category identified in the regulation, but this specifically highlights activities excluded from licensing such as research works and prototypes that are not intended for flight testing.[1125]

The first major category covers the types of work that require a license and includes four subcomponents. The first subcomponent focuses on the missile and space equipment itself, such as the type of rocket, the construction of the rocket, and the elements that comprise the system, including how the system functions overall.[1126] The second subcomponent covers the spacecraft and its elements.[1127] This includes whether it is automated or piloted, how it is fueled (solar, batteries, fuel, or combinations of energy sources), its methods of communication, as well as the life support systems for crewed craft.[1128] The third subcomponent covers the technical aspects of the land launch components (launch complex), including the equipment, devices, and systems of processing equipment and land infrastructure that supports the missile and space equipment.[1129] The final subcomponent covers 'miscellaneous' items that are otherwise not specifically identified in the prior three subcomponents or that are not principle to the spacecraft or missile system.[1130]

The second category requiring licensing is for services that are provided to implement the space activity. These are primarily focused on the support activities not related to the actual rocket or the spacecraft. For example, much of the focus is on the elements of preparation for injecting the rocket into outer space as well as the plan for its removal from space after mission, such as services focused on determining the trajectories of the rocket and spacecraft.[1131] Additionally, a second aspect of services focuses on the training required for space activity, in particular the training of the crew for those spacecraft which will be manned.[1132] Finally, activity such as the services for the land centers that manage the flights, inspection services covering the launch and control locations, as well as the services for development and testing of the equipment, are all covered aspects requiring licensing.[1133]

1124 *Id.* at Appendix, § II.
1125 *Id.* at Appendix, § III.
1126 *Id.* at Appendix, § I, para. 1.
1127 *Id.* at Appendix, § I, para. 2.
1128 *Id.*
1129 *Id.* at Appendix, § I, para. 3.
1130 *Id.* at Appendix, § I, para. 4.
1131 *Id.* at Appendix, § II, para. 7.
1132 *Id.* at Appendix, § II, para. 18.
1133 *Id.* at Appendix, § II, para. 13.

Compared to other licensing regimes, such as the United States, the Russian licensing regime is rather broad, allowing room for companies engaged in space operations to be more general in their descriptions. However, the ambiguity is also intended to encourage companies to provide the most information possible in the application for Roskosmos to analyze, versus the alternative. Additionally, the licensing regime should not be viewed in a vacuum. The parent document, 99-FZ, precludes licenses being issued for activity that would cause danger or damage to Russian values … including the environment.[1134] With this in mind, the descriptions a company must provide for licenses must also address the concerns expressed in 99-FZ that the environment not be damaged.[1135] Further, the 'environment' in 99-FZ is not limited to the confines of Earth.[1136] Therefore, since space activity requires licensing, the principles of 99-FZ apply to outer space as well.[1137] Thus, without specifically outlining a requirement to discuss the creation of space debris as part of the license request, it is fair to assume that debris is still a covered subject, even if not specifically enumerated.

3.3 *Principal Space Debris Regulation—GOST P 52925–2018*

To its credit, Russia has a specific regulation to inform space operators of the risk posed by space debris and the requirements for implementing space debris mitigation efforts. GOST P 52925-2018,[1138] *General Requirements for Space Assets to Limit Man-Made Clogging of Near-Earth Space,* sets forth the programmatic requirements, as the name implies, for reducing the amount of artificial material injected into space resulting from Russian activity.[1139] The standards contained in the 2018 version are not retroactive, and apply only to newly created and modernized space assets of 'scientific, socio-economic (including deep space exploration), commercial and special (defense) purposes.'[1140]

1134 федеральный закон рф о лицензировании отдельных видов деятельности [Federal Law of the Russian Federation About Licensing of Separate Types of Activity], *supra* note 1112 at art. 2(1).

1135 *Id.*

1136 *Id.*

1137 *Id.*

1138 GOST R 52925-2008 was originally approved on 9 June 2008, as "Space Technology Items. General Requirements for Mitigation of Near-Earth Space Debris Population." *See* GOST R 52925-2008, Space Technology Items. General Requirements for Mitigation of Near-Earth Space Debris Population, *available at* https://www.russiangost.com/p-61067-gost-r-52925-2008.aspx. It was superseded on 21 September 2018 by GOST R 52925-2018, "Space Technology Products. General Requirements for Space Assets to Limit Man-Made Clogging of Near-Earth Space."

1139 GOST P 52925-2018, *supra* note 1138 at § 1: Scope.

1140 *Id.*

Additionally, it applies to all stages of the operation of a space vehicle, from design to post-mission disposal.[1141]

Importantly, the regulation defines the Russian understanding of the parameters of space. Among them, defining near-Earth outer space at 100 km (referred to as the Karman Line,[1142] discussed earlier in Chapter 2, section 2.1.[1143] Additionally, a space object (referenced in the regulation as 'KO') is a body of artificial origin located in near-Earth space.[1144] It then provides clarity between functioning (active) and non-functioning (debris) objects. Space debris (referenced in the regulation as 'CM') is defined as all artificial space objects in LEO (including fragments or parts of such objects) that have finished their active functioning.[1145] Contrast that with the active operation of a space object which is the functioning of a space object in orbit in accordance with its intended purpose.[1146] Finally, man-made clogging is defined as the process of creating new objects that replenish the composition of existing space debris in near-Earth space.[1147]

3.3.1 Debris Reduction through Design

GOST P 52925-2018, Section 5, addresses the core cause of man-made debris in the perception of the Russians. The regulation lists out a series of debris-causing events that contribute to the clogging of the space environment. This includes explosions of space objects, self-destruction, ejection of materials in the course of operations (such as springs, pyro-bolts, et cetera.), collisions, unburned fuel emissions, material erosion of parts of the spacecraft into the atmosphere, and the ejection of materials as a result of supporting life and operations in manned spacecraft.[1148] To combat this formation, Section 5 outlines recommendations to minimize the amount of material that can cause debris to be injected into space. The regulation states that the goal is to exclude debris formation in the space environment.[1149]

1141 *Id.*

1142 Drake, *supra* note 191.

1143 GOST P 52925-2018, *supra* note 1138 at para. 3.1.

1144 *Id.* at para. 3.6.

1145 *Id.* at para. 3. 5. This definition is similar to those of most international bodies and debris mitigation guidelines. It also closely aligns with the US definition of "all man-made (read 'artificial') objects in orbit about Earth which no longer serve a useful purpose" (read '*which have finished their active functioning*'). For further comparison, refer to Chapter 1 discussion on 'What is Space Debris.'

1146 *Id.* at para. 3.6.

1147 *Id.* at para. 3.8.

1148 *Id.* at para. 5.1.

1149 *Id.* at para. 5.1.

Short of complete success, GOST P 52925-2018 establishes a series of expected actions to minimize debris creation. First, prevention of the formation of debris in the course of regular operations of the space object, likely implying through the design of the space object.[1150] Second, reducing the chance of explosion.[1151] Third, ensuring that post-mission disposal is accomplished by removing the objects from the working orbits of the space environment following the conclusion of their active life.[1152] Fourth, taking steps to prevent the possibility of collision with other objects.[1153] Last, reducing the ballistic duration, or the duration which the space object remains in orbit after its useful lifetime (or the point at which it enters the dense layers of the atmosphere[1154]).[1155]

Additionally, Section 5 provides that the design and technical development of the spacecraft must identify how each aspect of the spacecraft will meet the regulatory requirements.[1156] This includes a specific description of the design and operation of the spacecraft and the orbital stages and sources of fuel that could cause debris if an emergency happened.[1157] Especially challenging is a requirement that in the event of an explosion, the operator must hypothesize the potential expected number, mass, size, shape, and material of debris that will be created (if projected to be more than 1 mm in size) and the estimated duration that the debris will stay in outer space before entering the atmosphere (if at all).[1158]

3.3.2 Debris Reduction during Operations

While section 5 of the regulation primarily focuses on minimizing the possibility of debris through design, section 6 focuses on minimizing the possibility of debris during operations. Primarily, the regulation addresses the need to launch the space vehicle in a manner that avoids potential collisions with already orbiting spacecraft.[1159] Additionally, ensuring that if some contact

1150 *Id.* at para. 5.2.
1151 *Id.* at para. 5.2.
1152 *Id.* at para. 5.2.
1153 *Id.* at para. 5.2.
1154 *Id.* at para. 3.16 (for the formal definition of ballistic life and 3.17 for the dense layers of the atmosphere, defined as the area of the atmosphere for which a space object cannot make a full orbit around Earth).
1155 *Id.* at para. 5.2.
1156 *Id.* at para. 5.4.
1157 *Id.* at para. 5.4.
1158 *Id.* at para. 5.4.
1159 *Id.* at para. 6.3.1.

unfortunately occurs, the spacecraft is designed in a way to provide a reasonable amount of protection against complete destruction as a result.[1160]

Once in orbit, as part of preventing the formation of space debris during regular operations, the regulation outlines a series of expectations for mitigating the possibility debris is created.[1161] First, space vehicles should exclude the use of certain means of separation of the stages of the space vehicle to prevent debris fragments.[1162] This includes minimizing the use of explosives-based devices to prompt separation (e.g. pyro-bolts) of both the stage rockets and, if applicable, separate payloads later.[1163] Additionally, reducing the release of other associated spacecraft parts as well, including tethers during operations, nose cones, and nozzle stubs.[1164] Finally, ensuring that the fuel propelling the space object is eliminated to prevent combustion engine emissions into protected areas of space.[1165]

In addition to normal operations, Section 6 also sets out an expectation that failures during normal operations could inadvertently create debris. There is an expectation that the design and operation of the spacecraft accounts for this and predicts possible outcomes. As these failures can be identified, mitigations should be considered and plans drafted to allow for rapid passivation and removal of the space object if necessary.[1166] It should be noted that the regulation does not require a hypothesis of every possible failure, but only those 'likely failures that could lead to the accidental destruction' of a space object or tool.[1167]

In addition to unexpected failures of the spacecraft, the prevention of deliberate destruction is also paramount.[1168] The regulation demands that space vehicles are designed and developed in such a way to prevent deliberate destruction (that is, no self-destruction or the use of intentional collision or otherwise).[1169] The only identified exception is in the case where self-elimination is conducted in such a way that the space vehicle will reasonably

1160 *Id.* at para. 6.3.3.
1161 *Id.* at para. 6.3.
1162 *Id.* at para. 6.1.
1163 *Id.*
1164 *Id.*
1165 *Id.*
1166 *Id.* at para. 6.2.1.
1167 *Id.*
1168 *Id.*
1169 *Id.*

decelerate into the atmosphere for a timely natural decay (while still reducing the chance of large pieces of debris entering the atmosphere in-tact).[1170]

3.3.3 Debris Reduction during Post-mission Disposal

A host of options are outlined in the regulation to address post-mission disposal and passivation for those objects that will remain in orbit (that is, placed into graveyard orbit).[1171] First, required passivation. The regulation outlines the expectation that spacecraft will be voided of all fuel residues, including both the main tank(s) and the cavities of the space object to prevent accidental pressure build-up or chemical reactions over time that would cause explosions.[1172] Second, discharging the battery and separating the charging lines.[1173] Third, reducing or eliminating the pressure caused by gasses in any high-pressure cylinders to either a lower level of pressure or removal of pressure completely.[1174] Fourth, stopping the rotation of mechanical devices such as flywheels and gyroscopes within the space vehicle.[1175] Finally, the neutralization of pyrotechnic elements to prevent triggering as a result of unintended impact by space particles.[1176] For those spacecraft that will enter the atmosphere, it is expected that the deorbit will be safe, controlled, and result in the elimination of danger to the environment from the space object.[1177]

For those objects that, in addition to passivation, will be disposed of into a graveyard orbit, the regulation provides guidance that reflects international standards from the IADC Debris Mitigation Guidelines. According to the regulation, it is important that objects sent into graveyard orbits have sufficient remaining energy to complete the orbit change, should be placed above the geostationary orbit, and have a final perigee (point closest to Earth) at a height sufficient to prevent incursion to the protected geostationary orbit for at least 100 years.[1178]

If the space object is not put into such a high orbit, alternatives are allowed. In particular, any object which may remain in or pass through a useable orbit, but its design does not provide for changing the parameters of the orbit or maneuvering into a graveyard orbit at the end of operation, should not remain

1170 *Id.*
1171 *Id.* at para. 6.2.3.
1172 *Id.* at para. 6.2.3(a)(1).
1173 *Id.* at para. 6.2.3(a)(2).
1174 *Id.* at para. 6.2.3(a)(3).
1175 *Id.* at para. 6.2.3(a)(4).
1176 *Id.* at para. 6.2.3(b).
1177 *Id.* at para. 6.2.3.
1178 *Id.* at para, 6.4.2.

in the protected region in excess of 25 years.[1179] Finally, in the event that the space object contains radioactive, toxic, or other harmful substances on board, the withdrawal from orbit should utilize the Earth's atmosphere to destroy the contamination.[1180]

4 Conclusion

Russia has a long and proud history of space exploration and is currently demonstrating a renewed resurgence in advancing technologies to provide further access to space for the Russian people. Through their own efforts, agreements, and partnerships, the Russians have been looking for more opportunities to be a leader in space development, primarily to ensure their own continued interests are protected. In doing so, their most recent revisions of their regulations reflect an interest in strengthening the Government's role over the space economy and a recognition of the fragility of space. The continued advancements and updates to the mitigation requirements, as demonstrated in GOST P 52925-2018, indicate the importance that Russia places on addressing the threat of space debris. Additionally, the Russians have implemented many of the important aspects of debris mitigation efforts advanced by the international community. However, whether in practice these efforts will achieve their intended goal is yet to be determined. Primarily, the health of the Russian space program overall is unclear.

There is evidence that many of the original problems that plagued the Russian program when it was originally under exclusive government control persist. One report issued by the Rand Corporation, led by Brig. Gen. (Ret.) Bruce McClintock, points out at least five issues that are creating ongoing problems for the success of the overall space program. Among the most significant issues are corruption,[1181] multiple reorganizations with no real change,

---

1179 *Id.* at para. 6.4.4.

1180 *Id.* at para. 6.4.5.

1181 According to the United States Department of State, Russian corruption is considered widespread throughout all branches of government as well as at all levels, including its space program. "Its manifestations include bribery of officials, misuse of budgetary resources, theft of government property, kickbacks in the procurement process, extortion, and improper use of one's official position to secure personal profits." *See* CORY WELT, CONG. RSCH. SERV., R44775, RUSSIA: BACKGROUND AND U.S. POLICY 5–6 (Aug. 21, 2017) *available at* https://fas.org/sgp/crs/row/R44775.pdf. *See also* James Clay Moltz, *The Changing Dynamics of Twenty-First-Century Space Power*, 12 J. STRATEGIC STUD. 15 (2019).

reduced budgets, leadership turnover, and lack of substance to back up forward-looking vision statements.[1182] All of this while lacking a robust competitive private market of any real note.[1183]

At the same time, Russia has set lofty goals that will certainly increase the amount of debris the Russians create should they be successful. Among their goals, as outlined in their Federal Space Program for Russia 2016–2025,[1184] is the continued deployment of spacecraft in support of services that support the social, economic, and scientific interests of Russia.[1185] Specifically, Russia is exerting considerable effort toward creating constellations of satellites to support personal satellite communication systems, achieving a continuous presence on the Moon, deploying active debris removal technologies, and further contributions to ISS objectives.[1186]

However, whether their goals can overcome any commercial or government shortcomings presents a future that is not entirely clear. As far as debris mitigation is concerned, it is evident that the requirements for minimizing the creation of debris within Russia's goals are a crucial element of the Russian plan and are currently being executed.[1187] Whether the Russians can successfully achieve such lofty mitigation goals will take time to confirm.

1182 McClintock, *supra* note 1114 at 3. *See also* Zaborskiy, *supra* note 1030. *See also Challenges to Security in Space*, DEFENSE INTEL. AGENCY, 23–24 (2019), https://www.dia.mil/Portals/27/Documents/News/Military%20Power%20Publications/Space_Threat_V14_020119_sm.pdf. *See also* Yuri Karash, *Russian Space Program: Financial State, Current Plans, Ambitions and Cooperation with the United States*, 2016, THE SPACE CONGRESS PROCEEDINGS, (May 26, 2016, 6:00 PM), https://commons.erau.edu/cgi/viewcontent.cgi?article=3648&context=space-congress-proceedings. *See* TODD HARRISON, ET AL., SPACE THREAT ASSESSMENT 2018, REP. OF THE CENTER FOR STRATEGIC AND INT'L STUD. AEROSPACE SECURITY PROJECT, at 12 (Apr. 2018), https://csis-website-prod.s3.amazonaws.com/s3fs-public/publication/180823_Harrison_SpaceThreatAssessment_FULL_WEB.pdf.

1183 Zak, *supra* note 1046 at 3 (discussing the dissolution of the Federal Space Agency and establishing the Roskosmos State Corporation).

1184 Malyshev, *supra* note 1114.

1185 *Id.*

1186 *Id.*

1187 Most recently, China and Russia added emphasis to the point of the Russian plan for space operations, including not only international partnership, but development of "international space law and regulation in the field of space activities ... and will continue such cooperation on matters of mutual interest for the long-term sustainability of space activities ..." *See* Joint Statement of the Russian Federation and the People's Republic of China on the International Relations Entering a New Era and the Global Sustainable Development, Feb. 4, 2022, http://en.kremlin.ru/supplement/5770#sel=1:21:S5F,1:37:3jE (last visited Jun. 24, 2022).

CHAPTER 7

European Space Agency

1 Introduction

The years immediately following World War II were devastating for Europe. Having come out the other side of two world wars in just over 30 years, the physical and emotional tolls were extraordinary. Exacerbating the situation, most of the intellectual and scientific powerhouses that resided in Europe either fled in advance of the second war or ensconced mostly to the United States or the Soviet Union, where opportunities and financial backing, particularly for (rocket) engineers, was plentiful.[1188] This exodus left a vacuum in the collective scientific knowledge in Europe requiring a different approach to achieve success in many endeavors. Among them, the need to continue advancements toward accessing outer space.[1189] The Europeans recognized that their success in space was going to require pooling the remaining scientific knowledge to keep them competitive with the emerging superpowers.[1190]

1188 *History of Europe in Space*, EUROPEAN SPACE AGENCY, https://www.esa.int/About_Us/ESA_history/History_of_Europe_in_space. *See also* Emily Carney, *Space For Europe and for all humankind: A brief history of the ESA*, ARS TECHNICA (Dec. 31, 2015, 9:00 AM), https://arstechnica.com/science/2015/12/space-for-europe-and-for-all-humankind-a-brief-history-of-the-esa/. *See* Andrew Grant, *The Scientific Exodus from Nazi Germany*, PHYSICS TODAY (Sept. 26, 2018), https://physicstoday.scitation.org/do/10.1063/PT.6.4.20180926a/full/#:~:text=Thanks%20to%20such%20efforts%2C%20the,(see%20the%20accompanying%20article, discussing the pre-departure of many scientists as Adolf Hitler was ascending to power. Additionally, same subject, *see* Eric Weiss, *The Impact of the Intellectual Migration on the United States and Eastern Europe*, https://www.vanderbilt.edu/AnS/physics/brau/H182/Term%20Papers/Eric%20Weiss.html (last updated Apr. 27, 1998). The infamous Operation Paperclip was undertaken to bring German (Nazi) scientists to America after the war, *see* Laura Schumm, *What Was Operation Paperclip?*, History Stories (Jun. 2, 2014, updated Mar. 4, 2020), https://www.history.com/news/what-was-operation-paperclip.

1189 *History of Europe in Space*, *supra* note 1188. *See also* discussion of European motivation for collaboration, NAT'L RES. CTR., U.S. EUROPEAN COLLABORATION IN SPACE SCIENCE 16 (1998).

1190 *History of Europe in Space*, *supra* note 1188. *See also* Convention for the Establishment of a European Space Agency, Preamble, May 30, 1975, https://esamultimedia.esa.int/multimedia/publications/SP-1337/SP-1337_EN.pdf. The drafted language was a clear acknowledgment that the European countries would otherwise not be able to obtain peer status with the emerging space superpowers individually. Instead, a collective effort would be required. The Preamble stated, "The magnitude of the human, technical, and financial

© KONINKLIJKE BRILL NV, LEIDEN, 2023 | DOI:10.1163/9789004535848_009

By 1958, early collaboration began among European governments to advance the interests of all Europeans in space. Two figures in Europe, Pierre Auger[1191] of France and Edoardo Amaldi[1192] of Italy, recommended that a scientific organization be established to advance joint European interests in space.[1193] By 1960, both helped set up a commission among ten European countries to determine the feasibility of European cooperation in space.[1194] In moving forward, the commission settled on establishing the space program under the administration of two organizations. For launch management, the European Launch Development Organization (ELDO) was established.[1195] For spacecraft development, the European Space Research Organization (ESRO) was created.[1196] By 1965, both agencies had signed conventions and were officially established to advance European interests in space.[1197]

Over the next seven years, ESRO found success in its scientific developments and collaboration.[1198] However, its sister organization, ELDO, did not fare as well, plagued by technological problems, ballooning expenses, and

resources required for activities in the space field is such that these resources lie beyond the means of any single European Country." *See also* Comm. On the Peaceful Uses of Outer Space Legal Subcomm., on Its Fifty-Seventh Session, U.N. Doc. A/AC.105/C.2/2018/CRP.20, para. 1.1 (2018), https://www.unoosa.org/res/oosadoc/data/documents/2018/aac_105c_22018crp/aac_105c_22018crp_20_0_html/AC105_C2_2018_CRP20E.pdf.

1191 *Pierre Auger*, EUR. SPACE AGENCY, https://www.esa.int/About_Us/ESA_history/Pierre_Auger.

1192 *Eduardo Amaldi*, EUR. SPACE AGENCY, https://www.esa.int/About_Us/ESA_history/Edoardo_Amaldi.

1193 *History of Europe in Space*, *supra* note 1188.

1194 *Id.*

1195 *Id. See also* Alexander Badenoch, *ESRO and ELDO: Science vs. Technology*, INVENTING EUROPE, http://www.inventingeurope.eu/story/esro-and-eldo-science-vs-technology; Louis de Gouyon Matignon, *The First European Satellites*, SPACE LEGAL ISSUES (June 1, 2019), https://www.spacelegalissues.com/the-first-european-satellites/; HANDBOOK OF SPACE LAW, *supra* note 513 at ch. 4, para. 4.2.1, pgs. 208–209 (Frans von der Dunk & Fabio Tronchetti eds., 2015); Comm. On the Peaceful Uses of Outer Space Legal Subcomm., on Its Fifty-Seventh Session, U.N. Doc. A/AC.105/C.2/2018/CRP.20, para. 1.1 (2018), https://www.unoosa.org/res/oosadoc/data/documents/2018/aac_105c_22018crp/aac_105c_22018crp_20_0_html/AC105_C2_2018_CRP20E.pdf.

1196 *History of Europe in Space*, *supra* note 1188. *See also* Badenoch, *supra* note 1195; Matignon, *The First European Satellites*, *supra* note 1195; HANDBOOK OF SPACE LAW, *supra* note 513 at ch. 4, para. 4.2.1, pgs. 208–209; Comm. On the Peaceful Uses of Outer Space Legal Subcomm., on its Fifty-Seventh Session, *supra* note 1195 at para. 1.1.

1197 *History of Europe in Space*, *supra* note 1188.

1198 *Id.*

political disputes.[1199] To reconcile issues that the two organizations could not separately address, European discussions began on the feasibility of consolidating both under one organization.[1200] By 1974, ELDO was no more, and the merging of ELDO and ESRO responsibilities resulted in the creation of ESA by 1975.[1201] Its founding ten Member-States were Belgium, Germany, Denmark, France, the United Kingdom, Italy, the Netherlands, Sweden, Switzerland, and Spain, with Ireland also joining within a year under the ESA Convention.[1202]

2 ESA Today

Since its drafting, ESA's Convention has guided the organization in successful collaboration among European and partner Nations to launch satellites and engage in celestial scientific endeavors. The Convention states the purpose of ESA is to "promote, for exclusively peaceful purposes, cooperation among

1199 *Id. See also Europe: Is it Goodbye to ESRO and ELDO?*, 226 NATURE 226, 1011–1012 (1970), https://www.nature.com/articles/2261011a0; HANDBOOK OF SPACE LAW, *supra* note 513 atch. 4, para. 4.2.1, pgs. 210–211.

1200 *History of Europe in Space*, *supra* note 1188.

1201 *Id.* For additional discussion of the desire for autonomy of a European space program, *see* NAT'L RES. CTR., *supra* note 1189 at 18, discussing contributing underlying tensions between ESRO/ELDO and the US space programs. *See also* HANDBOOK OF SPACE LAW, *supra* note 513 at ch. 4, para. 4.2.1, pgs. 211–212. *See also* Frans von der Dunk, *The European Union and the Outer Space Treaty: Will the Twain Ever Meet?*, 89 SPACE, CYBER, & TELECOMM. L. PROGRAM FACULTY PUBLICATIONS 75, 76 (2017) discussing the shortcomings of ELDO/ESRO and the ultimate inception of ESA, https://digitalcommons.unl.edu/cgi/viewcontent.cgi?article=1089&context=spacelaw. *See also* II J. KRIGE, A. RUSSO & L. SEBESTA, A HISTORY OF THE EUROPEAN SPACE AGENCY 1973–1987 (2000), http://www.esa.int/esapub/sp/sp1235/sp1235v2web.pdf.

1202 *History of Europe in Space*, *supra* note 1188. For a list of dates for concurrence on the ESA Convention for each signatory, *see* Convention for the Establishment of a European Space Agency, *supra* note 1190. The last signatory, Ireland, signed on 31 December 1975. The ESA Convention entered into force on 30 October 1980. Interestingly, there was a five-year gap between the signatories and the ESA Convention entering into force. In that interim, the ESA Convention was applied 'de facto' and ESRO essentially continued its activities as the only legal personality under international law at the time, but under the name 'European Space Agency.' *See* G. Lafferanderie, *The European Space Agency and International Space Law*, Proceedings of the 3rd ECSL Colloquium on Int'l Org. & Space L., Perugia, 19, 20, para. 3 (May 6–7, 1999), http://adsabs.harvard.edu/pdf/1999ESASP.442...19L. The ESA Convention itself has since gone through revisions in 1995, 2001, 2005, and 2009. The most current version went into force 1 January 2010. *See* Convention for the Establishment of a European Space Agency, *supra* note 1190. *See also Key Dates 1960–2018*, EUROPEAN SPACE AGENCY, https://www.esa.int/About_Us/ESA_history/Key_dates_1960-2018.

European States ..."[1203] It provides the parameters to execute its stated mission through four objectives.[1204] First, by establishing a long-term European space policy to guide the efforts of Member-States and align their activities with those of other national and international organizations and institutions.[1205] Second, by advocating for space programs and taking the necessary steps to execute on those programs.[1206] Third, by coordinating and integrating Member-State national programs and the European space program, with special attention being paid to development of application satellites.[1207] Finally, advocating and implementing the industrial policies necessary to be able to carry out the program objectives among the Member-States.[1208] In addition to the main body, the convention consists of five annexes, which provide amplifying information on privileges and immunities, financial obligations,[1209] optional programs, internationalization of national programs, and industrial policy.[1210]

ESA's leadership consists of two main components; a Member Council and a Director-General assisted by a staff, created and described within the Convention.[1211] The Member Council consists of representatives of the

---

1203 Convention for the Establishment of a European Space Agency, *supra* note 1190 at art. II. *See also* Comm. On the Peaceful Uses of Outer Space Legal Subcomm., on its Fifty-Seventh Session, *supra* note 1195 at para. 1.1.

1204 For additional discussion, see Comm. On the Peaceful Uses of Outer Space Legal Subcomm., on its Fifty-Seventh Session, *supra* note 1195.

1205 Convention for the Establishment of a European Space Agency, *supra* note 1190 at art. II(a).

1206 *Id.* at art. II(b).

1207 *Id.* at art. II(c).

1208 *Id.* at art. II(d).

1209 For the financial obligations of each, see *ESA Convention*, EUROPEAN SPACE AGENCY, at art. XIII & Annex II. Additionally, for a thorough discussion of the financial requirements for optional programs, as well as the accompanying complications that may arise in determining payment for certain programs, particularly voluntary, see HANDBOOK OF SPACE LAW, *supra* note 513 atch. 4, para. 4.2.3.2.

1210 Convention for the Establishment of a European Space Agency, *supra* note 1190 at Annexes I–V.

1211 According to the ESA, as of 2018, ESA has approximately 2,300 staff in offices worldwide, a budget of approximately €5.60 Billion, developed and operated (in part) approximately 100 satellites and spacecraft, has six types of launchers it has developed, manages 60% of all of the spending that occurs on space-related endeavors in Europe, maintains approximately 95% of expenditures 'in-house' within the European industry, and has activities and programs covering all major space-related fields such as space science, robotic exploration, earth observation, navigation, telecommunication, et cetera. Additionally, it has almost 500 international agreements with governments, space agencies, and IGOs worldwide. For additional discussion, see Comm. On the Peaceful Uses of Outer Space Legal Subcomm., on its Fifty-Seventh Session, *supra* note 1195 at para. 1.10. *See also This is ESA*, EUROPEAN SPACE AGENCY,

Member-States and is responsible for providing the direction and guidance regarding the activities and programs of ESA, including approval, resource allocation, policies, and logistics involved with implementing and carrying out any approved activities.[1212] The vote count required for passing specific measures depends on the activities under consideration.[1213] The Director-General, elected by the Member-States to serve as the Chief Executive Officer for ESA, has corresponding duties for carrying out the direction of Member-States' activities as well as personnel, fiscal and administrative management of ESA.[1214] In addition to administrative and scientific efforts carried out by ESA, and its corresponding facility locations, ESA also maintains its launch facility in partnership with the French space program in Kourou, French Guiana.[1215]

---

https://esamultimedia.esa.int/docs/corporate/This_is_ESA_EN_LR.pdf; *One ESA*, EUROPEAN SPACE AGENCY, https://esamultimedia.esa.int/docs/corporate/One-ESA_brochure.pdf; Convention for the Establishment of a European Space Agency, *supra* note 1190 at art. X.

1212 Convention for the Establishment of a European Space Agency, *supra* note 1190 at art. XI. For specific roles and responsibilities of ESA's Council, including subgroups, *see* Comm. On the Peaceful Uses of Outer Space Legal Subcomm., on its Fifty-Seventh Session, *supra* note 1195 at para. 1.4.1.

1213 *ESA Convention*, *supra* note 1211 at art. XI. In addition to the variable number of votes required for passage depending on an activity, Canada also can contribute to the vote count in certain circumstances. Under a unique agreement between Canada and ESA, Canada retains limited rights to vote on questions relating to the programs in which it participates. However, that still does not carry over to the right to vote in Council on the budget or matters related to it. *See Canada-European Space Agency Cooperation Agreement*, GOVERNMENT OF CANADA, https://www.asc-csa.gc.ca/eng/funding-programs/canada-esa/about-cooperation-agreement.asp (modified Oct. 23, 2019).

1214 *ESA Convention*, *supra* note 1211 at art. XII. For specific roles and responsibilities of the Director-General, *see* Comm. On the Peaceful Uses of Outer Space Legal Subcomm., on its Fifty-Seventh Session, *supra* note 1195 at para. 1.4.2.

1215 Europe's spaceport is in French Guiana (Kourou) in South America. It was selected in 1964 by the French to launch their satellites because of its advantageous location. It sits positioned approximately 500 km north of the equator which allows launches into GEO without much need for changes in the rocket trajectory to reach its orbital position. Additionally, Earth's rotation during launch creates an effect that increases the speed of a launcher, allowing for reduced costs and fuel savings. This, in turn, can extend the operational life of the satellite. When ESA was established in 1975, the French government offered to allow ESA to utilize this facility, and ESA contributed funding to upgrade the facility in return. ESA continues to provide 2/3rds of the spaceport's annual funding. Today, it continues to be overseen by the French space program, the Centre National D'etudes Spatiales. *See Centre National D'Etudes Spatiales*, EUROPEAN SPACE AGENCY, https://www.esa.int/Enabling_Support/Space_Engineering_Technology/Centre_National_D_Etudes_Spatiales_CNES. *See Launch Site*, EUROPEAN SPACE AGENCY, https://www.esa.int/Applications/Telecommunications_Integrated_Applications/Hylas/Launch_site#:~:text=Hylas%2D1%20was%20launched%20from,which%20to%20launch%20its%20satellites.

2.1 ESA *Membership*

ESA membership has grown from the original 10 countries to the 22 countries that now sit on ESA's governing council.[1216] The 11 countries who have since joined the original members as full members are Austria (1986), Norway (1986), Finland (1995), Portugal (2000), Greece (2005), Luxembourg (2005), the Czech Republic (2008), Romania (2011), Poland (2012), Estonia (2015) and Hungary (2015).[1217] Collectively, ESA operates physical locations in France, Germany, Spain, Italy, the Netherlands and England.[1218]

In addition to full members, ESA also has several agreements with non-member partner countries that offer non-members some ESA business rights. A prime example is Canada. Canada's Cooperation Agreement allows the Canadian space sector to participate in ESA's decision-making process, allows Canadian companies to bid on ESA space contracts, and provides special industry alliances and access for Canadian technology and services.[1219] Again, all these rights are within the context that Canada is precluded from being an actual member of ESA by virtue of its geography (ESA membership requires being "European"). In return, Canada provides a degree of fiscal remuneration to ESA's general fund as well as collaboration for projects that Canada participates in.[1220]

1216 *Member States and Cooperating States*, EUROPEAN SPACE AGENCY, https://www.esa.int/About_Us/Corporate_news/Member_States_Cooperating_States. *See also* Elizabeth Howell, *European Space Agency: Facts & Information*, SPACE.COM, https://www.space.com/22562-european-space-agency.html.

1217 *ESA Member States, Canada, Latvia and Slovenia*, EUROPEAN SPACE AGENCY, https://www.esa.int/Education/ESA_Member_States_Canada_Latvia_and_Slovenia. For specific roles and responsibilities of the Director-General, *see* Comm. On the Peaceful Uses of Outer Space Legal Subcomm., on its Fifty-Seventh Session, *supra* note 1195 at para. 1.3.

1218 The ESA headquarters is in Paris, France, where the major policies and programs are developed. The European Astronaut Centre (EAC) is in Cologne, Germany, and is, as the name indicates, the home of ESA's astronaut training program. The European Space Astronomy Center (ESAC) is located near Madrid, Spain, and is the center for astronomy and space science in Europe. The European Space Operations Center (ESOC) is in Darmstadt, Germany and is ESA's primary mission control center. ESA's Centre for Earth Observation (ESRIN) is in Frascati, Italy, and serves as ESA's Earth observation center. The final two are the European Space Research and Technology Centre (ESTEC), in the Netherlands, and is the home of space technology and satellite testing for ESA. Finally, the European Centre for Space Applications and Telecommunications (ECSAT), located in Hartwell, England, focuses on space telecommunications. MasterClass Staff, *European Space Agency: History and Recent Missions*, MASTERCLASS (May 5, 2021), https://www.masterclass.com/articles/european-space-agency#a-brief-history-of-the-european-space-agency.

1219 *Canada-European Space Agency Cooperation Agreement*, *supra* note 1213.

1220 *Id.*

Other countries also have cooperation agreements in place, though geared more toward gaining eventual membership into ESA. These agreements establish membership-interested States first as associate members under the Plan for European Cooperating States (PECS).[1221] Associate status grants prospective ESA countries the right to participate in any of ESA optional programs except the science or technology programs.[1222] As associates, prospective countries benefit greatly from receiving direct ESA support for training, organization of events and advice.[1223]

Currently, Slovenia and Latvia are Associate Members having already joined under the PECS program.[1224] An additional four (Bulgaria, Cyprus, Lithuania, and Slovakia) are in the early stages under the PECS program, which requires a series of agreements, financial contributions, and five years under the PECS charter to pass before consideration for associate membership.[1225] Successful completion of PECS leads to associate membership, which last another five years.[1226] The successful completion of all stages in the membership process makes a prospective country potentially eligible for eventual full membership (or renewal for another five years as an associate member).[1227] Estonia, the Czech Republic, Hungary, Romania and Poland all completed both the PECS and associate membership stages before their accession.[1228]

2.2 *ESA Programs and Participant Requirements*

ESA Member-States have a series of requirements necessary to obtain membership and remain in good standing. Some of the provisions are mandatory, some voluntary, and some are referred to as operational activities, a hybrid of sorts. Within the agreement, the mandatory aspects consist of the requirements outlined in Section V of the ESA convention, *Activities and Programmes*.[1229] Mandatory requirements focus on several areas. Among them, collaboration

1221 *Programme for Associate Member States*, EUROPEAN SPACE AGENCY, https://www.esa.int/About_Us/Business_with_ESA/Programme_for_Associate_Member_States.

1222 *Id.*

1223 *Id.*

1224 *General Overview*, EUROPEAN SPACE AGENCY, https://www.esa.int/About_Us/Plan_for_European_Cooperating_States/General_overview.

1225 *Id.*

1226 *Programme for Associate Member States*, *supra* note 1221.

1227 *Slovenia Targets Full ESA Membership for 2024*, SLOVENIA TIMES (Oct. 20, 2020), https://sloveniatimes.com/slovenia-targets-full-esa-membership-for-2024/.

1228 *General Overview*, European Space Agency, *supra* note 1224.

1229 *ESA Convention*, *supra* note 1211 at art. V(1)(a), Activities and Programmes, p. 16. *See also* Comm. On the Peaceful Uses of Outer Space Legal Subcomm., on its Fifty-Seventh Session, *supra* note 1195 at para. 1.5.

and education between scientific programs, communication about ongoing and future scientific projects, and dissemination of relevant information pertinent to overall space programs.[1230] It is important to note that even in the case of 'mandatory activities', there are existing provisions within the agreement which provide for non-compliance without a country violating their membership requirements. These mandatory provisions are otherwise easily identified by their use of mandatory language such as 'shall', but the provisions still maintain a compliance 'escape-valve.' Article III of the ESA Convention, *Information and Data*, offers a prime example.[1231] It provides that Member-States shall "facilitate the exchange of scientific and technical information pertaining space research and technology."[1232] However, there is a caveat nullifying the requirement if any Member-State has reason to believe that doing so would be "inconsistent with the interests of its own security or agreements

---

1230 *ESA Convention*, *supra* note 1211 at art. V(1)(a), Activities and Programmes. *See also* HANDBOOK OF SPACE LAW, *supra* note 513 at ch. 4, para. 4.2.3.1, highlighting the approval of mandatory programs is by simple majority for the program itself, but then a second unanimous vote must be sought to determine the resources that will be dedicated to the program. Furthermore, Professor von der Dunk cites mandatory examples such as Mars Express (collaborating with NASA and Italy, to explore the atmosphere and surface of Mars from polar orbit since 2003, *see Mars Express* (*ESA*), NASA, https://mars.nasa.gov/mars-exploration/missions/express/), and the XMM-Newton Spacecraft (focusing on studying celestial X-ray sources to help inform on black holes and the origins of the universe, *see* Jeanette Kazmierczak, *X-Ray Satellite XMM-Newton Celebrates 20 Years in Space*, (Dec. 10, 2019), https://www.nasa.gov/feature/goddard/2019/x-ray-satellite-xmm-newton-celebrates-20-years-in-space), and the SOHO mission (*see* M.C.E. Huber, et al. *The History of the SOHO Mission*, ESA BULLETIN NR. 86 (May 1996), https://www.esa.int/esapub/bulletin/bullet86/huber86.htm#:~:text=The%20Solar%20and%20Heliospheric%20Observatory,Lagrangian%20point%2C%20L1%20(cf, describing the Solar and Heliospheric Observatory devoted to the study of the sun and its nearby environment). More recent programs, such as the Hera mission, will launch in October 2024 and is expected to arrive at the asteroid Didymos by 2026. There, it will observe a test of NASA's Double Asteroid Redirect Test (DART) spacecraft, which is intended to collide with a small moon of Didymos, called "Didymoon", to determine the ability of 'kinetic impactors' to change the orbit of an asteroid. *See* Jeff Foust, *Advocates Promote Planetary Defense Mission Ahead of ESA Ministerial*, SPACE NEWS (Nov. 18, 2019), https://spacenews.com/advocates-promote-planetary-defense-mission-ahead-of-esa-ministerial/. As an added example of the budget collaboration, ESA had requested €600 million for space safety programs, but only received €432 million. This is enough to fund the Hera mission, but other programs will need to be delayed. *See* Jeff Foust, *ESA Declares Success at Ministerial Meeting*, SPACE NEWS (Nov. 28, 2019), https://spacenews.com/esa-declares-success-at-ministerial-meeting/.

1231 *ESA Convention*, *supra* note 1211 at art. III(1), Activities and Programmes.

1232 *Id.*

with third parties" (or other agreements under which it was obtained).[1233] So, while a mandatory provision, Member-States only need to look to the exception and articulate a justifiable national-security reason to avoid compliance.

Optional activities are also outlined in Section V. Optional activities involve collaboration by voluntary participating members of ESA to advance particular efforts, such as designing, launching, and operating satellites in space or the creation of land-based launch facilities and support systems.[1234] Voluntary programs are similar to the mandatory programs for voting, with only a simple majority vote required for passage.[1235] However, in accordance with Annex III to the agreement, the optional nature of these projects allow them to be declined, provided the Member-State makes certain required notifications.[1236] Primarily, to opt-out, a desire to do so must be identified within three months and communicated to the other participating members.[1237]

Finally, the third type of activity executed by ESA is titled 'operational activities.'[1238] In accordance with the ESA Convention, ESA can carry out a wide range of activities on behalf of others outside of the normal membership within ESA.[1239] Accordingly, the ESA Convention allows for placing ESA facilities at the disposal of the others,[1240] launching and placing in orbit operational application satellites,[1241] or carrying out 'any other activity requested by users and approved by the council.'[1242] The caveat is that the costs are passed along directly to the requesting party.[1243]

1233 *Id.*

1234 *Id.* at art. V(1)(b), Activities and Programmes, 17. *See also* Comm. On the Peaceful Uses of Outer Space Legal Subcomm., on its Fifty-Seventh Session, *supra* note 1195 at para. 1.5.

1235 Convention for the Establishment of a European Space Agency, *supra* note 1190 at art. XI(5)(c).

1236 *Id.* at Annex III, art. I(2), 81.

1237 *Id.*

1238 *Id.* at art. V(2).

1239 *Id.* at art. V(2). *See also* HANDBOOK OF SPACE LAW, *supra* note 513 at para. 4.2.3.3. *See also* Comm. On the Peaceful Uses of Outer Space Legal Subcomm., on its Fifty-Seventh Session, *supra* note 1195 at para. 1.6.

1240 Convention for the Establishment of a European Space Agency, *supra* note 1190 at art. V(2)(a).

1241 *Id.* at art. V(2)(b).

1242 *Id.* at art. V(2)(c).

1243 *Id.* at art. V(2).

3 ESA and International Legal Standing and Authority

Since its inception in 1975, ESA chose the mechanism of an International Governmental Organization (IGO) for its establishment.[1244] This has created a construct under which ESA can participate in international space operations, as well as conduct required business functions.[1245] ESA's IGO status provides two key advantages. First, it has a recognized legal personality. This allows it to accomplish its most basic functions of existence. It can receive funds (through Member-States), create budgets,[1246] pay its obligations, hire personnel, operate centers and offices, and evolve its rules and regulations as appropriate to meet its mandates.[1247] Without the authority necessary to carry out these functions, the organization itself would not have the required infrastructure to carry out the goals on behalf of ESA's Member-States. Second, having established its authority to operate functionally, ESA, though its Convention, is also authorized on behalf of its Member-States, and acting through them, to specifically engage with external organizations and nations.[1248] It is true that, as an IGO, ESA has some limitations to engage fully in international agreements (for example, as suggested by the ICJ to establish treaties 'between nations').[1249] However, it still maintains the legal and contractual capacity of an IGO, giving it strong powers among its own Member-States, as well as provisions under its convention to act through its Member-States when engaging with the international community. In particular, Article XIV of ESA's Convention allows ESA, upon unanimous Council decision, to 'cooperate with other international organizations and institutions of non-Member-States and conclude an agreement with them to this effect.'[1250] This important power of ESA allows it to engage with the international community and, as appropriate, reach agreements which benefit the European community and ESA's Member-States.[1251]

1244 Comm. On the Peaceful Uses of Outer Space Legal Subcomm., on its Fifty-Seventh Session, *supra* note 1195 at para. 1.2.

1245 Comm. On the Peaceful Uses of Outer Space Legal Subcomm., on its Fifty-Third Session, U.N. Doc. A/AC.105/C.2/2014/CRP.28, 3 (2014), https://www.unoosa.org/pdf/limited/c2/AC105_C2_2014_CRP28E.pdf.

1246 Today, ESA has a budget of approximately €6.49 billion, for example. *ESA Budget 2021*, European Space Agency, Newsroom (Jan. 14, 2021), https://www.esa.int/Newsroom/ESA_budget_2021.

1247 Comm. On the Peaceful Uses of Outer Space Legal Subcomm., supra note 1245, para. 1.7.

1248 *Id.* at para. 1.2.

1249 *Id.* at para. 1.7.2 (citing ICJ Rep 249 [263] 2002).

1250 Convention for the Establishment of a European Space Agency, *supra* note 1190 at art. XIV(1).

1251 Comm. On the Peaceful Uses of Outer Space Legal Subcomm., supra note 1245, para. 2.3.

3.1 *ESA and International Agreements*

In sum, as best described by ESA itself, its IGO status is a construct by which states can "cooperate through ESA and ESA cooperates with other partners."[1252] As a result, it enjoys some degree of power in public international law and the authority necessary as an international legal personality.[1253] In exercising its legal recognition, ESA has become a 'party', to the maximum extent allowable, to treaties pertinent to the exploration and use of outer space. Specifically, ESA is a party to the Rescue Agreement, the Liability Convention, and the Registration Convention.[1254] However, unlike the three treaties above, the Outer Space Treaty does not provide any mechanism for an IGO to be a party to the treaty.[1255] Instead, ESA's Member-States are

---

1252 *Id.* at 3.

1253 "The Agency shall have legal personality." *See* Convention for the Establishment of a European Space Agency, *supra* note 1190 at art. XV, para. 1. *See also* Comm. On the Peaceful Uses of Outer Space Legal Subcomm., on its Fifty-Seventh Session, *supra* note 1195 at para. 1.2. *See also International Organizations (IGOs)*, HARV. L. SCHOOL, https://hls.harvard.edu/dept/opia/what-is-public-interest-law/public-service-practice-settings/public-international-law/intergovernmental-organizations-igos/, describing the fundamental purpose of an IGO, obligations, and rights, including that IGO's are, when formed by treaty, subject to international law and can enter into enforceable agreements among themselves or with States.

1254 It is important to distinguish that ESA is not a party to these three space agreements/conventions, but instead in a status as close as possible to being so. This is because the provisions of historical agreements typically did not allow for IGO membership, but after the Outer Space Treaty, new agreements did try to recognize IGOs as participating organizations. In doing so, the organization had to meet two specific requirements. First, it had to declare its acceptance of the provisions of the agreement, and second, a majority of the Member-States of the organization also had to be a part of the Convention and the Outer Space Treaty [actually these are two different requirements, so the 'total' would be three: there might well be a case where the majority of Member-States are party to the treaty at issue but not the Outer Space Treaty, or vice versa. In either case the declaration cannot be made/effective]. In this way, ESA was able to join the three agreements by meeting those two requirements (again, the Outer Space Treaty made no such concession). Therefore, ESA worked to establish proper wording for the declarations, since nothing specific was offered. Based on members meeting the second requirement's obligations, ESA lodged acceptance of the three agreements with the UN Secretary-General. The Rescue Agreement was lodged on 31 December 1975, the Liability Convention on 23 September 1976, and the Registration Convention on 2 December 1979. All three of these, originally adopted under the ESRO umbrella, were automatically assumed by ESA when its own convention went into effect in 1980. *See* Lafferanderie, *supra* note 1202 at 19, 20–21, paras. 3–4.

1255 G.A. Res. 2222 (XXI), *Treaty on Principles Governing the Activities of States in the Exploration and Use of Outer Space, Including the Moon and Other Celestial Bodies*, at art.

responsible for the activities of the IGO, including resolution of any issues that may arise.[1256]

The practical impact of ESA's treaty status is that while ESA has voluntarily subjected itself to international law, as have its individual Member-States, it is not itself a legislative governing body outside of ESA specific operations. It therefore cannot create international space law. At the same time, the nature of ESA still allows for all Member-States to individually participate in treaty development outside of ESA, as well as maintain the ability to sign on to international agreements or treaties as they see fit.[1257] Often, for ESA's Member-States, the lens from which they approach these treaties, and which they exert their influence, is reflective of the values of Europe as a whole. Therefore, regardless of ESA's lack of treaty 'Member status', ESA still exerts considerable indirect influence in the developing international law. Further, ESA evolves accordingly, either by direct adoption of the principles of these developed treaties, or by persuasion or adoption by Member-States of the treaty requirements into individual State's domestic law or practice.[1258]

3.2 *Creation of International Legal Norms—ESA Customary International Law*

International treaty law, recalling from earlier chapters, is a product of treaties developed by Nations to specify terms of a particular understanding.[1259] Among the 22 ESA Member-States, thousands of international agreements have been developed and signed bilaterally and multilaterally. In the case of

---

XIII (Dec. 19, 1966), https://www.unoosa.org/pdf/gares/ARES_21_2222E.pdf, Article XIII. *See* Lafferanderie, *supra* note 1202 at 19–20, para. 2.

1256 G.A. Res. 2222 (XXI), *Treaty on Principles Governing the Activities of States in the Exploration and Use of Outer Space, Including the Moon and Other Celestial Bodies*, at art. XIII (Dec. 19, 1966), https://www.unoosa.org/pdf/gares/ARES_21_2222E.pdf, which specifically opines activity of IGOs, but rests participation and membership resolution as a responsibility of the Member-States of the IGO who are also members of the Outer Space Treaty. Specifically, the first paragraph recognizes IGOs, such that it states, "The provisions of this Treaty shall apply to the activities of States Parties to the Treaty … whether such activities are carried on by a single State Party to the Treaty or jointly with other States, including cases where they are carried on within the framework of international intergovernmental organizations." However, the second paragraph makes clear that it is the States that must represent the IGO. Specifically, "any practical questions arising in connection with activities carried on by IGOs … shall be resolved by the States-Parties to the Treaty either with the appropriate IGO or with one or more States members of the IGO which are Parties to this Treaty."

1257 HANDBOOK OF SPACE LAW, *supra* note 513 at para. 4.2.5.

1258 *See* discussion *supra* Chapter 2, public international law.

1259 *Id.*

ESA, while it has become part of some of these agreements, it cannot create them independently. Where treaty law does not exist on a particular subject, customary international law can otherwise identify the prevailing rules for an activity.[1260] It is customary international law where ESA, as a large representative block, can exert enormous influence and leverage since its activities often reflect the consensus of the 22 Member-States for an activity.[1261] Or, conversely, the developments from ESA are taken back by the Member-States and often implemented in their practice if not specifically enumerated in their domestic law.

3.3 *ESA and Space Debris Legal Norms*

As discussed, the construct of ESA gives weight to its impact on international law by virtue of its membership. And among the important efforts of ESA, controlling the proliferation of space debris has been a consistent theme throughout ESA's history. As early as the 1980s, ESA began heightened efforts toward adoption of a series of measures and policies to address the increasing debris threat. Prompting, if not justifying, the heightened motivation, in 1986 an orbital stage of a French-owned Ariane rocket exploded in a sun-synchronous orbit releasing a total of 488 trackable debris objects.[1262] The following year, the Director-General of ESA, at the time Reimar Lust,[1263] had formed a Space

---

1260 *See* discussion *supra* Chapter 3, development of customary international law.

1261 It is worth noting that in the context of this book, the activities of ESA are utilized for the purposes of establishing its influence over customary international law among *all* nations. However, there is modern literature developing that acknowledges that organizations such as this could have, among its own member States, its own 'customary international law.' This concept is acknowledged even by the United Nations General Assembly as 'particular customary international law.' According to the United Nations, such customary international law is that which is 'a rule of customary international law that applies only among a limited number of States.' The same requirements for traditional customary international law apply, such that determining the existence of such a rule requires determining 'whether there is a general practice among the States concerned that is accepted by them as law (*opinio juris*) among themselves.' *See* G.A. Res. 73/203, part Seven, Conclusion 16 (Dec. 20, 2018).

1262 *Ariane Rocket Reported to Have Exploded*, N.Y. TIMES, Dec. 2, 1986, at C5, https://www.nytimes.com/1986/12/02/science/ariane-rocket-reported-to-have-exploded.html. *See also* Ray A. Williamson, *The Growing Hazard of Orbiting Debris*, 8 ISSUES IN SCI. & TECH. 77, 77 (Fall 1991), https://www-jstor-org.libproxy.unl.edu/stable/43311139?seq=1#metadata_info_tab_contents. *See also* H. Klinkrad et at., *Space Debris Activities in Europe*, in Proceedings of the Fourth European Conference on Space Debris, 18–20 April 2005 Darmstadt, Germany 25, para. 1 (August 2005).

1263 ESA Corporate News, *Prof. Dr. Reimar Lust was the Third Director General of ESA*, https://www.esa.int/About_Us/Corporate_news/Reimar_Luest (last visited Jun. 25, 2022).

Debris Working Group with the mandate to assess the space debris problem and make recommendations to curb the growth and effects.[1264] This group issued their report in 1988,[1265] resulting in an ESA Resolution, *Resolution on the Agency's Policy vis-à-vis the Space Debris Issue*, focused on addressing the concerns raised going forward.[1266]

The ESA resolution identified several objectives, including minimizing the creation of space debris, reducing the risk to Earth because of object re-entry, reducing the risk to GEO satellites, acquiring data to assess the overall threat, and studying the legal aspects of the threat.[1267] Reinforcing the importance of the subject matter, in December 2000, ESA again adopted another resolution specific to space debris, highlighting its importance to ESA and its Member-States. Resolution E/SA/C/(2000)93, *Resolution for a European Policy on the Protection of the Space Environment from Debris*, reiterated the previous concerns highlighted during the adoption of the earlier 29 June 1989 ESA Resolution (C/LXXXVII/Res.3).[1268] It expressed concern over the growing

---

1264 H.A. Baker, *The ESA and USS reports on Space Debris*, 6 SPACE POL'Y 332, 332 (1990).

1265 W. Flury, *Activities in Space Debris in Europe*, Proceedings of the 3d Eur. Conf. on Debris, ESOC, Darmstadt, Germany, 19–21 March 2001 (Aug. 2001) (citing ESA Space Debris Working Group, Space Debris, *The Report of the ESA Space Debris Working Group*, ESA SP-1009, (Nov. 1988)). *See also* Baker, *supra* note 1264.

1266 European Space Agency, *Resolution on the Agency's Policy vis-à-vis the Space Debris Issue*, ESA/C/LXXXVII/Res. 3 (final), approved ESA/C (89)24, rev. 1 (cited in W. Flury, *Activities in Space Debris in Europe*, Proceedings of the 3d Eur. Conf. on Debris, ESOC, Darmstadt, Germany, 19–21 March 2001, para. 1 (Aug. 2001)).

1267 Flury, *supra* note 1265 at para. 1 (ESA SP-472, August 2001, para. 1 (note article 26)). *See also* W. Flury, *European Activities on Space Debris*, Proceedings of the 2d Eur. Conf. on Space Debris, ESOC, Darmstadt, Germany, 17–19 March 1997, para. 1, (May 1997). Both citing to ESA Space Debris Working Group, *Space Debris-The Report of the ESA Space Debris Working Group*, ESA SP-1109 (Nov. 1988). Concurrently, the European Parliament also considered the importance of space access and operations and developed its own policy to guide the greater European community. At the same time, the policy was meant to recognize the importance of partnerships, building the groundwork laid by ESA. *See* Resolution on Community Participation in Space Research, No C 127/42, OFFICIAL J. OF THE EUR. COMMUNITIES, p. 19, para. 4. Significantly, it also states that the Commission should assist ESA in drawing up a 'comprehensive program to meet the likely requirements of the community Member-States for the next ten years and cooperating fully to implement it as efficiently as possible.' *Id.* at p. 19, para. 7.

1268 Comm. On the Peaceful Uses of Outer Space, National Research on Space Debris, *Safety of Space Objects with Nuclear Power Sources on Board and Problems of their Collisions with Space Debris*, U.N. Doc. A/AC.105/751/Add.1, 7–8 (Jan. 29, 2001) https://www.unoosa.org/pdf/reports/ac105/AC105_751Add1E.pdf (identifying the Dec. 20, 2000, European Space Agency's Resolution for a European Policy on the Protection of the Space Environment from Debris).

debris population, highlighted the urgency of specific measures to ensure accessibility of space for all Nations, and expressed great interest in the further development of the studies and implementation of current mitigation efforts, to include an ESA debris handbook, debris database development, and debris risk analysis tools.[1269]

4 Specific Efforts at Forming Legal Norms for Space Debris Mitigation and Prevention

4.1 *ESA Space Debris Mitigation Handbook*

The *ESA Space Debris Mitigation Handbook* (hereafter the ESA Debris Handbook) was a significant undertaking. First produced in 1999, the original version provided a background on the existing debris environment and its origins, followed by an outlook on the current and future collision risk analysis for orbits.[1270] It also offered an analysis of future actions which could prevent the growth of debris, including mitigation scenarios, passivation activities, deorbiting techniques and retrieval.[1271] Additional guidance was offered on overall vehicle design and recommended areas of improvement to respond to the future debris environment.[1272]

A principal goal of the ESA Debris Handbook was to provide a roadmap of best practices for space activities, from planning to operations, in light of current and future debris risks.[1273] Version two, produced in 2002 (published 2003), added to the accuracy of the ESA Debris Handbook by providing updated information on the developing debris space environment, as well as addressing new technologies to identify improvements in spacecraft shielding and overall debris protection solutions.[1274] This document was a non-regulatory, self-standing document, meant to provide technical information in support of European debris mitigation standards in conjunction with other ongoing

1269 *Id.* (identifying the Dec. 20, 2000, European Space Agency's Resolution for a European Policy on the Protection of the Space Environment from Debris).

1270 R. Walker, et al., *Update of the ESA Space Debris Mitigation Handbook*, Proceedings of the 3d Eur. Conf. on Debris, ESOC, Darmstadt, Germany, 19–21 March 2001, 1 (ESA SP-473, Aug. 2001) https://conference.sdo.esoc.esa.int/proceedings/sdc3/paper/10/SDC3-paper10.pdf.

1271 *Id.*

1272 *Id.* at § 2, p. 2.

1273 *Id.* at § 1, p. 1.

1274 *Id.*

efforts.[1275] It has not, since 2002, been updated, but as of today, it remains listed (though no longer available at ESA) on the ESA site.[1276] Instead, since it was supporting other documents such as the European Commission on Space Activities, it continues to serve as a valuable historical precursor to other ESA debris efforts.

4.2 *European Code of Conduct for Space Debris Mitigation*

Concurrent with the ESA Debris Handbook, ESA and other interested European space agencies worked on additional efforts to mitigate space debris. In 2004,[1277] ESA in conjunction with the Italian Space Agency (ASI), British National Space Center (BNSC), French Space Agency (CNES), and German Space Agency (DLR) published the *European Code of Conduct for Space Debris Mitigation* (hereafter European Debris Mitigation Code).[1278] Its structure was not intended to dictate how the specific actions to mitigate debris must be done, but instead to set out a broad view of what must be accomplished for success.[1279] One primary goal was to allow the maximum flexibility for space agencies to apply existing successful programs where able, but at the same time evolve and improve others in accordance with the guidance.[1280]

The European Debris Mitigation Code sets out three objectives. First, prevention of on-orbit breakups and collisions.[1281] Second, removal and subsequent disposal of spacecraft and orbital stages that have reached the end-of-mission operations from the useful densely populated orbital regions.[1282] Finally, limit the release of objects during normal operations.[1283] Accordingly,

---

1275 H. Klinkard, et al., *The ESA Space Debris Mitigation Handbook 2002*, 34 ADVANCES IN SPACE RSCH. 1251 (2004), https://www.sciencedirect.com/science/article/abs/pii/S0273117704001061. *See also* non-regulatory nature of the ESA Debris Handbook, discussed in N. Jasentuliyana, *Space Debris and International Law*, 26 J. of Space L. 139, 154 (1998) https://airandspace.confit.dev/pdfs/jsl-26-2.pdf.

1276 *Space Debris*, EUR. SPACE AGENCY, https://www.esa.int/About_Us/ECSL_-_European_Centre_for_Space_Law/Space_Debris3. For secondary source, *see* Update of the ESA Space Debris Mitigation Handbook, ESA Contract 14471/00/D/HK, July 2002, available at https://nebula.esa.int/sites/default/files/neb_study/423/C14471ExS.pdf (last visited 12 Dec 2021).

1277 While developed in 2004, it was officially signed by the parties in 2006. *See Mitigating Space Debris Generation*, EUR. SPACE AGENCY, https://www.esa.int/Safety_Security/Space_Debris/Mitigating_space_debris_generation.

1278 European Code of Conduct for Space Debris Mitigation 1 (June 28, 2004), https://www.unoosa.org/documents/pdf/spacelaw/sd/2004-B5-10.pdf.

1279 *Id.* at 2.

1280 *Id.*

1281 *Id.* at 4.

1282 *Id.*

1283 *Id.*

the document was structured to provide guidance that covered recommendations for each of these areas of space operations (minus launch, specifically not covered in this book) with the execution managed through a space debris mitigation plan led by a space debris manager.[1284] As a code of conduct, compliance was originally voluntary, absent implementation by individual states or organizations for mandatory compliance through domestic laws.[1285] However, on 1 April 2008, the requirements became mandatory for ESA and Member-States, as well as contractors providing services to them.[1286] As will be seen shortly, the European Debris Mitigation Code was short-lived as a viable document, superseded by the adoption of a series of space debris mitigation standards.

4.3 *European International Code of Conduct for Outer Space Activities*

That European Debris Mitigation Code was not the only code being proposed at the time in Europe. Around the same time, the European Union (EU) offered their own *European International Code of Conduct for Outer Space Activities* (hereafter European Outer Space Code).[1287] Their version, proposed between 2007 and 2008, while touching on the protection of the outer space environment as one aspect, spoke to a much larger desire for cooperation among spacefaring Nations in conducting space activities.[1288] The European Outer Space Code additionally focused on aspects of security, safety, and sustainability in space.[1289] But it did still have elements specifically focused on the control of debris. Recalling the Outer Space Treaty, the European Outer Space Code

---

1284 *Id.* Additionally, *see* European Code of Conduct for Space Debris Mitigation §§ 3.2 & 3.3 (June 28, 2004), https://www.unoosa.org/documents/pdf/spacelaw/sd/2004-B5-10.pdf.

1285 European Code of Conduct for Space Debris Mitigation 5 (June 28, 2004), https://www.unoosa.org/documents/pdf/spacelaw/sd/2004-B5-10.pdf.

1286 Louis de Gouyon Matignon, *Marine Pollution Caused by Space Debris*, SPACE LEGAL ISSUES (Jan. 29, 2020), https://www.spacelegalissues.com/marine-pollution-caused-by-space-debris/.

1287 The specific construct of the European Union and its relationship to lawmaking, particularly concerning ESA, is outside of a discussion focused on space debris and mitigation. However, that is not to say that the EU does not play an important role in providing input, guidance, and law through established treaties among members of the EU. For an excellent discussion on the topic of the EU and its relationship to the space activities of the EU and ESA, recommend *Chapter 4, in* HANDBOOK OF SPACE LAW, *supra* note 513, pgs. 239–267 (Frans von der Dunk & Fabio Tronchetti eds., 2015).

1288 *Id.*

1289 *Id.* One of the main objectives was focused on preventing space from becoming an area of conflict, not only because of the general security concerns, but also because of the environmental concerns. For a thorough discussion on the history and background of the drafting, *see* Wolfgang Rathgeber, Nina-Louisa Remus & Kai-Owe Schrogl, *Space Security*

implored states to implement policies and procedures that would reduce the possibility of accidents, collisions among space objects, or harmful interference with the use and exploration by fellow Nations.[1290] Additionally, in the conduct of space operations, States were expected to refrain from damaging or destroying each other's space objects by their actions, unless there was some unavoidable necessity.[1291]

As a code, like those before it, this was a non-binding instrument and currently has seen no further advancement toward adoption than it did when proposed originally in 2008.[1292] This is likely due to a lack of support from the major space-faring Nations. In particular, the United States did not endorse it (often a fatal reason by itself) because the United States was concerned that the European Outer Space Code would limit the ability of the US military to use space.[1293] And while most experts weighed in that it was unlikely to hinder US operations, it remained unsigned by the United States.[1294] Other important countries, such as Russia and China, also declined to endorse it, publicly stating that they objected since they felt they were not sufficiently consulted during development and believed that it would hinder future capabilities of space powers.[1295]

---

and the European Code of Conduct for Outer Space Activities, 4 DISARMAMENT FORUM 33 (2009), https://www.peacepalacelibrary.nl/ebooks/files/UNIDIR_pdf-art2909.pdf.

1290 Draft International Code of Conduct for Outer Space Activities, ERO. SPACE AGENCY, para. 4.1 (Mar. 31, 2014), https://eeas.europa.eu/sites/default/files/space_code_conduct_draft_vers_31-march-2014_en.pdf.

1291 *Id.* at para. 4.2. Examples within the code of unavoidable ('justified') reasons included 1) by imperative safety considerations, such as risk to life or health of humans, 2) to reduce the creation of debris, or 3) because of a response through the Charter of the United Nations, such as in individual or collective self-defense. Even if these actions are taken, the expectation is that they will be taken in a manner most proportional or with minimal damage created to the outer space environment. *Id.* at para. 4.2.

1292 *See Chapter 4*, *in* HANDBOOK OF SPACE LAW, *supra* note 513 at pgs. 239–267 (Frans von der Dunk & Fabio Tronchetti eds., 2015).

1293 Micah Zenko, *A Code of Conduct for Outer Space*, COUNCIL ON FOREIGN RELATIONS (Nov. 30, 2011), https://www.cfr.org/report/code-conduct-outer-space.

1294 *Id.*

1295 *Id.* It is likely that, in the case of Russia and China, this explanation was an excuse not to get on board with the European Outer Space Code, instead deciding to press forward with their own (Russia and China) proposals for a binding treaty that would allow weaponization of space. *See* the Outer Space Treaty, Rajwswari Pillai Rajagopalan, *The Outer Space Treaty*, COUNCIL ON FOREIGN RELATIONS (Feb. 23, 2021), https://www.cfr.org/report/outer-space-treaty, calling out that the failure to precoordinate, and then to try to renew coordination, was likely too overwhelming and 'the damage was already done' with Russia and China. *See also* Jeff Abramson, *EU Issues Space Code of Conduct*, ARMS CONTROL ASS'N https://armscontrol.org/act/2009-01/eu-issues-space-code-conduct.

Efforts on the European Outer Space Code continued through 2015, when in July of 2015, the European Outer Space Code failed again to secure the backing of the major spacefaring powers and to this day remains a draft.

Meanwhile, though, it was often refuted that it would hinder future capabilities of space powers, the counterarguments were to no avail. *See* Sergio Marchisio, *The Draft Code of Conduct for Outer Space Activities*, U.N. Thailand Workshop on Space Law 16–19 November 2010, 2, https://www.unoosa.org/pdf/pres/2010/SLW2010/02-10b.pdf. Even so, it was additionally declined by the United States and others. The United States specifically argued that compliance would be unverifiable and would not cover ground-based systems. Zenko, *supra* note 1293. By 2012, it was dead on arrival in the United States, though the United States indicated it would participate and advance a different version that might be more agreeable, with the European Outer Space Code version as a baseline. *See Draft International Code of Conduct for Outer Space Activities Fact Sheet*, SECURE WORLD FOUNDATION, https://swfound.org/media/83247/icoc_factsheet_may2013.pdf (updated May 2013). Other arguments indicate that the use of the word "European" versus "International" caused others to decline to participate. Zenko, *supra* note 1293. Latin America and Africa fretted over the language referencing the right to self-defense, arguing that acknowledging the need for self-defense could accelerate the trend toward weaponization. Rajeswari Pillai Rajagopalan, *Keep Space Code of Conduct Moving Forward*, SPACE NEWS (July 21, 2015), https://spacenews.com/op-ed-keep-space-code-of-conduct-moving-forward/. Some countries aside from the EU supported it, such as Canada, arguing that it was valuable and such a code for the rules of the road needed to be implemented. Paul Meyer, *Star-Crossed: An International Code of Conduct for Outer Space?*, OPEN CANADA (Aug. 31, 2015), https://opencanada.org/star-crossed-an-international-code-of-conduct-for-outer-space/. However, in 2010, in the face of overwhelming objections, additional updates to the European Outer Space Code tried to address the areas of contention, at least about the lack of pre-coordination. But, even the updated language resulted in friction, especially in the area of defense (advocating that states should provide to each other "information on national space policies and strategies, including basic objectives for security and defense-related activities"). Zenko, *supra* note 1293. Finally, as with all codes of conduct, the purely voluntary nature created no repercussions for signing up, reaping the benefits, but not actually taking any steps to comply with the tenets. *Id.* So, those likely to be bad actors could conduct activities as they wished, while those who did comply had no control over responding to the poor behavior of others. This turned out to be a bridge too far for many of the major space powers which would otherwise have no recourse mechanism. *Id.* Ultimately, especially for mature spacefaring Nations, the future of the European Outer Space Code is not likely to find a resurgence because of the disadvantage it may impose. For a post-mortem analysis of the 2015 failure, *see* Michael Listner, *The International Code of Conduct: Comments on Changes in the Latest Draft and Post-Mortem Thoughts*, SPACE REV. (Oct. 26, 2015), https://www.thespacereview.com/article/2851/1.

5 International Organization for Standardization Debris Mitigation Guidelines

Though by most accounts an unsuccessful effort, the European Outer Space Code, like the European Debris Mitigation Code, still served as a precursor to the identification and implementation of mandatory standards.[1296] Today, ESA and its Member-States have implemented debris mitigation guidance published by the International Organization for Standardization (ISO) as the law of the land for space operations.[1297] ISO is an independent, non-governmental international organization comprised of a federation of national standards bodies, with each member body comprising varied governmental and non-governmental international organizations.[1298] It originated in 1946 as a result of delegates from over 25 countries meeting for the first time to discuss the need for international standardization among a broad set of activities.[1299] By 1947, as an international organization, it was officially established and the first standard, ISO/R 1:1951,[1300] was published four years later.[1301]

The standardization work involved today is typically developed within the construct of ISO technical committees.[1302] The committees are comprised of a wide variety of experts from around the world, with any organization expressing an interest in the subject matter invited to participate within the committee.[1303] The intent is to bring together "experts to share knowledge and develop voluntary, consensus-based, market-relevant international standards that support innovation and provide solutions to global challenges."[1304] The result of these committees is generally focused on drafting international

1296 Zenkho, *supra* note 1293.

1297 *Mitigating Space Debris Generation*, *supra* note 1277. *See also* R. Nasca, *Space Debris Mitigation Compliance to ESA*, EURO. SPACE AGENCY, 3 (Mar. 20, 2019), https://conference.sdo.esoc.esa.int/proceedings/ecsl19/paper/8/ECSL19-paper8.pdf.

1298 INT'L STANDARDIZATION ORGANIZATION, SPACE SYSTEMS—SPACE DEBRIS MITIGATION REQUIREMENTS (24113:2011), https://www.iso.org/obp/ui/#iso:std:iso:24113:ed-2:v1:en.

1299 *Id.*

1300 This first standard set a reference point for industrial length measurements. Interestingly, this standard still exists today, now ISO 1:2002. *See A Brief History of ISO—the International Organization for Standardization*, PERRY JOHNSON REGISTRARS, INC., https://www.pjr.com/about-pjr/what-is-certification/history-of-iso#.

1301 *Id.*

1302 INT'L STANDARDIZATION ORGANIZATION (24113:2011), *supra* note 1298.

1303 *Id.*

1304 *About Us*, INT'L STANDARDIZATION ORGANIZATION, https://www.iso.org/about-us.html. *See also* Song Qiang, *ISO Standards and Space Debris*, China Academy of Launch Vehicle Technology (Cot. 2011), https://swfound.org/media/50900/song_iso.pdf.

standards which are circulated for a vote of approval to member bodies.[1305] At least 75% of member bodies must approve a proposal for it to be established and accepted as a standard.[1306] Acceptance, of course, does not mean that these standards are binding.[1307] As mentioned above, while 'all countries are encouraged to abide by' these standards, unless elements are adopted into specific domestic regulations or treaties, or implemented by an country or organization whole-cloth, they remain recommendations only as ISO standards.[1308]

5.1 *ISO and ESA Adoption of Debris Standards—ISO 24113:2010 through ISO 24113:2019*

Beginning in 2010, the first major comprehensive ISO standard specific to space debris was issued, ISO 24113:2010, *Space Systems—Space Debris Mitigation Requirements*.[1309] By May 2011, the standard had been updated, ISO 24113:2011, with improved specifications, focused on establishing the design and operations requirements to minimize the impact of space operations on the orbital environment.[1310] The usefulness of this iteration was recognized by the European Cooperation on Space Standardization (ECSS) organization. The ECSS is an organization comprised of interested European space agencies that coordinate a single set of user-friendly standards for use in all European space activities.[1311] In the case of debris mitigation efforts, the ECSS review

---

1305 INT'L STANDARDIZATION ORGANIZATION (24113:2011), *supra* note 1298.

1306 *Id.*

1307 *Id.*

1308 *Id.*

1309 *Id.*

1310 *Id.*

1311 As outlined, the ECSS goals include 1) providing a set of documents which are recognized and accepted by the European space community for use in space programs and projects, 2) achieving more cost-effective space programs and projects in Europe in terms of technical performance, life cycle cost-effectiveness, and on-time deliveries, 3) improving the competitiveness of the European space sector, 4) improving the quality and safety of space projects and products, 5) reducing the risk and guaranteeing interoperability and interface compatibility by applying proved and recognized requirements and methods, 6) facilitating clear and unambiguous communications between all parties involved in space systems development and operation, in a form suitable for inclusion in legally binding documents, 7) reflecting user needs and feedback from program experiences, projects and other appropriate sources to improve the ECSS standards, while preserving internal coherency of the ECSS system, and finally, 8) accounting for new practices, products, technologies, and missions. *See ECSS-P-003 Standardization Objectives, Policies and Organization*, EUR. COOPERATION SPACE STANDARDIZATION 10 (Mar. 22, 2013), https://ecss.nl/standard/ecss-p-00c-standardization-objectives-policies-and-organization-22march2013/ which outlines the objectives of the ECSS.

determined that the ISO 24113:2011 standards were the best standards for debris mitigation.[1312] Rather than develop an independent ECSS version, in 2012, the ECSS decided to simply adopt the ISO standard entirely as its own standard.[1313] In 2014, ESA's Director-General, acting similarly to and informed by the decision of the ECSS, determined that ESA would also officially adopt ISO 24113:2011 as ESA's standard to be applied to all ESA space operations.[1314] That continues to be the case today, with the ISO 24113 standard, now ISO 24113:2019, continuing as the applicable debris mitigation requirements to be applied to any ESA project.[1315]

In 2014, ESA's Director-General additionally set out the official *Space Debris Mitigation Policy for Agency Projects*.[1316] This new policy, beyond adopting ISO 24113:2011, established the scope of the application, the method of compliance assessment, and the roles and responsibilities of parties involved in the execution of the ISO standards.[1317] Additionally, there were two annexes.[1318] The first set out the requirement that a Space Debris Mitigation Plan (SDMP) must accompany projects to ensure compliance with the requirements would be met.[1319] Additionally, the annex required that a Space Debris Mitigation Report (SDMR) must be created, documenting and verifying the mitigation plan at each major project step.[1320] The second annex provided terms and definitions for the relevant parties and activities.[1321] Last, unaddressed in the ISO standard, was the maximum acceptable casualty risk.[1322] As such, the Director-General

1312 *Space Sustainability Adoption Notice of ISO 24113: Space Systems, Space Debris Mitigation Requirements*, EUR. COOPERATION FOR SPACE STANDARDIZATION, ECSS-U-AS-10C (Feb. 10, 2012). *See also Space Sustainability Adoption Notice of ISO 24113: Space Systems, Space Debris Mitigation Requirements*, EUR. COOPERATION FOR SPACE STANDARDIZATION, ECSS-U-AS-10C Rev. 1 (Dec. 3, 2019), which acknowledges and implements the new update as of 2019 of ISO standard 24113:2019, for application in the ECSS.

1313 *Id.*

1314 *Space Debris Mitigation Policy for Agency Projects*, EUR. SPACE AGENCY, ESA/ADMIN/IPOL(2014)2 (Mar. 28, 2014). *See also Space Debris: The ESA Approach*, EUR. SPACE AGENCY 10 (2017), https://download.esa.int/esoc/downloads/BR-336_Space_Debris_WEB.pdf.

1315 Vitali Braun, et al., *Exploiting Orbital Data and Observation Campaigns to Improve Space Debris Models*, 66 J. OF ASTRONAUTICAL SCI. 192, 194 (2019), https://link.springer.com/article/10.1007/s40295-019-00155-6 (by subscription).

1316 *Space Debris Mitigation Policy for Agency Projects*, EUR. SPACE AGENCY, ESA/ADMIN/IPOL(2014)2 (Mar. 28, 2014).

1317 *Id.*

1318 *Id.*

1319 *Id.*

1320 *Id.*

1321 *Id.*

1322 Casualty risk is defined as the probability of serious injury or death. *Id.* at 2, Annex 2.

used the opportunity presented by this policy to establish a 'best-effort'[1323] standard.[1324] However, for launches that occurred after the adoption of the policy, the standard was set not to exceed 1 in 10,000 casualties for any re-entry event, regardless of whether the re-entry was controlled or not.[1325]

5.1.1 ISO 24113:2019—Space Systems-Space Debris Mitigation Requirements

As discussed, ISO 24113:2019, serves as ESA's "primary space debris mitigation requirement standard for all elements of unmanned systems launched into, or passing through, near-Earth space, including launch vehicle orbital stages, operating spacecraft, and any objects released as part of normal operations."[1326] However, ISO 24113:2019 is only the 'top-level standard' between the primary space debris objectives and the actual standards and implementation reports that support compliance by the developer and operator.[1327] The below graph provides a visual depiction of the sub-regulations that attempt to comprehensively address the important aspects of mitigation for the lifecycle of space operations, including preventing orbital breakups, estimating lifetimes for the planning of deorbiting or disposal, limiting re-entry risks, and assessing survivability from debris impact to spacecraft (See Figure 3).[1328]

ISO 24113:2019, as the top-level document, sets out specific requirements for debris mitigation, beginning with defining debris. Space debris (also referenced as orbital debris) is defined as "objects of human origin in Earth's orbit or reentering the atmosphere, including fragments and elements thereof, that

1323 The policy did not define what the 'best-effort' standard required. However, 'best-effort' standards are generally understood to mean that, as a matter of contract law, the promising party owes all effort which can be expected of a reasonable party of the same kind in the same circumstance, considering the particular nature of the contract and interests of the parties. *See Best Efforts Undertakings*, TRANS-LEX.ORG, https://www.trans-lex.org/932000/_/best-efforts-undertakings/#.

1324 *Space Debris Mitigation Policy for Agency Projects*, *supra* note 1316, 2, para. 2(a).

1325 *Id.* at 2, para. 2(b).

1326 INT'L STANDARDIZATION ORGANIZATION, SPACE SYSTEMS—SPACE DEBRIS MITIGATION REQUIREMENTS, ISO 24113:2019, 1, para. 1 (3d ed. 2019), https://webstore.ansi.org/Standards/ISO/ISO241132019?gclid=Cj0KCQiAgomBBhDXARIsAFNyUqP-ZbeJHRfnMLnD6gHIw01gYVjbL24tAqKQTi9-qkGHFe-W1EpzuIcaAldkEALw_wcB.

1327 *Id.*

1328 H. Stokes, *Evolution of ISO's Space Debris Mitigation Standards*, 7 J. OF SPACE SAFETY ENGINEERING 325 (2020), https://reader.elsevier.com/reader/sd/pii/S2468896720300689?token=BA7DD482305A0E77AC715E8D66B87E2653A06BD55 CAC502562BB1C2B7380505AC3ABEC97E028644627E91DCC7C9D122C.

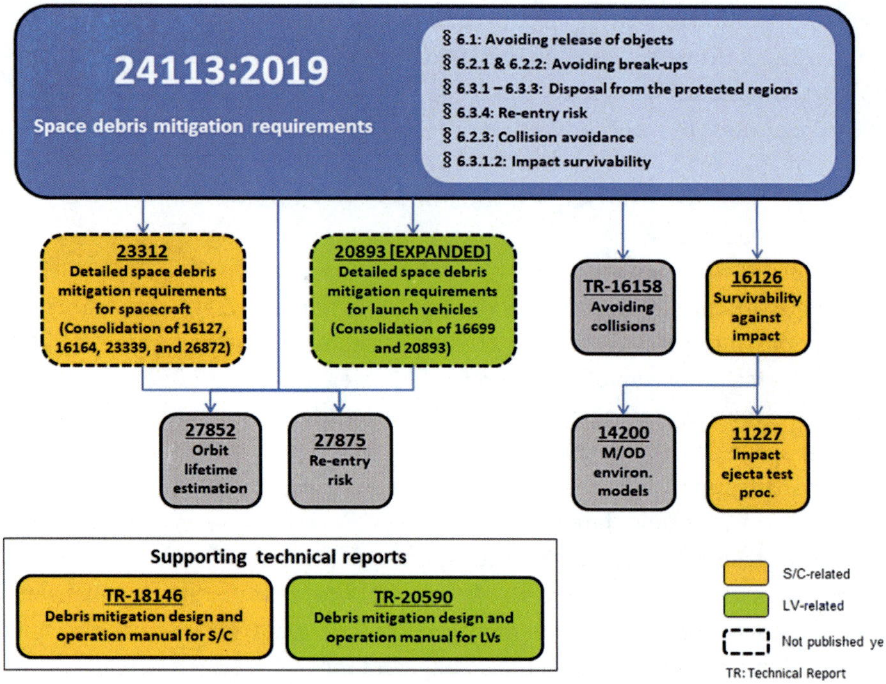

FIGURE 3 Visual depiction of the hierarchy of the ISO space debris mitigation standards. 24113:2019 provides the overarching guidance, with the lower regulations addressing specific vehicle types or activity.
SOURCE: DIAGRAM OBTAINED FROM H. STOKES ET AL., EVOLUTION OF ISO'S SPACE DEBRIS MITIGATION STANDARDS. *ID.* AT 328

no longer serve a useful purpose."[1329] It then sets out a specific list of top-level requirements and principles for the reduction of space debris. The regulation approaches the problem in phases, with requirements set out for each phase, within four major areas: the planning phase, the operational phase, dangers posed during the orbital lifetime, and end-of-mission expectations.[1330]

5.1.1.1 *ISO 24113:2019—Planning Phase Requirements*

The technical requirements set out during the planning phase require both a plan and ongoing attentiveness to prepare for potentially dangerous

1329 INT'L STANDARDIZATION ORGANIZATION (24113:2019), *supra* note 1326, 4, para. 3.23. Earth's orbit is defined as the bounded or unbounded Keplerian orbit with Earth at a focal point, or Lagrange point orbit which includes Earth as one of the two main bodies. *Id.* at 2, para. 3.8.

1330 *Id.* at para 3.23.

eventualities throughout the entire lifetime of the satellite. Beginning with the start of mission design, the expectation is that a SDMP will be developed that analyzes all phases of "design, manufacturing, launch, operation and disposal" to assess holistically the compliance of the activity with existing space debris mitigation requirements.[1331] Beyond applicability of mitigation requirements generally, there is also an expectation that a system is in place for verifying and validating whether the project is, and remains, compliant with mitigation expectations and any justifications in the event non-compliance for any reason is opined.[1332] Finally, the document remains 'living', such that there is an expectation that it will be reviewed and updated throughout all phases of operations, from inception to disposal.[1333] This overall plan, understandably, is not approved by ISO, which is only responsible for setting out the expectations (standards) of the plan and requirements for ongoing supervision. Instead, ISO 24113:2019 puts the burden on the approving agent for the plan, defined as the regulatory or licensing authority (whether national, international, or other delegated space agency) for which the activity is operating.[1334]

5.1.1.2 *ISO 24113:2019—Operational and Orbital Lifetime Phases Requirements*

Moving from the SDMP into actual execution, the operational guidelines of the ISO standard sets out expectations on spacecraft design and operation to prevent, or at worst mitigate, the release of debris into orbit through the activities of launch. In general, the policy is that no debris should be released.[1335] However, there are three specific exceptions that make some concessions for debris that are otherwise immediately unavoidable. The first acknowledges that space debris from pyrotechnics may occur, but should be designed to avoid release of space debris larger than 1 mm (in their largest dimension) in Earth's orbits.[1336] The second is that space debris from the solid rocket motors may occur, but the motors should be designed and operated so as also not to release space debris larger than 1 mm (in their largest dimension) in LEO or

1331 *Id.* at 9, para. 7.2.1.

1332 *Id.* at 9, paras. 7.2.2(c) & (e).

1333 *Id.* at 9, para. 7.2.4.

1334 *Id.* at 9, para. 7, planning requirements, regarding the SDMP specifically. *Id.* at 9–10, para. 7. *Id.* at 9–10, para. 7.2.3 for the requirement of approving agent and p. 1, para. 3.1 for the definition of approving agent.

1335 *Id.* at 6, para. 6.1.1.1.

1336 *Id.*

GEO protected regions.[1337] Finally, the launch vehicle orbital stage itself will understandably constitute debris, but it should be limited to one object.[1338] Pertinent to the orbital stage, there are additional restrictions based on where the stage will remain in outer space. If the orbital stage was for the placement of a man-made device into GEO orbit, then the stage after deployment should remain outside the GEO protected region for at least 100 years.[1339] If, on the other hand, the stage assisted in the placement of an object in LEO, it should have an orbital lifetime of no more than 25 years if it will orbit in, or cross through, LEO.[1340]

ISO 24113:2019 additionally addresses other aspects of operations for which debris can be created. This includes intentional destruction, accidental explosion, or accidental collisions of space objects (but does not necessarily consider fault for external events such as meteoroid or other debris impacts).[1341] Of course, the expectation for intentional destruction of a space object is

1337 *Id.* at 6, para. 6.2.2.2. ISO 24113:2019 defines protected regions as "regions in outer space that are protected with regard to the generation of space debris to ensure their safe and sustainable use in the future." *Id.* at 4, para. 3.21. ISO views the LEO protected region as a 'shell that extends from the surface of a spherical Earth … up to 2000 km.' *Id.* at 6, para. 5.2. ISO views the GEO protected region as 'a segment of a spherical shell which extends 200 km above and below the GEO altitude (35,786 km).' *Id.* at 6, para. 5.3.

1338 *Id.* at 6, para. 6.1.1.2.

1339 *Id.* at 6, para. 6.1.1.3(a).

1340 *Id.* at 6, para. 6.1.1.3(b). Importantly, INT'L STANDARDIZATION ORGANIZATION, SPACE SYSTEMS—ESTIMATION OF ORBIT LIFETIME, ISO 27852:2016, (2d ed., 2016) provides further amplifying specificity on how to appropriately model for ensuring compliance with the 25-year rule. In particular, it offers three specific processes that will be used in addition to any user-imposed constraints. *Id.* at para. 4.1. Notably, all three methods have benefits and drawbacks, appropriately outlined in each recommendation, but suggests that Method 1, high-precision numerical integration, is the best of the three options. ISO 24113:2019, para. 5.2., Method 1 primarily integrates a series of factors to attempt to account for predictable outcomes, even though not all of the factors can be definitively known (which also leads to its biggest drawback; imprecision). ISO 24113:2019, para. 5.2., Method 2 has the benefit of speed in calculation, but is less precise as a result of using an average ballistic coefficient versus an 'attitude-dependent' one specific to the object. ISO 24113:2019, para. 5.3., Method 3 provides a numerical table look-up analysis and fit formula evaluations, which is the result of using Methods 1 and 2 to allow analysts to estimate orbital lifetime for their particular space object. The margin of error varies between 10% and 25%. ISO 24113:2019; para. 5.4. In all methods, the standard identifies 25-year compliance success is reliant on utilization of a combination of "a) initial orbit selection, b) spacecraft vehicle design, c) spacecraft launch and early orbit concepts of operation which minimize LEO-crossing objects, d) spacecraft ballistic parameter modification at end-of-life, and e) spacecraft deorbit maneuvers." ISO 27852:2016, para. 4.1.

1341 INT'L STANDARDIZATION ORGANIZATION (24113:2019), *supra* note 1326, 7, para. 6.2.

zero.[1342] That said, accidental explosions and accidental collisions present unique challenges.

For accidental breakups, the regulation establishes that the probability of accidental breakup should be reduced to less than .001 (1 in 1,000) for the operational life of the object.[1343] As well, whether the object is planned for a controlled re-entry or not, it should be passivated to reduce any remaining onboard sources of energy to minimize the chance of an accidental explosion resulting in debris particles being dispersed.[1344] Finally, any object as part of its operational life should continually be monitored for any potential malfunctions which might otherwise result in destruction.[1345]

For accidental breakup caused by collision, the standard requires that spacecraft operating in GEO or LEO must have recurrent maneuver capability, with those in LEO having an additional expectation of continual supervision and active management to avoid collision.[1346] Interestingly, the specific collision risk threshold opined in this section is not set at any level. Instead the regulation defers to the approving agent to determine an appropriate level.[1347] However, if reached, the regulation requires ("shall") collision maneuvers be conducted to reduce the risk of collision to a level below the set threshold.[1348] There is also a planning element with an expectation that even though meteoroid impact is outside the control of the operators, spacecraft designers should incorporate this risk into designs to reduce the potential of breakups.[1349]

1342 *Id.* at 7, para. 6.2.1.

1343 *Id.* at 7, para. 6.2.2.1.

1344 *Id.* at 7, paras. 6.2.2.2 & 6.2.2.3.

1345 *Id.* at 7, paras. 6.2.2.5 & 6.2.2.6.

1346 *Id.* at 7, paras. 6.2.3.1 & 6.2.3.2. ISO Technical Report 16158:2013(E), *Space Systems—Avoiding Collisions with Orbiting Objects*, amplifies the relevant considerations for collision avoidance. Primarily, it describes the variables which must be analyzed in making the best plan of action for collision avoidance. This includes trajectory data to understand approaches to objects that could result in collisions, probabilities of the collision (and inherent inaccuracy), and the ability of each of the conjunction partners to be (or not be) able to conduct a maneuver. An even more strategic consideration also includes the very real possibility that an avoidance maneuver could result in an entirely new collision possibility with another object (which could be even more catastrophic than the first). *See* INT'L STANDARDIZATION ORGANIZATION, SPACE SYSTEMS—AVOIDING COLLISIONS WITH ORBITING OBJECTS, ISO/TR 16158:2013(E), Introduction (2013).

1347 INT'L STANDARDIZATION ORGANIZATION (24113:2019), *supra* note 1326, 7, para. 6.2.3.3.

1348 *Id.* at 7, para. 6.2.3.3.

1349 *Id.* at 7, para. 6.2.3.4. There is one primary sub-regulation to ISO 24113:2019 to address impact survivability, and an additional two ISO standards to provide amplifying information. INT'L STANDARDIZATION ORGANIZATION, SPACE SYSTEMS—ASSESSMENT OF SURVIVABILITY OF UNMANNED SPACE AGAINST SPACE DEBRIS AND METEOROID IMPACTS TO ENSURE SUCCESSFUL POST-MISSION DISPOSAL, ISO 16126:2014 (1st ed.

5.1.1.3 *ISO 24113:2019—End-of-Mission Requirements*

The final of the four phases involves the disposal of a spacecraft or launch vehicle orbital stage after the end-of-mission and addresses the requirements in three parts: general guidance, disposal in GEO, and disposal in LEO. General guidance requires that the probability of successful disposal of a spacecraft shall be at least 90% through end of the life.[1350] In addition, an assessment of the spacecraft for its ability to comply with the probability of successful disposal must be accomplished. This requires assessing variables such as its resistance to external impact, sufficient fuel for disposal maneuver (especially if there is a consideration for an extension of the original mission timeline),

---

2014) sets out a procedure for assessing survivability of unmanned spacecraft against debris and meteoroid impacts with the objective of ensuring the survival of critical components necessary for proper post-mission disposal. It also offers two impact risk analysis procedures to inform the likelihood of EOM disposal success in the event of impacts. *Id.* at para. 1. The analysis requires that a determination be made on the probability a spacecraft will (or not) be able to complete successful post-mission disposal. This is important because the risk analysis focuses on the condition of the spacecraft for disposal specifically; the analysis is not concerned with whether impact will prevent it from functioning for its intended mission purpose. If it will likely fail as a result of the impacts to the systems necessary for proper disposal, then additional protection on the spacecraft or design of the spacecraft must be readdressed. *Id.* at paras. 7.1.1 & 8.1.1. In attempting to determine what the population of meteoroids and other space debris is that will have an impact on the spacecraft, the INT'L STANDARDIZATION ORGANIZATION, SPACE ENVIRONMENT (NATURAL AND ARTIFICIAL)—GUIDE TO PROCESS-BASED IMPLEMENTATION OF METEOROID AND DEBRIS ENVIRONMENTAL MODELS (ORBITAL ALTITUDES BELOW GEO +2,000 KM), ISO 14200:2012(e) (1st ed. 2012), attempts to provide some guidance. ISO 14200:2012(e) acknowledges that there are many different models for impact risk assessment and attempts to give guidelines for the selection process for which model to use. *Id.* at para. 1. This involves a three-step approach: 1) Model selection agreement between the parties, 2) Model selection that is suitable to the project, and 3) implementation of the model on a project and the ability to properly obtain the necessary data from the selection. *Id.* at paras. 5.3.1.1–5.3.1.3. Finally, the analysis can help inform, based on the potential impacts, the material's vulnerability that is being considered for use in the spacecraft and launch vehicle. ISO 11227:2012 provides a ranking of materials and an assessment of what ejecta will result from hypervelocity impact. *See* INT'L STANDARDIZATION ORGANIZATION, SPACE SYSTEMS—TEST PROCEDURE TO EVALUATE SPACECRAFT MATERIAL EJECTA UPON HYPERVELOCITY IMPACT, AMENDMENT 1: OBLIQUE IMPACTS AND ANNEX C UPDATE, ISO 1227:2012 (2012), https://www.iso.org/standard/57535.html (only summary available), as well as INT'L STANDARDIZATION ORGANIZATION, SPACE SYSTEMS—TEST PROCEDURE TO EVALUATE SPACECRAFT MATERIAL EJECTA UPON HYPERVELOCITY IMPACT, AMENDMENT 1: OBLIQUE IMPACTS AND ANNEX C UPDATE, ISO 11227:2012/ DAM 1 (2020).

1350 INT'L STANDARDIZATION ORGANIZATION (24113:2019), *supra* note 1326, 7, para. 6.3.1.1.

continual spacecraft condition assessment, and whether disposal will be initiated manually or preprogrammed based on a set of criteria being met.[1351]

The second part of the disposal requirements address disposal for GEO objects. For a launch vehicle orbital stage, the expectation is that the object will not interfere with the GEO for at least 100 years after its end-of-life.[1352] For spacecraft operating within the GEO region, two options exist for disposal. The first is for the object to be placed in a graveyard orbit above GEO (as discussed earlier, generally an altitude 200 km above the protected GEO zone), or alternatively that the spacecraft is put in an altitude that will prevent it from entering GEO for at least 100 years after end-of-life.[1353]

For LEO, the expectation is similar, except the timeline is reduced from 100 to 25 years or less.[1354] The start of the 25-year count begins from one of three starting points. First, if the object cannot perform maneuvers, then the clock is measured from the time of the object's first entry into LEO orbit (if operating within LEO).[1355] If, however, the object has the ability to perform avoidance maneuvers, then the clock begins at the end of the mission.[1356] Or finally, if the object otherwise operates outside of LEO, the clock begins from the first time it enters LEO if within 100 years after the end-of-life of the object.[1357] The options for removal of the object from LEO, in order of preference of method, is by retrieval, controlled re-entry to a safe disposal location on the Earth's surface,[1358] natural decay within 25 years, maneuver in a controlled manner (again, within less than 25 years), or deployment of a device to assist in decay in less than 25 years.[1359] Should re-entry be considered, proper risk assessments

1351 *Id.* at 8, para. 6.3.

1352 *Id.* at 8, para. 6.3.2.1.

1353 *Id.* at 8, para. 6.3.2.2.

1354 *Id.* at 8, para. 6.3.3.1.

1355 *Id.* at 9, para. 6.3.3.1(a).

1356 *Id.* at 9, para. 6.3.3.1(b).

1357 *Id.* at 9, para. 6.3.3.1(c).

1358 For specific discussion/guidance on re-entry and risks, *see* INT'L STANDARDIZATION ORGANIZATION (24113:2019), *supra* note 1326, 9, para. 6.3.3.1(C). This ISO regulation provides a framework to "assess, reduce, and control the potential risks that spacecraft and launch vehicle orbital stages pose to people and the environment when those space vehicles re-enter the Earth's atmosphere and impact the earth's surface." *Id.* at para. 1. The ISO outlines the need for a Re-entry Risk Assessment and Mitigation Plan (RRAMP) to inform the re-entry procedure. *Id.* at para. 4.4.1. The RRAMP is informed by the risk magnitude expressed as an assessment of the combination of the severity of an object hitting something on Earth and the likelihood of its occurrence. *Id.* at para. 4.5. *See also Id.* at Annex B for different models and scoring schemes for each. *See also Id.* at 1, Annex B for the modified equation to obtain expected number of casualties (Ec).

1359 INT'L STANDARDIZATION ORGANIZATION (24113:2019), *supra* note 1326, 9, para. 6.3.3.2.

should be conducted within the thresholds as tolerable and established by the approving agent in control of the vehicle or object.[1360]

5.2 *Progeny of ISO 24113:2019—Debris Mitigation for Spacecraft and Launch Vehicles*

As stated in the beginning, ISO 24113:2019 is a parent regulation that sets out the broad expectations to address space debris mitigation. To provide detail in support of the standard, a series of sub-standards focus on specific aspects of space activities based on type. The first sub-category of regulations is focused on providing a detailed description of space debris mitigation requirements for spacecraft. At the time of this writing, there are four regulations focused on this area: ISO 16164:2015, ISO 26872:2019, ISO 23339:2012, and ISO 16127:2014.[1361] There is an expectation that eventually these four regulations will be consolidated under an omnibus ISO 23312.[1362] In addition to the requirements for spacecraft, there is also a complementary set of sub-regulations to ISO 24113:2019 that are focused on space debris mitigation requirements for launch vehicles, which includes ISO 16699:2015 and ISO 20893:2021. Similarly, at the time of this writing, those two ISO standards are the existing standards. However, a consolidation effort is ongoing to subsume both regulations into an 'expanded' ISO 20893. Each is taken in turn below.

5.2.1 Space Debris Mitigation Requirements for Spacecraft—ISO 16164:2015, ISO 26872:2019, ISO 23339:2012, ISO 16127:2014

For spacecraft, the first of the four regulations, ISO 16164:2015, *Space Systems—Disposal of Satellites Operating in or Crossing Low Earth Orbit*, deals exclusively with disposal of spacecraft operating in, or crossing through, LEO.[1363] It does

1360 *Id.* at 9, para. 6.3.4.

1361 It is important to note that while these relate to detailed space debris mitigation requirements for spacecraft, there is also an additional regulation pertinent to mitigation of debris for spacecraft: INT'L STANDARDIZATION ORGANIZATION, SPACE SYSTEMS—SPACE DEBRIS MITIGATION DESIGN AND OPERATION MANUAL FOR SPACECRAFT, TECHNICAL REPORT, ISO/TR 18146:2020 (2d ed. 2020). This technical manual is meant to assist engineers on both a review of the normative (mandatory) provisions of the ISO standards, as well as non-normative 'best-practices.' *Id.* at para. 1.

1362 Space Systems-Detailed Space Debris Mitigation Requirements for Spacecraft, INT'L STANDARDIZATION ORG. ISO/DIS 23312, Verified on Nov. 13, 2021, ISO 23112, ISO—ISO/DIS 23312—Space systems—Detailed space debris mitigation requirements for spacecraft (remains in 'under development' status).

1363 INT'L STANDARDIZATION ORGANIZATION, SPACE SYSTEMS—DISPOSAL OF SATELLITES OPERATING IN OR CROSSING LOW EARTH ORBIT, ISO 16164:2015(E) (1st ed. 2015).

not modify the basic requirements of ISO 24113:2019, but instead provides the granular details for spacecraft exclusively operating in LEO.[1364] Notably, in addition to the SDMP of ISO 24113:2019, ISO 16164:2015 requires the development of a plan specifically for post-mission disposal, the 'end-of-mission disposal plan' (EOMDP), which is meant to inform the overall SDMP for the entire operation.[1365] This assessment is comprehensive, incorporating not only the previously discussed requirement of a 90% success probability for any selected disposal method, but also guidance for specificity in each selection of disposal.[1366] In the event that the satellite will otherwise be disposed of in a way other than re-entry, specifics on passivation are also a requirement when all other activities for end-of-mission (EOM) are complete.[1367]

Similarly, ISO 26872:2019, *Space Systems—Disposal of Satellites Operating at Geosynchronous Altitude*,[1368] also deals exclusively with spacecraft. As its name suggests, ISO 26872:2019 outlines obligations for spacecraft exclusively within the GEO orbit. In addition, it sets out the guidelines for disposal specific to four major areas, considering that deorbit from GEO into Earth's atmosphere is (currently) entirely impractical.

First, the regulation addresses when the disposal action needs to be initiated.[1369] While the EOMDP requires planning for a successful determination, the regulation aptly points out that a series of variables may affect the actual moment when disposal actions should be initiated.[1370] As a result, a repeated assessment of the satellite must be conducted to determine the appropriate time when EOM is nearing. These factors include the remaining propellant in the satellite, the redundancy of systems and status of electrical power, redundancy and functioning of critical systems, and the time required to execute disposal actions.[1371] Independently, or in combination, these are all factors that could affect when disposal efforts should begin.[1372]

Second, the regulation establishes where the final disposal orbit should be. The regulation offers two options. The first is if the perigee of the final orbit

1364 *Id.* at 1, para. 1.
1365 *Id.* at 3, para. 6.2.
1366 *Id.* at 4, para. 6.3.
1367 *Id.* at 5, para. 6.7.
1368 INT'L STANDARDIZATION ORGANIZATION, SPACE SYSTEMS—DISPOSAL OF SATELLITES OPERATING AT GEOSYNCHRONOUS ALTITUDE, ISO 26872:2019 (2d ed. 2019).
1369 *Id.* at 6, para. 7.3.
1370 *Id.*
1371 *Id.*
1372 *Id.*

is above GEO at an altitude that will prevent the spacecraft from entering GEO within 100 years to avoid collisions with others. The alternative option is an orbit calculated such that the long-term perturbations will not cause the object to ever reenter the protected zone of GEO plus 200 km.[1373]

Third, the regulation requires that the operator ensure the disposal action is executed successfully (reflecting the 90% probability rule).[1374] This requires a design so the satellite will have sufficient energy to achieve the disposal orbit and be capable of receiving the commands to passivate the necessary systems upon disposal.[1375]

Finally, the regulation addresses ensuring passivation of the satellite to avoid debris creation because of an explosion at the EOM. The 'vehicle securing plan' involves depletion of propellants and on-board energy sources to ensure the satellite does not become dangerous debris within the GEO protected zone (or below), nor will the predicted final orbit be altered to create an otherwise unplanned orbital trajectory.[1376]

The third of the four sub-regulations focused on spacecraft is ISO 23339:2010, *Space Systems—Unmanned Spacecraft—Estimating the Mass of Remaining Usable Propellant*.[1377] Complementing the prior two regulations on the operations of spacecraft for end-of-life disposal planning, the focus here, as the title suggests, requires establishing the remaining usable propellant. This will help determine when to initiate EOM procedures, including how much fuel will be required to establish a graveyard orbit or re-entry, as well as how much propellant remains for passivation.[1378] Additionally, it informs the design of propellant measurement systems. What is particularly interesting is the acknowledgment of the imperfection of assessing the total remaining propellant. Because of the imprecision, both in the planning and operational phases of satellite operations, an estimate of the remaining propellant must include a sum large enough to account for the error probability.[1379] In other words, whatever the most conservative estimate of the remaining fuel is must control the decision-making for the satellite EOM initiation and deorbiting calculus.[1380]

1373 *Id.* at 7, para. 8.3.
1374 *Id.* at 6, para. 7.2.
1375 *Id.* at 6, para. 7.3.
1376 *Id.* at 8, para. 8.7.
1377 INT'L STANDARDIZATION ORGANIZATION, SPACE SYSTEMS—UNMANNED SPACECRAFT—ESTIMATING THE MASS OF REMAINING USABLE PROPELLANT, ISO 23339:2010 (1st ed. 2010).
1378 *Id.* at 2, para. 4.2.
1379 *Id.* at paras. 4.1–5.3.
1380 *Id.* at paras. 4.1–5.3.

The last of the four sub-regulations focused on spacecraft is ISO 16127:2014, *Space Systems—Prevention of Breakup of Unmanned Spacecraft*, which represents a culmination of much of the previous guidance to prevent avoidable debris causing events.[1381] This sub-standard addresses that to prevent a key debris-creating event such as a satellite breakup, a series of considerations should be evaluated to minimize the overall risk.[1382] However, this regulation is narrowly focused on only unmanned spacecraft, does not include nuclear power sources, and does not apply to fragmentations as a result of external impacts.[1383] It is specifically focused on design characteristics to reduce the risk of on-orbit breakup caused by an unplanned internal event or resulting from a failure to deplete all sources of stored energy.[1384]

Regarding an unplanned internal event, the expectation is that the design of the craft will otherwise factor in all the systems that could have a destructive fault and account for both redundancy and an ability to monitor the health of the system to determine risk.[1385] Regarding EOM activity, the expectation is that passivation should allow for all on-board sources of stored energy to be depleted once no longer required.[1386] This includes residual propellants, batteries, high-pressure vessels, self-destructive devices, flywheels, and momentum wheels at a minimum.[1387] Ultimately, the plan should be reviewed continually during design and through operation.[1388] It should also have processes and available tools that allow for monitoring the relevant parameters of each system of the satellite that could otherwise fail to prevent the occurrence or minimize the damage capacity and debris creation if the event is otherwise unavoidable.[1389]

5.2.2 Space Debris Mitigation Requirements for Launch Vehicles

The second sub-category under 24113:2019 are standards addressing detailed space debris mitigation requirements for launch vehicles. The first of two is

---

1381 INT'L STANDARDIZATION ORGANIZATION, SPACE SYSTEMS—PREVENTION OF BREAK-UP OF UNMANNED SPACECRAFT, ISO 16127:2014(E) (1st ed. 2014).

1382 INT'L STANDARDIZATION ORGANIZATION, SPACE SYSTEMS—UNMANNED SPACECRAFT—ESTIMATING THE MASS OF REMAINING USABLE PROPELLANT, ISO 23339:2010, 1, para. 1 (1st ed. 2010).

1383 *Id.*

1384 *Id.*

1385 *Id.* at 2, para. 4.1.

1386 *Id.*

1387 *Id.*

1388 *Id.* at 3, para. 4.3.1.

1389 *Id.*

ISO 16699:2015, *Space Systems—Disposal of Orbital Launch Stages*.[1390] Launch vehicles are among some of the more concerning objects that are released into space upon the delivery of the primary spacecraft.[1391] They are often large and contain residual propellants or other sources of energy that can cause explosion and debris release.[1392] As a result, the objective of this regulation is to provide guidance on the removal of launch stages from orbit or move them to non-threatening orbits at EOM.[1393] 16699:2015 provides guidance on removal through either re-entry into the atmosphere in as short a time as possible, or leaving the object in an orbit that will not intersect regions where it is likely to collide with other objects.[1394] The specific options for disposal of the stage rocket within this regulation cross-reference the options in ISO 24113:2019, including retrieval, decay, and manipulation to assist in decay.[1395] If the option of keeping the object in orbit is selected, passivation is a key component since the object could still pose a significant danger to other objects if it does not remain intact.[1396]

The second of the two regulations addressing detailed space debris mitigation requirements for launch vehicles is ISO 20893:2021, *Space Systems—Detailed Space Debris Mitigation Requirements for Launch Vehicle Orbital Stages*.[1397] This document provides a more in-depth discussion of avoidance

---

1390 INT'L STANDARDIZATION ORGANIZATION, SPACE SYSTEMS—DISPOSAL OF ORBITAL LAUNCH STAGES, ISO 16699:2015, v (1st ed. 2015).

1391 *Id.*

1392 *Id.*

1393 *Id.*

1394 *Id.*

1395 INT'L STANDARDIZATION ORGANIZATION (24113:2019), *supra* note 1326, 9, para. 6.3.3.2.

1396 INT'L STANDARDIZATION ORGANIZATION, SPACE SYSTEMS—DISPOSAL OF ORBITAL LAUNCH STAGES, ISO 16699:2015, 3, para. 5.2(c) (1st ed. 2015).

1397 INT'L STANDARDIZATION ORGANIZATION, SPACE SYSTEMS—DETAILED SPACE DEBRIS MITIGATION REQUIREMENTS FOR LAUNCH VEHICLE ORBITAL STAGES, ISO 20893:2021 (1st ed. 2021). It is important to note that ISO 20893:2021 and ISO 16699:2015 both relate to launch vehicle orbital stages. Those regulations are normative. However, additional recommended (non-normative) activities for the proper design and operation of orbital stages are otherwise not specifically captured in those two regulations. To fill the gap, ISO/TR 20590:2017(E), *Debris Mitigation Design and Operation Manual for Launch Vehicle Orbital Stages*, was produced. It targets engineers to help guide them in applying the normative standards from 24113:2019, 20893:2021, and 1699:2015. It also provides non-normative 'best practices' for design and operation of launch vehicles. ISO/TR 20590:2017(E), Introduction. For example, section 4 breaks down all the relevant ISO standards (normative) for each type of space-related element (launch vehicle, spacecraft, safety systems, et cetera.) and other relevant guidelines concerning debris (for example, the IADC guidelines; non-normative). INT'L STANDARDIZATION ORGANIZATION,

measures to prevent breakup of orbital stages. Primarily, it accomplishes this by addressing two major threats. The first is passivation, establishing specific requirements for removal of residual propellants, pressured gasses, and the depletion of battery power for example.[1398] Separately, the prevention of breakups because of collision.[1399] This is primarily accomplished by ensuring the proper removal after EOM to negate the threat through either re-entry into Earth's atmosphere or through the placement into outer space in an area that poses no danger to populated orbits.[1400] In all cases, planning ahead and vigilant monitoring during operations is key, with contingency planning for failures in either case amplifying the likelihood of success.[1401]

6 Beyond ESA ISO Standards

These ISO standards inform how ESA implements its requirements for spacecraft and space vehicle activities. However, these regulations are not the only guidepost from which ESA operates. The regulatory bodies of the European Union, namely the European Commission and Parliament, establish requirements through the legislative process for how the European Union will advance its interests in space. In addition to usual suspects, such as the advancement of economic interests in space, they have also undertaken to amplify the importance of space debris prevention and mitigation efforts. The primary method for advancing this message is through the European Commission Space Strategy for Europe. It is worth briefly discussing the relevant aspects here to touch on the high-level efforts and intention of the regulatory bodies.

6.1 *European Union Space Strategy for Europe*

In addition to the efforts of organizations like ESA and the ECSS, the European Union exerts its requirements and guidance over space matters, including debris, via the European Commission. The European Commission is the European Union's politically independent executive arm. Its responsibilities

Space Systems—Debris Mitigation Design and Operation Manual for Launch Vehicle Orbital Stages, ISO/TR 20590:2017(E), para. 4 (1st ed. 2017).

1398 Int'l Standardization Organization, Space Systems—Detailed Space Debris Mitigation Requirements for Launch Vehicle Orbital Stages, ISO 20893:2021, 2–3, para. 5 (1st ed. 2021).

1399 *Id.* at 3, para. 5.2.

1400 *Id.* at 2–3, para. 6.2.

1401 *Id.* at 2–3, para. 6.4.

include proposing new laws for adoption by Parliament and the Council of the European Union as well as drafting and advocating for support of strategies for important European Sectors.[1402] In 2016, the European Commission put forward the most recent Space Strategy for Europe, arguing that Europe needed to work together in space to promote its position as a leader, increase accesses and improve market-share in world space markets, as well as harness the benefits and advantages of space.[1403]

The strategy consists of four main goals.[1404] First, maximizing the benefits of space for society and the European economy.[1405] Second, fostering a globally competitive and innovative European space sector.[1406] Third, reinforcing Europe's autonomy in accessing and using space in a secure and safe environment.[1407] Last, strengthening Europe's role as a global actor and promoting international cooperation.[1408]

The third goal is particularly important for the discussion of space debris.[1409] It highlights the importance that the European Commission and European space efforts, writ large, place on good stewardship of the orbital environment. Specifically, it states that debris "remains the most serious risk to the sustainability of space activities."[1410] Furthermore, it must remain a topic of importance both within Europe, and among the international community. In addressing Europe's role, the European Commission highlighted SSA and tracking of debris as one of the services it now provides to better assess and address the vulnerabilities of space debris by more accurately identifying it.[1411] This, coupled with European standardizations for the minimization of

1402 *European Commission*, EUROPEAN UNION, https://europa.eu/european-union/about-eu/institutions-bodies/european-commission_en.

1403 *Communication from the Commission to the European Parliament, the Council, the European Economic and Social Committee and the Committee of the Regions*, at 3 COM (2016) 705 final (Oct. 26, 2016), eur-lex.europa.eu/legal-content/EN/TXT/PDF/?uri=CELEX:52016DC0705&from=EN. Earlier versions, as early as 2000, similarly focused on advancing the interests of Europe, including strengthening foundations for space activities, enhancing scientific knowledge, and utilizing the results to benefit society and the markets. Interestingly, the earliest of the versions mentions nothing about debris as a specific problem. *Id.*

1404 *Id.*

1405 *Id.*

1406 *Id.* at 5.

1407 *Id.* at 8.

1408 *Id.* at 11.

1409 *Id.* at 9, para. 3.3.

1410 *Id.*

1411 *Id.*

space debris, is an important contribution to ensure Europe's space aspirations maintain a focus on debris prevention and mitigation.

Going forward, while the 2016 strategy was an important contribution, the European Union recognizes that more needs to be done. The latest iteration of the European Space Strategy is under review and focuses not only on the improvement of the previous version but also on addressing new and emerging issues. Among the goals included are supporting new space exploration missions with a European-centric focus, maximizing existing systems to improve terrestrial connectivity, reducing international dependence for space programs and support elements, and finally, support for European entrepreneurship.[1412]

In the meantime, the European Council and Parliament are moving forward with approval for the adoption of the regulation to implement their strategy by establishing the European Union Space Program for the years 2021 to 2027.[1413] If passed, at least currently, the regulation will serve to enhance security and autonomy of the European Union, provide more leadership roles for the European Union in space, support space-related data and services, and result in more economic benefits for the European Union.[1414] Additionally, the regulation proposes a review, simplification, and streamlining of the existing European Union framework on space policy.[1415] Collectively, these efforts should allow the European Union to build on the previous space debris efforts and make advancements toward policies that improve the chances of reducing the amount of new debris going forward.

7 Conclusion

A multipronged approach to addressing the concerns associated with space debris is unquestionably critical to success, if not the solution. The continuing efforts of Europe in that direction, particularly through their regulatory implementation plans and policy guidance, are critical to any effective space debris program. In fact, an assessment of the existing European rules on mitigation of

1412 Sarah Harford, *4 Key Elements of the EU's New Space Strategy*, SILICONREPUBLIC (Jan. 13, 2021), https://www.siliconrepublic.com/innovation/eu-space-strategy-2021.

1413 Council of the EU Press Release Council Adopts Position on €14.8 Billion EU Space Programme for 2021–2027, EC, Council of the EU (Apr. 19, 2021), https://www.consilium.europa.eu/en/press/press-releases/2021/04/19/council-adopts-position-on-14-8-billion-eu-space-programme-for-2021-2027/.

1414 *Id.*

1415 *Id.*

space debris efforts would likely conclude that ESA and its Member-States are among the most committed in the international community to reducing space debris from the orbital environment. Moreover, while many of the previous countries and international organizations have significant principles or hard laws in effect, the ISO standards appear to be among the most comprehensive.

Additionally, ESA and its European partners are only following a historical trend of their own efforts.[1416] From early partners in the IADC, through their own codes of conduct and handbooks, the European Union has expended considerable effort to advance debris mitigation to the benefit of all international partners. Fortunately, there are at least some indications that European efforts are achieving success. The most recent environmental assessments conducted by ESA indicates that while the number of objects (including the total amount of mass) continues to increase in space, the amount of mission-related objects released into the space environment as debris is steadily declining.[1417]

It remains, however, that no binding international law has been forthcoming even despite the extensive efforts of Europe (and others). However, this result is not likely a fault of Europe, but instead an acknowledgment that there are so many disparate interests among international partners that any comprehensive reduction of debris or debris causing activities is likely to remain a struggle. But, one unique advantage Europe possesses, which will serve it well going forward, remains ESA membership. The importance of this fact cannot be understated. By virtue of having the participation of 22 countries and their individual space programs, ESA is better positioned to coordinate more effectively through its voting and consensus systems on approaches to debris and other space-related problems. While the rest of the international community is continually working to find partnerships for support, ESA has it 'built-in' by design. Going forward, this is likely to become more and more important as the expense and technology of projects (think Artemis[1418]) will almost mandate

---

1416 ESA is not the first to introduce a comprehensive set of debris mitigation guidelines. That accolade belongs to the United States (NASA) in 1995. However, the Europeans, led by ESA, have arguably been the most adamant about advocating internationally for principles and codes of conduct. *Space Debris Mitigation*, SPACE SAFETY MAGAZINE, http://www.spacesafetymagazine.com/space-debris/mitigation/#:~:text=The%20Requirements%20for%20Space%20Debris%20Mitigation%20for%20ESA,the%20mitigation%20measures%20helping%20protect%20especially%20active%20spacecraft.

1417 ESA Space Debris Office, ESA's Annual Space Environment Report, May 27, 2021, 88, https://www.sdo.esoc.esa.int/environment_report/Space_Environment_Report_latest.pdf.

1418 ESA has numerous partnerships in addition to the Member-States of ESA, and a long list of projects all of which will require a healthy space environment to operate in, making debris control a significant priority. In addition to collaboration with NASA on Artemis,

multi-national partnerships to be successful. This characteristic bodes well for the future of ESA, and for its efforts towards reducing the overall threat of debris in the most precious regions of space. Coupled with ESA's strict ISO standards that govern its space efforts, ESA (and the European Union writ large) will continue to be a lighthouse for space-related issues, especially debris prevention and mitigation.

ESA has upcoming missions in search of gravitational waves from space, seeking exoplanets through its Planetary Transits and Oscillations of Stars (PLATO) mission, and NASA's Transiting Exoplanet Survey Satellite (TESS) ongoing mission to search for an alien world. *See* Carolyn Collins Petersen, *The History of the European Space Agency*, THOUGHTCO (updated May 28, 2018), https://www.thoughtco.com/european-space-agency-4164062.

CHAPTER 8

Does Existing Space Debris Guidance Establish Customary International Law?

1 Introduction

Up to this point, this book has examined the major applicable space-related treaties and several existing guidelines and activities related to efforts to prevent the creation of space debris. Additionally, accepting that current technological developments still fall short of providing a solution to debris mitigation and prevention, this book examined efforts by the major spacefaring Nations to minimize the amount of debris created during operations. The primary mechanisms States have used to reduce debris has been through licensing and regulation of space operations.

Unfortunately, even when using licensing as the oversight method, most debris requirements by States remain unenforced guidelines after licenses are issued. In practice, the plans to obtain a license must be very detailed, describing all aspects of space operations, from design to post-mission disposal. However, once issued, there are no indications of any significant follow-up actions, particularly for post-mission disposal, if or when the plan fails. Furthermore, no international treaty law is violated nor associated repercussions against States that would necessarily motivate them to be more stringent in holding operators accountable for plan failures.

This absence of treaty law reflects the general lack of modern success in space treaties since the failure of the Moon Agreement to obtain binding commitments from the major space powers. Success has been elusive for numerous reasons. One obvious reason seems to be that States are hesitant to sign on to any treaties in space where they cannot easily predict the impact it may have on their future operations. Other reasons are less pragmatic and appear to be based more on legacy behaviors. Among them, suspicion between historical adversaries that any agreement proposed by one must somehow be at the expense of the other.[1419] Similarly themed, there is concern by advanced countries that agreeing to any limitations in space are only acceptable if one

1419 Newman, *supra* note 1094. *See also* HANDBOOK OF SPACE LAW, *supra* note 513 atch. 1, para. 2.1.3.

© KONINKLIJKE BRILL NV, LEIDEN, 2023 | DOI:10.1163/9789004535848_010

is at such a disadvantage that the only way to remedy the imbalance is to frame rules that 'hinder' both.[1420] This is very evident in the case of the United States. Its current technological leadership in many areas of space makes stringent rules in agreements so attractive to adversaries like Russia and China. Therefore, Russia and China are perceived by the United States to be attempting to 'box' the United States into a corner and take away any advantages the United States may have.[1421] Meanwhile, allegations abound that in the course of attempting to tie each other's hands, each is equally attempting to achieve

1420 *Id.* Specifically discussing that in the initial case of the United States and the Soviet Union when considering limitations on the use of space, "both superpowers apparently perceived the legal constraints under discussion to be restraining the opponent more than themselves," resulting in both the Soviet Union and the United States, based on their own (mis)perceptions of the strength of their opponent, giving way to a fundamental willingness on both sides to work together to develop an acceptable legal regime considering each other's own harbored (however inaccurate it might have been) sense of inferiority.

1421 Hoss Cartwright & Deborah Lee James, *The Space Rush: New US Strategy Must Bring Order, Regulation*, BREAKING DEFENSE (Mar. 26, 2021, 4:45 PM), https://breakingdefense.com/2021/03/the-space-rush-new-us-strategy-must-bring-order-regulation/. *See also* HANDBOOK OF SPACE LAW, *supra* note 513, atch. 1, para. 2.1.3. Such a situation is often reflective of the theory of the prisoner's dilemma, a theory designed by Melvin Dresher and Merill Flood, two RAND Corporation scientists (though the term 'prisoner's dilemma' was coined later by Albert W. Tucker). *See Prisoner's Dilemma*, CFI (updated Feb. 25, 2022), https://corporatefinanceinstitute.com/resources/knowledge/other/prisoners-dilemma/. The theory arises in situations "in which individualistic self-interested calculation of actors leads them to prefer joint decision-making because independent self-interested behavior can result in undesirable or suboptimal outcomes." *See* Arthur A. Stein, *Coordination and Collaboration: Regimes in an Anarchic World*, 36 INT'L ORG. 299, 304 (1982). This plays out in three scenarios in a situation between two people charged with a joint crime, but police only have evidence to secure a conviction against both on one minor crime. If neither talk, then both will get a light sentence on the charge. If one talks, but the other doesn't, the one that talks will go free and the other pays a high price. If both talk, both pay a moderate price. In such a scenario, the best outcome for each is to talk, because they face a medium sentence at worst, or a light one at best. In either case, they *do not* face a high price under any scenario if they at least talk. *See* LEPARD, *supra* note 511. Applied to the case at hand, such a scenario often is what drives the desire for States to come to, or drive the desire for, treaties or agreements between themselves. Doing so helps to avoid the unknown scenario presented by the prisoner's dilemma where each must act based on the lack of information on hand about how the other will act. Absent an agreement, they must act in a manner that they are almost guaranteed to lose 'something' versus coming to agreement where the potential is they lose a lot. How each party responds to such an outcome, however, is the issue presented here, such that the United States perception may be that its advantage is significant enough, and the drawbacks of non-cooperation small enough, that it is worth risking the worst potential outcomes of the prisoner's dilemma.

superiority over the space domain.[1422] At least one final consideration is that some countries, especially the United States, have laws that preclude some collaboration and technology sharing with adversaries such as China and Russia, affecting not just commerce and interactions generally, but often space agreements as well.[1423]

The result, particularly for major spacefaring countries like China, Russia, and the United States, is a prevailing view that 'all things are adversarial.' This has been persistently unproductive in advancing any new treaty opportunities. As noted by General (USMC, Ret.) Gen. James E. 'Hoss' Cartwright of the Atlantic Council, "If everybody that we talk to is the enemy, and there's a boogeyman behind every question and every opportunity, we're not going to go anywhere."[1424]

2 Beyond Legacy IADC and UN COPUOS—Recent Voluntary Space Debris Mitigation Guidelines

Absent any treaties on debris mitigation and prevention gaining traction, the vacuum has been filled by voluntary efforts, such as those of the IADC discussed previously. However, those are not the only guidelines. In response to changes in technology, such as the advent of easily accessible cube-satellite

---

1422 Bradley Bowan & Jared Thompson, *Russia and China Seek to Tie America's Hands in Space*, FOREIGN POLICY (Mar. 31, 2021, 11:31 AM), https://foreignpolicy.com/2021/03/31/russia-china-space-war-treaty-demilitarization-satellites/.

1423 Newman, *supra* note 1094. Specific limitations are contained in the 2013 'Wolf Amendment.' Introduced by US Representative Frank Wolf, this amendment prohibited NASA and the White House Office of Science and Technology Policy from spending any appropriated funds on anything related to space cooperation with China. A further amendment attempted to provide an 'escape clause' while still being somewhat draconian. Under the *Consolidated and Further Continuing Appropriations Act of 2015*, Representative Wolf passed language that stated that "no funds may be spent by NASA to develop, design, plan, promulgate, implement or execute a bilateral policy, program, or order or contract of any kind to participate, collaborate, or coordinate bilaterally in any way with China or any Chinese owned company unless such activities are specifically authorized by law after the date of the amendment of this act (later coined the 'Wolf Rule')." *See* Consolidated and Further Continuing Appropriations Act of 2015, Pub. L. No. 113–235, § 532, 128 Stat. 2130 (2015), https://www.congress.gov/113/plaws/publ235/PLAW-113publ235.pdf. *See also* Mathilde Minet, *Understanding the Wolf Agreement*, SPACE LEGAL ISSUES (Oct. 25, 2020), https://www.spacelegalissues.com/understanding-the-wolf-agreement/.

1424 Theresa Hitchens, *US Should Push New Space Treaty: Atlantic Council*, BREAKING DEFENSE (Apr. 12, 2021, 4:13 PM), https://breakingdefense.com/2021/04/us-should-push-new-space-treaty-atlantic-council/.

(hereafter cube-sat) technology, the international community has been further responsive with new suggestions to account for these technological developments. These new technologies are also prompting further calls for more thorough guidelines to stem the increase in debris growth.

To fully assess whether any customary international law has developed in debris mitigation efforts, in addition to the legacy IADC and UN COPUOS efforts, it is worth reviewing two additional recently developed guidelines. The first is the UN COPUOS Long-Term Sustainability Guidelines (hereafter UN COPUOS LTS Guidelines).[1425] The second is the Space Safety Coalition Best Practices for the Sustainability of Space Operations (hereafter SSC Sustainability Practices).[1426] Both of these have arisen as a result of technological advances in space and a community desire for better guidance to grapple with debris growth and risks. This book will review each in turn.

2.1 *Committee on the Peaceful Uses of Outer Space Guidelines for the Long-Term Sustainability of Outer Space Activities*

One of the most recent important voluntary guideline developments is the UN COPUOS LTS Guidelines. This effort originated in 2010, when the Working Group on the Long-Term Sustainability of Outer Space Activities was established by the United Nations (hereafter the LTS Working Group).[1427] Its mandate was to identify areas of concern for the long-term sustainability of outer space activities, offer solutions to improve sustainability, and finally, create a set of guidelines that could be used to reduce the risk to the long-term stability of the outer space environment.[1428] Among the primary themes, space debris and operations were of significant importance to the effort.[1429] By June of 2016,

1425 Guidelines for the Long-Term Sustainability of Outer Space Activities of the Committee on the Peaceful Uses of Outer Space, U.N. Office for Outer Space Affairs (2021), https://www.unoosa.org/res/oosadoc/data/documents/2021/stspace/stspace79_0_html/st_space79E.pdf.

1426 Best Practices for Space Operations, Space Safety Coalition (Sep. 16, 2019), https://spacesafety.org/wp-content/uploads/2021/04/Endorsement-of-Best-Practices-for-Sustainability_v40.pdf.

1427 *Long-Term Sustainability of Outer Space Activities*, supra note 1425.

1428 *Id.* For an in-depth description of the development and implementation of the program, *see* Peter Martinez, *The UN COPUOS Guidelines for the Long-term Sustainability of Outer Space Activities*, 8 J. SPACE SAFETY ENGINEERING 98 (2021), https://reader.elsevier.com/reader/sd/pii/S2468896721000094?token=F6C7F0EBC2FC22CBC5F07386B110380B62F3FF959ED959759283C395DCFD8688228C4A7E675501096C66719AA36726AD.

1429 *Id.*

the LTS Working Group had agreed to the first set of principles.[1430] This set of guidelines comprised 28 recommendations focused on the development of "policies, regulatory framework, and practices to support the long-term sustainability of outer space activities for Governments and IGO's authorizing or conducting space activities."[1431] Further development in 2018 resulted in an additional nine guidelines being added, though the report was not finalized due to disagreement among the LTS Working Group on the final product.[1432]

In 2019, the proposed guidelines were submitted to the United Nations. Among other issues at the time, there was a resurgence in the desire to discuss binding international agreements related to space debris. Much of this may have stemmed from concerns over the ASAT test conducted by India around the same time.[1433] In the delegation notes, it was expressed that there needed to be an "international, non-legally binding instrument covering the security, safety, and sustainability of outer space activities ... including a political commitment not to intentionally destroy space objects and to prevent any further generation of debris."[1434] However, despite these statements and evidence of a desire within the greater international community to establish more binding norms and agreements, meaningful steps in that direction remain elusive.[1435]

1430 Report of the Comm. on the Peaceful Uses of Outer Space on its Fifty-Ninth Session, U.N. Doc. A/71/20, at Annex "Guidelines for the Long-Term Sustainability of Outer Space Activities: First Set," (Aug. 16, 2016), https://www.unoosa.org/oosa/documents-and-resolutions/search.jspx?view=&match=A%2F71%2F20.

1431 *Id.* at Annex, sec. A.

1432 Report of the Comm. on the Peaceful Uses of Outer Space, Rep. of Sci. and Tech. Subcomm. on Its Fifty-Fifth Session, U.N. Doc. A/AC.105/1167, Annex 3 (Jan. 29—Feb. 9, 2018), *available at* https://www.unoosa.org/oosa/oosadoc/data/documents/2018/aac.105/aac.1051167_0.htm. In addition to the original guidelines, Guidelines 6, 11, 14, 15, 23, 24, 30, 31 and 32 were added. These provisions ranged from addressing enhanced registration of space objects to improving long-term sustainability through advanced information sharing.

1433 Tellis, *supra* note 81. On 27 March 2019, India successfully conducted an ASAT test earlier in the day, which struck and destroyed an Indian satellite in low sun-synchronous orbit at an altitude of 282 km. Fortunately, the test was conducted at an altitude that ensures some of the debris cloud would not linger in the atmosphere long. The missile intercept occurred on the downward trajectory of the impact missile, directing debris down to the atmosphere compared to further into outer space. It is estimated that the debris cloud eventually comprised 400 fragments, of which 270 will only remain for a few months. However, some pieces still were propelled to as high as 1,000 km, making their eventual decay significantly longer.

1434 Report of the Comm. on the Peaceful Uses of Outer Space, on Its Sixty-Second Session, U.N. Doc. A/74/20, at para. 36 (2019), *available at* https://www.unoosa.org/res/oosadoc/data/documents/2019/a/a7420_0_html/V1906077.pdf.

1435 *Id.* at para. 37.

Regardless, while still non-binding, the ultimate UN COPUOS LTS Guidelines still provide a useful contribution to the ongoing discussion of orbital debris mitigation and prevention best practices that could ultimately contribute to a treaty one day. As offered, the final 21 Guidelines are broken up into four major sections.

2.1.1 UN COPUOS LTS Guidelines—Policy and Regulatory Framework

The first section, *Policy and Regulatory Framework*, encourages implementing as many, if not all, of the provisions of the guidelines into national legislation.[1436] Recognizing the fact that these are voluntary guidelines, domestic implementation is the only viable way to materialize any of these provisions into mandatory actions on the part of spacefaring participants. This implementation recommendation is in addition to the obligations already agreed to under the Outer Space Treaty or as already implemented to reflect voluntary compliance with the IADC Debris Mitigation Guidelines and other preventive mitigation measures.[1437] Beyond that, the remaining provisions of the first section covers supervision of space activities with a particular focus on sustainability, respect for the equitable use of the frequency spectrum, and focused effort on the practice of registering objects and communication among Nations regarding their orbital locations.[1438] Registration is a 'key factor' in the safety and long-term sustainability of space activities.[1439]

2.1.2 UN COPUOS LTS Guidelines—Safety of Space Operations

The second major section, *Safety of Space Operations*, focuses on communication and dissemination of information among partners.[1440] In particular, it encourages communication to relay known and ongoing risks in the course of operations.[1441] This includes establishing a standard process of sharing risk information and improving the ability to identify space debris that would put operations of all Nations at risk.[1442] Additional sections discuss the need for accurate preflight conjunction assessments as well as ongoing assessments during operations to identify any need for avoidance measures as early as possible.[1443] This includes the need for foresight on potential uncontrolled

1436 *Id.* at Annex II, sec. A.1.(1–3).
1437 *Id.* at Annex II, sec. A.2.(1).
1438 *Id.* at Annex II, sec. A.5.(1).
1439 *Id.*
1440 *Id.* at Annex II, secs. B.1-B.10.
1441 *Id.* at Annex II, sec. B.1.
1442 *Id.* at Annex II, secs. B.2-B.3.
1443 *Id.* at Annex II, sec. B.5.

re-entry and the associated risks.[1444] Finally, to effectively accomplish many of these objectives, this section recommends improvements in the trackability of space objects to enhance the ability to keep oversight on them throughout their orbital lifetimes.[1445]

2.1.3 UN COPUOS LTS Guidelines—International Cooperation and Capacity Building and Awareness

The third section, *International Cooperation and Capacity Building and Awareness*, addresses that sustainability is likely dependent on aiding Nations beginning their journey into space, particularly with technological shortcuts. A historical problem with some suggestions of proposed space treaties is that they prevent the ability of new space entrants to learn through experience by prohibiting activities that mature Nations learned from conducting themselves. At the same time, these treaties typically do not incorporate obligations for making the technological know-how available to the new entrant to improve their capabilities and allow them to be responsible space sustainment partners. For example, some designs of spacecraft have enhanced anti-debris measures. However, this technology is usually proprietary and often developed through trial and error. Considerable amounts of space debris were created in the process of developing the technology. Without a mechanism (or willingness) to provide newer Nations with this information, treaties precluding Nations from 'learning by doing' face stiff resistance when the Nation lacks any other option to obtain the information. In other words, even if these Nations were willing or wanted to comply with the minimization expectations, they neither have the technological ability nor the historical experience to develop the technology without the same 'debris-creating' trial and error previously afforded to mature spacefaring Nations. Because of this, they begin their experimentation to learn, they decline to sign any treaties, and the result is further debris-producing events.

The UN COPUOS LTS Guidelines attempts to address these problems. First, it advocates for "facilitating international cooperation to enable all countries, in particular developing and emerging spacefaring countries, to implement these [LTS] guidelines."[1446] In doing so, it sets an expectation that "experience, expertise and information relating to the long-term sustainability of outer space activities" should be shared with these newer countries to enhance the

1444 *Id.* at Annex II, secs. B.4, B.9.

1445 *Id.* at Annex II, sec. B.8.

1446 *Id.* at Annex II, sec. C.1.

long-term sustainability of space activities.[1447] This includes recommending capacity building efforts between mature and emerging spacefaring Nations by giving these emerging Nations a head start on the 'knowledge on spacecraft design, flight dynamics, orbital data and tools for monitoring' that will make them partners in the preservation of the space environment.[1448] The final guideline in this section advocates for a campaign to raise awareness of the benefits of space activities and the importance that protecting the space environment has towards ensuring the environment remains available. The campaign should include outreach, sharing, cooperation, and partnership with government, non-governmental organizations, academia, and private interests.[1449]

2.1.4 UN COPUOS LTS Guidelines—Scientific and Technical Research and Development

The final category of the UN COPUOS LTS guidelines, *Scientific and Technical Research and Development*, focuses on promoting and supporting research into the sustainable exploration and use of outer space. Primarily, it advocates for supporting research that advances the 'social, economic, and environmental' interests of sustainable activities in space that will allow for the advancement of life on Earth.[1450] Key, of course, is finding new and innovative ways to manage space debris, through the prevention of its creation, the extension of operations for existing satellites, reducing the risks to satellites from collision (both functioning and non-functioning), and implementation of domestic and international legal and policy provisions to ensure outer space sustainability.[1451]

2.1.5 UN COPUOS LTS Guidelines—the Way Ahead

In adopting the UN COPUOS LTS guidelines, UN COPUOS acknowledged that much more work needs to be accomplished.[1452] Primarily, implementation of the principles into legal regimes at all levels.[1453] Beyond legal requirements, conversations must continue among relevant participants on how the next evolutions of the guidelines should be crafted.[1454] Specifically, a five-year

1447 *Id.* at Annex II, sec. C.2(1).
1448 *Id.* at Annex II, sec. C.3(1).
1449 *Id.* at Annex II, sec. C.4.
1450 *Id.* at Annex II, sec. AD.1.
1451 *Id.* at Annex II, sec. D.2.
1452 *Id.* at paras. 162–167.
1453 *Id.*
1454 *Id.*

workplan was developed to study the continuing challenges to long-term stability in space.[1455] In 2020, the committee decided that the working group would utilize the following framework to advance these objectives: 1) identify and study challenges for new guidelines for long-term sustainability, 2) share experiences and lessons learned from national implementation of the adopted guidelines, and 3) raise awareness and build capacity, particularly among new entrants to space operations.[1456] The efforts on this 'living document' continue.

2.2 *Background—Space Safety Coalition Best Practices for the Sustainability of Space Operations Guidelines*

The SSC Sustainability Practices is an initiative undertaken by interested space industry entities (60 by current count as of February 2023[1457]) to promote safe and efficient flight through technical means.[1458] Under this effort, the SSC created their own set of best practices covering all aspects of space flight loyal to the core principle of space sustainability.[1459] Again, it is a voluntary measure.[1460] However, where the SSC Sustainability Practices differ from the previous voluntary standards is that this effort attempts to focus on newer problems facing the orbital environments from debris.[1461] Namely, cube-sats and other small-satellites (hereafter small-sats) as well as large constellations of small-sats, that were not significantly envisioned under previous guideline efforts.[1462]

The primary concern regards the pure volume of constellation-satellite propositions from companies like OneWeb and SpaceX. In fact, an aggregate of information by Mr. Dan Oltrogge indicates that, based on applications with the FCC and ITU, 107,641 spacecraft applications have been submitted, which are projected to comprise at least 68 large constellation projects launched by 2029.[1463] If this number of satellites is placed into orbit, it is estimated that by 2030 we can expect up to 2.5 million close calls and approximately 40 satellite collisions annually.[1464] The potential impact of these collisions on the outer space environment could be catastrophic.[1465]

1455 *Id.*
1456 *Id.*
1457 Best Practices for Space Operations, *supra* note 1426. *See also* Oltrogge, *supra* note 18 at para. 1.
1458 *Id.* at para. 4.2.
1459 *Id.* at para. 1.
1460 *Id.* at para. 1.
1461 Oltrogge, *supra* note 18 at 3.
1462 *Id.* at para. 1.
1463 *Id.* at para. 3.
1464 *Id.*
1465 *Id.*

In response to this threat, the SSC has put forth a series of new principles to inform the existing guidelines. First, the global space community must establish a healthy and safe collaboration with the commercial sector.[1466] Second, the commercial community must ensure quick ability to exchange data with the international community on flight safety issues, and codify the best practices on how to do so.[1467] Finally, the United States and the United Kingdom, which are responsible for the bulk of these constellation applications, must lead this effort to ensure the necessary coordination and management occurs to avoid collisions as these satellites are launched.[1468]

2.2.1 SSC Sustainability Practices

The SSC Sustainability Practices themselves are proposed in two parts.[1469] The first part endorses the existing treaties and voluntary guidelines and standards of the existing governing bodies (IADC, UN, ISO).[1470] The second part, under five main categories, provides an additional 42 best practice proposals.[1471]

The first category advances the interests of information sharing for collision avoidance and space safety, advocating for heightened information sharing among spacecraft operators.[1472] The second category focuses on choosing launch service providers for contracts that have prioritized advanced space sustainability within their own core business model.[1473] In particular, this category advocates choosing launch service providers who have an exceptional track record for disposal reliability and who make efforts to go above and beyond typical disposal standards.[1474] Essentially, this argues for directing money toward those who are the best stewards of the environment, versus purely the most cost-effective. The third category puts heightened scrutiny on constellation designers and spacecraft operators, encouraging them to pay particular attention to the safety of space objects from collision by design.[1475] Spacing between satellites, accountability for failed satellites, heightened focus on failure rates, advanced testing, and similar concepts all provide evidence that the community needs to approach constellation-satellite proposals with a

1466 *Id.*
1467 *Id.*
1468 *Id.*
1469 *Id.* at para. 6.
1470 *Id.*
1471 *Id.*
1472 Best Practices for Space Operations, *supra* note 1426 at category 1.
1473 *Id.* at category 2.
1474 *Id.* at category 2(e).
1475 *Id.* at category 3.

heightened sense of responsibility.[1476] Simply put, constellation-satellites are a new concept, with maneuverability once in orbit often zero. Because of this, they need to be more resilient and have lower failure rates as a result of the sheer number of satellites being contemplated. The fourth category is focused on an increased disposal success rate, challenging the existing technology, and implementing a more stringent set of best practices for successful disposal (95% or better, closer to the 'goal' standard of the United States).[1477] This is especially true in higher LEO orbits (above 400 km) because of the slowed decay rate of debris at or above that altitude. Other mitigation measures, such as advanced and more reliable passivation functions are discussed and highly encouraged.[1478] Finally, the last category directly addresses the sustainability of the environment through collision avoidance measures and capabilities, close monitoring of spacecraft conditions, reiteration of acceptable disposal expectations (particularly in GEO), and shortened disposal and passivation activities at the end-of-mission.[1479]

The core purpose of these principles, with a focus on sustainability in the face of constellation-satellite projections, makes these principles a unique contributor to the body of sustainability guidelines for space. However, as indicated earlier, these remain not only voluntary but have yet to be adopted by any Nations or national organizations at the time of this writing. Until then, their value will remain limited. Meanwhile, they address a niche need in an area that will only see increasing investment by governments and commercial actors going forward.

3 Can Customary International Law Be Found as a Result of Nation-State Implementation of Orbital Debris Prevention and Mitigation Efforts?

Up to this point, we have reviewed how the major spacefaring Nations and ESA have implemented their own domestic orbital debris prevention and regulatory mitigation schemes. Additionally, we have reviewed at least four separate guidelines for debris mitigation. By themselves, these guidelines are not controlling, but they are certainly influential in the domestic programs of spacefaring Nations for orbital debris reduction and management. The key question

1476 *Id.*

1477 *Id.* at category 4.

1478 *Id.*

1479 *Id.* at category 5.

remains whether any of these domestic efforts, when compared with the other programs, meet the elements of customary international law and are therefore actually law in the eyes of the international community.

To answer this question, the following sections of this book identify seven themes arising out of the bulk of the proposed guidelines and practices. In examining those seven themes, this book then analyzes where, if at all, the major spacefaring Nations (the United States, Russia, and China) and ESA have implemented those themes within their own domestic law or practice. We can then compare and draw inferences whether there exists any commonality in practice and whether or not that rises to the level of customary international law.

As a reminder, the prerequisites for customary international law development, as seen in Chapter 3, are two-fold. The objective element of customary international law constitutes an understanding of settled practice. The subjective element requires that actors behave and act as though bound by that settled practice because they believe the settled practice is equivalent to actual law. The practice (the 'rule') has endurance as though it were a law and ensures a degree of maturity to exist as an understood rule even absent formal writing. Additionally, there is some element of time. The requisite time remains an issue of contention, with some scholars arguing extended periods, whereas others (including this author) argue that it can also come into existence instantly under the right circumstances.[1480] The circumstances are an important element of the time consideration.

Returning to the analysis, a degree of compilation is appropriate. In examining the four major spacefaring operators reviewed for this analysis, what is evident is that all four have made considerable efforts toward implementing debris minimization programs in their respective programs. The United States arguably operates the most diverse program, with multiple government and private organizations, including Congress, the FCC, NASA, and private corporations, et cetera., wielding considerable influence or regulatory power over the specific contours of the US debris mitigation program. On the other hand, ESA has taken the significant step of incorporating 'whole cloth' the ISO standards as their regulatory system for debris prevention and mitigation. While seemingly secretive overall in the information they proffer publicly related to their programs, Russia and China have still demonstrated competent regulatory schemes toward prevention and mitigation efforts. We must also acknowledge that while ESA and the United States mitigation rules and programs have

1480 *See generally* SCHARF, *supra* note 374.

mandatory aspects, the same does not appear evident for China and Russia. There is a body of evidence that indicates both mitigation programs of those two countries are implemented only as technical 'guidance.'

3.1 *The Seven Mitigation Themes*

This book proposes to answer whether customary international law has been established in debris mitigation and prevention practice among major spacefaring actors by comparing the practices and looking for similarities. The method employed groups the types of debris mitigation policies and practices by spacefaring actors under seven general mitigation and prevention themes of behavior. This allows for easier comparison among the different actors compared to the type of activity contemplated by the theme. If those practices are similar enough and treated by the actors as legally binding, a final analysis will be conducted to determine if the elements of customary international law have been met. Conclusions and recommendations will follow. The seven themes are as follows:[1481]

1. Debris mitigation is to be considered during all stages of a space project.
2. Release of space debris during normal operations is to be limited.
3. Efforts should be expended to avoid collisions in orbit.
4. Risk of breakups during operational phases is to be minimized.
5. The potential for post-mission breakups resulting from stored energy should be minimized by passivation.
6. If not destroyed by atmospheric methods, post-mission disposal of space objects away from LEO and GEO is to be arranged.
7. Intentional destruction and other harmful activities are to be avoided.

3.1.1 Theme 1—Debris Mitigation Is to Be Considered during All Stages of a Space Project

Each of the major debris mitigation efforts recommends that debris mitigation be part of the planning and execution process during all stages of a space endeavor. According to the IADC Debris Mitigation Guidelines, "during an

1481 These Themes are derived in whole, or part, from Lawrence Li, *Space Debris Mitigation as an International Law Obligation*, 17 INT'L COMM. L. REV. 297 (2015), https://heinonline.org/HOL/LandingPage?handle=hein.journals/intlfddb17&div=20&id=&page=. These predate the UN COPUOS Space Debris Mitigation Guidelines and the SSC Sustainability Practices, which were later applied by this author to the thematic concept.

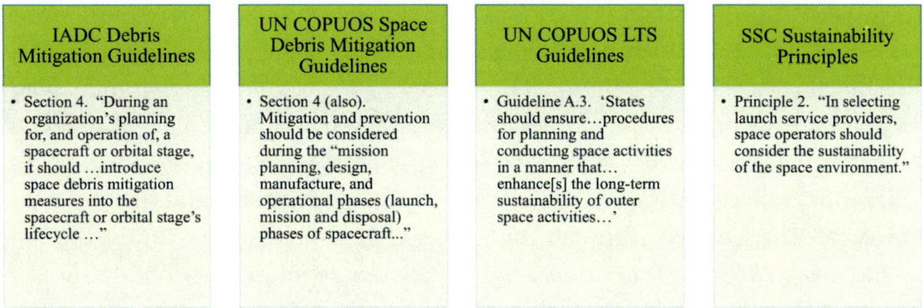

FIGURE 4 Summarized individual soft law references for Theme 1 (Debris mitigation is to be considered during all stages of a space project).

organization's planning for, and operation of, a spacecraft or orbital stage, it should take systematic action to reduce adverse effects on the orbital environment by introducing space debris mitigation measures into the spacecraft or orbital stage's lifecycle ..."[1482] The UN COPUOS Space Debris Mitigation Guidelines provides that "mitigation and prevention should be considered during the mission planning, design, manufacture, and operational phases (launch, mission and disposal) of spacecraft and launch vehicle orbital stages."[1483] The UN COPUOS LTS Guidelines say that "States should ensure that the entities under their jurisdiction or control that conduct outer space activities have the appropriate structures and procedures for planning and conducting space activities in a manner that supports the objective of enhancing the long-term sustainability of outer space activities, and that they have the means to comply with relevant national and international regulatory frameworks, requirements, policies, and processes in this regard."[1484] Finally, the SSC Sustainability Practices state that in the selection of launch service providers, space operators should consider the sustainability of the space environment (See Figure 4 Summary).[1485]

As reviewed in practice, the United States specifically reviews and addresses all flight profiles through its licensing requirements, but it is the ODMSP which designates the requirements that debris mitigation meet specific standards for spacecraft through all aspects of flight, from initiation to post-mission

1482 IADC SPACE DEBRIS MITIGATION GUIDELINES REV. 3, *supra* note 26 at para. 4.

1483 U.N. OFF. OF OUTER SPACE AFFAIRS, SPACE DEBRIS MITIGATION GUIDELINES OF THE COMMITTEE ON THE PEACEFUL USES OF OUTER SPACE, *supra* note 24 at III.

1484 Guidelines for the Long-Term Sustainability of Outer Space Activities, *supra* note 1425.

1485 Best Practices for Space Operations, *supra* note 1426 at practice 2.

disposal.[1486] Russia similarly imposes a review requirement from origination to post-mission disposal through Roskosmos and the space licensing regime.[1487] Specifically, Russian Regulation 99-FZ, *Law of the Russian Federation About Licensing of Separate Types of Activities*, and Russian Regulation No. 298, *About Licensing Space Activities*, discuss the specific details of submissions and consideration to authorize space activities, including environmental (debris) concerns.[1488] The Chinese, through their *Interim Measures on the Administration of Licensing the Project of Launching Civil Space* regulation, similarly set out requirements for licensing authorization requiring a review of all aspects of flight, including a heightened concern for the environment though prohibitions on activities that would cause 'irremediable danger to any future operations in space.'[1489] Finally, through the ISO standards, specifically ISO 24113:2019—*Space Systems*, ESA has established the requirements for operations, including orbital debris considerations, through all four major phases of space operations: planning, operations, orbital lifetime, and EOM.[1490] In sum, all four major space operators have implemented a standard that debris mitigation through each stage of a spacecraft lifecycle is a critical element of any space program (See Figure 5 Summary).

3.1.2 Theme 2—Release of Space Debris during Normal Operations Is to Be Limited

The IADC, as part of its fundamental principles, states that efforts should be made in the course of designing spacecraft and associated vehicle launches that limit the amount of objects that must be released as debris during the normal course of operations.[1491] Guideline 1 of the UN COPUOS Space Debris

1486 *U.S. Government Orbital Debris Mitigation Standard Practices, November 2019 Update, supra* note 585.

1487 Order of the Government of the Russian Federation About Licensing of Space Activities, *supra* note 1117 at Appendix, §§ I–II.

1488 Федеральный закон Российско Федерации о лицензировании отдельных видов деятельности [Federal Law of the Russian Federation About Licensing of Separate Types of Activities], *supra* note 1112 at art. 1(1.1). *See also* Order of the Government of the Russian Federation About Licensing of Space Activities, *supra* note 1117.

1489 Laws of the People's Republic of China, *Interim Measures on the Administration of Permits for Civil Space Launch Projects* (Nov. 21, 2002), http://www.asianlii.org/cn/legis/cen/laws/imotaopfcslp771/.

1490 INT'L STANDARDIZATION ORGANIZATION (24113:2019), *supra* note 1326, 4, para. 3.23. Earth's orbit is defined as the bounded or unbounded Keplerian orbit with Earth at a focal point, or Lagrange point orbit which includes Earth as one of the two main bodies. INT'L STANDARDIZATION ORGANIZATION (24113:2019), *supra* note 1326, 2, para. 3.8.

1491 Comm. on the Peaceful Uses of Outer Space, Sci. and Tech. Subcomm. on Its Fortieth Session, *Inter-Agency Space Debris Coordination Committee Space Debris Mitigation*

United States	Russia	China	ESA
• ODMSP, SPD-3, National policies. FAA/AST (51 U.S.C. §50922 & 14 C.F.R., Ch. III, 400-460, launch vehicles), FCC commercial satellite operations (47 C.F.R. Parts 5, 25, 97) and NASA government operations (NASA STD-8719.14C). U.S. licensing regimes 'requires limiting debris…through all aspects of flight, from initiation to post-mission disposal.'	• 99-FZ, *Law of the Russian Federation About Licensing of Separate Types of Activities* and Russian Regulation No. 298, *About Licensing Space Activities.* Requires debris mitigation consideration from 'origination to post-mission disposal.'	• Article 5, *Interim Measures on the Administration of Licensing the Project of Launching Civil Space.* Requires 'review of all aspects of flight…that would cause irremediable danger to any future operations in space.'	• Para 3.2.3, ISO 24113-2019-*Space Systems.* Requires consideration of orbital debris creation through…planning, operations, orbital lifetime, and end of mission.

FIGURE 5 Summarized relevant state/organization practice for Theme 1 (Debris mitigation is to be considered during all stages of a space project).

Mitigation Guidelines similarly states that "space systems should be designed not to release debris during normal operations."[1492] The UN COPUOS LTS Guidelines gives deference to compliance with the UN COPUOS Space Debris Mitigation Guidelines as well as the IADC Debris Mitigation Guidelines, and thus the debris release rules accordingly.[1493] However, it also independently advocates for pressure from governments to space actors to encourage 'not just prevention during normal operations, but also investigation of new measures to preclude collision and the creation of new debris.'[1494] Finally, the SSC Sustainability Practices, similarly reflecting the IADC and UN COPUOS efforts, also advocates for 'innovation and the need to limit the creation of new space debris, specifically focusing on pressure from space operators to choose those providers who include requirements that the release of debris during normal operations is both limited and, ideally, fully accounted for by destruction after release (See Figure 6 Summary).'[1495]

Guidelines, *supra* note 459. *See also* Comm. On the Peaceful Uses of Outer Space, Sci. and Tech. Subcomm. on Its Forty-Second Session, *Report of the Inter-Agency Space Debris Coordination Committee Activates on IADC Space Debris Mitigation Guidelines & Supporting Documents*, https://www.iadc-home.org/documents_public/file_down/id/4112; IADC Space Debris Mitigation Guidelines *Update*, *supra* note 461; IADC SPACE DEBRIS MITIGATION GUIDELINES REV. 3, *supra* note 26 at para. 5.1.

1492 U.N. OFF. OF OUTER SPACE AFFAIRS, SPACE DEBRIS MITIGATION GUIDELINES OF THE COMMITTEE ON THE PEACEFUL USES OF OUTER SPACE, *supra* note 24 at guideline 1.

1493 Guidelines for the Long-Term Sustainability of Outer Space Activities, *supra* note 1425 at Guidelines D.2(2) & A.2.2(f).

1494 *Id.* at Guideline D.2(3).

1495 Best Practices for Space Operations, *supra* note 1426 at practice 2.

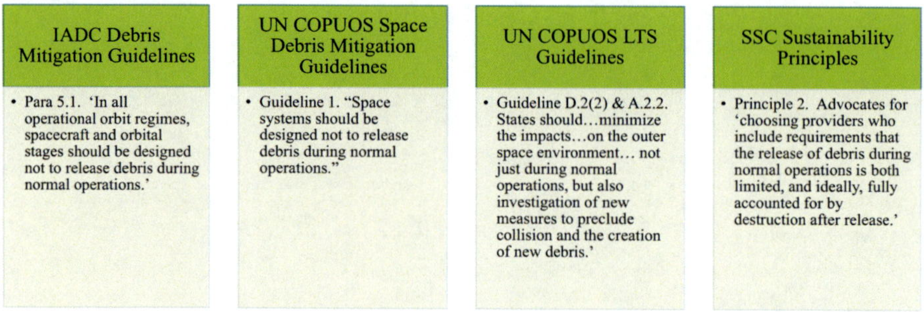

FIGURE 6 Summarized individual soft-law references for Theme 2 (Release of space debris during normal operations should be limited).

The United States, through SPD-3, addresses the concern of the release of debris during normal operations. It states that, absent some unavoidable reason for non-compliance, "spacecraft and upper stages should be designed to eliminate or minimize debris released during normal operations."[1496] China, like the United States, also requires operators to account for and control debris released during normal operations.[1497] Russia, similarly, also accounts for debris during normal operations, establishing that besides design, the primary focus during normal operations is to minimize the potential for collision with other spacecraft and protect against destruction from flying debris.[1498] Russia enforces this through a series of minimization procedures. For example, implementing requirements for activities like the method of separation of stage rockets (reduce the use of explosives, as well as reduction of the use of tethers and other parts that often result as debris).[1499] Finally ESA, through the ISO standard 24113:2019, specifies that the aim of debris mitigation is achieved by avoiding the intentional release of space debris.[1500] As such, "spacecraft shall be designed so as not to release space debris into Earth's orbit during normal operations."[1501] In sum, all four major space operators have implemented a

1496 *U.S. Government Orbital Debris Mitigation Standard Practices*, *supra* note 573 at para. 1–1.

1497 Laws of the People's Republic of China, *Interim Measures on the Administration of Permits for Civil Space Launch Projects* (Nov. 21, 2002), Arts. 6–7, http://www.asianlii.org/cn/legis/cen/laws/imotaopfcslp771/ (as discussed by Tronchetti, *supra* note 882 at 7; *see also* IADC SPACE DEBRIS MITIGATION GUIDELINES REV. 3, *supra* note 26 at para. 5.1.

1498 GOST P 52925-2018, *supra* note 1138 at paras. 5–6.

1499 *Id.*

1500 INT'L STANDARDIZATION ORGANIZATION (24113:2019), *supra* note 1326.

1501 *Id.* at 6, para. 6.1.1.1. To avoid confusion, it is not that there can be no release of debris. However, there are additional stringent rules on potentially debris causing components, such as pyrotechnics, which can be released, but the resulting debris can be no larger than 1 mm in its largest dimension, for example. *See Id.* at 6, para 6.1.2.

United States	Russia	China	ESA
• 14 C.F.R. A417.11(c)-(c)(1). Launch Vehicle. For all launch vehicles…that reach Earth orbit…debris generation does not result. • 47 CFR 25.114(d)(14)(i) Space Stations. Operators must provide a statement that the space station operator has "assessed and limited the amount of debris released in a planned manner during normal operations."	• GOST P 52925-2018, para's 5.2 and 6.1. 'Main measures to limit man-made clogging of the [space environment] are preventing the formation of [debris] in the course of regular operations of the [spacecraft].'	• Art's 6 & 7, China Interim Licensing Measures Laws of the People's Republic of China, *Interim Measures on the Administration of Permits for Civil Space Launch Projects.* Requires operators to 'account for, and control, debris during normal operations.'	• ISO standards, 24113:2019, para 6.1.1.1, *Space Debris Mitigation Requirements.* "Spacecraft shall be designed so as not to release space debris into Earth's orbit during normal operations."

FIGURE 7 Summarized relevant state/organization practice for Theme 2 (Release of space debris during normal operations should be limited).

standard that release of debris through normal operations should be extremely limited, if not eliminated entirely (See Figure 7 Summary).

3.1.3 Theme 3—Efforts Should Be Expended to Avoid Collisions in Orbit

The IADC Debris Mitigation Guidelines address reduction of on-orbit collision primarily by focusing on the design of the spacecraft.[1502] It sets out the expectation that a program or project should limit collision by obtaining the most reliable orbital data possible for avoidance maneuver, and if unavoidable, design the spacecraft in such a way that small debris will not cause total destruction.[1503] Similarly, the UN COPUOS Space Debris Mitigation Guidelines, Guideline 3, states that in developing the design and mission profile of a spacecraft, the probability of collision during launch and orbital lifetime should be estimated and, wherever possible, limited.[1504] In the event of a potential collision a maneuver should be considered for execution.[1505] The UN COPUOS LTS Guidelines address collisions under its safety of space operations section. It argues that states and intergovernmental organizations should establish appropriate means to enable timely coordination and positional information to avoid, or appropriately respond, to the threat of collisions, orbital breakups

1502 IADC SPACE DEBRIS MITIGATION GUIDELINES REV. 3, *supra* note 26 at para. 5.4.

1503 *Id.*

1504 U.N. OFF. OF OUTER SPACE AFFAIRS, SPACE DEBRIS MITIGATION GUIDELINES OF THE COMMITTEE ON THE PEACEFUL USES OF OUTER SPACE, *supra* note 24 at Guideline 3.

1505 U.N. OFF. OF OUTER SPACE AFFAIRS, SPACE DEBRIS MITIGATION GUIDELINES OF THE COMMITTEE ON THE PEACEFUL USES OF OUTER SPACE, *supra* note 24 at III.

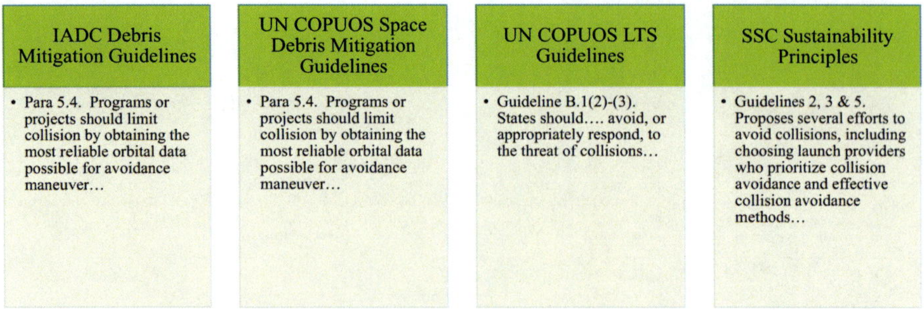

FIGURE 8 Summarized individual soft-law references for Theme 3 (Efforts should be expended to avoid collisions in orbit).

and other events that might increase the risk to the environment.[1506] Finally, the SSC Sustainability Practices propose several efforts to avoid collisions, including choosing launch providers who prioritize collision avoidance, effective collision avoidance methods (either active or passive), effective SSA and communication among operators, and implementation of passivation measures at the completion of its mission, if applicable (See Figure 8 Summary).[1507]

The United States sets out very specific requirements for collision avoidance, which must adhere to one of three criteria. During launch or re-entry, the operator must plan for a probability of collision by an object that reduces the likelihood of collision.[1508] Second, either during launch or re-entry, the object must maintain an ellipsoidal separation distance from other objects.[1509] Finally, the launching or reentering object must maintain a specific spherical separation distance from an object.[1510] Because one of these three criteria

1506 Guidelines for the Long-Term Sustainability of Outer Space Activities, *supra* note 1425 at Guidelines B.1(2)-(3).

1507 Best Practices for Space Operations, *supra* note 1426 at guidelines 2, 3 & 5.

1508 14 C.F.R. § 450.169(a)(1) (2021), *available at* https://www.ecfr.gov/cgi-bin/text-idx?SID=c839f88af39f5efe9fce08748e493dfb&mc=true&node=se14.4.450_1169&rgn=div8. The probability of collision parameters varies based on whether or not the opposing object is inhabited, operating, or orbital debris depending on size. It can be anywhere from .000001 for inhabitable to .00001 for debris of certain sizes.

1509 14 C.F.R. § 450.169(a)(2) (2021), *available at* https://www.ecfr.gov/cgi-bin/text-idx?SID=c839f88af39f5efe9fce08748e493dfb&mc=true&node=se14.4.450_1169&rgn=div8. The required ellipsoidal separation distance for inhabitable objects is 200 km in-track and 50 km cross-track and radially from the inhabitable object.

1510 14 C.F.R. § 450.169(a)(3) (2021), *available at* https://www.ecfr.gov/cgi-bin/text-idx?SID=c839f88af39f5efe9fce08748e493dfb&mc=true&node=se14.4.450_1169&rgn=div8. The spherical separation distance varies based on whether or not the opposing object is inhabited, operating, or orbital debris depending on size. It can be anywhere from 200 km for inhabited to 2.5 km for debris of certain sizes.

must be met, collision avoidance must inherently be part of the operational and planning efforts throughout the object's lifetime. China is not as specific on the parameters as the United States, but does require through its China Mitigation Measures that licensees have a duty to constantly monitor the risk of collision between their spacecraft and space debris.[1511] Furthermore, China has publicly stated that it prioritizes avoiding collisions and ensuring on-orbit safety of space objects through its network of space and land-based early warning systems.[1512] Russia similarly states the general requirement that space vehicles should be designed in such a way to prevent 'man-made clogging' of the space environment, with one of the main goals to limit the debris in space being to 'prevent collision in orbit.'[1513] To execute this goal, Russia requires that collision avoidance is factored in through all stages of the lifecycle of space vehicles, from mission inception to completion.[1514] Finally, ESA sets out its standards through ISO 24113:2019, specifically addressing collision avoidance through three primary lines of effort.[1515] At inception, spacecraft should be designed in a way that reduces the likelihood of destruction or break-up before its end-of-life.[1516] During operations, active management should be conducted to avoid collision with other objects.[1517] Last, spacecraft should have maneuver capability to ensure the ability to carry out avoidance measures if faced with the threat of collision.[1518] Interestingly, ESA continues to advance the concept of orbital collision safety in all its efforts. This is specifically evident from the language in the draft European Debris Mitigation Code, which points directly to the need to 'prevent on-orbit breakups and collisions.'[1519] In sum, all four programs have some provision to ensure that efforts are expended to avoid collisions in orbit (See Figure 9 Summary).

1511 Tronchetti, *supra* note 882 at 7, discussing the provisions of the Interim Instrument of Space Debris Mitigation and Management of 2010, Article 9.

1512 Statements by Chinese Delegation at the 55th Session of the Scientific and Technical Subcommittee of the Committee on the Peaceful Uses of Outer Space (Feb. 14, 2018), https://www.fmprc.gov.cn/ce/cgvienna/eng/hyyfy/t1535268.htm.

1513 GOST P 52925-2018, *supra* note 1138 at para. 5.2.

1514 *Id.* at para. 1.

1515 INT'L STANDARDIZATION ORGANIZATION (24113:2019), *supra* note 1326, 7, para. 6.

1516 *Id.* at 7, para. 6.

1517 *Id.*

1518 *Id.*

1519 European Code of Conduct for Space Debris Mitigation, para. 1 (June 28, 2004), https://www.unoosa.org/documents/pdf/spacelaw/sd/2004-B5-10.pdf.

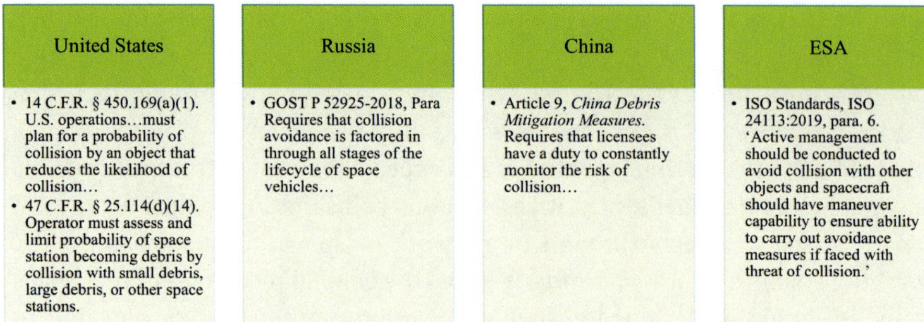

FIGURE 9 Summarized relevant state/organization practice for Theme 3 (Efforts should be expended to avoid collisions in orbit).

3.1.4 Theme 4—Risk of Breakups during Operational Phases is to be Minimized

The IADC Debris Mitigation Guidelines address the responsibility for minimizing the potential for breakups during operational phases.[1520] During design of both the spacecraft and the orbital stages, each project should demonstrate that there is 'no probable failure mode leading to accidental breakups.'[1521] If unavoidable, then all efforts should be expended to reduce the chance of their occurrence.[1522] Furthermore, the spacecraft or orbital stages should be regularly monitored to detect any potential problems that could result in a breakup and appropriate responses if such cases should arise.[1523] Similarly, the UN COPUOS Space Debris Mitigation Guidelines have specific provisions for minimizing the potential for breakups during the operational phase.[1524] According to the guidelines, the spacecraft and launch vehicle orbital stages should be designed to avoid failures that will result in breakups.[1525] Additionally, scenarios should be analyzed to reduce the probability a satellite breakup will cause catastrophic destruction, or if the catastrophe is unavoidable, that the destructive effects on the environment are minimized as much as possible.[1526] The UN COPUOS LTS Guidelines do not explicitly discuss expectations for reducing the probability

1520 IADC SPACE DEBRIS MITIGATION GUIDELINES REV. 3, *supra* note 26 at para. 5.2.

1521 *Id.*

1522 *Id.*

1523 *Id.*

1524 U.N. OFF. OF OUTER SPACE AFFAIRS, SPACE DEBRIS MITIGATION GUIDELINES OF THE COMMITTEE ON THE PEACEFUL USES OF OUTER SPACE, *supra* note 24 at Guideline 2.

1525 U.N. OFF. OF OUTER SPACE AFFAIRS, SPACE DEBRIS MITIGATION GUIDELINES OF THE COMMITTEE ON THE PEACEFUL USES OF OUTER SPACE, *supra* note 24 at Guideline 2.

1526 *Id.*

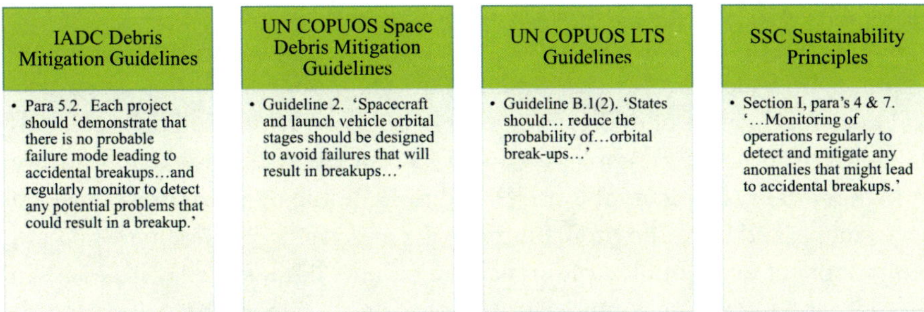

FIGURE 10 Summarized individual soft-law references for Theme 4 (Risk of breakups during operational phases should be minimized).

of orbital breakups.[1527] Instead, the UN COPUOS LTS Guidelines attempt to address and encourage proper coordination among governments and intergovernmental organizations should such a breakup occur.[1528] Primarily, the UN COPUOS LTS Guidelines advocate for exchange of relevant information between states and organizations that might otherwise affect the safety of all outer space operations.[1529] Finally, the SSC Sustainability Practices address breakups under the more general guidance that space operators should adopt concepts that enhance sustainability of the space environment as a whole.[1530] Again, addressing it post-design, the SSC Sustainability Practices encourage monitoring of operations regularly to detect and mitigate any anomalies that might lead to accidental breakups (See Figure 10 Summary).[1531]

The United States applies the principle of prevention of breakups as part of its flight safety analysis, which includes a debris analysis.[1532] A debris analysis must identify the inert, explosive, and other hazardous debris that could result from normal and malfunctioning launch vehicle flight.[1533] Specifically, a debris analysis must account for each potential cause of launch vehicle breakup, and must produce lists of predicted debris fragments for each cause

1527 Guidelines for the Long-Term Sustainability of Outer Space Activities, *supra* note 1425 at Guideline B.1(2).

1528 *Id.*

1529 *Id.*

1530 Best Practices for Space Operations, *supra* note 1426 at para. 5.

1531 *Id.* at para. 5(c).

1532 14 C.F.R. § 417.211 (2021), *available at* https://www.ecfr.gov/current/title-14/chapter-III/subchapter-C/part-417/subpart-C/section-417.211.

1533 14 C.F.R. §§ 417.211(b) & A417.11 (2021), *available at* https://www.ecfr.gov/current/title-14/chapter-III/subchapter-C/part-417/subpart-C/section-417.211.

of a breakup.[1534] For space stations, the operator must similarly make assessments of the design and operational strategies that will be used to mitigate orbital debris, including an assessment that "the probability the space station will become a source of debris as a result of collision with small debris" is calculated to be .01 (1 in 100) or less, using the NASA Debris Assessment Software or higher fidelity assessment tool.[1535] Additionally, the operator must make an assessment, and limit the probability during and after completion of mission operations, of accidental explosions or release of liquids that will persist in droplet form, including a demonstration that debris generation will not result from the conversion of energy sources on board the spacecraft into energy that fragments the spacecraft.[1536] Unfortunately, the available information for China does not demonstrate specific provisions regarding prevention of orbital breakup. It is likely that this is addressed in their regulatory standard, QJ3221–2005, revised in 2015, but the unavailability of the document makes specific citation challenging.[1537] Russia focuses on the design of the spacecraft to meet its own obligation for reducing the risk of breakups during the operational phase of flight.[1538] Specifically, the design should attempt to prevent the possible destruction of the space vehicle, including reducing the risk of

1534 14 C.F.R. § 417.211(c) (2021), *available at* https://www.ecfr.gov/current/title-14/chapter-III/subchapter-C/part-417/subpart-C/section-417.211.

1535 47 C.F.R. § 25.114 (d)(14)(II) (2020), *available at* https://www.ecfr.gov/current/title-47/chapter-I/subchapter-B/part-25.

1536 47 C.F.R. § 25.114 (d)(14)(III) (2020), *available at* https://www.ecfr.gov/current/title-47/chapter-I/subchapter-B/part-25.

1537 It is extremely important to note that China has at least eight regulations of varying governmental levels of importance relevant to space debris. Again, despite extensive effort, none of these became available nor were repeated inquiries into possible avenues for obtaining the information responded to. However, QJ3221-2005, revised 2015, is the China National Industry Standard, *Requirements for Orbital Debris Mitigation*, and is the overall controlling document. Below that are at least seven lower-level regulations, KJSP-T-1-01 chronologically through KJSP-T-1-06, and KJSP-M-1–01. *See* Gong, China Practices on Satellites Post-Mission Disposals Toward Space Long-Term Sustainability, *supra* note 927 at 19. However, secondary sources appear to conclude the Chinese debris regulations are based heavily on the UN COPUOS Debris Mitigation Guidelines and IADC Space Debris Mitigation Guidelines. *See PRC Standards System: Standards Used in China*, *supra* note 927. If that is the case, it is likely that China in some way reflects those regulations regarding prohibitions or minimization expectations for on-orbit breakups. Alternatively, there is some evidence that there is a national level standard which may be equivalent to ISO 24113-2019, though designated as voluntary; *Space Debris Mitigation Requirements*, The Standardization Administration of the People's Republic of China GB/T 34513-2017, which may contain the on-orbit breakup mitigation procedures.

1538 GOST P 52925-2018, *supra* note 1138 at para. 5.2.

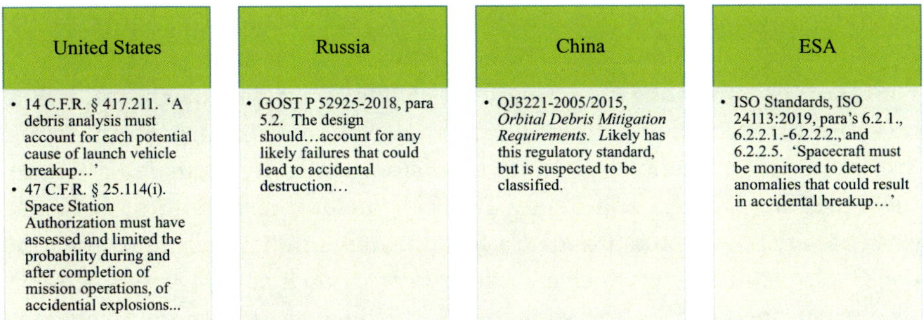

FIGURE 11 Summarized relevant state/organization practice for Theme 4 (Risk of breakups during operational phases should be minimized).

explosion.[1539] Additionally, the expectation is that the design and development of the space vehicle should include an analysis of the possible effects of the space environment on the space object and account for any likely failures that could lead to accidental destruction.[1540] Finally ESA, through ISO standard 24113:2019, has very specific standards for the avoidance of both intentional and accidental breakups.[1541] Obviously, intentional breakups are to be avoided.[1542] However, those are less likely a concern than accidental breakups, where the ISO standards are fairly stringent.[1543] Specifically, the probability of an accidental breakup should be less than .001 (or 1 in 1000) through its end-of-life, and this assessment should take into account all known failure possibilities that could cause an accidental breakup.[1544] Additionally, the standard requires that a spacecraft be monitored to detect anomalies that could result in accidental breakups, and if such is discovered, a contingency plan implemented to mitigate the risks.[1545] In sum, with the exception of China (which is simply unclear) the remaining programs have some provision to ensure that the risk of breakups during operational phases is assessed, and as much as possible, minimized (See Figure 11 Summary).

1539 *Id.* at para. 5.2.

1540 *Id.* at. para. 6.2.1. Additionally, addressing that design and development of space assets should preclude accidental and deliberate self-destruction. *See Id.* at para 6.2.2.

1541 INT'L STANDARDIZATION ORGANIZATION (24113:2019), *supra* note 1326, 7, para. 6.

1542 *Id.* at 6.2.1.

1543 *Id.* at 7, paras. 6.2.2.1–6.2.2.2.

1544 *Id.* at 7, para. 6.2.2.5.

1545 *Id.* at 7, para. 6.2.2.6.

3.1.5 Theme 5—the Potential for Post-mission Breakups Resulting from Stored Energy Should Be Minimized by Passivation

The IADC Debris Mitigation Guidelines address minimizing post-mission breakups through efforts directed at the passivation of the spacecraft.[1546] As discussed earlier, many spacecrafts have stores of energy remaining within their platforms at the end-of-life. This can include remaining propellants, extra battery power, pressure vessels, fly and momentum wheels, and other on-board sources of energy which can cause destruction if not properly 'safed.'[1547] As a result, the IADC Debris Mitigation Guidelines recommend implementation of passivation (depletion) processes for these energy sources as soon as doing so does not risk the payload or create subsequent risks in the process of passivation.[1548] The IADC Debris Mitigation Guidelines set out six activities which should be implemented for end-of-mission safety.[1549] First, deplete all propellants and fluids to avoid chemical reaction and destruction.[1550] Second, batteries should be 'safed' by deactivating charging lines.[1551] Third, high pressure vessels should be vented to avoid compression explosions.[1552] Fourth, self-destruct systems, if any, should be 'safed' to avoid activation.[1553] Fifth, fly and momentum wheels should have power removed.[1554] And finally, any remaining forms of energy should have mitigation measures applied.[1555] Similarly, the UN COPUOS Space Debris Mitigation Guidelines have a dedicated provision for avoiding post-mission breakups as a result of stored energy.[1556] These guidelines recommend all on-board energy should be depleted or made safe when it is no longer required for mission operations.[1557] These guidelines also make the observation that previous failures to passivate are likely the reason for the largest percentage of the catalogued space debris population.[1558] Notably, the UN COPUOS Space Debris Mitigation Guidelines highlight that failures to passivate among abandoned spacecraft, over a long enough period,

1546 IADC SPACE DEBRIS MITIGATION GUIDELINES REV. 3, *supra* note 26 at para. 5.2.1.
1547 *Id.*
1548 *Id.*
1549 *Id.*
1550 *Id.* at para. 5.2.1(1).
1551 *Id.* at para. 5.2.1(2).
1552 *Id.* at para. 5.2.1(3).
1553 *Id.* at para. 5.2.1(4).
1554 *Id.* at para. 5.2.1(5).
1555 *Id.* at para. 5.2.1(6).
1556 U.N. OFF. OF OUTER SPACE AFFAIRS, SPACE DEBRIS MITIGATION GUIDELINES OF THE COMMITTEE ON THE PEACEFUL USES OF OUTER SPACE, *supra* note 24 at Guideline 5.
1557 *Id.*
1558 *Id.*

often result in explosions that send debris throughout the space environment.[1559] The UN COPUOS LTS Guidelines demonstrate a preference to avoid the need for passivation by ideally investigating new methods of extending the operational lifetime of spacecraft instead.[1560] However, the UN COPUOS LTS Guidelines recognize passivation may still be necessary. If so, passivation should only be used (and the spacecraft kept in some orbit) if atmospheric re-entry is simply not an option (such as satellites in GEO).[1561] Finally, the SSC Sustainability Practices provide a 'twist' which slightly conflicts with the IADC Debris Mitigation Guidelines and the UN COPUOS Space Debris Mitigation Guidelines.[1562] Whereas those two recommend passivating as soon as practical, the SSC Sustainability Practices argues that passivation should be based on a 'tradeoff between the risk of debris generation due to breakup versus being due to collision with orbital debris over the passive deorbit period.'[1563] It is not that the SSC Sustainability Practices argue against passivation. Instead, it argues that passivation renders the object unable to be controlled.[1564] This is problematic for obvious reasons, and therefore passivating as soon as possible may not be the best plan in all cases. Instead, operators should strive to passivate once the need for collision avoidance is no longer necessary (for example, atmospheric re-entry).[1565] If re-entry is unlikely to be the method of disposal (such as opting for graveyard orbits) then passivation should only be considered when the object is finally placed into its post-mission orbit (See Figure 12 Summary).[1566]

The United States does not use the word 'passivation', instead opting for the word 'safed' to establish the requirement under the ODMSP that spacecraft must be passivated after their operational life.[1567] Specifically, the ODMSP

1559 *Id.*

1560 Guidelines for the Long-Term Sustainability of Outer Space Activities, *supra* note 1425 at Guideline D.2.

1561 *Id.* at Guideline D.2.

1562 Best Practices for Space Operations, *supra* note 1426 at para. 5(f).

1563 *Id.*

1564 *Id.* at para. 5(f)(II).

1565 *Id.*

1566 *Id.* at para. 5(f)(I)-(II).

1567 *U.S. Government Orbital Debris Mitigation Standard Practices, November 2019 Update, supra* note 585. *See also* 14 C.F.R. § 450.171 (a)(2)-(3) (2003), *available at* https://www.ecfr.gov/cgi-bin/text-idx?SID=4a429e4f34bf5f9c1dafa60edd3b8b50&mc=true&node=se14.4.450_1171&rgn=div8 (requiring that an operator must ensure that for any proposed launch for all vehicle stages or components that reach Earth orbit, "debris generation does not result from the conversion of energy sources into energy that fragments the vehicle or its components. Energy sources include chemical, pressure, and kinetic energy. For all vehicle stages or components that are left in orbit, stored energy is removed by depleting

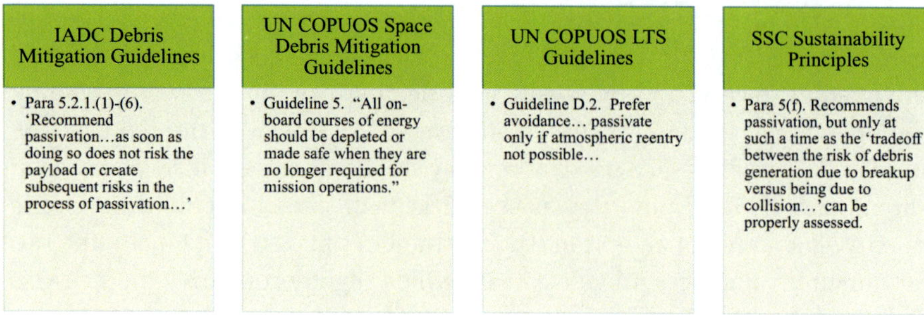

FIGURE 12 Summarized individual soft-law references for Theme 5 (The potential for post-mission breakups resulting from stored energy should be minimized by passivation).

states that all "on-board sources of stored energy of a spacecraft or upper stage should be depleted or 'safed' when they are no longer required for mission operations or post-mission disposal.[1568] Depletion should occur as soon as such an operation does not pose an unacceptable risk to the payload."[1569] Finally, it states that "propellant depletion burns and compressed gas releases should be designed to minimize the probability of a subsequent … accidental explosion."[1570] China implements passivation requirements for post-mission disposal as a subset of its national industry standard.[1571] According

residual fuel and leaving all fuel line valves open, venting any pressurized system, leaving all batteries in a permanent discharge state, and removing any source of stored energy."). *See also* 14 C.F.R. § 417.129, https://www.ecfr.gov/current/title-14/chapter-III/subchapter-C/part-417/subpart-B/section-417.129.

1568 *U.S. Government Orbital Debris Mitigation Standard Practices, November 2019 Update, supra* note 585 at § 2-2.

1569 *Id.*

1570 *Id.*

1571 Gong, China Practices on Satellites Post-Mission Disposals Toward Space Long-Term Sustainability, *supra* note 927 at 19. Though efforts to obtain the industry standard were unsuccessful, it is apparent based on the description of Professor Gong and the presentation that the standards align with the IADC expectations. Otherwise, the specific Chinese regulation is KJSP-T-1-01, *Rules of Spacecraft Passivation Design*, and also it appears that KJSP-T-0-06 may be applicable for determining the remaining propellant for launch vehicles. For spacecraft, KJSP-T-1-05, *Residual Propellant Measuring and Estimating of Spacecraft*, appears to be the controlling regulation. The implementation status of these sub-regulations is also unclear and may currently serve only as pre-approved guidance. However, it does appear that passivation remains a standard for Chinese space operations. Their policy guidance White Paper in 2016 specifically addressed passivation efforts, stating that China has made significant improvements in spacecraft design. Additionally, "all Long March carrier rockets have upper stage passivation, and discarded spacecraft

to Dr. Zizheng Gong, spacecraft passivation involves depletion of the residual propellants, discharging the batteries, relieving pressure vessels, disconnecting the self-destruct systems, and terminating fly and momentum wheels during disposal.[1572] For the launch vehicle, stage rockets are to complete passivation by depleting all residual propellants prior to proper disposal.[1573] The Russian standard for passivation is fairly comprehensive both during the planning and operational stages.[1574] Prior to operation, the Russian guidance requires that the design and development of the spacecraft should analyze the possible effects and likely failures that could lead to the accidental destruction of the spacecraft.[1575] Additionally, as part of the analysis, the operator must document the risk of destruction and loss of control, including activities involving withdrawal from the orbit by the spacecraft and its passivation.[1576] At the end of a spacecraft's mission, the Russian requirement provides extensive guidance on passivation steps.[1577] This includes removal of fuel residue and supercharged gasses, battery discharge and removal of charging lines, clearing high-pressure cylinders, halting flywheel, gyroscope, and other mechanical device movements, and preventing pyrotechnic triggering.[1578] ESA ISO standard 24113:2019 sets out the basic requirement that a 'spacecraft or launch vehicle orbital stage, for which a controlled re-entry has not been planned, shall be passivated in a safe and controlled manner before the end-of-life.[1579] Additionally, if for any reason a controlled planned re-entry cannot be accomplished, the item must also be capable of being passivated in a safe and controlled manner.'[1580] While

are moved out of orbit to protect the space environment." *See Full Text of White Paper on China's Space Activities in 2016*, *supra* note 994 at para. 9.

1572 Gong, China Practices on Satellites Post-Mission Disposals Toward Space Long-Term Sustainability, *supra* note 927 at 18. *See also* slide 27, providing a specific passivation procedure for the SINOSAT-3 spacecraft. First, the momentum wheels were stopped, followed by onboard active payload devices and heaters turned off. Next, the batteries were disconnected and the final status of the thrusters was set before it was deorbited. Upon completion, the downlink was cut off.

1573 Gong, China Practices on Satellites Post-Mission Disposals Toward Space Long-Term Sustainability, *supra* note 927 at 22.

1574 GOST P 52925-2018, *supra* note 1138.

1575 *Id.* at para. 6.2.1. It is worth noting that if the spacecraft will be deorbited into the atmosphere for total destruction, the requirements under 6.2.1. do not necessarily apply as a planning element since the spacecraft will not be deorbited into a graveyard orbit, but instead jettisoned into the atmosphere. *See Id.* at para 6.2.3.

1576 Id. at para. 6.2.1.

1577 *Id.* at para. 6.2.3.

1578 *Id.*

1579 INT'L STANDARDIZATION ORGANIZATION (24113:2019), *supra* note 1326, 7, para. 6.2.2.3.

1580 *Id.* at 7, para. 6.2.2.4.

the basic document does not give specifics on the steps for passivation, it does define passivation as the "act of permanently depleting, irreversibly deactivating, or making safe all on-board sources of stored energy capable of causing an accidental breakup."[1581] Examples of passivation includes the removal, disconnection, or release of residual propellants, batteries, high-pressure vessels, self-destruct devices, flywheels, and momentum wheels.[1582] In sum, all four programs address a requirement to minimize the potential for post-mission breakups resulting from stored energy (passivation) and provide comprehensive steps that should be accomplished. At the same time, there are differences between when passivation should occur and some preference for passivation versus atmospheric destruction among the major powers (See Figure 13 Summary).

3.1.6 Theme 6—If Not Destroyed by Atmospheric Methods, Post-mission Disposal of Space Objects Away from LEO and GEO Is to Be Arranged

The IADC Debris Mitigation Guidelines breaks the disposal of space objects from LEO and GEO into two different sections. For GEO, the IADC Debris Mitigation Guidelines set out that spacecraft should be maneuvered far enough from GEO so that it 1) will not cause interference with spacecraft or orbital stages still in GEO, and 2) the final orbital placement of the spacecraft should cause it to remain above the GEO protected[1583] region.[1584] Similarly, for LEO, spacecraft and orbital stages that are terminating in orbits that pass through LEO,

1581 *Id.* at 3, para. 3.19 (3d ed. 2019). For more granular detail, ISO 24113:2019 points to the specific ISO standards for each type of vehicle to be passivated; the spacecraft and the launch vehicle orbital stages hold additional requirements and specificity. *See* INT'L STANDARDIZATION ORGANIZATION, SPACE SYSTEMS—DETAILED SPACE DEBRIS MITIGATION REQUIREMENTS FOR LAUNCH VEHICLE ORBITAL STAGES, ISO 20893:2021 (1st ed. 2021). *See also* INT'L STANDARDIZATION ORGANIZATION, SPACE SYSTEMS—DISPOSAL OF ORBITAL LAUNCH STAGES, ISO 16699:2015, v (1st ed. 2015); INT'L STANDARDIZATION ORGANIZATION, SPACE SYSTEMS—DISPOSAL OF SATELLITES OPERATING AT GEOSYNCHRONOUS ALTITUDE, ISO 26872:2019 (2d ed. 2019); INT'L STANDARDIZATION ORGANIZATION, SPACE SYSTEMS—DISPOSAL OF SATELLITES OPERATING IN OR CROSSING LOW EARTH ORBIT, ISO 16164:2015(E) (1st ed. 2015); INT'L STANDARDIZATION ORGANIZATION, SPACE SYSTEMS—SPACE DEBRIS MITIGATION DESIGN AND OPERATION MANUAL FOR SPACECRAFT, TECHNICAL REPORT, ISO/TR 18146:2020 (2d ed. 2020).

1582 INT'L STANDARDIZATION ORGANIZATION (24113:2019), *supra* note 1326, 3, para. 3.19.

1583 For a definition of the protected region, *see* IADC guidelines, IADC SPACE DEBRIS MITIGATION GUIDELINES REV. 3, *supra* note 26 at paras. 5.3.1(1)-(2).

1584 *Id.* at para. 5.3.1.

United States	Russia	China	ESA
• 14 C.F.R. 417.129(c), Launch Vehicle. For all launch vehicle stages or components that reach Earth orbit "stored energy is removed by depleting…any remaining source of stored energy." • 47 C.F.R. § 25.114(ii), Spacecraft, Passivation demonstration 'that debris generation will not result from the conversion of energy sources on board that fragments the spacecraft…'	• GOST P 52925-2018, para's 6.2.1 & 6.2.3. 'Operator must document…activities involving withdrawal from the orbit by the spacecraft and its passivation.'	• KJSP-T-1-01, (spacecraft), KJSP-T-0-06 (launch vehicle). Launch vehicles and spacecraft are to complete passivation prior to proper disposal.	• ISO Standard 24113:2019, para's 6.2.2.3, 6.2.2.4, & 3.19. 'Spacecraft or launch vehicle orbital stage, for which a controlled re-entry has not been planned, shall be passivated in a safe and controlled manner before the end of life.'

FIGURE 13 Summarized relevant state/organization practice for Theme 5 (The potential for post-mission breakups resulting from stored energy should be minimized by passivation).

or might otherwise interfere with LEO, should be deorbited with a probability of success of at least 90% or otherwise retrieved for disposal.[1585] Finally, for all other orbits which spacecraft may be operating in, they should be maneuvered to reduce their orbital lifetime in accordance with the guidance for spacecraft in LEO, or relocated if they otherwise will cause interference with highly utilized orbital regions.[1586] The UN COPUOS Space Debris Mitigation Guidelines similarly bifurcate disposal for LEO and GEO.[1587] For LEO, Guideline 6 states that spacecraft and launch vehicles that pass through the LEO region should be removed at the 'termination' of their operational phases from orbit in a controlled fashion, or otherwise disposed of in orbits that prevent their long-term presence in the LEO regions.[1588] For GEO, Guideline 7 states that spacecraft and orbital stages that have terminated their operational phases in orbits that pass through GEO should be left in orbits that avoid their interference with the GEO region.[1589] The UN COPUOS LTS Guidelines defer in their recommendation to the UN COPUOS Space Debris Mitigation Guidelines. Specifically, the UN COPUOS LTS Guidelines state that spacecraft should "reach their intended graveyard orbit or deorbit appropriately, in accordance with the UN COPUOS

1585 *Id.* at para. 5.3.2.

1586 *Id.*

1587 U.N. OFF. OF OUTER SPACE AFFAIRS, SPACE DEBRIS MITIGATION GUIDELINES OF THE COMMITTEE ON THE PEACEFUL USES OF OUTER SPACE, *supra* note 24.

1588 *Id.* at Guideline 6.

1589 *Id.* at Guideline 7.

Space Debris Mitigation Guidelines."[1590] In addition, they encourage manufacturers and operators of space objects to design spacecraft in a way that "limits the long-term presence of space objects in protected regions of outer space after the end of their mission."[1591] The SSC Sustainability Practices align most closely to the IADC Space Debris Mitigation Guidelines. The SSC Sustainability Practices set out a series of recommendations broken into two parts.[1592] For upper stages, the SSC Sustainability Practices recommends that in LEO, upper stages should be deorbited, and in GEO, disposed of in a way where the upper stage will not enter the GEO protected region for 100 years of its end-of-life.[1593] In addition, the SSC Sustainability Practices recommends selection of service providers that can both meet the aforementioned standards, and also do so at a success rate of 90% or better.[1594] For spacecraft, the SSC Sustainability Practices recommends that a probability of successful disposal should be even higher than that of upper stages; 95% to be exact.[1595] For spacecraft in GEO, disposal should occur in a disposal orbit as soon as practical after the end of its service life and completion of the disposal maneuver and should remain outside of GEO for at least 100 years.[1596] For LEO, spacecraft should be disposed of by means of atmospheric re-entry as soon as possible after end-of-life, and those that use chemical or electric propulsion to deorbit should be deorbited in no more than five years (See Figure 14 Summary).[1597]

The ODMSP Objective 4 addresses post-mission disposal of space structures for the United States.[1598] The ODMSP requires a minimum probability reliability of post-mission disposal equivalent to the IADC Space Debris Mitigation Guidelines of 90%, while additionally imposing a goal of 99% or better.[1599] For spacecraft which will otherwise be utilizing atmospheric re-entry, the allowable timeframe is no more than 25 years after completion of mission.[1600] In

---

1590 *Id.* at para. B.7(5)(b).

1591 Guidelines for the Long-Term Sustainability of Outer Space Activities, *supra* note 1425 at para. B.8(2).

1592 Best Practices for Space Operations, *supra* note 1426.

1593 *Id.* at Guideline 2(c)-(d).

1594 *Id.* at Guideline 2.

1595 *Id.* at Guideline 4(a).

1596 *Id.* at Guideline 5(a).

1597 *Id.* at Guideline 5(f)-(h).

1598 *U.S. Government Orbital Debris Mitigation Standard Practices, November 2019 Update, supra* note 585 at objective 4. As a note, Objective 4 also discusses MEO in section 4–1(e), though I have not covered that as not germane to the main areas of discussion here for post-mission disposal of LEO and GEO in light of the entirety of the discussion.

1599 *Id.* at objective 4, para. 4–2.

1600 *Id.* at objective 4, para. 4–1(b).

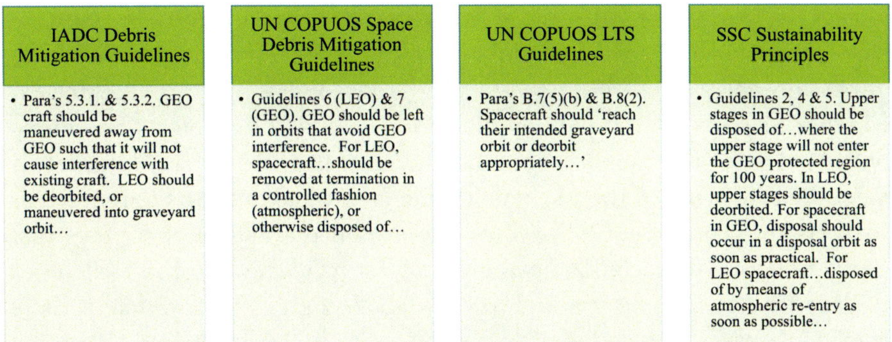

FIGURE 14 Summarized individual soft-law references for Theme 6 (If an object is not disposed of by atmospheric reentry, the space object should be disposed of away from LEO and GEO to avoid interference with those valuable orbits).

the event, however, that the spacecraft will be stored between LEO and GEO as the disposal method, Objective 4 provides two options.[1601] One, the object may be located where the perigee remains above the LEO zone (2000 km) for at least 100 years and the apogee remains below the GEO zone (35,586 km) for the same period of time (as well, time spent between 20,182 +/- 300 km is limited to 25 years or less over 200 years[1602]).[1603] Alternatively, the spacecraft must maneuver to a near circular disposal orbit to avoid crossing the GEO zone, the LEO zone, and the 20,182 km +/- 300 zone for at least 100 years and limit the risk to other operational craft by avoiding crossing the altitudes occupied by known constellation missions of ten or more spacecraft using near circular orbits for 100 years.[1604] Regarding storage above GEO, the craft must be maneuvered to an orbit with a perigee at least above 35,986 km sufficient enough to ensure the craft remains outside the GEO zone for at least 100 years.[1605] From the available data for China, it appears that for LEO, China

1601 *Id.* at objective 4, para. 4–1(c).

1602 This specific altitude is called out because it is the altitude at which Global Positioning System satellites orbit. *See* The Interoperable Global Navigation Satellite Systems Space Service Volume, U.N. Doc. E.19.IV.1, (2018), https://www.unoosa.org/res/oosadoc/data/documents/2018/stspace/stspace75_0_html/st_space_75E.pdf. *See also U.S. Government Orbital Debris Mitigation Standard Practices, November 2019 Update, supra* note 585 at objective 4, para. 4–1(c)(I).

1603 *U.S. Government Orbital Debris Mitigation Standard Practices, November 2019 Update, supra* note 585 at objective 4, para. 4–1(c)(I).

1604 *Id.* at objective 4, para. 4–1(c)(II).

1605 *Id.* at objective 4, para. 4–1(d).

follows the IADC Debris Mitigation Guidelines and similarly the ESA ISO standards for removal of spacecraft and orbital stages that have reached their end-of-mission operations within 25 years.[1606] Additionally, for GEO, it is unclear whether or not China strictly applies a 100-year rule for objects remaining outside of GEO after mission completion, but it is evident that China recognizes the sensitivity of the GEO environment and makes efforts to remove its spacecrafts accordingly.[1607] Based on the evidence available, it appears that China utilizes a protected zone above GEO for its graveyard orbit that varies in distance between 60 km and 328 km above GEO.[1608] Additionally, there is evidence that China adheres to the UN COPUOS Space Debris Mitigation Guidelines, which would presumably invoke previously discussed Guideline 6 and Guideline 7.[1609] That might also explain why there is no specific reference to the GEO 100-year guidance which is found in some other guidelines and programs, since the UN COPUOS Space Debris Mitigation Guidelines do not contain such a provision.[1610] Russia's requirements for disposal match the IADC Debris Mitigation Guidelines fairly closely with the exception of the probability of success for disposal.[1611] For GEO, spacecraft and orbital stages should be removed at the end of operation in a way that does not allow them to interfere with GEO or return into GEO for 100 years after initial withdrawal.[1612] Regarding the parameters of the GEO protected region, the Russian formula matches the formula of the IADC Debris Mitigation Guidelines exactly.[1613] For LEO, all spacecraft and orbital stages that have completed their mission, or are passing through LEO, must either be diverted to a graveyard orbit where they will not interfere with LEO for 100 years, or if unable to be controlled, should remain within LEO for no more than 25 years.[1614] ESA ISO standard 24113:2019

1606 Gong, China Practices on Satellites Post-Mission Disposals Toward Space Long-Term Sustainability, *supra* note 927 at 17.

1607 *Id.* at 24.

1608 *Id.* at 25.

1609 U.N. Off. of Outer Space Affairs, Space Debris Mitigation Guidelines of the Committee on the Peaceful Uses of Outer Space, *supra* note 24 at guidelines 6–7.

1610 Gong, China Practices on Satellites Post-Mission Disposals Toward Space Long-Term Sustainability, *supra* note 927 at 29.

1611 The requirement for successful disposal for the IADC should be at least 90%, whereas the probability of success for Russian craft is at least 80%. *See* GOST P 52925-2018, *supra* note 1138 at para. 6.4.1.

1612 *Id.* at para. 6.4.2.

1613 *Id.* at para. 3.1.2. Defining GEO at 35,786, with lower/upper altitude equal to 'GEO +/- 200 km and +/1 15 degrees latitude.' *See also* IADC Space Debris Mitigation Guidelines Rev. 3, *supra* note 26 at para. 3.3.2.(2).

1614 GOST P 52925-2018, *supra* note 1138 at para. 6.4.4.

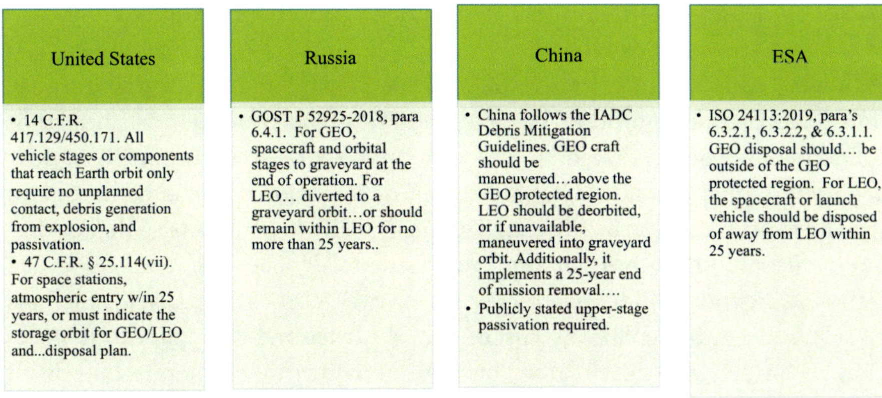

FIGURE 15 Summarized relevant state/organization practice for Theme 6 (If an object is not disposed of by atmospheric reentry, the space object should be disposed of away from LEO and GEO to avoid interference with those valuable orbits).

establishes that disposal of a spacecraft or launch vehicle orbital stages after end-of-mission should have a disposal probability of success of at least 90% through the end-of-life.[1615] For disposal of craft in GEO, disposal should ensure that the object will not reenter the GEO protected region within 100 years after its end-of-life and the graveyard orbit should be outside of the GEO protected region.[1616] For LEO, the spacecraft or launch vehicle should be disposed of away from LEO within 25 years beginning at either 1) the orbit injection epoch (initial injection) if the object has no collision avoidance capability, or 2) at the end-of-mission epoch if it otherwise can perform collision avoidance, or finally, 3) the epoch of the first intersection of the orbit with the LEO protected region within 100 years after the end-of-life if the craft otherwise operates outside of the LEO protected region.[1617] In sum, all four programs have provisions addressing that space objects at the end of their mission life should be properly disposed of, offering varying preferred options and methods to do so (See Figure 15 Summary).

1615 INT'L STANDARDIZATION ORGANIZATION (24113:2019), *supra* note 1326, 8, para. 6.3.1.1.

1616 *Id.* at 8, paras. 6.3.2.1–6.3.2.2. Note also that para. 6.3.2.2. specifically discusses the conditions for a spacecraft operating in GEO to remain outside of the GEO protected region.

1617 *Id.* at 8, para. 6.3.3.1.

3.1.7 Theme 7—Intentional Destruction and Other Harmful Activities Are to Be Avoided

The IADC Debris Mitigation Guidelines specifically address avoiding intentional destruction and other harmful activities. The IADC Debris Mitigation Guidelines advocate that activities that may increase collision risks, self-destruction of spacecraft or orbital stages, or intentional breakups should be 1) avoided entirely, or 2) if conducted, done in such a low altitude so that orbital fragments are short-lived in the environment.[1618] The UN COPUOS Space Debris Mitigation Guidelines reflect the IADC Debris Mitigation Guidelines closely, stating that collisions, intentional destruction of any on-orbit spacecraft or launch vehicle, or other harmful activities that generate long lived debris should be avoided.[1619] Similarly, if unavoidable, they should be conducted at sufficiently low altitudes to limit the orbital lifetime of remaining fragments.[1620] The UN COPUOS LTS Guidelines do not have a specific provision for avoidance of harmful activities.[1621]

However, a major tenet of the UN COPUOS LTS Guidelines is to promote behavior that is not otherwise adverse to other spacefaring countries or the environment.[1622] For example, the UN COPUOS LTS Guidelines encourage States and IGO's to promote research and development of sustainable technologies, processes and services for sustainable exploration and use of outer space (read 'do no harm').[1623] Furthermore, the UN COPUOS LTS Guidelines advocate for IGO's to consider appropriate safety measures to protect Earth and the space environment from harmful contamination (such as activities which might otherwise result in debris creating events like collisions, self-destruction, et cetera.).[1624] Additionally, the UN COPUOS LTS Guidelines advocate for State behavior that promotes security, such as compliance with the ITU radio regulations and transparent standards for exchange of data to avoid collisions or other harmful events in outer space.[1625] Again, while not specific, the UN COPUOS LTS Guidelines encourage overall behaviors that support sustainable activities in space. Finally, the SSC Sustainability Practices,

1618 IADC SPACE DEBRIS MITIGATION GUIDELINES REV. 3, *supra* note 26 at para. 5.2.3.

1619 U.N. OFF. OF OUTER SPACE AFFAIRS, SPACE DEBRIS MITIGATION GUIDELINES OF THE COMMITTEE ON THE PEACEFUL USES OF OUTER SPACE, *supra* note 24 at Guideline 4.

1620 *Id.*

1621 Guidelines for the Long-Term Sustainability of Outer Space Activities, *supra* note 1425 at para. B.8(2).

1622 *Id.* at para. B.8(2).

1623 *Id.* at para. D.1(3).

1624 *Id.* at para. D.1(4).

1625 *Id.* at para. C.4(4).

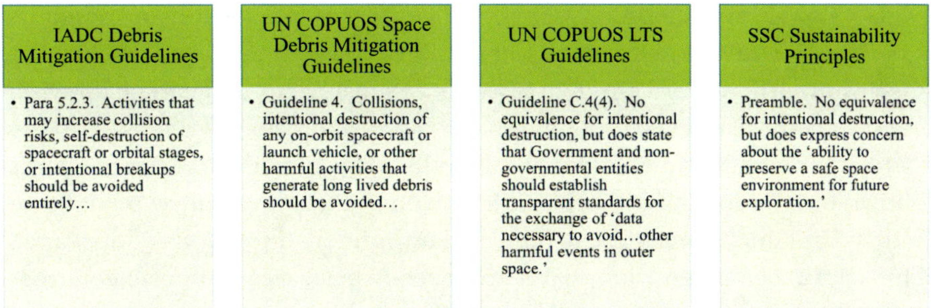

FIGURE 16 Summarized individual soft-law references for Theme 7 (Intentional destruction of space objects and other harmful activities are to be avoided).

as a general matter, expresses that there are concerns about the ability to preserve a safe space environment for future exploration and the need to limit the creation of new space debris to ensure the ability to operate in the future.[1626] It advocates that all space actors must implement best practices to ensure the safety and accessibility of the space environment.[1627] Additionally, the SSC Sustainability Practices outline clear expectations to preserve the space environment, including proper spacecraft design, collision avoidance maneuvers to be coordinated with other space actors once operational, consistent monitoring of spacecraft during operations to avoid potential disasters, and finally, attention to proper disposal techniques.[1628] All of this in the interest of ensuring space accessibility well into the future (See Figure 16 Summary).

The preamble from the ODMSP of the United States addresses the requirements for avoidance of harmful activities.[1629] It says that it is in the interest of all States to minimize new debris and mitigate the effect of existing debris.[1630] The ODMSP also implores all space participants to promote an efficient and effective set of space safety practices to "contribute to safe space operations and the long-term sustainability of space activities."[1631] The practice of the United States has been consistent with this theme, specifically in the case of intentional destruction of satellites and, if conducting such activity, doing so in a manner that reduces the time of any remaining debris in orbit. Notably, the

1626 Best Practices for Space Operations, *supra* note 1426 at 8.
1627 *Id.* at 9.
1628 *Id.* at Guidelines 4–5.
1629 *U.S. Government Orbital Debris Mitigation Standard Practices, November 2019 Update, supra* note 585 at 1.
1630 *Id.*
1631 *Id.*

USA-193 spacecraft shootdown by the United States in 2008 demonstrated its adherence to avoiding damaging activity when its ASAT test was conducted at such a low altitude (250 km) that it was both sensitive to, and compliant with, the UN COPUOS and IADC guidelines.[1632] China indicates an adherence to the IADC Debris Mitigation Guidelines as well as the UN COPUOS Space Debris Mitigation Guidelines, both of which reference the avoidance of harmful activity and intentional destruction.[1633] Furthermore, in its 2016 White Paper, China advanced its position that it approaches space as a responsible partner and "takes effective measures to protect the space environment ... and guarantee that its space activities benefit the whole of mankind."[1634] While China was publicly called out for its environmentally disastrous 2007 ASAT test, discussed earlier, China has since not engaged in similar destructive behavior.[1635] Russia specifically addresses preventing deliberate destruction of space assets, requiring that spacecraft should be designed and developed in such a way as to exclude deliberate destruction (either self-destruction or destruction as a result of collision), as well as other actions of destruction that could lead to the formation of debris and significantly increase the risk of collision with other spacecraft.[1636] However, concerns of intentional 'self-destruction' do not apply to destruction as a result of proper post-mission disposal by atmospheric re-entry.[1637] Unfortunately, while Russia had not conducted a destructive ASAT test since 1983, that changed on 15 November 2021 when United States Space Command (USSPACECOM) confirmed the 'successful' test by Russia of

1632 Space Debris Assessment for USA-193, Presentation to the 45th Session of the Sci. & Tech. Subcomm., Comm. Peaceful Uses of Outer Space (Feb. 11–22, 2008), https://www.unoosa.org/pdf/pres/stsc2008/tech-16.pdf. The assessment indicated that more than 50% of the debris created would not be orbital and would enter Earth's atmosphere within 45 minutes of destruction. Furthermore, over 99% of the remaining debris would fall out of orbit within one week of the event (which assumed a worst-case scenario).

1633 Gong, China Practices on Satellites Post-Mission Disposals Toward Space Long-Term Sustainability, *supra* note 927 at 29.

1634 *Full Text of White Paper on China's Space Activities in 2016*, *supra* note 994 at para. 3.

1635 This is not to say that it does not still conduct ASAT tests, nor that its program does not continues to develop. The United States suspects that as late as 2013 the Chinese government authorized firing the Dong Ning-2, which China argued was for scientific purposes. The United States appeared unconvinced, and believed that the missile was actually an ASAT kinetic-kill vehicle that could reach as far as GEO. However, it remains that while their program continues to develop, and while they may continue to engage in potential ASAT-like tests, they have not engaged in the destructive behavior of the 2007 ASAT test. *See* Aachary Keck, *China Secretly Tested an Anti-Satellite Missile*, THE DIPLOMAT (Mar. 19, 2014), https://thediplomat.com/2014/03/china-secretly-tested-an-anti-satellite-missile/.

1636 GOST P 52925-2018, *supra* note 1138 at para. 6.2.2.

1637 *Id.* at para. 6.2.2.

a direct-ascent anti-satellite (DA-ASAT) missile against the defunct Russian Cosmos 1408 satellite.[1638] ESA, through ISO 24113:2019, addresses intentional breakups, noting in clear terms that "in Earth's orbit, intentional breakup of a spacecraft or launch vehicle orbital stages shall be avoided."[1639] Furthermore, in respect to activities that could otherwise cause an intentional breakup, such as ASAT tests, no current ESA member country has the capability to conduct an ASAT test, thus negating the concern of the capability or need to address such activity within its regulations.[1640] In sum, with the exception of China,

---

1638 Pavel Podvig, *Russian Military Space Capabilities, in* ENSURING AMERICA'S SPACE SECURITY 125, *available at* https://fas.org/pubs/_docs/10072004164624.pdf. Until November of 2021, Russia had continued to test ASAT capabilities, most recently on April 15, 2020, with the Russian Nudol interceptor, though these tests had previously been non-destructive. *See* Mike Wall, *Don't Panic About Russia's Recent Anti-Satellite Test, Experts Say*, SPACE.COM (Apr. 30, 2020), https://www.space.com/russia-anti-satellite-weapon-fears-overblown.html. *See also* Raju, *supra* note 15 at 4 (discussing the early tests of Russia were likely very destructive, but the Nudol tests appear to have simply completed several orbits before returning to Earth). However, the test against Cosmos 1408 was particularly destructive because of the risk it additionally placed to the ISS. *A Russian Anti-Satellite Missile Test Puts the ISS in Peril*, THE ECONOMIST (Nov. 18, 2021), https://www.economist.com/science-and-technology/2021/11/18/a-russian-anti-satellite-missile-test-puts-the-iss-in-peril. The test required an early-morning notification to the astronauts on the ISS to take refuge within the Soyuz and Dragon capsules, docked to the space station (interestingly the four crew on the ISS included two Russians). Chelsea Gohd, *Russian Anti-Satellite Test a "Dangerous and Irresponsible" Act that Threatens Astronauts, US Says*, SPACE.COM (Nov. 15, 2021), https://www.space.com/russia-asat-test-space-debris-dangerous-irresponsible. The Chinese taikonauts on their own Tiangong space station were also warned about the danger to their station. Kelsey D., *This Week's Destroyed Russian Satellite Created Even More Dangerous Space Debris*, POPULAR SCIENCE (Nov. 16, 2021), https://www.popsci.com/technology/russian-missile-destroys-russian-satellite/. The Russians deny that any threat was posed to the ISS, and the Russian Defense Ministry issued a statement calling criticism of Russia hypocritical. The statement said that "the U.S. knows for certain that the resulting fragments, in terms of test time and orbital parameters, did not and will not pose a threat to orbital stations, spacecraft and space activities." Elizabeth Howell, *Russia Defends Anti-satellite Test Amid US Criticism*, SPACE.COM (Nov. 16, 2021), https://www.space.com/russia-defends-anti-satellite-test-amid-criticism. Cosmos 1408 operated somewhere around 650 km. At this altitude, the resulting debris is likely to remain for at least years, and possibly decades according to USSPACECOM. Tereza Pultarova, *Space Debris from Rusian Anti-Satellite Test will be a Safety Threat for Years*, SPACE.COM (Nov. 16, 2021), https://www.space.com/russia-anti-satellite-test-space-debris-threat-for-years.

1639 INT'L STANDARDIZATION ORGANIZATION (24113:2019), *supra* note 1326, 7, para. 6.2.1.

1640 At least at the unclassified level, it appears the only ASAT capable countries are the United States, China, Russia, India, and potentially Israel. *See* Ajai Shukla, *India Successfully Tests ASAT Missile, Joins Space Superpower Club*, BUSINESS STANDARD (Apr. 3, 2019), https://www.business-standard.com/article/current-affairs/india-successfully-tests-asat-miss

United States	Russia	China	ESA
• ODMSP, Preamble. The "USG recognizes that it is in the interest of all nations to minimize new debris and mitigate effects of existing debris."	• GOST P 52925-2018, para 6.2.2. Spacecraft should be designed and developed in such a way as to 'exclude deliberate destruction (either self-destruction or destruction as a result of collision), as well as other actions of destruction that could lead to the formation of debris and significantly increase the risk of collision with other spacecraft.'	• China indicates an adherence to the IADC Debris Mitigation Guidelines as well as the UN COPUOS Space Debris Mitigation Guidelines, both of which reference the avoidance of harmful activity and intentional destruction.	• ISO 24113:2019, para 6.2.1. "In Earth's orbit, intentional breakup of a spacecraft or launch vehicle orbital stage shall be avoided."

FIGURE 17 Summarized relevant state/organization practice for Theme 7 (Intentional destruction of space objects and other harmful activities are to be avoided).

all three other major spacefaring actors have provisions addressing that they should refrain from activities that cause intentional destruction and other harmful conduct in space (even if Russia now appears to have a very loose interpretation of their prohibited activities). And while no specific provision is obvious in the Chinese program, they do still publicly state their position as such. Unlike the Russians, China has refrained since 2007 from any further ASAT tests providing further evidence that they believe doing so is unwise (See Figure 17 Summary).

4 Do Any Similarities in the Way Nations Implement the Standards Represented within the Themes Meet the Standards of Customary International Law?

What we find from this comparison boils down to two major points. The first is that, when approached as themes, there is significant commonality between the provisions of the major spacefaring Nations, including ESA. All four have implemented some form of regulation or guidance, albeit not always mandatory, that establishes that the only functional way to operate in space is to approach activities with the 'end in mind' and avoid unnecessary creation of space debris. We can see that all four have determined, as a fundamental principle, that release of space debris during normal operations should be limited. Furthermore, accidents (including collisions and breakups) should be

ile-joins-space-superpower-club-119032800048_1.html. *See also* Main-moderator, *ASAT-Anti Satellite Weapon Systems*, WITANWORLD (Jul. 19, 2020), https://witanworld.com/article/2020/07/19/asat-anti-satellite-weapon-systems/.

minimized through either constant monitoring or communication with other spacefaring Nations through SSA tools. Planning for the worst possible eventuality is key. Not only is there some degree of expectation that the post-mission disposal will be successful, but it is also bifurcated to account for objects which cannot be deorbited atmospherically and must alternatively be placed into a non-interfering orbit. In addition, there is consensus that if the objects are to remain in some orbit, they should be neutralized as a threat. This is done by precluding their return into highly utilized orbits and by passivating the remaining energy from batteries, flywheels, et cetera., to maximize the chance the craft does not become a dangerous debris field.

The second point is that while the themes have some consistency, there are important nuances to some. Additionally, even those areas with general commonality are not necessarily approached by all four in the same manner, particularly in program distinctions between what constitutes 'guidance' and what are actually 'hard rules.' ESA and the United States arguably have the most stringent programs with clear regulatory lines. And the United States has, at least for GEO, a specific regulatory enforcement requirement in the United States Code stating that "a space station authorized to operate in GEO ... *shall* be relocated at the end of its useful life, barring catastrophic failure of satellite components ..."[1641] Russia and China also have what appear to be required submissions for debris mitigation plans, but lack enforcement mechanisms and their regulatory guidance appears to be limited to just that ... 'guidance.' However, even when considering the stringent programs of the United States compared to Russia and China, there is no evidence in any of the four programs that there is a 'stick in addition to the carrot.' For example, the compliance expectation for successful post-mission disposal, as discussed above, for the ESA and China is 90%. The United States has the same baseline expectation, but also establishes a goal of 99% or better. Russia, on the other hand, sets a success expectation of only 80% for post-mission disposal.

However, more to the point is that even if all the actors treated these compliance rates as 'hard rules', none of those programs specifically identify what will occur in the event of non-compliance. There is no specific remedy for an operator that fails to meet this disposal requirement. We can certainly presume that if there is continued bad behavior, via the licensing process, States might otherwise get 'wise' to bad actors and potentially deny them a license for future endeavors. Or we might presume that if a post-mission disposal plan

1641 47 C.F.R. § 25.283, *available at* https://www.law.cornell.edu/cfr/text/47/25.283. This provision also requires passivation for any space stations upon completion of the maneuver as well.

submitted during the licensing stage seems too optimistic, the reviewer might otherwise get suspicious and investigate further. However, there is no specific evidence that this has occurred either. Absent any repercussions, it is hard to establish that States would perceive an understood practice to evolve into, or in fact be, a hard rule.

Accordingly, the four major spacefaring actors surveyed have programs that recognize the importance of mitigating space debris and the threat that space debris presents to current and future operations of space. However, they also have the most to lose from non-compliance to any standard. In response, the United States, Russia, China, and ESA have exerted efforts to address the problem of space debris through various mechanisms from which they advocate their positions: public statements, established domestic laws and adopted regulations, and behaviors consistent with understanding the importance of environmental management to name a few. The common thread throughout continues to be that each spacefaring Nation has demonstrated a keen awareness of the fragility of the space environment and an obligation to preserve it.

Despite that recognition, and corresponding efforts on behalf of the major spacefaring Nations, the variances in practices are notable enough that both a subjective and objective assessment would likely determine that customary international law has not been definitively established. Additionally, some of the characteristics that you might otherwise find desirable for 'law' to exist are also not necessarily evident. For example, there is not consistency across the board for either minimum standards or specific goals, nor are there particular enforcement mechanisms for failure to adhere to the standards once the spacecraft is in operation (and fails to comply post-mission with their licensing expectations).[1642] On the other hand, there is hope that as technology becomes more advanced, as cooperation becomes more necessary, and as the private sector takes over more and more responsibilities, more consistent practices will solidify. At that point, hopefully, some of the more traditional accompanying expectations of law, enforceability, and specific standards will take shape to support customary understanding among Nations.

4.1 *The 25 Year 'Rule'*

While the seven themes previously discussed may not suffice to establish a specific principle(s) which, whether now or in the future, will develop into customary (or treaty) law, this book previously touched at varying points on the

1642 Scott Michael Steele, *Can International Law Provide a Basis for Actively Removing Space Debris?*, Advanced Maui Optical and Space Surveillance Technologies Conference, para. 2.3. (2020).

'25-year' LEO guideline as one of the long-standing tenets of debris mitigation found in some fashion in most space programs. As such, it is at least worth a brief re-examination of whether this principle, on its own, might suffice to establish a rule in customary international law.

In brief review, the 25-year 'rule' is a guideline adopted by many international organizations and spacefaring Nations which encourages those entities with objects in LEO to ensure their objects will decay and reenter Earth's atmosphere within 25 years (typically of mission completion). Its first major appearance as a 'rule' was as early as 1995 when NASA included it as a standard in NASA Safety Standard 1740.14.[1643] Since that time, efforts through the IADC and other voluntary debris mitigation guidelines have pushed the concept into the mainstream. Incorporation of the 'rule' is now evident in the domestic guidance of major spacefaring countries as well as some other smaller space participants. By the time the IADC had officially published version 1 of the IADC Debris Mitigation Guidelines, the argument put forth by the IADC was that the available research, including its own efforts, established that 25 years was a 'reasonable and appropriate' lifetime limit for space objects to remain in the LEO region.[1644]

In response, the major space operators that had not already made some reference to this rule began to do so (and continue to this day to reference the guidepost).[1645] However, though very commonly referenced and reflected in

1643 NASA Safety Standard 1740.14, *supra* note 543 at 36, para 6. "In general, the post-mission disposal options are ... (2) maneuver to an orbit for which atmospheric draft will remove the structure within 25-years ...".

1644 IADC SPACE DEBRIS MITIGATION GUIDELINES, INTER-AGENCY SPACE DEBRIS COORDINATION COMMITTEE, REV. 1 para. 5.3.2 (2007) https://www.unoosa.org/documents/pdf/spacelaw/sd/IADC-2002-01-IADC-Space_Debris-Guidelines-Revision1.pdf. For background, *see also* J.C. Liou & Nicholas Johnson, *A LEO satellite Postmission Disposal Study using LEGEND*, 57 ACTA ASTRONAUTICA 324 (2005).

1645 The 2021 current version, Version 3, can be found for download here: IADC SPACE DEBRIS MITIGATION GUIDELINES REV. 3, *supra* note 26. The rule is found in IADC Debris Mitigation Guideline 5, *Mitigation Measures*, para. 5.3.2., *Objects Passing Through the LEO Region*, "spacecraft or orbital stages ... should be deorbited ... with an expected residual orbital lifetime of 25 years or shorter." The UN COPUOS Space Debris Mitigation Guidelines do not specifically call out the 25-year rule, but arguably advocate for an even shorter period of time. Guideline 6 states that "spacecraft ... that have terminated their operational phases in orbits that pass through the LEO region should be removed from orbit in a controlled fashion." The implication is that they should be removed 'immediately as possible upon mission completion' versus as long as 25 years. Similarly, the UN COPUOS LTS Guidelines, Guideline A.5.(6), mirrors the UN COPUOS Space Debris Mitigation Guidelines. *See* Guidelines for the Long-Term Sustainability of Outer Space Activities, *supra* note 1425. "Spacecraft ... that have terminated their operational phases in orbits that pass through LEO should be removed from orbit in a controlled fashion."

space programs, it is difficult to assess whether it is a rule under customary international law. Two major arguments have arisen that undermine whether there is even consensus on the value of the guideline to begin with.

The first major argument is that the 25-year rule is, in fact, not followed sufficiently enough to establish that anyone realistically treats it as a 'law.'[1646]

Again, '*upon mission completion*' indicates an 'immediacy.' Finally, SSC Sustainability Practices, Best Practices for Space Operations, Space Safety Coalition Guideline 3(b)(III), states that "precautions should be taken to safeguard the environment ... which includes launch into and initial operation in orbits that comply with a natural orbit lifetime of fewer than 25 years." Best Practices for Space Operations, *supra* note 1426 at Guideline 3(b)(III). Additionally, the SSC Sustainability Practices state, as a general overview, that "spacecraft manufacturers ... [should strive] to avoid any spacecraft from becoming derelict in an orbit which will not passively decay to re-entry within 25 years." *Id.* In practice, the United States has incorporated the rule in three places in the ODMSP. *U.S. Government Orbital Debris Mitigation Standard Practices, November 2019 Update, supra* note 585. Paragraph 1–1 implies applicability with a rule that non-compliance with debris deorbit must be justified; "each instance of planned release of debris larger than 5 mm in any dimensions that remain in orbit for more than 25 years should be evaluated and justified." *See also Id.* at para. 4–1(b), Atmospheric Re-entry; "leave the structure in an orbit which ... atmospheric drag will limit the lifetime to as short as practicable but no more than 25 years after completion of mission." *See also Id.* at para. 5–2(a); "Any spacecraft in LEO should be limited to an orbital lifetime as short as practicable but no more than 25 years after completion of mission (referencing specifically small-sats)." For Russia, *see* GOST P 52925-2018, *supra* note 1138 at § 6, para. 6.4.3, "the estimated duration of passive ballistic existence by the forces of the [object] does not exceed 25 years." *See also* GOST P 52925-2018, *supra* note 1138 at § 6, para. 6.4.4, "Orbital means, whose design does not provide for the possibility of changing parameters of the orbit or maneuvering after the end of their operation, should be put into orbits ... with an estimated time of passive ballistic existence no more than 25 years." For ESA, *see* INT'L STANDARDIZATION ORGANIZATION (24113:2019), *supra* note 1326, 8, para. 6.3.1.1. "The orbit lifetime of a spacecraft or launch vehicle orbital stage shall be less than 25 years ..." For China, *see* Gong, China Practices on Satellites Post-Mission Disposals Toward Space Long-Term Sustainability, *supra* note 927, "Design and practice of lifetime 25-years limit of LEO space System."

1646 Dr. Liou estimates that the current compliance to the 25-year guideline is likely below 50%. Jeff Foust, *Orbital Debris Mitigation Guidelines Still Useful, if Complied with*, SPACE NEWS (Jan. 15, 2020), https://spacenews.com/orbital-debris-mitigation-guidelines-still-useful-if-complied-with/. In fact, it was noted that ESA's annual environmental report stated that for satellites at altitudes that would otherwise not decay on their own within 25 years, the compliance rate was likely closer to as low as 15-25%. Jeff Foust, *Incentives and Requirements may be Needed to Enhance Space Sustainability*, SPACE NEWS (Sept. 20, 2019), https://spacenews.com/incentives-and-requirements-may-be-needed-to-enhance-space-sustainability/. *See also* Kevin Conole, Senior Program Specialist in the Office of International and Interagency Relations at NASA, Statement at the 58th Session of the UN COPUOS Scientific and Technical Subcommittee: Space Debris (Apr. 20, 2021), available at https://vienna.usmission.gov/2021-copuos-stsc-space-debris/, reiterating the lack of compliance by global operators with the 25-year post-mission rule in LEO, stating that

Importantly, a 27 January 2021 report was issued by the NASA Office of Inspector General which reviewed the compliance of satellite operators globally with the 25-year rule. That report found that "although NASA's compliance rate for end-of-mission disposal within 25 years stands at approximately 96 percent over the last decade, the global compliance rate has only averaged between 20 to 30 percent—much lower than the 90 percent required to slow the rate at which debris is generated in LEO."[1647] Dr. Liou has parroted that the 25-year rule is adequate … if followed.[1648] However, Dr. Liou has also noted that the evidence demonstrates that the compliance rate is particularly low and we "are just not doing a very good job globally to implement those policies, practices, and requirements to limit the generation of orbital debris."[1649] He cites that less than 50% of satellites have been properly disposed of in accordance with the rule.[1650]

A second major argument is that the 25-year rule is actually too long a period. There is considerable literature indicating that many believe the 25-year rule should be reduced.[1651] Some global industry experts argue that satellites should be deorbited out of LEO in less than 10 years, or in more extreme cases, five years or less, from the expiration of operational life.[1652] Jan Woerner, former Director-General of ESA, was quoted as saying, "I believe this [25-year

---

not only was the compliance low, but that "every year, tens of upper stages and spacecraft end their mission operations in LEO but are left in long-lived orbits."

1647 Office of the Inspector General, Report No. IG-21-011, NASA's Efforts to Mitigate the Risk Posed by Orbital Debris 3 (2021), https://oig.nasa.gov/docs/IG-21-011.pdf.

1648 This perspective was noted earlier in this book by Dr. Liou. However, an amplified discussion demonstrates that as applied to the 25-year rule, if not complied with at all, the result over 200 years would be a 330% increase in debris. If the standard of 90%, advocated by many space programs for compliance with the 25-year rule is followed, however, then the increase in orbital debris is reduced by 2/3rds, to 110% growth over the same period. In the event that the rule is reduced to 5 years as some have advocated, including former Director-General of ESA, Mr. Jan Woerner, assuming the same compliance of 90% to the 25-year rule, Dr. Liou noted that the growth in objects improves to only 100% growth over 200 years. In short, 'statistically insignificant.' Foust, *Orbital Debris Mitigation Guidelines Still Useful, if Complied With*, *supra* note 1646.

1649 Foust, *Orbital Debris Mitigation Guidelines Still Useful, if Complied With*, *supra* note 1646.

1650 Jeff Foust, *Will We Hit the Snooze Button on an Orbital Debris Wakeup Call?*, The Space Review, (Feb. 17, 2020), https://www.thespacereview.com/article/3885/1 (last visited Jul. 24, 2020).

1651 J.-C. Liou, M. Kieffer, A. Drew & A. Sweet, *The 2019 U.S. Government Orbital Debris Mitigation Standard Practices*, 24 Orbital Debris Q. News 5 (2020), https://orbitaldebris.jsc.nasa.gov/quarterly-news/pdfs/odqnv24i1.pdf.

1652 Foust, *Orbital Debris Mitigation Guidelines Still Useful, if Complied With*, *supra* note 1646.

rule] is too long" and that "we have to work on a shorter period."[1653] One of the primary drivers of this perspective is the belief that with the advent of more and more constellation satellite systems,[1654] both their size and number will require a stricter adherence to removal guidelines to avoid increased collision probabilities.[1655]

Other experts express concern that even if reduced, constellation satellite owners are not fully appreciating the prospect of leaving defunct satellites in space for extended periods of time after operational termination, much less 25 years.[1656] Specifically, many of the constellation operators appear to be establishing the operational lifetime of their satellite constellations at less than five years, but are doing so without plans to deorbit them immediately (nor do the small-sats commonly have the inherent capability to do so anyway).[1657] As a result, while the normal rate of orbital decay would reduce these satellites into lower orbit within 25 years, the sheer number of satellites simply makes the rule insufficient to control the proliferation of debris and increased risk of 'Kessler-like' outcomes. Concerns exist that proposed constellation operators like SpaceX and others have taken the position that they will solve the problem created by the debris of their constellations later down the line after their constellations are in place; a prospect which may not be forthcoming.[1658]

Interestingly, the NASA Office of Inspector General report did not recommend reducing the 25-year rule. Instead, it recommended that NASA, in collaboration with "Congress, other federal agencies, and partners from the private and public sectors [should] adopt national and international guidelines … and strategies for increasing global compliance rates for timely removal of spacecraft at the end-of-mission."[1659] Furthermore, in 2020, NASA published

---

1653 *Id.*

1654 These systems are becoming more and more popular because of reduced cost of building and launching them because of their size, but also because they enable faster and more flexible deployments also because of their small size. Larger, more complex, and expensive spacecraft have a much higher investment in time, effort, and money, and a failure of any kind can be catastrophic from a business perspective. Contrasted with the loss of one small-sat among 100, the differences are obvious. *See* Steinar Lag, *Mega-Constellation Satellites on the Horizon*, DNV, https://www.dnv.com/to2030/technology/mega-constellation-satellites-on-the-horizon.html.

1655 Foust, *Orbital Debris Mitigation Guidelines Still Useful, if Complied With*, *supra* note 1646.

1656 Theresa Hitchens, *Satellite Firms Debate New Commerce Space Safety Rules*, Breaking Defense (Apr. 26, 2019, 2:24 PM), https://breakingdefense.com/2019/04/satellite-firms-debate-new-commerce-space-safety-rules/.

1657 *Id.*

1658 *Id.*

1659 Office of the Inspector General, Report No. IG-21-011, NASA's Efforts to Mitigate the Risk Posed by Orbital Debris 4 (2021), https://oig.nasa.gov/docs/IG-21-011.pdf. Importantly, the report goes on to minimize the importance of the 25-year rule

a separate report indicating that while reducing the 25-year rule might result in some reduction in orbital debris overall, it is 'statistically insignificant.'[1660] The report went on to say that in light of the increases in costs for fuel and other factors relevant to reduction, doing so simply was not actually beneficial.[1661] NASA has taken the position that the "25-year rule appears to still be a good balance between cost and benefit."[1662] Finally, the FCC also reviewed whether or not to reduce the 25-year rule, and acknowledged that many of the commentators to its notice of proposed rule-making recommended doing so for commercial systems.[1663] However, the FCC also declined to make modifications to the 25-year 'benchmark' as it called it.[1664]

Even within the United States there is no outright consensus on whether the 25-year rule is sufficient or should be shortened. Government interagency partners including the FCC, NASA, and the DoD have all aired competing concerns. For NASA's part, as discussed above with Dr. Liou, the approach appears

overall in light of the report's advocacy that the only real solution likely lies in the active removal of debris. Specifically, according to the report, it found that "even if global spacefaring entities achieve a 90% compliance rate with post-mission disposal … it will not be sufficient to slow the growth of orbital debris without the active debris removal of at least five defunct spacecraft a year, beginning in the year 2020." OFFICE OF THE INSPECTOR GENERAL, REPORT NO. IG-21-011, NASA'S EFFORTS TO MITIGATE THE RISK POSED BY ORBITAL DEBRIS 23 (2021), https://oig.nasa.gov/docs/IG-21-011.pdf.

1660 J.-C. Liou, M. Kieffer, A. Drew & A. Sweet, *The 2019 U.S. Government Orbital Debris Mitigation Standard Practices*, 24 ORBITAL DEBRIS Q. NEWS 5 (2020), https://orbitaldebris.jsc.nasa.gov/quarterly-news/pdfs/odqnv24i1.pdf.

1661 *Id.*

1662 *Id.*

1663 Mitigation of Orbital Debris in the New Space Age, Fact Sheet, F.C.C., 42, paras. 98–102 (Apr. 2, 2020), *available at* https://docs.fcc.gov/public/attachments/DOC-363486A1.pdf.

1664 Mitigation of Orbital Debris in the New Space Age, Fact Sheet, F.C.C., 42, paras. 98–102 (Apr. 2, 2020), *available at* https://docs.fcc.gov/public/attachments/DOC-363486A1.pdf. Specifically, the FCC noted that it was implementing a requirement that all space stations that operate above 400 km have maneuverability, indicating that they would be able to achieve post-mission disposal prior to 25 years anyway (such as at the end of operations). Mitigation of Orbital Debris in the New Space Age, Fact Sheet, F.C.C., 42, para. 99 (Apr. 2, 2020), *available at* https://docs.fcc.gov/public/attachments/DOC-363486A1.pdf. Otherwise, those operating below 400 km would, by default, decay into the atmosphere within 25 years regardless. Mitigation of Orbital Debris in the New Space Age, Fact Sheet, F.C.C., 42, para. 99 (Apr. 2, 2020), *available at* https://docs.fcc.gov/public/attachments/DOC-363486A1.pdf. As such, the FCC found reason to readdress the 25-year benchmark as a redundant activity to what would already occur by existing requirement or nature.

to be that compliance is the problem, not the rule.[1665] The FCC appears to trend towards some favorable attitude regarding the 25-year rule generally, but recently has indicated an openness to revisiting shorter timelines.[1666] Finally, the DoD, who has enjoyed the luxury of waivers for many of its compliance requirements under the 25-year rule, also appears receptive to possible reductions in the timeline to protect the debris environment on which it is so dependent.[1667] On the other hand, the increased costs of compliance make the DoD wary, coupled with a feeling that the United States is the only superpower really following the rules.[1668] The gyrations within the US Government mirror much of the international inconsistency in both applications, and willingness, to adhere to any binding mitigation rules pertaining to the 25-year rule.

Additionally, since compliance with the 25-year rule appears fairly low, despite its reflection in many spacefaring Nation's guidelines, programs, or laws, the compliance in practice does not appear consistent enough to declare the 25-year 'rule' an actual international law norm of any sort. And there really is no impetus for compliance other than a somewhat abstract risk of polluting space and repercussions that may hypothetically arise sometime in the future. Take a scenario of a satellite that inadvertently exhausts its fuel before executing maneuvers to remove it from LEO. Has a violation occurred? From an international perspective, no law has been broken. No treaty requires adherence to the 25-year rule. As to some domestic laws, while the licensing requirements require a plan be implemented for mitigation and passivation, there is still the question of enforcement. No specific repercussions appear outlined in any program, and even any which may be implemented in the future are still subject to the discretion of the government to enforce.

Complicating matters, the current 25-year rule does not account for the possibility of on-orbit-servicing (OOS). It is worth noting that the 25-year rule might need additional nuance in the future, such that the time that tolls should only begin subject to some timeline when OOS might occur. For example, at this moment, a satellite that runs out of fuel would qualify as debris under the most widely accepted definitions of space debris. However, there may come a time where OOS could return the satellite to functioning status. That could render the 25-year rule moot at worst, or the time in which it begins

1665 Brian Weeden, *The United States is Losing its Leadership Role in the Fight Against Orbital Debris*, THE SPACE REVIEW (Feb. 24, 2020), https://www.thespacereview.com/article/3889/1.

1666 *Id.*

1667 *Id.*

1668 *Id.*

to toll ambiguous at best, because of advancements in technology. The result is that the expectation for compliance might be 25 years after orbital life is exhausted unless OOS can be conducted within a specific timeframe. Or, if OOS can be performed within 25 years, then the clock begins from the day that the OOS contract for service is set to begin. However, the danger is that in any of these scenarios, the object will most likely remain in the highly utilized orbit significantly longer than 25 years. This presents a danger because of the lack of control over the object in the interim, and the ensuing increase in collision probability. The point is, there may be so many necessary caveats to the 25-year rule because of advancing technologies that the rule itself would be inadequate even if it could currently be viewed as a legitimate rule.

5 Conclusion

'At least for now' it does not appear that there is sufficient space debris mitigation and prevention behaviors across the major spacefaring Nations to constitute cognizable customary international law. As discussed in this book, there are themes that run throughout each of the major spacefaring national programs that resemble, if not mirror, each other. And for a good reason. Absent any efforts, the evidence demonstrates that the growth of debris, under even the best circumstances, is likely to double in the next 200 years.[1669] In the worst case, the scenario could be at least 3-fold that amount. And, with the advent of constellation satellites just beginning, it is possible that the current models are not even yet sufficient to address the potential problem properly.

The sum of what has been discovered from the prior examination of the programs, without going into repetitive depth on each of the respective countries and ESA, is that all Nations appear to acknowledge that the most valuable orbits must be protected from debris. But while this is the case, the fact is that practical adherence by Nations to make this a reality remains elusive. While there may be domestic guidelines and principles, and in rare cases such as the United States and ESA a few legally binding standards, the formation of any specific customary international law appears to fall short of the requirements to establish it.

And, while it might otherwise be ideal to have rules of the road that fill in gaps since the Moon Agreement, it is also worth considering that our advances in space are still so juvenile that there may be a reason to resist attempts to

---

1669 Foust, *Orbital Debris Mitigation Guidelines Still Useful, if Complied With*, *supra* note 1646.

establish customary international law or rigid requirements at this point. One reason could simply be that even if customary international law could be established, States do not want the risk of being held accountable when debris is created. But that doesn't seem to be the case. There appears to be at least a consensus that is strong enough to acknowledge that the major spacefaring countries greatly fear the inaccessibility of space for future operations, though the degree is largely based on their own technological advancements. For example, it is commonly acknowledged that the United States is, at least currently, the *de facto* leader in the need for space accessibility. Its civilian commercial enterprises are heavily dependent on space as is its national security apparatus to maintain air and space dominance and so its concerns are heightened for debris. For others, as they are near peers or becoming so in their need for space access like the United States, they have been equally hesitant to take reckless steps toward mismanagement of space. Also, countries that are not yet mature spacefaring Nations, either starting out or with high hopes for the use of space in the future, do not want to see access hindered because of the negligence of others before them. It is a fleeting resource, and once abused, there is a tipping point for which coming back (if even possible) will take herculean efforts (and for which the technology still is largely nascent).

Interestingly, another argument against customary international law is that if Nations wanted these rules, customary international law is not necessarily the best way to do it. When taken as a whole, there have been extensive national and international discussions regarding managing orbital debris. Additionally, there have been numerous efforts at non-binding guidelines in the hopes that consensus will arise by continuing to advocate for adoptions of these guidelines. Essentially, Nations are already very well 'educated and informed' on the available information and impact that all our activities have on the space environment. If there were rules that Nations wanted to agree on, there would be little reason why they would need to turn to customary international law to establish them. Treaty law could be drafted, and Nations could become signatories.

Looking to the next and final chapter, there are additional arguments that customary international law is simply not the answer for space debris. In addressing this issue further, this book will also examine alternative ways that Nations attempt to address the debris problem if neither customary international law is appropriate nor is treaty law likely.

CHAPTER 9

Where Do We Go from Here?

1 Introduction

The research and results from the previous chapter demonstrates that while there are some similarities in practice among the major spacefaring actors, there currently does not appear to be sufficient evidence that these similarities have met the requisite elements of customary international law to constitute legally recognizable obligations. That said, the answer still cannot be to hope the existing practices will reduce the number of debris. We know this wont work. Acknowledging that means more will have to be done in the future to stem the increase. Therefore, this final chapter will look to address options that might be added to our current efforts to help alleviate the problem as we go forward. First, this chapter will briefly examine whether using soft law is sufficient to solve the debris problem to begin with. If not, whether alternatives may address the issue instead, such as a new governance model. Beyond governance, the issue remains whether there are solutions that, for better or worse, might circumvent the need for a formal treaty by addressing the problem using technology. However, even if technology provides the ultimate solution, new legal issues will still arise. But, at least those will be pertinent to addressing the actual debris problem. Finally, this chapter will suggest a few common principles that might be relevant to the discussion regardless of the ultimate solutions.

2 Is Soft Law Appropriate to Address the Space Debris Issue at All?

One of the more in-depth analyses on the benefits and drawbacks of soft law as it relates to space debris has recently been proffered by Professor Jack Beard of the University of Nebraska. He proposes that there exists a series of flaws in the use of soft law for the development and acceptance of space debris codes of conduct and similar efforts, and that these efforts can actually be counterproductive to the development of solutions for space debris.[1670] One issue he

1670 Jack Beard, *Soft Laws Failure on the Horizon: The International Code of Conduct for Outer Space Activities*, 38 U. Pa. J. Int'l L. 335 (2017).

© KONINKLIJKE BRILL NV, LEIDEN, 2023 | DOI:10.1163/9789004535848_011

raises is that that the use of soft law skirts the natural robust political debate that should accompany finding solutions for challenging problems.[1671] Without that debate, soft law often does not fully examine many of the considerations which would create a better, and hopefully legally enforceable, outcome.[1672] The natural push and pull of ideas, debated in open forums, the nuances that are identified, understood, and formulated into an agreement, and then proffered to international partners (or in concert with) to come to agreement, are likely to result in the best and most enduring commitments and solutions.[1673] On the other hand, utilizing soft law to establish some consensus bereft of any

---

1671 *Id.* at 345.

1672 *Id.* This problem is not unique to space debris of course. See similar arguments for development of quasi-binding norms in human rights through similar non-transparent and non-accessible processes because of skirting the normal rule-making domestic processes of Nations. *See* European Center for Not-for-Profit Law (United Nations Special Rapporteur on the Promotion and Protection of Human Rights and Fundamental Freedoms while Countering Terrorism), *Counter-Terrorism & Human Rights: Soft Law, Hard Consequences*, available at https://www.ohchr.org/Documents/Issues/Terrorism/SR/UNSRCTbrieferSoftLaw.pdf. On the other hand, some argue it does have its benefits, allowing for non-traditional, non-State actors to take part in the process of global governance through their influential actions, such as non-governmental actors, social movements, corporate sector entities, and individuals, versus hard law reserved to Nations. *See* Kumaravadivel Guruparan & Jennifer Zerk, *Influence of Soft Law Grows in International Governance*, CHATHAM HOUSE (Jun. 17, 2021), https://www.chathamhouse.org/2021/06/influence-soft-law-grows-international-governance. Still, even more recent events such as the COVID-19 crisis have awakened renewed criticism of the soft law approach. *See* Mariaolina Eliantonio & Oana Stefan, *The Elusive Legitimacy of EU Soft Law: An Analysis of Consultation and Participation in the Process of Adopting COVID-19 Soft Law in the EU*, 12 EUR. J. RISK REGU. 159 (2021) https://www.cambridge.org/core/journals/european-journal-of-risk-regulation/article/elusive-legitimacy-of-eu-soft-law-an-analysis-of-consultation-and-participation-in-the-process-of-adopting-covid19-soft-law-in-the-eu/ED1F587B4FEBFD593C010F81833F5A3C (addressing the criticism in the EU to soft law as circumventing decision-making formalities of Parliament and other formal EU governing institutions, as well as encroachment on areas which otherwise would be reserved for Member-State decision and management).

1673 Beard, *supra* note 1670 at 361. *See also generally U.S Treaties & Agreements—The Process*, INT'L LEGAL RES. TUTORIAL, https://law.duke.edu/ilrt/treaties_3.htm. *See also*, THE UNITED NATIONS UNIVERSITY, ENVIRONMENTAL CHANGE AND INTERNATIONAL LAW: NEW CHALLENGES AND DIMENSIONS Section 2(B) (Edith Brown Weiss ed., 1992) https://archive.unu.edu/unupress/unupbooks/uu25ee/uu25ee09.htm, discussing the treaty-making process generally; *International Agreements*, U.S. DEP'T OF HEALTH & HUMAN SERVICES, SCIENCE SAFETY SECURITY, https://www.phe.gov/s3/law/Pages/International.aspx (last reviewed Feb. 15, 2018), highlighting the importance that only the treaty text is legally binding, reinforcing the importance of the development process to be inclusive to not leave 'interpretation' where possible from the four corners of the document.

contentious issues within them leave them without detail and lacking tangible understanding.[1674]

A related problem is a conflict that occurs between what Professor Beard calls 'top-down diplomatic approaches' versus 'bottom up' approaches to development of soft law.[1675] A 'top-down diplomatic approach' involves development of soft law at a high level by diplomats of States and international organizations.[1676] Contrast this with the 'bottom-up' approach, which involves best practices developed by specialized government agencies and commercial operators, academic institutions, and other technical experts.[1677] Real conflict between the two approaches emerges as both attempt to solve the same problem but from two different perspectives.[1678] In the best case, the two efforts align.[1679] More likely, however, is disparate outcomes which create confusion among actual practitioners and policy makers, inconsistency in practice, or ultimately abandonment for varying reasons all together.[1680] As a result, instead of enhancing security and cooperation among Nations, the exact opposite can occur.

Other problems compound the previously mentioned ones. For example, democratically open and transparent societies typically suffer under such soft arrangements because they are disadvantaged by meeting the 'spirit' of the rules.[1681] Democratic countries, in light of the ambiguities, often interpret the meaning of the soft law to be far more limiting and binding.[1682] Meanwhile,

---

1674 Beard, *supra* note 1670 at 345.

1675 *Id.* at 345.

1676 *Id.* at 353 (proposing examples such as the UN General Assembly '*Outer Space Transparency and Confidence Building Measures*' (TCBMS).

1677 *Id.* at 348, n. 44 (quoting Gregory L. Schulte & Audrey M. Schaffer, *Enhancing Security by Promoting Responsible Behavior in Space*, 6 STRATEGIC STUD. Q. 9, 14 (Spring 2012)).

1678 *Id.* at 385.

1679 *Id.*

1680 *Id. See also*, for example, 'abandonment' by the United States of the Convention on the Rights of Persons with Disabilities (CRPD), modeled after the US *Americans with Disabilities Act*. The CRPD, signed by President Obama, was not ratified by 39 US Senators (all Republicans) and therefore was abandoned by the United States because of fear and confusion over US sovereignty. *See* Jeffrey D. Sachs, *The High Costs of Abandoning International Law*, BOSTON GLOBE (Mar. 5, 2017), https://www.bostonglobe.com/opinion/2017/03/05/the-high-costs-abandoning-international-law/OXGzXIJP3th3Fc9EGNsXTN/story.html.

1681 Beard, *supra* note 1670 at 374–76.

1682 *Id. See also* Michael Williams, *Filling the Void: Why Existing International Law is not Suited to Mitigate Space Debris*, 42 MICH. J. INT'L L. ONLINE, http://www.mjilonline.org/filling-the-void-why-existing-international-law-is-not-suited-to-mitigating-space-debris/ (highlighting that soft law has proven insufficient because Member-States who wish

less democratic countries can use this to their advantage to exploit the shortcomings of soft law to their advantage while still not violating any international laws.[1683] In short, under soft law developments, democratic countries typically tie their hands, and less democratic ones use that as an opportunity to expand their own reach and grip.

Finally, regardless of the specifics in the particular soft law proposal, the language that is typically used is "vague, imprecise, ambiguous, or otherwise indeterminate" in an attempt to find agreement among otherwise adversarial (or at best disinterested) international partners.[1684] The result is that confirming compliance among participants is typically very difficult because of the ambiguity of the rules.[1685] And, as these soft-law efforts are ultimately voluntary, repercussions (if any) for 'cheating' cannot be directly imposed as a result of perceived violations.[1686] Collectively, in the current environment, the proliferation of soft-law efforts specific to space debris has the potential to cloud

not to comply, but still benefit from the compliance of others, have no incentive to comply since there is no penalty for behaving in such a manner.)

1683 Beard, *supra* note 1670 at 374–76.

1684 *Id.* at 361. *See also*, Andrew T. Guzman & Timothy Meyer, *International Soft Law*, 2 J. LEGAL ANALYSIS 171 (2010) (discussing that in soft law, obligations are, to a large extent, in the eye of the beholder and legal texts, particularly in soft law, are often imprecise and "ambiguous and thus reasonable minds may differ of what a legal obligation requires.").

1685 Beard, *supra* note 1670 at 361.

1686 *Id.* As a point of discussion, it is not to say that this problem is unique to soft law or customary international law by any means. As recently as 2019, the Russian Federation submitted to the UN General Assembly the "*Survey of the Problem of Discretion Exercised by States in Interpreting Basic Legal Principles and Norms Related to Safety and Security in Outer Space.*" Comm. on the Peaceful Uses of Outer Space, *Survey of the Problem of Discretion Exercised by States in Interpreting Basic Legal Principles and Norms Related to Safety and Security in Outer Space*, U.N. Doc. A/AC.105/L.319 (Apr. 4, 2019), https://www.unoosa.org/oosa/oosadoc/data/documents/2019/aac.105l/aac.105l.319_0.html. In that paper, the Russian Federation highlighted that even the provisions of the 1967 Outer Space Treaty were subject to the interpretation and discretion of each individual State to determine its compliance. *Id.* at para. 2. The Russian Federation provided the example that Article IX of the Outer Space Treaty prescribing the requirement to avoid potentially harmful interference with the space activities of other States lacks specificity. *Id.* The Russian Federation argues that a method that would make it possible to "measure the harmful nature of interference objectively and absolutely may, in a decisive way, promote relevant agreed understanding." *Id.* In other words, even the treaty language creates ambiguity in their mind. The Russian Federation further argued that beyond Article IX, the Outer Space Treaty generally contains definite commitments based on solid ethical standards designed to promote conditions of stability in outer space. *Id.* at para. 5. However, it argues that the way States uphold the spirit of relevant legal provisions depends to a decisive degree on the States themselves. *Id.*

the field with 'too many' ideas, dilute the relevant points, or divert time and attention from the truly hard work of treaty development which would likely solve many of the debris issues if established.

Though that criticism is supportable, it is not the end of the story. It would be unrealistic not to find some positive aspects of soft law in space operations. Contrasting the criticisms, soft law certainly offers an opportunity for Nations to rapidly establish consensus on certain behaviors without formality. Soft law can also be credited with providing an impetus to begin discussions that often absolutely must occur. Finally, soft law can provide the contours for hard law in the long run.

For example, this book presented several attempts to create soft law, including the IADC Debris Mitigation Guidelines, the UN COPUOS Space Debris Mitigation Guidelines, the SSC Sustainability Practices, the European Code of Conduct and the EU Outer Space Code. While these did not result in the formulation of any specific debris treaties, they still have a huge impact on the operation of major spacefaring Nations. ISO, for example, employed many of the IADC Debris Mitigation Guidelines in its ultimate proffer of space debris mitigation standards and practices. In turn, ESA ultimately incorporated all the ISO requirements as their own for all space operations conducted by ESA. So, there are many elements of soft law that are still directly influential on space operations throughout Europe.

Furthermore, the technology is demonstrating, particularly for cube-sats and micro-sats, that the existing debris guidelines of many Nations will likely have to evolve rapidly to be successful. These soft law mechanisms have value in acting like a crystal ball of sorts, projecting out the potential risks facing future operations and laying the groundwork for necessary discussions on adapting existing rules to be responsive to technologically changing times. In some cases, the soft law discussions will inevitably influence the outcome of any legal modifications. As offered by Professor Beard, the balance is unfavorably tipped when soft law 'substitutes' for the hard work necessary to develop critical understandings in space.[1687] When that occurs, the criticisms of soft law become much more pertinent.

2.1 *Though Soft Law Is Not a Likely Solution, Treaty Law Is Equally Elusive to Solve the Problem*

It is hard to envision a successful solution to the debris problem without a formal treaty among spacefaring Nations. Such a comprehensive treaty would

1687 Beard, *supra* note 1670 at 385.

acknowledge space debris for the danger it is and result in spacefaring States investing in truly binding solutions. This treaty would be reviewed, approved, and signed by the major spacefaring countries (and ratified by States where necessary). The result should cause stagnation in the growth of debris, if not actually reduce the annual injections. It would also ideally have sufficient detail to pave the way for technical and political cooperation on the problem. However, the reality is that a full treaty concluded between major space powers, let alone a larger group, is unlikely.[1688] On a sliding scale, reasons previously discussed vary anywhere from probably the least culpable, lack of technological know-how, to the most culpable, competitive and political hegemony. The result is that any recommendations on an omnibus plan have been dead on arrival to the debate floor. Alternatively, there has been a boom in proffering ever-more niche non-binding agreements to address increasingly discrete debris problems in space.

We know this is likely the case because this has been the experience of Nations. It is well known that efforts toward a singular treaty to solve much of the debris problems have been tried … and thus far failed. And the collective has largely accepted that such an effort is probably unrealistic. The failure of the Moon Agreement is a case in point. While adopted by the UN General Assembly and opened for signature in 1979, today only 18 countries have ratified it since then.[1689] Meanwhile, arguably the most important countries, the United States, Russia, China, as well as ESA, have not taken any meaningful steps toward advancing it as a realistic international treaty.[1690]

Among the key issues hindering the Moon Agreement is that it states the Moon and other celestial bodies[1691] should be used exclusively for peaceful purposes,[1692] that the environments should not be disrupted,[1693] and that the United Nations should be made aware of the location and purpose of any

---

1688 Specifically, *see* Chapter 8, Section 1, discussing States' hesitancy to limit their options, suspicion of motivations, technological superiority, developmental concerns, and legal limitations on technological sharing to name a few.

1689 Official Records of the General Assembly, Thirty-fourth Session, Chapter XXIV, Outer Space, https://treaties.un.org/Pages/ViewDetails.aspx?src=IND&mtdsg_no=XXIV-2&chapter=24&clang=_en (status as of 12-31-2021, 1015 EDT).

1690 Michael Listner, *The Moon Treaty: Failed International Law or Waiting in the Shadows?*, THE SPACE REVIEW, (Oct. 24, 2011), https://www.thespacereview.com/article/1954/1.

1691 UNGA Resolution 34/68, Agreement Governing the Activities of States on the Moon and Other Celestial Bodies (a.k.a. Moon Agreement), Annex, Article 1, ARES_34_68E.pdf (unoosa.org).

1692 *Id.* at Annex, Article 3(1).

1693 *Id.* at Annex, Article 7(1).

stations emplaced on celestial bodies.[1694] It also prevents ownership of any extraterrestrial property by any organization or private person unless that organization is international and governmental and meets sharing expectations among all States Parties.[1695] Again, the geopolitical environment seems disinterested in the potential sacrifices that would be necessary to explore truly cooperative efforts that could result in widespread agreement.[1696] This simply isn't the direction countries appear to be moving in today for their operations in space.

In the meantime, absent developments in customary international law, acknowledging the limited usefulness of soft-law, and accepting the elusiveness of treaty law in this area, are there options that might still help address the debris problem? It would appear the most likely solutions moving forward are twofold. One, a recognition that the hierarchical method of regulation of space and activities, and the original treaties which regulated that activity, are likely becoming archaic and insufficient to address the growing debris problem.[1697] Instead, a new governance model may be needed, involving much higher levels of communication and cooperation among Nations, and their respective private sector entities, to avoid a tragedy of the commons. Second, aggressive collective efforts should be advanced to reduce the number of debris currently cluttering space, specifically through advocacy, support, and implementation of ADR as soon as technologically feasible. And, while these two recommendations may not solve all debris issues, they still present significant and timely opportunities to solve some problems. Understanding a new way to view space governance can then inform how we can better approach some of the political and legal challenges to ADR once the technical issues are resolved.

1694 *Id.* at Annex, Article 5(1).

1695 *Id.* at Annex, Article 12.

1696 Interview by Japan Aerospace Exploration Agency with Michiru Nishida, Ministry of Foreign Affairs of Japan (Apr. 26, 2017), https://global.jaxa.jp/article/2017/special/debris/nishida.html (suggesting in particular that the only successful path for a treaty is likely through the United Nations because of its legitimacy, and that any actions pursued by developed countries unilaterally would not achieve much support).

1697 Outer Space Treaty, at Rajwswari Pillai Rajagopalan, *The Outer Space Treaty*, COUNCIL ON FOREIGN RELATIONS (Feb. 23, 2021), https://www.cfr.org/report/outer-space-treaty (arguing that the treaties of the 1960's and 1970's are ill-suited for addressing contemporary challenges, in particular because of their expansive legal interpretations).

3 Is New Governance the Answer? Evolving Space Governance—Past, Present and Future

If soft law is not specifically suited to address the problem, a new way to look at space governance may be an important part of the solution. Whether efforts such as ADR or other debris removal and mitigation efforts will be successful in the future will depend on whether the current space governance model(s) can grow, adapt, and provide flexibility to meet the needs of both public and private space operators. Whatever the new evolution is will likely require a regime constructed of 'rational-choices' among actors, such that actors with similar goals can establish relationships in stable and mutually beneficial ways that advance the longer-term objectives of all parties.[1698] Prior to discussing ADR as one of the most likely solutions, a brief discussion about the accompanying

1698 Robert O. Keohane, *The Demand for International Regimes*, 36 INT'L ORG. 325, 330 (1982). Keohane's concept under regime theory of rational-choice, which he refers to as 'constraint-choice' seeks to develop models that will help to explain trends or tendencies towards which patterns of behavior will converge that ultimately helps to provide a predictable pattern of why self-interested actors in world politics, for example, would establish an international regime through mutual agreement. *Id.* at 325–26. Among the many benefits of such regimes, are to help establish stable mutual expectations about others' patterns of behavior and develop working relationships that will allow parties to orient to new situations. *Id.* at 331. The end goal is to help establish, through the use of international regimes, the prevention of anarchy among actors that leads to a complete 'war of all against all.' *Id.* at 332. *See also* Anu Bradford, *Regime Theory*, MAX PLANCK ENCYCLOPEDIA OF PUB. INT'L L. (Feb. 2007), utilizing the definition of SD Krasner to define a regime as a set of 'principles, norms, rules, and decision-making procedures around which actors' expectations converge in a given area of international relations' (citing INTERNATIONAL REGIMES (Stephen D. Krasner ed. 1983)) with the expectation that such regimes will mitigate anarchy that would otherwise prevail and thereby facilitate cooperation amount States. As a result of the assumption that States are rational, unitary actors who seek to maximize self-interest, regimes can help create an understanding among States of areas of mutually beneficial behavior, stability, reduction of transaction costs, uncertainty reduction, and an increase in the guarantees of compliance to commitments. *Id.* Within the context of regime theory, there are competing theories, even if the result of self-interest is the same. One theory, the 'liberal institutionalists', argues that cooperation between States with mutual interests will result in a degree of cooperation because of absolute gains for all. On the other hand, the more cynical view is that of the realists, or 'neo-realists', who argue that some States have a comparative advantage over others and will cooperate as long as the result is that neither gains more power or resources over the others, such as arms treaties that are both cooperative and limiting at the same time. *See* Stoyan Stoyanov, *Why are Regimes and Regime Theory Accepted by Realists and Liberals*, E-INTERN'L RELATIONS (Aug. 17, 2012), https://www.e-ir.info/2012/08/17/why-are-regimes-and-regime-theory-accepted-by-realists-and-liberals/.

space governance regime that will most suitably support debris efforts going forward is worthwhile.

Space Governance, as the name suggests, is the collection of "international, regional, or national laws as well as regulatory institutions and actions, manners, and processes of governing or regulating space-related affairs or activities."[1699] Space governance includes a wide range of "codes of conduct, confidence-building measures, safety concepts, international institutions, international treaties and other agreements, regulations, procedures, and standards."[1700] In action, space governance is the convergence of understanding and action on a given issue by space actors as a result of space actors applying the relevant "principles, norms, rules, and decision-making procedures" to space activities.[1701]

As indicated by its definition and discussed more below, space governance has historically been static, requiring a clear set of rules to be promulgated by some governing body which space operators then utilize to go about the business of space utilization and exploration. However, whether that model can remain relevant considering the advent of increased privatization in space operations, while still under the licensing and purview of States, remains to be seen. However, more modern thought on space governance argues that future governance success will demand a more flexible model, referred to by some as 'adaptive governance.'[1702] While not completely shedding the rigidity of previous governance models, adaptive governance models propose an evolution

---

1699 Global Space Governance: An International Study 7 (Ram S. Jakhu & Joseph N. Pelton eds., 2017). By no means the only definition, *see also* Michael R. Migaud, Robert A. Greer & Justin B. Bullock, *Developing an Adaptive Space Governance Framework*, 55 Space Pol'y 101400 (2021) (defining governance as "the set of regulatory processes, mechanisms, and organizations through which political actors influence environmental actions and outcomes").

1700 The Montreal Declaration 2014, Inst. Air & Space L. (May 31, 2014), https://www.mcgill.ca/iasl/gsg/montrealdeclaration.

1701 Oltrogge & Christensen, *supra* note 566 at 432, Section 1. For discussion of origins of governance in space, *see* Frans von Der Dunk, *Structuring the Governance of Space Activities Worldwide*, 48 Georgia J. Int'l & Comparative L. 645 (2020) Section II, discussing Article VI of the Outer Space Treaty, originating the responsibility for governmental and non-governmental entities to the States Parties to the Treaty for their domestic activities.

1702 Oltrogge & Christensen, *supra* note 566 at Section 6. *See also* Scott Shakelford, *Ostrom Workshop Expands Study of Governance in Outer Space*, Indiana University, Space Governance Rsch., https://research.impact.iu.edu/our-strengths/social-sciences/space-governance.html (arguing that current space governance is a "Cold War Remnant" and needs to change in light of the fact that the commercial sector now leads with new technologies, activities, and business models, which create further ambiguities in space law and strain already outdated legal governance systems).

of rules and norms to better enable collaboration among actors across diverse interests, sectors, and institutional arrangements allowing for increased flexibility and responsiveness to changes.[1703] This is particularly suited to environments and activities that are still developmentally juvenile so as not to impose restrictive rules to activities which have parameters that are not yet well known and whose development would be hindered by overly-aggressive regulatory schemes 'stifling innovation.'[1704] Specific to space activities, modern arguments for space governance are particularly sensitive to advocating for any regime that would attempt to regulate that which is currently unknown, but still acknowledges that some regulation is needed to provide legal certainty and common rules to satisfy international obligations.[1705] As such, a static system is detrimental, instead preferring a system that allows for rapid regulatory changes, adjusting incrementally as situations arise, and responsive to an ever changing environment.[1706] As Mr. Oltrogge puts it, a 'governance philosophy' more than a specific regulatory structure or approach is needed.[1707] Whether or not such a model is possible requires an understanding of original governance model frameworks, where we tend to stand today, and where we might otherwise be able to go in the future to achieve such flexibility.

3.1 *Space Governance—Where We Were*

Upon the advent of space activities, the original space governance model of treaties began to form, led by the efforts of the only two spacefaring States at the time, the Soviet Union and the United States. Some scholars refer to this as the 'traditional model' of space governance, characterized as a top-down model that developed the original space laws using treaties.[1708] Arguably this first period, somewhere between the 1960s and 1990s, saw elements of the Cold War spill over into space activities.[1709] The United States and Soviet Union battled for supremacy and position in space, consolidating the ability to operate in space among NASA and Roscosmos (at the time RSA).[1710] Because of the

1703 Oltrogge & Christensen, *supra* note 566 at Section 6. *See also* Steve Hatfield-Dodds, Rohan Nelson & David C. Cook, Adaptive Governance: An Introduction and Implications for Public Policy, ANZSEE Conference, Noosa Australia (Jul. 4–5, 2007) (arguing that the processes of social learning and collective choice set the guidelines for governance though legislation and social norms).

1704 Oltrogge & Christensen, *supra* note 566 at Section 6.

1705 Oltrogge & Christensen, *supra* note 566 at Section 6.

1706 Oltrogge & Christensen, *supra* note 566 at Section 6.

1707 *Id.*

1708 Migaud, Greer & Bullock, *supra* note 1699 at Section 2.

1709 *Id.*

1710 *Id.*

financial, technical, and legal sophistication required, the ability to operate in space remained exclusively the purview of governmental agencies until the 1990s.[1711]

Around the 1990s, and through the mid-2000s, governments began to change how they engaged in space activity, with the United States making particular efforts to begin shifting from an exclusively government model of space exploration to a public-private partnership.[1712] This was also the result of additional countries advancing their own space interests.[1713] The tension required domestic legal adaptation of domestic laws and an international recognition that some cooperation was going to be required.[1714] This period, sometimes referred to as the 'transitional model/period', was characterized by this newfound need to cooperate internationally[1715] and to provide the groundwork for the growth of private industry to support national goals.[1716] However, the hierarchical approach was still the preeminent model among Nation-States.[1717] This was relatively easy to maintain, particularly considering that even while additional States were achieving success in space, there still remained very few space powers with an 'overweight' influence on international policy.[1718]

This structure maintained itself well during the years between the 1960s and 2000s, since any legal issues that arose could be negotiated on a global basis between the major spacefaring powers. As necessary, these negotiations were incorporated into domestic law to bind the government as appropriate, or provide the parameters to contracting private companies in support of the government.[1719] Brian Israel refers to the law of this period as 'Space Law 1.0', reflecting national legislatures as the preeminent rule-making authority, coordinated through the international community, and providing nearly exclusive top-down guidance.[1720] As a model, when very few space-operators existed

1711 *Id.*

1712 *Id.*

1713 *Id.*

1714 *Id.*

1715 Notably, international cooperation in space made leaps and bounds during this time, with the establishment of the first segment of the international space station launching in 1998 in partnership with the Russians, and building from there as an international cooperative, eventually adding partners like Japan and ESA. *History and Timeline of the ISS*, ISS NAT'L LAB'Y., CENTER FOR THE ADVANCEMENT OF SCI. IN SPACE, https://www.issnationallab.org/about/iss-timeline/.

1716 Migaud, Greer & Bullock, *supra* note 1699 at Section 2.

1717 *Id.*

1718 *Id.*

1719 Brian Israel, *Space Governance 3.0*, 48 GA. J. INT'L & COMP. L. 715, 718 (2020).

1720 *Id.*

(and those that did had overweight influence over minority opinions) this model worked as an original rigid governance model.[1721]

3.2 *Space Governance—Where We Are*

'Space Law 2.0' is a concept used by Brian Israel to describe a status of space law that is not completely disassociated from Space Law 1.0, but instead is a parallel development where national legislatures are put in a precarious position as a result of the evolution from exclusively Nation-State activity to concurrent activity with private companies.[1722] Whereas the first iterations of space law and governance reflected rigid top town legislation and activity in support of regimented Nation-State endeavors, the concept of Space Law 2.0, and corresponding governance, is characterized by private space missions going beyond what governments are doing in space.[1723] The rapid growth of private space activity requires legislatures to come up with legal solutions in parallel (at best) with evolving international legal interpretation or ahead (at worst) of international consensus.[1724] In other words, private companies are engaging in novel activity requiring legislatures to look at existing space law to

1721 *Id.*

1722 *Id.*

1723 Israel, *supra* note 1719 at 719. *See also* Brian Kennedy & Mark Strauss, *Many in U.S. Have Confidence in What Private Space Companies will Accomplish*, PEW RSCH. CTR. (Jun. 22, 2018), https://www.pewresearch.org/fact-tank/2018/06/22/many-in-u-s-have-confidence-in-what-private-space-companies-will-accomplish/.

1724 Israel, *supra* note 1719 at 719. *See also* Kennedy & Strauss, *supra* note 1723. Israel discusses that NASA, as early as 2018, was already investing over $6.8 billion USD in developing commercial launch systems for astronauts to go to space and eventually to Mars. Some of the constructs that NASA sets up include supporting them by paying for at least 25% of a program cost if aligned with NASA goals, allowing NASA to steer the development of space technology while still saving money were it to develop the program itself. This program is known as 'Tipping Point', and as of 2019, had contributed over $120 million towards these development projects. *See* Michael Sheetz, *How NASA is Evolving through Partnerships with Private Space Companies*, CNCC (Nov. 30, 2019) https://www.cnbc.com/2019/11/30/how-nasa-is-evolving-through-partnerships-with-private-space-companies.html. Other contracts, such as those to launch astronauts from lunar orbit to the surface of the Moon, are much larger contracts, divesting NASA of the responsibility and instead allowing the private company to provide the entire support. For example, NASA has recently provided a contract to SpaceX for $2.9 Billion to take astronauts from lunar orbit to the surface of the Moon. *See* Kenneth Chang, *SpaceX Wins NASA $2.9 Billion Contract to Build Moon Lander*, N.Y. TIMES (Apr. 16, 2021), https://www.nytimes.com/2021/04/16/science/spacex-moon-nasa.html#:~:text=NASA%20announced%20on%20Friday%20that%20it%20had%20awarded,ferry%20people%2C%20cargo%20and%20robotic%20explorers%20to%20space.

determine their legality and trying to reconcile, often during or after the fact, the activities with the national obligations under existing treaty law.[1725]

For the record, Space Law 2.0 is not considered to be a 'net-positive' but instead a dysfunction of the Space Law 1.0 system requiring governments to be well out ahead of the typical legislative process and international engagement.[1726] Fortunately, the existing obligations can be broadly interpreted to support much of the current activity. However, not too far in the foreseeable future certain activity will not be entirely accounted for or rules sufficiently pre-drafted to cover the activity.[1727] One such case is the obligations under the Outer Space Treaty for environmental protections, and the likelihood of private enterprise beginning aggressive mining activities in space which will demand rapid legal evolution.[1728] The concept of space mining is already a very contentious international issue, both from a legal obligation perspective and because there will likely be States who will not directly benefit from the activity. Space mining has the potential to create very contentious issues for the international community going forward.

Meanwhile, in practice, there are still strong similarities between the 'traditional/1.0' governance and legal model and the more current 'transitional/2.0' model.[1729] The result has been a further fracturing of the governance model into a more challenging, convoluted method of governance. For example, since the early 2000's, the United States' ability to engage in most space activities requires the coordination or rule-making of at least some combination of the FAA, FCC, NASA, Department of Commerce, DoD, domestic legislative and

1725 Israel, *supra* note 1719 at 719.

1726 *Id.* at 720.

1727 *Id.*

1728 Louis de Gouyon Matignon, *The Future Space Legal Issues*, SPACE LEGAL ISSUES (Sept. 24, 2019), https://www.spacelegalissues.com/the-future-space-legal-issues. Matignon discusses that that mining resources on celestial bodies is likely to run into immediate conflict when the technology arrives because of obligations under the Outer Space Treaty, Article II, which does not allow for 'national appropriation of the Moon and other celestial bodies, by claim of sovereignty, by means of use or occupation, or by any other means.' However, the United States is currently on a trajectory to create a conflict with its Outer Space Treaty obligations because of its 2015 *Space Resource Exploration and Utilization Act*, which currently contemplates private companies exploiting and selling the resources of celestial bodies. While on the one hand it is impressive that the legislative process is at least structurally arranged for such activities, the actual issues that will arise are likely well ahead of the actual boundaries provided for in the law.

1729 Migaud, Greer & Bullock, *supra* note 1699 at Sections 2–3. Migaud discussing that there is still heavy government hierarchical involvement, but transitioning. Meanwhile, the aging treaties are becoming less and less responsive to the changing needs of space operators for clear rules of expected behavior.

policy bodies, as well as coordination with international bodies such as the ITU and the United Nations.[1730] This creates dizzying prospects for any attempts to reconcile governance structures that are intended to be responsive, flexible, and adaptive.

The last evolution of the Space Law '1.0/2.0' concept is reflected in the last decade; what Brian Israel describes as the 'network mode.'[1731] This reflects a huge shift to partnership between government and private companies fully supporting joint efforts, and considerable sharing of technology.[1732] There is also a shift to a lack of exclusivity of ownership with the government for emerging technologies.[1733] Much of it appears as a government model of 'fee for services', with the role of government largely reflecting rule-based support and licensing in accordance with domestic and international requirements, but private companies taking the most significant roles away from government entirely; from development of rockets to launching astronauts into space and delivery of goods to the ISS.[1734] This has also forced governments to take an

1730 Thomas Percy, *Investigation of National Policy Shifts to Impact Orbital Debris Environments*, 30 SPACE POL'Y 23 (2014). *See also* Oltrogge & Christensen, *supra* note 566 at 5. Percy discusses that the US system demonstrates no centralized licensing activity authorization, instead requiring multiple authorities and interagency approaches.

1731 Migaud, Greer & Bullock, *supra* note 1699 at Section 2.

1732 *Id.* However, it is worth noting that while this may present acceptable sharing within government and companies, this gets particularly complicated for sharing of technology related to space objects when partnerships might work with separate sovereign governments and companies. There is often concern about compromising technologies to the disadvantage of the sharing country. *See* Melissa S. Hersh & Ajey Lele, *A Code of Conduct for Space*, THE DIPLOMAT (Feb. 17, 2014), https://thediplomat.com/2014/02/a-code-of-conduct-for-space/.

1733 Migaud, Greer & Bullock, *supra* note 1699 at Section 2.

1734 *Id.* As discussed in other footnotes and here, we are seeing this developing already. For example, NASA and ESA, in partnership, are awarding contracts to private companies to largely execute the planned Artemis effort (towards putting a long-term presence on the Moon among other goals), including contracting out the development of the Lunar Gateway habitat module, as well as the European System Providing Refueling, Infrastructure and Telecommunications ((ESPRIT) refueling and communications model. Jeff Foust, *ESA Awards Contracts for Moon and Mars Exploration*, SPACE NEWS Oct. 15, 2020), https://spacenews.com/esa-awards-contracts-for-moon-and-mars-exploration/. NASA last month (September 2021) awarded additional contracts in support of Artemis to eventually provide regular astronaut transportation from lunar orbit to the surface of the Moon. *See* Eric Brothers, *NASA Selects Five US Companies to Mature Artemis Lander Concepts*, AEROSPACE MANUFACTURING AND DESIGN (Sept. 27, 2021), https://www.aerospacemanufacturinganddesign.com/article/nasa-selects-five-us-companies-mature-artemis-lander/.

even more active role in coordinating internationally to achieve specific objectives in support of domestic space agendas.[1735]

3.3 *Space Governance—Do We Need a Different Governance Model (Where Are We Going)?*

The question of whether debris in space is increasing is well settled: it is. That being the case, whether current efforts toward debris mitigation are resulting in an adequate reduction in debris accumulation is also currently settled: it isn't. So, does addressing debris require a new governance model? It is certainly worth entertaining the possibility. The current governance regime, reflecting a fairly rigid hierarchical model, with almost exclusively non-binding efforts internationally, have not been successful in reducing the overall debris accumulation. What is more, the advent of micro-satellites (hereafter micro-sats) and satellite constellations demonstrate how access to space is being contemplated by a much broader host of actors. Meanwhile, there is little to no legal recourse for failure to adhere to debris guidelines. Furthermore, if we are going to support ADR efforts fully, a more flexible system of governance may be beneficial, if not actually required.

Considerations for the construct of a new model abound.[1736] Proposed by Michael Migaud are five principles to guide the crafting of a new governance model.[1737] First, any model must prioritize collaboration and cooperation in space exploration to expand global understanding of the universe beyond Earth's atmosphere.[1738] Second, values of each space actor are likely different, and must be appreciated if conflict is to be avoided.[1739] Third, interactions in the space environment by humans will rapidly change our understanding of

---

1735 Migaud, Greer & Bullock, *supra* note 1699 at Section 2.

1736 Inkoo Kang, *The Future of Global Space Governance for the New Commercial Era*, ATLANTIC COUNCIL (Jun. 4, 2021), https://www.atlanticcouncil.org/blogs/geotech-cues/global-space-governance-in-the-commercial-era/. In addition to the discussions here, Kang delves into five separate possible governance models. A new space order of global principles which subordinates countries (wildly unpopular) to a governing regime. Second, capabilities-based regime which distinctly separates military (threatening) activity from commercial purposes and creates a new regime to address the threats. Third, bilateral agreements for advancements. Fourth, much like bilateral agreements between countries, commercial arrangements via legally enforceable contracts. Finally, deterrence activities, such as policies and activities which, if infringed upon, risk the repercussions of Mutually Assured Destruction. There are pro's and cons to each, but Kang effectively sets out some of the overarching additional governance concepts and options.

1737 Migaud, Greer & Bullock, *supra* note 1699.

1738 *Id.* at Section 5.1.

1739 *Id.* at Section 5.2.

operations and the consequences of the environment.[1740] The result is that a particularly flexible system must be developed that can rapidly change to an adapting environment.[1741] Fourth, the number of stakeholders with interests in space development is growing exponentially, and the governance structure must address how resources are used and governed in space among an ever increasing number of resource users.[1742] Simply put, the days of just big Nations and the United Nations using and influencing resource allocation are dwindling and we must secure additional forums for resolution of resource allocation issues and management.[1743] Finally, the management of these interactions and resource allocations will require oversight from institutions oriented to manage the increased level of demand, and address conflicts as they arise, resulting from the influx of space actors and organizations.[1744]

However, what Migaud proposes are only principles for a new governance model, not an actual one. Therefore, having space law 1.0 and 2.0 as a backdrop, Brian Israel does offer a future governance model 'Space Governance 3.0.'[1745] Space Governance 3.0 takes the principles of Migaud and other scholars, but views the new governance model as outside the typical governance purview of States. Instead, it is a model that relies on a system of contractual obligations agreed to by interested parties to adjudicate all of the relevant issues, versus a national or international legislature.[1746] This provides the flexibility demanded of the rapidly moving space sector, meets the business interests of operators, and establishes necessary rules of the road among operators.[1747] At the same time, it rids the governance model of the weighty processes and lack of flexibility of governments and their intractability.[1748] Space Governance 3.0 is inter-operator-centric and operator-driven governance model.[1749] The principal attribute for its success, as stated by Brian Israel, is that it creates a "private law regime, constructed from contracts between spacecraft operators in which all space actors, public and private, play on a level playing field."[1750]

1740 *Id.* at Section 5.3.
1741 *Id.*
1742 *Id.*
1743 *Id.* at Section 5.4.
1744 *Id.* at Section 5.5.
1745 Israel, *supra* note 1719 at 721.
1746 *Id.* at 722.
1747 *Id.*
1748 *Id.*
1749 *Id.*
1750 *Id.*

Space Governance 3.0 proposes a mass of private satellite operators agreeing among themselves on a set of rules and self-regulation of their own actions, including accountability and corresponding repercussion for failures to comply.[1751] This takes after the Ostrom model of interested self-regulation among users.[1752] For example, in the case of space debris, operators would agree among themselves to a series of rules. These rules would be memorialized in contracts, committed among each other, prescribing the rules for end-of-life spacecraft actions, and consequences for any transgressions.[1753] However, instead of traditional contractual agreements, requiring national legal systems for enforcement and jurisdiction, Space Governance 3.0 proposes the contractual regime be built upon blockchain networks, such as Ethereum, which can be self-executing (referred to as 'smart-contracts'); there are no national enforcement or legal systems required.[1754] Instead, the consequences of non-compliance are hard-coded and only require an objective determination of breach to trigger the validation of a contractual breach.[1755] The result will be an immediate corresponding transfer of some valuable consideration as previously agreed to.[1756]

Again, assuming the necessary mass of operators is willing to sign on to such a method, then Nation-States are only required to provide the umbrella compliance and licensing authorization for launches and operations.[1757] But the rules of the contract would already meet the low threshold of international obligations.[1758] The benefit to all is that the resource (outer space in this case) is protected for the future use of the operators by their own design, under their own control, responsive to their own needs, and adaptable as new information becomes available.[1759] It also uses methods like blockchain technology

---

1751 *Id.*

1752 *The Swiss Village that Changed Ecology—Twice*, House of Switzerland (Mar. 28, 2018), https://houseofswitzerland.org/swissstories/environment/swiss-village-changed-ecology-twice, recalling the earlier discussion on the CPR argument that that tragedy of the commons can be avoided if measures are enacted among groups which are self-initiated and governed, thereby alleviating the need for private ownership.

1753 Israel, *supra* note 1719 at 722.

1754 *Id.*

1755 *Id.*

1756 *Id.*

1757 *Id.* at 723.

1758 *Id.*

1759 *Id.* at 725. Chiu proposes a similar concept of 'space governance without government.' *See* S.W. Chiu, *Promoting International Cooperation in the Age of Global Space Governance—A study on On-Orbit Servicing*, 161 ACTA ASTRONAUTICA 375 (2019). Chiu argues that the current international regime, in which States are all 'equal' is insufficient to the task of managing resources, since there is not an international body that independently has

which is largely beyond the control of governments, such as the example of Ethereum.[1760] If a critical mass determines their interests are better served inside the regime than out, then the governance model suddenly becomes quite viable.[1761]

Certainly, this proposal is only one of many, which Brian Israel acknowledges. He also suggests that a launch tax is one option contemplated to prompt, and pay for, an orbital debris removal market.[1762] However, countering the tax argument is that there is no incentive to refrain from polluting, only a cost for launching to begin with.[1763] The problem of debris is not solved nor the risk of damage reduced. Another is the possibility of a 'security-deposit' for a license, in which case if the actor does not properly dispose of the satellite, then the money can be used to either 1) pay for removal, 2) pay costs of fuel usage by other actors to avoid impacting the debris, or 3) remuneration as a

---

'seniority' over all others, e.g., the United Nations is not superior to all States, but instead has powers only as conceded by some degree from States (such as the members of the UN Security Council). *Id.* Chiu recalls in his work the argument of Garret Hardin (and predicate William Forster Lloyd) of the tragedy of the commons. *Id.* The tragedy of the common's theory holds that individuals make the best decisions for their personal situation regardless of the impact on others, believing that others will act in the same manner. *See* Alexandra Spiliakos, *Tragedy of the Commons: What it is and 5 Examples*, HARVARD BUS. SCH., BUS. INSIGHTS BLOG (Feb. 6, 2019), https://online.hbs.edu/blog/post/tragedy-of-the-commons-impact-on-sustainability-issues. *See also* Nodir Adilov, Peter J. Alexander & Brendan Cunningham, *An Economic Analysis of Earth Orbit Pollution*, 60 ENV'T & RES. ECON. 81, 83 (2015). Hence, when using a resource, individuals will act with their short-term interest in mind, absent some influence, consuming an unsustainable product regardless of the greater harm it may do to the environment or the public. *See* Alexandra Spiliakos, *Tragedy of the Commons: What it is and 5 Examples*, HARVARD BUS. SCH., BUS. INSIGHTS BLOG (Feb. 6, 2019), https://online.hbs.edu/blog/post/tragedy-of-the-commons-impact-on-sustainability-issues. An example is a farmer, grazing cows in a common meadow, who increases his number of cows, as do others, regardless of the resource dwindling until the resource is complexly expired. *See* Stever Robbins, *The Tragedy of the Commons Explained*, STEVER ROBBINS, INC. https://www.steverrobbins.com/articles/tragedyofthecommons/. *See also* Adilov, Alexander & Cunningham, 60 ENV'T & RES. ECON. at 83. However, there is a counter to the argument recognized by Chiu, as proposed by Elinor Ostrom's work termed "Common Pool Resources" (CPR). *See The Swiss Village that Changed Ecology—Twice*, *supra* note 1752. The CPR argument stated that tragedy of the commons can be avoided if measures are enacted among groups which are self-initiated and governed, thereby alleviating the need for private ownership. *See also* Chiu, *supra* note 1759 at para. 2.2.

1760 Israel, *supra* note 1719 at 723.

1761 *Id.* at 724.

1762 *Id.* at 725.

1763 *Id.*

result of inadvertent contact in the worst case scenario.[1764] Otherwise, if properly disposed of, the money is returned, providing the incentive to comply.[1765] However, who governs and manages this process becomes an entirely separate question. The issues can become overwhelming, including agreement among spacefaring nations regarding the costs, who manages the program, some method of adjudication for partial compliance, et cetera. The likelihood of these potential options being enacted is not zero, but it does raise the question that if there were this degree of appetite for such solutions, a treaty should be equally welcome instead. Since the international community has yet to arrive at such a conclusion, these alternative options seem unlikely.

4 One Key Option to Solve the Debris Problem—Active Debris Removal and Legal Challenges

Within the existing governance model of Nation-State licensing and compliance with the international treaties and the international law regime, ADR remains among the most promising opportunities to alleviate, if not largely address, the major problems posed by space debris. Assuming there is some consensus that ADR is among the more effective solutions once technologically feasible, this discussion now turns to what ADR options are available, and what legal impediments exist to implementing ADR successfully within the current governance model.

ADR is most commonly defined as the "means to remove objects from orbit above and beyond the currently-adopted mitigation measures."[1766] More specifically, ADR has been defined holistically as "the purchase of a service by a customer in which an ADR service provider works alongside the customer to remove from orbit or move to a graveyard orbit a piece of space debris."[1767]

1764 *Id.* at 726.

1765 *Id.*

1766 J.-C. Liou, *An Active Debris Removal Parametric Study for LEO Environmental Remediation on Using Active Debris Removal for LEO Environment Remediation*, 47 ADVANCES IN SPACE RSCH. 1865, 1865 (2011). Other more specific definitions have been developed from this earlier definition, to broaden the scope. Offered by Christopher May at the center for Space Policy and Strategy, ADR is 'the removal of obsolete spacecraft (satellites and rockets) or fragments of spacecraft that have broken off satellites and rockets, through an external disposal method (defined as safely de-orbiting, maneuvering into graveyard orbits, or complete destruction).' *See* Christopher R. May, Triggers and Effects of an Active Debris Removal Market, CENTER FOR SPACE & STRATEGY, GAME CHANGER, 2 (Jan. 2021), https://aerospace.org/sites/default/files/2021-01/adr%20paper.pdf.

1767 May, *supra* note 1766 at 2.

ADR options come in many forms and proposals and success depends on a variety of factors, such as the size of the debris, the location of the debris, and the potential functionality of the debris. ADR can also arguably be an omnibus enough term to include the concept of OOS, such that what was once technically non-functioning debris could be serviced back to functionality, thus 'actively removing' it from the category of debris.

ADR has seen encouraging advocacy from both private and government entities. While the European Union Space Strategy makes no specific mention of ADR in its current space policy,[1768] both the European Union and ESA have a history of ongoing projects and support of ADR. For example, the European Union, through its 'Seventh Framework' program,[1769] had supported testing ADR concepts to help advance the research and technology required to identify key areas of development for successful ADR in the future.[1770]

ESA has similarly taken steps to encourage exploration of ADR options, providing criteria for selection of the 'right' pieces that should be planned for removal to lower the overall debris threats.[1771] ESA's selection criteria includes

---

1768 *Communication from the Commission to the European Parliament, the Council, the European Economic and Social Committee and the Committee of the Regions*, *supra* note 1403. Instead of discussing ADR, the European Union Policy focuses on efforts toward enhancing the SST support framework for the avoidance of collisions and the corresponding creation of debris.

1769 This was not a specific space-based effort, but instead borne out of a European Union agreement to fund research and development efforts within the European Union with the specific purpose of "contribut[ing] to the Union becoming the world's leading research area." This requires the Framework Program to be strongly focused on promoting and investing in world-class state-of-the-art research, based primarily upon the principle of excellence in research. *See* Decision of the European Parliament and of the Council of 18 December 2006 Concerning the Seventh Framework Program of the European Community for Research, technological development and demonstration activities 2006 O.J. (L. 412) 1, Preamble, para. 4, https://eur-lex.europa.eu/legal-content/EN/TXT/?uri=CELEX%3A32006D1982. The seventh framework ran until 2013. *See* https://www.researchitaly.it/en/seventh-framework-programme-fp7/.

1770 *RemoveDebris Mission*, SHARING EARTH OBSERVATION RESOURCES, https://directory.eoportal.org/web/eoportal/satellite-missions/r/removedebris. Specifically, the model is to launch a micro-sat called 'RemoveSAT' which will release, capture, and deorbit two space debris targets, called 'DebrisSats' in sequence using various rendezvous, capture, and deorbiting technologies to demonstrate key ADR technologies for future missions. *Id. See also* Jason L. Forshaw, et al. *The RemoveDebris ADR Mission: Preparing for an International Space Station Launch*, Proc. 7th European Conference on Space Debris, Darmstadt, Germany (Apr. 18–21, 2017), https://conference.sdo.esoc.esa.int/proceedings/sdc7/paper/173/SDC7-paper173.pdf.

1771 *Active Debris Removal*, EUR. SPACE AGENCY, https://www.esa.int/Safety_Security/Space_Debris/Active_debris_removal.

that objects should have high mass (such that they would have the greatest impact upon collision), they should have high collision probabilities (that is, reside in densely populated areas), and be in high altitudes (where natural decay is unlikely in a reasonable period of time).[1772] Additionally, ESA has taken tangible steps by committing significant funds to space debris removal startups.[1773]

The United States can argue a longer formal recognition of the importance of ADR, with the NSP's of the United States since as early as 2010 acknowledging the need for ADR as one facet of the space debris remediation effort.[1774] Specifically, NASA and the Secretary of Defense were mandated ('the United States shall') to pursue research and development of technologies and techniques … to mitigate and remove on-orbit debris.'[1775] Not to be left out, Russia and China are also developing their own programs, recognizing that space sustainability will require the removal of debris and development of technologies to advance that goal.[1776]

1772 *Id. See also* Benjamin Bastide Virgili & Holger Karg, Criteria for the Selection of Targets for Active Debris Removal, 4th CEAS Air & Space Conference (2013) available at https://www.researchgate.net/publication/266556868_Criteria_for_the_Selection_of_Targets_for_Active_Debris_Removal.

1773 One of the most significant commitments was the €86 million Euro contract with Swiss space startup "ClearSpace SA" to initiate the first active debris removal mission by the company by 2025 (using a capture method). Associated Press, *Europe Signs $102M Deal to Bring Space Trash Home*, PBS News Hour (Nov.26, 2020), https://www.pbs.org/newshour/world/europe-signs-102m-deal-to-bring-space-trash-home.

1774 National Space Policy of the United States of America, June 28, 2010, 11 http://marshall.wpengine.com/wp-content/uploads/2013/09/National-Space-Policy-of-the-United-States-of-America-June-28-2010.pdf.

1775 *Id.* For an additional extensive discussion of the US efforts and development toward ADR, *see also* Brian Weeden, US Space Policy, Organizational Incentives, and Orbital Debris Removal, SPACE R. (Oct. 30, 2017), https://www.thespacereview.com/article/3361/1.

1776 Russia is developing a novel ADR system to turn space junk into fuel which can be used by the capturing satellite to fuel its next mission, and so on. *See Russia Creates Space Junk Recycling System to Turn Fuel*, TASS, RUSSIAN NEWS AGENCY, https://tass.com/science/1050699. China has also recognized the ADR importance, developing its own programs through laser proposals as well as satellites with robotic arms (Roaming Dragon), capable of capturing debris and plunging them back into the atmosphere. *See* Stephen Chen, *Is China Militarizing Space? Experts Say New Junk Collector could be used as Anti-Satellite Weapon*, SOUTH CHINA MORNING POST (Jun. 28, 2016), https://www.scmp.com/news/china/diplomacy-defence/article/1982526/china-militarising-space-experts-say-new-junk-collector. *See also* David Axe, *Is China's Mysterious New Satellite Really a Junk Collector—or a Weapon?*, DAILY BEAST (Apr. 13, 2017 3:27 PM), https://www.thedailybeast.com/is-chinas-mysterious-new-satellite-really-a-junk-collectoror-a-weapon.

4.1 *Background on Modern ADR Efforts*

Recognizing the importance of ADR, international efforts through both private and public partnerships have pursued several methods of ADR. Some are advanced and in various stages of execution. Others remain at the concept and initial development or testing stages. And while none have seen mainstream adoption or success, a few have seen some limited initial operational success in outer space. Before addressing the challenges faced by these ADR efforts, a brief overview of some of the ongoing efforts is useful. It is important to note that the efforts reviewed involve those that will remove debris currently in orbit. Debris that are attached as part of debris mitigation in the development stage (such as solar sails, magnetics, and tethers[1777]) are not considered for this

1777 These are excluded for the fact that they are included in the development of space-based systems prior to launch and are considered part of the obligations under domestic laws and agreements of countries to attempt to minimize the creation of debris beforehand by methods and techniques to ensure that satellites do not 'become' debris. For the purposes here, we are examining the issues with debris currently in orbit and ADR aimed at the removal of existing debris. Tethers, some pre-attached sail concepts, 'terminator tape' and other concepts are consent-based, operative on satellites at end-of-mission, and meant to comply with existing rules. They help prevent the creation of more debris but are not solutions for removing existing debris that is opined for the purposes of this discussion. For a good discussion on tethers, *see* Jeremy Hsu, *The U.S. Space Mission Aims to Demonstrate Technology that could Someday Help Clean up Space Junk*, Scientific American (Nov. 4, 2019), https://www.scientificamerican.com/article/kilometer-long-space-tether-tests-fuel-free-propulsion/. Terminator tape at Tethers Unlimited, Inc., *Taking Out the Space Trash: Tethers Unlimited Announces Successful Operation of Space-Debris Removal Device*, TETHERS UNLIMITED (Jan. 16, 2020), https://www.tethers.com/taking-out-the-space-trash-tethers-unlimited-announces-successful-operation-of-space-debris-removal-device/. Solar sails at D. Romagnoli & S. Theil, *De-Orbiting Satellites in Leo Using Solar Sails*, 4 J. Aerospace Engineering Sci. & Applications 49 (2012), https://issfd.org/ISSFD_2011/S12-Orbit.Dynamics.3-ODY3/S12_P3_ISSFD22_PF_038.pdf. Finally, magnetics are included in this so much as they have been considered for 'docking' to a deorbiting satellite such that both the satellite and the deorbiting satellite must have been already situated to have magnetics of opposite poles already present on the spacecraft. A 'deorbiting' satellite would then be deployed, magnetically connecting to the other satellite, and then thrust it into the atmosphere. Again, based on the pre-launch mitigation requirement of the setup, this is not included as an ADR measure for the purposes of this discussion. *See* Morgan McFallen-Johnsen, *A Spacecraft that could Grab Dead Satellites with Magnets is About to Test a New Way to Clean up Space Junk*, Business Insider (Mar. 23, 2021, 9:28 AM), https://www.businessinsider.com/astroscale-mission-to-clean-up-space-junk-magnets-2021-3. One other note is that OOS is also not considered in this concept of ADR, such that the targets for OOS are arguably not debris, though they may not be currently functioning. Since they can be brought back to operation by refueling or some repair, they are outside of the discussions of this concept. These operations have already begun as early as 2019 for launch and 2020 for execution. For example, the Northrop Grumman Innovation Systems

ADR discussion.[1778] The current 'usual-suspects' include efforts with ground and space-based lasers, harpoons, grappling arms, and system capture and containment (nets).

4.2 *Current Major* ADR *Efforts*

4.2.1 Lasers

Ground-based lasers have been used for removal of space debris for at least the past 25 years.[1779] To be an effective tool against debris, lasers are repeatedly focused on the surface of a debris object causing material ablation or an orbital velocity reduction. Typically, for slightly larger debris particles,

---

Mission Extension Vehicle (MEV-1) was launched in 2019 and successfully docked with a client (Intelsat IS-901) satellite in 2020, with a second Northrop Grumman MEV-2 launching and docking with Intelsat IS-1002 on 12 April 2021. *See Space Logistics*, NORTHROP GRUMMAN, https://www.northropgrumman.com/space/space-logistics-services/.

1778 This is by no means an exhaustive list. Other concepts abound, such as the use of foam to 'splatter' and cover the debris into a growing ball, at which point the ball begins to decay naturally into the atmosphere at a more rapid rate. *See* M. Andrenucci, P. Pergola & A. Ruggiero, *Expanding Foam Application for Active Debris Removal*, EUROPEAN SPACE AGENCY (Feb. 21, 2011), https://www.esa.int/gsp/ACT/doc/ARI/ARI%20Study%20Report/ACT-RPT-MAD-ARI-10-6411-Pisa-Active_Removal_of_Space_Debris-Foam.pdf. Another idea is to distribute dust into narrow bands of orbits that will collect on floating debris increasing the mass and, in turn, causing it to deorbit more rapidly. See Mark Priyant & Surekha Kamath, *Review of Active Space Debris Removal Methods*, 47 SPACE POL'Y 194, para. 2.7 (2019). Additionally, concepts of a magnetic field which pushes debris into lower orbits as the debris passes the magnet, changing its trajectory. *Id.* Suggestions of using Aerogel and other low-density material to 'catch' small debris objects in the gel causing increased mass and decelerating it into the atmosphere. *See* Marlon Sorge & Glenn Peterson, *How to Clean Space: Dispose and Active Debris Removal*, 16 Crosslink 46, 49 (2015), https://aerospace.org/sites/default/files/2019-04/Crosslink%20Fall%202015%20V16N1%20.pdf. *See also* Thierry Woignier, et at., *Aerogels Materials as Space Debris Collectors*, ADVANCES IN MATERIALS SCIENCE & ENGINEERING (2016).

1779 David Neely, et al., *Energy Coupling in Short Pulse Laser Solid Interactions and Its Impact for Space Debris Removal*, 53 APPLIED OPTICS 141, 141 (2014). Also, the activity is commonly referred to as LODR, or Laser Orbital Debris Removal. For specifics of energy required, and the technical specifications, *see* Claude Phipps, *Clearing Space Debris with Lasers*, SPIE (Jan. 20, 2012), https://spie.org/news/4076-clearing-space-debris-with-lasers?SSO=1. Specifically, the article highlights the diminished effectiveness from a distance, such that to get a telescope to focus a laser down to a 30 cm diameter circle on a target 1000 km away overshoots much of the laser but is still capable of hitting the target. For each pulse on the target, the laser is capable of slowing small debris approximately 10 cm per second for each pulse. At higher powers, some targets can be slowed even more, requiring less contact time because the deceleration required to send the object into Earth's orbit is less than other objects at higher speeds. *Id. See also* Sorge & Peterson, *supra* note 1778 at 50.

lasers are effective at deceleration and redirection of material toward the atmosphere.[1780] For smaller debris particles, lasers can be effective at eliminating the debris entirely if not otherwise causing the remainder to decelerate.[1781] Once decelerated, they will begin to fall toward the atmosphere in a faster period of time than if they were otherwise left to decelerate on their own.[1782] The most common target size for lasers against debris is 1–10 cm for two reasons. First, debris smaller than 1 cm typically does not present a risk to spacecraft due to existing shielding on space systems. Similarly, larger than 10 cm pieces are typically too large for lasers to deflect or decelerate effectively. Instead, pieces larger than 10 cm are more effectively avoided by maneuvers of the spacecraft since debris of that size can be effectively tracked and assessed for their potential risk.[1783]

While most of the research is currently focused on ground-based systems, these systems have limits to their effectiveness. Among the issues is the obvious distance between the laser and the target making the object hard to track, especially for debris that is only a few centimeters.[1784] Additionally, to concentrate an effective laser on the target, a very large beam director mirror is needed to obtain the proper density on the target for both ablation and course change.[1785] Finally, over such a distance, much of the laser power is wasted, requiring either repeated targeting of the debris over multiple orbital revolutions, or multiple lasers acting sequentially globally, to be effective.[1786]

1780 Shen Shuanyan, Jin Xing & Chang Hao, *Cleaning Space Debris with a Space-Based Laser System*, 27 Chinese J. of Aeronautics 805, 806 (2014). In some cases, it may be that the object cannot be directly targeted back into the atmosphere. However, it is generally accepted that any redirection of the object that might otherwise prevent a collision with existing material/spacecraft in space would be an acceptable outcome. *See* Neil Savage, *Lasers Could Clear Space Junk from Orbit*, IEEE Spectrum (May 14, 2021), https://spectrum.ieee.org/laser-could-clear-space-junk-from-orbit.

1781 Shuanyan, Xing & Hao, *supra* note 1780 at 806.

1782 Neely et al., *supra* note 1779 at para. 1.

1783 Shuanyan, Xing & Hao, *supra* note 1780 at 805.

1784 *Id.* at 806. Advancements in this area include more precise targeting to overcome this shortfall. For example, Electro-Optic Systems unveiled a new technology in 2021 whereby it utilizes two lasers; one for tracking and improving the ability to determine the required measurements more quickly and easily for a piece of debris, followed by a second laser which then utilizes the information to be able to maneuver the debris. *See* Liam Garman, *EOS Unveils New Space Debris Threat Mitigation Laser*, Space Connect, Apr. 9, 2021), https://www.spaceconnectonline.com.au/operations/4828-eos-unveils-new-space-debris-threat-mitigation-laser.

1785 Shuanyan, Xing & Hao, *supra* note 1780 at 806.

1786 *Id.*

Space-based lasers are not yet in use, but are currently in conceptual development.[1787] Current experiments include both attachment to existing large satellite or space systems (such as the ISS) or stand-alone systems with the laser and accompanying radar detection system being part of one space system.[1788] The advantage over ground-based systems include far more effective detection and identification of debris as well as far less laser energy waste.[1789] The expectation is that over the next few years, a proof of concept will be placed on the ISS consisting of a prototype laser and tracking system to determine the effectiveness of a space-based system.[1790]

4.2.2 Solar Sails

Distinct from the type of solar sails which are attached pre-launch as a post-mission removal technique, there are also proposals to utilize sails to be able to maneuver ADR satellites that will remove existing debris.[1791] The primary concept involves the launch of several ADR cube-sats.[1792] These cube-sats would be equipped with capture robotics to intercept and attach to rogue debris and then, deploying a sail, would leverage solar pressure radiation to bring the junk down to lower altitudes and ultimately for destruction in the atmosphere.[1793] The technology of the sails allow for the Sun's radiation to help maneuver the cube-sat based on orientation of the sail, facing the sail either toward or away from the Sun, with variation between both causing deceleration into the atmosphere.[1794] Ultimately, this method would allow for these cube-sats to remain in space with little to no chemical energy onboard, extending the life of the cube-sat limited only by the resilience of the hardware itself against the harsh space environment.[1795]

Solar sail proposals also envision satellites which are primarily a solar sail themselves to be utilized to rendezvous and attach with defunct larger

---

1787 Charles Q. Choi, *Space Station Could Get Laser Cannon to Destroy Orbital Debris*, SPACE.COM (Apr. 30, 2015), https://www.space.com/29271-space-station-laser-cannon-orbital-debris.html.

1788 *Id.*

1789 *Id.*

1790 *Id.*

1791 Ginger Pinholster, *Solar-Propelled Invention Design to Clean Up Space Trash*, EMBRY RIDDLE AERONAUTICAL UNIVERSITY (Jun. 17, 2021, 8:34 AM), https://news.erau.edu/headlines/solar-propelled-invention-designed-to-clean-up-space-trash.

1792 *Id.*

1793 *Id.*

1794 *Id.*

1795 *Id.*

debris.[1796] Once the solar sail cube-sat attaches to the larger piece of debris, the solar sail can then deploy creating drag on the large piece of debris.[1797] As before, this drag will ultimately cause deceleration and deorbiting into Earth's atmosphere until it either burns up or predictably hits Earth in a safe manner and location.[1798]

4.2.3 Harpoons

As the word conceptually implies, the harpoon method of debris removal involves a satellite armed with a harpoon and tether which orients toward a piece of debris.[1799] When in close proximity to the debris, the satellite fires the harpoon into the object.[1800] Once the object is successfully captured, the satellite itself then makes a deorbit maneuver into the atmosphere dragging the debris with it.[1801]

The first successful use of a harpoon to remove debris was conducted in 2018 by the *RemoveDebris* effort, supported by the European Union.[1802] *RemoveDebris* was a low-cost mission aiming to test key ADR technology, including the viability of harpoons for capturing orbital debris.[1803] A satellite armed with a harpoon[1804] fired into an aluminum target board held at the end

1796 Jeremy Hsu, *Solar Sails Could Clean Up Space Junk*, SPACE.COM (Apr. 28, 2010), https://www.space.com/8296-solar-sails-clean-space-junk.html.

1797 *Id.*

1798 *Id.* Additional concepts using the solar sail include using a solar sail to create photon pressure to move space junk toward the atmosphere. *See also* Darren McKnight, *Pay Me Now or Pay Me More Later: Start the Development of Active Orbital Debris Removal Now*, Advanced Maui Optical and Space Surveillance Technologies Conference (Sept 14–17, 2010). Another variation is to envelop an object with a solar sail with combination tethers attached, like a wrap, that would then cause drag. *See also* Louis Viasgie & Theodoros Theodorou, *Hybrid Solar Sails for Active Debris Removal*, Final Report, EUR. SPACE AGENCY (2011).

1799 Tereza Pultarova, *Watch a Satellite Fire a Harpoon in Space in Wild Debris-Catching Test (Video)*, SPACE.COM (Feb. 18, 2019), https://www.space.com/space-junk-harpoon-removedebris-satellite-video.html.

1800 *Id.*

1801 *Id.*

1802 Tereza Pultarova, *This Space Junk Removal Experiment Will Harpoon & Net Debris in Orbit*, SPACE.COM (Apr. 6, 2018), https://www.space.com/40221-space-junk-debris-sweeper-experiment.html.

1803 Vaios J. Lappas et al., *RemoveDebris: An EU Low Cost Demonstration Mission to Test ADR Technologies*, Int'l Astronautical Congress (Sept. 2014), https://core.ac.uk/download/pdf/48182494.pdf.

1804 There are technical analyses related to the type of harpoon which is ideal, with concerns about the loss of the debris in the event that the harpoon is so designed that it either 1) doesn't sufficiently penetrate the debris, 2) passes through the debris entirely

of a boom set up to test the harpoon.[1805] According to reports, the harpoon effectively penetrated the board, knocking it off the boom, at which point the harpoon deployed barbs to prevent the test board from floating away.[1806] And, while the experiment caused the satellite to begin to spin as a result of the thrust and impact of the harpoon on the debris, the spacecraft was able to return to its normal orientation by maneuver commands from the ground controlling station.[1807]

4.2.4 Grappling Arms/Claws

Similar to the harpoon concept, *ClearSpace-1* is an effort targeted for 2025 led by ESA, allegedly the size of a washing machine and possessing a four-armed claw, that will capture and dispose of a piece of orbiting space debris.[1808] The first expected target is one of ESA's own debris, a Vega rocket, which launched in 2013 to place two satellites into orbit.[1809] That now makes this a perfect target for its simplicity and similarity to a small-sat.[1810] Once in position with the target, the *CleanSpace-1* mission will rapidly determine the orientation and characterization of the object before deploying the claw to capture it.[1811] If all

---

and becomes problematic on the other side, or 3) passes through and as a result of the hold, cuts the tether of the harpoon thus creating even more debris. *See* Yuto Tamaki & Hiroaki Tanaka, *Penetration Characteristics of Metal Harpoons with Various Tip Shapes for Capturing Space Debris*, 8th Eur. Conference on Space Debris (Apr. 20-23, 2021), https://conference.sdo.esoc.esa.int/proceedings/sdc8/paper/60/SDC8-paper60.pdf.

1805 Jonathan Amos, *Space Harpoon Skewers 'Orbital Debris'*, BBC NEWS (Feb. 15, 2019), https://www.bbc.com/news/science-environment-47252304.

1806 *Id.*

1807 *Id.* For an additional in-depth discussion of the experiment, *see* Lappas et al., *supra* note 1803.

1808 Daniel Clery, *Europe Plans Space Claw to Capture Orbiting Junk*, SCIENCE (Dec. 1, 2020), https://www.science.org/news/2020/12/europe-plans-space-claw-capture-orbiting-junk.

1809 *Id.*

1810 *Id.*

1811 *Id.* There is a race with other companies who are generally targeting the same timeline. Astroscale, for example, is currently in development to use its developmental debris removal satellite, ADRAS-J, to connect with a rocket body, take over maneuverability, and then bring the rocket into the atmosphere. *See* Dominic Bliss, *Millions of Pieces of Debris from Defunct Satellites and Spacecraft Litter the Earth's Orbit. Disaster Looms if we Don't Start Cleaning it Up. But How?*, MS AMLIN (Nov. 12, 2020), https://www.msamlin.com/en/chart-hub/english/cleaning-up-space-debris.html. Recently (September 2021), Rocket Lab USA won a contract with Astroscale to launch the ADRAS-J to test phase 1, which is the rendezvous and characterization of the rocket body, in preparation for future missions to remove the debris. *Rocket Lab Receives an Astroscale Contract to Launch the ADRAS-J Smallsat*, SATNEWS (Sept. 22, 2021), https://news.satnews.com/2021/09/22/rocket-lab-receives-an-astroscale-contract-to-launch-the-adras-j-smallsat/.

goes well, once captured, the entire system will maneuver into the atmosphere for destruction.[1812]

4.2.5 System Capture and Containment

Principally referred to as a 'tethered-net', this method of ADR involves capturing a target with a net, as the name implies, but is primarily advantageous because it avoids many of the elements that have limited other efforts.[1813] Specifically, it is capable of capturing a target regardless of the cooperative nature of the target, the surface geometry of the target, the material from which the target is made, or its angular rates.[1814] It can also adjust the size of the net and the connected tether.[1815] As such, it is increasingly becoming a favored concept. What is especially advantageous is that as the net is deployed around the object, the net begins to dampen the non-cooperative spin of the object without much risk of damage or potential 'co-tumble' vulnerabilities.[1816] As with other concepts, once harnessed by the net, the capturing ADR satellite will then thrust the entire system into the atmosphere.[1817]

4.3 *Legal Challenges to Implementation of ADR*

While the options for ADR continue to develop, it still faces some considerable legal headwinds. Specifically, the legal issues surrounding removal of debris in the event an owner of the debris cannot be identified. Alternatively, there

---

1812 Clery, *supra* note 1808. It is unclear if this is the first true attempt or if the Chinese, or other similarly governed countries that might be much less 'public' with their information, have already successfully attempted this. For example, according to Kevin Pollpeter, China has been testing robotic arm technologies to build a 'floating space robot' consisting of an arm on a satellite to capture micro-sats. It would appear that this might have been accomplished as early as 2013. *See* Kevin Pollpeter, *China's Space Robotic Arm Programs*, SITC BULLETIN ANALYSIS (Oct. 2013), https://escholarship.org/content/qt2jsoc5r8/qt2jsoc5r8_noSplash_308ba05cdedfb90ab23d648da59e3bb6.pdf. It is suspected that this test might be the Chinese SJ-7 mission, which has been observed changing orbits unexpectedly and significantly (one change in orbit lowered it by 150 km) several times since being orbited. *See* Marcia Smith, *Surprise Chinese Satellite Maneuvers Mystify Western Experts*, SPACEPOLICYONLINE.COM (Aug. 19, 2013, 12:00 AM), https://spacepolicyonline.com/news/surprise-chinese-satelllite-maneuvers-mystify-western-experts/.

1813 K. Stadnyk, K. Hovell & L. Brewster, *Space Debris Removal with Sub-Tethered Net: A Feasibility Study and Preliminary Design*, 8th Eur. Conference on Space Debris (Apr. 20–23, 2021), https://conference.sdo.esoc.esa.int/proceedings/sdc8/paper/304/SDC8-paper304.pdf.

1814 *Id.* at para. 1.3.

1815 *Id.*

1816 *Id.*

1817 *Id.*

are challenging legal issues where a debris owner can be identified, but the owner refuses to consent to removal. Briefly as follows is a discussion of the ramifications of those two scenarios and possible ways to overcome them. It is worth noting that a comprehensive review of these legal issues is not necessarily possible, since no legal cases have resulted from the removal of debris from a non-consenting owner. However, conceptually, the issues that may arise still have potential pathways to favorable resolution. There is legal precedent that would support arguments to non-consensually remove debris under the right circumstances.

Primarily, the biggest legal issue revolves around the ownership of debris and consent based on that ownership. For many of the ADR proposals, such as OOS, consent is a 'given.' It is unlikely anyone (at least privately) would invest and provide OOS to a satellite if they did not have the consent and fees for services rendered, not to mention the technology or information necessary to rendezvous with the satellite successfully. In fact, this consent issue has been so complicated that many of the early test cases had to bring their own debris with them as part of the plan to avoid the specific ownership legal issue.[1818] Other technologies, such as those that use a net, are by their very nature less discriminate, proposing to capture or slow to the point of destroying any debris that comes along their path. That will render the legal issues surrounding non-consensual removal immediately on point.

Consent, then, must be overcome if a true effort toward utilizing ADR technology to remove hazardous debris is to be successful. The consent argument is generally as follows: the jurisdiction and control of a space object belongs to the State which has registered the space object. There is currently no method for transfer of registration (though you can contractually bind separate liability issues). Space debris is not currently internationally accepted as distinct from space objects for ownership purposes. Space objects are owned, under the current international legal regime, in perpetuity by the registering State. The result is that removal of space debris is removal of a space object, and as such, requires the permission of the State which owns the registered space object.[1819]

1818 Adilov, Alexander & Cunningham, *supra* note 1759.

1819 *See supra* Chapter 3, discussing the registration of space objects and the resulting ownership in perpetuity and responsibility for objects launched into space by the State which has launched it. Collectively, *see* Articles VI, VII, and VIII of the Outer Space Treaty. Outer Space Treaty, *supra* note 234. For liability concerns with ADR, *see* Chapter 2, para. 3.1.3., discussing that under Article VII of the Outer Space Treaty, each 'State Party from whose territory or facility an object is launched is internationally liable for damage to another States Party to the Treaty …' Outer Space Treaty, *supra* note 234. *See also* Chapter 2, section

Needless to say, there is no obvious case of any State advocating for the removal of their own debris absent their complete and total agreement to do so. Because of this, the proposals in ADR for many of the models must obtain or knowingly assume consent for removal by the space object owner. Now, it is likely that with the right coordination, there will be a receptiveness among some States to consent to removing their debris. For example, damaged or destroyed satellites with little hope of future OOS revitalization, such as the Iridium 33/Cosmos 2251 satellites[1820] not 'recoverable' by OOS, or large rocket bodies which make up the most important removal efforts in the near term, might not find heavy resistance to removal from some, though certainly not all, States.

But there will come a time when we may feel compelled to go beyond just those consensual pieces. There are a host of possible reasons why, including that those additional pieces represent a direct danger to existing functional objects. An alternative possibility is that less cooperative States may be using the debris as a military orbital denial tool. Another objection could arise as a result of an objection by a third-party whose debris might otherwise be captured as part of a separate consent-based effort between two other parties (think foam that captures unintended pieces of other objects as part of the process). Raising a claim such as in the scenario of foam is, however, unlikely. It would require that some third-party was aware of its debris embedded in the principal object or otherwise caught by the foam. The third-party would then somehow have to prove that allegation, and furthermore, likely have to prove it to such a degree that its 'incorporation' into the principal object somehow affected the rights afforded to the registering country of the object.

Take an actual situation currently practiced with laser ablation and passivation. There are no indications that actors are seeking out permission from some countries to force a collision avoidance maneuver by affecting small debris with a laser from the ground. Whether that argument is sufficient is unlikely to be adjudicated since no one is likely to be on the other side of the legal claim. This also raises the issue that although consent is otherwise required, there is no established rule for removal of a space object that has no known registering State (or registry itself). And though future technology may be able to determine owners better than we can today, it still does not forge a

---

5, discussing that even transferring rights does not relieve liability of at least one State (launching) from still being liable. *Id.* at art. VIII.

1820 Brian Weeden, *1009 Iridium-Cosmos Collision Fact Sheet*, SECURE WOLRD FOUNDATION (updated Nov. 10, 2010), https://swfound.org/media/6575/swf_iridium_cosmos_collision_fact_sheet_updated_2012.pdf.

path for determining an owner of debris generally smaller than 10 cm. This scenario creates a danger to existing space objects but lacks any solution. Acting through ADR activities could help address the problem. Previously published literature on this point proposes ways of addressing these problems, which will not be repeated in its entirety here. However, suffice it to say, suggestions have included at least two possible ways around consent prohibitions, with smaller debris (approximately less than 10 cm) providing a good roadmap for success.

The first way to avoid the consent argument is simple. If we cannot determine the originator of the material, we should not feel encumbered by legal prohibitions associated with known owners to remove the material. The simple fact is that if we remove unidentifiable material, there is no adversarial party opposite the removing actor to make an allegation of some breach of property rights requiring their consent. For example, were we to release a foam ball in space and capture passing small debris in the foam, and then jettison that into the atmosphere where it burns up, who could challenge such a notion if an owner is indeterminate? And were there to be a general challenge from 'all' objecting parties, in which forum would that be held? Now, that is not to say that the behavior might be politically chastised in international forums, but that is different than an actual legal risk. The issue here is that there is simply no aggrieved party to bring a claim.

The second way to avoid consent concerns is to challenge the right for an adverse claimant to object to the removal of debris in the first place. This scenario does contemplate that, either through historical tracking from SSA or some other method, some originator can be determined. Take a hypothetical such as a piece of debris 10 cm or smaller, which is known to populate an orbit, trackable back to say, a Chinese ASAT test in 2007. The question becomes on what grounds would the owner have to claim that there is no right to remove the debris? Certainly, the Chinese could claim that there is some 'value' to the property; maybe components were platinum or something similar. However, this would likely be a 'de-minimis' value for such a small piece and likely insufficient to show definitive proof of the value. To the question of rights to decline to clean up a 'common area' free to all, the question would be 'does the State have some precedent which would preclude a claim of wrongdoing against them for removal of such debris?'

One argument in support of the removing State would be the defense offered by the 'clean-hands' doctrine. Generally, the clean hands doctrine proposes that "a party to a dispute is precluded from invoking another party's responsibility when the former has in fact been guilty of violating a reciprocal obligation."[1821] While this doctrine has been used in various complaints, its influence and receptiveness in the international community and Courts waxes and wanes depending on the case to which it is applied.[1822] However, where Courts have been particularly receptive is in such cases where there is a violation of a reciprocal obligation.[1823] For example, in the case of the Outer Space Treaty, ratifying States have obligations, discussed earlier, for responsibility to the other parties, including registration requirements, continuous supervision of their activities, and to conduct their activities with regard for corresponding interests of each other ... in accordance with international law.[1824]

Such reciprocal obligations were demonstrated in international law in the *Diversion of Water from the Meuse* case.[1825] In dismissing both the claim of the Netherlands and the counterclaim of Belgium for misuse of the Meuse river, the PCIJ stated that it "finds it difficult to admit that the Netherlands are now warranted in complaining of the construction and operation of a lock of which

---

1821 Ori Pomson & Yonatan Horowitz, *Humanitarian Intervention and the Clean Hands Doctrine in International Law*, 48 ISRAEL L. REV. 219 (2015).

1822 *See generally* Rahim Moloo, *A Comment on the Clean Hands Doctrine in International Law*, TDM 1 (2011), in which he notes that the International Court of Justice has not been receptive to the clean hands doctrine in all cases, such as diplomatic protection, but it has found safe harbor in several cases. The author discussed two cases considered extremely influential; the Diversion of Water from Meuse (*Neth. v. Belg.*), Judgment, 1937 P.C.I.J. (ser. A/B) No. 70, at 76–78 (June 28) and the Military and Paramilitary Activities in and Against Nicaragua (*Nicar. V. U.S.*), Judgment, 1986 I.C.J. Rep. 14 (June 27). In both those cases, there was a reference to wrongdoing by the complainants in the case prior to coming to the courts for relief.

1823 This book discussed these earlier obligations among Outer Space Treaty signatory States. Under the Outer Space Treaty, Article I, States are obligated to ensure that space shall be 'free for exploration by all States.' *See* Outer Space Treaty, *supra* note 234 at art. I. Article III binds States to execute their activities in space in accordance with international law. *Id.* at art. III. Under Article IX, the relevant excerpts state that 'in the exploration and use of outer space ... States Parties to the treaty ... shall conduct all their activities in outer space, including the Moon and other celestial bodies, with due regard to the corresponding interests of all other States Parties to the Treaty.' *Id.* at art. IX. Finally, and to some lesser degree, Article XI states, in part, that to promote the peaceful exploration of outer space, States agree to notify the United Nations and the international scientific community of the "nature, conduct, locations and results of" their exploration activities. *Id.* at art. XI. Collectively, the point is that as signatories of the Outer Space Treaty, major spacefaring nations have a requisite legal obligation to each other, and a violation of that obligation should allow for the potential for a 'reciprocal' violation through Active Debris Removal to remediate the threat under the clean hands doctrine and other principles discussed herein.

1824 *Id.*

1825 Diversion of Water from Meuse (Neth. v. Belg.), Judgment, 1937 P.C.I.J. (ser. A/B) No. 70, at 76–78 (June 28).

they themselves set an example in the past."[1826] As was evident, this was a reflection of recognition by the PCIJ of the clean-hands doctrine in international law.[1827] As discussed earlier, under the Outer Space Treaty Articles I, III, IX, and XI, as signatories of the Outer Space Treaty, major spacefaring nations have a requisite legal obligation to each other, and a violation of that obligation should allow for the potential for a 'reciprocal' violation through ADR to remediate the threat under the clean hands doctrine and other principles discussed herein.[1828] Therefore, in a case where a space actor is attempting to hinder removal of debris, the clean hands doctrine would make a worthy argument to support limited, if any, claims against an ADR actor removing the debris. The very existence of the debris could be viewed as a reciprocal violation of their own treaty obligations under international law.

Assuming there is precedent, and assuming the technology for ADR is available, should a nation endeavor to remove such debris or continue to argue for some form of consent against an objecting nation? The evidence from this book surmises that the State should not wait if the technology is available. Instead, the State should remove the debris, and then determine whether any claims are made against them. The State and the actor will likely find there is little, if any, resistance to such removal. And, in the event there is no objection, there would be the added benefit that the groundwork for the development of traditional customary international law would be initiated. Or, even better, the possibility that instant customary international law would be developed. As seen in the next section, there is certainly precedence that instant customary international law could form from such behavior.

1826 Pomson & Horowitz, *supra* note 1821 at 228.

1827 *See generally Id.* at 228, 231, 233 & 235. Pomson and Horowitz provide additional examples of cases where the clean hands doctrine was also recognized in the international forum in addition to the *Meuse* and *Nicaragua* cases. These include *Nullus Commodum Capere de Sua Injria Propria* (no advantage may be gained from one's own wrong) found in the Factory at Chorzow case (*Factory at Chorzów* (*Ger. v. Pol*)), Jurisdiction, 1927 P.C.I.J. (ser. A) No 9 (Jul. 26); *Ex Delicto non Oritur Actio* (an unlawful act cannot serve as the basis of an action in law), found in the Greenland case (*Legal Status of Eastern Greenland*) 1933 P.C.I.J. Rep (ser. A/B) No. 53, at 95 (Apr. 5); and Provocation, such that the conduct was merely a response to the defendants activities, as demonstrated in the Tehran Hostages case, United States Diplomatic and Consular Staff in Tehran (*United States v. Iran*), Judgment, 1980 I.C.J. Rep 3 (May 24). All of these doctrines exemplify that while not universally applicable, there are instances in international law which allow for serious discussions on the possible application of the clean-hands doctrine.

1828 Outer Space Treaty, *supra* note 234 at art. I, III, IX & XI.

4.4 *Recommendations to Address Debris Removal Legal Challenges*

This book addressed earlier how customary international law is formed. This book also initially raised the concept of 'instant' customary international law in Chapter 3.[1829] One of the proposed advances in solving the orbital debris problem may involve bold action by challenging the notions of existing law and removing debris without specific consent, at least for material in outer space which has no function nor hope of revitalization. This section proposes that a basis, and legal support for removal of such debris without consent, lies in the concept of 'instant customary international law', particularly for debris which is neither 'functioning nor can be brought back into operation in a reasonable amount of time.' The concept of instant customary international law has all the tenets of traditional customary international law, with the exception of the time requirement. In other words, it is based on an activity which, when conducted, is accepted immediately by all other (relevant) Nations as being sound and having the force of law. Essentially, if every principal Nation is on the same page for a behavior or conduct immediately, why is there a need to toll time for time's sake? Such examples exist in international law, as demonstrated in three cases below.

4.4.1 Instant Customary International Law in Practice

The first example here of instant customary international law was demonstrated by the act of Harry Truman, referenced earlier,[1830] when addressing the continental shelf of the United States. As discussed, prior to 1945 maritime law was considered '*res communis*' with use being open and communal.[1831] President Truman upended that understanding with his continental shelf proclamation, claiming control of an extensive portion of the continental shelf "contiguous to the coast of the United States and under its jurisdiction and control."[1832]

The response from the international community was relatively mute, and likely for good reason. This change made sense to other countries and was advantageous to them. Additionally, it was replicable, and it did not require States to take any affirmative action to implement the new understanding. Thus, the change was relatively 'instant' and in short order the understanding of ownership of the continental shelf was changed entirely.[1833]

1829 *See supra* Chapter 3, sections 2–3.
1830 *See supra* Chapter 3, section 2.1.3.
1831 BUZAN, *supra* note 370 at 2.
1832 Proclamation No. 2667, 10 Fed. Reg.12, 305 (Sept. 28, 1945).
1833 SCHARF, *supra* note 374 at 109.

The second instance was the Soviet flyover of Sputnik. Also discussed earlier,[1834] the Soviets demonstrated a similar resolve to act as an 'instant' customary international law pioneer. Before Sputnik, flying through the airspace (or 'over' in this case) of any one of the countries Sputnik passed over would have required authorization from the country whose airspace was transited. In the case of the Soviets, they did not seek this permission and Sputnik travelled around the world without any permission. This arguably established instant customary international law because of the lack of objection from States.[1835] Instead of approaching the Soviets or the United Nations with complaints about their behavior, States instead appeared to acquiesce to the activity. As a result, as appropriately summarized by Judge Lachs, "… freedom of movement

1834 *See supra* Chapter 3, section 3.1.

1835 If there had been some objection, this might otherwise have constituted persistent objector status. However, some scholars have questioned how 'overt' this objection must be for recognition. Some scholars, such as Professor Brian Lepard have argued that persistent objector status can only be achieved by a clear indication of the objection. He states, "we should presume in the absence of other evidence that the community of states requires that a defecting State object *explicitly* on principled grounds to any imposition of the rule on any other objecting State to be qualified to exempt itself from the rule. Explicit objection can take several forms, but it must be clear and unambiguous." *See* LEPARD, *supra* note 511 at 238. *See also* G.A. Res. 73/203 (Dec. 20, 2018), discussing persistent objectors, stating that "where a State has objected to a rule … that rule is not opposable to the State concerned for so long as it maintains its objections … [but] the objection must be clearly expressed, made known to other States, and maintained persistently." G.A. Res 73/203, Conclusion 15 (Dec. 20, 2018). Other scholars have indicated that there are instances in which a State must make clear its decision to 'opt-in', otherwise it is a persistent objector 'by default.' For example, J. Patrick Kelly argues this in the case of a newly formed State. In such a case, he argues that "[i]f, as is frequently argued, this consent notion I premised on sovereignty, then new states need not accept limitations on their sovereignty without their consent." Since new States, at their inception, "neither consented to, nor participated in, the formation of custom" prior to their existence Kelly appears to argue that contrary to the 'explicit' opt-out proposal of Professor Lepard, new States could constitute persistent objectors simply by virtue of not "opting-in." *See* Kelly, *supra* note 358 at 80. Still other scholars see even more fault with relying on the absence of any overt statement or act because the underlying reason may betray their true beliefs regarding the rule. Malcolm Shaw, for example, argues that States "fail to protest for many reasons … [they may not wish to give offense gratuitously or it might wish to reinforce political ties to other diplomatic and political considerations." He also outlines that States may find it too burdensome to "expect every State to react to every single act of every other State" that the first State may object to in an attempt to avoid customary formation. In short, Malcolm Shaw argues that the requisite behavior "will depend to a great extent on the facts of the situation and the view of the international community." *See* MALCOLM SHAW, INTERNATIONAL LAW 76–77 (9th ed. 2021).

into outer space, and in it, came to be established ... in a remarkably short period of time."[1836]

The third, and most recent, demonstration occurred after the Al-Qaeda attacks against the United States on 11 September 2001. Shortly after the attacks, President G. W. Bush declared that the "terrorists who committed the acts of 9/11 and anyone who harbors them will be considered one and the same."[1837] In response, the UN General Assembly and the UN Security Council both adopted resolutions[1838] (the UN Security Council being binding) on 12 September 2001, reflecting the position of President G.W. Bush and the United States.[1839] In doing so, and in accordance with the requirements of customary international law, both an objective State practice (or usage) and the "*opinio juris*" (that there is a sense of legal obligation by the State) existed at that moment that organizers and sponsors of the 9/11 terrorist attacks and those responsible for aiding, supporting or harboring the perpetrators, organizers and sponsors of these acts would be regarded as a 'hostile regime.'[1840] Hence, this demonstrated an event where a position was taken by one Nation (the United States), accepted by the UN General Assembly and UN Security Council, and followed up with action.[1841] Therefore, customary international law was instantly (or nearly

1836 McWhinney, *supra* note 387 at 230. For the full quote of judge Lachs, *see* Chapter 3, para. 3.1.

1837 Presidential Statement in his Address to the Nation, The White House (Sept. 11, 2001, 8:30 PM), http://georgewbush-whitehouse.archives.gov/news/releases/2001/09/20010911-16.html.

1838 G.A. Res. 56/1 (Sept. 18, 2001), in which the body stated that it "also urgently calls for international cooperation to prevent and eradicate acts of terrorism, and stresses that those responsible for aiding, supporting or harboring the perpetrators, organizers and sponsors of such acts will be held accountable." *See also* S.C. Res. 1368 (Sept. 12, 2001) in which the body stated that it "calls on all States to work together urgently to bring to justice the perpetrators, organizers and sponsors of these terrorist attacks and stresses that those responsible for aiding, supporting or harboring the perpetrators, organizers and sponsors of these acts will be held accountable."

1839 Department of State, The Global War on Terrorism: The First 100 Days, https://2001-2009.state.gov/s/ct/rls/wh/6947.htm, stating that "The Presidents policy puts the world on notice that any nation that harbors or supports terrorism will be regarded as a hostile regime." See further that "136 countries have offered a diverse range of military assistance; 46 multilateral organizations have declared their support." Additionally, "196 countries support the financial war on terror; 142 countries have acted to freeze terrorist assets."

1840 Benjamin Langille, *It's "Instant Custom": How the Bush Doctrine Became Law After the Terrorist Attacks of September 11, 2001*, 26 B.C. Int'l & Comp. L. Rev. 145, 153 (2003).

1841 *Id.* at 154–55. Langille makes note of the fact that within three weeks of the passage of the UN Resolutions, 46 multilateral declarations of support had been signed from States including Great Britain, India, Russia, Pakistan, Japan, China, Australia, and South Korea and that these States also acted accordingly, such as Great Britain taking on an active

instantly) established. It is fair to say that the resolution of the UN Security Council the following day (referenced above) was binding law, and that any customary international law was rendered moot since the law became codified. However, in the time between the statement of President G.W. Bush and the resolution codification by the UN Security Council, there is an argument that instant customary international law was created.

This concept, of course, is not without its critics. For example, Robert Jennings wrote that the modern interpretation of instant customary international law "is not only not customary law, it does not even faintly resemble a customary law."[1842] The resistance to the development of instant customary international law is understandable, considering that the development of customary law, as mentioned above, has historically been arduous and developed only over long periods of time. Hence, a classic approach to the development of customary international law, and its most ardent supporters, would invariably resist the removal of one of the main tenets of the original doctrine.

Also, it is fair to say that laws that develop over time and survive the test of time often make for better laws than those made quickly and sometimes only in response to significant events. However, this ignores the modern evolution of international operations and makes no room to recognize what is occurring irrespective of resistance to modern change. As such, if there is an opportunity for State practice and behavior to arise to reinforce an agreement and understanding between countries, particularly if it is narrowly tailored to those countries most affected, then the lack of such reinforcement does not undermine the existence of the parties' understanding.

5 A Need to "Go It Alone" to Establish Customary International Law?

Based on the opportunities that are presented by instant customary international law, and the potential defenses that exist even against possible claims for debris removal, it may be time for at least one of the most interested spacefaring

military role, Pakistan allowing the safe passage of coalition forces and weapons through its airspace, and countries such as Saudi Arabia severing ties with the Taliban regime. All of this demonstrated that it was not mere acquiescence by the states in light of the statements made by President Bush, but in fact active involvement following the declaration by the United States.

1842 *See generally* Niels Petersen, *Customary Law Without Custom? Rules, Principles and the Role of State Practice in International Norm Creation*, 23 AM. U. INT'L L. REV. 275, 282 (citing BIN CHENG, INTERNATIONAL LAW: TEACHING AND PRACTICE (1982)).

actors to consider acting, independently if necessary.[1843] No treaty addressing space debris has been signed, nor have any mandatory measures been implemented. It is also unlikely, shy of some catastrophic event which forces the hand of States, that any mitigation or ADR measures will be established in international law through treaty. However, instant customary international law, carrying the same force as regular law, can provide one possible option to overcome these problems. Based on this, there is no reason why States cannot, by statement and by act, establish instant customary international law pertaining to how ADR will be utilized in space and its effectiveness.

Much like the acceptance of the flyover of Sputnik, the rules establishing space-overflight not requiring consent was the result of an immediate act (Sputnik flyover) followed by acquiescence by States. No treaty was signed in 1957 allowing for such flyover or defining the rules pertaining to it. So too could an act, reinforced by stated policy, potentially be accomplished for the non-consensual removal of debris based on one or more ADR technologies with low risk of international legal repercussions.

Specific to the legal concerns applied to the case at hand, Article VIII of the Outer Space Treaty, discussed previously, establishes the requirement that "a State Party to the Treaty on whose registry an object launched into outer space is carried shall retain jurisdiction and control over such object, and over any personnel thereof, while in outer space or on a celestial body."[1844] This is the point at which the clean hands doctrine and the Outer Space Treaty intersect, such that debris which is no longer 'functioning, nor can be brought back into operation in a reasonable amount of time' is not under the control of a country. It is also not maneuverable as a result. It may also be of a size so small that it is not regularly accountable by modern tracking systems. Therefore, any 'owners' of debris (particularly of small sizes) are arguably, by the very existence of these pieces in outer space, in violation of their international treaty obligations. Were a modern ADR activity to be exercised over a debris piece, absent consent, any claim against the ADR operator would inevitably be coming from a State which had failed to fulfill its own obligations. The "clean hands doctrine" could have very strong defensive merits against any claimant State.

1843 Megan Ansdell, *Active Space Debris Removal: Needs Implications and Recommendations for Today's Geopolitical Environment*, 21 PRINCETON J. PUB. & INT'L AFFAIRS 7 (2010) (stating "international cooperation in space has rarely resulted in cost-effective or expedient solutions, especially in politically-charged areas of uncertain technological feasibility.").

1844 Outer Space Treaty, *supra* note 234 at art. VIII.

Second, in many cases, particularly with the most dangerous smaller debris, it is unlikely a nation of origin could be identified anyway. The logic then follows that if there is no one to claim rights over a piece of debris, what claims could possibly be levied against a State who removed it. And how would any claimant do so without invoking their own culpability under the clean hands doctrine. Furthermore, what is the possibility that any country is aware of where so many of these hundreds of thousands of potential pieces exist that belonged to them from 10, 20, 30, or more years ago? The answers to these questions support the argument that if a nation is willing to do what others won't (or can't) and take the lead in ADR activities, particularly against debris of unknown origin, why shouldn't they? Furthermore, who would be able to claim a legitimate right against doing so?

Third is the issue of ownership. In the case of electrodynamic tethers, a nation deploying such an ADR measure is not actually capturing anything. Instead, the tether creates a magnetic field which can slow the speed of an object passing it. Over time, the friction as it nears the atmosphere will eventually cause it to burn up. In such a scenario, no property rights have been exchanged and no capture has occurred. It would be hard for a State to claim, even if it was somehow possible to identify that its debris was artificially slowed, that the ADR equipment was somehow wrong to do so. The debris had no purpose to begin with and per our qualification, was neither 'functioning, nor can be brought back into operation in a reasonable amount of time.'

Last, even if a State were to be able to identify a piece that was theirs and they were tracking it, then the question arises as to what their future expectation is for the debris. If they intended for it to be deorbited into the atmosphere, there should not be extensive debate against some other State advancing the same outcome. On the other hand, if the object were to be able to be captured and returned to Earth by some other form of ADR, it could easily be returned to the owner if the owner could provide identifying information indicating it was theirs (though a highly unlikely scenario). And last, what claim could any State make that they want the debris to remain in outer space orbiting above Earth or even more so that they should be allowed by the international community to do so? There is no apparent legal justification under any treaty that could support such a position so the issue would be moot.

In sum, it is possible that a nation acting independently to pursue several potential ADR options would be free of at least legal liability to do so. There would likely be little legal justification to make a claim against another country for doing so. Further, it would be politically difficult for a state to claim they had been wronged and somehow had a right to leave their debris floating up there 'just because.' As discussed, the outcome could be that if most stakeholders acquiesce to the behavior, customary international law could begin to form. In the best-case scenario, instant customary international law might be established. Again, conceding there are nuances here that should be fleshed out further, the point is simply to identify the advantages and potential pitfalls to acting independently and without consent. In the right circumstances, it may not be as legally treacherous as may have historically been believed.

5.1 *"Going It Alone"—Principles for Successful Independent ADR Activity*

There is no doubt that pursuing ADR independently is rarely the ideal way to address problems that affect the entire international community. And, whether there is an appetite for supporting removal can remain a point of conversation. However, debating whether debris needs to be removed to preserve the space environment is not a subject of legitimate discourse. Therefore, should the time arrive where a State decides it must act first, and independently, to non-consensually remove debris, a few principles could make doing so at least more politically palatable and pave the way toward greater acceptance earlier in the process. A few principles provided here are offered as a starting point for the discussion.

First, the approach to space debris removal efforts must be pragmatic. There are genuine and legitimate legal concerns with non-consensual debris removal. But States must be encouraged to accept that there should be some ability to arrive at a consensus, if for nothing else then at least for the removal of debris for which no owner can be identified. From there, it may be possible to argue that pieces of a certain size, which cannot possibly be serviced for repair (returned to function in a reasonable amount of time) should be the next iteration to be removed without the need to seek consent. The point is that there are, at least on their face, some areas where cooperation and agreement should be achievable even if the larger objects remain elusive. Suppose there is success, even with the smaller pieces. That could constitute a huge win for international cooperation and begin the reduction of one of the most dangerous categories of debris.

Second, this book acknowledges that the legal issues that arise are most certainly not the only problems facing the larger space debris problem. Whether we can solve or even find some common ground to legally overcome or avoid the consent argument, we still lack a regime to encourage the development and execution of these ADR technologies on a large scale. There currently is no mechanism to pay for these technologies beyond consent-based models. Governments will either have to come to some agreement to support funding or import and translate an existing regime that will allow for accumulation of necessary funds to pay for this type of activity.[1845] Unfortunately, the debris that is among the most desirable for removal, if not done by consent, will likely lack funding support from the objecting party. As such, fiscal complications must be addressed which go well beyond the legal issues raised here.

Finally, if you can reach consensus with the major spacefaring States, your chances of success increase exponentially with each new major partner. We know this from examining the 'lack of success' of the Moon Agreement. In the event of non-consensual removal of debris, some understanding will be necessary with the major spacefaring States even if not to an exacting degree. This is not to say that non-consensual removal cannot still occur if the actor is willing to take on the potential political and economic risks. But if customary international law is to be formed, an understanding or reasonable prediction of how the major spacefaring actors will react after the act is critically important. Again, this is not meant to discourage the decision to act independently, only that if there are opportunities for early conditioning for some eventual act, it should be exploited if possible.

6 Conclusion

The original premise of this effort, discussed at the beginning of this chapter, was to examine whether there was existing customary international law that would otherwise provide for already adjudicated rules for space debris prevention and mitigation. As it turns out, the research found in this book demonstrates that there does not yet appear to be a clear formulation.

Arriving at that conclusion involved a three-part process. First, examining the basis for international law as it pertains to space debris. Primarily, treaty

1845 While outside the scope of this book, some regimes which may provide the groundwork and a funding model include the International Seabed Authority (ISA), which proposes a voluntary funding model comprised of members of the international community who have ratified the UN Convention on the Law of the Sea and therefore achieved membership in the ISA. *See* About ISA, INT'L SEABED AUTHORITY, https://www.isa.org.jm/about-isa. *See also* Jordan Wolman, *The World is Set to Debate Seabed Mining Regulations, but the U.S. will be on the Outside Looking In*, POLITICO (Mara. 22, 2022, 9:58 am), https://www.politico.com/news/2022/03/22/seabed-mining-regulations-00019005. Others, such as USAF Maj Edwin Kisiel, have proposed that existing environmental laws provide opportunity for a remedy to the outer space environment. Under the Comprehensive Environmental Response, Compensation, and Liability Act (CERCLA) of 1980, a superfund was created via taxes on petroleum and chemical companies to clean up hazardous waste contamination. Those funds then reimburse response cleanup actions. Kisiel argues such a model is translatable to orbital debris cleanup. *See* Kisiel, *supra* note 261.

law and how it is formed, customary international law (including instant customary international law) and its formation elements, and third, soft law as it is used to guide current efforts. This book then examined how the United States, Russia, China, and ESA approached debris mitigation and prevention within their jurisdictions, as well as private and international efforts which influenced those laws. Finally, the book examined whether there were similarities among the four major spacefaring powers that would, if sufficient, rise to the level of customary international law in the absence of any treaty law.

The assessment of this book, that there were enough inconsistencies in practice to preclude declaring customary international law to exist in this area, then concluded by asking the question that in the absence of any specific international consensus, where do we go from here? One suggestion is a different regulatory scheme. Another, or potentially concurrent effort, is to develop ADR efforts further, and as possible, act when the technology is available. Where consent is available, this should provide an easy legal solution once the technological and fiscal issues are overcome. Where consent is absent, the legal challenges must be addressed. But those challenges are not insurmountable, and a degree of courage and risk-acceptance for the greater good by at least one State has the potential to overwhelm the dam of resistance that seems to pervade much of the current conversation.

In the meantime, as discussed in the body of this book, it remains critical that efforts to tighten regulatory oversight, and ultimately compliance once in orbit, will be critical to stem the amount of mass that continues to accumulate in space. At least the major spacefaring States do have licensing and registration authority over operators within their jurisdiction which they can use to wield considerable power. Small changes, such as reducing the amount of contracts awarded to space-actors who fail to strictly comply with post-mission disposal requirements, could go a long way to motivate companies to do everything possible to be compliant.

In sum, the solution to space debris will involve a concerted effort by the international community to address the problem holistically. The solution must include the convergence of legal, technological, fiscal, and political efforts. The legal realm will have to continue to find ways to be adaptable and responsive and take on hard questions. This includes further discussion if a new definition for space debris versus space objects or determining when a space object officially 'lacks functionality'? These issues will be critical to the success of potential nonconsensual removal of larger pieces. The technological realm will have to continue to develop the craft that will be able to carry out these extraordinary feats of removal, from approach to destruction. The fiscal realm will have to find a way to create support from the public and private sector to establish markets that can sustain companies as they develop the technological solutions for removal. And finally, a political appetite to work together internationally when possible. Where not possible, the fortitude to move forward alone if necessary. Meanwhile, the political will to act will still have to contest with an environment of extraordinary polarization, both domestically and internationally.

None of this will be easy, but it also will not be solved with simple verbal machinations or handwringing. Some State will likely need to step up and act, and the first to do so, as seen in the early space race, will likely be the one to have the greatest influence on the way that activity is carried out, and the corresponding rules, going forward. Who will that be?

References

Books

18TH SPACE CONTROL SQUADRON. LAUNCH CONJUNCTION ASSESSMENT HANDBOOK (Dec. 2018), https://www.space-track.org/documents/LCA_Handbook.pdf.

Alexandrowicz, C.H. AN INTRODUCTION TO THE HISTORY OF THE LAW OF NATIONS IN THE EAST INDIES (1967).

Aliberti, Marco. WHEN CHINA GOES TO THE MOON (2015).

Allan, Duncan, et al. MYTHS AND MISCONCEPTIONS IN THE DEBATE ON RUSSIA: HOW THEY AFFECT WESTERN POLICY, AND WHAT CAN BE DONE (2021).

Anz-Meador, Phillip D., et al. HISTORY OF ON-ORBIT SATELLITE FRAGMENTATIONS (5th ed. 2018).

Baiocchi, Dave & William Welser IV. CONFRONTING SPACE DEBRIS: STRATEGIES AND WARNINGS FROM COMPARABLE EXAMPLES INCLUDING DEEPWATER HORIZON (2010).

Benzing, Markus. INTERNATIONAL ORGANIZATIONS OR INSTITUTIONS, SECONDARY LAW (2007), *reprinted in* THE MAX PLANCK ENCYCLOPEDIA OF PUBLIC INTERNATIONAL LAW 74 (Rudiger Wolfrum, ED., 2012).

Bradford, Anu. *Regime Theory, in* MAX PLANCK ENCYCLOPEDIA OF PUB. INT'L L. (Feb. 2007).

Buzan, Barry. SEABED POLITICS (1976).

Catledge, Burton "Ernie" & Jeremy Powell. *Space History, in* AU-18 SPACE PRIMER (2009).

Chapter VII: Special Provisions for Radio, in COLLECTION OF THE BASIC TEXTS OF THE INTERNATIONAL TELECOMMUNICATIONS UNION ADOPTED BY THE PLENIPOTENTIARY CONFERENCE (2019).

Chapter 8, in HANDBOOK OF SPACE LAW (Frans von der Dunk & Fabio Tronchetti eds., 2015).

Cheng, Bin. INTERNATIONAL LAW: TEACHING AND PRACTICE (1982).

COMM. FOR THE ASSESSMENT OF NASA'S ORBITAL DEBRIS PROGRAMS, ET AL. LIMITING FUTURE COLLISION RISK TO SPACECRAFT: AN ASSESSMENT OF NASA'S METEOROID AND ORBITAL DEBRIS PROGRAMS (2011).

Danilenko, Gennady M. IMPLEMENTATION OF INTERNATIONAL LAW IN RUSSIA AND OTHER CIS STATES (1998).

Dobbins, Dorothy L. & Xiaoping Pan, *Neurological Effects and Mechanisms of Blast Overpressure Injury, in* HANDBOOK OF TOXICOLOGY OF CHEMICAL WARFARE AGENTS (Ramesh C. Gupta ed., 2d ed., 2015).

GLOBAL SPACE GOVERNANCE: AN INTERNATIONAL STUDY (Ram S. Jakhu & Joseph N. Pelton eds., 2017).

Goedhuis, Daniel. *Conflicts of Law and Divergencies in the Legal Regimes of Air Space and Outer Space, in* ACADEMIE DE DROIT INTERNATIONAL [ACAD. OF INT'L L.], RECUEIL DES COURS [COLLECTION OF COURSES] (1963).

HANDBOOK OF SPACE LAW (Frans von der Dunk & Fabio Tronchetti eds., 2015).

Harrison, Todd, et al. *Others, in* SPACE THREAT ASSESSMENT 2019 (2019).

Harrison, Todd, et al. SPACE THREAT ASSESSMENT 2018: REP. OF THE CTR. FOR STRATEGIC AND INT'L STUD. AEROSPACE SEC. PROJECT (Apr. 2018).

Hart, H.L.A. THE CONCEPT OF LAW (1961).

Hemenway, Brett, et al. ACHIEVING HIGHER-FIDELITY CONJUNCTION ANALYSIS USING CRYPTOGRAPHY TO IMPROVE INFORMATION SHARING (2014).

INTERNATIONAL REGIMES (Stephen D. Krasner ed., 1983).

INTERNATIONAL STANDARDIZATION ORGANIZATION, SPACE SYSTEMS—SPACE DEBRIS MITIGATION REQUIREMENTS (2011), https://www.iso.org/obp/ui/#iso:std:iso:24113:ed-2:v1:en.

INTERNATIONAL STANDARDIZATION ORGANIZATION, SPACE SYSTEMS—TEST PROCEDURE TO EVALUATE SPACECRAFT MATERIAL EJECTA UPON HYPERVELOCITY IMPACT, AMENDMENT 1: OBLIQUE IMPACTS AND ANNEX C UPDATE, ISO 1227:2012 (2012).

INTERNATIONAL STANDARDIZATION ORGANIZATION, SPACE ENVIRONMENT (NATURAL AND ARTIFICIAL)—GUIDE TO PROCESS-BASED IMPLEMENTATION OF METEOROID AND DEBRIS ENVIRONMENTAL MODELS (ORBITAL ALTITUDES BELOW GEO +2,000 KM), ISO 14200:2012(E) (1st ed., 2012).

INTERNATIONAL STANDARDIZATION ORGANIZATION, SPACE SYSTEMS—ASSESSMENT OF SURVIVABILITY OF UNMANNED SPACE AGAINST SPACE DEBRIS AND METEOROID IMPACTS TO ENSURE SUCCESSFUL POST-MISSION DISPOSAL, ISO 16126:2014 (1st ed., 2014).

INTERNATIONAL STANDARDIZATION ORGANIZATION, SPACE SYSTEMS—AVOIDING COLLISIONS WITH ORBITING OBJECTS, ISO/TR 16158:2013(E), Introduction (2013).

INTERNATIONAL STANDARDIZATION ORGANIZATION, SPACE SYSTEMS—DEBRIS MITIGATION DESIGN AND OPERATION MANUAL FOR LAUNCH VEHICLE ORBITAL STAGES, ISO/TR 20590:2017(E) (1st ed., 2017).

INTERNATIONAL STANDARDIZATION ORGANIZATION, SPACE SYSTEMS—DETAILED SPACE DEBRIS MITIGATION REQUIREMENTS FOR LAUNCH VEHICLE ORBITAL STAGES, ISO 20893:2021 (1st ed., 2021).

INTERNATIONAL STANDARDIZATION ORGANIZATION, SPACE SYSTEMS—DISPOSAL OF SATELLITES OPERATING AT GEOSYNCHRONOUS ALTITUDE, ISO 26872:2019 (2d ed., 2019).

INTERNATIONAL STANDARDIZATION ORGANIZATION, SPACE SYSTEMS—DISPOSAL OF ORBITAL LAUNCH STAGES, ISO 16699:2015 (1st ed., 2015).

INTERNATIONAL STANDARDIZATION ORGANIZATION, SPACE SYSTEMS—DISPOSAL OF SATELLITES OPERATING IN OR CROSSING LOW EARTH ORBIT, ISO 16164:2015(E) (1st ed., 2015).

INTERNATIONAL STANDARDIZATION ORGANIZATION, SPACE SYSTEMS—ESTIMATION OF ORBIT LIFETIME, ISO 27852:2016 (2d ed., 2016).

INTERNATIONAL STANDARDIZATION ORGANIZATION, SPACE SYSTEMS—SPACE DEBRIS MITIGATION DESIGN AND OPERATION MANUAL FOR SPACECRAFT, TECHNICAL REPORT, ISO/TR 18146:2020 (2d ed., 2020).

INTERNATIONAL STANDARDIZATION ORGANIZATION, SPACE SYSTEMS—SPACE DEBRIS MITIGATION REQUIREMENTS, ISO 24113:2019 (3d ed., 2019).

INTERNATIONAL STANDARDIZATION ORGANIZATION, SPACE SYSTEMS—REENTRY RISK MANAGEMENT FOR UNMANNED SPACECRAFT AND LAUNCH VEHICLE ORBITAL STAGES, ISO 27875:2019(E) (2d ed., 2019).

INTERNATIONAL STANDARDIZATION ORGANIZATION, SPACE SYSTEMS—UNMANNED SPACECRAFT—ESTIMATING THE MASS OF REMAINING USABLE PROPELLANT, ISO 23339:2010 (1st ed., 2010).

Jankowitsch, Peter, et al. JOURNAL OF SPACE LAW (Harold Berger, et al. EDS., 1998).

Johnson-Freese, Joan. THE CHINESE SPACE PROGRAM: A MYSTERY WITHIN A MAZE (1988).

Johnson, Nicholas. ARES BIENNIAL REPORT: ORIGIN OF THE INTER-AGENCY SPACE DEBRIS COORDINATION COMMITTEE (2012).

Kelly, J. Patrick. *Customary International Law in Historical Context, in* REEXAMINING CUSTOMARY INTERNATIONAL LAW 47 (Brian D. Lepard, ed., 2017).

Krige J., et al. A HISTORY OF THE EUROPEAN SPACE AGENCY 1973–1987 (2000).

Lepard, Brian D. CUSTOMARY INTERNATIONAL LAW: A NEW THEORY WITH PRACTICAL APPLICATIONS (2010).

Lowe, Vaughan. INTERNATIONAL LAW (2015).

Majsova, Natalija. *Neither Rupture nor Continuity: Memorializing the Dawn of the Space Age in Contemporary Russian Cinematography, in* THE TWENTIETH CENTURY IN EUROPEAN MEMORY: TRANSCULTURAL MEDIATION AND RECEPTION 198 (Tea Sindbaek Andersen & Barbara Tornquist-Plewa, eds., 2017).

Malkov, Sergey P. & Catherine Doldirina. *Regulation of Space Activities in the Russian Federation, in* NATIONAL REGULATION OF SPACE ACTIVITIES (Ram S. Jakhu ed., 2010).

Malysheva, Nataliia R. *Federal Space Program of Russia for 2016–2017, in* SPACE LAW AND POLICY IN THE POST-SOVIET STATES (2018).

Malysheva, Nataliia R. SPACE LAW AND POLICY IN THE POST-SOVIET STATES (2018).

Mateesco, Nicolas M. La Coutume Dans Les Cycles Juridiques Internationaux [Custom in International Legal Cycles] (2d ed., 1947).

Matte, Nicolas Mateesco. *Outer Space Treaty*, *in* Encyclopedia of Public International Law 836 (R. Bernhardt, ed., 1992).

Mcwhinney, Edward. Judge Manfred Lachs and Judicial Law-Making (1995).

Mendelson, Maurice H. *Formation of Customary International Law*, *in* 272 Recueil Des Cours [Collection of Courses] (1998).

Mieczkowski, Yanek. Eisenhower's Sputnik Moment: The Race for Space and World Prestige (2013).

Morell, James B. The Law of the Sea: A Historical Analysis of the 1982 Treaty and Its Rejection by the United States (2013).

nat'l res. ctr. U.S. European Collaboration in Space Science (1998).

Newell, Jr., Homer E. Beyond the Atmosphere: Early Years of Space Science (2010).

Nussbaum, Arthur. Principles of Private International Law (1943).

O'Connell, D.P. The International Law of the Sea (1983).

Podvig, Pavel. *Russian Military Space Capabilities*, *in* Ensuring America's Space Security.

Ramcharan, B.G. The International Law and Practice of Early-Warning and Preventive Diplomacy: The Emerging Global Watch (1991).

Reexamining Customary International Law (Brian D. Lepard ed., 2017).

Revelations from the Russian Archives, Perestroika, *in* Library of Cong. Soviet Archives.

Rodriguez, Roberto. The Space Program of the People's Republic of China (2011).

Rose, Frank A. Managing China's Rise in Outer Space (Apr. 2020).

Safety Design for Space Operations (Firooz A. Allahdadi & Tommaso Sgobba eds., 2013).

Scharf, Michael P. Customary International Law in Times of Fundamental Change: Recognizing Grotian Moments (2013).

Shaw, Malcolm. International Law (9th ed., 2021).

staff of the comm. On Astronautics and Space Exploration. 58th Con. Rep. on Space Handbook: Astronautics and its Applications at Section iv. Astronautics in Other Countries.

the space found. The Space Briefing Book: A Reference Guide to Modern Space Activities (2019) (ebook).

The U.N. Univ. Environmental Change and International Law: New Challenges and Dimensions (Edith Brown Weiss ed., 1992).

Tronchetti, Fabio. *Space Law and China*, *in* Oxford Res. Encyclopedia, Planetary Sci. (Feb. 2019).

Tsunjino, Teruhisa. *Chapter 4: Role of Space Development in the National Security of China, in* INTERNATIONAL SYMPOSIUM ON SECURITY AFFAIRS (2015).

Journal Articles

Adams, Benjamin. *Cooperation in Space: An International Comparison for the Benefit of Emerging Space Agencies*, 162 ACTA ASTRONAUTICA 409 (2019).

Adilov, Nodir, et al. *An Economic Analysis of Earth Orbit Pollution*, 60 ENV'T & RES. ECON. 81 (2015).

Alby, F. et al. *The European Space Debris Safety and Mitigation Standard*, 34 ADVANCES IN SPACE RSCH. 1260 (2004).

Ansdell, Megan. *Active Space Debris Removal: Needs Implications and Recommendations for Today's Geopolitical Environment*, 21 PRINCETON J. PUB. & INT'L AFFAIRS 7 (2010).

Bai, Zhili & Juan Liu. *China's Governance Model and System in Transition*, 9 J. CONTEMP. E. ASIA STUD. 65 (Mar. 24, 2020).

Baker, H.A. *The ESA and USS Reports on Space Debris*, 6 SPACE POL'Y 332 (1990).

Beard, Jack. *Soft Laws Failure on the Horizon: The International Code of Conduct for Outer Space Activities*, 38 UNIV. PA. J. INT'L L. 335 (2017).

Benko, Marietta & Kai-Uwe Schrogl, *History and Impact of the 1996 UN Declaration on Space Benefits*, 13 SPACE POL'Y 139 (1997).

Bockstiegel, Karl-Heinz. *ILA Draft Convention on Space Debris*, 44 GERMAN J. AIR & SPACE L. 29 (1995).

Boris, Krivokapic. *On the Issue of So-Called 'Instant' Customs in International Law*, 9 ACTA UNIVERSITATIS DANUBIUS 81 (2017).

Braun, Vitali, et al. *Exploiting Orbital Data and Observation Campaigns to Improve Space Debris Models*, 66 J. OF THE ASTRONAUTICAL SCIS. 192 (2019).

Chansoria, Monika. *The Political History of China's Nuclear Bomb*, 6 CLAWS J. 79 (2013).

Character, Essence, Origin and Content of the Jus Gentium According to Vico and Suares, 16 PERIODICALS ARCHIVE ONLINE 167 (Jan. 1, 1936).

Charney, Jonathan I. *Universal International Law*, 87 AM. J. INT'L L. 529 (1993).

Cheng, Bin. *Properly Speaking, Only Celestial Bodies Have Been Reserved for Use Exclusively for Peaceful (Non-Military) Purposes, but Not Outer Void Space*, 75 INT'L L. STUD. 81 (2000).

Cheng, Bin. *United Nations Resolutions on Outer Space: "Instant" International Customary Law?*, 5 INDIAN J. INT'L L. 23 (1965).

Chiu, S.W. *Promoting International Cooperation in the Age of Global Space Governance—A Study On On-Orbit Servicing*, 161 ACTA ASTRONAUTICA 375 (2019).

Chrysaki, Margarita. *The Sustainable Commercialisation of Space: The Case for a Voluntary Code of Conduct for the Space Industry*, 52 SPACE POL'Y 5 (2020), https://doi.org/10.1016/j.spacepol.2020.101375.

Conklin, William. *Myth of Primordialism*, 23 LEIDEN J. INTL'L L. 479 (2010).

Cui, Jing, et al. *Tangling and Instability Effect Analysis of Initial In-Plane/Out-of-Plane Angles on Electrodynamic Tether Deployment Under Gravity Gradient*, 34 CHINESE J. OF AERONAUTICS 1 (2021).

D'Amato, Antony. *Groundwork for International Law*, 108 AMER. J. INT'L L. 4 (2014).

Dembling, Paul G. & Daniel M. Arons. *The Evolution of the Outer Space Treaty*, 33 J. AIR L. & COM. 419 (1967).

DFH-1, ASTRONAUTIX, http://www.astronautix.com/d/dfh-1.html (last accessed Jan. 10, 2021).

Eliantonio, Mariaolina & Oana Stefan. *The Elusive Legitimacy of EU Soft Law: An Analysis of Consultation and Participation in the Process of Adopting COVID-19 Soft Law in the EU*, 12 EUR. J. RISK REGUL. 159 (2021).

Europe: Is it Goodbye to ESRO and ELDO?, 226 NATURE 226 (1970).

Flury, Walter & Jean-Michel Contant. *The Updated IAA Position Paper on Orbital Debris*, 2 PROC. OF THE THIRD EUR. CONF. ON SPACE DEBRIS 841 (2001).

Gangale, Thomas. *The Non Karman Line: An Urban Legend of the Space Age*, 41 J. SPACE L. 151 (2017).

Gorove, Stephen. *Contamination and the Outer Space Treaty*, 14 PROC. ON L. OUTER SPACE 63 (1971).

Gorove, Stephen. *Interpreting Article II of the Outer Space Treaty*, 37 FORDHAM L.R. 349 (1969).

Guzman, Andrew T. *The Design of International Agreements*, 16 EUR. J. OF INT'L L. 579 (2005).

Guzman, Andrew T. & Timothy Meyer. *International Soft Law*, 2 J. LEGAL ANALYSIS 171 (2010).

Helfer, Lance & Ingrid Wuerth. *CIL as an Instrument Choice Perspective*, 37 MICH. J. INT'L L. 563 (2016).

He, Qizhi. *Main Features of Space Law Teaching in China*, 29 PROC. ON L. OUTER SPACE 272 (1986).

Hilborne, Mark. *China's Rise in Space and US Policy Responses: A Collision Course?*, 29 SPACE POL'Y 121 (2013).

Hwang, Feng-tai. *China's Development of Space Warfare and Its Operational Applications*, 3 FLETCHER SEC. REV. 85 (2017).

Israel, Brian. *Space Governance 3.0*, 48 GA. J. INT'L & COMPAR. L. 715 (2020).

Jasentuliyana, N. *Space Debris and International Law*, 26 J. OF SPACE L. 139 (1998).

Jing Jing, Nie & Yang Hui. *Revisit the Concept of International Custom in International Space Law*, 54 PROC. INT'L INST. OF SPACE L. 348 (2013).

Johnson-Freese, Joan. *China's Space Ambitions*, 15 GEO. J. INT'L L. 139 (2014).

Johnson, Nicolas L. *Saving Space: The Multilateral Approach to Orbital Debris*, 15 GEO. J. INT'L AFFAIRS 130 (2014).

Johnson, N. *Origin of the Inter-Agency Space Debris Coordination Committee*, 16 ORBITAL DEBRIS Q. NEWS 4 (2012).

Kadens, Emily. *The Medieval Law Merchant: The Tyranny of Construct*, 7 J. LEGAL ANALYSIS 251 (2015).

Keohane, Robert O. *The Demand for International Regimes*, 36 INT'L ORG. 325 (1982).

Kessler, Donald J. & Burton G. Cour-Palais. *Collision Frequency of Artificial Satellites: The Creation of a Debris Belt*, 83 J. OF GEOPHYSICAL RES. (June 1, 1978).

Kirgis, Frederic L. *Custom on a Sliding Scale*, 81 AM. J. INT'L L. 146 (1987).

Kisiel, Edwin. *Law as an Instrument to Solve the Orbital Debris Problem*, 51 ENV'T L. 223 (2021).

Klinkrad, H., et al. *The ESA Space Debris Mitigation Handbook 2002*, 34 ADVANCES IN SPACE RSCH. 1251 (2004).

Kuan, Yang. *Chinese Perspective on An International Regime of Space Traffic Management*, 6 J. OF SPACE SAFETY ENG'G 156 (2019).

Langille, Benjamin. *It's "Instant Custom": How the Bush Doctrine Became Law After the Terrorist Attacks of September 11, 2001*, 26 B.C. INT'L & COMPAR. L. REV. 145 (2003).

Lauterpacht, Hersch. *Sovereignty Over Submarine Areas*, 27 BRIT. Y.B. INT'L L. 376 (1950).

Li, Bin & Haifeng Zhao. *Governmental Regulations on Commercial Aspects of China's Space Activities*, 3 INDIAN J. OF INT'L ECON. L. 28 (2010).

Li, Lawrence. *Space Debris Mitigation as an International Law Obligation*, 17 INT'L COMM. L. REV. 297 (2015).

Liou, J.C. & Nicholas Johnson. *A LEO Satellite Postmission Disposal Study Using LEGEND*, 57 ACTA ASTRONAUTICA 324 (2005).

Liou, J.C. *An Active Debris Removal Parametric Study for LEO Environmental Remediation on Using Active Debris Removal for LEO Environment Remediation*, 47 ADVANCES IN SPACE RSCH. 1865 (2011).

Liou, J.C., et al. *The 2019 U.S. Government Orbital Debris Mitigation Standard Practices*, 24 ORBITAL DEBRIS Q. NEWS 5 (2020).

Lipson, Leon S. *The Soviet View on International Law*, 61 INT'L L. STUD. 101 (1980).

Liu, Irina, et al. *Evaluation of China's Commercial Space Sector*, SCI. & TECH. POL'Y INST. 11 (Sept. 2019).

Maclay, T. & D. Mcknight. *Space Environment Management: Framing the Objective and Setting Priorities for Controlling Orbital Debris Risk*, 8 J. OF SPACE SAFETY ENG'G 93 (2021).

Martinez, Peter. *The UN COPUOS Guidelines for the Long-term Sustainability of Outer Space Activities*, 8 J. SPACE SAFETY ENG'G 98 (2021).

Ma, Tianming, et al. *Research on Pointing Correction Algorithm of Laser Ranging Telescope Oriented to Space Debris*, 32 J. of Laser Applications 012004-1 (2020).

Mccall, Gene H. & John H. Darrah. *Space Situational Awareness: Difficult, Expensive—and Necessary*, 28 Air & Space Power J. 6 (2014).

McClintock, Bruce. *The Russian Space Sector: Adaptation, Retrenchment, and Stagnation*, 10 Space & Def. 3 (2017).

McDougal, M.S. & N.A. Schlei. *The Hydrogen Bomb Tests in Perspective: Lawful Measures for Security*, 64 Yale L. J. 648 (1955).

Mcdowell, Jonathan C. *The Edge of Space: Revisiting the Karman Line*, 151 Acta Astronautica 668 (2018).

Mejia-Kaiser, Martha. *Removal of Non-Functional Space Objects without Prior Consent*, 50 Proc. on L. Outer Space 293 (2007).

Migaud, Michael R., et al. *Developing an Adaptive Space Governance Framework*, 55 Space Pol'y 101400 (2021).

Mineiro, Michael C. *FY-1C and USA-193 ASAT Intercepts: An Assessment of Legal Obligations under Article IX of the Outer Space Treaty*, 34 J. Space L. 321 (2008).

Mirmina, Steven A. *The Regulation of Orbital Debris through National Measures*, 29 Air & Space L. 137 (2004).

Moltz, James Clay. *The Changing Dynamics of Twenty-First-Century Space Power*, 12 J. Strategic Stud. 15 (2019).

Moloo, Rahim. *A Comment on the Clean Hands Doctrine in International Law*, Inter Alia 39 (2010).

Muelhaupt, Theodore J., et al. *Space Traffic Management in the New Space Era*, 6 J. of Space Safety Eng'g 80 (2019).

Muntoni, Giacomo, et al. *Space Debris Detection in Low Earth Orbit with the Sardinia Radio Telescope*, 6 Elecs. 59 (2017).

Mu, Rongping & Yonggang Fan. *An Overview of Chinese Space Policy*, *in* Handbook of Space Security 413 (2015).

Neely, David, et al. *Energy Coupling in Short Pulse Laser Solid Interactions and Its Impact for Space Debris Removal*, 53 Applied Optics 141 (2014).

Niemirowicz, Z. *A Marriage to COSPAR: Part 1—1957–1967*, 1993 COSPAR Info. Bull. 77 (1993).

Odermatt, Jed. *The Development of Customary International Law by International Organizations*, 66 Int'l & Compar. L. Q. 491 (2017).

Oltrogge, Daniel L. & Ian A. Christensen. *Space Governance in the New Space Era*, 7 J. Space Safety Eng'g 6 (2020).

Percy, Thomas. *Investigation of National Policy Shifts to Impact Orbital Debris Environments*, 30 Space Pol'y 23 (2014).

Petersen, Niels. *Customary Law Without Custom? Rules, Principles and the Role of State Practice in International Norm Creation*, 23 Am. Univ. Int'l L. Rev. 275 (2007).

Pomson, Ori & Yonatan Horowitz. *Humanitarian Intervention and the Clean Hands Doctrine in International Law*, 48 ISR. L. REV. 219 (2015).

Priyant, Mark & Surekha Kamath. *Review of Active Space Debris Removal Methods*, 47 SPACE POL'Y 194 (2019).

Rathgeber, Wolfgang, et al. *Space Security and the European Code of Conduct for Outer Space Activities*, 4 DISARMAMENT FORUM 33 (2009).

Resolution on Community Participation in Space Research, No C 127/42, OFF. J. OF THE EUR. CMTYS.

Reynolds, Glenn H. & Robert P. Merges. *The Role of Commercial Development in Preventing War in Outer Space*, 25 JURIMETRICS 130 (1985).

Reynolds, R.C., et al. *Issues Arising from the NASA Safety Standard to Control Orbital Debris*, 19 ADVANCES IN SPACE RSCH. 381 (1997).

Robinson, George S. *Article IX of the Outer Space Treaty: Extraterrestrial Bank Contamination, the U.S. Constitution, and the "Politics" of U.S. Regulatory Authority*, 53 PROC. INT'L INST. SPACE L. 646 (2010).

Romagnoli, D. & S. Theil. *De-Orbiting Satellites in Leo Using Solar Sails*, 4 J. AEROSPACE ENG'G SCI. & APPLICATIONS 49 (2012).

Scharf, Michael P. *Accelerated Formation of Customary International Law*, 20 ILSA J. INT'L & COMPAR. L. 305 (2014).

Shaskova, A.V., et al. *Questioning State Corporations as Special Forms of Legal Entities*, 1 INT'L J. ECON. & BUS. ADMIN. 186 (2019).

Shuanyan, Shen. et al. *Cleaning Space Debris with a Space-Based Laser System*, 27 CHINESE J. OF AERONAUTICS 805 (2014).

Sloss, David. *Non-Self-Executing Treaties: Exposing a Constitutional Fallacy*, 36 U.C. DAVID L. REV. 1 (2002).

Sohn, Louis B. *Stockholm Declaration on Human Environment*, 14 HARV. INT'L L.J. 423 (1973).

Sorge, Marlon & Glenn Peterson. *How to Clean Space: Dispose and Active Debris Removal*, 16 CROSSLINK 46 (2015).

Steer, Casandra. *Global Commons, Cosmic Commons: Implications of Military and Security Uses of Outer Space*, 18 GEO. J. INT'L AFFAIRS 9 (2017).

Stein, Arthur A. *Coordination and Collaboration: Regimes in an Anarchic World*, 36 INT'L ORG. 299 (1982).

Stokes, H. *Evolution of ISO's Space Debris Mitigation Standards, H. Stokes*, 7 J. OF SPACE SAFETY ENG'G 325 (2020).

Su, Jinyuan, & Zhu Lixin. *The European Union Draft Code of Conduct for Outer Space Activities: An Appraisal*, 30 SPACE POL'Y 34 (2014).

Thompson, Cort S. *Avoiding Pyrrhic Victories in Orbit: A Need for Kinetic Anti-Satellite Arms Control in the Twenty-First Century*, 85 J. AIR L. & COM. 105 (2020).

Tunkin, Gregory I. *Remarks on the Juridical Nature of Customary Norms in International Law*, 49 CAL. L. R. 419 (1961).

Vedda, James A. *National Space Council, History and Potential*, CTR. FOR SPACE POL'Y & STRATEGY POL'Y PAPER 2 (Nov. 2016).

Von Der Dunk, Frans G. *Space Debris and the Law*, 3 EUR. CONFS. ON SPACE DEBRIS 863 (2001).

Von der Dunk, Frans G. *The European Union and the Outer Space Treaty: Will the Twain Ever Meet?*, 89 SPACE, CYBER, & TELECOMM. L. PROGRAM FACULTY PUBL'N 75 (2017).

Von der Dunk, Frans G. *The Origins of Authorization: Article VI of the Outer Space Treaty and International Space Law*, 69 SPACE, CYBER & TELECOMM. L. PROGRAM, FACULTY PUBL'N (2011).

Williams, Andrew. *France and the Origins of the United Nations, 1944–1945: "Si La France ne compte plus, qu'on nous le dise"*, 28 DIPL. & STATECRAFT 215 (2017).

Williams, Michael. *Filling the Void: Why Existing International Law Is Not Suited to Mitigate Space Debris*, 42 MICH. J. INT'L L. ONLINE.

Williamson, Ray A. *The Growing Hazard of Orbiting Debris*, 8 ISSUES IN SCI. & TECH. 77 (Fall 1991).

Wi, Xiaodan. *China's Lunar Exploration and Utilization: Positive Energy for International Law or Not?*, 15 ANUARIO MEXICANO DE DERECHO INTERNACIONAL [MEX. Y.B. OF INT'L L.] 137 (2015).

Woignier, Thierry, et al. *Aerogels Materials as Space Debris Collectors*, ADVANCES IN MATERIALS SCI. & ENG'G (2016).

Wu, Xiaodan. *China and Space Security: How to Bridge the Gap Between Its Stated and Perceived Intentions*, 33 SPACE POL'Y 20 (2015).

Yang, Caixia & Guozhu Gai, *Overview of the Current Situation and Improvement of Chinese Space Legislation*, 38 ANNALS OF AIR & SPACE L. 385 (2013).

Yeshchuk, Olga & Anna Vasina, *Chinese Space Law: Problems and Areas of Reforming*, 3 ADVANCED SPACE L. 140 (2019).

Zhao, Yun. *National Space Law in China; An Overview of the Current Situation and Outlook for the Future*, 10 STUD. IN SPACE L. 42 (2015).

Website Articles and Online PDFs

About ISA, INT'L SEABED AUTH., https://www.isa.org.jm/about-isa.

About the European Space Agency, EUR. SPACE AGENCY https://www.esa.int/Newsroom/About_the_European_Space_Agency.

About the Office of Commercial Space Transportation, FED. AVIATION ADMIN. (last updated July 6, 2020), https://www.faa.gov/about/office_org/headquarters_offices/ast.

About Us, INT'L STANDARDIZATION ORG., https://www.iso.org/about-us.html.

Abramson, Jeff. *EU Issues Space Code of Conduct*, ARMS CONTROL ASS'N, https://armscontrol.org/act/2009-01/eu-issues-space-code-conduct.

A Brief History of ISO—the International Organization for Standardization, PERRY JOHNSON REGISTRARS, INC., https://www.pjr.com/about-pjr/what-is-certification/history-of-iso#.

Active Debris Removal, EUR. SPACE AGENCY, https://www.esa.int/Safety_Security/Space_Debris/Active_debris_removal.

Active Debris Removal Technologies, SMALL BUS. INNOVATION RES., https://www.sbir.gov/content/active-debris-removal-technologies.

Agreement Governing the Activities of States on the Moon and Other Celestial Bodies, U.N. OFF. OF OUTER SPACE AFFAIRS https://www.unoosa.org/oosa/en/ourwork/spacelaw/treaties/intromoon-agreement.html.

Amos, Jonathan. *Space Harpoon Skewers 'Orbital Debris'*, BBC NEWS (Feb. 15, 2019), https://www.bbc.com/news/science-environment-47252304.

Andrenucci, M. et al. *Expanding Foam Application for Active Debris Removal*, EUR. SPACE AGENCY (Feb. 21, 2011), https://www.esa.int/gsp/ACT/doc/ARI/ARI%20Study%20Report/ACT-RPT-MAD-ARI-10-6411-Pisa-Active_Removal_of_Space_Debris-Foam.pdf.

Anthropogenic, FREE DICTIONARY, https://www.dictionary.com/browse/anthropogenic.

ASAT-Anti Satellite Weapon Systems, WITANWORLD (July 19, 2020), https://witanworld.com/article/2020/07/19/asat-anti-satellite-weapon-systems.

ASTERANK, http://www.asterank.com.

Atherton, Kelsey D. *This Week's Destroyed Russian Satellite Created Even More Dangerous Space Debris*, POPULAR SCI. (Nov. 16, 2021), https://www.popsci.com/technology/russian-missile-destroys-russian-satellite.

A Timeline of the Exploration and Peaceful Use of Outer Space, U.N. OFF. OF OUTER SPACE AFFAIRS, http://www.unoosa.org/oosa/en/timeline/index.html.

Attorney: Constitutional Amendment on International Law Could Give Russia a "Red Button", CURRENT TIME (June 25, 2020), https://en.currenttime.tv/a/30690618.html.

Axe, David. *Is China's Mysterious New Satellite Really a Junk Collector—or a Weapon?*, DAILY BEAST (Apr. 13, 2017, 3:27 PM), https://www.thedailybeast.com/is-chinas-mysterious-new-satellite-really-a-junk-collectoror-a-weapon.

Badenoch, Alexander. *ESRO and ELDO: Science vs. Technology*, INVENTING EUR., http://www.inventingeurope.eu/story/esro-and-eldo-science-vs-technology.

Ban, Xiao. *Current and Former Chinese Communist Party Members Explain their Motivations for Joining*, ABC NEWS (July 24, 2020, 3:33 PM), https://www.abc.net.au/news/2020-07-25/chinese-communist-party-members-motive-join-us-travel-ban/12485530.

Benson, Thor. *Space Force Says Its New 'Space Fence' Will Protect Us in Space*, INVERSE (Apr. 1, 2020, 9:00 AM), https://www.inverse.com/innovation/space-fence-is-now-operational.

Best Efforts Undertakings, TRANS-LEX.ORG, https://www.trans-lex.org/932000/_/best-efforts-undertakings.

Best Practices for Space Operations, SPACE SAFETY COAL. (Sep. 16, 2019), https://spacesafety.org/wp-content/uploads/2021/04/Endorsement-of-Best-Practices-for-Sustainability_v40.pdf.

Billing, Chloe. *There's a Parking Crisis in Space—and You Should be Worried About it*, THE CONVERSATION (Sept. 29, 2017, 9:40 AM), https://theconversation.com/theres-a-parking-crisis-in-space-and-you-should-be-worried-about-it-83479.

Bliss, Dominic. *Millions of Pieces of Debris from Defunct Satellites and Spacecraft Litter the Earth's Orbit. Disaster Looms if we Don't Start Cleaning It Up. But How?*, MS AMLIN (Nov. 12, 2020), https://www.msamlin.com/en/chart-hub/english/cleaning-up-space-debris.html.

Bowan, Bradley & Jared Thompson, *Russia and China Seek to Tie America's Hands in Space*, FOREIGN POL'Y (Mar. 31, 2021, 11:31 AM), https://foreignpolicy.com/2021/03/31/russia-china-space-war-treaty-demilitarization-satellites.

Brief History of Rockets, NASA, https://www.grc.nasa.gov/www/k-12/TRC/Rockets/history_of_rockets.html.

Briz-M Core Stage Fragments Near Geosynchronous Orbit, ORBITAL DEBRIS Q. NEWS, Apr. 2016, https://orbitaldebris.jsc.nasa.gov/quarterly-news/pdfs/odqnv20i1-2.pdf.

Broker, Tyler. *Space Law Can Only Be Libertarian Minded*, ABOVE THE LAW (Jan. 14, 2020, 10:32 AM), https://abovethelaw.com/2020/01/space-law-can-only-be-libertarian-minded.

Brothers, Eric. *NASA Selects Five US Companies to Mature Artemis Lander Concepts*, AEROSPACE MFG. & DESIGN (Sept. 27, 2021), https://www.aerospacemanufacturinganddesign.com/article/nasa-selects-five-us-companies-mature-artemis-lander.

Bullmer, Joe. *The Power of a Picture: The Wright Brothers Take Off*, AIR FORCE TIMES (Dec. 17, 2018).

Carney, Emily. *Space For Europe and for All Humankind: A Brief History of the ESA*, ARS TECHNICA (Dec. 31, 2015, 9:00 AM), https://arstechnica.com/science/2015/12/space-for-europe-and-for-all-humankind-a-brief-history-of-the-esa.

Cartwright, Hoss & Deborah Lee James. *The Space Rush: New US Strategy Must Bring Order, Regulation*, BREAKING DEF. (Mar. 26, 2021, 4:45 PM), https://breakingdefense.com/2021/03/the-space-rush-new-us-strategy-must-bring-order-regulation.

Celine. *Difference Between Soviet Union and Russia*, DIFFERENCEBETWEEN.NET, http://www.differencebetween.net/miscellaneous/politics/political-institutions/difference-between-soviet-union-and-russia.

Centre National D'Etudes Spatiales, EUR. SPACE AGENCY, https://www.esa.int/Enabling_Support/Space_Engineering_Technology/Centre_National_D_Etudes_Spatiales_CNES.

Challenges to Security in Space, DEF. INTEL. AGENCY (2019), https://www.dia.mil/Portals/27/Documents/News/Military%20Power%20Publications/Space_Threat_V14_020119_sm.pdf.

Chen, Stephen. *Is China Militarizing Space? Experts Say New Junk Collector Could Be Used As Anti-Satellite Weapon*, S. CHINA MORNING POST (June 28, 2016), https://www.scmp.com/news/china/diplomacy-defence/article/1982526/china-militarising-space-experts-say-new-junk-collector.

China Plans Space Debris Monitoring and Research Program, MOOD DAILY (Mar. 7, 2001), https://www.moondaily.com/reports/China_Plans_Space_Debris_Monitoring_and_Research_Program.html.

China National Space Administration (CNSA), GLOBALSECURITY.org, https://www.globalsecurity.org/space/world/china/cnsa.htm.

China's Space Activities in 2006, CHINA NAT'L SPACE ADMIN. (Dec. 12, 2006), http://www.cnsa.gov.cn/english/n6465645/n6465648/c6477657/content.html.

Chinese Anti-Satellite Test Creates Most Severe Orbital Debris Cloud in History, ORBITAL DEBRIS Q. NEWS, April 2007, at 1–3, http://orbitaldebris.jsc.nasa.gov/newsletter/pdfs/ODQNv11i2.pdf.

Chinese Nuclear Program, ATOMIC HERITAGE FOUND. (July 19, 2018), https://www.atomicheritage.org/history/chinese-nuclear-program.

Choi, Charles Q. *Space Station Could Get Laser Cannon to Destroy Orbital Debris*, SPACE.COM (Apr. 30, 2015), https://www.space.com/29271-space-station-laser-cannon-orbital-debris.html.

Clark, Colin. *Chinese ASAT Test was "Successful:" Lt. Gen. Raymond*, BREAKING DEF. (Apr. 14, 2015, 6:34 PM), https://breakingdefense.com/2015/04/chinese-asat-test-was-successful-lt-gen-raymond.

Clery, Daniel. *Europe Plans Space Claw to Capture Orbiting Junk*, SCI. (Dec. 1, 2020), https://www.science.org/news/2020/12/europe-plans-space-claw-capture-orbiting-junk.

Coldewey, Devin. *LeoLabs and Its High-Fidelity Space Radar Track Orbital Debris Better Than Ever—From New Zealand*, TECHCRUNCH (Oct. 14, 2019, 5:14 PM), https://techcrunch.com/2019/10/14/leo-labs-and-its-high-fidelity-space-radar-track-orbital-debris-better-than-ever-from-new-zealand.

Commercial Space Transportation Assistance Tool, FED. AVIATION ADMIN. (last updated June 11, 2020), https://www.faa.gov/space/licensing_process.

Committee on the Peaceful Uses of Outer Space [COPUOS] and its Subcommittees, U.N. OFF. OF OUTER SPACE AFFAIRS, http://www.unoosa.org/oosa/en/ourwork/copuos/comm-subcomms.html.

Committee on the Peaceful Uses of Outer Space [*COPUOS*] *History*, U.N. OFF. OF OUTER SPACE AFFAIRS, http://www.unoosa.org/oosa/en/ourwork/copuos/index.html.

Conjunction Summary Message Guide, SPACE-TRACK.ORG, https://www.space-track.org/documents/CSM_Guide.pdf.

Council of the EU Press Release Council Adopts Position on €14.8 Billion EU Space Programme for 2021–2027, COUNCIL OF THE EU (Apr. 19, 2021), https://www.consilium.europa.eu/en/press/press-releases/2021/04/19/council-adopts-position-on-14-8-billion-eu-space-programme-for-2021-2027.

Curtis E. Lemay Center, *Space Situational Awareness*, https://www.doctrine.af.mil/Portals/61/documents/Annex_3-14/3-14-D04-SPACE-SSA.pdf (last updated Aug. 27, 2018).

David, Leonard. *China's Chang'e 5 Moon Samples are Headed to the Lab*, SPACE.COM https://www.space.com/china-chang-e-5-moon-samples-lab.

David, Leonard. *Ugly Truth of Space Junk: Orbital Debris Problem to Triple by 2030*, SPACE.COM, https://www.space.com/11607-space-junk-rising-orbital-debris-levels-2030.html.

DMSP—Block 5D-3 Spacecraft Overview, SPACEFLIGHT101.COM, http://spaceflight101.com/spacecraft/dmsp-block-5d-3/.

Draft International Code of Conduct for Outer Space Activities, EUR. SPACE AGENCY (Mar. 31, 2014), https://eeas.europa.eu/sites/default/files/space_code_conduct_draft_vers_31-march-2014_en.pdf.

ECSS-P-003 Standardization Objectives, Policies and Organization, EUR. COOP. SPACE STANDARDIZATION (Mar. 22, 2013), https://ecss.nl/standard/ecss-p-00c-standardization-objectives-policies-and-organization-22march2013.

Eduardo Amaldi, EUR. SPACE AGENCY, https://www.esa.int/About_Us/ESA_history/Edoardo_Amaldi.

Ephemeris, WIKIPEDIA, https://en.wikipedia.org/wiki/Ephemeris.

Environmental Protection Law of the People's Republic of China, CHINA.ORG.CN, http://www.china.org.cn/english/environment/34356.htm.

ESA Budget 2021, EUR. SPACE AGENCY NEWSROOM (Jan. 14, 2021), https://www.esa.int/Newsroom/ESA_budget_2021.

ESA Convention, EUR. SPACE AGENCY, https://esamultimedia.esa.int/multimedia/publications/SP-1337/SP-1337_EN.pdf.

ESA Member States, Canada, Latvia and Slovenia, EUR. SPACE AGENCY, https://www.esa.int/Education/ESA_Member_States_Canada_Latvia_and_Slovenia.

Ethiopia Celebrates Launch of First Satellite, PHYS.ORG (Dec. 20, 2019), https://phys.org/news/2019-12-ethiopia-celebrates-satellite.html.

Ethiopia Competitiveness Rank, TRADING ECONOMICS, https://tradingeconomics.com/ethiopia/competitiveness-rank.

Ethiopia in Space, GLOBALSECURITY.ORG, https://www.globalsecurity.org/space/world/ethiopia/index.html.

Ethiopia, THE WORLD BANK DATA, https://data.worldbank.org/country/ET.

Erwin, Sandra. *Pentagon Report: China's Space Program "Continues to Mature Rapidly"*, SPACE NEWS (Aug. 20, 2018), https://spacenews.com/pentagon-report-chinas-space-program-continues-to-mature-rapidly.

Erwin, Sandra. *U.S. Space Command Eager to Hand Over Space Traffic Duties to Commerce Department*, SPACE NEWS (Nov. 17, 2019), https://spacenews.com/u-s-space-command-eager-to-hand-over-space-traffic-duties-to-commerce-department.

European Commission, EUR. UNION, https://europa.eu/european-union/about-eu/institutions-bodies/european-commission_en.

European Space Agency: History and Recent Missions, MASTERCLASS (May 5, 2021), https://www.masterclass.com/articles/european-space-agency#a-brief-history-of-the-european-space-agency.

Europe Signs $102M Deal to Bring Space Trash Home, PBS NEWS HOUR (Nov. 26, 2020), https://www.pbs.org/newshour/world/europe-signs-102m-deal-to-bring-space-trash-home.

Express Web Desk, *What is Mission Shakti—ASAT?*, THE INDIAN EXPRESS, (Mar. 27, 2019, 3:44 PM), https://indianexpress.com/article/what-is/mission-shakti-asat-missile-5645166.

Fact Sheet #1, UNITED NATIONS, 2011 Treaty Event Towards Universal Participation and Implementation, https://treaties.un.org/doc/source/events/2011/Press_kit/fact_sheet_1_english.pdf.

Fact Sheet—Commercial Space Transportation Activities, FED. AVIATION ADMIN. (June 19, 2020), https://www.faa.gov/news/fact_sheets/news_story.cfm?newsId=19074.

Fact Sheet: Presidential Directive on National Space Policy, THE WHITE HOUSE, OFF. OF THE PRESS SEC'Y 4 (Feb. 11, 1988), https://aerospace.org/sites/default/files/policy_archives/National%20Space%20Policy%20Feb88.pdf.

Fact Sheet: Presidential Directive on National Space Policy, THE WHITE HOUSE, OFF. OF THE PRESS SEC'Y 4 (Nov. 16, 1989), https://aerospace.csis.org/wp-content/uploads/2019/02/NSPD-1-Bush-I-National-Space-Policy.pdf.

Fact Sheet: National Space Policy, THE WHITE HOUSE, NAT'L SCI. & TECH. COUNCIL 12 (Sept. 19, 1996), https://aerospace.org/sites/default/files/policy_archives/National%20Space%20Policy%20Sep96.pdf.

Failure Mode and Effect Analysis (FMEA) and Failure Modes, Effects and Criticality Analysis (FMECA), WEIBULL.COM, https://www.weibull.com/basics/fmea.htm.

FCC Updates Satellite Orbital Debris Mitigation Rules, FC NEWS FROM THE F.C.C. (Apr. 23, 2020), https://docs.fcc.gov/public/attachments/DOC-363947A1.pdf.

Flight Assurance Procedure P-302-720, Performing a Failure Mode and Effects Analysis, The Elsmar Cove Mission, https://elsmar.com/pdf_files/FMEA%20Examples/FMEA_Nasa_spacecraft.pdf.

Foust, Jeff. *Advocates Promote Planetary Defense Mission Ahead of ESA Ministerial*, Space News (Nov. 18, 2019), https://spacenews.com/advocates-promote-planetary-defense-mission-ahead-of-esa-ministerial.

Foust, Jeff. *ESA Awards Contracts for Moon and Mars Exploration*, Space News (Oct. 15, 2020), https://spacenews.com/esa-awards-contracts-for-moon-and-mars-exploration.

Foust, Jeff. *ESA Declares Success at Ministerial Meeting*, Space News (Nov. 28, 2019), https://spacenews.com/esa-declares-success-at-ministerial-meeting.

Foust, Jeff. *Incentives and Requirements may be Needed to Enhance Space Sustainability*, Space News (Sept. 20, 2019), https://spacenews.com/incentives-and-requirements-may-be-needed-to-enhance-space-sustainability.

Foust, Jeff. *NASA Receives more than $19.6 Billion in 2017 Omnibus Spending Bill*, Space News (May 1, 2017), https://spacenews.com/nasa-receives-more-than-19-6-billion-in-2017-omnibus-spending-bill.

Foust, Jeff. *Orbital Debris Mitigation Guidelines Still Useful, if Complied with*, Space News (Jan. 15, 2020), https://spacenews.com/orbital-debris-mitigation-guidelines-still-useful-if-complied-with.

Foust, Jeff. *U.S. Government Updates Orbital Debris Mitigation Guidelines*, Space News (Dec. 9, 2019), https://spacenews.com/u-s-government-updates-orbital-debris-mitigation-guidelines.

Foust, Jeff. *Will We Hit the Snooze Button on an Orbital Debris Wakeup Call?*, The Space Rev. (Feb. 17, 2020), https://www.thespacereview.com/article/3885/1.

Fragmentation of Fregat Upper Stage Debris, Orbital Debris Q. News (Apr. 2016), https://orbitaldebris.jsc.nasa.gov/quarterly-news/pdfs/odqnv20i1-2.pdf.

Frequently Asked Questions: Orbital Debris, NASA Orbital Debris Program Off., https://orbitaldebris.jsc.nasa.gov/faq.

Full Text of White Paper on China's Space Activities in 2016, English.gov.cn (last updated Dec. 28, 2016), http://english.www.gov.cn/archive/white_paper/2016/12/28/content_281475527159496.htm.

Full Text of White Paper on China's Space Activities in 2021, English.gov.cn (last updated Jan. 28, 2022), http://english.www.gov.cn/archive/whitepaper/202201/28/content_WS61f35b3dc6d09c94e48a467a.html.

Functions and Powers of the NPC, The Nat'l People's Cong. for the People's Republic of China, http://www.npc.gov.cn/englishnpc/c2846/201903/b149298c33b24f1e8aaa7b8b0e45fa77.shtml.

Functions and Powers of the Standing Committee, THE NAT'L PEOPLE'S CONG. FOR THE PEOPLE'S REPUBLIC OF CHINA, http://www.npc.gov.cn/englishnpc/c2847/201903/bcc988763e4140d298515047a9c1549a.shtml.

Garman, Liam. *EOS Unveils New Space Debris Threat Mitigation Laser*, SPACE CONNECT (Apr. 9, 2021), https://www.spaceconnectonline.com.au/operations/4828-eos-unveils-new-space-debris-threat-mitigation-laser.

General Overview, EUR. SPACE AGENCY, https://www.esa.int/About_Us/Plan_for_European_Cooperating_States/General_overview.

GEO vs LEO—Quick Facts, AVANT, https://www.avantiplc.com/wp-content/uploads/2020/09/GEO-vs-LEO_Quick-Facts_Avanti-Communications.pdf.

Gohd, Chelsea. *Russian Anti-Satellite Test a "Dangerous and Irresponsible" Act that Threatens Astronauts, US Says*, SPACE.COM (Nov. 15, 2021), https://www.space.com/russia-asat-test-space-debris-dangerous-irresponsible.

Government Space Budgets: Russian Government Space Budget, THE SPACE REP. ONLINE, https://www.thespacereport.org/?taxonomy=topic&term=russian-government-space-budget.

Grant, Andrew. *The Scientific Exodus from Nazi Germany*, PHYSICS TODAY (Sept. 26, 2018), https://physicstoday.scitation.org/do/10.1063/PT.6.4.20180926a.

Grush, Loren. *An Out-of-Control Rocket May Have Dumped Debris in Africa After Falling from Space*, THE VERGE (May 13, 2020, 9:28 PM), https://www.theverge.com/2020/5/13/21256484/china-rocket-debris-africa-uncontrolled-reentry-long-march-5b.

Grush, Loren. *More than 50 Pieces of Debris Remain in Space after India Destroyed its own Satellite in March*, THE VERGE (Aug. 8, 2019, 1:27 PM), https://www.theverge.com/2019/8/8/20754816/india-asat-test-mission-shakti-space-debris-tracking-air-force.

Gruss, Mike. *Pentagon Says 2013 Chinese Launch May Have Tested Antisatellite Technology*, SPACE NEWS (May 14, 2015), https://spacenews.com/pentagon-says-2013-chinese-launch-may-have-tested-antisatellite-technology.

Guidelines and Assessment Procedures for Limiting Orbital Debris, NASA OFF. OF SAFETY AND MISSION ASSURANCE (Aug. 1995), https://ntrs.nasa.gov/archive/nasa/casi.ntrs.nasa.gov/19960020946.pdf.

Guruparan, Kumaravadivel & Jennifer Zerk. *Influence of Soft Law Grows in International Governance*, CHATHAM HOUSE (June 17, 2021), https://www.chathamhouse.org/2021/06/influence-soft-law-grows-international-governance.

Handl, Gunther. *Declaration of the United Nations Conferences on the Human Environment & Rio Declaration on Environment and Development*, AUDIOVISUAL LIBRARY OF INT'L L. https://legal.un.org/avl/ha/dunche/dunche.html.

Harford, Sarah. *4 Key Elements of the EU's New Space Strategy*, SILICON REPUBLIC (Jan. 13, 2021), https://www.siliconrepublic.com/innovation/eu-space-strategy-2021.

Hersh, Melissa S. & Ajey Lele. *A Code of Conduct for Space*, THE DIPLOMAT (Feb. 17, 2014), https://thediplomat.com/2014/02/a-code-of-conduct-for-space.

History and Timeline of the ISS, ISS Nat'l Lab'y, Ctr. for the Advancement of Sci. in Space, https://www.issnationallab.org/about/iss-timeline.

History, Int'l Telecomm. Union, https://www.itu.int/en/about/Pages/history.aspx#:~:text=ITU%20was%20founded%20in%20Paris,agency%20of%20the%20United%20Nations.

History of Europe in Space, Eur. Space Agency, https://www.esa.int/About_Us/ESA_history/History_of_Europe_in_space.

History of the United Nations, U.N., https://www.un.org/en/sections/history/history-united-nations (last accessed Feb. 17, 2020).

Hitchens, Theresa. *NRL's LARADO Project Hopes to Track Tiny Space Debris*, Breaking Def. (Apr. 18, 2019, 4:26 PM), https://breakingdefense.com/2019/04/nrls-larado-project-hopes-to-track-tiny-space-debris.

Hitchens, Theresa. *NSC Memo May Spell End of National Space Council*, Breaking Def. (Feb. 5, 2020, 12:11 PM), https://breakingdefense.com/2021/02/nsc-memo-may-spell-end-of-national-space-council.

Hitchens, Theresa. *Satellite Firms Debate New Commerce Space Safety Rules*, Breaking Def. (Apr. 26, 2019, 2:24 PM), https://breakingdefense.com/2019/04/satellite-firms-debate-new-commerce-space-safety-rules.

Hitchens, Theresa. *SPACECOM to Write New Ops War Plan: 100km and Up*, Breaking Def. (Sept. 16, 2019, 11:23 AM), https://breakingdefense.com/2019/09/spacecom-to-write-new-ops-war-plan-100km-and-up.

Hitchens, Theresa. *US Should Push New Space Treaty: Atlantic Council*, Breaking Def. (Apr. 12, 2021, 4:13 PM), https://breakingdefense.com/2021/04/us-should-push-new-space-treaty-atlantic-council.

Hodgkins, Kelly. *Space Force: U.S. Government's $1.5 Billion Space Fence Is Now Operational*, iDrop News (Mar. 30, 2020), https://www.idropnews.com/news/fast-tech/space-force-u-s-governments-1-5-billion-space-fence-is-now-operational/132471.

Howell, Elizabeth. *European Space Agency: Facts & Information*, Space.com https://www.space.com/22562-european-space-agency.html.

Howell, Elizabeth. *Explorer 1: The First U.S. Satellite*, Space.com (Aug. 11, 2017), http://www.space.com/17825-explorer-1.html.

How Far do Tectonic Plates Move Each Year?, Reference (Mar. 27, 2020), https://www.reference.com/science/far-tectonic-plates-move-year-822add27f707b0cf.

Hsu, Jeremy. *Solar Sails Could Clean Up Space Junk*, Space.com (Apr. 28, 2010), https://www.space.com/8296-solar-sails-clean-space-junk.html.

Info. Off. of the State Council of the People's Republic of China. *Environmental Protection in China*, Permanent Mission of the People's Republic of China to the U.N. Off. at Geneva and Other Int'l Orgs. in Switz. (June 1996), https://www.mfa.gov.cn/ce/cegv//eng/bjzl/t176940.htm.

Insinna, Valerie. *With Biden's "Full Support," the Space Force is Officially Here to Stay*, DEF. NEWS (Feb. 3, 2021), https://www.defensenews.com/space/2021/02/03/with-the-full-support-of-the-biden-adminisration-the-space-force-is-officially-here-to-stay.

In Situ Measurements, ORBITAL DEBRIS PROGRAM OFF., https://orbitaldebris.jsc.nasa.gov/measurements/in-situ.html.

Interim Measures on the Administration of Permits for Civil Space Launch Projects, LAWS OF THE PEOPLE'S REPUBLIC OF CHINA (Nov. 21, 2002), http://www.asianlii.org/cn/legis/cen/laws/imotaopfcslp771.

International Agreements, U.S. DEP'T OF HEALTH & HUMAN SERVS., SCI. SAFETY SEC., https://www.phe.gov/s3/law/Pages/International.aspx.

International Law, ENCYCLOPEDIA BRITANNICA, https://www.britannica.com/topic/international-law/Historical-development.

International Legal Agreements Relevant to Space Weapons, UNION OF CONCERNED SCIENTISTS (Feb. 11, 2004), https://www.ucsusa.org/resources/legal-agreements-space-weapons.

International Organizations (IGOs), HARV. L. SCH., https://hls.harvard.edu/dept/opia/what-is-public-interest-law/public-service-practice-settings/public-international-law/intergovernmental-organizations-igos.

Int'l Space Activities. *Launching Countries,* SPACEPOLICYONLINE.COM (Dec 9, 2020, 5:22 PM), https://spacepolicyonline.com/topics/international-space-activities.

Is MEO Poised for New Growth as Satellite Market Shifts?, KRATOS, https://www.kratosdefense.com/constellations-podcast/articles/is-meo-poised-for-new-growth-as-satellite-market-shifts.

Johnston, Robert. *High-Altitude Nuclear Explosions* (last updated Jan. 28, 2009), http://www.johnstonsarchive.net/nuclear/hane.html.

Kang, Inkoo. *The Future of Global Space Governance for the New Commercial Era*, ATL. COUNCIL (June 4, 2021), https://www.atlanticcouncil.org/blogs/geotech-cues/global-space-governance-in-the-commercial-era.

Karash, Yuri. *Russian Space Program: Financial State, Current Plans, Ambitions and Cooperation with the United States*, THE SPACE CONG. PROCS. (May 26, 2016, 6:00 PM), https://commons.erau.edu/cgi/viewcontent.cgi?article=3648&context=space-congress-proceedings.

Kazmierczak, Jeanette. *X-Ray Satellite XMM-Newton Celebrates 20 Years in Space*, NASA (Dec. 10, 2019), https://www.nasa.gov/feature/goddard/2019/x-ray-satellite-xmm-newton-celebrates-20-years-in-space.

Keck, Zachary. *China Secretly Tested an Anti-Satellite Missile*, THE DIPLOMAT (Mar. 19, 2014), https://thediplomat.com/2014/03/china-secretly-tested-an-anti-satellite-missile.

Kennedy, Brian & Mark Strauss. *Many in U.S. Have Confidence in What Private Space Companies Will Accomplish*, PEW RSCH. CTR. (June 22, 2018), https://www.pewresearch.org/fact-tank/2018/06/22/many-in-u-s-have-confidence-in-what-private-space-companies-will-accomplish.

Key Dates 1960–2018, EUR. SPACE AGENCY, https://www.esa.int/About_Us/ESA_history/Key_dates_1960-2018.

Kidwai, Saman Ayesha. *Tracing Strategy in China's Militarization of Space—Analysis*, EURASIA REV. (Feb. 28, 2020), https://www.eurasiareview.com/28022020-tracing-strategy-in-chinas-militarization-of-space-analysis.

Kimball, Daryl. *The Outer Space Treaty at a Glance, Fact Sheets & Briefs*, ARMS CONTROL ASS'N (last updated Oct. 2020), https://www.armscontrol.org/factsheets/outerspace#:~:text=UN%20Resolution%201962%20set%20out,General%20Assembly%20in%20June%201966.

Konstantin E. Tsiolkovsky, NASA (Sept. 22, 2010), https://www.nasa.gov/audience/foreducators/rocketry/home/konstantin-tsiolkovsky.html.

Kramer, Leslie. *What is GDP and Why is it So Important to Economists and Investors?*, INVESTOPEDIA (Dec. 2, 2019), https://www.investopedia.com/ask/answers/what-is-gdp-why-its-important-to-economists-investors.

Krebs, Gunter D. *West Ford Needles*, GUNTER'S SPACE PAGE, https://space.skyrocket.de/doc_sdat/westford.htm (last accessed Dec. 7, 2021).

L5 News: UN Moon Treaty Falling to US Opposition Groups, NAT'L SPACE SOC'Y (Mar. 1982), https://space.nss.org/l5-news-un-moon-treaty-falling-to-us-opposition-groups.

Lag, Steinar. *Mega-Constellation Satellites on the Horizon*, DNV, https://www.dnv.com/to2030/technology/mega-constellation-satellites-on-the-horizon.html.

Laskai, Lorand. *Civil Military Fusion and the PLA's Pursuit of Dominance in Emerging Technologies*, CHINA BRIEF (Apr. 9, 2018), https://jamestown.org/program/civil-military-fusion-and-the-plas-pursuit-of-dominance-in-emerging-technologies.

Launch or Reentry Vehicles, FED. AVIATION ADMIN. (last updated June 27, 2016), https://www.faa.gov/about/office_org/headquarters_offices/ast/licenses_permits/launch_reentry.

Launch Site, EUR. SPACE AGENCY, https://www.esa.int/Applications/Telecommunications_Integrated_Applications/Hylas/Launch_site#:~:text=Hylas%2D1%20was%20launched%20from,which%20to%20launch%20its%20satellites.

Lederer, S. M., et al. *NASA's Optical Program on Ascension Island: Bringing MCAT to Life as the Eugene Stansbury-Meter Class Autonomous Telescope (ES-MCAT)*, NASA ORBITAL DEBRIS PROGRAM OFF., https://ntrs.nasa.gov/archive/nasa/casi.ntrs.nasa.gov/20170008560.pdf.

Lew, Su-Yin. *Rules Needed to Stop Arms Race in Space*, AUSTL. STRATEGIC POL'Y INST. (Jan. 23, 2020), https://www.aspistrategist.org.au/rules-needed-to-stop-arms-race-in-space.

Lex Generalis, Oxford Reference, https://www.oxfordreference.com/view/10.1093/acref/9780195369380.001.0001/acref-9780195369380-e-1243?rskey=OB8GGU&result=7.

Lex Specialis Law and Legal Definition, USLegal, https://definitions.uslegal.com/l/lex-specialis.

Listner, Michael. *The International Code of Conduct: Comments on Changes in the Latest Draft and Post-Mortem Thoughts*, Space Rev. (Oct. 26, 2015), https://www.thespacereview.com/article/2851/1.

Listner, Michael. *The Moon Treaty: Failed International Law or Waiting in the Shadows?*, The Space Rev. (Oct. 24, 2011), https://www.thespacereview.com/article/1954/1.

Long, Wei. *China Celebrates 30th Anniversary of First Satellite Launch*, Space Daily (Apr. 25, 2000), https://www.spacedaily.com/news/china-00u.html.

Lyons, Kim. *China's Chang'e 5 Completes Docking Mission on Its Way Back to Earth*, The Verge (Dec. 5, 2020, 5:54 PM), https://www.theverge.com/2020/12/5/22156311/china-change-5-docking-mission-moon-lunar-samples.

Major Problems Facing Ethiopia Today, Africa w, https://www.africaw.com/major-problems-facing-ethiopia-today.

Mansfield, Bill. *Law of the Seas*, Te Ara (June 12, 2006), http://www.teara.govt.nz/en/law-of-the-sea/page-1.

Mao Tse-tung, Biography (last updated Sept. 1, 2020), https://www.biography.com/political-figure/mao-tse-tung.

Marcus Tullius Cicero, History.com (Dec. 16, 2009, last updated June 10, 2019), https://www.history.com/topics/ancient-history/marcus-tullius-cicero.

Mars Express (ESA), NASA, https://mars.nasa.gov/mars-exploration/missions/express.

Matignon, Louis de Gouyon. *Marine Pollution Caused by Space Debris*, Space Legal Issues (Jan. 29, 2020), https://www.spacelegalissues.com/marine-pollution-caused-by-space-debris.

Matignon, Louis de Gouyon. *Orbital Slots and Space Congestion*, Space Legal Issues (June 8, 2019), https://www.spacelegalissues.com/orbital-slots-and-space-congestion.

Matignon, Louis de Gouyon. *Parking Orbit and Graveyard Orbit*, Space Legal Issues (May 7, 2019), https://www.spacelegalissues.com/parking-orbit-and-graveyard-orbit.

Matignon, Louis de Gouyon. *Sputnik and the Birth of Space Law*, Space Legal Issues (Jan. 16, 2019), https://www.spacelegalissues.com/space-law-sputnik-and-the-birth-of-space-law.

Matignon, Louis de Gouyon. *The First European Satellites*, Space Legal Issues (June 1, 2019), https://www.spacelegalissues.com/the-first-european-satellites.

Matignon, Louis de Gouyon. *The Future Space Legal Issues*, Space Legal Issues (Sept. 24, 2019), https://www.spacelegalissues.com/the-future-space-legal-issues.

Matney, Mark. *Measuring Small Debris—What You Can't See Can Hurt You*, NASA Orbital Debris Program Off., https://ntrs.nasa.gov/archive/nasa/casi.ntrs.nasa.gov/20160011226.pdf.

May, Christopher R. *Triggers and Effects of an Active Debris Removal Market*, Ctr. for Space & Strategy, Game Changer (Jan. 2021), https://aerospace.org/sites/default/files/2021-01/adr%20paper.pdf.

McFallen-Johnsen, Morgan. *A Spacecraft That Could Grab Dead Satellites with Magnets Is About to Test a New Way to Clean up Space Junk*, Bus. Insider (Mar. 23, 2021, 9:28 am), https://www.businessinsider.com/astroscale-mission-to-clean-up-space-junk-magnets-2021-3.

McKinnon, Mika. *A History of Garbage in Space*, Gizmodo (May 7, 2014, 7:00 pm), http://space.gizmodo.com/a-history-of-garbage-in-space-1572783046.

Medium Earth Orbit Satellites, Capacity (Dec. 31, 2010, 7:00 pm), https://www.capacitymedia.com/article/29ot47zfua7b7uq4z7g1s/news/medium-earth-orbit-satellites.

Meet the People: Yang Liwei, Encyclopedia Britannica, https://www.britannica.com/explore/space/yang-liwei.

Member Agencies, Inter-Agency Space Debris Coordination Comm., https://www.iadc-home.org.

Member States & Cooperating States, Eur. Space Agency, https://www.esa.int/About_Us/Corporate_news/Member_States_Cooperating_States.

Memorandum on National Space Traffic Management Policy, Daily Comp. Pres. Doc. (June 18, 2018), https://www.govinfo.gov/content/pkg/DCPD-201800430/pdf/DCPD-201800430.pdf.

Meyer, Paul. *Star-Crossed: An International Code of Conduct for Outer Space?*, Open Can. (Aug. 31, 2015), https://opencanada.org/star-crossed-an-international-code-of-conduct-for-outer-space.

Mgaloblishvili, Anastasia. *Russian Interference in Georgia's Elections. How Will the Government Respond*, New E. Eur. (Sept. 28, 2020), https://neweasterneurope.eu/2020/09/28/russian-interference-in-georgias-elections-how-will-the-government-respond.

MIDAS 6, NASA Space Sci. Data Coordinated Archive, https://nssdc.gsfc.nasa.gov/nmc/spacecraft/display.action?id=1963-014A.

Minet, Mathilde. *Understanding the Wolf Agreement*, Space Legal Issues (Oct. 25, 2020), https://www.spacelegalissues.com/understanding-the-wolf-agreement.

Mitigating Space Debris Generation, Eur. Space Agency, https://www.esa.int/Safety_Security/Space_Debris/Mitigating_space_debris_generation.

Mitigation of Orbital Debris in the New Space Age, Fact Sheet, F.C.C. (Apr. 2, 2020), https://docs.fcc.gov/public/attachments/DOC-363486A1.pdf.

Monzon, Inigo. *Did A Russian Spy Satellite Break Apart In Orbit?*, INT'L BUS. TIMES (Jan. 14, 2020, 8:52 PM), https://www.ibtimes.com/did-russian-spy-satellite-break-apart-orbit-2902562.

NASA. *Orbital Debris Management and Risk Mitigation*, https://www.nasa.gov/pdf/692076main_Orbital_Debris_Management_and_Risk_Mitigation.pdf.

NASA. ORBITAL DEBRIS Q. NEWS, 1–4 (Apr. 2016), https://orbitaldebris.jsc.nasa.gov/quarterly-news/pdfs/odqnv20i1-2.pdf.

NASA. *Satellite Collision Leaves Significant Debris Cloud*, ORBITAL DEBRIS Q. NEWS (Apr. 2009), https://orbitaldebris.jsc.nasa.gov/quarterly-news/pdfs/odqnv13i2.pdf.

NASA Technical Standard, Process for Limiting Orbital Debris, NASA (Nov. 5, 2021), https://standards.nasa.gov/standard/nasa/nasa-std-871914.

Nasca, R. *Space Debris Mitigation Compliance to ESA*, EURO. SPACE AGENCY (Mar. 20, 2019), https://conference.sdo.esoc.esa.int/proceedings/ecsl19/paper/8/ECSL19-paper8.pdf.

Nat'l Audubon Soc'y. *The Migratory Bird Treaty Act, Explained*, AUDUBON (Jan. 26, 2018), https://www.audubon.org/news/the-migratory-bird-treaty-act-explained.

National Space Policy of the United States of America, THE WHITE HOUSE (June 28, 2010), https://obamawhitehouse.archives.gov/sites/default/files/national_space_policy_6-28-10.pdf.

National Space Transportation Policy, THE WHITE HOUSE (Nov. 21, 2013), https://obamawhitehouse.archives.gov/sites/default/files/microsites/ostp/national_space_transportation_policy_11212013.pdf.

Newman, Christopher. *Artemis Accords: Why Many Countries are Refusing to Sign Moon Exploration Agreement*, THE CONVERSATION (Oct. 19, 2020, 7:45 AM), https://theconversation.com/artemis-accords-why-many-countries-are-refusing-to-sign-moon-exploration-agreement-148134.

Northern Expedition, ENCYCLOPEDIA BRITANNICA (last updated Dec. 29, 2020), https://www.britannica.com/place/China/The-Northern-Expedition.

NSS 1740.14, NASA Safety Standard: Guidelines and Assessments for Limiting Orbital Debris (Aug 1995), EVERY SPEC, http://everyspec.com/NASA/NASA-NSS-PUBS/NSS_1740--14_2276/.

One ESA, EUR. SPACE AGENCY, https://esamultimedia.esa.int/docs/corporate/One-ESA_brochure.pdf.

Overpressure, WIKIPEDIA, https://en.wikipedia.org/wiki/Overpressure.

Pedroncelli, Peter. *10 African Countries Which Have Launched Satellites Into Space*, THE MOGULDOM NATION (Jun. 20, 2019), https://moguldom.com/207725/10-african-countries-which-have-launched-satellites-into-space.

Petersen, Carolyn Collins. *A Short History of Roscosmos and the Soviet Space Program*, THOUGHTCO (July 3, 2019), https://www.thoughtco.com/soviet-space-program-history-4140631.

Petersen, Carolyn Collins. *The History of the European Space Agency*, ThoughtCo (last updated May 28, 2018), https://www.thoughtco.com/european-space-agency-4164062.

Phipps, Claude. *Clearing Space Debris with Lasers*, SPIE (Jan. 20, 2012), https://spie.org/news/4076-clearing-space-debris-with-lasers?SSO=1.

Pierre Auger, Eur. Space Agency, https://www.esa.int/About_Us/ESA_history/Pierre_Auger.

Pickrell, Ryan. *The U.S. Has Been Getting "It's Ass Handed To It" in War Games Simulating Fights Against Russia and China*, Bus. Insider (Mar. 8, 2019, 10:26 AM), https://www.businessinsider.com/the-us-apparently-gets-its-ass-handed-to-it-in-war-games-2019-3.

Pinholster, Ginger. *Solar-Propelled Invention Design to Clean Up Space Trash*, Embry Riddle Aeronautical Univ. (June 17, 2021, 8:34 AM), https://news.erau.edu/headlines/solar-propelled-invention-designed-to-clean-up-space-trash.

Pollpeter, Kevin. *China's Space Robotic Arm Programs*, SITC Bull. Analysis (Oct. 2013), https://escholarship.org/content/qt2js0c5r8/qt2js0c5r8_noSplash_308ba05cdedfb90ab23d648da59e3bb6.pdf.

PRC Standards System: Standards Used in China, Am. Nat'l Standards Inst., https://www.standardsportal.org/usa_en/prc_standards_system/standards_used_in_china.aspx.

Presidential Statement in his Address to the Nation, The White House (Sept. 11, 2001, 8:30 PM), http://georgewbush-whitehouse.archives.gov/news/releases/2001/09/20010911-16.html.

President Trump Reestablishes National Space Council, Space News (June 30, 2017), https://spacenews.com/breaking-president-trump-reestablishes-national-space-council.

Prisoner's Dilemma, CFI (last updated Feb. 25, 2022), https://corporatefinanceinstitute.com/resources/knowledge/other/prisoners-dilemma.

Prof. Dr. Reimar Lust was the Third Director General of ESA, ESA Corporate News, https://www.esa.int/About_Us/Corporate_news/Reimar_Luest.

Programme for Associate Member States, Eur. Space Agency, https://www.esa.int/About_Us/Business_with_ESA/Programme_for_Associate_Member_States.

Project West Ford, NASA Space Sci. Data Coordinated Archive, https://nssdc.gsfc.nasa.gov/nmc/experiment/display.action?id=1961-028A-03.

Pruitt, Sarah. *China Makes Historic Landing on 'Dark Side' of the Moon*, Hist. (Jan. 3, 2019), https://www.history.com/news/china-plans-historic-landing-on-dark-side-of-the-moon.

Pultarova, Tereza. *Space Debris from Russian Anti-Satellite Test will be a Safety Threat for Years*, Space.com (Nov. 16, 2021), https://www.space.com/russia-anti-satellite-test-space-debris-threat-for-years.

Pultarova, Tereza. *This Space Junk Removal Experiment Will Harpoon & Net Debris in Orbit*, SPACE.COM (Apr. 6, 2018), https://www.space.com/40221-space-junk-debris-sweeper-experiment.html.

Pultarova, Tereza. *Watch a Satellite Fire a Harpoon in Space in Wild Debris-Catching Test (Video)*, SPACE.COM (Feb. 18, 2019), https://www.space.com/space-junk-harpoon-removedebris-satellite-video.html.

Radarsat-1, WIKIPEDIA, https://en.wikipedia.org/wiki/Radarsat-1 (last updated Apr. 4, 2020).

Rajagopalan, Rajeswari Pillai. *Keep Space Code of Conduct Moving Forward*, SPACE NEWS (July 21, 2015), https://spacenews.com/op-ed-keep-space-code-of-conduct-moving-forward.

Recent NOAA-16 Satellite Breakup, ORBITAL DEBRIS Q. NEWS (Apr. 2016), https://orbitaldebris.jsc.nasa.gov/quarterly-news/pdfs/odqnv20i1-2.pdf.

Recommendation ITU-R S.1003, Environmental Protection of the Geostationary-Satellite Orbit, INT'L TELECOMM. UNION (Dec. 2010), https://www.itu.int/rec/R-REC-S.1003/en.

Remarks on Signing a Memorandum on National Space Traffic Management Policy, DAILY COMP. PRES. DOC. (June 18, 2018), https://www.govinfo.gov/content/pkg/DCPD-201800430/pdf/DCPD-201800430.pdf.

RemoveDebris Mission, SHARING EARTH OBSERVATION RESS., https://directory.eoportal.org/web/eoportal/satellite-missions/r/removedebris.

Resumption of Fighting, ENCYCLOPEDIA BRITANNICA (last updated Dec. 29, 2020), https://www.britannica.com/place/China/Resumption-of-fighting.

Riebeek, Holli. *Catalog of Earth Satellite Orbits*, NASA EARTH OBSERVATORY (Sept. 4, 2009), http://earthobservatory.nasa.gov/Features/OrbitsCatalog.

Robbins, Steve. *The Tragedy of the Commons Explained*, STEVE ROBBINS, INC., https://www.steverrobbins.com/articles/tragedyofthecommons.

Rocket Lab Receives an Astroscale Contract to Launch the ADRAS-J Smallsat, SATNEWS (Sept. 22, 2021), https://news.satnews.com/2021/09/22/rocket-lab-receives-an-astroscale-contract-to-launch-the-adras-j-smallsat.

Russia Adopts Major Amendments to its Constitution, MORGAN LEWIS & BOCKIUS LLP (July 13, 2020), https://www.lexology.com/library/detail.aspx?g=9173f461-a6e0-4b5d-9964-c2632abc2fc6.

Russia Creates Space Junk Recycling System to Turn Fuel, TASS, RUSS. NEWS AGENCY, https://tass.com/science/1050699.

Russia Doesn't Just Violate International Law—It Follows and Shapes it Too, THE CONVERSATION (Mar. 23, 2018, 10:38 AM), https://theconversation.com/russia-doesnt-just-violate-international-law-it-follows-and-shapes-it-too-92700.

Russian Federation's Constitution of 1993 with Amendments Through 2008, CONSTITUTEPROJECT.ORG (1993), https://www.constituteproject.org/constitution/Russia_2008.pdf.

Russian Revolution, Hist. (Nov. 9, 2009), https://www.history.com/topics/russia/russian-revolution.

Russian SOZ Unit Breaks Up in March, Orbital Debris Q. News (Apr. 2016), https://orbitaldebris.jsc.nasa.gov/quarterly-news/pdfs/odqnv20i1-2.pdf.

Sachs, Jeffrey D. *The High Costs of Abandoning International Law*, Boston Globe (Mar. 5, 2017), https://www.bostonglobe.com/opinion/2017/03/05/the-high-costs-abandoning-international-law/OXGzXIJP3th3Fc9EGNsXTN/story.html.

Safety: The Foundation of Everything We Do, Fed. Aviation Admin. (last updated Nov. 6, 2019), https://www.faa.gov/about/safety_efficiency.

Salter, Alexander. *Space Debris: A Law and Economics Analysis of the Orbital Commons*, Mercatus Ctr.—George Mason Univ. (Sep. 23, 2015), https://www.mercatus.org/publications/technology-and-innovation/space-debris-law-and-economics-analysis-orbital-commons.

Satellites by Countries and Organizations, N2YO.com, https://www.n2yo.com/satellites/?c=&t=country.

Savage, Neil. *Lasers Could Clear Space Junk from Orbit*, IEEE Spectrum (May 14, 2021), https://spectrum.ieee.org/laser-could-clear-space-junk-from-orbit.

Scanning and Observing, Euro. Space Agency, https://www.esa.int/Safety_Security/Space_Debris/Scanning_and_observing2.

Schumm, Laura. *What Was Operation Paperclip?*, Hist. Stories (June 2, 2014), https://www.history.com/news/what-was-operation-paperclip.

Sheetz, Michael. *How NASA is Evolving through Partnerships with Private Space Companies*, CNBC (Nov. 30, 2019), https://www.cnbc.com/2019/11/30/how-nasa-is-evolving-through-partnerships-with-private-space-companies.html.

Shukla, Ajai. *India Successfully Tests ASAT Missile, Joins Space Superpower Club*, Bus. Standard (Apr. 3, 2019), https://www.business-standard.com/article/current-affairs/india-successfully-tests-asat-missile-joins-space-superpower-club-119032800048_1.html.

Singer, Karen. *100th Space Sharing Agreement Signed, Romania Space Agency Joins*, U.S. Strategic Command (Apr. 26, 2019), https://www.stratcom.mil/Media/News/News-Article-View/Article/1825882/100th-space-sharing-agreement-signed-romania-space-agency-joins.

Sloss, David. *Domestic Application of Treaties*, Santa Clara L. Digital Commons (Apr.29,2011),https://digitalcommons.law.scu.edu/cgi/viewcontent.cgi?article=1620&context=facpubs#:~:text=Used%20in%20this%20sense%2C%20dualist,to%20give%20effect%20to%20them.

Slovenia Targets Full ESA Membership for 2024, Slovn. Times (Oct. 20, 2020), https://sloveniatimes.com/slovenia-targets-full-esa-membership-for-2024.

Smith, Marcia. *Surprise Chinese Satellite Maneuvers Mystify Western Experts*, SpacePolicyOnline.com (Aug. 19, 2013, 12:00 AM), https://spacepolicyonline.com/news/surprise-chinese-satelllite-maneuvers-mystify-western-experts.

Smith, Marcia. *U.S. Accuses China of Conducting Another ASAT Test*, SPACEPOLICYONLINE.COM (July 25, 2014, 12:00 AM), https://spacepolicyonlinc.com/news/u-s-accuses-china-of-conducting-another-asat-test.

Soft Law, USLEGAL, https://definitions.uslegal.com/s/soft-law.

Sokok, Sam. *Russian Disinformation Distorted Reality in Ukraine. Americans Should Take Note*, FOREIGN POL'Y (Aug. 2, 2019, 4:40 PM), https://foreignpolicy.com/2019/08/02/russian-disinformation-distorted-reality-in-ukraine-americans-should-take-note-putin-mueller-elections-antisemitism.

Sonkar, Sunil. *The 1916 Migratory Bird Convention*, FUNENDER.COM (Sept. 15, 2018), https://funender.com/wildlife/the-1916-migratory-bird-convention.html.

Space Agencies and Their Budgets, RADIO FREE EUR. RADIO LIBERTY (Feb. 12, 2019), https://www.rferl.org/a/space-agencies-and-their-budgets/29766044.html.

Space Debris 101, AEROSPACE, https://aerospace.org/article/space-debris-101.

Space Debris, EUR. SPACE AGENCY, https://www.esa.int/About_Us/ECSL_-_European_Centre_for_Space_Law/Space_Debris3.

Space Data Center, SPACE DATA ASS'N, https://www.space-data.org/sda/space-data-center-3.

Space Debris by the Numbers, EUR. SPACE AGENCY, https://www.esa.int/Safety_Security/Space_Debris/Space_debris_by_the_numbers (last updated July 11, 2022).

Space Debris from Anti-Satellite Test to "Vanish" in 45 Days: Defence Research Body Chief, NDTV (Mar. 28, 2019, 6:03 PM), https://www.ndtv.com/india-news/mission-shakti-space-debris-from-anti-satellite-test-to-vanish-in-45-days-defence-research-body-chie-2014301.

Space Debris: The ESA Approach, EUR. SPACE AGENCY (2017), https://download.esa.int/esoc/downloads/BR-336_Space_Debris_WEB.pdf.

Space Law Treaties and Principles, U.N. OFF. FOR OUTER SPACE AFFAIRS, http://www.unoosa.org/oosa/en/ourwork/spacelaw/treaties.html.

Space Logistics, NORTHROP GRUMMAN, https://www.northropgrumman.com/space/space-logistics-services.

Space Threat 2018: China Assessment, AEROSPACE (Apr. 12, 2018), https://aerospace.csis.org/space-threat-2018-china.

Spacey, John. *What is the Karman Line*, SIMPLICABLE (May 14, 2016), https://simplicable.com/new/karman-line.

Spiliakos, Alexandra. *Tragedy of the Commons: What it is and 5 Examples*, HARV. BUS. SCH., BUS. INSIGHTS BLOG (Feb. 6, 2019), https://online.hbs.edu/blog/post/tragedy-of-the-commons-impact-on-sustainability-issues.

Sputnik and the Dawn of the Space Age, NASA, http://history.nasa.gov/sputnik (last updated Oct. 10, 2007).

Sputnik Launched, HIST. (2009), http://www.history.com/this-day-in-history/sputnik-launched.

SSA Programme Overview, EUR. SPACE AGENCY, https://www.esa.int/Safety_Security/SSA_Programme_overview.

Standard for Performing a Failure Mode and Effects Analysis (FMEA) and Establishing a Critical Items List (CIL), NASA RAPID SPACECRAFT DEV. OFF., https://rsdo.gsfc.nasa.gov/documents/Rapid-III-Documents/MAR-Reference/GSFC-FAP-322-208-FMEA-Draft.pdf.

State Administration for Science, Technology and Industry for National Defense (SASTIND), NUCLEAR THREAT INITIATIVE (last updated July 13, 2012), https://www.nti.org/learn/facilities/781.

State Institutions, THE NAT'L PEOPLE'S CONG. FOR THE PEOPLE'S REPUBLIC OF CHINA,http://www.npc.gov.cn/englishnpc/statestructure2019/201911/fa2deebf75264effa68df01cfecfb60c.shtml.

Statement about the Karman Line, FÉDÉRATION AÉRONAUTIQUE INTERNATIONALE [INT'L AERONAUTICAL FOUND.] (Nov. 30, 2018), https://www.fai.org/news/statement-about-karman-line.

Stephens, Dale. *Military Space Operations and International Law: The Woomera Manual Project—Part 1*, JUST SECURITY (Mar. 2, 2020), https://www.justsecurity.org/68815/military-space-operations-and-international-law.

Stoyanov, Stoyan. *Why are Regimes and Regime Theory Accepted by Realists and Liberals*, E-INT'L RELS. (Aug. 17, 2012), https://www.e-ir.info/2012/08/17/why-are-regimes-and-regime-theory-accepted-by-realists-and-liberals.

Su, Jinyuan. *How Far is China from the European Code of Conduct for Outer Space Activities?*, E-INT'L RELS. (July 30, 2012), https://www.e-ir.info/2012/07/30/how-far-is-china-from-the-european-code-of-conduct-for-outer-space-activities.

Sun-synchronous orbit, THE FREE DICTIONARY, https://www.thefreedictionary.com/sun-synchronous+orbit.

Sveda, Andrew. *The U.S. Military's Achilles Heel*, OBSERVER (Sept. 23, 2019), https://ndsmcobserver.com/2019/09/the-u-s-militarys-achilles-heel.

Svetlicinii, Alexandra. *Can Russia's Constitution Be Above International Law*, CGTN (Jan 20, 2020, 7:13 PM), https://news.cgtn.com/news/2020-01-20/Can-Russia-s-Constitution-be-above-international-law--NppxZNaSTS/index.html.

Taking Out the Space Trash: Tethers Unlimited Announces Successful Operation of Space-Debris Removal Device, TETHERS UNLIMITED (Jan. 16, 2020), https://www.tethers.com/taking-out-the-space-trash-tethers-unlimited-announces-successful-operation-of-space-debris-removal-device.

Tellis, Ashley J. *India's ASAT Test: An Incomplete Success*, CARNEGIE ENDOWMENT FOR INT'L PEACE (Apr. 15, 2019), https://carnegieendowment.org/2019/04/15/india-s-asat-test-incomplete-success-pub-78884.

The Collapse of the Soviet Union, U.S. DEP'T OF STATE, OFF. OF THE HISTORIAN, https://history.state.gov/milestones/1989-1992/collapse-soviet-union.

The Federal Communications Commission, NAT'L TELECOMM. AND INFO. ADMIN., https://www.ntia.doc.gov/book-page/federal-communications-commission-fcc.

The Global War on Terrorism: The First 100 Days, U.S. DEP'T OF STATE, https://2001-2009.state.gov/s/ct/rls/wh/6947.htm.

The Nuclear Rainbow Bomb Parties of 1962, KNOWLEDGENUTS (June 16, 2014), https://knowledgenuts.com/2014/06/16/the-nuclear-rainbow-bomb-parties-of-1962.

The Outer Space Treaty, COUNCIL ON FOREIGN RELS. (Feb. 23, 2021), https://www.cfr.org/report/outer-space-treaty.

The Swiss Village that Changed Ecology—Twice, HOUSE OF SWITZ. (Mar. 28, 2018), https://houseofswitzerland.org/swissstories/environment/swiss-village-changed-ecology-twice.

This Day in History, March 9, 1918, Russian Bolshevik Party Becomes the Community Party, HIST. (Nov. 6, 2019), https://www.history.com/this-day-in-history/russian-bolshevik-party-becomes-the-communist-party.

This Day in History: October 4, HIST., https://www.history.com/this-day-in-history/sputnik-launched.

This is ESA, EUR. SPACE AGENCY, https://esamultimedia.esa.int/docs/corporate/This_is_ESA_EN_LR.pdf.

Torkelson, Ashley. *Defining the Line: Why the Department of Defense Should Reconsider United States Space Command's Area Of Responsibility*, OVER THE HORIZON: MULTI-DOMAIN OPERATIONS & STRATEGY (Jan. 30, 2020), https://othjournal.com/2020/01/30/defining-the-line-why-the-department-of-defense-should-reconsider-united-states-space-commands-area-of-responsibility.

Treaties and International Agreements, Univ. OF RICHMOND SCH. OF L., https://law-richmond.libguides.com/treaties (last updated Jun. 18, 2019, 11:57am).

Types of Orbits, Geostationary Orbit (GEO), EUR. SPACE AGENCY (Mar. 30, 2020), https://www.esa.int/Enabling_Support/Space_Transportation/Types_of_orbits#GEO.

Update: High-Risk Satellite Conjunction Passes Without Incident, SPACEFLIGHT101.COM (Jan. 7, 2017, 11:15PM), http://spaceflight101.com/close-orbital-encounter-january-7-2017.

UCS Satellite Database, UNION OF CONCERNED SCIENTISTS (last updated Jan. 1, 2022), https://www.ucsusa.org/resources/satellite-database.

UNIV. OF ARIZ. *The Trouble with Space Junk*, FLANDRAU SCI. CTR. & PLANETARIUM (Feb. 10, 2019), https://flandrau.org/news/2019/02/trouble-space-junk.

UN Resolutions, U.N. Library, http://research.un.org/en/docs/resolutions.

U.S. GDP, Google, https://www.bing.com/search?q=us+gdp&form.

U.S. Government Orbital Debris Mitigation Standard Practices, NASA ASTROMATERIALS RSCH. & EXPL. SCI., ORBITAL DEBRIS PROGRAM OFF., https://www.hsdl.org/?abstract&did=722493.

U.S. Government Orbital Debris Mitigation Standard Practices, November 2019 Update, NASA ASTROMATERIALS RSCH. & EXPL. SCI., ORBITAL DEBRIS PROGRAM OFF., https://orbitaldebris.jsc.nasa.gov/library/usg_orbital_debris_mitigation_standard_practices_november_2019.pdf.

U.S. National Space Policy, AERO SPACE, https://aerospace.org/sites/default/files/policy_archives/Natl%20Space%20Policy%20fact%20sheet%2031Aug06.pdf.

U.S. Strategic Command Fact Sheet, COMBINED SPACE OPERATIONS CTR., https://www.stratcom.mil/Portals/8/Documents/CSpOC_Factsheet_2018.pdf.

U.S Treaties & Agreements—The Process, INT'L LEGAL RES. TUTORIAL, https://law.duke.edu/ilrt/treaties_3.htm.

Vaios J. Lappas et al. *RemoveDebris: An EU Low Cost Demonstration Mission to Test ADR Technologies*, INT'L ASTRONAUTICAL CONG. (Sept. 2014), https://core.ac.uk/download/pdf/48182494.pdf.

Van Allen Radiation Belt, ENCYCLOPEDIA BRITANNICA, https://www.britannica.com/science/Van-Allen-radiation-belt.

Wall, Mike. *Don't Panic About Russia's Recent Anti-Satellite Test, Experts Say*, SPACE.COM (Apr. 30, 2020), https://www.space.com/russia-anti-satellite-weapon-fears-overblown.html.

Wall, Mike. *Trump Unveils New National Space Policy for US Leadership off the Earth*, SMALL.COM (Dec. 10, 2020), https://www.space.com/trump-unveils-national-space-policy-us-leadership.

Wang, Brian. *China's Space Budget is Nearly Triple Russia's Budget about Far Less than the USA Budget*, NEXT BIG FUTURE (July 24, 2019), https://www.nextbigfuture.com/2019/07/chinas-space-budget-is-nearly-triple-russias-budget-but-far-less-than-usa.html.

Wang, Liheng. *China Aerospace Science and Technology Corporation* (CASC), FED'N OF AM. SCIENTISTS (Sept. 8, 2020), https://fas.org/nuke/guide/china/contractor/casc.htm.

Weeden, Brian. *2009 Iridium-Cosmos Collision Fact Sheet*, SECURE WORLD FOUND., http://swfound.org/media/6575/swf_iridium_cosmos_collision_fact_sheet_updated_2012.pdf (last updated Nov. 10, 2010).

Weeden, Brian. *Anti-Satellite Tests in Space—The Case of China*, SECURE WORLD FOUND., https://swfound.org/media/115643/china_asat_testing_fact_sheet_aug_2013.pdf (last updated Aug. 16, 2013).

Weeden, Brian. *Space Situational Awareness Fact Sheet*, SECURE WORLD FOUND., https://swfound.org/media/205874/swf_ssa_fact_sheet.pdf (last updated May 2017).

Weeden, Brian. *The United States Is Losing Its Leadership Role in the Fight Against Orbital Debris*, THE SPACE REV. (Feb. 24, 2020), https://www.thespacereview.com/article/3889/1.

Weeden, Brian. *US Space Policy, Organizational Incentives, and Orbital Debris Removal*, Space Rev. (Oct. 30, 2017), https://www.thespacereview.com/article/3361/1.

What's Behind the China-Taiwan Divide?, BBC News (Sept. 28, 2020), https://www.bbc.com/news/world-asia-34729538.

What We Do, Fed. Aviation Admin., https://www.faa.gov/about/mission/activities.

What We Do, U.S. Dept. of Transp., https://www.transportation.gov/about.

White Paper on China's Space Activities in 2011, Chinese Embassy (Dec. 30, 2011), http://bg.chineseembassy.org/eng/dtxw/t891870.htm.

White Paper on China's Space Activities Published, China.org.cn (Oct. 12, 2006), http://www.china.org.cn/english/2006/Oct/183588.htm.

Wolman, Jordan. *The World is Set to Debate Seabed Mining Regulations, But the U.S. will be on the Outside Looking In*, Politico (Mar. 22, 2022, 9:58 AM), https://www.politico.com/news/2022/03/22/seabed-mining-regulations-00019005.

Wood, Danielle. *Changing How We Build Satellites Could Do More Than Reduce Space Junk*, Space.com (Jan. 24, 2019), https://www.space.com/43098-satellite-design-engineering-equity-justice.html.

Xi, Jinping. *Strengthening the Party's Leadership Over the Rule of Law in a Comprehensive Manner*, (Feb. 15, 2019), http://www.xinhuanet.com/politics/2019-02/15/c_1124120391.htm.

Zaborskiy, Victor. *Russia: From Space Programs to Space Strategy*, Space News (May 2, 2012), https://spacenews.com/russia-space-programs-space-strategy.

Zak, Anatoly. *The Russian Space Agency, Roskosmos*, RussiaSpaceWeb.com (last updated Sept. 18, 2018), http://russianspaceweb.com/roskosmos.html.

Zeese, Kevin, & Margaret Flowers. *Keeping War, Environmental Degradation and Profit Out of Space*, New Age (Feb. 16, 2020, 00:00 AM), https://www.newagebd.net/article/99667/keeping-war-environmental-degradation-and-profit-out-of-space.

Zenko, Micah. *A Code of Conduct for Outer Space*, Council on Foreign Rels. (Nov. 30, 2011), https://www.cfr.org/report/code-conduct-outer-space.

Zhu, Sirui. *China's Long March to Space*, Reuters Graphics (July 24, 2019), https://graphics.reuters.com/SPACE-EXPLORATION-MOON/0100B0BH0NZ/index.html?fbclid=IwAR1kdi84loyGvILV0vsPxaOFYTulH8Wn2L1HcUBMP2hY3jvvtO5LAa2us6g.

Magazine/Newspaper Articles

Abrams, Abigail. *Here's What we Know so Far About Russia's 2016 Meddling*, Time (Apr. 18, 2019, 8:20 AM), https://time.com/5565991/russia-influence-2016-election.

Ariane Rocket Reported to Have Exploded, N.Y. Times (Dec. 2, 1986), https://www.nytimes.com/1986/12/02/science/ariane-rocket-reported-to-have-exploded.html.

A Russian Anti-Satellite Missile Test Puts the ISS in Peril, THE ECONOMIST (Nov. 18, 2021), https://www.economist.com/science-and-technology/2021/11/18/a-russian-anti-satellite-missile-test-puts-the-iss-in-peril.

Broad, William J. & David E. Sanger, *China Tests Anti-Satellite Weapon, Unnerving U.S.*, N.Y. TIMES (Jan. 18, 2007), https://www.nytimes.com/2007/01/18/world/asia/18cnd-china.html.

Campbell, Charlie. *From Satellites to the Moon and Mars, China is Quickly Becoming a Space Superpower*, TIME (July 17, 2019), https://time.com/5623537/china-space.

Chang, Kenneth. *SpaceX Wins NASA $2.9 Billion Contract to Build Moon Lander*, N.Y. TIMES (Apr. 16, 2021), https://www.nytimes.com/2021/04/16/science/spacex-moon-nasa.html.

David, Emmanuelle. *Compliance of Rocket Upper Stages in GTO with Space Debris Mitigation Guidelines*, SPACE SAFETY MAG. (July 18, 2013), HTTP://WWW.SPACESAFETYMAGAZINE.COM/SPACE-DEBRIS/MITIGATION/COMPLIANCE-ROCKET-UPPER-STAGE-GTO-SPACE-DEBRIS-MITIGATION-GUIDELINES.

Drake, Nadia. *Where, Exactly, is the Edge of Space? It Depends on Who You Ask*, NAT'L GEOGRAPHIC (Dec. 20, 2018), https://www.nationalgeographic.com/science/2018/12/where-is-the-edge-of-space-and-what-is-the-karman-line.

Dunietz, Jesse. *Space Law Needs to Catch Up with Asteroid Mining*, SCI. AM. (Aug. 28, 2017), https://www.scientificamerican.com/article/floating-treasure-space-law-needs-to-catch-up-with-asteroid-mining.

Higgins, Andrew. *The Theatrical Method in Putin's Vote Madness*, N.Y. TIMES (July 1, 2020), https://www.nytimes.com/2020/07/01/world/europe/putin-referendum-vote-russia.html.

Hsu, Jeremy. *The U.S. Space Mission Aims to Demonstrate Technology that could Someday Held Clean up Space Junk*, SCI. AM. (Nov. 4, 2019), https://www.scientificamerican.com/article/kilometer-long-space-tether-tests-fuel-free-propulsion.

Huber, M.C.E., et al. *The History of the SOHO Mission*, ESA BULL. NR. 86 (May 1996).

Koren, Marina. *What Happens to the Space Force Now?*, THE ATL. (Jan. 26, 2021), https://www.theatlantic.com/science/archive/2021/01/space-force-trump-biden/617812.

Mayfield, Mandy. *SATELLITE 2020 NEWS: Commerce Department Tackles Space Congestion with Air Force*, NAT'L DEF. (Mar. 11, 2020), https://www.nationaldefensemagazine.org/articles/2020/3/11/commerce-department-wargaming-with-air-force-to-address-space-congestion.

Mesert, Elias. *Ethiopia's First Satellite Launch into Space by China*, ASSOCIATED PRESS NEWS (Dec. 20, 2019), https://apnews.com/37baf3f65b352e8b6480b43246ccbf77.

O'Callaghan, Jonathan. *SpaceX Declined to Move a Starlink Satellite at Risk of Collision with a European Satellite*, FORBES (Aug. 22, 2018), https://www.forbes.com/sites/jonathanocallaghan/2019/09/02/spacex-refused-to-move-a-starlink-satellite-at-risk-of-collision-with-a-european-satellite/#36e043e11f62.

Routh, Adam. *Near-Earth Space Holds Economic Value—But We Need International Space Governance*, THE HILL (Jan. 10, 2020, 8:00 AM), https://thehill.com/opinion/energy-environment/477240-near-earth-space-holds-economic-value-but-we-need-international.

Space Debris Mitigation, SPACE SAFETY MAG., http://www.spacesafetymagazine.com/space-debris/mitigation.

Wines, Michael. *Qian Xuesen, Father of China's Space Program, Dies at 98*, N.Y. TIMES (Nov. 3, 2009), https://www.nytimes.com/2009/11/04/world/asia/04qian.html#:~:text=BEIJING%20%E2%80%94%20Qian%20Xuesen%2C%20a%20brilliant,died%20on%20Saturday%20in%20Beijing.

Wischer, Gregory. *A Proposal to Counter the Greatest Space Threat*, INT'L POL'Y DIGEST (Feb. 4, 2020), https://intpolicydigest.org/2020/02/04/a-proposal-to-counter-the-greatest-space-threat.

International Agencies' Reports and Resolutions

ESA Space Debris Off. ESA's Annual Space Environment Report, May 27, 2021, https://www.sdo.esoc.esa.int/environment_report/Space_Environment_Report_latest.pdf.

ESA Space Debris Working Group, *Space Debris—The Report of the ESA Space Debris Working Group*, ESA SP-1109 (Nov. 1988).

European Code of Conduct for Space Debris Mitigation (June 28, 2004), https://www.unoosa.org/documents/pdf/spacelaw/sd/2004-B5-10.pdf.

European Space Agency, *Resolution on the Agency's Policy vis-à-vis the Space Debris Issue*, ESA/C/LXXXVII/Res. 3 (final), approved ESA/C (89)24, rev. 1.

Eur. Space Agency, Resolution on the Long-Term Space Policy Committee (1999).

Inter-Agency Space Debris Coordination Comm. [IADC], *20 Years of IADC: 51st Session of the Scientific and Technical Subcommittee* (Feb. 2014).

Inter-Agency Space Debris Coordination Comm. [IADC], *IADC Space Debris Mitigation Guidelines*, Revision 3 (2021), https://www.iadc-home.org/documents_public/file_down/id/5251.

Inter-Agency Space Debris Coordination Comm. [IADC], *Stability of the Future LEO Environment*, IADC-12-08 Revision 1 (Jan. 2013).

National Security Law of the People's Republic of China, promulgated by the Standing Comm. Nat'l People's Cong., July 1, 2015.

Remler, Philip. *Russia at the United Nations: Law, Sovereignty, and Legitimacy*, CARNEGIE ENDOWMENT FOR INT'L PEACE (Jan 22, 2020).

Space Debris Mitigation Policy for Agency Projects, EUR. SPACE AGENCY, ESA/ADMIN/IPOL(2014)2 (Mar. 28, 2014).

Space Sustainability Adoption Notice of ISO 24113: Space Systems, Space Debris Mitigation Requirements, EUR. COOP. FOR SPACE STANDARDIZATION, ECSS-U-AS-10C (Feb. 10, 2012).

Space Sustainability Adoption Notice of ISO 24113: Space Systems, Space Debris Mitigation Requirements, EUR. COOP. FOR SPACE STANDARDIZATION, ECSS-U-AS-10C Rev. 1 (Dec. 3, 2019).

The Montreal Declaration 2014, INST. AIR & SPACE L. (May 31, 2014), https://www.mcgill.ca/iasl/gsg/montrealdeclaration.

Viasgie, Louis & Theodoros Theodorou. *Hybrid Solar Sails for Active Debris Removal*, Final Report, EUR. SPACE AGENCY (2011).

U.N. Resolutions, Reports and Documents

China: Accession to Outer Space Treaty, U.N. Off. for Disarmament Affairs (Dec. 30, 1983), http://disarmament.un.org/treaties/a/outer_space/china/acc/washington.

Comm. on the Peaceful Uses of Outer Space, National Research on Space Debris, *Safety of Space Objects with Nuclear Power Sources on Board and Problems of their Collisions with Space Debris*, U.N. Doc. A/AC.105/751/Add.1 (Jan. 29, 2001).

Comm. on the Peaceful Uses of Outer Space, Rep. of Sci. & Tech. Subcomm. on Its Twenty-Seventh Session, U.N. Doc. A/AC.105/456 (Mar. 12, 1990).

Comm. on the Peaceful Uses of Outer Space, Rep. of Sci. & Tech. Subcomm. on Its Thirty-Second Session, U.N. Doc. A/AC.105/605 (Feb. 24, 1995).

Comm. on the Peaceful Uses of Outer Space, Rep. of Sci. and Tech. Subcomm. on Its Fortieth Session, *Inter-Agency Space Debris Coordination Committee Space Debris Mitigation Guidelines*, U.N. Doc. A/AC.105/C.1/L.260 (Nov. 29, 2002).

Comm. on the Peaceful Uses of Outer Space, Rep. of Sci. & Tech. Subcomm. on Its Forty-Second Session, *Draft Report of the Working Group on Space Debris*, U.N. Doc. A/AC.105/C.1/SD/2005/L.1 (Mar. 3, 2005).

Comm. on the Peaceful Uses of Outer Space, Rep. of Sci. & Tech. Subcomm. on Its Forty-Second Session, U.N. Doc. A/AC.105/848 (Feb. 7, 2005).

Comm. on the Peaceful Uses of Outer Space, Rep. of Sci. & Tech. Subcomm. on Its Forty-Third Session, *Progress Report of the Working Group on Space Debris, submitted by the Chairman of the Working Group*, U.N. Doc. A/AC.105/C.1/L.284 (Feb. 28, 2006).

Comm. on the Peaceful Uses of Outer Space, Rep. of Sci. and Tech. Subcomm. on Its Forty-Fifth Session, U.N. Doc. A/AC.105/786 (Mar. 15, 2002).

Comm. on the Peaceful Uses of Outer Space, Rep. of Sci. and Tech. Subcomm. on Its Forty-Eighth Session, *Intersessional Meeting of the Working Group on Space Debris of the Scientific and Technical Subcommittee*, U.N. Doc. A/AC.105/2005/CRP.8 (June 10, 2005).

Comm. on the Peaceful Uses of Outer Space, Rep. of Sci. & Tech. Subcomm. on Its Forty-Ninth Session, U.N. Doc. A/AC.105/C.1/2012/CRP.16 (2012).

Comm. on the Peaceful Uses of Outer Space, Rep. of the Int'l Interdisc. Cong. on Space Debris Remediation and On-Orbit Satellite Servicing on Its Forty-Ninth Session, *Active Debris Removal—An Essential Mechanism for Ensuring the Safety and Sustainability of Outer Space*, U.N. Doc. A/AC.105/C.1/2012/CRP.16 (Jan. 27, 2012).

Comm. on the Peaceful Uses of Outer Space, Rep. of Sci. & Tech. Subcomm. on Its Fiftieth Session, U.N. Doc. A/AC.105/890 (Mar. 6, 2007).

Comm. on the Peaceful Uses of Outer Space, Legal Subcomm. on Its Fifty-Third Session, U.N. Doc. A/AC.105/C.2/2014/CRP.28 (2014).

Comm. on the Peaceful Uses of Outer Space, Rep. of Sci. & Tech. Subcomm. on Its Fifty-Fifth Session, U.N. Doc. A/AC.105/1167 (2018).

Comm. on the Peaceful Uses of Outer Space, Legal Subcomm. on Its Fifty-Seventh Session, U.N. Doc. A/AC.105/C.2/2018/CRP.20 (2018).

Comm. on the Peaceful Uses of Outer Space, Rep. of Sci. & Tech. Subcomm., U.N. Doc. A/AC.105/720 (1999).

Comm. on the Peaceful Uses of Outer Space Rep. to U.N.G.A., Supplement, U.N. Doc. A/49/20 (Aug. 12, 1994).

Comm. on the Peaceful Uses of Outer Space, *Survey of the Problem of Discretion Exercised by States in Interpreting Basic Legal Principles and Norms Related to Safety and Security in Outer Space*, U.N. Doc. A/AC.105/L.319 (Apr. 4, 2019).

Comm. on the Peaceful Uses of Outer Space, Union of Soviet Socialist Republics: Draft Declaration of the Basic Principles Governing the Activities of States Pertaining to the Exploration and Use of Outer Space on Its Seventeenth Session, U.N. Doc. A/AC.105/L.2 (1962).

Conole, Kevin. Statement at the Fifty-Eighth Session of the UN COPUOS Scientific and Technical Subcommittee: Space Debris (Apr. 20, 2021).

Continental Shelf Convention, June 10, 1964, 499 U.N.T.S. 311.

Convention on the Territorial Sea and the Contiguous Zone, Apr. 29, 1958, 516 U.N.T.S. 205.

G.A., *Agenda Item 28: International Co-operation in the Peaceful Uses of Outer Space* (1963).

G.A., Rep. of Comm. on the Peaceful Uses of Outer Space, U.N. Doc. A/5785 (Nov. 13, 1964).

G.A., Rep. of Comm. on the Peaceful Uses of Outer Space on Its Fifty-Seventh Session, U.N. Doc. A/69/20 (June 2014).

G.A., Rep. of Comm. on the Peaceful Uses of Outer Space on Its Sixty-Second Session, U.N. Doc. A/62/20 (2007).

G.A. Res. 34/68 (Dec. 5, 1979).

G.A. Res. 44/46 (Dec. 6, 1988).

G.A. Res. 45/72 (Dec. 8, 1989).

G.A. Res. 46/45 (Dec. 9, 1991).

G.A. Res. 48/39 (Feb. 10, 1994).

G.A. Res. 51/122 (Dec. 13, 1996).

G.A. Res. 56/1 (Sept. 18, 2001).

G.A. Res. 73/203 (Jan. 11, 2019).

G.A. Res. 1348 (Dec. 13, 1958).

G.A. Res. 1721 (Dec. 20, 1961).

G.A. Res. 1963 (Dec. 13, 1963).

G.A. Res. 2222 (Dec. 19, 1966).

G.A. Res. 3235 (Jan. 14, 1975).

G.A., U.N. Doc. A/6431 (Sept. 22, 1966).

G.A., U.N. Doc. A/C.1/L.363/REV.1 (Dec. 18, 1965).

Gong, Zizheng. *CASC Efforts on Dealing with Space Debris Toward Space Long Term Sustainability*, UN COPUOS Sci. & Tech. Subcomm., Fiftieth Session, Vienna (Feb. 11–22, 2013).

Gong, Zizheng. *China Practices on Satellites Post-Mission Disposals Toward Space Long-Term Sustainability*, UN COPUOS Sci. & Tech. Subcomm., Fifty-Third Session, Vienna (Feb. 15–26, 2016).

Guidelines for the Long-Term Sustainability of Outer Space Activities of the Committee on the Peaceful Uses of Outer Space, U.N. Off. for Outer Space Affairs (2021).

Hudson, Manley O. *Article 24 of the Statute of the International Law Commission*, 2 Y.B. INT'L L. COMM'N 24, U.N. Doc. A/CN.4/16 (1950).

Int'l Law Comm'n, Third Rep. on Identification of Customary International Law, Michael Wood, Special Rapporteur, U.N. Doc. A/CN.4/682 (Mar. 27, 2015).

Int'l Law Comm'n, Rep. on the Work of its Seventieth Session, Supplement No. 10 (1/73/10), U.N. Doc. A/73/10 (2018).

Ma, Xinmin. *China's Space Diplomacy: Policies and Practices*, UNISPACE+50, High Level Forum (HLF), Dubai, (Nov. 20–24, 2016).

Meaning of the Expressions "in Consultation with" and "after consultation with" in the Practice of the United Nations, 1962 U.N. JURID. Y.B. 268, U.N. Doc. ST/LEG/8.

Off. of Outer Space Affairs, Space Debris Mitigation Guidelines of the Comm. on the Peaceful Uses of Outer Space, U.N. Sales No. V.09-8857 (2010).

Off. Recs. of the G.A., Thirty-Fourth Session, Chapter XXIV, Outer Space (last updated Dec. 31, 2021, 10:15 AM).

Rep. of Comm. on the Peaceful Uses of Outer Space on Its Forty-Fifth Session, U.N. Doc. A/45/20 (Aug. 31, 1990).

Rep. of Comm. on the Peaceful Uses of Outer Space on Its Forty-Eighth Session, U.N. Doc. A/58/20 (2003).

Rep. of Comm. on the Peaceful Uses of Outer Space on Its Fiftieth Session, U.N. Doc. A/50/20 (1995).

Rep. of Comm. on the Peaceful Uses of Outer Space on Its Fifty-Seventh Session, U.N. Doc. A/57/20 (2002).

Rep. of Comm. on the Peaceful Uses of Outer Space on Its Fifty-Ninth Session, U.N. Doc. A/71/20 (Aug. 16, 2016).

Rep. of Comm. on the Peaceful Uses of Outer Space, on Its Sixty-Second Session, U.N. Doc. A/74/20 (2019).

Rep. of Comm. on the Peaceful Uses of Outer Space, U.N. Doc. A/48/20 (Aug. 16, 1993).

Rep. of Comm. on the Peaceful Uses of Outer Space, U.N. Doc. A/55/49 (Sept. 24, 1963).

REP. OF THE U.N. CONFERENCE ON THE HUMAN ENVIRONMENT, U.N. DOC. A/CONF.48/14/REV.1 (1972).

S.C. RES. 1368 (Sept. 12, 2001).

Status of International Agreements Relating to Activities in Outer Space as of 1 January 2020, U.N. Off. of Outer Space Affairs.

The Interoperable Global Navigation Satellite Systems Space Service Volume, U.N. Doc. E.19.IV.1 (2018).

Treaty Banning Nuclear Weapon Tests in the Atmosphere, in Outer Space, and Under Water, Oct. 15, 1963, 480 U.N.T.S. 43.

Treaty on Principles Governing the Activities of States in the Exploration and Use of Outer Space, Including the Moon and other Celestial Bodies, Jan. 27, 1967, 610 U.N.T.S. 205.

U.N. CHAIRMAN, *Opening Statement*, U.N. Doc. A/5482 (1963).

U.N. CHARTER ART. 13(1)(A).

U.N. Conference on Environment and Development, *Rio Declaration on Environment and Development*, U.N. Doc. A/CONF. 151/26/Rev. 1 (Vol. I) (Aug. 12, 1992).

U.N. Conference on the Human Environment, U.N. Doc. A/CONF.48 (1972).

U.N. Convention on the Law of the Sea, Dec. 10, 1982, 1833 U.N.T.S. 397.

U.N./Int'l Inst. of Air & Space L. Workshop on Capacity Building in Space L., U.N. Doc. ST/Space/14 (2003).

U.N. OFF. FOR OUTER SPACE AFFAIRS, UNITED NATIONS TREATIES AND PRINCIPLES ON OUTER SPACE AND RELATED GENERAL ASSEMBLY RESOLUTIONS, U.N. Sales No. E.08.I.10 (2008).

U.N. Secretariat, Consideration by the Inter-Agency Space Debris Coordination Committee of the Comments Received from Member States of the Committee on the Peaceful Uses of Outer Space on the Proposals on Space Debris Mitigation and Results of the Consultative Meeting of the Inter-Agency Space Debris Coordination Committee and the Committee on the Peaceful Uses of Outer Space held in Vancouver, Canada, on 4 October 2004, Notes by the Secretariat, Comm. on the Peaceful Uses of Outer Space, U.N. Doc. A/AC.105/C.1/L.277 (Feb. 7, 2005).

U.N. Secretariat, National Research on Space Debris Safety of Nuclear-Powered Satellites: Problems of Collisions of Nuclear-Power Sources with Space Debris, Notes by the Secretariat, Comm. on the Peaceful Uses of Outer Space, U.N. Doc. A/AC.105/593 (Dec. 1, 1994).

U.N. Secretariat, National Research on Space Debris Safety of Nuclear-Powered Satellites: Problems of Collisions of Nuclear-Power Sources with Space Debris, Notes by the Secretariat, Comm. on the Peaceful Uses of Outer Space, U.N. Doc. A/AC.105/731 (Dec. 20, 1999).

Vienna Convention on the Law of Treaties, 1969, 1155 U.N.T.S. 331.

Wang, Guoyu. *China's Space Regulations: Registration and Licensing*, UN COPUOS Legal Subcomm., Fifty-Third Session, Vienna (Mar. 2014).

Papers/Essays

Baudet, Lucille, & Manon Ruffiot. Active Debris Removal: From the Main Barriers to the Definition of a Business Model (Feb. 3, 2016) (Master's dissertation, Toulouse Business School).

Hatfield-Dodds, Steve, et al. *Adaptive Governance: An Introduction, and Implications for Public Policy* (Austl. Agric. & Res. Econs. Soc'y, Working Paper No. 0701, 2007).

Parisi, Franceso & Daniel Pi. The Emergence and Evolution of Customary International Law (Sept. 20, 2012) (Univ. of Minn. L. Sch. Legal Rsch. Paper Series, Research Paper No. 12–40).

Mund, Brian Zachary. In Defense of Sovereignty: An Analysis of Russian Voting Behavior in the United Nations Security Council (1995–2012) (Apr. 1, 2013) (B.A. thesis, Univ. of Pa.).

Raju, Nivedita. *A Proposal for a Ban on Destructive Anti-Satellite Testing: A Role for the European Union?*, NON-PROLIFERATION & DISARMAMENT PAPERS, no. 74, April 2021.

Weiss, Eric. *The Impact of the Intellectual Migration on the United States and Eastern Europe* (Apr. 27, 1998) (Term paper, Vand. Univ.).

Conference Papers

Air Sovereignty and the Legal Status of Outer Space, Rep. of the Forty-Eighth Conf. of the Int'l L. Assoc., 324 (1958).

Breccia, Pierfrancesco. Article III of Outer Space Treaty and Its Relevance in the International Space Legal Framework (Sixty-Seventh Int'l Astronautical Cong., 2016).

Carroll, Joseph A. Bounties on Orbital Debris? (First Int'l Orbital Debris Conf., 2019).

Chatterjee, Joyeeta. Legal Issues Relating to Unauthorized Space Debris Remediation (Sixty-Fifth Int'l Astronautical Cong., 2014).

Comm. on the Formation of Customary Int'l L. Rep. of the Sixty-Ninth Conf. of the Int'l L. Assoc. (2000).

Forshaw, Jason L., et al. The RemoveDebris ADR Mission: Preparing for An International Space Station Launch (Procs. of the Seventh Eur. Conf. on Space Debris, 2017).

Flury, W. Activities in Space Debris in Europe (Procs. of the Third Eur. Conf. on Debris, 2001).

Flury, W. European Activities on Space Debris (First Eur. Conf. on Space Debris, 1993).

Hatfield-Dodds, Steve, et al. Adaptive Governance: An Introduction and Implications for Public Policy (ANZSEE Conf., 2007).

Int'l L. Assoc. Statement of Principles Applicable to the Formation of General Customary International Law (London Conf., 2000).

Jim, Rui Lin & Win Liu. Environmental Policy and Legislation in China (Procs. of the Sino-American Conf. on Env't L., 1987).

Kelso, T.S. Analysis of the 2007 Chinese ASAT Test and the Impact of its Debris on the Space Environment (Advanced Maui Optical & Space Surveillance Techs. [AMOS] Conf., 2007).

Kerrest, Armel. New Development and the Legal Framework Covering the Exploitation of the Resources of the Moon (Procs. of the Forty-Seventh Colloquium on the L. of Outer Space, 2005).

Klinkrad, H., et al. Space Debris Activities in Europe (Procs. of the Fourth Eur. Conf. on Space Debris, 2005).

Lafferanderie, G. The European Space Agency and International Space Law (Procs. of the Third ECSL Colloquium on Int'l Org. & Space L., 1999).

Lewis, Hugh G. Understanding Long-Term Orbital Debris Population Dynamics (First Int'l Orbital Debris Conf., 2019).

Loesch, M., et al. Economic Approach for Active Space Debris Removal Services (Int'l Symp. on A.I., Robotics, & Automatic in Space, 2010).

Marchisio, Sergio. National Jurisdiction for Regulating Space Activities of Governmental and Non-Governmental Entities (U.N./Thai. Workshop on Space L., 2010).

Marchisio, Sergio. The Draft Code of Conduct for Outer Space Activities (U.N./Thai. Workshop on Space L., 2010).

Matney, M., et al. The NASA Orbital Debris Engineering Model 3.1: Development, Verification, and Validation (First Int'l Orbital Debris Conf., 2019).

McKnight, Darren. Pay Me Now or Pay Me More Later: Start the Development of Active Orbital Debris Removal Now (Advanced Maui Optical & Space Surveillance Techs. [AMOS] Conf., 2010).

Nester, Olusoji. Africa in Space: Legal Issues and Responsibilities Related to Space Technology Development (U.N./S. Afr. Symp. On Basic Space Tech., 2017).

Oltrogge, Daniel L. The Contributions of Commercial Best Practices to the Global Space Governance Continuum (Advanced Maui Optical & Space Surveillance Techs. [AMOS] Conf., 2020).

Sloan, John. FAA International Workshops on Commercial Space Transportation (Sixty-Eighth Int'l Astronautical Conf., Sept. 2017).

Stadnyk, K., et al. Space Debris Removal with Sub-Tethered Net: A Feasibility Study and Preliminary Design (Eighth Eur. Conf. on Space Debris, 2021).

Steele, Scott Michael. Can International Law Provide A Basis for Actively Removing Space Debris? (Advanced Maui Optical & Space Surveillance Techs. [AMOS] Conf., 2020).

Tamaki, Yuta & Hiroaki Tanaka. Penetration Characteristics of Metal Harpoons with Various Tip Shapes for Capturing Space Debris (Eighth Eur. Conf. on Space Debris, 2021).

Virgili, Benjamin Bastide & Holger Karg. Criteria for the Selection of Targets for Active Debris Removal (Fourth CEAS Air & Space Conf., 2013).

Von Der Dunk, Frans G. Two New National Space Laws: Russia and South Africa (Procs. of the Forty-Eighth Colloquium on the L. of Outer Space, 1995).

Walker, R., et al. Update of the ESA Space Debris Mitigation Handbook (Procs. of the Third Eur. Conf. on Debris, 2001).

Cases

Asylum (Colom. v. Peru), Judgment, 1950 I.C.J. 7 (Nov. 20).

Connecticut Comm. Against Pay TV v. F.C.C., 301 F.2d 835 (D.C. Cir. 1962).

Diversion of Water from Meuse (Neth. v. Belg.), Judgment, 1937 P.C.I.J. (ser. A/B) No. 70 (June 28).

Factory at Chorzów (Ger. v Pol), Jurisdiction, 1927 P.C.I.J. (ser. A) No. 9 (July 26).

Fisheries Jurisdiction (U.K. v. Ice.), Judgment, 1951 I.C.J. 55 (Feb. 1973).

Legal Status of Eastern Greenland, 1933 P.C.I.J. Rep (ser. A/B) No. 53 (Apr. 5).

Missouri v. Holland, 252 U.S. 416 (1920).

Nat'l Broadcasting Co. v. U.S., 63 S. Ct. 997 (1943).

North Sea Cont'l Shelf (Ger. v. Den. & Ger. v. Neth.), Judgment, 1969 I.C.J. Nos. 51 & 52 (Feb. 20).

SS *"Lotus"* (Fr. v. Turk.), Judgment, 1927 P.C.I.J. No. 9 (Sept. 7).

U.S. Diplomatic and Consular Staff in Tehran (U.S. v. Iran), Judgment, 1980 I.C.J. Rep 3 (May 24).

Federal Agency Reports

BOWE, ALEXANDER. CHINA'S PURSUIT OF SPACE POWER STATUS AND IMPLICATIONS FOR THE UNITED STATES, U.S.-CHINA ECON. & SEC. REV. COMM'N (Apr. 11, 2019).

CONG. RSCH. SERV., R. 45416, COMMERCIAL SPACE: FEDERAL REGULATION, OVERSIGHT AND UTILIZATION 19–20, https://fas.org/sgp/crs/space/R45416.pdf (updated Nov. 29, 2018).

Consolidated and Further Continuing Appropriations Act of 2015, Pub. L. No. 113–235, 128 Stat. 2130 (2015).

KAN, SHIRLEY. CONG. RSCH. SERV., RS22652, CHINA'S ANTI-SATELLITE WEAPON TEST (2007).

MCCALL, STEPHEN M. CONG. RSCH. SERV., IF10337, CHALLENGES TO THE UNITED STATES IN SPACE (2020).

MORGAN, DANIEL. CONG. RSCH. SERV., R45416, COMMERCIAL SPACE: FEDERAL REGULATION, OVERSIGHT AND UTILIZATION (last updated Nov. 29, 2018).

MULLIGAN, STEPHEN P. CONG. RESEARCH SERV., RL 32528, INTERNATIONAL LAW AND AGREEMENTS: THEIR EFFECT UPON U.S. LAW (updated Sept. 19, 2018).

OFF. OF THE INSPECTOR GEN., REP. NO. IG-21-011, NASA'S EFFORTS TO MITIGATE THE RISK POSED BY ORBITAL DEBRIS (2021).

Proclamation No. 2667, 10 Fed. Reg. 12 (Sept. 28, 1945).

Processing Applications in the Digital Broadcast Satellite Service, 86 Fed. Reg. 49484 (Sept. 3, 2021) (to be codified at 47 C.F.R. § 25.114 (d)(14)(1)).

Mitigation of Orbital Space Debris in the New Space Age, 85 Fed. Reg. 52452 (Aug. 25, 2020).

The National Space Policy, 85 Fed. Reg. 81755 (2020).

WELT, CORY. CONG. RSCH. SERV., R44775, RUSSIA: BACKGROUND AND U.S. POLICY (Aug. 21, 2017).

United States Code

Asteroid Resource & Space Resource Rights, 51 U.S.C. § 51303.

Chapter 5: Wire or Radio Communications, 47 U.S.C. §§ 151–614.

Commercial Space Competitiveness: Definitions, 51 U.S.C. § 50501.

Commercial Space Launch Activities: Consultation, 51 U.S.C. § 50918.

Commercial Space Launch Activities: Definitions, 51 U.S.C. § 50902.

Commercial Space Launch Activities: Regulations, 51 U.S.C. § 50922.

Space Situational Awareness Services and Information: Provision to non-United States Government Entities, 10 U.S.C. § 2274.

Applications & Licenses: Applications for Space Station Authorizations, 47 C.F.R. § 25.114 (2020).
Applications & Licenses: Applications for Streamlined Small Spacecraft Authorization, 47 C.F.R. § 25.123 (2020).
Applications & Licenses: Applications for Streamlined Small Space Station Authorization, 47 C.F.R. § 25.122 (2020).
Applications & Licenses: License Term & Renewals, 47 C.F.R. § 25.121 (2014).
Applications & Licenses: Special Provisions for Satellite Systems, 47 C.F.R. § 5.64 (2013).
Flight Hazard Area Analysis for Aircraft & Ship Protection: Aircraft Hazard Areas Analysis, 14 C.F.R. APP. § B417.9 (2006).
Flight Hazard Area Analysis for Aircraft & Ship Protection: Land Hazard Areas Analysis, 14 C.F.R. § B417.13 (2006).
Flight Hazard Area Analysis for Aircraft & Ship Protection: Ship Hazard Areas Analysis, 14 C.F.R. app. § B417.11 (2006).
Flight Safety Analysis: Debris Analysis, 14 C.F.R. § 417.211 (2006).
Forfeiture, Termination, & Reinstatement of Station Authorization: Surety Bonds, 47 C.F.R. § 25.165 (2018).
General & License Terms & Conditions: Registration of Space Objects, 14 C.F.R. § 417.19 (2006).
Launch Safety: Continuing Accuracy of License Application; Application for Modification of License, 14 C.F.R. APP. § A417.11 (2016).
Launch Safety Responsibilities: Flight Safety, 14 C.F.R. § 417.107 (2016).
Launch Safety Responsibilities: Launch Plans, 14 C.F.R. § 417.111 (2006).
Launch Safety Responsibilities: Launch Safety Rules, 14 C.F.R. § 417.113 (2006).
Launch Safety Responsibilities: Safety at End of Launch, 14 C.F.R. § 417.129 (2006).
License Application Procedures: Pre-Application Consultation, 14 C.F.R. § 413.15 (2012).
License Application Procedures: Issuing A License or Permit, 14 C.F.R. § 413.19 (2007).
Organization & Definitions: Definitions, 14 C.F.R. § 401.5 (2003).
Payload Review & Determination: Payloads Not Subject to Review, 14 C.F.R. § 415.53 (2012).
Policy Review & Approval: General, 14 C.F.R. § 415.21 (2012).
Policy Review & Approval: Policy Review, 14 C.F.R. § 415.23 (2012).
Safety Requirements: Launch & Reentry Collision Avoidance Analysis Requirements, 14 C.F.R. § 450.169 (2021).
Safety Review & Approval for Launch from a Federal Launch Range: General, 14 C.F.R. § 415.31 (2006).
Special Operations: Space Station, 47 C.F.R. § 97.207 (2020).
Technical Operations: Control of Transmitting Stations, 47 C.F.R. § 25.271 (2020).
Technical Operations: End-of-Life Disposal, 47 C.F.R. § 25.283 (2004).

Other/Unpublished/Foreign Language Materials

Canada-European Space Agency Cooperation Agreement, GOV'T OF CAN., https://www.asc-csa.gc.ca/eng/funding-programs/canada-esa/about-cooperation-agreement.asp (last updated Oct. 23, 2019).

China Nat'l Space Admin. CHINA'S SPACE ACTIVITIES, A WHITE PAPER (Nov. 22, 2000).

Communication from the Commission to the European Parliament, the Council, the European Economic and Social Committee and the Committee of the Regions, COM (2016) 705 final (Oct. 26, 2016).

Convention for the Establishment of a European Space Agency, Preamble, May 30, 1975, https://esamultimedia.esa.int/multimedia/publications/SP-1337/SP-1337_EN.pdf.

Federal Law of the Russian Federation, About Licensing of Separate Types of Activity, No. 99-FZ, May 4, 2011 (as amended on 31 July 2020), https://cis-legislation.com/document.fwx?rgn=43154.

E-mail from Paul Maley to John C. Broman, Jr. (June 26, 1996, 3:02 PM), http://www.satobs.org/seesat/Jun-1996/0299.html.

Exec. Order No. 12465, 49 Fed. Reg. 7211 (Feb. 24, 1984).

Establishment of Domestic Communications-Satellite Facilities by Nongovernmental Entities, 22 F.C.C.2d 86 (1970) (report and order).

General Requirements for Space Assets to Limit Man-Made Clogging of Near-Earth Space, P 52925-2018 Space Technology Products.

GOST R 52925-2008, Space Technology Items. General Requirements for Mitigation of Near-Earth Space Debris Population, https://www.russiangost.com/p-61067-gost-r-52925-2008.aspx.

GOST P 52925-2018, Space Technology Products. General Requirements for Space Assets to Limit Man-Made Clogging of Near-Earth Space, Russian Federation's National Standard Space Products.

Interview with Michiru Nishida, Ministry of Foreign Affairs of Japan (Apr. 26, 2017).

Joint Statement of the Russian Federation and the People's Republic of China on the International Relations Entering a New Era and the Global Sustainable Development, Feb. 4, 2022.

LETTER FROM TED WACKLER, ACTING DIRECTOR OF THE OFF. OF SCI. & TECH. POL'Y, TO CONG. (AUG. 14, 2017) (ON FILE WITH THE WHITE HOUSE ARCHIVES).

Mitigation of Orbital Debris, 19 F.C.C.R. 11567 (2004).

Mitigation of Orbital Debris in the New Space Age, No. 18–313, 2020 W.L. 2740496 *8 (F.C.C. Apr. 23, 2020), https://docs.fcc.gov/public/attachments/FCC-20-54A1.pdf.

NAT. RES. COUNCIL, COMM. FOR THE ASSESSMENT OF NASA'S ORBITAL DEBRIS PROGRAMS, LIMITING FUTURE COLLISION RISK TO SPACECRAFT: AN ASSESSMENT OF NASA'S METEOROID AND ORBITAL DEBRIS PROGRAMS (2011).

Order of the Government of the Russian Federation About Licensing of Space Activities, No. 160 (Feb. 22, 2012).

Order of the Government of the Russian Federation About Licensing of Space Activities, No. 298 (Mar. 18, 2020, effective Apr. 18, 2020).

Qiang, Song. *ISO Standards and Space Debris*, China Academy of Launch Vehicle Technology (Cot. 2011), https://swfound.org/media/50900/song_iso.pdf.

Shakelford, Scott. *Ostrom Workshop Expands Study of Governance in Outer Space*, Ind. Univ., Space Governance Rsch., https://research.impact.iu.edu/our-strengths/social-sciences/space-governance.html.

Update of the ESA Space Debris Mitigation Handbook, ESA Contract 14471/00/D/HK, July 2002.

Федеральный закон Российской Федерации о космической деятельности [The Law of the Russian Federation About Space Activities], ukazy [Decrees] Aug. 20, 1993 (as amended Apr. 15, 2019), No 5663–1.

федеральный закон рф о лицензировании отдельных видов деятельности [Federal Law of the Russian Federation About Licensing of Separate Types of Activity] Sobranie Zakonodatel'stva Rossiĭskoĭ Federatsii [SZ RF] [Russian Federation Collection of Legislation] 2011, No. 99-FZ (as amended July 31, 2020).

Constitutions

Konstitutsiia Rossiĭskoĭ Federatsii [Konst. RF] [Constitution] (Russ.).

U.S. Const.

Index

Printed in the United States
by Baker & Taylor Publisher Services